Research Methods for Business

Research Methods for Business

A Skill-Building Approach

EIGHTH EDITION

Roger Bougie

and

Uma Sekaran

VP AND EDITORIAL DIRECTOR	Mike McDonald
EXECUTIVE EDITOR	Lise Johnson
EDITORIAL MANAGER	Judy Howarth
CONTENT MANAGEMENT DIRECTOR	Lisa Wojcik
CONTENT MANAGER	Nichole Urban
SENIOR CONTENT SPECIALIST	Nicole Repasky
PRODUCTION EDITOR	Mathangi Balasubramanian
PHOTO EDITOR	Anindita Adiyal
COVER PHOTO CREDIT	© Eugene Onischenko/Shutterstock

This book was set in 10/12 Times LT Std by SPi Global and printed and bound by Quad Graphics.

Founded in 1807, John Wiley & Sons, Inc. has been a valued source of knowledge and understanding for more than 200 years, helping people around the world meet their needs and fulfill their aspirations. Our company is built on a foundation of principles that include responsibility to the communities we serve and where we live and work. In 2008, we launched a Corporate Citizenship Initiative, a global effort to address the environmental, social, economic, and ethical challenges we face in our business. Among the issues we are addressing are carbon impact, paper specifications and procurement, ethical conduct within our business and among our vendors, and community and charitable support. For more information, please visit our website: www.wiley.com/go/citizenship.

Evaluation copies are provided to qualified academics and professionals for review purposes only, for use in their courses during the next academic year. These copies are licensed and may not be sold or transferred to a third party. Upon completion of the review period, please return the evaluation copy to Wiley. Return instructions and a free of charge return shipping label are available at: www.wiley.com/go/returnlabel. If you have chosen to adopt this textbook for use in your course, please accept this book as your complimentary desk copy. Outside of the United States, please contact your local sales representative.

ISBN: 978-1-119-56122-4 (PBK)
ISBN: 978-1-119-60925-4 (EVAL)

Library of Congress Cataloging-in-Publication Data

LCCN: 2019030449

The inside back cover will contain printing identification and country of origin if omitted from this page. In addition, if the ISBN on the back cover differs from the ISBN on this page, the one on the back cover is correct.

Printed and bound by CPI Group (UK) Ltd, Croydon, CR0 4YY

C9781119663706_220923

Contents

6   Theoretical Framework and Hypothesis Development   83

7   Elements of Research Design   103

8   Interviews   117

9   Observation   129

10 Administering Questionnaires 143

11 Experimental Designs 164

12 Measurement of Variables: Operational Definition 190

13 Measurement of Variables: Scaling, Reliability and Validity 198

14 Sampling   221

15 Quantitative Data Analysis   254

18 Conclusions 323

19 The Research Report 337

About the Authors

Roger Bougie is Associate Professor at the TIAS School for Business and Society (Tilburg University, The Netherlands), where he teaches executive courses in Business Research Methods. He has received a number of teaching awards, including the Best Course Award for his course on Business Research Methods. Dr Bougie's main research interests are in marketing, consumer behaviour, organizational change and managerial decision making. Dr Bougie authored or co-authored numerous papers published in peer-reviewed journals such as the *Journal of the Academy of Marketing Science*, *Journal of Social Marketing* and the *Journal of Promotion Management*, books, book chapters and cases in the area of Marketing and Business Research Methods. Dr Bougie is ad hoc reviewer for the *Journal of Business Research*, the *Journal of Marketing Research*, the *Journal of Service Research* and *Marketing Letters*.

Uma Sekaran was Professor Emerita of Management, Southern Illinois University at Carbondale (SIUC), Illinois. She obtained her MBA degree from the University of Connecticut at Storrs and her PhD from UCLA. She was the Chair of the Department of Management and also the Director of University Women's Professional Advancement at SIUC when she retired from the University and moved to California to be closer to her family. Professor Sekaran authored or co-authored eight books, 12 book chapters and more than 55 refereed journal articles in the management area and presented more than 70 papers at regional, national and international management conferences. She also won recognition for significant research contributions to cross-cultural research from US and international professional organizations. She received Meritorious Research Awards both from the Academy of Management and SIUC and was conferred the Best Teacher Award by the University.

Preface

Previous editions of this book have been used in various research methods courses with great success. For many years the book has helped thousands of my own students (undergraduate students, graduate students and executive students), as well as many more around the world, to carry out their research projects. The great strength of *Research Methods for Business* is that students find it clear, informal, easy to use and unintimidating. I have tried to maintain these strengths in this eighth edition.

CHANGES IN THE EIGHTH EDITION

The eighth edition of *Research Methods for Business* has been thoroughly revised.

- Two new chapters (on Defining the Management Problem and on Drawing Conclusions) are included in this new edition of the book. Changes have been made in every chapter of the book.
- Chapter 2 (The scientific approach and alternative approaches to investigation), Chapter 4 (Defining the Research Problem), as well as the chapters on Interviews, Measurement of Variables and Sampling have been substantially modified and updated in this edition.
- Examples, exercises and other pedagogical features have been revised and updated in all the chapters.
- The structure of the book has not changed, but the storyline has been further improved. As in previous editions, the accessible and informal style of presenting information has been maintained and the focus on practical skill building preserved.
- Chapter 2 introduces and discusses alternative approaches to research. New in this chapter is a detailed discussion of a pragmatic approach to research. Subsequent chapters follow up on this by reviewing a range of topics (such as the definition of the management problem and the research problem) from a pragmatic perspective. The discussion of various approaches to research allows the readers to recognize and develop their *personal ideas* on research and how it should be done, to determine which kinds of research questions are important to them and what methods for collecting and analysing data will give them the best answers to their research questions.

As in previous editions, the book provides numerous examples to illustrate the concepts and points presented. Readers will also note a variety of examples from different areas of the world as well as different areas of business – human resources management, strategic management, operations management, management control, marketing, finance, accounting and information management.

Most chapters in the book include managerial implications of the contents discussed, emphasizing the need for managers to understand research. The ethical considerations involved in conducting research are also clearly brought out. The dynamics of cross-cultural research in terms of instrument development, surveys and sampling are discussed, which, in the context of today's global economy, will be useful to students.

We expect that students and instructors alike will enjoy this edition. Students should become effective researchers, helped by the requisite knowledge and skills acquired through this book. Finally, it is hoped that students will find research interesting, unintimidating and of practical use.

HOW TO USE THIS EIGHTH EDITION

You can read this book in a variety of ways, depending on your reasons for using this book.

If the book is part of a Business Research Methods course, the order in which you read the chapters will be prescribed by your instructor.

If you are reading the book because you are engaged in a project (a consultancy project, a research project or a dissertation), then the order in which your read the chapters is your own choice. However, we recommend that you follow the structure of the book rather closely. This means that we advise you to start with reading the first four chapters that introduce research, various approaches to what makes good research and the development of a management problem, research problem and a research proposal. Based on the type of research questions and whether, as a result of your research questions, your study is qualitative or quantitative, you may decide to read the book in the following way.

In the case of qualitative research:

5	The critical literature review
7	Research design
8, 9, and/or 10	Data collection methods
14	Sampling
17	Qualitative data analysis
19	The research report

In the case of quantitative research:

5	The critical literature review
6	Theoretical framework
7	Research design
10	Questionnaires
11	Experimental designs
12 and 13	Measurement and Scaling
14	Sampling
15 and 16	Quantitative data analysis
19	The research report

COMPANION WEBSITE AND ENHANCED EBOOK

Lecturers have a dedicated companion website available at www.wiley.com/go/bougie/research-methodsforbusiness8e.

Lecturers will find a range of bespoke video material, developed by the author to provide extra explanation on difficult topics. The website also houses additional case studies related to each chapter. There is also an extensive test bank for lecturers, a comprehensive set of Power-Point slides in addition to a image gallery and an instructor's manual, which offers an up-to-date and valuable additional teaching aid.

Students who use the enhanced ebook will have access to the videos, a glossary, flashcards, which are useful for self-study and revision and self-test quizzes with over 250 questions for students to use while studying outside the classroom.

ACKNOWLEDGEMENTS

Working on the eighth edition of *Research Methods for Business* has been a positive and rewarding experience. Many people have contributed to this in many different ways. Thank you colleagues at Tilburg University and the TIAS School for Business and Society for your feedback on earlier versions of this book. Thank you for providing me with a pleasant, professional and inspiring work environment. Thank you dear students for the lively and inspiring discussions we have had during the past 20 years; I have learned a lot from these discussions. Thanks everybody at John Wiley & Sons, for your support, your patience and your confidence. Thank you reviewers for your constructive and insightful comments on earlier drafts of this book.

ROGER BOUGIE

Introduction to Research

LEARNING OBJECTIVES

After completing Chapter 1, you should be able to:

1. Describe and define business research.

2. Distinguish between applied and basic research, giving examples, and discussing why they fall into one or the other of the two categories.

3. Explain why managers should know about research and discuss what managers should and should not do in order to interact effectively with researchers.

4. Identify and fully discuss specific situations in which a manager would be better off using an internal research team, and when an external research team would be more advisable, giving reasons for the decisions.

5. Discuss what research means to you and describe how you, as a manager, might apply the knowledge gained about research.

6. Demonstrate awareness of the role of ethics in business research.

INTRODUCTION

Just close your eyes for a minute and utter the word *research* to yourself. What kinds of images does this word conjure up for you? Do you visualize a laboratory where scientists working with Bunsen burners and test tubes, or an Einstein-like character writing a dissertation on some complex subject such as 'behavioural heterogeneity in economic institutions' or someone analysing large amounts of scanner data to assess the impact of a price reduction on sales? Most certainly, all these images do represent different aspects of research. However, research is not necessarily characterized by Bunsen burners, Einstein-like characters or Big Data. **Research**, a somewhat intimidating term for some, is simply the process of finding solutions to a problem after a targeted and systematic study and analysis of materials and sources. Along these lines, people (consumers, investors, managers) constantly engage themselves in exploring and examining issues – and hence are involved in some form of research activity – as they want to change mobile phone providers, buy a new car, go to the movies, invest in a business start-up or increase advertising expenditures in their role as a manager.

Research, in some form or another, may help *managers* in organizations to make decisions at the workplace. As we all know, sometimes they make good decisions, sometimes they make poor decisions and on occasions they make such colossal blunders that they get stuck in the mire. The difference between making good decisions and committing blunders often lies in how we go about the decision-making process. In other words, good decision-making fetches a 'yes' answer to the following questions: Do we identify where exactly the problem lies? Do we correctly recognize the relevant factors in the situation needing investigation? Do we know what types of information are to be gathered and how? Do we know how to make use of the information so collected and draw appropriate conclusions to make the right decisions? And, finally, do we know how to implement the results of this process to solve the problem? This is the essence of research, and to be a successful manager it is important to know how to go about making the right decisions by being knowledgeable about the various steps involved in finding solutions to problematic issues of interest to the organization and/or its stakeholders. This is what this book is all about.

BUSINESS RESEARCH

Business research can be described as a systematic and organized effort to investigate a specific decision problem encountered in the work setting, which needs a solution. It comprises a series of steps that are designed and executed with the goal of finding answers to the issues that are of concern to the manager in the work environment. This means that the first step in research is to know where the problem area exists in the organization and to identify as clearly and specifically as possible the problem that needs to be studied and resolved. Once the management problem is clearly defined, a research objective and research questions can be developed. From there, steps can be taken with regard to the planning, collection and analysis of data. Based on the data collected and analysed, an informed judgment with regard to (a solution to) the organizational problem can ultimately be drawn.

The entire process by which we attempt to solve problems is called research. Thus, research involves a series of well-thought-out and carefully executed activities that enable the manager to know how organizational problems can be solved, or at least considerably minimized. Research encompasses the processes of inquiry, investigation, examination and sometimes experimentation. These processes have to be carried out systematically, diligently, critically, objectively and logically. The expected end result would be a conclusion that helps the manager to deal with the problem situation.

Identifying the critical issues, gathering relevant information, analysing the data in ways that help decision-making and implementing the right course of action are all facilitated by understanding business research. After all, decision-making is simply a process of choosing from among alternative solutions to resolve a problem and research helps to generate viable alternatives for effective decision-making. Knowledge of research thus enables you to undertake research yourself in order to solve the smaller and bigger problems that you will encounter in your (future) job as a treasurer, controller, brand manager, product manager, marketing manager, IT auditor, project manager, business analyst or consultant. What's more, it will help you to discriminate between good and bad studies published in (professional) journals, to discriminate between good and bad studies conducted by research agencies, to discriminate between good and bad research proposals of research agencies and to interact more effectively with researchers and consultants.

We can now define business research as an *organized, systematic, data-based, critical, objective, inquiry or investigation into a specific problem*, undertaken with the purpose of finding answers or solutions to it. In essence, research provides the necessary information that guides managers to make *informed* decisions to successfully deal with problems. The information provided could be the result of a careful analysis of *primary* data gathered first-hand or of *secondary* data that are already available (in the company, industry, archives, etc.). These data can be *quantitative* (quantitative data are data in the form of numbers as generally gathered through structured questions) or *qualitative* (qualitative data are data in the form of words) as generated from the broad answers to questions in interviews, or from responses to open-ended questions in a questionnaire, or through observation or from already available information gathered from various sources such as the Internet.

RESEARCH AND THE MANAGER

Instructors can visit the companion website at **www.wiley.com/go/bougie/researchmethods forbusiness8e** for **Author Video: Research and the manager.**

An experience common to all organizations is that the managers thereof encounter problems, big and small, on a daily basis, which they have to solve by making the right decisions. In business, research is usually primarily conducted to resolve problematic issues in, or interrelated among, the areas of accounting, finance, management and marketing. In *accounting*, budget control systems, practices and procedures are frequently examined. Inventory costing methods, accelerated depreciation, time-series behaviour of quarterly earnings, transfer pricing, cash recovery rates and taxation methods are some of the other areas that are researched. In *finance*, the operations of financial institutions, optimum financial ratios, mergers and acquisitions, leveraged buyouts, intercorporate financing, yields on mortgages, the behaviour of the stock exchange, the influence of psychology on the behaviour of financial practitioners and the subsequent effect on markets, and the like become the focus of investigation. *Management* research could encompass the study of employee attitudes and behaviours, human resources management, the impact of changing demographics on management practices, production operations management, strategy formulation, information systems and the like. *Marketing* research could address issues pertaining to consumer decision-making, customer satisfaction and loyalty, market segmentation, creating a competitive advantage, product image, advertising, sales promotion, marketing channel management, pricing, new product development and other marketing aspects.

Exhibit 1.1 gives an idea of some commonly researched topical areas in business.

EXHIBIT 1.1 Some Commonly Researched Areas in Business

1. Employee behaviours such as performance, absenteeism and turnover
2. Employee attitudes such as job satisfaction, loyalty and organizational commitment
3. Supervisory performance, managerial leadership style and performance appraisal systems
4. Employee selection, recruitment, training and retention
5. Validation of performance appraisal systems
6. Human resource management choices and organizational strategy
7. Agile organizations
8. The dynamics of rating and rating errors in the judgment of human performance
9. Strategy formulation and implementation
10. Just-in-time systems, continuous-improvement strategies and production efficiencies
11. Updating policies and procedures in keeping with latest government regulations and organizational changes
12. Organizational outcomes such as increased sales, market share, profits, growth and effectiveness
13. Consumer decision-making
14. Customer relationship management
15. Consumer satisfaction, complaints, customer loyalty and word-of-mouth communication
16. Complaint handling
17. Delivering and performing service
18. Product life cycle, new product development and product innovation
19. Market segmentation, targeting and positioning
20. Product image, corporate image
21. Cost of capital, valuation of firms, dividend policies and investment decisions
22. Risk assessment, exchange rate fluctuations and foreign investment
23. Tax implications of reorganization of firms or acquisition of companies
24. Blockchain technology
25. Banking strategies
26. Behavioural finance: overconfidence, bounded rationality and home-bias
27. Executive compensation
28. Mergers and acquisitions
29. Portfolio and asset management
30. Financial reporting
31. Cash flow accounting
32. Accounting standards
33. Outsourcing of accounting

34. Sustainability reporting

35. The implications of social networks on the capital markets

36. Corporate governance

37. Development of effective cost accounting procedures

38. Installation of effective management information systems

39. Advanced manufacturing technologies and information systems

40. Auditor behaviour

41. Approaches and techniques of auditing

42. The use of technology in auditing

43. Decision-making in auditing

44. Installation, adaptation and updation of computer networks and software suitable for creating effective information systems for organizations

45. Installation of an effective data warehouse and data mining system for the organization

46. The acceptance of new computer programs

47. Tax audits

48. Internal auditing

49. Accounting fraud and auditor liability

50. Cryptocurrencies

Not only are the issues within any sub-area related to many factors within that particular system, but they must also be investigated in the context of the external environment facing the business. For example, economic, political, demographic, technological, competitive and other relevant global factors could impinge on some of the dynamics related to the firm. These have to be scrutinized as well to assess their impact, if any, on the problem being researched.

TYPES OF BUSINESS RESEARCH: APPLIED AND BASIC	Research can be undertaken for two different purposes. One is to solve a decision problem faced by the manager in the work setting, demanding a timely solution. For example, a particular product may not be selling well and the manager might want to find the reasons for this to take corrective action. Such research is called **applied research**. The other is to generate a body of knowledge by trying to comprehend how certain problems that occur in organizations can be solved. This is called **basic**, **fundamental** or **pure research**.

It is quite possible that some organizations may, at a later stage, apply the knowledge gained by the findings of basic research to solve their own problems. For instance, a university professor may be interested in investigating the factors that contribute to absenteeism as a matter of mere academic interest. After gathering information on this topic and analysing the data, the professor may identify factors such as inflexible work hours, inadequate training of employees and low morale are primarily influencing absenteeism. Later on, a manager who encounters absenteeism of employees in his organization may use this information to determine if these factors are relevant to that particular work setting.

In sum, research done with the intention of applying the results of the findings to solve specific problems currently being experienced in an organization is called applied research. Research done chiefly to make a contribution to existing knowledge is called basic, fundamental or pure research. The findings of such research contribute to the building of knowledge in the various functional areas of business; they teach us something we did not know before. Such knowledge, once generated, is usually later applied in organizational settings for problem solving.

APPLIED RESEARCH

The following two examples, situations cited in *Businessweek* and *The New York Times*, should provide some idea of the scope of business research activities.

1. Globally, colas account for more than 50% of all sodas sold. The challenge for the $187 billion soft drink industry is giving consumers in developed markets the sugary taste they want without giving them the mouthful of calories they don't. Concerns about obesity and health have led to nine years of falling U.S. soda consumption. The soda giants can't rely on existing diet versions of their namesake colas, as consumers are shying away from the artificial sweeteners they contain. Critics have blamed the ingredients – rightly or not – for everything from weight gain to cancer. Diet Coke is losing U.S. sales at 7% a year, almost double the rate of decline of American cola sales overall. So Coke and Pepsi are turning to research to save their cola businesses, which take in about two-thirds of the industry's U.S. sales. 'If you can crack the perfect sweetener, that would be huge', says Howard Telford, an analyst at researcher Euromonitor International.

Source: Stanford, D. (2015, March 19). *Scientists Are Racing to Build a Better Diet Soda*. Retrieved from http://www.bloomberg.com/news/articles/2015-03-19/coke-pepsi-seek-diet-soda-s-perfect-sweetener

2. In classical mythology, Aquila is the eagle carrying Jupiter's thunderbolts skyward. At Facebook, it is the code name for a high-flying drone, indicative of the social networking company's lofty ambitions. The V-shaped unmanned vehicle, which has about the wingspan of a Boeing 767 but weighs less than a small car, is the centerpiece of Facebook's plans to connect with the 5 billion or so people it has yet to reach. Taking to the skies to beam Internet access down from solar-powered drones may seem like a stretch for a tech company that sells ads to make money. The business model at Facebook, which has 1.4 billion users, has more in common with NBC than Boeing. But in a high-stakes competition for domination of the Internet, in which Google wields high-altitude balloons and high-speed fiber networks and Amazon has experimental delivery drones and colossal data centers, Facebook is under pressure to show that it, too, can pursue projects that are more speculative than product. One of those offbeat ideas, or so the thinking goes, could turn out to be a winner. 'The Amazons, Googles and Facebooks are exploring completely new things that will change the way we live', said Ed Lazowska, who holds the Bill and Melinda Gates Chair in Computer Science and Engineering at the University of Washington.

Source: Hardy, Q. & Goel, V. (2015, March 26). *Drones Beaming Web Access are in the Stars for Facebook*. Retrieved from http://www.nytimes.com/2015/03/26/technology/drones-beaming-web-access-are-in-the-stars-for-facebook.html

These examples illustrate the benefits of applied research. An example of basic or fundamental research is provided next.

BASIC OR FUNDAMENTAL RESEARCH

Right from her days as a clerical employee in a bank, Sarah had observed that her colleagues, though extremely knowledgeable about the nuances and intricacies of banking, were expending very little effort to improve the efficiency and effectiveness of the bank in the area of customer relations and service. They took on the minimum amount of work, availed themselves of long tea and lunch breaks and seemed unmotivated in their dealings with the customers and the management. That they were highly knowledgeable about banking policies and practices was clearly evident from their discussions as they processed applications from customers. Sarah herself was very hardworking and enjoyed her work with the customers. She always used to think what a huge waste it was for talented employees to goof off rather than to work hard and enjoy their work. When she left the bank and did the dissertation for her PhD, her topic of investigation was Job Involvement, or the ego investment of people in their jobs. The conclusion of her investigation was that the single most important contributory factor to job involvement is the fit or match between the nature of the job and the personality predispositions of the people engaged in performing it. For example, challenging jobs allowed employees with high capabilities to get job-involved, and people-oriented employees got job-involved with service activities. Sarah then understood why the highly intelligent bank employees could not get job-involved or find job satisfaction in the routine jobs that rarely called for the use of their abilities.

Subsequently, when Sarah joined the Internal Research Team of a Fortune 500 company, she applied this knowledge to solve problems of motivation, job satisfaction, job involvement and the like in organizations.

The above is an instance of basic research, where knowledge was generated to understand a phenomenon of interest to the researcher. Most research and development departments in various industries, as well as many professors in colleges and universities, do basic or fundamental research so that more knowledge is generated in particular areas of interest to industries, organizations and researchers. Though the objective of engaging in basic research is primarily to equip oneself with additional knowledge of certain phenomena and problems that occur in several organizations and industries with a view to finding solutions, the knowledge generated from such research is often applied later for solving organizational problems.

As stated, the primary purpose of conducting basic research is to generate more knowledge and understanding of the phenomena of interest and to build theories based on the research results. Such theories subsequently form the foundation of further studies on many aspects of the phenomena. This process of building on existing knowledge is the genesis for theory building, particularly in the management area.

Several examples of basic research can be provided. For instance, research into the causes and consequences of global warming will offer many solutions to minimize the phenomenon and lead to further research to determine if and how global warming can be averted. Although research on global warming might primarily be for the purpose of understanding the nuances of the phenomenon, the findings will ultimately be applied and useful to, among others, the agricultural and building industries.

Many large companies, such as Apple, BMW, General Electric, Google, Microsoft and Shell, also engage in basic research. For instance, fundamental research carried out at the German BMW facilities is aimed at further reducing the fleet's greenhouse gas emissions and promoting electromobility innovations. High-tech companies such as Apple, Microsoft, Google and Facebook study online behaviour and interactions to gain insights into how social and technological forces interact. This allows them to build new forms of online experiences around communities of interest and to increase their understanding of how to bring people together.

University professors engage in basic research in an effort to understand and generate more knowledge about various aspects of businesses, such as how to improve the effectiveness of information systems, integrate technology into the overall strategic objectives of an organization, assess the impact of marketing action, increase the productivity of employees in service industries, monitor sexual harassment incidents at the workplace, increase the effectiveness of small businesses, evaluate alternative inventory valuation methods, change the institutional structure of the financial and capital markets and the like. These findings later become useful for application in business situations.

As illustrated, the main distinction between applied and basic business research is that the former is specifically aimed at solving a currently experienced problem within a specific organization, whereas the latter has the broader objective of generating knowledge and understanding of phenomena and problems that occur in various organizational settings. Despite this distinction, both types of research may benefit from targeted and systematic inquiry to arrive at solutions to problems.

WHY MANAGERS NEED TO KNOW ABOUT RESEARCH

In this book, we will primarily focus on applied research. Managers with knowledge of research have an advantage over those without. Though you yourself may not be doing any major research as a manager, you will have to understand, predict and control events that are dysfunctional within the organization. For example, a newly developed product may not be 'taking off', or a financial investment may not be 'paying off' as anticipated. Such disturbing phenomena have to be *understood* and explained. Unless this is done, it will not be possible to *predict* the future of that product or the prospects of that investment and how future catastrophic outcomes can be *controlled*. A grasp of research methods enables managers to understand, predict and control their environment.

A thought that may cross your mind is that, because you will probably be bringing in researchers to solve problems instead of doing the research yourself, there is no need to bother to study research. The reasons for its importance become clear when one considers the consequences of failing to do so. With the ever-increasing complexity of modern organizations, and the uncertainty of the environment they face, the management of organizational systems now involves constant troubleshooting in the workplace. It would help if managers could sense, spot and deal with problems *before* they got out of hand. Knowledge of research and problem-solving processes helps managers to identify problem situations before they get out of control. Although minor problems can be fixed by the manager, major problems warrant the hiring of outside researchers or consultants. The manager who is knowledgeable about research can interact effectively with them. Knowledge about research processes, design and interpretation of data also helps managers to become discriminating recipients of the research findings presented and to determine whether or not the recommended solutions are appropriate for implementation.

Another reason why professional managers today need to know about research methods is that they will become more discriminating while sifting through the information disseminated in business journals. Some journal articles are more scientific and objective than others. Even among the scientific articles, some are more appropriate for application or adaptation to particular organizations and situations than others. This is a function of the sampling design, the types of organizations studied and other factors reported in the journal articles. Unless the manager is able to grasp fully what the published empirical research really conveys, she or he is likely to err in incorporating some of the suggestions such publications offer. By the same token, managers can handle with success their own problems at considerable cost savings by studying the results of published research that has addressed similar issues.

There are several other reasons why professional managers should be knowledgeable about research and research methods in business. First, such knowledge sharpens the sensitivity of managers to the myriad variables operating in a situation and reminds them frequently of the multicausality and multifinality of phenomena, thus avoiding inappropriate, simplistic notions of one variable 'causing' another. Second, when managers understand the research reports about their organizations handed to them by professionals, they are equipped to take intelligent, educated and calculated risks with known probabilities attached to the success or failure of their decisions. Research then becomes a useful decision-making tool rather than generating a mass of incomprehensible statistical information. Third, if managers become knowledgeable about research, vested interests inside or outside the organization will not automatically prevail. For instance, an internal research group within the organization will not be able to distort information or manipulate the findings to their advantage if managers are aware of the biases that can creep into research and know how data are analysed and interpreted. As an example, an internal research team might state that a particular unit to which it is partial (for whatever reason) has shown increased profits and hence should be allocated more resources to buy sophisticated equipment to further enhance its effectiveness. However, the increased profit could have been a one-time windfall phenomenon due to external environmental factors such as market conditions, bearing no relation whatever to the unit's operating efficiency. Thus, awareness of the different ways in which data may be camouflaged will help the manager to make the right decision. Fourth, knowledge about research helps the manager to relate to and share pertinent information with the researcher or consultant hired for problem solving.

In sum, being knowledgeable about research and research methods helps professional managers to:

1. Identify and effectively solve minor problems in the work setting.

2. Know how to discriminate good from bad research.

3. Appreciate and be constantly aware of the multiple influences and multiple effects of factors impinging on a situation.

4. Take calculated risks in decision-making, knowing fully well the probabilities associated with the different possible outcomes.

5. Prevent possible vested interests from exercising their influence in a situation.

6. Relate to hired researchers and consultants more effectively.

7. Combine experience with evidence while making decisions.

THE MANAGER AND THE CONSULTANT–RESEARCHER

Managers often need to engage a consultant to study some of the more complex, time-consuming problems that they encounter, as in the case of Facebook mentioned earlier. It is thus important to be knowledgeable about how to effectively interact with the consultant (the terms researcher and consultant are used interchangeably), what the manager–researcher relationship should be and the advantages and disadvantages of internal versus external consultants.

During their careers, it often becomes necessary for managers to deal with consultants. In such cases, the manager must not only interact effectively with the research team but must also explicitly delineate the roles for the researchers and the management. The manager has to inform the researchers what types of information may be provided to them and, more importantly, which of their records will *not* be made available to them. Such records might include the personnel files of the employees, or certain trade secrets. Making these facts explicit at the very beginning can save a lot of frustration for both parties. Managers who are very knowledgeable about research can more easily foresee what information the researchers might require, and if certain documents containing such information cannot be made available, they can inform the research team about this at the outset. It is vexing for researchers to discover, at a late stage, that the company will not let them have certain information. If they know the constraints right from the beginning, the researchers might be able to identify alternative ways of tackling the problems and to design the research in such a way as to provide the needed answers.

Beyond specifying the roles and constraints, the manager should also make sure that there is congruence in the value systems of management and the consultants. For example, the research team might very strongly believe and recommend that reduction of the workforce and streamlining would be the ideal way to significantly cut down operating costs. Management's consistent philosophy, however, might be *not* to fire employees who are experienced, loyal and senior. Thus, there might be a clash of ideologies between management and the research team. Research knowledge will help managers to identify and explicitly state, even at the outset, the values that the organization holds dear, so that there are no surprises down the road. Clarification of the issue offers the research team the opportunity to either accept the assignment and find alternative ways of dealing with the problem, or regret its inability to undertake the project. In either case, both the organization and the research team will be better off having discussed their value orientations, thus avoiding potential frustration on both sides.

Exchange of information in a straightforward and forthright manner also helps to increase the rapport and trust levels between the two parties, which in turn motivates the two sides to interact effectively. Under this setup, researchers feel free to approach the management to seek assistance in making the research more purposeful. For instance, the research team is likely to request that management inform the employees of the ensuing research and its broad purpose to allay any fears they might entertain.

To summarize, while hiring researchers or consultants the manager should make sure that:

1. The roles and expectations of both parties are made explicit.

2. Relevant philosophies and value systems of the organization are clearly stated and constraints, if any, are communicated.

3. A good rapport is established with the researchers, and between the researchers and the employees in the organization, enabling the full cooperation of the latter.

INTERNAL CONSULTANTS/RESEARCHERS

INTERNAL VERSUS EXTERNAL CONSULTANTS/ RESEARCHERS

Some organizations have their own consulting or research department, which might be called the Management Services Department, the Organization and Methods Department, R&D (research and development department), or some other name. This department serves as the **internal consultant** to subunits of the organization that face certain problems and seek help. Such a unit within the organization, if it exists, is useful in several ways, and enlisting its help might be advantageous under some circumstances, but not others. The manager often has to decide whether to use internal or external researchers. To reach a decision, the manager should be aware of the strengths and weaknesses of both, and weigh the advantages and disadvantages of using either, based on the needs of the situation. Some of the advantages and disadvantages of both internal and external teams are now discussed.

Advantages of Internal Consultants/Researchers

There are at least four advantages in engaging an internal team to do the research project:

1. The internal team stands a better chance of being readily accepted by the employees in the subunit of the organization where research needs to be done.

2. The team requires much less time to understand the structure, the philosophy and climate and the functioning and work systems of the organization.

3. They are available to implement their recommendations after the research findings have been accepted. This is very important because any 'bugs' in the implementation of the recommendations may be removed with their help. They are also available to evaluate the effectiveness of the changes and to consider further changes if and when necessary.

4. The internal team might cost considerably less than an external team for the department enlisting help in problem solving, because they will need less time to understand the system due to their continuous involvement with various units of the organization. For problems of low complexity, the internal team would be ideal.

Disadvantages of Internal Consultants/Researchers

There are also certain disadvantages to engaging internal research teams for the purposes of problem solving. The four most critical ones are:

1. In view of their long tenure as internal consultants, the internal team may quite possibly fall into a stereotyped way of looking at the organization and its problems. This inhibits any fresh ideas and perspectives that might be needed to correct the problem. This is definitely a handicap for situations in which weighty issues and complex problems are to be investigated.

2. There is scope for certain powerful coalitions in the organization to influence the internal team to conceal, distort or misrepresent certain facts. In other words, certain vested interests could dominate, especially in securing a sizable portion of the available scant resources.

3. There is also a possibility that even the most highly qualified internal research teams are not perceived as 'experts' by the staff and management, and hence their recommendations may not get the consideration and attention they deserve.

4. Certain organizational biases of the internal research team might, in some instances, make the findings less objective and consequently less persuasive.

EXTERNAL CONSULTANTS/RESEARCHERS

The disadvantages of the internal research teams turn out to be the advantages of the external teams, and the former's advantages work out to be the disadvantages of the latter. However, the specific advantages and disadvantages of the external teams may be highlighted.

Advantages of External Consultants/Researchers

The advantages of the external team are as follows:

1. The external team can draw on a wealth of experience from having worked with different types of organizations that have had the same or similar types of problems. This wide range of experience enables them to think both divergently and convergently rather than hurry to an instant solution on the basis of the apparent facts in the situation. They are able to ponder over several alternative ways of looking at the problem because of their extensive problem-solving experience in various other organizational setups. Having viewed the situation from several possible angles and perspectives (divergently), they can critically assess each of these, discard the less viable options and alternatives and focus on specific feasible solutions (think convergently).

2. The external teams, especially those from established research and consulting firms, might have more knowledge of current sophisticated problem-solving models through their periodic training programs, which the teams within the organization may not have access to. Because knowledge obsolescence is a real threat in the consulting area, external research institutions ensure that their members are conversant with the latest innovations through periodic organized training programs. The extent to which internal team members are kept abreast of the latest problem-solving techniques may vary considerably from one organization to another.

Disadvantages of External Consultants/Researchers

The major disadvantages in hiring an external research team are as follows:

1. The cost of hiring an external research team is usually high and is the main deterrent, unless the problems are critical.

2. In addition to the considerable time the external team takes to understand the organization being researched, they seldom get a warm welcome, nor are readily accepted by employees. Departments and individuals likely to be affected by the research study may perceive the study team as a threat and resist them. Therefore, soliciting employees' help and enlisting their cooperation in the study is a little more difficult and time-consuming for external researchers than for internal teams.

3. The external team also charges additional fees for their assistance in the implementation and evaluation phases.

Keeping in mind these advantages and disadvantages of internal and external research teams, the manager who desires research services has to weigh the pros and cons of engaging either before making a decision. If the problem is a complex one, or if there are likely to be vested interests, or if the very existence of the organization is at stake because of one or more serious problems, it would be advisable to engage external researchers despite the increased costs involved. However, if the problems that arise are fairly simple, if time is of the essence in solving moderately complex problems, or if there is a system-wide need to establish procedures and policies of a fairly routine nature, the internal team would probably be the better option.

Knowledge of research methods and appreciation of the comparative advantages and disadvantages of external and internal teams help managers to make decisions on how to approach problems and determine whether internal or external researchers are the appropriate choice to investigate and solve the problem.

KNOWLEDGE ABOUT RESEARCH AND MANAGERIAL EFFECTIVENESS

As already mentioned, managers are responsible for the final outcome by making the right decisions at work. This is greatly facilitated by research knowledge. Knowledge of research heightens the sensitivity of managers to the innumerable internal and external factors operating in their work and organizational environment. It also helps to facilitate effective interactions with consultants and comprehension of the nuances of the research process.

In today's world, a multitude of instruments and theories, (big) data, and sophisticated technology is available to model and analyse a wide range of issues such as business processes, consumer behaviour, investment decisions, and the like. The recommendations of the external consultant who is proficient in research and urges the application of particular models, instruments or statistical techniques in a particular situation may make no sense to, and might create some misgivings in, the manager not acquainted with research. Even superficial knowledge of research helps the manager to deal with the consultant/researcher in a mature and confident manner, so that dealing with 'experts' does not result in discomfort. As the manager, *you* will be the one to make the final decision on the implementation of the recommendations made by the research team. Remaining objective, focusing on problem solutions, fully understanding the recommendations made and why and how they have been arrived at, make for good managerial decision-making. Although company traditions are to be respected, there may be occasions where today's rapidly changing turbulent environment demands the substitution or re-adaptation of some of these traditions, based on research findings. Thus, knowledge of research greatly enhances the decision-making skills of the manager.

ETHICS AND BUSINESS RESEARCH

Ethics in business research refers to a code of conduct or expected societal norms of behaviour while conducting research. Ethical conduct applies to the organization and the members that sponsor the research, the researchers who undertake the research and the respondents who provide them with the necessary data. The observance of ethics begins with the person instituting the research, who should do so in good faith, pay attention to what the results indicate and, surrendering the ego, pursue organizational rather than self-interests. Ethical conduct should also be reflected in the behaviour of the researchers who conduct the investigation, the participants who provide the data, the analysts who provide the results and the entire research team that presents the interpretation of the results and suggests alternative solutions.

Thus, ethical behaviour pervades each step of the research process – data collection, data analysis, reporting and dissemination of information on the Internet, if such an activity is undertaken. How the subjects are treated and how confidential information is safeguarded are all guided by business ethics. We will highlight these as they relate to different aspects of research in the relevant chapters of this book.

There are business journals such as the *Journal of Business Ethics* and the *Business Ethics Quarterly* that are mainly devoted to the issue of ethics in business. The American Psychological Association has established certain guidelines for conducting research, to ensure that organizational research is conducted in an ethical manner and the interests of all concerned are safeguarded. As stated, we will discuss the role of ethics in the chapters that follow, insofar as it is relevant to the various steps in the research process.

SUMMARY	• **Learning objective 1: Describe and define business research.** Research is the process of finding solutions to a problem after a targeted and systematic study and analysis of materials and sources. Business research is an organized, systematic, data-based, critical, objective, inquiry or investigation into a specific problem, undertaken with the purpose of finding answers or solutions to it. In essence, business research provides the necessary information that guides managers to make informed decisions to successfully deal with problems. In one form or another, both theory and information play an important role in research.

• **Learning objective 2: Distinguish between applied and basic research, giving examples, and discussing why they fall into one or the other of the two categories.** Research can be undertaken for different purposes. One is to solve a decision problem faced by the manager in the work setting, demanding a timely solution. Such research is called applied research. The other is to generate a body of knowledge by trying to comprehend how certain problems that occur in organizations can be solved. This is called basic, fundamental or pure research. The findings of such research teach us something we did not know before. Such knowledge, once generated, is usually later applied in organizational settings for problem solving.

• **Learning objective 3: Explain why managers should know about research and discuss what managers should and should not do in order to interact effectively with researchers.** Managers with knowledge of research have an advantage over those without. A grasp of research methods enables managers to understand, predict and control their environment and/or to effectively communicate with external researchers or consultants. While hiring external researchers/consultants the manager should ensure that the roles and expectations of both parties are made explicit; relevant philosophies and value systems of the organization are clearly stated and constraints are communicated; and, a good rapport is established with the researchers.

• **Learning objective 4: Identify and fully discuss specific situations in which a manager would be better off using an internal research team, and when an external research team would be more advisable, giving reasons for the decisions.** The manager often has to decide whether to use internal or external researchers. To reach a decision, the manager should be aware of the strengths and weaknesses of both, and weigh the advantages and disadvantages of using either, based on the specific needs of the situation.

• **Learning objective 5: Discuss what research means to you and describe how you, as a manager, might apply the knowledge gained about research.** As the manager, *you* will be the one to make the final decision on the implementation of the recommendations made by the researcher or the research team. Remaining objective, focusing on problem solutions, fully understanding the recommendations made, and why and how they have been arrived at make for good managerial decision-making. Knowledge of research greatly enhances the decision-making skills of the manager.

- **Learning objective 6: Demonstrate awareness of the role of ethics in business research.**   Ethics in business research refers to a code of conduct or expected societal norms of behaviour while conducting research. Ethical conduct applies to the organization and the members that sponsor the research, the researchers who undertake the research and the respondents who provide them with the necessary data. Ethical behaviour pervades each step of the research process. We will highlight these as they relate to different aspects of research in the relevant chapters of this book.

DISCUSSION QUESTIONS

1. Describe a situation where you used research in order to inform thinking, decisions and/or actions in relation to a personal issue of interest such as buying a new mobile phone or going to the movies. Provide information about the purpose of your research, the problem, the information you collected, how you collected this information, the role of theory and the solution to the problem.

2. Why should a manager know about research when the job entails *managing* people, products, events, environments, and the like?

3. For what specific purposes is basic research important?

4. When is applied research, as distinct from basic research, useful?

5. Why is it important to be adept in handling the manager–researcher relationship?

6. Explain, giving reasons, which is more important, applied or basic research.

7. Give two specific instances where an external research team would be useful and two other scenarios when an internal research team would be deployed, with adequate explanations as to why each scenario is justified for an external or internal team.

8. Describe a situation where research will help you as a manager to make a good decision.

9. Given the situations below:
   a. Discuss, with reasons, whether they fall into the category of applied or basic research.
   b. For Scenario 1, explain, with reasons, who will conduct the research.

Scenario 1 To Acquire or Not to Acquire: That Is the Question

Companies are very interested in acquiring other firms, even when the latter operate in totally unrelated realms of business. For example, Coca-Cola has announced that it wants to buy China Huiyuan Juice Group in an effort to expand its activities in one of the world's fastest-growing beverage markets. Such acquisitions are claimed to 'work miracles'. However, given the volatility of the stock market and the slowing down of business, many companies are not sure whether such acquisitions involve too much risk. At the same time, they also wonder if they are missing out on a great business opportunity if they fail to take such risks. Some research is needed here!

Scenario 2 Reasons for Absenteeism

A university professor wanted to analyse in depth the reasons for absenteeism of employees in organizations. Fortunately, a company within 20 miles of the campus employed her as a consultant to study that very issue.

Scenario 3 Effects of Service Recovery on Customer Satisfaction

A research scientist wants to investigate the question: What is the most effective way for an organization to recover from a service failure? Her objective is to provide guidelines for establishing the proper 'fit' between service failure and service recovery that will generalize across a variety of service industries.

CASE	The Laroche Candy Company

In 1864 Henricus Laroche started making high-quality chocolate in his kitchen in Ooigem, Belgium. Henricus learned his trade at a famous chocolate shop in Paris, and he and his wife began to make chocolate in bars, wafers and other shapes soon after Henricus had returned to Belgium to start his own business. The Belgian people loved Laroche's chocolate and the immediate success soon caused him to increase his production facilities. Henricus decided to build a chocolate factory in Kortrijk, a nearby city in the Flemish province West Flanders. With mass-production, the company was able to lower the per-unit costs and to make chocolate, once a luxury item, affordable to everybody. The Laroche Candy Company flourished, expanded its product lines and acquired related companies during the following decades. Within a century, the company had become Belgium's leading candy-manufacturer, employing over 2,500 people.

Today, The Laroche Candy Company is one of the biggest manufacturers of chocolate and non-chocolate confectionery products in Europe. Under the present leadership of Luc Laroche, the company has become truly innovative. What's more, the company has adopted a very proactive approach to marketing planning and is therefore a fierce competitor in an increasingly global marketplace. The number of products the company produces and markets has increased dramatically; at this moment there are more than 250 Laroche Candy items distributed internationally in bulk, bags and boxes.

Luc Laroche, born in 1946, is the fifth generation of his family to lead The Laroche Candy Company. He is the great-great-grandson of company founder Henricus Laroche and the current chairman and CEO of the company. But Luc is nearing retirement. He has planned to stop working in two to three years. Whereas stepping back from power is a very difficult thing to do for a lot of people, it is an easy thing to do for Luc: He is looking forward to spending time with his grandchildren and to driving his Harley-Davidson across Europe. What's more, he has never found the time to play golf, and he is planning to spend 'three whole summers learning it' if necessary. And yet, even though 'letting go' is not a problem for Luc, he still has his worries about his imminent retirement.

As in most family businesses, Luc's two children spent their share of summers working for the company. Luc's oldest son Davy has repeatedly worked for the accounting department, whereas Davy's younger brother Robert has infrequently worked in the field. However, they have never shown a serious interest in the business. Davy, who is 35, currently works as an associate professor of management accounting at a reputable university in Belgium. Robert, aged 32, lives in Paris and has been working as a photographer for the past ten years. About twelve years ago, Robert told his dad, 'I know you'd like me to come into the business, but I've got my own path to travel'. Luc recalls responding that he respects that and that he does not want Robert to feel constrained; 'I just want you to be happy', is what he told Robert on that particular occasion.

Ever since this conversation with Robert, Luc has put his hopes on Davy. A few days ago, Luc invited Davy to have dinner at the famous In de Wulf restaurant in Dranouter, Belgium, to discuss the future of The Laroche Candy Company. He wants to talk about his retirement and a succession plan for the company with Davy, who has serious doubts about taking over the company. Davy knows that for his dad the company is his life and, like his dad, he wants the company to be successful in the future; but he just does not know whether it is a good idea to take over from his father. In an effort to maintain a balanced perspective on the issue, Davy has done some research on it. Hence, he has become very familiar with statistics about the failure rate of family transitions. These statistics have triggered numerous concerns and fears about taking over the company from his father.

Luc and Davy discuss the future of the company during a memorable dinner in Dranouter. Luc tells Davy that he wants his son to take over the company, but Davy explains that he has qualms. He brings up his doubts and fears and alternatives such as going public, selling to a strategic acquirer or investor, or selling to employees through an employee stock ownership plan. Luc hardly listens to Davy's concerns and strikes a blow for family business.

'History is full of examples of spectacular ascents of family business', he said after the waiter has refilled his glass for the fourth time in just over an hour, 'the Rothschilds, the Murdochs, the Waltons and the Vanderbilts, to name only a few. The Rothschilds, for instance, not only accumulated the largest amount of private wealth the Western world has ever seen, they also changed the course of history by financing kings and monarchs. Did you know that they supported Wellington's armies, which ultimately led to the defeat of Napoleon at Waterloo? I bet you didn't'.

Davy raised an eyebrow. 'I didn't. But what I do know', he replied, 'is that only fifty years after the death of Cornelius Vanderbilt, who created a fortune in railroads and shipping, several of his direct descendants were flat broke. Apparently the Vanderbilts had both a talent for acquiring and spending money in unmatched numbers. Seriously, dad, I do believe that strong family values are very important but I also feel that they may place restraints on the development of the company. It is commonly known that familism in Southern Italy is one of the main reasons for the slower economic development of the south relative to the north'.

Luc sighed and looked at his son. 'So, what does this all mean?'

'Well, I think that the key question is whether family firms evolve as an efficient response to the institutional and market environment, or whether they are an outcome of cultural norms that might be harmful for corporate decisions and economic outcomes', Davy replied with a gentle smile. 'Don't you think so?'

'I . . . um . . . I guess I do'. Luc smiled back at his son. 'I am not sure that I understand what you mean, but it sounds great. Let's throw some money at it and hire a consultant who knows something about this. I'll call McKinsey first thing tomorrow morning. Cheers'.

'Cheers dad', Davy echoed lifting his glass.

Two weeks later, Paul Thomas Anderson, a senior McKinsey consultant, put forward the following problem statement in a meeting with Luc Laroche: What are the implications of family control for the governance, financing, and overall performance of The Laroche Candy Company?

CASE QUESTIONS

1. What is business research?

2. Why is the project that Mr. Anderson is doing for The Laroche Candy Company a *research* project?

3. Which steps will the consultant take now that he has clearly defined the problem that needs attention?

4. Luc Laroche has decided to hire an external consultant to investigate the problem. Do you think that this is a wise decision or would it have been better to ask his son Davy or an internal consultant to do the research project?

5. What can (or should) Luc do to assist Mr. Anderson to yield valuable research results?

6. How can basic or fundamental research help Mr. Anderson to solve the specific problem of The Laroche Candy Company?

7. Try to find relevant books, articles and research reports relating to this issue. Use, among others, electronic resources of your library and/or the Internet.

CHAPTER 2

The Scientific Approach and Alternative Approaches to Investigation

LEARNING OBJECTIVES

After completing Chapter 2, you should be able to:

1. Explain what is meant by scientific investigation, giving examples of both scientific and non-scientific investigations.

2. Discuss the seven steps of the hypothetico-deductive method, using an example of your own.

3. Discuss alternative perspectives on what makes good research.

INTRODUCTION

Managers frequently face issues that call for critical decision-making. Managerial decisions based on the results of 'good' research tend to be effective. In Chapter 1, we defined research as the process of finding solutions to a problem after a targeted and systematic study and analysis of materials and sources. In this chapter, we will focus on what makes 'good' research. For many people, good research is scientific in nature. That is why both basic and applied research are often carried out in a *scientific* way. It is therefore important to understand what the term scientific means. Scientific research focuses on solving problems and pursues a step-by-step logical, organized and rigorous method to identify the problems, gather data, analyse them and draw valid conclusions from them. Thus, scientific research is not based on hunches, experience and intuition (though these may play a part in final decision-making), but is purposive and rigorous. Because of the rigorous way in which it is done, scientific research enables all those who are interested in researching and knowing about the same or similar issues to come up with comparable findings when the data are analysed. Scientific research also helps researchers to state their findings with accuracy and confidence. Furthermore, **scientific investigation** tends to be more objective than subjective.

Do researchers always take a scientific approach to research? No. Sometimes, researchers have a different perspective on what makes good research and how research should be done. We will have more to say about this later in this chapter. In an applied research context, the scientific method, which is aimed at testing hypotheses (as we will explain later on in this chapter) does not necessarily pertain to the problem that has set off the research process. For instance, if a manager simply wants to know how satisfied employees are with their jobs, and thus simply wants to *describe* a phenomenon (job satisfaction), hypothesis testing is irrelevant. In some cases, managers may even reject the idea of doing research completely, for instance, because the problem is so simple that it does not call for elaborate research, and past experience might offer the necessary solution (we will have more to say about different types of problems that do and do not call for research in Chapter 3). Finally, exigencies of time (where quick decisions are called for), unwillingness to expend the resources needed for doing good research, lack of knowledge and other factors might prompt businesses to try to solve problems based on hunches. However, the probability of making wrong decisions in such cases is high. Even such business 'gurus' as Richard Branson and Steve Jobs have confessed to making big mistakes due to errors of judgment. *Business week*, *Fortune* and the *Wall Street Journal*, among other business periodicals and newspapers, feature articles from time to time about organizations that face difficulties because of wrong decisions made on the basis of hunches and/or insufficient information. Many implemented plans fail because not enough research has preceded their formulation. Let us now take a closer look at scientific research.

The hallmarks or main distinguishing characteristics of scientific research may be listed as follows:

THE HALL-MARKS OF SCIENTIFIC RESEARCH

1. Purposiveness
2. Rigor
3. Testability
4. Replicability
5. Precision and confidence
6. Objectivity
7. Generalizability
8. Parsimony

Each of these characteristics can be explained in the context of a concrete example. Let us consider the case of a manager who is interested in investigating how employees' commitment to the organization can be increased. We shall examine how the eight hallmarks of science apply to this investigation so that it may be considered 'scientific'.

PURPOSIVENESS

The manager has started the research with a definite aim or purpose. The focus is on increasing the commitment of employees to the organization, as this will be beneficial in many ways. An increase in employee commitment will translate into lower turnover, less absenteeism and probably increased performance levels, all of which will definitely benefit the organization. The research thus has a *purposive* focus.

RIGOR

A good theoretical base and a sound methodological design add **rigor** to a purposive study. Rigor connotes carefulness, scrupulousness and the degree of exactitude in research investigations. In the case of our example, let us say the manager of an organization asks 10 to 12 of its employees to indicate what would increase their level of commitment to it. If, solely on the basis of their responses, the manager reaches several conclusions on how employee commitment can be increased, the whole approach to the investigation is unscientific. It lacks rigor for the following reasons:

1. The conclusions are based on the responses of just a few employees whose opinions may not be representative of those of the entire workforce.
2. The manner of framing and addressing the questions could have introduced bias or incorrectness in the responses.
3. There might be many other important influences on organizational commitment that this small sample of respondents did not or could not verbalize during the interviews, and the researcher has therefore failed to include them.

Therefore, conclusions drawn from an investigation that lacks a good theoretical foundation, as evidenced by reason 3, and methodological sophistication, as evident from 1 and 2, are unscientific. Rigorous research involves a good theoretical base and a carefully thought-out methodology. These factors enable the researcher to collect the right kind of information from an appropriate sample with the minimum degree of bias and facilitate suitable analysis of the data gathered. The following chapters of this book address these theoretical and methodological issues.

TESTABILITY

Testability is a property that applies to the hypotheses of a study. In Chapter 6, we will define a **hypothesis** as a tentative, yet testable, statement, which predicts what you expect to find in your empirical data. Hypotheses are derived from theory, which is based on the logical beliefs of the researcher and on (the results of) previous research – we will have more to say about these matters in Chapter 6.

A scientific hypothesis must be *testable*. Not all hypotheses can be tested. Non-testable hypotheses are often vague statements, or they put forward something that cannot be tested experimentally. A famous example of a hypothesis that is not testable is the hypothesis that God created the earth.

If, after talking to a random selection of employees of the organization and study of the previous research done in the area of organizational commitment, the manager or researcher develops certain hypotheses on how employee commitment can be enhanced, then these can be tested by applying certain statistical tests to the data collected for the purpose. For instance, the researcher might hypothesize that those employees who perceive greater opportunities for participation in decision-making will have a higher level of commitment. This is a hypothesis that can be tested when the data are collected.

Scientific research thus lends itself to testing logically developed hypotheses to see whether or not the data support the educated conjectures or hypotheses that are developed after a careful study of the problem situation. **Testability** thus becomes another hallmark of scientific research.

REPLICABILITY

Replication is made possible by a detailed description of the design details of the study, such as the sampling method and the data collection methods that were used. This information should create the possibility to replicate the research. Replicability is the extent to which a restudy is made possible by the provision of the design details of the study in the research report. **Replicability** is another hallmark of scientific research.

PRECISION AND CONFIDENCE

In management research, we seldom have the luxury of being able to draw 'definitive' conclusions on the basis of the results of data analysis. This is because we are unable to study the universe of items, events or population we are interested in, and have to base our findings on a sample that we draw from the universe. In all probability, the sample in question may not reflect the exact characteristics of the phenomenon we are trying to study (these difficulties are discussed in greater detail in Chapter 14). Measurement errors and other problems are also bound to introduce an element of bias or error in our findings. However, we would like to design the research in a manner that ensures that our findings are as close to reality (i.e., the true state of affairs in the universe) as possible, so that we can place reliance or confidence in the results.

Precision refers to the closeness of the findings to 'reality' based on a sample. In other words, precision reflects the degree of accuracy or exactitude of the results on the basis of the sample, to what really exists in the universe. For example, if I estimated the number of production days lost during the year due to absenteeism at between 30 and 40, as against the actual figure of 35, the precision of my estimation compares more favourably than if I had indicated that the loss of production days was somewhere between 20 and 50. You may recall the term *confidence interval* in statistics, which is what is referred to here as precision.

Confidence refers to the probability that our estimations are correct. That is, it is not merely enough to be precise, but it is also important that we can confidently claim that 95 percent of the time our results will be true and there is only a 5 percent chance of our being wrong. This is also known as the *confidence level*.

The narrower the limits within which we can estimate the range of our predictions (i.e., the more precise our findings) and the greater the confidence we have in our research results, the more useful and scientific the findings become. In social science research, a 95 percent confidence level – which implies that there is only a 5 percent probability that the findings may *not* be correct – is accepted as conventional, and is usually referred to as a significance level of 0.05 ($p = 0.05$). Thus, precision and confidence are important aspects of research, which are attained through appropriate scientific sampling design. The greater the precision and confidence we aim at in our research, the more scientific is the investigation and the more useful are the results. Both precision and confidence are discussed in detail in Chapter 14 on Sampling.

OBJECTIVITY

The conclusions drawn through the interpretation of the results of data analysis should be as objective as possible; that is, they should be based on the facts of the findings derived from actual data, and not on our own subjective or emotional values. For instance, if we had a hypothesis that stated that greater participation in decision-making would increase organizational commitment, and this was not supported by the results, it would make no sense if the researcher continued to argue that increased opportunities for employee participation would still help! Such an argument would be based not on the factual, data-based research findings, but on the subjective opinion of the researcher. If this was the researcher's conviction all along, then there was no need to do the research in the first place!

The more objective the interpretation of the data, the more scientific the research investigation becomes. Though managers or researchers might start with some initial subjective values and beliefs, their interpretation of the data should be stripped of personal values and bias. If managers attempt to do their own research, they should be particularly sensitive to this aspect. **Objectivity** is thus another hallmark of scientific investigation.

GENERALIZABILITY

Generalizability refers to the scope of applicability of the research findings in one organizational setting to other settings. Obviously, the wider the range of applicability of the solutions generated by research, the more useful the research is to different types of users. However, not many *applied* research findings can be generalized to other settings, situation or organizations.

PARSIMONY

Simplicity in explaining the phenomena or problems that occur, and in generating solutions for the problems, is always preferred to complex research frameworks that consider an unmanageable number of factors. For instance, if two or three specific variables in the work situation are identified, which when changed would raise the organizational commitment of the employees by

45 percent, that would be more useful and valuable to the manager than if it were recommended that he should change ten different variables to increase organizational commitment by 48 percent. Such an unmanageable number of variables might well be totally beyond the manager's control to change. Therefore, the achievement of a meaningful and parsimonious, rather than an elaborate and cumbersome, model for problem solution becomes a critical issue in research.

Economy in research models is achieved when we can build into our research framework a lesser number of variables that explain the variance far more efficiently than a complex set of variables that only marginally add to the variance explained. **Parsimony** can be introduced with a good understanding of the problem and the important factors that influence it. Such a good conceptual theoretical model can be realized through unstructured and structured interviews with the concerned people, and a thorough literature review of the previous research work in the particular problem area.

THE HYPOTHETICO-DEDUCTIVE METHOD	Scientific research pursues a step-by-step, logical, organized and rigorous method (a scientific method) to find a solution to a problem. The *scientific method* was developed in the context of the natural sciences, where it has been the foundation of many important discoveries. Although there have been numerous objections to this method and to using it in social and business research (we will discuss some of these later in this chapter), it is still the predominant approach for generating knowledge in natural, social and business sciences. The hypothetico-deductive method, popularized by the Austrian philosopher Karl Popper, is a typical version of the scientific method. The hypothetico-deductive method provides a systematic approach for generating knowledge to solve basic and managerial problems. This systematic approach is discussed next.

THE SEVEN-STEP PROCESS IN THE HYPOTHETICO-DEDUCTIVE METHOD

The **hypothetico-deductive method** involves the seven steps listed and discussed next.

1. Observation
2. Preliminary information gathering
3. Theory formulation
4. Hypothesizing
5. Data collection
6. Data analysis
7. Interpretation of data

Observation

A drop in sales, frequent production interruptions, incorrect accounting results, low-yielding investments, disinterestedness of employees in their work, customer switching and the like could attract the attention of the manager and catalyse the research project. A problem is defined and research questions are developed.

Preliminary Information Gathering

Preliminary information gathering involves the seeking of information in depth, of what is observed (for instance, the observation that our company is losing customers). This could be done by a literature review (literature on customer switching) or by talking to several people in the work setting, to clients (why do they switch?), or to other relevant sources, thereby gathering information on what is happening and why. Through any of these methods, we get an idea or a 'feel' for what is transpiring in the situation. This allows us to develop a theory on (or in other words, an explanation for) what is happening.

Theory Formulation

In this step, variables are examined to ascertain their contribution or influence in explaining why the problem occurs and how it can be solved. The network of associations identified among the variables is then theoretically woven, together with justification as to why they might influence the problem. From a theorized network of associations among the variables, certain hypotheses or educated conjectures can be generated.

Hypothesizing

For instance, at this point, we might hypothesize that specific factors such as overpricing, competition, inconvenience and unresponsive employees affect customer switching.

A scientific hypothesis must meet two requirements. The first criterion is that the hypothesis must be *testable*. We have discussed the testability of hypotheses earlier in this chapter. The second criterion, and one of the central tenets of the hypothetico-deductive method, is that a hypothesis must also be *falsifiable*. That is, it must be possible to disprove the hypothesis. According to Karl Popper, this is important because a hypothesis cannot be confirmed; there is always a possibility that future research will show that it is false. Hence, failing to falsify (!) a hypothesis does not prove that hypothesis: it remains provisional until it is disproved. Hence, the requirement of falsifiability emphasizes the tentative nature of research findings: we can only 'prove' our hypotheses until they are disproved.

The development of hypotheses and the process of theory formulation are discussed in greater detail in Chapter 6.

Data Collection

After we have developed our hypotheses, data with respect to each variable in the hypothesis need to be obtained. These data then form the basis for data analysis. Data collection is extensively discussed in Chapters 8 to 13.

Data Analysis

In the data analysis step, the data gathered are statistically analysed to see if the hypotheses that were generated have been supported. For instance, to see if unresponsiveness of employees affects customer switching, we might want to do a correlational analysis to determine the relationship between these variables.

Hypotheses are tested through appropriate statistical analysis, as discussed in Chapter 16.

Interpretation of Data

Now we must decide whether our hypotheses are supported or not by interpreting the meaning of the results of the data analysis. For instance, if it was found from the data analysis that increased responsiveness of employees was negatively related to customer switching (say, 0.3), then we can deduce that if customer retention is to be increased, our employees have to be trained to be more responsive. Another inference from this data analysis is that responsiveness of our employees accounts for (or explains) 9 percent of the variance in customer switching (0.3^2). Based on these deductions, we are able to make recommendations on how the 'customer switching' problem may be solved (at least to some extent); we have to train our employees to be more flexible and communicative.

REVIEW OF THE HYPOTHETICO-DEDUCTIVE METHOD

The hypothetico-deductive method involves the seven steps of identifying a observation, preliminary data gathering, theory formulation, hypothesizing, data collection, data analysis and the interpretation of the results. The scientific method uses **deductive research** to *test a theory* (to a scientist, a theory is an organized set of assumptions that generates testable predictions) about a topic of interest. In deductive research, we work from the more general to the more specific. We start out with a general *theory* and then narrow down that theory into specific hypotheses we can test. We narrow down even further when we collect specific *observations* to test our hypotheses. Analysis of these specific observations ultimately allows us to confirm (or refute) our original theory.

Inductive research works in the opposite direction: it is a process where we observe specific phenomena and on this basis arrive at general conclusions. Hence, in inductive research, we work from the more specific to the more general. The observation of a first, second and third white swan (this is a very famous example) may lead to the proposition that 'all swans are white'. In this example, the repeated observation of a white swan has led to the general conclusion that all swans are white. According to Karl Popper it is not possible to 'disprove' a hypothesis by means of *induction*, because no amount of evidence assures us that contrary evidence will not be found. Observing 3, 10, 100 or even 10,000 white swans does not justify the conclusion that 'all swans are white' because there is always a possibility that the next swan we observe will be black. That is why Popper proposed that (proper) science is accomplished by *deduction*.

However, despite Popper's criticism on induction, both inductive and deductive processes are often used in both fundamental and applied research. Indeed, many researchers have argued that theory generation (induction) *and* theory testing (deduction) are essential parts of the research process.

Induction and deduction are often used in a sequential manner. John Dewey describes this process as 'the double movement of reflective thought'. Induction takes place when a researcher observes something and asks, 'Why does this happen?' In answer to this question, the researcher may develop a provisional explanation – a hypothesis. Deduction is subsequently used to test this hypothesis. The following example illustrates this process.

This example shows how inductive and deductive processes can be applied in a research project. Although both deductive and inductive processes can be used in quantitative and qualitative research, deductive processes are more often used in causal and quantitative studies, whereas inductive research processes are regularly used in exploratory and qualitative studies.

Example	A manager may notice that frequent price promotions of a product have a negative effect on product sales. Based on this observation, the manager may wonder why price promotions have a negative – instead of a positive – effect on sales. Interviews with customers indicate that frequent price promotions have a negative effect on sales because frequent price promotions negatively affect the reputation or image of the product. Based on these interviews, the manager develops a new theory about why price promotions have a negative effect on sales – because frequent price promotions have a negative effect on the reputation of the product! Accordingly, the manager hypothesizes that frequent price promotions negatively affect the reputation of the product and hence product sales. The manager may verify this hypothesis by means of deduction.

ALTERNATIVE APPROACHES TO RESEARCH	Instructors can visit the companion website at **www.wiley.com/go/bougie/researchmethods forbusiness8e** for **Author Video: Alternative approaches to research**.

Following a scientific approach to research should help the researcher to get to the truth about the subject of the research. But is there such a thing as *the* truth? Or is the truth subjective; something that we have only constructed in our minds? All research is based on beliefs about the world around us (the philosophical study of what can be said to exist is called **ontology**) and what we can possibly discover by research. Different researchers have different ideas about these issues.

The disagreement about the nature of knowledge or how we come to know (the appropriate name for these matters is **epistemology**) has a long history and it is not restricted to research in business. Questions such as 'What exists?', 'What is knowledge?' and 'How do we acquire knowledge?' have fascinated philosophers and researchers in many fields for over 2,000 years. At this point, we will briefly discuss the most important perspectives for contemporary research in business. We will successively deal with **positivism**, **constructionism**, **critical realism** and **pragmatism**. Note that in order to make our point we will sometimes exaggerate the descriptions of these research perspectives. For this reason, experts on these matters may sometimes disapprove on what we have to say.

POSITIVISM

In a *positivist* view of the world, science and scientific research is seen as the way to get at *the* truth – indeed, positivists believe that there is an objective truth out there – to understand the world well enough so that we are able to predict and control it. For a positivist, the world operates by laws of cause and effect that we can discern if we use a *scientific approach* to research. Positivists are concerned with the rigor and replicability of their research, the reliability of observations and the generalizability of findings. They carry out deductive research by putting forward theories that they can test by means of a fixed, predetermined research design and objective measures. The key approach of positivist researchers is the experiment, which allows them to test cause-and-effect relationships through manipulation and observation. Some positivists believe that the goal of research is to only describe phenomena that one can directly observe and objectively measure. For them, knowledge of anything beyond that – such as emotions, feelings and thoughts – is impossible.

CONSTRUCTIONISM

A completely different approach to research and how research should be done is constructionism. Constructionism criticizes the positivist belief that there is an objective truth. Constructionists hold the opposite view, namely that the world (as we know it!) is fundamentally mental or mentally constructed. For this reason, constructionists do not search for the objective truth. Instead, they aim to understand the rules people use to make sense of the world by investigating what happens in people's minds. Constructionism thus emphasizes how people construct knowledge; it studies the accounts people give of issues and topics and how people get to these accounts. Constructionists are particularly interested in how people's views of the world result from interactions with others and the context in which they take place. The research methods of constructionist researchers are often qualitative in nature. Focus groups and unstructured interviews allow them to collect rich data, oriented to the contextual uniqueness of the world that is being studied. Indeed, constructionists are often more concerned with understanding a specific case than with the generalization of their findings. This makes sense from the viewpoint of the constructionist; there is no objective reality to generalize about.

CRITICAL REALISM

Between these two opposed views on research and on how research should be done, there are many intermediary viewpoints. One of these viewpoints is critical realism. Critical realism is a combination of the belief in an external reality (an objective truth) with the rejection of the claim that this external reality can be objectively measured; observations (especially observations on phenomena that we cannot observe and measure directly, such as satisfaction, motivation, culture) will always be subject to interpretation. The critical realist is thus *critical* of our ability to understand the world with certainty. Where a positivist believes that the goal of research is to uncover the truth, the critical realist believes that the goal of research is to progress towards this goal, even though it is impossible to reach it. According to the critical realist viewpoint, measures of phenomena such as emotions, feelings and attitudes are often subjective in nature and the collection of data is, generally speaking, imperfect and flawed. The critical realist also believes that researchers are inherently biased. They argue that we therefore need to use *triangulation* across multiple flawed and erroneous methods, observations and researchers to get a better idea of what is happening around us.

PRAGMATISM

A final viewpoint on research that we will discuss here is pragmatism. Pragmatists do not take on a particular position on what makes good research. They feel that research on both objective, observable phenomena and subjective meanings can produce useful knowledge, depending on the problem that initiated the study. The focus of pragmatism is on practical, applied research where different viewpoints on research and the subject under study are helpful in solving a (business) problem. Pragmatism describes research as a process where concepts and meanings (theory) are generalizations of our past actions and experiences and of interactions we have had with our environment. Pragmatists thus emphasize the socially constructed nature of research; different researchers may have different ideas about, and explanations for, what is happening around us. For the pragmatist, these different perspectives, ideas and theories help us to gain an understanding of the world; pragmatism thus endorses *eclecticism* and *pluralism*. Another important feature of pragmatism is that it views the current truth as *tentative* and changing over time. In other words, research results should always be viewed as provisional truths. Pragmatists stress the relationship between theory and practice. For a pragmatist, theory is derived from practice (as we have just explained) and then applied back to practice to achieve *intelligent* practice. Along these lines, pragmatists see theories and concepts as important tools for finding our way in the world that surrounds us. For a pragmatist, the value of research lies in its practical relevance; the purpose of theory is to inform practice.

A PRAGMATIC APPROACH TO RESEARCH

Although the scientific method has laid the foundation for many great discoveries in the past and the present, it is not *necessarily* the most suitable method in an *applied* research context. An important reason for this is that in many cases, managers and researchers are not interested in testing hypotheses in a research project that is aimed at solving a problem in a work setting. This is because very often (some people say more often than not) the problem of the client organization does not call for causal research, but for other types of research – research that is exploratory or descriptive in nature (exploratory, descriptive and causal research are discussed in Chapter 4 of this book). For instance, if a manager wants to know what percentage of the population prefers a Samsung mobile phone over an iPhone or a Huawei, or how customers make decisions, or how competitors position their products in the market or how satisfied employees of the organization are with their work, causal research – research that aims to explain and thus to understand whether or not certain variables produce changes in other variables – does not apply.

Another point that may help to explain why some researchers are taking a different approach to research than a scientific approach is related to the idea of 'good' research. It goes without saying that applied research should be 'good'; if the information that the researcher collects is not 'good' (accurate, reliable, representative for the population and valid), the conclusions of the researcher *cannot* be good (or valid) and the recommendations provided to the client organization will, in all probability, be misleading. However, taking a scientific approach to good research may turn out to be problematic in many cases. If the research project is exploratory or descriptive in nature, many hallmarks of scientific research, such as *testability* and *precision and confidence*, do not (necessarily) apply for obvious reasons (one does not test any hypotheses). Earlier in this chapter, we have already explained why another hallmark of scientific research, *generalizability*, also does not necessarily apply when research is aimed at solving a specific problem in a work setting. That is why many researchers feel that in an applied research context, the scientific approach does not always provide clear guidance on shaping the research effort. In those cases, the researcher may benefit from taking a different approach to good research to make sure that the research project is targeted, systematic, organized, logical and rigorous. A *pragmatic approach* is often used to help the researcher to produce useful knowledge that informs thinking, decision-making and/or actions of managers. From a pragmatic perspective, the research effort is closely related to the type of problem that has triggered the research process, as we will detail next.

RESEARCH IN ORGANIZATIONS

One way to look at a business is as a collection of three principal activities: intelligence, operations and strategy development. *Intelligence* amounts to any activity devoted to the collection or depiction of information for use in operational or strategic decisions. *Operations* relates to the current focus of a business, including manufacturing, finance, marketing programs and the like. *Strategy development* includes activities such as research & development and long-range planning. Research is often needed to serve the information needs of both operations and strategy development. For instance, monitoring phenomena such as customer satisfaction, sales and market share provide managers with data for evaluating programmes, products and services. More sophisticated research might apply to the evaluation of alternative programmes (such as testing alternative operating procedures, websites or advertising campaigns). The most ambitious types of research are related to organizational change and the creation of new business opportunities, discussed next.

'FIXING SITUATIONS THAT ARE BROKEN'; ORGANIZATIONAL CHANGE

A change process is often set in motion when a manager notices that the existing situation is not in line with a desired situation or with a certain norm or standard. When this is the case, a manager has an *action problem*. An *action problem* is called an action problem because (in the end) there is only one way to solve the problem: to take action. In other words, an intervention to fix the situation is needed. Let us, before discussing the role of research in these situations, present some examples of action problems to provide you with a feel for what an action problem is.

- Staff turnover is much higher (14 percent) than the average staff turnover (6 percent) in the industry. This bothers the manager because staff turnover results in a loss of experienced employees. What's more, turnover negatively affects productivity, brings about extra costs (such as replacement costs) and leads to less profits. That is why the manager wants to reduce staff turnover.

- Customers are not satisfied with the services of the organization. A manager finds this problematic because dissatisfied customers engage in negative word-of-mouth communication and switching behaviour. For these reasons, the manager wants to improve customer satisfaction.

- The company's market share is lower than required. This precludes the organization to benefit from economies of scale, brand-name dominance and greater bargaining power with suppliers, distributors and customers. The manager wants to increase the company's market share.

- An audit has revealed that the organization is not in control. This is problematic because organizational activities are inconsistent, ineffective and inefficient. The manager wants to regain control.

In the above situations, the organization (business unit, department) is in some kind of trouble and the manager needs to find a way out. Changes are needed. A manager should take care of an undesirable and, sometimes, complicated situation. With the existing situation (for instance, 14 percent staff turnover) as a starting point, the manager needs to develop an organizational objective (for instance, 6 percent staff turnover). In order to achieve this objective, the manager eventually needs to intervene, to take action and to fix the problem. In this action stage, relevant issues must be improved. The idea is that the actions taken solve the problem and do not lead to the recurrence of the problem identified or create new problems; if they do, the actions haven't been effective.

An obvious question that you may have at the moment is: what has *research* got to do with the aforementioned situations? The answer is not too difficult: when the manager wants to reach a specific objective (think for instance, 6 percent staff turnover), *but does not know how* he or she can (best) reach this objective, research is needed. Such research is generally aimed at finding solutions to the problem or at finding the most effective solution to the problem. Along these lines, research informs the manager about the actions that can be taken or about which specific actions are more effective than other actions to solve the problem. This type of research is called *action-oriented research* (not to be confused with action research).

BOX 2.1	A NOTE ON THE NECESSITY OF ACTION-ORIENTED RESEARCH

Notice that action-oriented research is not *always* needed when the existing situation is not in line with the desired situation or with a certain norm or standard. Sometimes the solution to the problem is clear as soon as the problem has been identified; in such cases the manager – or an expert commissioned by the manager – will be able to solve the problem *without* having to engage in (action-oriented) research. The problem is a routine problem and the manager – or the expert – has enough knowledge and experience to solve the problem. Such problems are called *technical* or *routine problems*. We will have more to say about different types of action problems, including technical problems, in the next chapter.

In sum, if the managerial (action) problem is clear but the solution to the problem is not (because the solution is not straightforward or it is unclear what is the most effective solution to the problem), further research is needed. After the management problem has been identified, the manager has an *information problem* (because he or she does not *know* how to effectively rectify the situation). This is where research comes in.

BOX 2.2	MANAGERS OFTEN HAVE A NOSE FOR PROBLEMS

Managers are often very sensitive to situations that are undesirable or to situations where information about something important is needed. Triggers coming from others (clients, employees, the boss) or from situations beyond one's control (such as new regulations affecting the organization) may also bring an issue to the manager's attention.

CREATING NEW BUSINESS OPPORTUNITIES

The foregoing section illustrated how many organizational problems are imposed on managers from the outside. Consumer preferences are changing, new entrants are coming into the market, regulations are changing and the like. As a consequence, the market share of the organization might be dropping or the sales figures of the organization might be moving downwards; an action problem manifests itself. But there is no law that states that managers must wait for problems to be forced upon them. *They* can take the initiative and create new opportunities *before* a problem even arises. Along these lines, a second situation that often calls for more complex research can be created – a situation where managers create their own decision problems.

For instance:

- A manager is thinking about entering a certain market. However, it is unclear whether entering this market is a wise decision. That is why the manager wants to know the long-term profitability of that specific market.

- A manager wants to introduce a new product to the market. In order to make a decision on whether and how to introduce the product in the market, she is interested in consumer decision-making. She wants to know who the potential customers are, what they buy, why, where and how they buy and so on.

- A manager wants to make a decision on how, when, where and how much capital will be spent on investment opportunities. That is why she is interested in determining the costs and returns for each option.

- A manager is thinking about repositioning a product tightly around a unique product benefit in a particular segment. However, it is unclear what the needs and wants of (potential) customers in that particular segment are and how these consumers make buying decisions. That is why it is unclear whether it is a smart move to reposition the product.

What the above cases have in common is that – in contrast to situations where organizations have an action problem – everything is still good. There is no loss in market share, no high employee turnover and no large proportion of dissatisfied customers. Instead, the managers in the above examples are *proactively* looking for decision opportunities. Instead of waiting for a situation that is imposed upon them, they are taking the initiative. For a variety of reasons (see Box 2.3), research is often a logical first step in the above situations.

BOX 2.3	**DIFFERENT REASONS TO COLLECT INFORMATION**

1. For decision-making
   a. Appropriate use (evidence-based decision-making)
   b. Inappropriate/biased use (selective use of information to support position)

2. To obtain knowledge
   a. About a phenomenon (long-term profitability, employee motivation, customer satisfaction, risk aversion)
   b. About a process (market entry, manufacturing process, customer decision-making)

3. For political purposes

   a. Include others in decision process/change process
   b. Tradition/policy
   c. Signal importance
   d. Impress others

4. To increase comfort
   a. Reduce uncertainty about a decision
   b. Feeling that one has done a thorough job

Menon and Varadarajan (1992) thus make a distinction between use for decision-making versus use for the decision-maker (gain knowledge, political purposes, increase comfort).

In sum, we have presented two (often rather complex) situations that may (or may not) call for applied research: (1) situations where a manager feels that the existing situation is not in line with a desired situation or standard or norm (and sees this as problematic) and (2) a situation where a manager is proactively looking for decision opportunities. Next, we want to introduce two slightly different but nonetheless related processes that managers and researchers may go through in both situations in order to make effective decisions. Since the process in the first situation (the manager is in trouble and needs to find a way out) is somewhat more sophisticated than the process in the second situation (the manager is proactively looking for decision opportunities), we will focus on the process of the first situation in the next sections. The boxes exemplify the second situation, where a manager is proactively looking for business opportunities.

THE INITIAL STAGES: THE MANAGER STARTS EXPLORING

A manager noticed that staff turnover has increased over the last few years. However, it is not clear to the manager whether the situation is problematic; in other words, the exact nature and size of the problem is unclear to the manager. Based on available or easily obtainable information and/or an initial exchange of ideas with (a selection of) stakeholders, the manager aims to provide an answer to the question of whether the discomfort with the existing situation should lead to further action. Based on this *exploration stage*, the manager may decide to reappraise the situation; to re-interpret the situation and accept it as it is. Alternatively, the manager may decide to make a project out of it.

| Example | A sales manager might observe that customers are perhaps not as pleased as they used to be. The manager may not be certain that this is really the case but may experience uneasiness among consumers and observe that the number of customer complaints has increased recently. This process of observation or sensing of the phenomena around us is what gets most research – whether applied or basic – started. The next step for the manager is to determine whether there is a real problem and, if so, how serious it is. This problem identification calls for some exploration. The manager might talk casually to a few customers to find out how they feel about the products and customer service. During the course of these conversations the manager might find that the customers like the products but are upset because many of the items they need are frequently out of stock, and they perceive the salespersons as not being helpful. From discussions with some of the salespersons, the manager might discover that the factory does not supply the goods on time and promises new delivery dates that it fails, on occasion, to keep. Salespersons might also indicate that they try to please and retain the customers by communicating the delivery dates given to them by the factory.

Integration of the information obtained through the informal and formal interviewing process helps the manager to determine that a problem does exist. |
| --- | --- |
| **The Manager Explores** | |

If the manager decides to make a (change) project out of it, an internal or external party is often called in and put on the project. In that case, 'the problem' is presented to this internal or external party (the researcher), and this party is then instructed to further investigate the situation.

BOX 2.4   SEEKING AREAS FOR IMPROVEMENT: THE MANAGER EXPLORES

To further increase the sales of the organization, a manager is thinking about selling their products in a new market. Before implementing such a market development strategy, the manager wants to know how attractive the designated market is in the long run. The manager has already collected some easily obtainable information about this market and talked about the idea of entering this new market with a selection of stakeholders. Based on the results of this exploration, she decides to put an external party on the project.

THE INITIAL STAGES: BRIEFING THE RESEARCHER

The research process is usually set in motion when a member of the client organization contacts a researcher about helping to solve an organizational issue. The **briefing** that follows typically involves a clarification of the organizational issue. This 'problem' may be presented in a more specific (increased staff turnover, a decreased market share) or a more general way ('we need to make fast changes'). Note that in a lot of cases, the presented problem is (only) a symptom of an underlying problem. On other occasions, the presented problem includes an implied or specified solution ('we need to downsize' or 'we need to cut costs'). That is why it is important that the researcher realizes that the presented problem is usually nothing more than a rough draft (see examples below).

---

1. Long and frequent delays lead to much frustration among airline passengers.
2. Staff turnover is higher than anticipated.
3. The current instrument for the assessment of potential employees for management positions is imperfect.
4. Minority group members in organizations are not advancing in their careers.
5. The newly installed information system is not being used by the managers for whom it was primarily designed.
6. The introduction of flexible work hours has created more problems than it has solved.
7. Young workers in the organization show low levels of commitment to the organization.

Example

Examples of tentative definitions of Problems

More often than not, the client has merely *explored* the problem, but has not been able to put enough time and energy into a more extensive analysis of the situation and/or into a diagnosis.

BOX 2.5	**SEEKING AREAS FOR IMPROVEMENT: BRIEFING**

The manager presents the information problem to two researchers working for a professional research agency. She explains: 'We are thinking about entering this new market with our current products, but we do not know whether this is a good idea. We need information about the long-term profitability of that specific market and any other information that will help us to make an informed decision with regard to entering or not entering that market'.

THE PRELIMINARY STAGES OF THE RESEARCH PROCESS: EXPLORATION AND (IN SOME CASES) DIAGNOSES

We have just explained why many organizational problems are not quite what they seem at first sight. Managers often perceive a situation through a filter of assumptions and expectations. That is why the first step in the *research* process involves *exploration*; the collection of preliminary information about the organization and the potential problem. The information collected in this stage should come from a wide variety of sources (a wide variety of people and documents) and should help both the researcher and the client organization to determine whether they should carry on with the process.

The next stage in the research process (if the problem is an action problem) is called diagnosis. *Diagnosis* is a collaborative process, involving both managers and researchers in collecting relevant data & analysing these data, aimed at *defining the organizational problem* (Cummings and Worley, 2015). The diagnosis stage is an extremely important stage in many applied research projects. If this stage is not executed well, there is a chance of misdiagnosing the problem, especially when the problem is complex. If a research project is based on the wrong problem, its 'solutions' will not solve the actual problem of the organization and might even make matters worse. We will have more to say about exploration and diagnosis in the next chapter.

| BOX 2.6 | **SEEKING AREAS FOR IMPROVEMENT: THE RESEARCHERS EXPLORE** |

The researchers spend the next few days talking a wide variety of people in the organization. How do *they* feel about the idea of entering this new market? They also collect information via internal and external documents, the Internet and the like about the organization, its history, its culture, structure and strategy, as well as their motivation to enter this new market. They also gather some preliminary information on the potential new market. They present their understanding of the project and their definition of the organizational problem along with their ideas on how to move on with the project to the client organization. Based on the potential usefulness of the research results and the monetary costs and benefits of the project, a decision is made on whether to carry on with the research process.

THE PRELIMINARY STAGES OF THE RESEARCH PROCESS: A FIRST REVIEW OF THE LITERATURE

A *first review of the literature* runs parallel to the stages of exploration and diagnosis. The literature – the body of knowledge available to the researcher – may help researchers in different ways during the preliminary stages of the research process. For example, it may help them to think about and/or better understand the organization and the problem of the organization since it provides them with a wide range of models and tools to look at the organization and the organizational problem. A careful review of textbooks, journal articles, conference proceedings and other published and unpublished materials (see Chapter 5 for a detailed discussion on how to review the literature) ensures that researchers have a thorough awareness and understanding of current work and viewpoints on issues related to the subject area. This helps them to structure the preliminary stages of the research processes on work already done. A first literature review will also provide access to instruments and tools that may help the researcher to explore and diagnose. A first review of the literature thus helps researchers to subsequently define the management problem and the research problem (the research objective and research questions). A first review of the literature may also help researchers to make an informed decision about their research approach.

| BOX 2.7 | **SEEKING AREAS FOR IMPROVEMENT: A FIRST REVIEW OF THE LITERATURE** |

A first review of the literature provides the researchers with useful tools to collect information about the organization and the new market the organization aims to enter. It also helps the researchers to define the management problem and the research problem.

THE START OF THE RESEARCH PROCESS: DEVELOPING A RESEARCH PROPOSAL

After the initial stages of exploration, diagnosis (if the problem is an action problem) and a first review of the literature, the researcher is ready to *develop a research proposal*. A research proposal serves as an agreement between the client organization and the researcher. It contains information about the management problem, the research problem, the methodology to be used, the duration of the project, the costs and the like. We will have more to say about the research proposal in Chapter 4.

FINDING SOLUTIONS TO THE PROBLEM: THE PLANNING, COLLECTION AND ANALYSES OF DATA

Once the research problem has been defined (that is the research objective has been developed and specific research questions have been specified) the researcher is ready to start thinking about solutions to the problem. A *second review of the literature* (discussed in Chapter 4) and the *planning* (Chapter 7), *collection* (Chapters 8 to 14) and *analysis* (Chapters 15, 16 and 17) *of empirical data* allows the researcher to solve the decision problem of the client organization.

PROVIDING FEEDBACK TO THE CLIENT ORGANIZATION

On the basis of the data that the researcher has collected and the analysis of these data, one is ready to develop an informed judgment with regard to (a solution to) the problem of the client organization. In other words, the researcher is ready to *draw conclusions* (discussed in Chapter 18). These conclusions might relate to how satisfied or dissatisfied employees are with the organization, how attractive a specific industry is in the long run, how competitors are positioning their products in a specific market segment or how the client organization is able to improve its market share (customer satisfaction, employee turnover and the like). The researcher subsequently develops *recommendations* based on these conclusions. With that, the researcher has achieved the objective of the research project. Thus, the researcher has made his or her contribution to solving the problem of the client organization.

THE FINAL STAGES: THE MANAGER MAKES A DECISION AND ACTS

With the conclusions and recommendations, the researcher gives the project back to the manager. Now it is up to the manager to *make a decision and take further action*. What the manager will do and whether the manager will follow the advice of the researcher depends on the quality of the research project and on how convincing the conclusions and recommendations are.

CONCLUSION

You may have asked yourself repeatedly, 'Why do I need to know different perspectives on research and what makes good research?' One answer is that we believe that it is important for you to know that there is more than one viewpoint on what makes good research. Knowledge of epistemology may help you to relate to and understand the research of others and the choices that were made in this research. Different researchers have different ideas about the nature of knowledge or on how we come to know (indeed, *the scientific approach* to research is only one – albeit important – view on what 'good' research is). These different ideas translate into different approaches that are taken to research, into different research designs and into different choices regarding the research methods used.

Another answer to the question 'Why do I need to know this?' is that you will probably have noticed that *you* prefer one research perspective over the other perspectives. Understanding your personal ideas on research and how it should be done allows you to determine which kinds of research questions are important to you and what methods for collecting and analysing data will give you the best answer to these questions. It will also help you to make informed decisions during the research process, to have a clear understanding about what the findings of your study (do and do not) mean and to understand the type of conclusions that your research approach allows you to draw. Like this, it helps you to put your research and research findings in perspective.

In sum, your viewpoint on the nature of knowledge and on how we come to know will have a strong influence on, among other things, the research questions you ask, your research design and the research methods you will use. The rest of this book is primarily concerned with the identification and definition of the organizational problem, the development of research questions, research design and research methods and much less with the foregoing philosophical issues. However, it is important that every so often you consider the philosophical underpinnings of your research questions, your research design, your research methods and the like. This is important since the value of your research findings and with that the value of your conclusions and recommendations depends on how well they relate to the methods you have used, the design you have chosen, the questions you have asked and the research perspective you have taken.

SUMMARY	• **Learning objective 1: Explain what is meant by scientific investigation, giving examples of both scientific and non-scientific investigations.** *Scientific research* focuses on solving problems and pursues a step-by-step, logical, organized and rigorous method to identify the problems, gather data, analyse them and draw valid conclusions from them. The hallmarks or main distinguishing characteristics of scientific research are purposiveness, rigor, testability, replicability, precision and confidence, objectivity, generalizability and parsimony.

• **Learning objective 2: Discuss the seven steps of the hypothetico-deductive method, using an example of your own.** The hypothetico-deductive method is a typical version of the scientific method. This method provides a useful, systematic approach for generating knowledge to solve basic and managerial problems. The hypothetico-deductive method involves seven steps: (1) identify a broad problem area; (2) define the problem statement; (3) develop hypotheses; (4) determine measures; (5) collect data; (6) analyse data and (7) interpret data. The scientific method uses deductive reasoning to test a theory about a topic of interest.

• **Learning objective 3: Discuss alternative perspectives on what makes good research.** All research is based on beliefs about the world around us and what we can possibly discover by research. Different researchers have different ideas about these issues. *Your* viewpoint on the nature of knowledge and on how we come to know things will have a strong influence on the research questions you ask, your research design and the research methods you will use.

In the rest of this book these matters are discussed in more detail.

> Instructors can visit the companion website at **www.wiley.com/go/bougie/researchmethods forbusiness8e** for **Case Study: The Pacific Futures Trading Company**.

DISCUSSION QUESTIONS	1. Describe the hallmarks of scientific research.

2. What are the steps in hypothetico-deductive research? Explain them, using your own example.

3. One hears the word *research* being mentioned by several groups such as research organizations, college and university professors, doctoral students, graduate assistants working for faculty, graduate and undergraduate students doing their term papers, research departments in industries, newspaper reporters, journalists, lawyers, doctors and many other professionals and non-professionals. In the light of what you have learned in this chapter, which among the aforementioned groups of people do you think may be doing 'scientific' investigations in the areas of basic or applied research? Why?

4. Explain the processes of deduction and induction, giving an example of each.

5. Discuss the following statement: 'Good research is deductive in nature'.

6. Discuss the following statement: 'The hallmarks of scientific research do not/cannot apply to inductive research'.

7. If research in the management area cannot be 100 percent scientific, why bother to do it at all? Comment on this question.

8. What is epistemology and why is it important to know about different perspectives on research and how it should be done?

9. Discuss the most important differences between positivism and pragmatism.

10. Is there a specific perspective on research that appeals to you? Why?

11. Some people think that you should choose a particular research perspective based on the research questions of your study. Others feel that a particular research perspective 'chooses' you. That is, they believe that you will have a rather strong preference for one particular research perspective; in turn, this will have an influence on the type of questions you ask. How do you feel about this matter?

12. Critique the following research done in a service industry as to the extent to which it meets the hallmarks of scientific investigation discussed in this chapter.

The Mobile Phone Company

The Mobile Phone Company has been named as the most complained-about mobile phone company, narrowly beating 3G, which has shot to the top of the table as the worst landline provider.

According to the latest figures from the regulator, Ofcom, the Mobile Phone Company was the most complained-about mobile provider – with 0.15 complaints per 1,000 – in the last three months of 2014. It saw its complaint figures rise substantially in the last quarter of 2014. The company wanted to pinpoint the specific problems and take corrective action.

Researchers were called in, and they spoke to a number of customers, noting the nature of the specific problems they faced. Because the problem had to be attended to very quickly, they developed a theoretical base, collected relevant detailed information from a sample of 100 customers and analysed the data. The results promise to be fairly accurate with at least an 85 percent chance of success in problem solving. The researchers will make recommendations to the company based on the results of data analysis.

| **Defining the Management Problem**

LEARNING OBJECTIVES

After completing Chapter 3, you should be able to:

1. Identify problem areas that are likely to be studied in organizations.

2. Explain why it is important to distinguish between two different types of situations that may or may not lead to a research project.

3. Carry out an exploration.

4. Make a Diagnosis.

5. Distinguish between different types of action problems: technical problems, information problems, consensus problems and a combination of information and consensus problems.

6. Define the management problem.

INTRODUCTION

There are many reasons to carry out applied research. The common theme is that every *research project* starts with a problem (an information problem) that a researcher wants to address. In the previous chapter, two situations were introduced, related to organizational change, that are commonly associated with more complex forms of research in an applied context. As explained earlier, research is often needed when managers are proactively looking for *decision opportunities*. For example, a manager might be thinking about entering a new market (but she does not know whether it is a good idea) or about introducing a new product into the market (but she wants to involve consumers in the process of developing that product). Another manager might be committed to maintaining the overall competitiveness of the organization (but he has little insight into the competitive environment of the organization). Indeed, unless managers understand what is going on in such situations, they cannot make effective decisions. Applied research may also result from a specific situation that a manager wants to *change* (for instance, staff turnover is 20 percent and for some reason the manager finds this problematic). If a manager wants to solve the (action) problem, but does not know how or if it is unclear which intervention is more effective compared to other interventions, research is needed. Such research will help managers to make effective decisions to solve the problems.

This chapter discusses both situations. We first examine situations where managers are proactively looking for decision opportunities. After that, we will pay attention to situations where (in the manager's perspective) the existing situation is not in line with a desired situation; situations where the manager has an action problem. In both cases, we pay attention to the first step(s) of the research process ('exploration' and 'exploration and diagnosis', respectively) and think about how one can best define the management problem. In the next chapter, we look at how the researcher can develop a research problem from the management problem.

A multitude of decisions must be made in organizations. Even in situations where there are no immediate problems such as a loss in market share, dissatisfied personnel or disgruntled consumers, effective managers are constantly *looking for decision opportunities* or areas for improvement. Instead of waiting for a situation that is imposed upon them, they show initiative. Along these lines, there are many potential applications for research. These applications include the following:

LOOKING FOR DECISION OPPORTUNITIES OR AREAS FOR IMPROVEMENT

- *Monitoring performance* (sales, margins, market share, employee satisfaction, turnover, customer satisfaction and different types of audits) may help managers to obtain useful feedback for decision-making.

- *Identifying market opportunities and constraints* is often an important starting point for developing effective strategies.

- Firms that are considering *new product introductions or entries into new markets* will benefit from obtaining information on issues such as long-term profitability of a market, competitors and consumers.

- *Customer analysis* helps managers to understand needs and wants of customers, to develop effective segmentation strategies, position a product in the market and the like.

- Research on the organization's *competitive environment* is key to maintaining and improving an organization's overall competitiveness.

- *Industry evaluation* may help managers to identify whether the organization is effective in maximizing the benefits to the organization (in terms of, for instance, sales, market share and profits) from available opportunities.

- *Idea generation* through extensive research may lead to successful introductions of new products.

The above examples illustrate that research often plays an important role in situations where a manager is proactively looking for decision opportunities or areas for improvement. Research may help the manager to make decisions, gain knowledge, reduce uncertainty about a decision and/or include stakeholders in the decision process.

THE FIRST STEP OF THE RESEARCH PROCESS: EXPLORATION

To Conduct Research or Not

After having been briefed by the manager, the researcher is ready to start. A logical starting point for exploration in situations where a manager is proactively looking for decision opportunities or areas for improvement is the issue of whether to conduct research. Four factors influence the decision to conduct research: (1) the potential usefulness of the research results, (2) the resources available for implementing the research results, (3) the attitude of various stakeholders towards the project and (4) the costs and benefits of the project (Lehmann, Gupta & Steckel, 1998; Parasuraman, Grewal & Krishnan, 2004).

The potential usefulness of a research project is the extent to which its findings contribute to decision-making and action. It is related to the extent to which the research findings reduce a decision-maker's uncertainty and provide additional insights into a given situation. A project with little potential usefulness should not be executed.

Research is also futile if an organization lacks the *resources* (money, time and staff) to *follow up on research results*. For instance, if research to uncover market opportunities reveals that a specific market is very attractive, but the organization does not have the resources to increase the capacity, the research project is useless.

Stakeholders must look at a proposed research project with an open mind if the research project is to be successful. If stakeholders have negative feelings about a project, if they are not willing to cooperate or if they do not accept the results of a project, efforts will be worthless. The questions in Box 3.1 will help you to assess the position of stakeholders.

| BOX 3.1 | USEFUL QUESTIONS TO ASSESS THE POSITION OF STAKEHOLDERS |

Who are the key stakeholders?

How important do they think the project is and why?

What type of information do we need from various stakeholders?

Are they willing and able to provide us with the necessary information?

What are their objectives, tasks and responsibilities?

What are their objectives in relation to the project?

What are their ideas and feelings about the project?

Are they open to change?

Are they emotionally involved?

What do various stakeholders have to lose in the course of the project?

Will that lead to resistance? How problematic is that? How will this affect the process?

All the factors discussed so far are, in one way or another, related to the costs and benefits of a research project. Indeed, they all focus on whether it is worthwhile to set a research project in motion. In addition, it is important to look at the *monetary costs and benefits* of a project. This may avoid the perils of a research project that costs more than its worth. Note that it is often relatively easy to quantify the costs of a research project; on the other hand, making an accurate prediction of the benefits of a research project is not so straightforward. Decision trees are often presented as a means to make a quantitative assessment of the value of information. Although the conceptual use of decision trees is widespread, its practical application is nonetheless quite limited, primarily because managers find them hard to apply.

| BOX 3.2 | ASSESSING THE VALUE OF INFORMATION |

In order to assess the value of information, several considerations are taken into account (Lehmann, Gupta & Steckel, 1998):

1. Time pressure: under what kind of time pressure is the manager?

2. How easy is it to collect information?

3. What is the cost of a bad decision?

4. How do the viable alternatives differ?

5. How likely is it that more information will change the decision?

Note that considerations 1 and 2 are related to the costs of information, 3 and 4 to the relative results of alternative decisions and 5 to the relative odds of making a good decision with and without more information.

Defining the Management Problem

In order to be able to evaluate the costs and benefits of a research project, the researcher needs information on the 'what' and the 'why' of the project. What does the manager want to find out and why? In other words, the management 'problem' has to be defined. It is often helpful to define the management problem in terms of the following (Kapteyn, 1999):

1. The existing situation

2. Why this situation is problematic (the change motive or the motive for doing research)

3. The desired situation (the management objective)

In a situation where a manager is proactively looking for decision opportunities or areas for improvement, we might formulate the management problem as follows:

1. *The existing situation*
   In order to grow, we are considering to enter a new market. However, it is unclear how attractive this market is in the long run.

2. *Why this situation is problematic*
   This is problematic because we want to make a market entry decision.

3. *The desired situation (the management objective)*
   Obtaining insights into the long-term attractiveness of the market.

From this management problem, the researcher should be able to define the *research* problem (*research* objectives and research questions). The formulation of the research problem is discussed in the next chapter. In the rest of this chapter, we focus on the second situation that may call for research – a situation where an organization is in trouble and the manager needs to find a solution.

A manager's important tasks are to ensure that the organization's objectives are realized and that the organization is functioning efficiently. If organizational objectives are not achieved or if the organization is not operating in the best possible manner, it is the manager's task to solve the problems. A problem-solving process is often set in motion if a manager finds that the existing situation is undesirable or the situation does not meet a certain norm or standard.

FIXING SITUATIONS THAT ARE BROKEN

For instance, a manager may find it problematic when the company's employee turnover rate is higher than the average rate in the industry, customers are not satisfied with the services of the organization or the company's market share is lower than required. When a manager finds that the gap between the existing and desired situation is too big and sees or foresees major negative consequences as a result of this gap, the manager will initiate actions aimed at finding a way out of the existing situation. A *research* process is set in motion when the manager commissions a researcher to help to solve the organizational issues. Exploration and diagnosis will help the researcher to (eventually) define the management problem.

THE FIRST STEP OF THE RESEARCH PROCESS: EXPLORATION

After having been briefed by the manager, researchers are ready to start. The first step that must be taken by the researcher is exploration, that is, the researcher tries to find more about the core issue: 'what is happening?' and 'why is it problematic?' are two important questions that need a provisional answer at this stage. It is also useful to explore the conditions for solving the problem. For instance, in some cases, there is so much speed required that it does not make sense to turn the problem into a change project. Such a project would simply take too much time. An assessment of the costs and benefits of the potential project, the issue's importance to the organization and potential sensitivities that might get in the way of the project may also help the researcher to assess the viability of the project. Based on the results of the exploration stage, the researcher should be able to make an informed decision whether to carry on with the process of problem solving or not. Since making a diagnosis is the logical next step, the first decision that has to be made in this respect is: 'are we going to invest in diagnosis or not?' There are two scenarios that the researcher would like to avoid (Kapteyn, 1999):

1. Overestimating the problem: deciding to invest time and energy in diagnosis when the problem is trivial and insignificant

2. Underestimating the problem: deciding not to diagnose when there is a potential problem and change is needed

If the researcher and the client organization decide to carry on with the project, it becomes important to think about how one wants to approach the diagnosis stage: Who needs to get involved and in which role (participant, informant or expert)? How much and what type of resources are needed? Do we have access to relevant information? It is often useful to settle such issues with the client organization before the researcher enters the diagnosis stage.

The questions in Box 3.3 may help you organize the exploration stage.

BOX 3.3   USEFUL QUESTIONS FOR EXPLORATION

First Exploration of the Problem

What is happening? Why is that bad? What has caused the client to notice the problem? How important is it? In which way? To whom? Do other people also believe that there exists a problem? Who? Why? What information is already available on the problem? How do I get access to this information? How will the project contribute to decision-making and action? Does the client have enough resources (money, time and staff) to follow up on possible solutions? Are there any constraints in this respect? What are the monetary costs and benefits of the project?

Conditions for Doing Research/Solving the Problem

Who are the key stakeholders? Do they think that there is a problem? What is their relation to the problem? Are they open to change? Is it possible to influence them? Are they willing to provide us with the information that we need from them? Are they emotionally involved? What are *their* objectives in relation to the problem? Are there many phenomena that are related to the problem and to each other? What are these phenomena? How are these phenomena related to each other and to the problem? Has somebody already tried to solve the problem? How? Why have these efforts not been successful? What do we need to solve the problem (in terms of people and other resources)? Is the issue important? To whom? How? Is it worthwhile to solve the problem? At what costs? How much time, money and effort will be needed to solve the problem? Is speed required (when it comes to solving the problem)? How does that affect the process? Is research an option? What specific aspects should we take into account (emotions, regulations, confidentiality, culture and other issues)? Do we need help? What kind of help? From whom? At what stage of the process? How does this affect the problem solving/research process?

Provisional Definition of the Problem

What is happening? Why is that problematic? How big is the problem?

Regarding the Diagnosis

Are we going to diagnose? Who will do what in the diagnosis stage? What do we need to be able to diagnose (people, resources)? What type of information do we need in the diagnosis stage and how are we going to collect this information? From people? Which people? In which role (respondent, expert, informant)? From documents? Which documents?

For many researchers, the exploration stage is a difficult one mainly because there is a lot of uncertainty. Common pitfalls are the desire to achieve quick results, tunnel vision and the tendency to confuse interpretations with facts. Box 3.4 provides some helpful suggestions regarding the exploration stage that may help you to avoid such pitfalls.

THE SECOND STEP OF THE RESEARCH PROCESS: DIAGNOSIS

The exploration stage will go over into the next stage, making a diagnosis, if the researcher, after having consulted with the client organization, is convinced that further investigation of the issue is worthwhile. The diagnosis stage is, in many ways, the most important stage of the change process. In the diagnosis stage, the researcher will delve deeper into the problem, in order to profusely understand the situation. The problem and the constraints of the solution need to be thoroughly defined. This is not a straightforward task. It is crucial that the researcher makes sure that the right problem is addressed and that the problem is solved in the right way.

BOX 3.4   **SUGGESTIONS FOR EXPLORATION**

- Keep an open mind.
- Do not focus too quickly: a broad scope is better than a narrow one at this stage.
- Do not jump to conclusions.
- Make sure that your information comes from many different sources (people and documents).
- Distinguish facts from interpretations.
- Uncertainty is an important characteristic of this stage. This makes it difficult for many people.
- There is no need to come up with a final definition of the problem at this stage. You may want to formulate one or more *preliminary* problem definition(s).

- Keep everything flexible.
- Do not accept predefined solutions.
- Try to make a realistic assessment of the severity of the problem.
- Think about the organization of next stage: diagnosis. What do you need from whom?
- You may come to the conclusion that the process ends here.
- Do not continue if the issue is not worth investigating.

Table 3.1   Relationship between Level of Diagnosis and Broad Topic

Topic	Level of diagnosis
Organizational performance, stakeholder satisfaction	Organizational level
Team effectiveness, quality of work	Group level
Job satisfaction, personal development	Individual level

Diagnosis can take place at different levels in an organization. For instance, a diagnosis process can take place at the level of the organization, a department or strategic business unit (SBU) or at the level of the individual, such as an employee or a client. Diagnosis can be aimed at all these levels but also at one of these levels. Table 3.1 provides some examples of the relationship between the level at which the diagnosis could take place and the broad topic of a change project.

There are many valuable instruments and tools that can help you to diagnose, and the majority of these instruments are analytical in nature (they help you to separate the issue into constituent parts or elements). These instruments may help you to structure your activities and organize the collection of information in the diagnosis stage. Instruments that may come in handy are the McKinsey 7S Framework or a Tichy matrix, reworked by Peter Camp (see Box 3.5). Some instruments, such as a fishbone diagram or a root cause analysis (also known as '5 times why'), emphasize cause and effect. Needless to say, the instrument that one uses should be in line with the level at which the diagnosis takes place and the intricacies of the situation at hand. Examples of a Tichy Matrix and a root cause analysis are provided in Box 3.5.

The Tichy matrix, reworked by Peter Camp, aims to support organizational change. It is based on theory developed by Noël Tichy on the coherent development of three important organizational issues: policy, organization and staff. Tichy argued that within organizations three features exert influence on organizational performance: technical, political and cultural features. This has led to a matrix with nine cells, each with a specific point of interest for change. Note that there are often strong relations between the specific elements in the nine cells.

Besides the aforementioned instruments, the questions in Box 3.6 may help you to shape the diagnosis stage.

BOX 3.5	TICHY MATRIX, REWORKED BY PETER CAMP

Technical features	**Objectives and strategy**	**Tasks and responsibilities**	**Expertise**
	• Objectives	• Organization	• Qualification demands
	• Strategy	• Division of tasks	• Team composition
	• Research	• Consultation	• Expertise
	• Budget	• Procedures	• Rewards
Political features	**Policy influencers**	**Decision-making**	**Autonomy**
	• Leaders	• Participation	• Degree of freedom
	• Contractors	• Contracting	• Needs and wants
	• Stakeholders	• Negotiation	• Perspectives
	• Investors	• Regulations	• Risks
Cultural features	**Culture**	**Cooperation**	**Attitude**
	• Quality standards	• Planning	• Competencies
	• Involvement	• Team building	• Willingness
	• Perceptions	• Idea generation	• Creativity
	• Habits	• Methods	• Improvization

Example	
Problems versus Symptoms of Problems	It is very important that symptoms of problems are not defined as the real problem. For instance, a manager might have tried to decrease the employee turnover (the best people are leaving the organization) by increasing wages, but with little success. Here, the real problem may be something else such as low motivation of employees who feel they do not have enough control over their work. The high turnover rate may merely be a symptom of deep-rooted motivational problems. Under these conditions, in the long run, higher salary will not affect employees' intentions to leave. Thus, finding the 'right' answer to the 'wrong' problem definition will not help. Hence, it should be recognized that correct problem identification is extremely critical for finding solutions to vexing issues.

Frequently, managers tend to describe a problem in terms of symptoms. Rather than accepting it as described, the researcher needs to identify the problem more accurately. One way of determining that the problem, rather than the symptom, is being addressed is a technique called '*5 Whys*' or '*5 times why*'. 5 Whys is a fairly straightforward approach that will help you to find the root cause (the most basic cause) of a problem (via preliminary research). Developed by the Japanese industrialist Sakichi Toyada, the idea is to keep asking 'why?' until the most basic cause is arrived at.

Let's go back to our example to illustrate this approach.

My best employees are leaving the organization.

Why?   Because they are not satisfied with their jobs.

Why?   Because they do not find a challenge in their jobs.

Why?   Because they do not have control over their work.

Why?   Because they do not have a lot of influence over planning, executing and evaluating the work they do.

Why?   Because we have been reluctant to delegate.

Note that the number five is a general guideline for the number of why's needed to get to the root cause level, but asking 'why?' five times versus three, four or six times is not a strict requirement. *What matters is that we investigate recurring problems by addressing true causes and not symptoms of these causes.*

BOX 3.6   USEFUL QUESTIONS FOR DIAGNOSIS

Stakeholders

Who are the 'key stakeholders'? Do they think that there is a problem? How do they define the problem? How important do they think the problem is and why? What are their ideas, feelings about the problem? What are their objectives, tasks and responsibilities? How does this affect their views and feelings about the problem?

Information

What information is already available? How was this information collected?

Causes and Consequences of the Problem

When did this problem come to light? How long has this problem been persisting? What factors contribute to the existing situation? What are the consequences of the issue? Is a root cause analysis helpful? How? Are there other instruments that we could use? Is there any other information or other 'evidence' that underlines the relevance of the issue?

Complexity of the Problem

Is the situation simple or complex? In which way? In a 'cognitive' way? Politically? Is the problem part of a bigger system? What information is available on contributing, related factors?

Problem Definition

What is the existing situation (the facts)? Why is it bad? What does the client want to achieve? Is there consensus on these issues?

Conditions

What are the constraints of the solution? Resources? Rules and regulations? Policy? Values? Is there consensus on these issues?

Stakeholders – Revisited

Is there consensus on what the problem is? The management objective? Constraints? What do various stakeholders have to lose in the course of the project? Will that lead to resistance? How problematic is that? How will this affect the process?

Type of Problem

How can we classify the problem? Is it an information problem or another type of problem? How simple, complicated, complex is the problem? What information is needed to reach the managerial objective? Do we have access to the necessary information? How?

One of the primary objectives of diagnosis is to define the management problem. Again, the management problem can best be defined in terms of the following (Kapteyn, 1999):

1. The existing situation

2. Why this situation is problematic (in this case, the change motive)

3. The desired situation (the management objective)

A description of the existing situation and the desired situation plays an important role in a problem definition. Both the existing situation and the desired situation are preferably formulated in terms of factual events or circumstances. Formulating the existing situation in terms of facts is often a good idea because it is difficult to disagree with facts (e.g, 'sick leave is 12 percent'). On the other hand, a mix of facts and interpretations ('sick leave is too high') may lead to misunderstandings and/or disagreements between various stakeholders. The formulation of the management objective should also be specific and clear (see Box 3.7). This reduces the chance of misunderstandings, and it helps the manager to easily communicate the objective to various stakeholders.

Again, it is important to note that facts (e.g, a staff turnover of 12 percent or a Net Promoter Score of +35) have no meaning in themselves. They become meaningful when they are placed in the context of a certain change motive. That is why a change motive (or an answer to the question 'Why is this problematic?') is a third important element of the problem definition. The motive reflects *why* change is deemed necessary and forms the logical connection between the existing situation and the desired situation. This can be explained by an example.

BOX 3.7	**SMART OBJECTIVES**

A change project is considered to be successful if the management objectives set are achieved. The first step towards success is well-formed and formulated objectives. Many books, articles and websites have advocated the development of goals that are SMART to reduce the risk of setting vague or unclear objectives that are unlikely to be achieved. SMART is an acronym that has come to mean different things to different people.

- Specific (some people say simple, sensible)
- Measurable (motivating, meaningful)
- Achievable (attainable, agreed upon)
- Realistic (reasonable)
- Time-bound (time based, time limited)

The first known use of the term SMART is by Doran (1981, in *Management Review*). The criteria are nonetheless commonly attributed to Drucker.

Example of a definition of the management problem:

1. *Existing situation*
   The undesirable turnover of personnel who have been in service for less than a year is, on average, 18 percent over the past three calendar years.

2. *Why this is problematic (the motive to change the existing situation)*
   The high turnover rate among employees who have been working for the organization for less than a year leads to dissatisfaction, demotivation and dropping out of colleagues who have chosen not to leave; to frustration with regard to supporting inexperienced and inefficient recruits; to extra management time needed to deal with the negative consequences of turnover and to high recruitment costs.

3. *Desired situation (the management objective)*
   To reduce the undesirable turnover of personnel who have been in service for less than a year with 50 percent.

As we have already explained, it is helpful to describe the existing situation in terms of facts rather than interpretations. It is therefore better to state that 'the undesirable employee turnover is 18 percent' than to state that 'the undesirable employee turnover is too high'. After all, what is too high might be a matter of opinion. The motive to change the existing situation (or the answer to the question 'why is this problematic?') indicates why the manager wants to change (in other words, it represents the change motive); feelings of dissatisfaction, demotivation and the dropping out of colleagues who have chosen to stay, frustration with supporting inexperienced and inefficient recruits, high replacement costs and the like form the logical connection between the existing situation and the articulated management objective. The management objective (or desired situation) is the logical starting point for the development of the research problem, at least in situations where research is needed at a later stage of the problem-solving process (we will come back to this in a moment). Note that the management objective is formulated in terms of behaviour: *to reduce* the undesirable turnover of personnel who have been in service for less than a year with 50 percent.

THE CONSTRAINTS OR PRECONDITIONS THAT SHOULD BE TAKEN INTO ACCOUNT

Before one can start to think about solving the action problem, one needs to define not only the management problem but also the constraints or the preconditions that the solution to the problem must meet. Constraints relate to matters that do not arise directly from the problem definition but are important in the context of achieving the management objective. Such restrictive conditions might relate to resources (such as time and money), laws and regulations or, for instance, an organization's policy. In the example of undesirable staff turnover, constraints might relate to what the solution may cost (in terms of time, money and energy) and to legal requirements, employment regulations and/or the HRM policy of the organization. Insight into and a definition of these constraints prevents that in the end recommendations are provided (solutions are presented) that cannot be carried out because they are too expensive, because they do not meet the (possibly divergent) wishes of the parties involved or because they are forbidden by the law.

BOX 3.8   DEFINING THE MANAGEMENT PROBLEM

In the early stages of the research process you will have to spend time alternating between preliminary research (e.g., exploration, diagnosis and a first review of the literature) and (re)defining the management problem. Until you have developed a first tentative problem definition, you cannot decide what information is useful. However, the awareness and understanding of current work and viewpoints in the subject area as well as the results of your exploration and diagnosis may change your perspective on what the problem is and encourage you to refine and redefine the management problem; a more refined problem definition may trigger the need to collect further information, which may inspire you to reframe the problem definition and so on.

DIFFERENT TYPES OF PROBLEMS AND SOLUTIONS TO THESE PROBLEMS

Diagnosis is aimed at defining the management problem and the constraints of the solution. That is why diagnosis is a crucial stage (some people say, the most important stage) in the problem-solving process. But diagnosis is not always easy; some problems are easier to define than others. Indeed, some problems are complex and difficult to grasp; there is a multitude of interrelated phenomena, which are undesirable for various reasons. In other situations, it might be difficult or even impossible to gather enough information to be able to understand what is going on. And sometimes, stakeholders disagree on whether there is a problem to begin with, on what the problem is and/or on the constraints of the solution. Sometimes, problems are so complex that one can safely speak of a mess. All these matters affect the solvability of the problem.

The solvability of a problem is *positively* influenced if it is possible to clearly define the problem and the constraints of the solution. If there is consensus on these issues and if the stakeholders think that it is possible to reach the managerial objective within the constraints that have been formulated, one can start thinking about solving the problem.

In general, the solvability of a problem is determined by two factors (Douglas & Wildavsky, 1982):

- the degree of consensus on whether there is a problem, on what the problem is and on the constraints that should be met by the solution;
- the extent to which relevant knowledge is available on how the problem can be solved.

Based on these factors, four types of action problems can be distinguished (Table 3.2).

Let's have a closer look at these different types of problems. If the management problem is a **technical** or **routine problem**, there is clarity and agreement on what the problem is and the constraints of the solution. Moreover, there is sufficient knowledge and experience on how to solve the problem, either within or outside (an expert that can be commissioned to solve the problem) the organization, for example, because the solution is obvious or because previously implemented solutions can be used. Solving the problem is therefore a matter of planning and action. This category includes all routine problems.

Table 3.2 Types of Action Problems

Consensus on the problem and the constraints that the solution should meet	Presence of available knowledge with regard to how the problem can be solved	
	Present	**Not present**
High	Technical/routine problem *Planning, action*	Information problem *Research*
Low	Consensus problem *Negotiation, persuasion*	Information and consensus problem (messy problem) *Leadership*

Based on Douglas and Wildavsky (1982) and Kapteyn (1999).

Example

A general medical practice wants to improve its digital accessibility. A representative of the medical practice has asked the organization 'Indispensable Accessibility', an expert on this issue to come up with a plan for carrying out the necessary changes.

If the problem can be defined as an **information problem**, there is also agreement about what the problem is and the constraints of the solution. But in contrast to routine problems, it is *not* clear how the problem can (best) be solved (here is the information problem). There are alternative courses of action, one course of action is more effective than the other and it is initially unclear which alternative is the most effective one. The solution to such problems can be found by doing research aimed at informing the manager on how the problem can (best) be solved. Such research is called action-oriented research.

Example

A marketing manager wants to improve customer loyalty, but does not know how.

In some cases, stakeholders do not agree on what the problem is and/or the constraints of the solution. Sometimes, there is sufficient knowledge about how to solve the problem, but due to, for example, conflicting interests or different value systems, beliefs or ethical standpoints, every viable solution to the problem is blocked. Such **consensus problems** frequently occur in organizations. Negotiation, persuasion and/or making use of one's authority are more common ways to arrive at a solution. In some cases, consensus problems may lead to politically motivated research, where the conclusions of the study are clear from the outset. Note that undertaking such research is never a good idea.

Example

A human resources professional has been instructed to change the bonus system of a financial institution. However, many people in the organization (especially those who receive a bonus) do not think that changes are needed. There is an open revolt against the plans to change the system.

If a problem is a combination of an information and a consensus problem, there is little or no knowledge about how the problem can be solved, but there is also insufficient agreement about what the problem is and/or about the constraints that the solution must meet. In this situation, there is often disagreement about the desired direction of change. This stands in the way of gathering information on how the problem can be solved. The problem is therefore seemingly unsolvable. In many cases, it is difficult to determine which steps must be taken to arrive at a common problem definition and a management objective that is acceptable to everyone. There are several ways to break the deadlock; charismatic and authoritarian leadership are most often mentioned.

Many big problems we are facing at the moment (such as environmental problems, global health problems, refugee crises and the like) are combinations of information and consensus problems. It should therefore not come as a surprise that it is very difficult to solve these problems. A very nice example of this type of problem in an organizational context is the 'fishing game'. Details can be found here: https://economics-games.com/tragedy-commons.

Example

All these four types of problems regularly occur in organizations. As explained in Table 3.2, (action-oriented) research is not *always* the most obvious path towards a solution to the problem. Depending on the specific characteristics of the problem, planning and action, negotiation and persuasion or different forms of leadership may help the manager to deal with an undesirable situation instead. If the problem is a technical or routine problem, research with regard to how the problem can (best) be solved is not necessary; all the relevant information that is needed to solve the problem is readily available. The problem can be solved by planning (identifying the costs of intervening, establishing baselines or performance measures, allocation of resources, the development of a realistic timetable and the like) and taking action. If the problem is a consensus problem, consultation in the form of a dialogue or discussion, or if needed the use of authority, is a crucial first step towards defining and solving the management problem. Charismatic and authoritarian leadership may break the deadlock if the problem is a combination of a consensus and information problem.

Since research is not always the most obvious path to finding a solution to an action problem, it is very important that the researcher is focused not only on defining the management problem and the constraints of the solution during the diagnosis stage but also on determining the characteristics of the problem and with that, the type of problem. Only if the researcher comes to the conclusion that the problem is[1] an information problem – when it is clear what the problem is, but not how the problem can (best) be solved – (action-oriented) research is needed. In such situations, the researcher can start thinking about formulating the *research problem* and developing a research proposal. In other situations where the action problem is not an information problem, the job of the researcher has come to an end at the diagnosis stage.

The diagnosis stage is often even more difficult than the exploration stage. Box 3.9 aims to provide helpful suggestions with regard to making a diagnosis process.

BOX 3.9   SUGGESTIONS FOR DIAGNOSIS

Leave prejudice behind.

Do not judge too quickly.

Do not think in solutions yet.

Look at the situation from different perspectives. Talk to various stakeholders. Develop your own viewpoint on the issue.

Collect more information.

Do not forget about the constraints.

Benefit from existing literature and the like. Do not try to reinvent the wheel. Use existing tools and instruments to diagnose.

Use the right instruments.

Use the instruments in the right way.

A root cause analysis and a fishbone diagram are often useful tools but not the only tools you can use.

Assign meaning to the large amount of data you gather (often qualitative, chaotic and contradicting each other).

Connect your findings to the literature in order to be able to benefit from existing ideas and insights.

Is the problem a technical problem, an information problem, a consensus problem or messy? How does that affect the next stages of the problem-solving process?

---

[1]Note that this is never clear from the outset. Diagnosis is needed to determine the type of problem.

PROVIDING FEEDBACK TO THE CLIENT ORGANIZATION	An important step in the initial stages of the research process is providing feedback to the client organization. Feedback is typically provided in a meeting or (even better) in a series of meetings. Having meetings provide the client organization with the opportunity to discuss the results of the exploration and/or diagnosis stage, to draw conclusions and to devise action plans. The provision of feedback thus ensures ownership of the problem-solving and/or decision-making process, arouses organizational action and directs energy towards organizational problem solving and decision-making. Several characteristics of effective feedback have been provided in the literature (Folkman, 2006):

1. Relevance. The data that are fed back to the client organization should be meaningful to members of the client organization and reduce uncertainty about pertinent issues that relate to the exploration and diagnosis stage. The data should be related to the problem.

2. Comprehensible. The feedback must be presented comprehensibly. Sometimes, data are difficult to interpret without a benchmark. In such cases, it might be helpful to provide data from comparative groups.

3. Verifiable. Feedback data should be accurate, representative, reliable and valid. Members of the client organization should be able to verify the data.

4. Timely. Feedback should be provided as quickly as possible after the relevant data have been collected and analysed.

5. Limited. Do not overload the client with information.

6. Provisional. Feedback can be a stimulus for further discussion, further exploration and further diagnosis.

MANAGERIAL IMPLICATIONS	In situations where there are no immediate problems such as a loss in market share, dissatisfied personnel or disgruntled consumers, effective managers are constantly looking for decision opportunities or areas for improvement. Instead of waiting for a situation that is imposed upon them, they are taking the initiative. Managers should understand how, why and under which circumstances research may play a role in these situations.

If organizational objectives are not attained or if the organization, strategic business unit or department is not operating in the best possible manner, it is the manager's task to solve the problem. A problem-solving process is often set in motion if a manager finds an existing situation undesirable or finds that the situation does not meet a certain norm or standard. Based on available or easily obtainable information and/or an initial exchange of ideas with (a selection of) stakeholders, the manager should provide an answer to the question of whether the discomfort with the existing situation should lead to further action. Based on this first exploration, the manager may decide to reappraise the situation or to make a project out of it. If the manager decides to make a (change) project out of it, an internal or external party is often called in and involved in the project. In that case, 'the problem is presented to the internal or external party (the researcher), and this party is then instructed to further investigate the situation'. A *research* process is set in motion when the manager commissions a researcher to help to solve the organizational issue. The manager is responsible for an adequate briefing of the researcher.

It is also important that a manager understands what the first stages of the research process are all about. The researcher needs a lot of information in the preliminary stages of the research process, and it is important that the manager provides the researcher with access to this information. Without information, the researcher will not be able to (1) adequately define the management problem and (2) assess the costs and benefits of a research project.

An understanding of different types of action problems helps the manager to understand that it is not always easy to define the problem. What's more, knowledge of different types of action problems may help the manager to select and implement an effective strategy to solve the problem.

- **Learning objective 1: Identify problem areas that are likely to be studied in organizations.** A research process is often set in motion when managers notice that they find themselves in one of the following two situations: (1) the manager is proactively looking for decision opportunities or areas for improvement and (2) the existing situation is not in line with a desired situation or with a certain norm or standard. This bothers the manager for some reason. In other words, the manager has an action problem.

- **Learning objective 2: Explain why it is important to distinguish between two different types of situations that may or may not lead to a research project.** It is important to distinguish between two different types of situations (proactive and reactive) that may or may not lead to a research project because the management objective is different and because the function of research is different. This may lead to different types of research questions and methods.

- **Learning objective 3: Carry out an exploration.** After researchers have been briefed by the manager, they are ready to start. The first step that must be taken by the researcher is to explore. The idea is that the researcher tries to find out more about the potential issue: 'what is happening?' and 'why is that problematic?' are two important questions that need a provisional answer at this stage. It is also useful to explore the conditions for solving the problem/doing research.

- **Learning objective 4: Make a Diagnosis.** If the management problem is an action problem, the exploration stage will go over into the next stage, making diagnosis, if further investigation of the issue is worthwhile. The diagnosis stage is, in many ways, the most important stage of the change process. The problem and the constraints for the solution need to be thoroughly defined. Diagnosis can take place at different levels in an organization. For instance, diagnosis can take place at the level of the organization, a department or SBU or at the level of the individual, such as an employee or a client. Diagnosis can be aimed at all these levels but also at one of these levels. There are many valuable instruments and tools that can help you to diagnose. The majority of these instruments are analytical in nature.

- **Learning objective 5: Distinguish between different types of action problems: Technical problems, information problems, consensus problems and a combination of information and consensus problems.** If the management problem is a *technical* or *routine problem*, there is clarity and agreement on what the problem is and the constraints of the solution. Moreover, there is sufficient knowledge and experience on how to solve the problem, either within or outside (an expert that can be commissioned to solve the problem) the organization, for example, because the solution is obvious or because previously implemented solutions can be copied. Solving the problem is therefore a matter of planning and action. If the problem can be defined as an *information problem*, there is also agreement about what the problem is and the constraints of the solution. But in contrast to routine problems, it is not clear how the problem can (best) be solved (here is the information problem). There are alternative courses of action, one course of action is more effective than the other and it is initially unclear which alternative is the most effective one. The solution to such problems can be found by doing research aimed at informing the manager on how the problem can (best) be solved. Such research is called action-oriented research. In some cases, stakeholders do not agree on what the problem is and/or the constraints of the solution. Sometimes, there is sufficient knowledge about how to solve the problem, but for example, due to conflicting interests or different value systems, beliefs or ethical standpoints, every viable solution to the problem is blocked. Such *consensus problems* frequently occur in organizations. Negotiation, persuasion and/or making use of one's authority are more common ways to arrive at a solution. In some cases, consensus problems may lead to politically motivated research, where the conclusions of the study are clear from the outset. Note that undertaking such research is never a good idea. If a problem is a *combination of an information and a consensus problem*, there is little or no knowledge about how the problem can be solved, but there is also insufficient agreement about what the problem is and/or about the constraints that the solution must meet. In this situation, there is often disagreement about the desired direction of change. This hinders gathering information on how the problem can be solved. The problem is therefore seemingly unsolvable. In many cases, it is difficult to determine which steps must be taken to arrive at a common problem definition and a management objective that is acceptable to everyone. There are several ways to break the deadlock; charismatic and authoritarian leadership are most often mentioned.

- **Learning objective 6: Define the management problem.** The management problem should be defined in terms of the following:
  - The existing situation
  - Why this situation is problematic (the change motive or the motive for doing research)
  - The desired situation (the management objective)

Instructors can visit the companion website at **www.wiley.com/go/bougie/researchmethods forbusiness8e** for **Author Video: The Inter Magnus Group**.

DISCUSSION QUESTIONS

1. Define 'problem' and provide an example of a problem you have encountered in your daily life. Discuss how you have solved the problem? Have you used research at any moment in the problem-solving process? When and why? Have you used any other problem-solving strategies such as negotiation, leadership and/or planning and action? Why (why not)?

2. Describe the functions of exploration if a manager is proactively looking for decision opportunities.

3. Describe the function of exploration and diagnosis if a manager has an action problem.

4. Use the Internet to find more information about the '5 times why' approach. Discuss this approach using an example provided on the Internet.

5a. Provide three examples of situations where a manager is proactively looking for decision opportunities.

5b. Under which circumstances, is it wise to do research?

6. Provide an example of an action problem.

7. Compare technical and information problems. Provide an example of both.

8. Are technical problems always simple problems or do you think that technical problems could also be complicated? Explain.

9. Provide a description and an example of a consensus problem.

10. Describe action-oriented research in your own words.

11. Below is the gist of an article from *Businessweek*. After reading it:
    a. Identify the broad problem area.
    b. Explain how you would proceed further.

    Two years ago, Electronic Arts, the second-largest U.S. video game company, ran on promises. Developers pitching a feature for a big game had to produce a cool video to win approval from the bosses. They were then left alone for months, until it was too late to fix any problems, says Ian Milham, one of the company's creative directors. He describes the philosophy as 'make a trailer that promises a lot and then don as o f anyone until itthat promi'. Often it wasnitthat promises a lot and then don as o fix any problems, says Ian Milham, one of the companytching a f were so bug-ridden on release that they crashed game servers and were essentially unplayable for days or weeks before they were fixed. EA servers and were essentially unplayable foram, one of the videos of glitches trapping digital athletes in anatomically impossible positions.

    Burger, D. (2015, March 12) *EA Tries Selling Video Games That Work.* Retrieved from http://www.bloomberg.com/news/articles/2015-03-12/electronic-arts-delays-game-releases-to-fix-bugs-for-a-change

Background Information on the Organization

Information gathered on relevant contextual factors will be useful in talking knowledgeably with managers and other employees in the company and raising the appropriate issues related to the problem. Background information might include, among other things, the contextual factors listed below, which may be obtained from various sources:

1. The origin and history of the company – when it came into being, business is in rate of growth, ownership and control and so on

2. Size in terms of employees, assets or both

3. Charter – purpose and ideology

4. Location – regional, national or other

5. Resources – human and others

6. Interdependent relationships with other institutions and the external environment

7. Financial position during the previous five to ten years and relevant financial data

8. Information on structural factors (for instance, roles and positions in the organization and number of employees at each job level, communication channels, control systems and workflow systems)

9. Information on the management philosophy

Depending on the situation, the type of problem investigated and the nature of some initial responses received, certain aspects may have to be explored in greater depth than others.

The contextual information mentioned may be obtained through various primary and/or secondary data collection methods, such as interviews and a review of company records and archives. Data gathered through existing sources are called secondary data. **Secondary data** are data that have been collected by others for another purpose than the purpose of the current study. Some secondary sources of data are statistical bulletins, government publications, published or unpublished information available from either within or outside the organization, company websites and the Internet. The nature and the value of secondary data should be carefully evaluated before it is used. Box 3.10 provides an overview of the key criteria for evaluating secondary data.

The collection of secondary data is very often quite helpful in the early stages of the research process, but in some cases, information is best obtained by other methods such as interviewing people, observation or by administering questionnaires to individuals. Such data that the researcher gathers first hand for the specific purpose of the study are called **primary data**. Four principal methods of primary data collection (interviews, observation, administering questionnaires and experiments) are discussed in Chapters 8 to 11.

Note that it is often beneficial to simultaneously gather primary and secondary data in the early stages of the research process. On the one hand, secondary data can help you to focus (further) interviews more meaningfully on relevant aspects pertaining to the problem; on the other hand, interviews may help you to search for relevant information in secondary sources.

BOX 3.10   CRITERIA FOR EVALUATING SECONDARY DATA

Timeliness of the data. *When were the data collected?* It is important that the data are up-to-date. Check the dates on all of your secondary data to make sure that you have the newest information available.

Accuracy of the data. *What was the purpose of (presenting) the data?* Web pages are created with a specific purpose in mind. Commercial organizations often post information online that might favour them in some way or represent their own interests. *Who collected the data? How were the data collected? What are the author's credentials on this subject?* The accuracy of data can be impacted by who collected it and how the data were collected. *Are the data consistent with data from other sources?* If specific information varies from source to source, you need to find out which information is more accurate.

Relevance of the data. Not all of the secondary data you find will be relevant to your particular needs. Data may be accurate and up-to-date but not applicable to your research objective(s) and research questions.

Costs of the data. How much do the data cost? Do the benefits outweigh the costs? Are you better off collecting other data? Are you better off using other (primary) methods of data collection?

Defining the Research Problem

LEARNING OBJECTIVES

After completing Chapter 4, you should be able to:

1. Narrow down the management problem into a research problem.
2. Develop a good research problem.
3. Develop a research proposal.
4. Be aware of the role of the manager in the early stages of the research process.
5. Be aware of the role of ethics in the early stages of the research process.

INTRODUCTION

In the last chapter, we have explained that there are two types of situations that may (or may not) call for research: situations where managers are proactively looking for decision opportunities and situations where something is 'broken that needs to be fixed' (a manager wants to increase customer loyalty, employee motivation and the like). We have explained that in both situations, a management problem needs to be defined in terms of the existing situation, why that situation is problematic, and the management objective. In this chapter, we will look at defining the *research* problem. We will introduce two important components of the research problem; the research objective (the 'why' of the research project) and research questions (the 'what' of the research project). We will also discuss the development of a research proposal and explain that the management problem and the research problem are two important elements of a research proposal.

THE MANAGE-MENT PROBLEM

Applied research starts with a management problem. In the previous chapter, we have explained that a management problem can be defined in terms of:

- The existing situation
- Why this situation is problematic (the change motive or the motive for doing research)
- The desired situation (the management objective)

A well-defined management provides the foundation for defining the research problem. Indeed, if research is the logical next step in the decision-making or problem-solving process, we need a research problem to guide our actions as a researcher.

DEFINING THE RESEARCH PROBLEM

After defining the management problem, the researcher is in a position to define the research problem. It is critical that the **research problem** is unambiguous, specific and focused, and that the problem is addressed from a specific academic perspective. No amount of good research can find solutions to the situation if the research problem is not clearly pinpointed.

WHAT MAKES A GOOD PROBLEM STATEMENT?

Instructors can visit the companion website at **www.wiley.com/go/bougie/researchmethods forbusiness8e** for **Author Video: What makes a good problem statement?**

A good problem statement includes both a statement of the **research objective(s)** and the **research question(s)**. In Chapter 2, we have explained that good research has a purposive focus. Whereas the purpose of fundamental (or basic) research in business is related to expanding knowledge (of processes) of business and management in general, the ultimate aim of applied research is often to inform decision-making and action of managers. For instance, a manager might be interested in improving employee commitment, since an increase in employee commitment may translate into lower staff turnover, less absenteeism and increased performance levels, all of which will benefit the organization. A research objective – determining the factors that increase employee commitment to the organization – can be derived from the management objective. The purpose or objective of the study explains *why* the study is being done. The statement of the research objective(s) should be brief, but nonetheless communicate clearly the focus of the project.

Example	
Examples of Research Objectives	• To find out what motivates consumers to buy a product online. • To study the effect of leadership style on employees' job satisfaction. • To investigate the relationship between capital structure and profitability of the firm. • To establish success factors regarding the adoption and use of information systems. • To determine the optimal price for a product. • To investigate the influence of the in-store shopping environment on impulse buying. • To establish the determinants of employee involvement. • To understand the causes of employee absence. • To investigate the long-term profitability of a certain market (obviously the market has to be specified). • To identify market segments. • To determine the level of employee commitment. • To find out whether the organization is in control.

Once the purpose of the study has been identified, one is able to formulate the research question(s) of the study. The inclusion of one or more research questions in the problem statement further clarifies the issue to be resolved. The research question(s) specify *what* you want to learn about the topic. They guide and structure the process of collecting and analyzing information to help you to attain the purpose of your study. In other words, research questions are the translation of the problem of the organization into a specific need for information. Box 4.1 provides an example of the process of defining the research problem. Note that both the research objective and the research questions of the study are detailed in this example.

The research problem discussed in Box 4.1 addresses both the research objectives and the research questions of the study. The research objective and the research questions are strongly related; it would have been impossible to adequately detail the research questions if the research objective had been unclear, unspecified or ambiguous. What's more, the research questions have been clarified to the extent that it is possible to relate them to existing literature in the areas of waiting, service evaluations and mood theory. Hence, the management problem area has been transformed into a researchable topic for study.

Box 4.2 summarizes the management problem and the research problem of the research project discussed in Box 4.1.

BOX 4.1   EXAMPLE OF A PROBLEM STATEMENT

CAA Airlines carries out charter and regular flights to medium-haul destinations – such as the Mediterranean, North Africa and the Red Sea – and to long-haul destinations such as the Caribbean. Today, CAA's fleet consists of three (new) Boeing 737-800s and four (outdated) Boeing 767-300s. Because the Boeing 767s are rather outdated they need more maintenance than the average airplane. Despite an intensive maintenance program, these planes have a lot of technical problems. Consequently, the long-haul fleet of CAA has needed to deal with a lot of delays recently. New long-haul planes have been ordered, but these planes will not be delivered before 2016. This means that more delays will inevitably occur. This may translate into much frustration among airline passengers, to switching behaviour and to negative word-of-mouth communication. These feelings and behaviours of consumers may eventually have negative effects on the performance and the profitability of the firm. The management objective is to improve the customers' waiting experience, customer satisfaction and service evaluations.

Prior research has claimed that service waits can be controlled by two techniques: operations management and management of perceptions. For CAA Airlines, it is very difficult to obtain 'zero defects' (no delays). Hence, this project will focus on managing the perceptions of the wait experience: because CAA Airlines cannot control the actual amount of delays and the duration, the company must focus on managing the customers' perception of the waiting experience. The purpose of this study is twofold: (1) to identify the factors that influence the passengers' waiting experience and (2) to investigate the possible impact of waiting on customer satisfaction and service evaluations.

Therefore, this project focuses on the following research questions:

1. What are the factors that affect the perceived waiting experience of airline passengers and to what extent do these factors affect the perception of waiting times?

2. What are the affective consequences of waiting and how does affect mediate the relationship between waiting and service evaluations?

3. How do situational variables (such as filled time) influence customer reactions to the waiting experience?

Drawing from prior research in the areas of waiting, service evaluations and mood theory, hypotheses are generated regarding the relationships among a delay, the waiting experience, affect and service evaluations. The hypothesized relationships are tested in a field setting involving delayed CAA airline passengers.

BOX 4.2   MANAGEMENT PROBLEM TRANSLATED INTO RESEARCH PROBLEM

		Research problem
Management objective	Research objective	Research questions
To improve the customers' waiting experience, customer satisfaction and service evaluations.	The purpose of this study is twofold: (1) to identify the factors that influence the passengers' waiting experience and (2) to investigate the possible impact of waiting on customer satisfaction and service evaluations.	1. What are the factors that affect the perceived waiting experience of airline passengers and to what extent do these factors affect the perception of waiting times? 2. What are the affective consequences of waiting and how does affect mediate the relationship between waiting and service evaluations? 3. How do situational variables (such as filled time) influence customer reactions to the waiting experience?

By now, it should be clear that a research problem addresses both the 'why' (the specific aim or purpose of the study) and the 'what' (the central research question or a set of research questions) of the research. There are three key criteria to assess the quality of a problem statement: it should be relevant, feasible and interesting.

A research problem is relevant if it is meaningful from a managerial perspective, an academic perspective or both. From a *managerial* perspective, research is *relevant* if it relates to (1) an information problem that currently exists in an organizational setting or (2) an area that a manager believes needs to be improved in the organization.

Example **Academic Relevance**	From an *academic* perspective, research is *relevant* if: (1) nothing is known about a topic, (2) much is known about the topic, but the knowledge is scattered and not integrated, (3) much research on the topic is available, but the results are (partly) contradictory, or (4) established relationships do not hold in certain situations. If you base your research report on the 'nothing is known' argument, you will have to prove that your claim is right. The observation that much is known about a topic, but that the knowledge is scattered and not integrated also provides a good basis for a research report. Your task is, however, a difficult one, since it is expected that you will present an integrated overview of the topic. A research project that aims to reconcile contradictory findings or to establish boundary conditions is also a real challenge.

A good research problem is relevant but also *feasible*. A problem statement is feasible if you are able to answer the research questions within the restrictions of the research project. These restrictions are possibly related to time and money, but also to the availability of respondents, the expertise of the researcher (a problem statement may be too difficult to answer) and the like. A frequent problem in terms of feasibility is that the problem statement is both unclear (the research objective and research questions are not precise enough and/or ambiguous) and too broad in scope. Indeed, it is important that you develop a narrowly defined research question that can be investigated within a reasonable amount of time, and with a reasonable amount of money and effort. For instance, the question 'How do consumers behave?' is far too general to investigate.

Example **Bringing clarity and focus to the problem**	The 'secret' to bringing *clarity* and *focus* to your research problem is to isolate the key ideas in the first version of the problem statement. A broad, first statement of the problem often includes several words and/or phrases that need definition. Check out the following research objective: *To find out why Minority group members in organizations are not advancing in their careers.* To identify the key terms in your research problem, look for the subjects (careers), verbs (advancing) and objects (minority group members) in your statement. Definitions of key terms must be precise in order to identify the subject of the research and to gain access to relevant academic literature. Precise definitions will allow you to explore the literature. The literature review will help you to refine your research objective(s) and research questions and thus to develop a feasible topic for research.

The selection of a particular (academic) perspective on the problem will also enhance the feasibility of a research project since it allows us to draw upon a rich body of literature to help us to formulate the research problem. This is exemplified by the following example.

Consider the following problem: '*Long and frequent delays lead to much frustration among airline passengers. These feelings may eventually lead to switching behaviour, negative word-of-mouth communication, and customer complaints*'. That is why the airline company aims to reduce negative feelings of passengers associated with waiting times. Preliminary research on this issue suggests that service waiting times are typically controlled by two techniques: operations management, to decrease actual, objective waiting times (perspective 1) and management of perceptions, which will help service providers to manage the customers' subjective waiting experience (perspective 2). The selection of a particular academic perspective on the problem (for instance, *management of perceptions* in the foregoing example of long and frequent delays) provides us with a vast body of knowledge that will help us to shape our own thinking and spark valuable insights on the problem under study.

Example

How the Selection of an Academic Perspective Will Help Us to Narrow Down Our Research

A third characteristic of a good research problem is that it is *interesting* to you. Research is a time-consuming process and you will go through many ups and downs before you present the final version of your research report. It is therefore vital that you are genuinely interested in the problem statement you are trying to answer, so that you can stay motivated throughout the entire research process.

1. To what extent do the structure of the organization and type of information systems installed account for the variance in the perceived effectiveness of managerial decision-making?
2. To what extent has the new advertising campaign been successful in creating the high-quality, customer-centred corporate image that it was intended to produce?
3. How has the new packaging affected the sales of the product?
4. Has the new advertising message resulted in enhanced recall?
5. How do price and quality rate on consumers' evaluation of products?
6. Is the effect of participative budgeting on performance moderated by control systems?
7. Does better automation lead to greater asset investment per dollar of output?
8. Does expansion of international operations result in an enhancement of the firm's image and value?
9. What are the effects of downsizing on the long-range growth patterns of companies?
10. What are the specific factors to be considered in creating a data warehouse for a manufacturing company?

Example

Well-defined Research Questions

BASIC TYPES OF QUESTIONS: EXPLORATORY DESCRIPTIVE AND CAUSAL QUESTIONS

Instructors can visit the companion website at **www.wiley.com/go/bougie/researchmethods forbusiness8e** for **Author Video: Purpose of the study.**

Earlier in this chapter, we explained that the research problem includes both a statement of the research objective(s) and the research questions. There are three *basic types of questions* that research projects can address: exploratory, descriptive and causal questions. We will now look at each of these in some detail.

Exploratory Research Questions

Exploratory research questions are typically developed when: (a) not much is known about a particular phenomenon; (b) existing research results are unclear or suffer from serious limitations; (c) the topic is highly complex; or (d) there is not enough theory available to guide the development of a *theoretical framework* (discussed in Chapter 6). **Exploratory research** often relies on qualitative approaches to data gathering such as informal discussions (with consumers, employees, managers), interviews, focus groups and/or case studies (discussed in Chapters 7 and 8). As a rule, exploratory research is flexible in nature. Indeed, the activities of the researcher in exploratory research are quite similar to the activities of Inspector Lewis, Inspector Wallander, Sergeant Hunter, Detective Dee or the South Florida team of forensic investigators from 'CSI Miami', who use old-fashioned police work, cutting-edge scientific methods or both to solve murder crimes. Whereas the focus of the research is broad at first, it becomes increasingly narrower as the research proceeds. The results of exploratory studies are typically not generalizable to the population.

The following is an example where exploratory research would be necessary.

Example	The manager of a multinational corporation is curious to know if the work ethic values of employees working in its subsidiary in Pennathur City are different from those of Americans. There is very little information about Pennathur (except that it is a small city in southern India), and since there is considerable controversy about what work ethic values mean to people in other cultures, the manager's curiosity can be satisfied only by an exploratory study, interviewing the employees in organizations in Pennathur. Religion, political, economic and social conditions, upbringing, cultural values and so on play a major role in how people view their work in different parts of the world. Here, since very little is known about work ethic values in India, an exploratory study will have to be undertaken.

Descriptive Research Questions

The objective of a **descriptive study** is to obtain data that describes the topic of interest. For instance, if we want to know what percent of the population likes Coca-Cola better than Pepsi in a double-blind test, we are interested in describing consumers' taste preferences. Descriptive studies are often designed to collect data that describe characteristics of objects (such as persons, organizations, products or brands), events or situations. Descriptive research is either quantitative or qualitative in nature. It may involve the collection of quantitative data such as satisfaction ratings, production figures, sales figures or demographic data, but it may also entail the collection of qualitative information. For instance, qualitative data might be gathered to describe how consumers go through a decision-making process or to examine how managers resolve conflicts in organizations.

Sometimes the researcher is interested in associations among variables to describe populations, events or situations. For instance, a researcher might be interested in the relationship between job involvement and job satisfaction, arousal-seeking tendency and risk-taking behaviour, self-confidence and the adoption of innovative products or goal clarity and job performance. Such studies are correlational in nature. **Correlational studies** describe relationships between variables. While correlational studies can suggest that there is a relationship between two variables, finding a correlation does not mean that one variable *causes* a change in another variable.

Descriptive studies may help the researcher to:

1. Understand the characteristics of a group in a given situation (for instance, the profile of a specific segment in a market).

2. Think systematically about aspects in a given situation (for instance, factors related to job satisfaction).

3. Offer ideas for further probing and research.

4. Help make certain (simple) decisions (such as decisions related to the use of specific communication channels depending on the customer profile, opening hours, cost reductions, staff employment and the like).

Below are examples of situations warranting a descriptive study.

A bank manager wants to have a profile of the individuals who have loan payments outstanding for six months and more. The profile will include details of their average age, earnings, nature of occupation, full-time/part-time employment status and the like. This might help him to elicit further information or decide right away on the types of individuals who should be made ineligible for loans in the future.

A CEO may be interested in having a description of how companies in her industry have incorporated corporate social responsibility into the business strategy of the organization. Such information might allow comparison later of the performance levels of specific types of companies.

Example

Causal Research Questions

Causal studies test whether or not one variable causes another variable to change. In a **causal study**, the researcher is interested in delineating one or more factors that are causing a problem. Typical examples of causal research questions are: 'What is the effect of a reward system on productivity?' and 'How does perceived value affect consumer purchase intentions?' The intention of the researcher conducting a causal study is to be able to state that variable X (the independent variable) causes variable Y (the dependent variable). So, when variable X is removed or altered in some way, problem Y is solved (note that quite often, however, it is not just one variable that causes a problem in organizations). In Chapter 6, we will explain that in order to establish a causal relationship, the following conditions should be met:

1. The independent and the dependent variable should covary.

2. The independent variable (the presumed causal factor) should precede the dependent variable.

3. In order to establish causality, the researcher should control for the effects of 'extraneous' variables to make sure that variation in the dependent variable is not due to factors or variables other than the independent variable included in the experiment. An extraneous variable is a variable that has an unintended influence on the results of a study. Extraneous variables confound the results when they are allowed to change systematically along with the two variables being studied. Hence, such variables distort the results and make it impossible to draw meaningful conclusions from the results as they allow for alternative explanations for the results.

Because of the time sequence condition, experimental designs, discussed in Chapter 6 and in more detail in Chapter 11, are often used to establish causal relationships.

Examples of causal studies are given below.

| Example | A marketing manager wants to know if the sales of the company will increase if he increases the advertising budget. Here, the manager would like to know the nature of the relationship that may be established between advertising and sales by testing the hypothesis: 'If advertising is increased, then sales will also go up'. |

A marketing manager wants to know if the sales of the company will increase if he increases the advertising budget. Here, the manager would like to know the nature of the relationship that may be established between advertising and sales by testing the hypothesis: 'If advertising is increased, then sales will also go up'.

A prevalent theory is that the diversity of the workforce increases organizational effectiveness. A manager wants to know if this relationship holds for her organization.

A manager wants to test the hypothesis that stress experienced in the job negatively affects the job satisfaction of employees.

A researcher is interested in testing the hypothesis that women are more motivated for their jobs than men.

Researchers often aim to answer different types of research questions in a single project. For this reason, it is quite common to conduct exploratory research before moving to descriptive or causal studies in order to develop a thorough understanding of the phenomenon under study. Indeed, the three types of research (exploratory, descriptive and causal) are often viewed as building blocks, where exploratory research lays the foundation for descriptive research and causal research builds on descriptive research.

BOX 4.3   THE POSITIVIST VIEW

Causal studies are at the heart of the scientific approach. For a positivist, the world operates by laws of cause and effect that can be discerned if a scientific method to research is used. Exploratory research is needed when there is not enough knowledge available to guide the development of a theoretical framework. In such cases, exploratory research needs to be done to understand what is going on. Based on this – in the eyes of the positivist – preliminary work, we will be able to set up more rigorous (read: causal) designs for further investigation.

After you have defined the research problem, you are ready to start your research. First, however, you need to communicate the problem statement and a number of other important aspects of the study – such as the scope of the study, the procedures to be followed, the time frame and the budget – to all the parties involved.

| THE RESEARCH PROPOSAL | Before any research study is undertaken, there should be an agreement between the person who authorizes the study and the researcher as to the management problem, the research problem to be investigated, the methodology to be used, the duration of the study and its cost. This ensures that there are no misunderstandings or frustrations later for either party. This is usually accomplished through a research proposal, which the researcher submits and gets approved by the sponsor, who issues a letter of authorization to proceed with the study. |

The **research proposal** drawn up by the investigator is the result of a planned, organized and careful effort, and basically contains the following:

1. A working title.

2. Background of the study.

3. The management problem:
   If the management problem is an action problem: the constraints or preconditions that the solution must meet.

4. The research problem:

   a. The purpose of the study

   b. Research questions.

5. The scope of the study.

6. The relevance of the study.

7. The research design, offering details on:

   a. Type of study – exploratory and descriptive

   b. Data collection methods

   c. The sampling design

   d. Data analysis.

8. Time frame of the study, including information on when the written report will be handed over to the sponsors.

9. The budget, detailing the costs with reference to specific items of expenditure.

10. Selected bibliography.

MODEL 4.1	Research Proposal to Study Retention of New Employees

Management Problem

Employee turnover is 40 percent within the first three years of recruitment. This is undesirable since turnover has a negative effect on productivity, it brings about extra costs, and it leads to less profits. The management objective is to reduce undesirable employee turnover with 50 percent within the next 12 months.

Purpose of the Study

To find a solution to the recurring problem of 40 percent employee turnover within the first three years of their recruitment, and more specifically to:

1. draw up a profile of the employees who quit;

2. assess if there are any special needs of the new recruits that require to be met;

3. determine the reasons for employees leaving the organization in the first three years.

Research Question

How can small- to medium-sized firms increase the organizational commitment of their employees?

(Continued)

(Continued)

Scope of the Study

This research analyzes the problem of high turnover of employees within *small- to medium-sized firms*.

Relevance of the Study

The cost of employee turnover to firms has been estimated to be up to 150 percent of the employees' remuneration package (Schlesinger & Heskett, 1991). There are both direct and indirect costs involved. Direct costs relate to leaving costs, replacement costs and transition costs, while indirect costs relate to the loss of production, reduced performance levels, unnecessary overtime and low morale. The results of this study provide managers with the means to decrease the costs of employee turnover.

The Research Design (i.e., Details of the Study)

Survey instruments. First, we will interview a small number of employees who have joined the company in the previous three years. Based on these exploratory findings, we will administer a questionnaire to all of the employees who have joined the company in the past three years.

Data collection. The interviews will be conducted during office hours in the conference hall of the organization at a prearranged time convenient to the interviewees. The questionnaire will be given to the employees to be completed by them in their homes and returned anonymously to the box set up for the purpose by the specified date. They will all be reminded two days before the due date to return their questionnaires, if not already done.

Time Frame

The time frame necessary for completion of this research project is approximately five months. During these five months, periodic reports will be provided on the progress being made.

Budget

The budget for this project is in Appendix A.[1]

Selected Bibliography

Bateman, T. S. & Strasser, S. (1984) A longitudinal analysis of the antecedents of organizational commitment. *The Academy of Management Journal*, 27(1), 95–112.

Lachman, L. & Aranya, N. (1986) Evaluation of alternative models of commitments and job attitudes of professionals. *Journal of Occupational Behavior*, 7, 227–243.

Meyer, J. & Allen, N. (1997) *Commitment in the workplace: Theory, research and application.* Thousand Oaks: Sage.

Meyer, J., Stanley, D., Herscovitch, L. & Topolnytsky, L. (2002) Affective, continuance and normative commitment: a meta-analysis of antecedents, correlates and consequences. *Journal of Vocational Behavior*, 63, 20–52.

Schlesinger, L. & Heskett, J. (1991) The service-driven service company. *Harvard Business Review*, 69, 71–81.

Vandenberghe, C., Bentein, K. & Stinglhamber, F. (2002) Affective commitment to the organization, supervisor and work group: antecedents and outcomes. *Journal of Vocational Behavior*, 64, 47–71.

[1]Please note that Appendix A has not been included as Model 4.1 is an example only.

Such a proposal containing the above features is presented to the manager, who might seek clarification on some points, want the proposal to be modified in certain respects or accept it in to. An excerpt of a research proposal to study the frequent turnover of newly recruited employees is presented below.

Once the proposal is accepted, the researcher conducts the research, going through the appropriate steps discussed in the research design process.

| **MANAGERIAL IMPLICATIONS** | Managers' inputs help researchers to define the management problem and to narrow down the management problem into a feasible topic for research. Managers who realize that a correct **definition** of both the management and the research problem is critical to ultimate |

problem solving and decision-making do not begrudge the time spent in working closely with researchers, particularly at the early stages of the research project.

A well-developed research proposal allows managers to judge the relevance of the proposed study. However, to make sure that the objectives of the study are actually being achieved, managers must stay involved throughout the *entire* research process. Information exchange between the manager and the researcher during all the important stages of the research process will definitely enhance the managerial relevance and the quality of the research effort.

ETHICAL ISSUES IN THE PRELIMINARY STAGES OF INVESTIGATION

Preliminary information is gathered by the researcher define the management and the research problem. In many cases, the researcher interviews decision makers, managers and other employees to gain knowledge of the situation so as to better understand the problem. Once a management problem is specified and a research problem is defined, the researcher needs to assess his or her research capabilities; if the researcher does not have the skills or resources to carry out the project, he or she should decline the project. If the researcher decides to carry out the project, it is necessary to inform all the employees – particularly those who will be asked to participate in the study – of the proposed study (though it is not necessary to acquaint them with the actual reasons for the study, because this might bias responses). The element of unpleasant surprise will thus be eliminated for the employees. It is also necessary to assure employees that their responses will be kept confidential by the interviewer/s and that individual responses will not be divulged to anyone in the organization. These two steps make the employees comfortable with the research undertaken and ensure their cooperation. Employees should not be forced to participate in the study. When employees are willing to participate in the study, they have the right to be protected from physical or psychological harm. They also have a right to privacy and confidentiality. Attempts to obtain information through deceptive means should be avoided at all costs.

Example

Checklist for Dealing with Ethical Considerations and Dilemmas During the First Stages of the Research Process

- Why is this research project worth doing?
- How does the organization benefit from this project?
- What impact, if any, does your research have on the organization?
- Do you have the skills and resources to carry out this research project?
- Have you informed all the employees of the research project? Why not?
- Do you explain the purpose of your research to the participants? Why not?
- Are participants given the opportunity to decline participation?
- Are participants able to withdraw their consent at any point? How?
- Does the research cause you to have access to sensitive information? How will you ensure the confidentiality of this information?
- How will you ensure individual respondents cannot be identified from any research reports or papers that are produced?
- Are there any possible negative effects (long or short term) on your participants (including any physical or psychological harm)?
- How will you report back from the research to your participants?
- Where ethical dilemmas have arisen, what steps have you taken to resolve these?

SUMMARY	• **Learning objective 1: Define a research problem based on the management problem.** A management problem does not provide researchers with enough information to embark on their research journey. That is why the management problem has to be transformed into a *researchable topic* for investigation. The research problem (the research objective and research questions) needs to be (a) specific and precise and (b) needs to have clear boundaries. Finally, the researcher needs to select a (c) perspective from which the organizational problem is investigated. Preliminary research should help the researcher to arrive at a specific research problem.

• **Learning objective 2: Develop a good research problem.** There are three key criteria to assess the quality of a research problem: it should be relevant, feasible and interesting. A good research problem includes both a statement of the research objective(s) and the research question(s). The research objectives and the research questions are strongly related. There are three *basic types of questions* that research projects can address: exploratory, descriptive and causal questions.

• **Learning objective 3: Develop a research proposal.** Before any research study is undertaken, there should be an agreement between the sponsor of the study and the researcher as to the management problem and the research problem, the methodology, the duration of the study and its cost. This is usually accomplished through a research proposal, which the researcher submits and has approved by the sponsor, who issues a letter of authorization to proceed with the study.

• **Learning objective 4: Be aware of the role of the manager in the early stages of the research process.** Managers must stay involved in a research project throughout the entire research process. This will enhance the managerial relevance and the quality of the research effort.

• **Learning objective 5: Be aware of the role of ethics in the early stages of the research process.** The checklist provided in this chapter will help the researcher to deal with ethical considerations and dilemmas during the first stages of the research process.

In the next chapter, we will examine the next step in the research process: the critical literature review.

Instructors can visit the companion website at **www.wiley.com/go/bougie/researchmethods forbusiness8e** for **Case Study: CAP Airlines**.

DISCUSSION QUESTIONS	**1a.** Under which circumstances do we still have to transform the following management objective into a researchable topic for investigation?

> *To reduce sick leave with 40 percent within the next 12 months.*

1b. Develop a relevant and feasible research objective from this management objective.

2. 'The problem definition stage (definition of the management and the research problem) is perhaps more critical in the research process than the problem solution stage'. Discuss this statement.

3. 'The "secret" to bringing *clarity* and *focus* to your research problem is to isolate the key ideas in the first version of the problem statement'. What are the subjects, verbs and objects in the following research objective?

> *To provide insight in why managers do not use the newly installed information system.*

4. Offer a clearly focused research objective in the broad area of corporate culture, job satisfaction *or* risk-seeking behaviours of investors.

5. A typical example of a research questions is: 'What is the effect of reward system on productivity?' What is the problem here, according to the researcher?

And what is a possible solution to the problem, according to the same researcher?

Often it wasn't. Several of EA's biggest 2013 releases, including entries in its SimCity and Battlefield franchises, were so bug-ridden on release that they crashed game servers and were essentially unplayable for days or weeks before they were fixed. EA's sports games have become Internet punch lines, thanks to videos of glitches trapping digital athletes in anatomically impossible positions.

Burger, D. (2015, March 12) *EA Tries Selling Video Games That Work.* Retrieved from http://www.bloomberg.com/news/articles/2015-03-12/electronic-arts-delays-game-releases-to-fix-bugs-for-a-change

6. Define a possible management objective and research objective in the following situation:

Employee loyalty

Companies benefit through employee loyalty. Crude downsizing in organizations during the recession crushed the loyalty of millions. The economic benefits of loyalty embrace lower recruitment and training costs, higher productivity of workers, customer satisfaction, and the boost to morale of fresh recruits. In order that these benefits are not lost, some companies, while downsizing, try various gimmicks. Flex leave, for instance, is one. This helps employees receive 20 percent of their salary, plus employer-provided benefits, while they take a 6- to 12-month sabbatical, with a call option on their services. Others try alternatives like more communication, hand holding, and the like.

The Critical Literature Review

LEARNING OBJECTIVES

After completing Chapter 5, you should be able to:

1. Discuss the functions of a literature review.

2. Write a literature review on any given topic, documenting the references in the prescribed manner.

3. Discuss the ethical issues of documenting the literature review.

INTRODUCTION

In Chapter 2, we explained that a first review of the academic literature will help you to define the problem of the organization and to develop a clear and specific research problem. But mere definition of a problem does not solve it. How, then, does one proceed further? One answer is by going through the process as shown in the research process model in Figure 5.1. This figure illustrates that the next step, after you have developed a research proposal, is a critical literature review. This step is indicated by the shaded portion in the figure.

The aim of this chapter is to introduce you to the process of carrying out a critical **literature review**. The chapter begins with a definition of the critical literature review, followed by a discussion of its functions. Then it explains that a critical literature review is a step-by-step process that involves the identification of published and unpublished work from secondary data sources on the topic of interest, the evaluation of this work in relation to the problem and the documentation of this work. Finally, this chapter discusses two pitfalls you have to be aware of when you document the literature review: misrepresenting others and plagiarism.

To help the organization to solve its problem, you have to become an expert on your topic. A second review of the literature, or **critical literature review**, is therefore essential in most research projects. A literature review is 'the selection of available documents (both published and unpublished) on the topic, which contain information, ideas, data and evidence written from a particular standpoint to fulfil certain aims or express certain views on the nature of the topic and how it is to be investigated, and the effective evaluation of these documents in relation to the research being proposed' (Hart, 1998, p. 13).

In general, a literature review ensures that:

1. The research effort is positioned relative to existing knowledge and builds on this knowledge.

2. You do not run the risk of 'reinventing the wheel', that is, wasting effort on trying to rediscover something that is already known.

3. The research effort can be contextualized in a wider academic debate. In other words, it allows you to relate your findings to the findings of others.

4. You are able to introduce relevant terminology and to define key terms used in your writing. This is important because the same term may have different meanings, depending on the

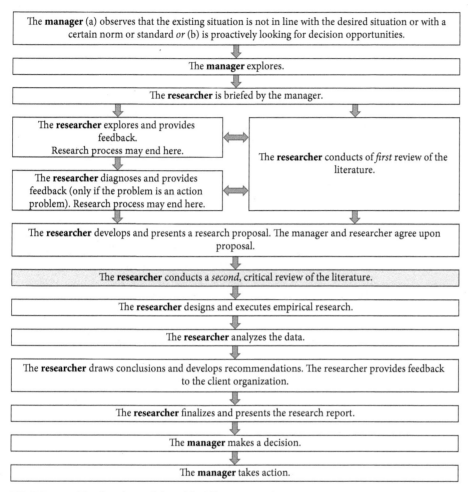

FIGURE 5.1   The functions of the critical literature review

DEFINING WAITING FOR SERVICE

Waiting for service refers to the time between the point a customer is ready to receive a service and the point the service starts (Taylor, 1994). A customer may have to wait before, during or after a transaction. In other words, there are three kinds of waits: pre-process waits, in-process waits and post-process waits (Dubé-Rioux, Schmitt & LeClerc 1988; Miller, Kahn & Luce, 2008). To make these different kinds of waits more concrete, imagine you are flying with an airline from point A to B. You may have to wait before you can board the plane (a *pre-process wait*), because the plane you are in does not have permission to land (an *in-process wait*), and because you cannot disembark immediately (a *post-process wait*).

context in which it is used. Definitions will also help you to give structure to your essay, article or report (see Box 5.1 for an example).

5. You obtain useful insights of the research methods that others have used to provide an answer to similar research questions.

Since the research questions of your study serve as the starting point for your critical review of the literature, some of the functions of a critical literature review depend on the type of study and the specific research approach that is taken, as illustrated by the examples in Box 5.2.

SPECIFIC FUNCTIONS OF A LITERATURE REVIEW

Emma is involved in a *descriptive* study that aims to describe how a major player in the pharmaceutical industry delivers valuable products to the market. A critical review of the literature should help her to come up with a comprehensive overview of the relevant perspectives on value, a guiding definition of value and an in-depth overview of frameworks, instruments and analytical tools (such as Michael Porter's value chain) that will help her to *describe* how the organization can create value and competitive advantage.

George's fundamental research project is *inductive* and *exploratory* in nature. A review of the literature has helped him to develop a theoretical background, which provides an overview of the literature pertinent to the specific topic he is studying. Relevant research findings, methodological issues and major conclusions of earlier and more recent work are put forward, the logical continuity between earlier and more recent work is clarified, and controversial issues, when relevant, are addressed. George explains that despite the valuable work of others, exploratory research is needed. He argues that although earlier research findings provide a wide variety of potential explanations for the problem under study, they are often conflicting and industry-specific, which limits the generalizability of these findings.

Jim's applied study is *deductive* in nature. A second review of the literature has allowed him to develop a theoretical background. This has helped him to obtain a clear idea as to what *variables* (different types of variables are discussed in Chapter 6) will be important to consider in his theoretical framework, why they are considered important, how they are related to each other, and how they should be measured to solve the problem. A critical review of the literature has also helped him to provide arguments for the relationships between the variables in his conceptual causal model and to develop hypotheses. Along these lines, a second review of the literature provides Jim with a framework for his own work. It ensures that no important variable that has in the past been found (repeatedly) to have an impact on the problem is ignored in the research project. Indeed, if there are variables that are not identified but influence the problem critically, then research done without considering them is an exercise in futility. In such a case, the true reason for the problem will remain unidentified and the research project will not help the manager to solve the problem. To avoid such possibilities Jim has delved into all the important research relating to the problem under study.

A critical review of the literature has helped Emma, George and Jim (check Box 5.2) to become familiar with relevant knowledge related to the problem that they aim to solve. The examples in Box 5.2 illustrate that a critical review of the literature is vital in nearly all research projects, regardless of the type of study, but also that the specific functions of the literature review may vary per project. Indeed, familiarity with the literature on your subject area is beneficial in exploratory, descriptive and causal research. A literature review is helpful in both an academic (or fundamental) and a non-academic (or applied) context. In both cases, a good theoretical base will add rigor to the study.

In sum, a critical review of the literature will spark many useful insights on your research topic; it will allow you to work in an expert manner, to make informed decisions and to benefit from existing knowledge in many different ways. Let us now turn to how you can approach the literature review.

HOW TO APPROACH THE LITERATURE REVIEW

The first step of a literature review involves the identification of the various published and unpublished materials that are available on the topic of interest, and gaining access to these.

DATA SOURCES

The quality of a literature review depends on a cautious selection and reading of books, academic and professional journals, theses, conference proceedings, unpublished manuscripts and the like. Academic books and journals are, in general, the most useful sources of information. However, other sources such as professional journals, reports and even newspapers may also be valuable because they can provide you with specific, real-world information about markets, industries or companies. Therefore, as a rule, you will need to use a combination of information resources. The precise combination of resources depends on the nature and the objectives of your research project.

Textbooks

Textbooks are a useful source of theory in a specific area. An advantage of textbooks is that they can cover a broad range of topics. What's more, textbooks can cover a topic much more thoroughly than articles can. Hence, textbooks offer a good starting point from which to find more detailed sources such as journal articles, theses and unpublished manuscripts. A downside of textbooks is that they tend to be less up to date than journals.

Journals

Both academic and professional journals are important sources of up-to-date information. Articles in academic journals have generally been peer-reviewed: this means that the articles have been subject to the scrutiny of experts in the same field before being accepted for publication. *Review articles* (that may or may not contain a meta-analysis: a type of data analysis in which the results of several studies are combined and analyzed as if they were the results of one large study) summarize previous research findings to inform the reader of the state of existing research. Review articles are very useful because they provide an overview of all the important research in a specific area. *Research articles* are reports of empirical research, describing one or a few related studies. The conceptual background section of a research article provides a compact overview of relevant literature. Research articles also provide a detailed description of the purpose of the study, the method(s) used, the results of the study and the implications of these findings for researchers and practitioners.

Articles in professional journals are a valuable source of recent developments in the field and of facts and figures. What's more, they may provide you with a feel for the practical relevance of a problem.

Theses

PhD theses often contain an exhaustive review of the literature in a specific area. Most PhD theses include several empirical chapters. These chapters often have the same structure and characteristics as academic journal articles. Note that not every empirical chapter of a thesis is eventually published in an academic journal.

Conference Proceedings

Conference proceedings can be useful in providing the latest research, or research that has not (yet) been published. Conference proceedings are very up to date, and for this reason this information source is quite valuable if you are working in a relatively new area or domain. Not every manuscript presented at a conference is eventually published in an academic journal; hence you must critically assess the quality of this information source.

Unpublished Manuscripts

The APA defines an unpublished manuscript as any information source that is not 'officially' released by an individual, publishing house or other company. Examples of unpublished manuscripts may include papers accepted for publication but still 'in press', data from an unpublished study, letters, manuscripts in preparation and personal communications (including e-mails). Unpublished manuscripts are often very up to date.

Reports

Government departments and corporations commission carry out a large amount of research. Their published findings provide a useful source of specific market, industry or company information.

Newspapers

Newspapers provide up-to-date business information. They are a useful source of specific market, industry or company information. Note that opinions in newspapers are not always unbiased.

The Internet

The amount of information that can be found on the Internet is enormous. You can search for (the details of) books, journals and journal articles and conference proceedings, as well as for specialized data such as company publications and reports. The number of newspapers, magazines and journals that are available electronically is massive.

Note that the Internet is unregulated and unmonitored. Moreover, developing an Internet page is easy and cheap. For this reason, the Internet provides exceptional challenges in determining the usefulness and reliability of information. An instrument that may help you to assess the quality of online information is the RADAR (Rationale, Authority, Date, Accuracy and Relevance) system (Mandalios, 2011). You can find useful information on this instrument on the Internet itself; what's more, several universities have developed useful guidelines to assess the quality of information found online (check, for instance, http://guides.lib.berkeley.edu/evaluating-resources).

Search engines such as Google can help you to find relevant information. For instance, Google Scholar, which can be accessed from the Google homepage, can help you to identify academic literature, such as peer-reviewed papers, theses, books, abstracts and articles from academic publishers, universities and other scholarly organizations.

SEARCHING FOR LITERATURE

Instructors can visit the companion website at **www.wiley.com/go/bougie/researchmethods forbusiness8e** for **Author Video: Searching for literature**.

Not too long ago, one had to manually go through several bibliographical indexes that are compiled periodically, listing the journals, books and other sources in which published work in the area of interest could be found. With modern technology, locating sources where the topics of interest have been published has become much easier. Every library today has computer online systems to locate published information. Computerized databases provide a number of advantages. First, they save enormous amounts of time. Second, they are comprehensive in their listing and review of references. Third, gaining access to them is relatively inexpensive. For these reasons you can focus on material most central to the research effort.

You will benefit from spending some time on becoming familiar with the online resources that your library provides. Most libraries have the following electronic resources at their disposal: Annual reports, (E-)Books, Book reviews, (E-)Journals, Journal Articles, Theses and the like.

Some important databases available on the Internet are also provided in the appendix. Databases include, among others, listings of journal articles, books in print, census data, dissertation abstracts, conference papers and newspaper abstracts that are useful for business research.

EVALUATING THE LITERATURE

Accessing the online system and searching for literature in the area of interest will provide a comprehensive bibliography on the subject. Because the search for literature can sometimes provide as many as 100 or more results, you will have to carefully select relevant books and articles. Two important criteria in this respect are relevance and quality.

A glance at the *titles* of the articles or books will indicate which of them may be pertinent and which others are likely to be peripheral to the contemplated study. The *abstract* of an article usually provides an overview of the study purpose, general research strategy, findings and conclusions. A good abstract thus provides you with enough information to help you to decide whether an article is relevant for your study. An article's *introduction* also provides an overview of the problem addressed by the research and specific research objectives. The introduction often ends with a summary of the research questions that guide the study. The problem statement, research questions and/or the research objectives give you a feel for what the researcher is studying and thus for the relevance of the article to your study. In a similar fashion, the *table of contents* and the *first chapter of a book* may help you to assess the relevance of the book.

A good literature review needs to include references to the key studies in the field. For this reason, articles and books that are often cited by others must be included in your literature review, even if these articles and books were written twenty or even thirty years ago. Of course, more recent work should also be incorporated in your literature survey, since recent work will build on a broader and more up-to-date stream of literature than older work.

To assess the quality of *recent* research (indeed, in this case you cannot use the number of citations as an indicator of the quality of an article), you could ask the following questions:

- Is the main research question or problem statement presented in a clear and analytical way?
- Is the relevance of the research question made transparent?
- Does this study build directly upon previous research?
- Will the study make a contribution to the field?
- Is there a theory that guides the research?
- Is the theory described relevant and is it explained in an understandable, structured and convincing manner?
- Are the methods used in the study explained in a clear manner (description of methods)?
- Is the choice of certain methods motivated in a convincing way (justification of methods)?
- Is the sample appropriate?
- Are the research design and/or the questionnaire appropriate for this study?
- Are the measures of the variables valid and reliable?
- Has the author used the appropriate quantitative and/or qualitative techniques?
- Do the conclusions result from the findings of the study?
- Do the conclusions give a clear answer to the main research question?
- Has the author considered the limitations of the study?
- Has the author presented the limitations in the article?

The quality of the journal that published an article can also be used as an indicator of the quality of an article. Important questions in this respect are: 'Is the journal peer-reviewed; that is, do all articles have to undergo a review process before they are published?' and 'What is the impact factor of the journal?' The impact factor of a journal can be viewed as the average number of citations in a year given to those papers in the journal that were published during a given period (usually the two preceding years). Because important articles are cited more often than articles that are not important, the impact factor of a journal is frequently used as a proxy for the importance of that journal to its field.

In sum, some criteria for assessing the value of articles or books are: the relevance of the issues that are addressed in the article or book, the importance of a book or article in terms of citations, the year of publication of the article or book and the overall quality of the article or book.

All the articles considered relevant to your study can be listed as references, using the appropriate referencing format, which is discussed in the appendix to this chapter.

DOCUMENTING THE LITERATURE REVIEW

As stated earlier, the purpose of the literature review is to help the researcher to build on the work of others and to make informed decisions during the various stages of the research project. A review of the literature identifies and highlights relevant themes and documents significant findings, frameworks and/or instruments from earlier research that will serve as the foundation for the current project. Documenting the literature review is important to convince the reader that the researcher is knowledgeable about the problem area and has done the preliminary homework that is necessary to conduct the research.

Murray and Hughes (2008) identify a number of clearly distinguishable functions of academic writing: definition, description, comparing and contrasting, classifying, explaining causes and effects and developing an argument. Knowledge of these functions of academic writing may help you to determine what you are looking for when you are carrying out your literature review and aiming for when you are documenting your literature review. Note that depending on the specific characteristics of your project (for instance, depending on whether the project is exploratory, descriptive or causal in nature), some of these functions might be important, whereas other functions might be less important or not important at all.

- Defining: Assigning meaning to the key terms of one's writing. Note that this function is always important, regardless of the type of project.
- Describing: Description can take on many forms in a research project. Murray and Hughes explain that it may involve (a) an explanation of how to do something (e.g., how to conduct an experiment), (b) an explanation of the different elements of which something is composed (e.g., some experts have argued that the elements that make up employee well-being are job demands and job resources) or (c) a description of time sequence, the order in which events unfold in time.
- Comparing and contrasting: A consideration of the similarities and differences between two or more things (e.g., between two instruments aimed at making a portfolio analysis or two approaches to customer satisfaction).
- Classifying: Organizing items, instruments, definitions and the like into clearly distinguishable groups.
- Explaining causes and effects: The discussion of causal relationships is aimed at explaining why things happen (e.g., why the morale of employees is low or why customers are not satisfied).
- Developing an argument: As we will explain in Chapter 18 an argument is a set of statements that includes a conclusion and evidence which supports that conclusion.

A point to note is that the literature survey should bring together all relevant information in a cogent and logical manner instead of presenting all the studies in chronological order with bits and pieces of uncoordinated information. A literature review is intended to *synthesize* (and not necessarily to summarize) relevant research on your topic. To synthesize is to combine two or more elements to form a new whole. In your literature review, the *elements* are the findings of the literature you select and read; the *new whole* is the conclusion you draw from these findings.

There are several accepted methods of citing references in the literature survey section and using quotations. The *Publication Manual of the American Psychological Association* (2019) offers detailed information regarding citations, quotations, references and so on and is one of the accepted styles of referencing in the management area. Other formats include *The Chicago Manual of Style* (2017) and the *Harvard Format Citation Guide* (2016). As stated earlier, details of the referencing style and quotations based on the APA *Manual* are offered in the appendix at the end of this chapter.

To conclude, let us take *a portion* of a completed literature review and examine how this review has helped to (1) introduce the subject of study and (2) to build on previous research to offer the basis from which to get to the next steps of the research process.

EXAMPLE

The Impact of Racial Bias on Decision-making

A recent stream of research has documented the existence of in-group racial biases in the employment, criminal, judicial and educational settings (Bertrand et al., 2005; Donohue & Levitt, 2001; Giuliano et al., 2011; Stoll et al., 2004). While social and legal changes have eliminated many institutionalized forms of racial discrimination, the same policy tools may have less leverage against the implicit racial stereotypes that underpin in-group favouritism. An example of the continued impact of racial bias on decision-making is evident in recent research analysing the behaviour of National Basketball Association (NBA) referees (Price and Wolfers, 2010). Using NBA data from 1991 to 2003, Price and Wolfers found that white and black players receive relatively fewer personal fouls when most of the referees officiating the game are their own race. The in-group favouritism displayed by NBA referees was large enough to have an appreciable impact on game outcomes and is consistent with a broader literature documenting in-group biases.

In this study, we exploit a particularly unusual natural experiment that occurred in May 2007 when the results of the Price and Wolfers study received widespread media attention and examine whether this increased awareness of in-group favouritism among NBA referees subsequently impacted the observed bias. The media attention associated with the release of this study included front-page coverage in the New York Times and many other newspapers, extensive coverage on the major news networks, ESPN and talk radio and in the sports media, including comments from star players LeBron James, Kobe Bryant and Charles Barkley, and then NBA Commissioner David Stern. We consider the greater awareness of racial bias that resulted from this to be a quasi-experimental treatment.

From the above extract, several insights can be gained. The literature review (1) introduces the subject of study (racial bias), (2) summarizes the work done so far on the topic and (3) introduces the objective of the study. With that, the authors have carefully paved the way for the next step, which is to introduce the research method and discuss the empirical results of the study.

ETHICAL ISSUES

Earlier in this chapter we have explained that research involves building on the work of others. When you summarize, add to, or challenge the work of others, there are two important pitfalls that you have to beware of:

1. Purposely misrepresenting the work of other authors – that is, their viewpoints, ideas, models, findings, conclusions, interpretations and so on.

2. Plagiarism – the use of another's original words, arguments or ideas as though they were your own, even if this is done in good faith, out of carelessness or out of ignorance.

Both purposely misrepresenting the work of others and plagiarism are considered to be fraud. In today's information age, copying and pasting information from online sources into your own research paper has become very simple. This may create a temptation to copy (significant) portions of text into your work. Your task is to resist this temptation. Plagiarism is a type of fraud that is taken very seriously in the academic world, mainly because using the work of others as if it were your own does not convey much respect for the efforts that other people have put into their work. Two other reasons to take plagiarism very seriously are provided by IJzermans and Van Schaaijk (2007). They point out that:

1. Plagiarism makes it is difficult for the reader to verify whether your claims about other authors and sources are accurate.

2. You are participating in a scientific debate. You need to make your position in this debate clear by designating the authors whose work you are building on or whose ideas you are challenging.

There are many forms of plagiarism above and beyond copying and pasting text into your own work. Box 5.3 provides an overview of common forms of plagiarism. This overview may help you to avoid the pitfall of plagiarism.

Note that many universities use software such as Turnitin or Ephorus to detect plagiarism. To avoid plagiarism, you need to observe the rules for referencing sources, detailed in the appendix of this chapter. You may also benefit from examining the plagiarism guidelines of your own university or from checking out the integrity handbook of the Massachusetts Institute of Technology at http://web.mit.edu/academicintegrity/handbook/handbook.pdf

---

| BOX 5.3 | **COMMON FORMS OF PLAGIARISM** |

Sources not cited

1. **'The Ghost Writer'**
The writer turns in another's work, word-for-word, as his or her own.

2. **'The Photocopy'**
The writer copies significant portions of text straight from a single source, without alteration.

3. **'The Potluck Paper'**
The writer tries to disguise plagiarism by copying from several different sources, tweaking the sentences to make them fit together while retaining most of the original phrasing.

4. **'The Poor Disguise'**
Although the writer has retained the essential content of the source, he or she has altered the paper's appearance slightly by changing key words and phrases.

5. **'The Labor of Laziness'**
The writer takes the time to paraphrase most of the paper from other sources and make it all fit together, instead of spending the same effort on original work.

6. **'The Self-Stealer'**
The writer 'borrows' generously from his or her previous work, violating policies concerning the expectation of originality adopted by most academic institutions.

Sources cited (but still plagiarized)

1. **'The Forgotten Footnote'**
The writer mentions an author's name for a source, but neglects to include specific information on the location of the material referenced. This often masks other forms of plagiarism by obscuring source locations.

2. **'The Misinformer'**
The writer provides inaccurate information regarding the sources, making it impossible to find them.

3. **'The Too-Perfect Paraphrase'**
The writer properly cites a source, but neglects to put in quotation marks text that has been copied word-for-word, or close to it. Although attributing the basic ideas to the source, the writer is falsely claiming original presentation and interpretation of the information.

4. **'The Resourceful Citer'**
The writer properly cites all sources, paraphrasing and using quotations appropriately. The catch? The paper contains almost no original work! It is sometimes difficult to spot this form of plagiarism because it looks like any other well-researched document.

5. **'The Perfect Crime'**
Well, we all know it doesn't exist. In this case, the writer properly quotes and cites sources in some places, but goes on to paraphrase other arguments from those sources without citation. This way, the writer tries to pass off the paraphrased material as his or her own analysis of the cited material.

Reprinted with permission from: What Is Plagiarism? (n.d.), retrieved June 22, 2011, from http://www.plagiarism.org/learning_center/what_is_plagiarism.html

- **Learning objective 1: Discuss the functions of a literature review.** A literature review is the selection of available documents on a topic, which contain information, ideas, data and evidence written from a particular standpoint to fulfil certain aims or express certain views on the nature of the topic and how it is to be investigated and the effective evaluation of these documents in relation to the research being proposed. A literature review ensures that the research effort is positioned relative to existing knowledge and builds on this knowledge. A literature review has many other functions. Because the research questions of a study serve as the starting point for the literature review, some of these functions depend on the type of research questions the researcher develops.

- **Learning objective 2: Write a literature review on any given topic, documenting the references in the prescribed manner.** The first step of a literature review involves the identification of the materials that are available on the topic of interest and gaining access to these. Searching for literature in the area of interest will provide a comprehensive bibliography on the subject. That is why the researcher will have to carefully select relevant material. Some criteria for assessing the value of materials are: the relevance of the issues that are addressed, the importance in terms of citations, the year of publication and overall quality. Documenting the literature review is important to convince the reader that the researcher is knowledgeable about the problem area and has done the preliminary homework that is necessary to conduct the research.

- **Learning objective 3: Discuss the ethical issues of documenting the literature review.** When researchers document their literature review, there are two important pitfalls that they have to beware of: (1) purposely misrepresenting the work of other authors and (2) plagiarism – the use of another's original words, arguments or ideas as though they were your own, even if this is done in good faith, out of carelessness or out of ignorance. Both purposely misrepresenting the work of others and plagiarism are considered to be fraud.

The appendix to this chapter offers information on (1) online databases, (2) bibliographical indexes, (3) the APA format for references and (4) notes on referencing previous studies and quoting original sources in the literature review section.

> | **SUMMARY** |

Instructors can visit the companion website at **www.wiley.com/go/bougie/researchmethods forbusiness8e** for **Case Study: The Literature Review.**

| **DISCUSSION QUESTIONS** |

1. What is the purpose of a critical literature review?

2. 'The exact purpose of a critical literature review depends on the research approach that is taken'. Discuss this statement.

3. Provide at least two distinctive definitions of two of the following terms:
   - Leadership
   - Job satisfaction
   - Organizational effectiveness
   - Service quality
   - Auditor liability
   - Cash flow

4. How would you go about doing a literature review in the area of corporate social responsibility?

5. Find two or more sources with contrasting viewpoints on the same issue. Discuss the main differences between these sources.

6. After studying and extracting information from all the relevant work done previously, how does the researcher know which particular references, articles and information should be given prominence in the literature review?

7. Why is appropriate citation important? What are the consequences of not giving credit to the source from which materials are extracted?

PRACTICE PROJECT	Do the project assigned below, following the step-by-step process outlined:

Compile a bibliography on any one of the following topics, or any other topic of interest to you, from a business perspective: (a) service quality; (b) product development; (c) blockchain technology; (d) information systems; (e) agile leadership; (f) assessment centres; (g) transfer pricing.

From this bibliography, select five to seven references that include books, academic journals and professional journals.

Based on these five to seven references, write a literature review using different forms of citation, as described in the appendix.

Some Online Resources Useful for Business Research

ONLINE DATABASES

Databases contain raw data stored in a variety of ways. Computerized databases can be purchased that deal with statistical data, financial data, texts and the like. Computer network links allow the sharing of these databases, which are updated on a regular basis. Most university libraries have computerized databases pertaining to business information that can be readily accessed. Some of the databases useful for business research are listed below:

1. **ABI/INFORM Global** and **ABI/INFORM** provide the capability to search most major business, management, trade and industry and scholarly journals from 1971 onwards. The information search can be made by keying in the name of the author, periodical title, article title or company name. Full texts from the journals and business periodicals are also available on CD-ROM and electronic services.

2. **Dow Jones Factiva** products and services provide business news and information. The collection of more than 14,000 sources includes the *Wall Street Journal*, *Financial Times*, Dow Jones and Reuters newswires and the Associated Press, as well as Reuters Fundamentals and D&B company profiles.

3. **EconLit** is a comprehensive index of journal articles, books, book reviews, collective volume articles, working papers and dissertations.

4. **IMF eLibrary (Data).** Access to Marco-economic and financial data.

5. **IMF eLibrary (Publications).** The IMF eLibrary delivers the IMF's publications, research, analytical papers, reports and data as a one-stop resource for IMF content.

6. **MUSE.** Access to digital humanities and social science content for the scholarly community.

7. **Orbis.** Comprehensive information on companies worldwide.

8. **PsycINFO** is an abstract database of psychological literature from the 1800s to the present. PsycINFO contains bibliographic citations, abstracts, cited references and descriptive information of scholarly publications in the behavioural and social sciences.

9. **RePEc** (**Re**search **P**apers in **Ec**onomics) is a collaborative effort of volunteers in 63 countries to enhance the dissemination of research in economics. The heart of the project is a decentralized database of working papers, journal articles and software components.

10. **SSRN (Social Science Research Network)** is devoted to the rapid worldwide dissemination of social science research and is composed of a number of specialized research networks in each of the social sciences.

11. **Web of Science provides access to international research journals.** Access to: Science Citation Index, Social Sciences Citation Index and Arts & Humanities Citation Index.

12. **Web of Stories** contains video archive of interviews with today's greatest scientists, writers, filmmakers and craftspeople about their work. Once-only registration required for a personalized view of the website.

13. **World Development Indicators (World Bank)** is a database, produced by the World Bank, containing statistical data from 1970 onwards on the economic and social development of 223 countries.

14. **Zephyr** contains information on M&A, IPO, private equity and venture capital deals.

The following databases can also be accessed through the Internet: Business and Industry Database, Guide to Dissertation Abstracts, Periodicals Abstract, Social Science Citation Index, STAT-USA.

   Note: A cumulated annotated index to articles on accounting and in business periodicals arranged by subject and by author is also available. The Lexis-Nexis Universe provides specific company and industry information including company reports, stock information, industry trends, and the like.

ON THE WEB

Some of the many websites useful for business research are provided below.

General

Bureau of Census: http://www.census.gov

Business Information on the Internet: http://www.rba.co.uk/sources. A selection of key business Information Sites on the Internet, compiled by Karen Blakeman.

Business Researcher's Interests: http://www.brint.com/interest.html

Businessweek Online: http://www.bloomberg.com/businessweek. The journal *Businessweek* online from 1995 until now.

China & World Economy: http://en.iwep.org.cn/publications/publications_china_world_economy

Company Annual Reports: http://www.annualreports.com

Corporate Information: http://www.corporateinformation.com. Starting point to find corporate information from around the world.

Economic Journals on the Web: http://www.oswego.edu/~economic/journals.htm

Euromoney Publications: http://www.euromoney.com. The journal *Euromoney* online from 1995 until now. Registration required.

European Business Directory: http://www.europages.com/home-en.html

Eurostat: http://ec.europa.eu/eurostat. Eurostat is the site of the Statistical Office of the European Community. It provides direct access to the latest and most complete statistical information available on the European Union, the EU members, the euro-zone and other countries.

Fortune: http://www.fortune.com. Also contains the Fortune 500 List (500 American companies and 500 global companies with financial data and their home pages).

Forbes Magazine: http://www.forbes.com/forbes. The journal *Forbes Magazine* online from August 1997 until now.

FT.com. TotalSearch: http://news.ft.com/home/europe. FT.com's TotalSearch gives you access to more than ten million free newspaper and magazine articles alongside results gathered from leading online news sources. TotalSearch also incorporates a definitive Web guide in association with Business.com, a leader in business website classification. You can search in the *Financial Times*, the *Guardian* and *Wall Street Journal* from 1996 until now, or you can refine your search for the *Financial Times* only.

globalEDGE: http://globaledge.msu.edu. A directory of international business resources categorized by specific orientation and content. Each resource has been selected and reviewed by the globalEDGE TM Team.

Institute of Finance & Management (IOFM): www.iofm.com. This site links to business resources that include financial management, legal resources, small business, human resources and Internet marketing.

Kompass: http://www.kompass.com. Addresses and business information of 1.5 million companies worldwide.

List of Economics Journals:

http://en.wikipedia.org/wiki/List_of_economics_journals

STAT-USA: http://www.usa.gov/statistics

Wall Street Executive Library: http://www.executivelibrary.com. Business sites on newspapers, magazines, government, financial markets, company and industry, law, marketing and advertising, statistics, etc.

Wall Street Journal: http://online.wsj.com/public/us

Accounting

ARN: http://www.ssrn.com/en/index.efm.arn. The Accounting Research Network (ARN) was founded to increase communication among scholars and practitioners of accounting worldwide. ARN encourages the early distribution of research results by publishing abstracts of top quality research papers in three journals: *Auditing, Litigation and Tax Abstracts*, *Financial Accounting Abstracts*, and *Managerial Accounting Abstracts*. The journals publish abstracts of articles dealing with empirical, experimental and theoretical research in financial and managerial accounting, auditing and tax strategy. ARN is a division of the Social Science Research Network (SSRN).

Accounting terminology guide: https://www.nysscpa.org/professional-resources/accounting-terminology-guide#sthash.krYdJ7QM.dpbs

AuditNet: http://www.auditnet.org/. A global resource for auditors.

Internal Auditing World Wide Web (IAWWW): http://www.bitwise.net/iawww. A warehouse of information and knowledge pertaining to the internal auditing profession and functions across all associations, industries and countries.

Management

Academy of Management: http://www.aomonline.org

Harvard Business Review: https://hbr.org

Society for Human Resource Management: www.shrm.org

Sloan Management Review: http://sloanreview.mit.edu

Financial economics

Behavioural Finance: http://www.behaviouralfinance.net

CNN financial network: http://money.cnn.com

The Financial Economic Network (FEN) is a division of the Social Science Research Network (SSRN): http://www.ssrn.com/update/fen/index.cfm/fen

FINWeb: http://finweb.com. FINWeb is a financial economics website managed by James R. Garven. The primary objective of FINWeb is to list Internet resources providing substantive information concerning economics and finance-related topics.

MFFAIS: http://www.mffais.com. Mutual Fund Facts About Individual Stocks. A reference site that shows you (among other things) which and how many mutual funds sold shares in a specific company. And the only one that lists more than just the top ten fundholders of a company.

Morningstar, Inc. is a leading provider of independent investment research in North America, Europe, Australia and Asia: http://www.morningstar.com

Standard & Poor's Ratings Services provides market intelligence in the form of credit ratings, research: http://www.standardandpoors.com

Marketing

The Marketing Science Institute is a non-profit, membership-based organization dedicated to bridging the gap between academic marketing theory and business practice: http://www.msi.org

Links to academic marketing journals: http://www.sfu.ca/~mvolker/biz/journal1.htm

KnowThis: http://www.knowthis.com. Marketing virtual library, offering an objective and unbiased resource for marketing basics, market research, Internet marketing, marketing plans, advertising and much more.

APA FORMAT FOR REFERENCING RELEVANT ARTICLES

A distinction has to be made between a bibliography and references. A **bibliography** is a listing of work that is relevant to the main topic of research interest arranged in alphabetical order of the last names of the authors. A **reference list** is a subset of the bibliography, which includes details of all the citations used in the literature review and elsewhere in the paper, arranged, again, in alphabetical order of the last names of the authors. These citations have the goals of crediting the authors and enabling the reader to find the works cited.

At least three modes of referencing are followed in business research. These are based on the format provided in the *Publication Manual of the American Psychological Association* (APA) (2019), the *Chicago Manual of Style* (2017) and Turabian's *Manual for Writers* (2018). Each of these manuals specifies, with examples, how books, journals, newspapers, dissertations and other materials are to be referenced in manuscripts. Since the APA format is followed for referencing by many journals in the management area, we will use this below to highlight the distinctions in how books, journals, newspaper articles, dissertations and so on are referenced. In the following section we will discuss how these references should be cited in the literature review section. All the citations mentioned in the research report will find a place in the References section at the end of the report.

SPECIMEN FORMAT FOR CITING DIFFERENT TYPES OF REFERENCES (APA FORMAT)

Book by a single author
Leshin, C.B. (1997). *Management on the World Wide Web*. Englewood Cliffs, NJ: Prentice Hall.

Book by more than one author
Diener, E., Lucas, R., Schimmack, U., & Helliwell, J.F. (2009). *Well-being for public policy*. New York: Oxford University Press.

Book review

Nichols, P. (1998). A new look at Home Services [Review of the book Providing Home Services to the Elderly by Girch, S.]. *Family Review Bulletin*, 45, 12–13.

Chapter in an edited book

Riley, T., & Brecht, M.L. (1998). The success of the mentoring process. In R. Williams (Ed.), *Mentoring and career success*, pp. 129–150. New York: Wilson Press.

Conference proceedings publication

Sanderson, R., Albritton B., Schwemmer R., & Van de Sompel, H. (2011). Shared canvas: A collaborative model for medieval manuscript layout dissemination. Proceedings of the Eleventh ACM/IEEE Joint Conference on Digital Libraries, pp. 175–184. Ottawa, Ontario.

Doctoral dissertation

Hassan, M. (2014). *The Lives of micro-marketers: Why do some differentiate themselves from their competitors more than others?* Unpublished doctoral dissertation, University of Cambridge.

Edited book

Pennathur, A., Leong, F.T., & Schuster, K. (Eds.) (1998). *Style and substance of thinking.* New York: Publishers Paradise.

Edited book, digital, with DOI (Digital Object Identifier)[1]

Christiansen, S. (Ed.). (2007). Offenders' memories of violent crimes. doi: 10.1002/7980470713082.

Journal article

Jeanquart, S., & Peluchette, J. (1997). Diversity in the workforce and management models. *Journal of Social Work Studies*, 43 (3), 72–85.

Deffenbacher, J.L., Oetting, E.R., Lynch, R.S., & Morris, C.D. (1996). The expression of anger and its consequences. *Behavior Research and Therapy*, 34, 575–590.

Journal article in press

Van Herpen, E. Pieters, R. & Zeelenberg, M. (2009). When demand accelerates demand: Trailing the bandwagon, *Journal of Consumer Psychology*.

Journal article with DOI

López-Vicente, M., Sunyer, J., Forns, J., Torrent, M. & Júlvez, J. (2014). Continuous Performance Test II outcomes in 11-year-old children with early ADHD symptoms: A longitudinal study. *Neuropsychology*, 28, 202–211. http://dx.doi.org/10.1037/neu0000048

More than one book by the same author in the same year

Roy, A. (1998a). *Chaos theory.* New York: Macmillan Publishing Enterprises.

Roy, A. (1998b). *Classic chaos.* San Francisco, CA: Jossey-Bass.

Newspaper article, no author

QE faces challenge in Europe's junk bond market (2015, March 27). *Financial Times*, p. 22.

Paper presentation at conference

Bajaj, L.S. (1996, March 13). Practical tips for efficient work management. *Paper presented at the annual meeting of Entrepreneurs*, San Jose, CA.

Unpublished manuscript

Pringle, P.S. (1991). *Training and development in the '90s.* Unpublished manuscript, Southern Illinois University, Diamondale, IL.

REFERENCING NON-PRINT MEDIA

App

Skyscape. (2010). *Skyscape Medical Resources (Version 1.9.11) [Mobile application software].* Retrieved *from* http://itunes.apple.com/

---

[1] A Digital Object Identifier is a unique alphanumeric string assigned by a registration agency (the International DOI Foundation) to identify an object (such as an electronic document) and provide a persistent link to its location on the Internet. A publisher assigns a DOI when an article is published and made available electronically.

Conference proceeding from the Internet

Balakrishnan, R. (2006, March 25–26). *Why aren't we using 3d user interfaces, and will we ever?* Paper presented at the IEEE Symposium on 3D User Interfaces. doi:10.1109/VR.2006.148

Dictionary

Motivation. (n.d.). In Merriam-Webster's online dictionary (12th ed.). Retrieved from http://www.merriam-webster.com/dictionary/motivation

E-book

Diener, E., Lucas, R., Schimmack, U., & Helliwell, J.F. (2009). *Well-being for public policy* (New York: Oxford University Press). Retrieved from http://books.google.com

Electronic journal article

Campbell, A. (2007). Emotional intelligence, coping and psychological distress: A partial least squares approach to developing a predictive model. *E-Journal of Applied Psychology, 3* (2), 39–54. Retrieved from http://ojs.lib.swin.edu.au/index.php/ejap/article/view/91/117

Message posted to online forum or discussion group

Davitz, J.R. (2009, February 21). How medieval and renaissance nobles were different from each other [Msg 131]. Message posted to http://groups.yahoo.com/group/Medieval_Saints/message/131

Online document

Frier, S. (2015, March 19). *Facebook shares hit record amid optimism for ads business*. Retrieved from http://www.bloomberg.com/news/articles/2015-03-19/facebook-shares-hit-record-amid-optimism-for-ads-business

Online document, no author identified, no date

GVU's 18th WWW customer survey. (n.d.). Retrieved 2009, March 24, from http://www.bb.gotech.edu/gvu/user-surveys/survey-2008-10/

Podcast

Raz, G. (TED Radio Hour Host). (2015, February 27). *Success (R)* [Audio podcast]. Retrieved from http://podbay.fm/show/523121474/e/1425015000?autostart=1

Report from private organization, available on organization's website

Philips UK. (2009, March 23). U.S. Department of Energy honors Philips for significant advancement in LED lighting. Retrieved March 2009, 24, from http://www.philips.co.uk/index.page

Streaming video (for instance from YouTube)

How2stats (2011, September 15). Cronbach's Alpha – SPSS (part 1) [Video file]. Retrieved from https://www.youtube.com/watch?v=2gHvHm2SE5s

Tweet

TIAS (@TIASNews). "Cooperative banks make the financial system more stable, says Professor Hans Groeneveld", buff.ly/1BwXNhR. 13 March 2015, 19.24 p.m. Tweet.

Wikipedia

Game theory (n.d.). In *Wikipedia*. Retrieved 2015, November 6, from http://en.wikipedia.org/wiki/Game_theory

REFERENCING AND QUOTATION IN THE LITERATURE REVIEW SECTION

Cite all references in the body of the paper using the author–year method of citation; that is, the surname of the author(s) and the year of publication are given in the appropriate places. Examples of this are as follows:

1. Todd (2015) found the more motivated students are . . .

2. More recent studies of transformational leadership (Hunt, 2014; Osborn, 2013) focus on . . .

3. In a follow-up study from 2013, Green demonstrates . . .

As can be seen from the above, if the name of the author appears as part of the narrative as in the case of 1, the year of publication alone has to be cited in parentheses. Note that in case 2, both the author and the year are cited in parentheses, separated by a comma. If the year and the author are a part of the textual discussion as in 3 above, the use of parentheses is not warranted.

Note also the following:

1. Within the same paragraph, you need not include the year after the first citation so long as the study cannot be confused with other studies cited in the article. An example of this is:
   - Lindgren (2009, p. 24) defines satisfaction as 'the customer's fulfillment response. It is the judgment that a . . . service . . . provides a pleasurable level of consumption-related fulfillment'. Lindgren finds that . . .

2. When a work is authored by *two* individuals, always cite both names every time the reference occurs in the text, as follows:
   - As Tucker and Snell (2014) pointed out . . .
   - As has been pointed out (Tucker & Snell, 2014), . . .

3. When a work has *more than two* authors but fewer than six authors, cite all authors the first time the reference occurs, and subsequently include only the surname of the first author followed by '*et al.*' as per the example below:
   - Bougie, Pieters, and Zeelenberg (2003) found . . . (first citation) Bougie *et al.* (2003) found . . . (subsequent citations)

4. When a work is authored by *six or more* individuals, cite only the surname of the first author followed by *et al.* and the year for the first and subsequent citations. Join the names in a multiple-author citation in running text by the word *and*. In parenthetical material, in tables, and in the reference list, join the names by an ampersand (&).

5. When a work has no author, cite in text the first two or three words of the article title. Use double quotation marks around the title of the article. For example, while referring to the newspaper article cited earlier, the text might read as follows:
   - There are limits to how risky investors want to get ("QE faces challenge," 2015), . . .

6. When a work's author is designated as 'Anonymous', cite in text the word *Anonymous* followed by a comma and the date: (Anonymous, 2014). In the reference list, an anonymous work is alphabetized by the word *Anonymous*.

7. When the same author has several works published in the same year, cite them in the same order as they occur in the reference list, with the in press citations coming last. For example:
   - Research on Corporate Social Responsibility (Long, 1999, 2003, in press) indicates . . .

8. When more than one author has to be cited in the text, these should be in the alphabetical order of the first author's surname, and the citations should be separated by semicolons as per the illustration below:
   - In the job design literature (Aldag & Brief, 2007; Alderfer, 2009; Beatty, 1982; Jeanquart, 1999), . . .

9. Personal communication through letters, memos, telephone conversations and the like should be cited in the text only and not included in the reference list since these are not retrievable data. In the text, provide the initials as well as the surname of the communicator together with the date, as in the following example:
   - T. Peters (personal communication, June 15, 2013) feels . . .

In this section we have seen different modes of citation. We will next see how to include quotations from others in the text.

QUOTATIONS IN TEXT

Quotations should be given exactly as they appear in the source. The original wording, punctuation, spelling and italics must be preserved even if they are erroneous. The citation of the source of a direct quotation should always include the page number(s) as well as the reference.

Use double quotation marks for quotations in text. Use single quotation marks to identify the material that was enclosed in double quotation marks in the original source. If you want to emphasize certain words in a quotation, underline them and immediately after the underlined words, insert within brackets the words: *italics added*. Use three ellipsis points (. . .) to indicate that you have omitted material from the original source. See the example that follows below.

If the quotation is of more than 40 words, set it in a free-standing style starting on a new line and indenting the left margin a further five spaces. Type the entire quotation double spaced on the new margin, indenting the first line of paragraphs five spaces from the new margin, as shown below.

For instance, Weiner (1998, p. 121) argues that:

> *Following the outcome of an event, there is initially a general positive or negative reaction (a "primitive" emotion) based on the perceived success or failure of that outcome (the "primary" appraisal). (. . .) Following the appraisal of the outcome, a causal ascription will be sought if that outcome was unexpected and/or important. A different set of emotions is then generated by the chosen attributions.*

If you intend publishing an article in which you have quoted extensively from a copyrighted work, it is important that you seek written permission from the owner of the copyright. Make sure that you also footnote the permission obtained with respect to the quoted material. Failure to do so may result in unpleasant consequences, including legal action taken through copyright protection laws.

Theoretical Framework and Hypothesis Development

LEARNING OBJECTIVES

After completing Chapter 6, you should be able to:

1. Discuss the need for a theoretical framework in deductive research.

2. Describe four main types of variables and identify and label variables associated with any given situation.

3. Develop a theoretical framework that includes all relevant components.

4. Develop a set of hypotheses to be tested.

5. Demonstrate awareness of the manager's role in the development of a theoretical framework.

INTRODUCTION

A discussion of causal relationships, and with that the development of a theoretical framework and hypotheses, is needed when a researcher (a) aims to understand *why* things happen (for instance, why the consumers of the client organization are dissatisfied or why staff turnover in the client organization is high) and/or (b) seeks to assess the effects of a certain intervention (e.g., an activity, a project, a new policy or a new program). In order to present causes and effects clearly to the reader, researchers often develop a theoretical framework. A theoretical framework represents one's beliefs on how certain phenomena are related to each other and an explanation of why one believes that these variables are related to each other.

BOX 6.1   THE THEORETICAL FRAMEWORK AND THE HYPOTHETICO-DEDUCTIVE METHOD

A theoretical framework is the foundation of the *hypothetico-deductive method* as it is the basis of the hypotheses that you will develop. Recall that this method involves the seven steps of identifying a broad problem area, defining the problem statement, hypothesizing, determining measures, data collection, data analysis and the interpretation of the results. The method is used to test a theory – an explanation of why things happen – about a topic of interest.

Theoretical frameworks are usually associated with a deductive approach to research (see Box 6.1). As we have seen in Chapter 2, a deductive approach moves towards hypothesis testing, after which the beliefs of the researcher are confirmed, refuted or modified.

From a pragmatic point of view, the development of a theoretical framework and hypotheses is needed only if the research questions that have been developed by the researcher are causal in nature. If one, on the other hand, undertakes research that is exploratory or descriptive in nature, one does *not* develop or test hypotheses. Box 6.2 provides two examples of situations that call for the development of a theoretical framework and one example of a situation that does not require the development of a theoretical framework.

Before hypotheses can be tested, they first have to be generated. This chapter explains how a theoretical framework is developed. The process of building a theoretical framework, different types of variables and the development of hypotheses are discussed in some detail.

THE NEED FOR A THEORETICAL FRAMEWORK

A **theoretical framework** represents your beliefs on *how* certain phenomena (or variables or concepts) are related to each other (a model) and an explanation of *why* you believe that these variables are associated with each other (a theory). Both the model and the theory flow logically from the documentation of previous research in the problem area and the results of qualitative (exploratory or descriptive) research that precedes the causal study.

The process of building a theoretical framework includes the following:

1. Introducing definitions of the concepts or variables in your model

2. Developing a conceptual model that provides a descriptive representation of your theory

3. Coming up with a theory that provides an explanation for relationships between the variables in your model

From the theoretical framework, then, testable hypotheses can be developed to examine whether your ideas are valid or not. The hypothesized relationships can thereafter be tested through appropriate statistical analyses.

Since a theoretical framework involves the identification of the network of relationships among the variables considered important to the study of any given problem situation, it is essential to understand what a variable means and what the different types of variables are.

A **variable** is anything that can take on differing or varying values. The values can differ at various times for the same object or person or at the same time for different objects or persons. Examples of variables are production units, absenteeism and motivation.

VARIABLES

Example

Production units: One worker in the manufacturing department may produce one widget per minute, a second might produce two per minute, a third might produce five per minute. It is also possible that the same member might produce one widget the first minute and five the next minute. In both cases, the number of widgets produced has taken on different values and is therefore a variable.

Absenteeism: Today, three members in the sales department may be absent; tomorrow, six members may not show up for work; the day after, there may be no one absent. The value can thus theoretically range from 'zero' to 'all' being absent, on the absenteeism variable.

Motivation: The levels of motivation of members to learn in the class or in a work team might take on varying values ranging from 'very low' to 'very high'. An individual's motivation to learn from different classes or in different work teams might also take on differing values.

Four main types of variables are discussed in this chapter[1]:

1. The dependent variable (also known as the criterion variable)

2. The independent variable (also known as the predictor variable)

3. The moderating variable

4. The mediating variable

Each of these variables can be discrete (e.g., male/female) or continuous (e.g., the age of an individual). Associated scale levels of variables are discussed in Chapter 13.

DEPENDENT VARIABLE

The **dependent variable** is the variable of primary interest to the researcher. The researcher's goal is to understand and describe the dependent variable, or to explain its variability, or predict it. In other words, it is the main variable that lends itself for investigation. From a pragmatic point of view, it is where the problem lies. For instance, if we were interested in investigating the problem of staff turnover, our dependent variable would be staff turnover. Through the analysis of the dependent variable (i.e., finding what variables influence it), it is possible to find answers or solutions to the problem. For this purpose, the researcher will be interested in quantifying and measuring the dependent variable, as well as the other variables that influence this variable.

---

[1] Extraneous variables that confound cause-and-effect relationships are discussed in Chapter 11, Experimental Designs.

Example	A manager is concerned that the sales of a new product, introduced after test marketing it, do not meet with his expectations. The dependent variable here is 'sales'. Since the sales of the product can vary – they can be low, medium or high – it is a variable; since sales is the main focus of interest to the manager, it is the dependent variable.

A basic researcher is interested in investigating the debt-to-equity ratio of manufacturing companies in southern Germany. Here, the dependent variable is the ratio of debt to equity.

A vice president is concerned that the employees are not loyal to the organization and, in fact, seem to switch their loyalty to other institutions. The dependent variable in this case is 'organizational loyalty'. Here again, there is variance found in the levels of organizational loyalty of employees. The vice president might want to know what accounts for the variance in the loyalty of organizational members with a view to controlling it. If he finds that increased pay levels would ensure their loyalty and retention, he can then offer inducement to employees by way of pay rises, which will help control the variability in organizational loyalty and keep them in the organization.

It is possible to have more than one dependent variable in a study. For example, there is always a tussle between quality and volume of output, low-cost production and customer satisfaction and so on. In such cases, the manager is interested to know the factors that influence all the dependent variables of interest and how some of them might differ in regard to different dependent variables. These investigations may call for multivariate statistical analyses.

Now do Exercises 6.1 and 6.2.

EXERCISE 6.1	Research in behavioural finance has shown that overconfidence can cause investors to under-react to new information. What is the dependent variable in this case?

EXERCISE 6.2	A marketing manager believes that limiting the availability of a product increases product desirability. What is the dependent variable here?

INDEPENDENT VARIABLE

It is generally conjectured that an **independent variable** is one that influences the dependent variable in a certain (positive or negative, linear or non-linear) way. That is, when the independent variable is present, the dependent variable is also present, and with each unit of increase in the independent variable, there is an increase or decrease in the dependent variable. In other words, the variation in the dependent variable is accounted for by variation in the independent variable. From a pragmatic point of view, the independent variables represent possible solutions to the problem. To establish that a change in the independent variable *causes* a change in the dependent variable, *all three* of the following conditions should be met:

1. The independent and the dependent variable should covary: in other words, a change in the dependent variable should be associated with a change in the independent variable.

2. The independent variable (the presumed causal factor) should precede the dependent variable. In other words, there must be a time sequence in which the two occur: the cause must occur before the effect.

3. In order to establish causality, the researcher should control for the effects of 'extraneous' variables to make sure that variation in the dependent variable is not due to factors or variables other than the independent variable included in the experiment. An extraneous variable is a

variable that has an unintended influence on the results of a study. Extraneous variables confound the results when they are allowed to change systematically along with the two variables being studied. Hence, such variables distort the results and make it impossible to draw meaningful conclusions from the results as they allow for alternative explanations for the results.

Because of the time sequence condition, experimental designs, described in Chapter 11, are often used to establish causal relationships.

<table>
<tr><td></td><td>Example</td></tr>
</table>

Research studies indicate that successful new product development has an influence on the stock market price of the company. That is, the more successful the new product turns out to be, the higher will be the stock market price of that firm. Therefore, the 'success of the new product' is the *independent variable* and 'stock market price' the *dependent variable*. The degree of perceived success of the new product developed will explain the variance in the stock market price of the company. This relationship and the labelling of the variables are illustrated in Figure 6.1.

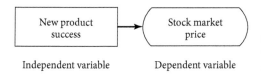

FIGURE 6.1   Diagram of the relationship between the independent variable (new product success) and the dependent variable (stock market price)

Cross-cultural research indicates that managerial values govern the power distance between superiors and subordinates. Here, power distance (i.e., egalitarian interactions between the boss and the employee, versus the high-power superior in limited interaction with the low-power subordinate) is the subject of interest and hence the dependent variable. Managerial values that explain the variance in power distance comprise the independent variable. This relationship is illustrated in Figure 6.2.

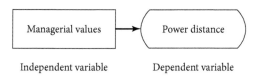

FIGURE 6.2   Diagram of the relationship between the independent variable (managerial values) and the dependent variable (power distance)

Now do Exercises 6.3 and 6.4. List the variables in these two exercises individually, and label them as dependent or independent, explaining why they are so labelled. Create diagrams to illustrate the relationships.

An investor believes that more information increases the accuracy of his forecasts.

EXERCISE 6.3

A marketing manager believes that selecting physically attractive spokespersons and models to endorse their products increases the persuasiveness of a message.

EXERCISE 6.4

MODERATING VARIABLE

Instructors can visit the companion website at **www.wiley.com/go/bougie/researchmethods forbusiness8e** for **Author Video: The mediating variable**.

The **moderating variable** is one that has a *contingent* effect on the independent variable–dependent variable relationship. That is, the presence of a third variable (the moderating variable) modifies the original relationship between the independent and the dependent variables. This becomes clear through the following examples.

Example

It has been found that there is a relationship between the availability of reference manuals that manufacturing employees have access to and the product rejects. That is, when workers follow the procedures laid down in the manual, they are able to manufacture products that are flawless. This relationship is illustrated in Figure 6.3(a). Although this relationship can be said to hold true generally for all workers, it is nevertheless contingent on the inclination or urge of the employees to look in the manual every time a new procedure is to be adopted. In other words, only those who have the interest and urge to refer to the manual every time a new process is adopted will produce flawless products. Others who do not consult the manual will not benefit and will continue to produce defective products. This influence of the attributes of the worker on the relationship between the independent and the dependent variables can be illustrated as shown in Figure 6.3(b).

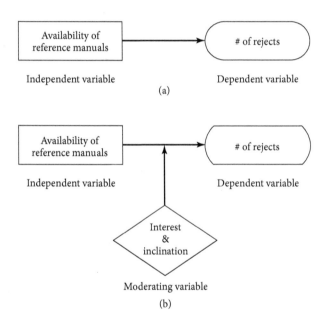

FIGURE 6.3   (a) Diagram of the relationship between the independent variable (availability of reference manuals) and the dependent variable (rejects); (b) diagram of the relationship between the independent variable (availability of reference materials) and the dependent variable (rejects) as moderated by the moderating variable (interest and inclination)

As in the above case, whenever the relationship between the independent variable and the dependent variable becomes contingent or dependent on another variable, we say that the third variable has a moderating effect on the independent variable–dependent variable relationship. The variable that moderates the relationship is known as the moderating variable. From a pragmatic point of view, moderating variables help us to explain that a specific intervention may be less effective (or even ineffective or counterproductive) in some situations or for some of our objects (for instance, employees or consumers).

The Distinction Between an Independent Variable and a Moderating Variable

At times, confusion is likely to arise as to when a variable is to be treated as an independent variable and when it becomes a moderating variable. For instance, there may be two situations as follows:

1. A research study indicates that the better the quality of the training programs in an organization and the greater the growth needs of the employees (i.e., where the need to

Example

Let us take another example of a moderating variable. A prevalent theory is that the diversity of the workforce (comprising people of different ethnic origins, races and nationalities) contributes more to organizational effectiveness because each group brings its own special expertise and skills to the workplace. This synergy can be exploited, however, only if managers know how to harness the special talents of the diverse work group; otherwise they will remain untapped. In the above scenario, organizational effectiveness is the dependent variable, which is positively influenced by workforce diversity – the independent variable. However, to harness the potential, managers must know how to encourage and coordinate the talents of the various groups to make things work. If not, the synergy will not be tapped. In other words, the effective utilization of different talents, perspectives and eclectic problem-solving capabilities for enhanced organizational effectiveness is contingent on the skill of the managers in acting as catalysts. This managerial expertise then becomes the moderating variable. These relationships can be depicted as in Figure 6.4.

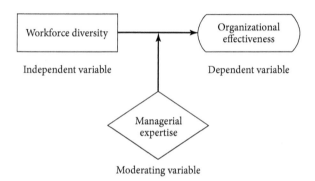

FIGURE 6.4 Diagram of the relationship among the three variables: workforce diversity, organizational effectiveness and managerial expertise

develop and grow on the job is strong), the greater is their willingness to learn new ways of doing things.

2. Another research study indicates that the willingness of the employees to learn new ways of doing things is *not* influenced by the quality of the training programs offered by the organizations to *all* people without any distinction. Only those with high growth needs seem to have a yearning to learn to do new things through specialized training.

In the above two situations, we have the same three variables. In the first case, the training programs and growth need strength are the independent variables that influence employees' willingness to learn, this latter being the dependent variable. In the second case, however, the quality of the training program is the independent variable, and while the dependent variable remains the same, growth need strength becomes a moderating variable. In other words, only those with high growth needs show a greater willingness and adaptability to learn to do new things when the quality of the training program is improved. Thus, the relationship between the independent and dependent variables has now become contingent on the existence of a moderator. Whether you would include growth needs as an independent or moderating variable in your model depends on your ideas on how the variables in your model are related to each other.

Figure 6.5 makes it clear that even though the variables used are the same, the decision as to whether to label them dependent, independent or moderating depends on the researcher's ideas about how they affect one another. The differences between the effects of the independent and the moderating variables may be visually depicted as in Figures 6.5(a) and 6.5(b). Note the steep incline of the top line and the relative flatness of the bottom line in Figure 6.5(b).

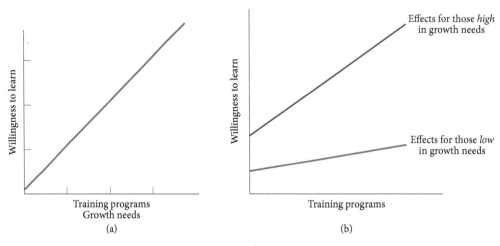

FIGURE 6.5 (a) Illustration of the influence of independent variables on the dependent variable when no moderating variable operates in the situation; (b) illustration of the influence of independent variables on the dependent variable when a moderating variable is operating in the situation

Now do Exercises 6.5 and 6.6. List and label the variables in these two exercises and explain and illustrate by means of diagrams the relationships among the variables.

EXERCISE 6.5

A manager finds that off-the-job classroom training has a great impact on the productivity of the employees in her department. However, she also observes that employees over 60 years of age do not seem to derive much benefit and do not improve with such training.

EXERCISE 6.6

A manager of an insurance company finds that 'fear appeals' in commercials are positively associated with consumers' behavioural intentions to insure their house. This effect is particularly strong for people with a high inherent level of anxiety.

MEDIATING VARIABLE

Instructors can visit the companion website at **www.wiley.com/go/bougie/researchmethods forbusiness8e** for **Author Video: The moderating variable**.

A **mediating variable** (or **intervening variable**) is one that surfaces between the time the independent variables start operating to influence the dependent variable and the time their impact is felt on it. There is thus a temporal quality or time dimension to the mediating variable. In other words, bringing a mediating variable into play helps you to model a *process*. The mediating variable surfaces as a function of the independent variable(s) operating in any situation and helps to conceptualize and explain the influence of the independent variable(s) on the dependent variable. The following example illustrates this point.

It would be interesting to see how the inclusion of the moderating variable, 'managerial expertise' in the foregoing example, would change the model or affect the relationships. The new set of relationships that would emerge in the presence of the moderator is depicted in Figure 6.7. As can be seen, managerial expertise moderates the relationship between workforce diversity and creative synergy. In other words, creative synergy will not result from the multifaceted problem-solving skills of the diverse workforce unless the manager is capable of harnessing that synergy

Example

In the previous example, where the independent variable (workforce diversity) influences the dependent variable (organizational effectiveness), the mediating variable that surfaces as a function of the diversity in the workforce is 'creative synergy'. This creative synergy results from a multi-ethnic, multiracial and multinational (i.e., diverse) workforce interacting and bringing together their multifaceted expertise in problem solving. This helps us to understand how organizational effectiveness can result from having diversity in the workforce. Note that creative synergy, the mediating variable, surfaces at time t_2, as a function of workforce diversity, which was in place at time t_1, to bring about organizational effectiveness in time t_3. The mediating variable of creative synergy helps us to conceptualize and understand how workforce diversity brings about organizational effectiveness. The dynamics of these relationships are illustrated in Figure 6.6.

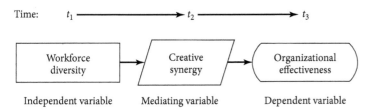

FIGURE 6.6   Diagram of the relationship among the independent, mediating and dependent variables

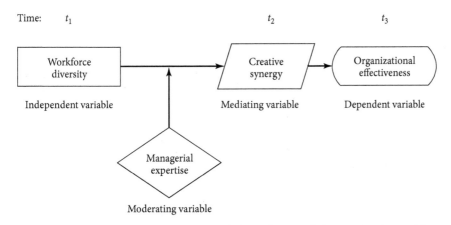

FIGURE 6.7   Diagram of the relationship among the independent, mediating, moderating and dependent variables

by creatively coordinating the different skills. If the manager lacks the expertise to perform this role, then no matter how many different problem-solving skills the diverse workforce might have, synergy will just not surface. Instead of functioning effectively, the organization might just remain static, or even deteriorate.

It is now easy to see what the differences are among an independent variable, a mediating variable and a moderating variable. The **independent variable** helps to *explain* the variance in the dependent variable; the **mediating variable** *surfaces at time t_2* as a function of the independent variable, which also helps us to conceptualize the relationship between the independent and dependent variables; and the **moderating variable** has a *contingent effect* on the relationship between two variables. To put it differently, while the independent variable explains the variance in the dependent variable, the mediating variable does not add to the variance already explained by the independent variable, whereas the moderating variable has an interaction effect with the independent variable in explaining the variance. That is, unless the moderating variable is present, the theorized relationship between the other two variables considered will not hold.

Whether a variable is an independent variable, a dependent variable, a mediating variable or a moderating variable should be determined by a careful reading of the dynamics operating in any given situation. For instance, a variable such as motivation to work could be a dependent variable, an independent variable, a mediating variable or a moderating variable, depending on the theoretical model that is being advanced.

Now do Exercises 6.7 to 6.9.

EXERCISE 6.7 Make up three different situations in which motivation to work would be an independent variable, a mediating variable and a moderating variable.

EXERCISE 6.8 Failure to follow accounting principles causes immense confusion, which in turn creates a number of problems for the organization. Those with vast experience in bookkeeping, however, are able to avert the problems by taking timely corrective action. List and label the variables in this situation, explain the relationships among the variables and illustrate these by means of diagrams.

EXERCISE 6.9 A store manager observes that the morale of employees in her supermarket is low. She thinks that if their working conditions are improved, pay scales raised and the vacation benefits made more attractive, the morale will be boosted. She doubts, however, if an increase in pay scales would raise the morale of all employees. Her conjecture is that those who have supplemental incomes will just not be 'turned on' by higher pay, and only those without side incomes will be happy with increased pay, with a resultant boost in morale. List and label the variables in this situation. Explain the relationships among the variables and illustrate them by means of diagrams. What might be the problem statement or problem definition for the situation?

HOW THEORY IS GENERATED

Having examined the different kinds of variables that can operate in a situation and how the relationships among these can be established, it is now possible to see how we can develop the theoretical framework for our research.

The theoretical framework is a logically developed, described and elaborated network of associations among the variables deemed relevant to the problem situation. It is identified through a critical review of the literature and qualitative research (e.g., via interviews, observation and/or a content analysis of documents). Indeed, a literature review provides a solid foundation for developing a theoretical framework. It will help the researcher to identify the variables that might be important to solving the problem, to specify the theory underlying these relations and to describe the nature and direction of the relationships. Qualitative research allows the researcher to take the specific context of the organization into account and to further refine his or her ideas with regard to possible solutions to the problem.

It becomes evident at this stage that, to arrive at good solutions to the problem, one should first correctly identify the problem (the dependent variable in your model), and then the variables that contribute to it (the independent variables in our model, representing potential solutions to the problem) and possibly moderating and mediating variables. The importance of doing a thorough literature review and conducting exploratory and qualitative research now becomes clear. After identifying the appropriate variables, the next step is to elaborate the network of associations among the variables, so that relevant hypotheses can be developed and subsequently tested. The results of hypothesis testing provide the researcher with information on whether and to what extent different interventions contribute to solving the problem. Developing and testing a theoretical framework might thus be seen as an important step in the research process.

THE COMPONENTS OF THE THEORETICAL FRAMEWORK

A good theoretical framework identifies and defines the important variables in the situation that are relevant to the problem and subsequently describes and explains the interconnections among these variables. The relationships among the independent variables, the dependent variable(s), and, if applicable, the moderating and mediating variables are elaborated. Should there be any moderating variable(s), it is important to explain how and what specific relationships they moderate. An explanation of why they operate as moderators should also be offered. If there are any mediating variables, a discussion on how or why they are treated as mediating variables is necessary. Any interrelationships among the independent variables themselves, or among the dependent variables themselves (in case there are two or more dependent variables), should also be clearly spelled out and adequately explained. Note that a good theoretical framework is not necessarily a complex framework.

Earlier in this chapter, we have already explained that there are three basic features that should be incorporated in any theoretical framework:

1. A clear definition of the variables considered relevant to the study

2. A conceptual model that describes the relationships between the variables in the model

3. A clear explanation of why we expect these relationships to exist

It is not always easy to come up with generally agreed-upon conceptual *definitions* of the relevant variables. More often than not, there are many definitions available in the literature (for instance, there are literally dozens of definitions of 'brand image', 'customer satisfaction' and 'service quality' available in the marketing literature). Still, well-chosen guiding definitions of concepts are needed, because they will help you to provide an explanation for the relationships between the variables in your model. What's more, conceptual definitions will also serve as a basis for the operationalization or measurement of your concepts in the data collection stage of the research process. Hence, you will have to choose a useful definition from the literature (do not use dictionary definitions, they are usually too general). It is also important that you explain why you have chosen a particular definition as your guiding definition.

A *conceptual model* helps you to structure your discussion of the literature. A conceptual model describes your ideas about how the concepts (variables) in your model are related to each other. A schematic diagram of the conceptual model helps the reader to visualize the theorized relationships between the variables in your model and thus to obtain a quick idea about how you think that the management problem can be solved. Hence, conceptual models are often expressed in this form. Both a schematic diagram of the conceptual model and a description of the relationships between the variables in words will help the reader to comprehend the theorized relationships. This facilitates and stimulates discussion about the relationships between the variables in your model. It is therefore important that your model is based on a sound theory.

A theory or a clear explanation for the relationships in your model is the last component of the theoretical framework. A theory attempts to explain relationships between the variables in your model: an explanation should be provided for all the important relationships that are theorized to exist among the variables. If the nature and direction of the relationships can be theorized on the basis of the findings of previous research and/or your own ideas on the subject, then there should also be an indication as to whether the relationships should be positive or negative and linear or non-linear. From the theoretical framework, then, testable hypotheses can be developed to examine whether the theory formulated is valid or not.

Note that you do not necessarily have to 'invent' a new theory every time you are undertaking a research project. In an applied research context, you apply existing theories to a specific context. This means that arguments can be drawn from previous research. However, in a basic research context you, will make some contribution to existing theories and models. In such a case, it is not (always) possible to use existing theories or explanations for relationships between variables. As a result, you will have to rely on your own insights and ideas.

Now do Exercise 6.10.

EXERCISE 6.10   Avatars are virtual characters that can be used as representatives of a company that is using the Internet as a distribution channel. For instance, avatars can be used as shopping assistants, website guides or identification figures. A manager of an online company believes that avatar-mediated communication will have a positive effect on satisfaction with her company and on purchase intentions of consumers, because avatars enhance the value of information provided on the website and increase the pleasure of the shopping experience. She also believes that the positive effect of the perceived information value on satisfaction with the company and purchase intentions is stronger when customers are highly involved. Develop a theoretical framework for this situation after stating what the problem definition of the researcher would be in this case.

HYPOTHESIS DEVELOPMENT   Once we have identified the important variables in a situation and established the relationships among them through logical reasoning in the theoretical framework, we are in a position to test whether the relationships that have been theorized do, in fact, hold true. By testing these relationships scientifically through appropriate statistical analyses, or through negative case analysis in qualitative research (described later in the chapter), we are able to obtain reliable information on what kinds of relationships exist among the variables operating in the problem situation. The results of these tests offer us some clues as to what could be changed in the situation to solve the problem. Formulating such testable statements is called *hypothesis development*.

DEFINITION OF A HYPOTHESIS

A **hypothesis** can be defined as a tentative, yet testable, statement, which predicts what you expect to find in your empirical data. Hypotheses are derived from the theory on which your conceptual model is based and are often relational in nature. Along these lines, hypotheses can be defined as logically conjectured relationships between two or more variables expressed in the form of testable statements. By testing the hypotheses and confirming the conjectured relationships, it is expected that solutions can be found to correct the problem encountered.

Example   Several testable statements or hypotheses can be drawn from the example depicted in Figure 6.4. One of them might be:

Workforce diversity has a positive effect on organizational effectiveness.

The above is a testable statement. By measuring the extent of workforce diversity and organizational effectiveness, we can statistically examine the relationship between these two variables to see if there is a significant (positive) correlation between the two. If we do find this to be the case, then the hypothesis is substantiated. If a significant correlation is not found, then the hypothesis has not been substantiated. By convention in the social sciences, to call a relationship 'statistically significant', we should be confident that 95 times out of 100 the observed relationship will hold true. There should be only a 5 percent chance that the relationship will not be detected.

STATEMENT OF HYPOTHESES: FORMATS

If–then Statements

As already stated, a hypothesis can be defined as a testable statement of the relationship among variables. A hypothesis can also test whether there are differences between two groups (or among several groups) with respect to any variable or variables. To examine whether or not the conjectured relationships or differences exist, these hypotheses can be set either as propositions or in the form of *if–then statements*. The two formats can be seen in the following two examples.

Young women will be more likely to express dissatisfaction with their body weight, when they are more frequently exposed to images of thin models in advertisements.

If young women are more frequently exposed to images of thin models in advertisements, then they will be more likely to express dissatisfaction with their body weight.

DIRECTIONAL AND NONDIRECTIONAL HYPOTHESES

If, in stating the relationship between two variables or comparing two groups, terms such as *positive*, *negative*, *more than*, *less than* and the like are used, then these are **directional hypotheses** because the direction of the relationship between the variables (positive/negative) is indicated, as in the first example below, or the nature of the difference between two groups on a variable (more than/less than) is postulated, as in the second example.

The greater the stress experienced in the job, the lower the job satisfaction of employees.
Women are more motivated than men.

On the other hand, **nondirectional hypotheses** are those that do postulate a relationship or difference, but offer no indication of the direction of these relationships or differences. In other words, though it may be conjectured that there is a significant relationship between two variables, we may not be able to say whether the relationship is positive or negative, as in the first example below. Likewise, even if we can conjecture that there will be differences between two groups on a particular variable, we may not be able to say which group will be more and which less on that variable, as in the second example.

There is a relation between arousal-seeking tendency and consumer preferences for complex product designs.

There is a difference between the work ethic values of American and Asian employees.

Nondirectional hypotheses are formulated either because the relationships or differences have never been explored, and hence there is no basis for indicating the direction, or because there have been conflicting findings in previous research studies on the variables. In some studies, a positive relationship might have been found, while in others a negative relationship might have been traced. Hence, the current researcher might only be able to hypothesize that there is a significant relationship, but the direction may not be clear. In such cases, the hypotheses can be stated nondirectionally. Note that in the first example there is no clue as to whether arousal-seeking tendency and preferences for complex product designs are positively or negatively correlated, and in the second example we do not know whether the work ethic values are stronger in Americans or in Asians. However, it would have been possible to state that arousal-seeking tendency and preferences for complex product designs are positively correlated, since previous research has indicated such a relationship. Whenever the direction of the relationship is known, it is better to develop directional hypotheses for reasons that will become clear in our discussions in a later chapter.

NULL AND ALTERNATE HYPOTHESES

We have just explained that a hypothesis is a statement that represents your predictions (or deductions). It is sometimes written as H_1, whereas its opposite – the null hypothesis – is written as H_0. For instance, if you would predict that advertising has an effect on sales (your H_1), your H_0 would be that advertising does *not* have an effect on sales. When used, the null hypothesis (stating that there is no effect) is presumed true until statistical evidence, in the form of a hypothesis test, indicates otherwise. The null hypothesis is thus a hypothesis set up to be rejected in order to support the alternate (alternative) hypothesis, labelled H_1 (your prediction).

The development of null hypotheses is preferred when contradictory evidence is more convincing than confirmatory evidence, for instance, when you make unrestricted generalizations; statements to the effect that every, each, all or any object of some kind has a particular property (for instance, all swans are white) or stand in some relation to something (for instance, all cats like fish). The great difficulty is that no amount of favourable observations (ten, a hundred or even a thousand white swans) is sufficient to prove your hypothesis that all swans are white. On the other hand, the observation of a single black swan would disprove your hypothesis. The idea is thus that some predictions cannot be verified, they can only be falsified.

Let's have look at some examples to illustrate the development of a null and alternate hypothesis. The *null* hypothesis in respect of group differences stated in the example '*Women are more motivated than men*' would be

$$H_0: \mu_M = \mu_W$$

or

$$H_0: \mu_M - \mu_W = 0$$

where H_0 represents the null hypothesis, μ_M is the mean motivational level of men and μ_W is the mean motivational level of women.

The *alternate* for the above example would statistically be set as follows:

$$H_A: \mu_M < \mu_W$$

which is the same as

$$H_A: \mu_W > \mu_M$$

where H_A represents the alternate hypothesis and μ_M and μ_W are the mean motivation levels of men and women, respectively.

For the nondirectional hypothesis of mean group differences in work ethic values in the example '*There is a difference between the work ethic values of American and Asian employees*', the null hypothesis would be

$$H_0: \mu_{AM} = \mu_{AS}$$

or

$$H_0: \mu_{AM} - \mu_{AS} = 0$$

where H_0 represents the null hypothesis, μ_{AM} is the mean work ethic value of Americans and μ_{AS} is the mean work ethic value of Asians.

The alternate hypothesis for the above example would statistically be set as

$$H_A: \mu_{AM} \neq \mu_{AS}$$

where H_A represents the alternate hypothesis and μ_{AM} and μ_{AS} are the mean work ethic values of Americans and Asians, respectively.

The null hypothesis for the relationship between the two variables in the example '*The greater the stress experienced in the job, the lower the job satisfaction of employees*', would be H_0: There is no relationship between stress experienced on the job and the job satisfaction of employees. This would be statistically expressed by

$$H_0: \rho = 0$$

where ρ represents the correlation between stress and job satisfaction, which in this case is equal to 0 (i.e., no correlation).

The alternate hypothesis for the above null, which has been expressed directionally, can be statistically expressed as

$$H_A: \rho < 0 \text{ (The correlation is negative.)}$$

For the example *'There is a relationship between age and job satisfaction'*, which has been stated nondirectionally, the null hypothesis would be statistically expressed as

$$H_0: \rho = 0$$

whereas the alternate hypothesis would be expressed as

$$H_A: \rho \neq 0$$

After the null and alternate hypotheses have been formulated, the appropriate statistical tests (*t*-tests, *F*-tests) can then be applied, which indicate whether or not support has been found for the alternate hypothesis – that there is a significant difference between groups or that there is a significant relationship between variables, as hypothesized.

The steps to be followed in hypothesis testing are as follows:

1. State the null and the alternate hypotheses.

2. Choose the appropriate statistical test depending on whether the data collected are parametric or nonparametric.

3. Determine the level of significance desired ($p = 0.05$, or more, or less).

4. See if the output results from computer analysis indicate that the significance level is met. If, as in the case of Pearson correlation analysis in Excel software, the significance level is not indicated in the printout, look up the critical values that define the regions of acceptance on the appropriate table (i.e., (t, F, χ^2) – see the statistical tables at the end of this book). This critical value demarcates the region of rejection from that of acceptance of the null hypothesis. When the resultant value is larger than the critical value, the null hypothesis is rejected, and the alternate accepted. If the calculated value is less than the critical value, the null is accepted and the alternate rejected.

Note that null hypotheses are rarely presented in research reports or journal articles.

Now do Exercises 6.11 to 6.13.

EXERCISE 6.11

Create a diagram to illustrate the relationships between the relevant variables in Exercise 6.9 and develop five different hypotheses.

EXERCISE 6.12

A production manager is concerned about the low output levels of his employees. The articles that he has read on job performance frequently mention four variables as being important to job performance: (1) skills required for the job, (2) rewards, (3) motivation and (4) satisfaction. In several of the articles, it was also indicated that only if the rewards were (attractive) to the recipients did motivation, satisfaction and job performance increase, not otherwise. Given this situation:

1. Define the problem.
2. Create a diagram.
3. Develop at least six hypotheses.

| EXERCISE 6.13 | A recent study has investigated the effect of corporate social responsibility (CSR) on the market value of the firm. This study developed and tested a conceptual framework, which posits that (1) customer satisfaction mediates the relationship between CSR and the market value of the firm, and (2) two firm factors ('innovativeness capability' and 'product quality') moderate the relationship between CSR and customer satisfaction. For this situation, define the problem, draw a schematic diagram and formulate the hypotheses. |

Hypothesis testing is strongly associated with designing experiments and the collection of quantitative data. However, as exemplified by Box 6.4, hypotheses can also be tested with qualitative data.

BOX 6.4   HYPOTHESIS TESTING WITH QUALITATIVE RESEARCH: NEGATIVE CASE ANALYSIS

Hypotheses can also be tested with qualitative data. For example, let us say that, after extensive interviews, a researcher has developed the theoretical framework that unethical practices by employees are a function of their inability to discriminate between right and wrong, or due to a dire need for more money, or the organization's indifference to such practices. To test the hypothesis that these three factors are the primary ones that influence unethical practices, the researcher should look for data to refute the hypothesis. When even a single case does not support the hypothesis, the theory needs revision. Let us say that the researcher finds one case where an individual is deliberately engaged in the unethical practice of accepting kickbacks (despite the fact that he is knowledgeable enough to discriminate right from wrong, is not in need of money and knows that the organization will not be indifferent to his behaviour), simply because he wants to 'get back' at the system, which 'will not listen to his advice'. This new discovery, through disconfirmation of the original hypothesis, known as *the negative case method*, enables the researcher to revise the theory and the hypothesis until such time as the theory becomes robust.

We have thus far seen how a critical literature review is done, theoretical frameworks are formulated, and hypotheses developed. Let us now illustrate this logical sequence through a small example where a researcher wants to examine the organizational factors influencing women's progress to top management positions. The literature review and the number of variables are deliberately kept small, since the purpose is merely to illustrate how a theoretical framework is developed from the literature review and how hypotheses are developed based on the theoretical framework.

Example	
Literature Review, Theoretical Framework, and Hypothesis Development	**INTRODUCTION** 'Fewer large companies are run by women than by men named John, a sure indicator that the glass ceiling remains firmly in place in corporate America' (Wolfers, 2015). Despite the spectacular increase in the number of managerial women during the last decades, the number of women in top management positions continues to be very small and static, suggesting a glass-ceiling effect that women still face (Lückerath-Rovers, 2013; Morrison, White & Vura, 1999; O'Neil, Hopkins & Bilimoria, 2008; Van Velsor, 2000). Given the demographics of the workplace, which projects that more and more women will enter the workforce in the future, it becomes important to examine the factors that might facilitate the advancement of women to top executive positions. This study is an effort to identify the factors that currently impede women's advancement to the top in organizations. **A BRIEF LITERATURE REVIEW** It is often declared that since women have only recently embarked on careers and entered the managerial ranks, it will take more time for them to rise to top executive positions. However, many

women in higher middle-management positions feel that there are at least two major stumbling blocks to their advancement: gender role stereotypes and inadequate access to critical information (Daniel, 1998; Koenig et al., 2011; Schein, 2007; Welch, 2001).

Gender stereotypes, or sex-role stereotypes as they are also known, are societal beliefs that men are better suited for taking on leadership roles and positions of authority and power, whereas women are more suited for taking on nurturing and helping roles (DeArmond et al., 2006; Eagly, 1989; Kahn & Crosby, 1998; Smith, 1999). These beliefs influence the positions that are assigned to organizational members. Whereas capable men are given line positions and developed to take on higher responsibilities and executive roles in the course of time, capable women are assigned to staff positions and dead-end jobs. With little exposure to management of budgets and opportunities for significant decision-making, women are seldom groomed for top-level positions.

Women are also excluded from the 'old boys' network because of their gender. Information exchange, development of career strategies, clues regarding access to resources and such important information vital to upward mobility are thus lost to women (*The Chronicle*, 2000). While many other factors impinge on women's upward mobility, the two variables of gender-role stereotypes and exclusion from critical information are particularly detrimental to women's advancement to senior level positions.

THEORETICAL FRAMEWORK

The dependent variable of advancement of women to top management positions is influenced by gender-role stereotyping and access to critical information. These two variables are also inter-related as explained below.

Gender-role stereotypes adversely impact on women's career progress. Since women are perceived as ineffective leaders but good nurturers, they are not assigned line positions in their early careers but offered staff responsibilities. It is only in line positions that managers make significant decisions, control budgets and interact with top-level executives who have an impact on their future careers. These opportunities to learn, grow and develop on the job and gain visibility in the system help managers to advance to top-level positions. However, since women in staff positions do not gain these experiences or have the visibility to be identified as key people in the organization with the potential to be successful top managers, their advancement to top-level positions is never considered by the system and they are always overlooked. Thus, gender-role stereotypes hinder the progress of women to the top.

Gender-role stereotypes also hinder *access to information*. If women are not considered to be decision-makers and leaders, but are perceived merely as support personnel, they will not be apprised of critical information essential for organizational advancement, since this is not seen as relevant for them. Exclusion from the networks where men informally interact with one another (golf courses, bars and so on) precludes women from gaining access to crucial information and resources vital for their advancement. For example, many of the significant organizational changes and current events are discussed informally among men outside the work setting. Women are generally unaware of the most recent developments since they are not a part of the informal group that interacts and exchanges information away from the workplace. This definitely is a handicap. For example, knowledge of an impending vacancy for an executive position enables one to strategize to occupy that position. One can become a key contender by procuring critical information relevant to the position, get prepared to present the appropriate credentials to the right people at the right time and thus pave the way for success. Thus, access to critical information is important for the progress of all, including women. When women do not have the critical information that is shared in informal networks, their chances of advancement to top positions also get severely restricted.

The foregoing relationships are shown schematically in Figure 6.8.

FIGURE 6.8
Schematic
diagram of the
example relating
to women
in manage-
rial positions

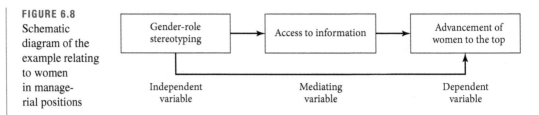

Gender-role stereotyping	Access to information	Advancement of women to the top
Independent variable	Mediating variable	Dependent variable

HYPOTHESES

1. *The greater the extent of gender-role stereotyping in organizations, the fewer will be the number of women at the top.*
2. *The effect of gender-role stereotyping on advancement of women to the top is partially mediated by access to information.*

MANAGERIAL IMPLICATIONS

Knowledge of how and for what purpose the theoretical framework is developed, and the hypotheses are generated, enables the manager to be an intelligent judge of the research report submitted by the consultant. At this juncture, it becomes clear that once the problem is defined, a good grasp of the concepts 'independent variable' and 'dependent variable' broadens the understanding of managers as to how multiple factors (the independent variables in the model) may provide possible solutions to the problem (the dependent variable in the model). An understanding of the concept 'moderating variable' may allow the manager to understand that some of the proposed solutions may not solve the problem for everybody or in every situation. Likewise, knowledge of what significance means, and why a given hypothesis is either accepted or rejected, helps the manager to persist in or desist from following hunches, which, while making good sense, do not work. If such knowledge is absent, many of the findings through research will not make much sense to the manager and decision-making will bristle with confusion.

SUMMARY

- **Learning objective 1: Discuss the need for a theoretical framework in deductive research.** A theoretical framework represents a researcher's beliefs on how certain phenomena (or variables or concepts) are related to each other (a model) and an explanation of why he or she believes that these variables are associated with each other (a theory). From a theoretical framework, testable hypotheses can be developed to examine whether a theory is valid or not.

- **Learning objective 2: Describe four main types of variables and identify and label variables associated with any given situation.** Since a theoretical framework involves the identification of a network of relationships among the variables considered important to the study of any given problem situation, it is essential to understand what a variable means and what the different types of variables are. A variable is anything that can take on differing or varying values. Four main types of variables discussed in this chapter are (1) the dependent variable; (2) the independent variable; (3) the moderating variable and (4) the mediating variable.

- **Learning objective 3: Develop a theoretical framework that includes all the relevant components.** Three basic features that should be incorporated in any theoretical framework:

  - The variables considered relevant to the study should be clearly defined.

  - A conceptual model that describes the relationships between the variables in the model should be given.

  - There should be a clear explanation of why we expect these relationships to exist.

  Just as the literature review usually in combination with qualitative research, sets the stage for a good theoretical framework, this in turn provides the logical base for developing testable hypotheses.

- **Learning objective 4: Develop a set of hypotheses to be tested.** Hypotheses are derived from the theory on which a conceptual model is based. They are often relational in nature. Along these lines, hypotheses can be defined as logically conjectured relationships between two or more variables expressed in the form of testable statements. By testing the hypotheses and confirming the conjectured relationships, it is expected that solutions can be found to correct the problem encountered.

- **Learning objective 5: Demonstrate awareness of the role of the manager in the development of a theoretical framework.** Knowledge of how and for what purpose the theoretical framework is developed and the hypotheses are generated enables the manager to be an intelligent judge of the research report submitted by the researcher.

In the next chapter, we will examine a number of basic research design issues.

Instructors can visit the companion website at **www.wiley.com/go/bougie/researchmethods forbusiness8e** for **Case Study: The Social Network.**

DISCUSSION QUESTIONS

1. 'Because literature review is a time-consuming exercise, a good, in-depth interview should suffice to develop a theoretical framework'. Discuss this statement.

2. 'Good models are complex. What's more, a good model should include both moderating and mediating variables'. Discuss this statement.

3. 'Academic researchers usually develop more complex and elaborate models than applied researchers'. Discuss this statement.

4. 'In an applied research context you do not need to explain the relationships between the variables in your conceptual model'. Discuss this statement.

5. There is an advantage in stating the hypothesis both in the null and in the alternate; it adds clarity to our thinking of what we are testing. Explain.

6. It is advantageous to develop a directional hypothesis whenever we are sure of the predicted direction. How will you justify this statement?

7. In recent decades, many service markets have been liberalized. For this reason, incumbent service firms are facing new competitors and must address customer switching. You are discussing the determinants of customer switching with a service firm manager. She believes that product quality, relationship quality and switching costs are important determinants of customer switching. You agree with the contention that product quality and relationship quality are important determinants of switching. However, you believe that switching costs *moderate* the relationships between product quality, relationship quality and customer switching. Provide arguments for this contention.

8. For the following case:
   a. Identify the problem.
   b. Develop a diagram representing the conceptual model.
   c. Develop the hypotheses.

   Concerned about her current customer base, manager Andersen started to think of factors that might affect the attractiveness of an auditing firm. Of course, the service quality provided and the fees charged by the auditor seem two important factors. Next, she decides that the reputation of the auditing firm also needs to be included in the framework as an independent variable. As illustrated by the dramatic effects of recent auditing scandals, reputation seems especially important for large auditors (i.e., auditing firms that are large in size). Finally, the manager also thinks that the proximity of the auditing firm to the customer is another variable to be included as an independent variable. Proximity very likely affects the possibility for the client to personally meet with the auditors on a regular basis and she knows from her own contact with customers that they perceive personal interactions as quite important.

9. Develop a conceptual model for the below scenario.

   Incidence of smoking in movies has started to increase again, after having declined for several decades. According to the National Cancer Institute, smoking is seen in at least three out of four contemporary box-office hits as well as in many Netflix productions. What's more, identifiable cigarette brands appeared in about one-third of all movies in 2008. Exposure to smoking in movies is an important predictor of adolescent smoking initiation: smoking in movies has been shown to affect adolescents' intentions to start smoking. In turn, the intentions to start smoking are determined by a more positive attitude towards smoking after seeing a film character smoke. Recent research has revealed that the relationship between seeing a film character smoke and the attitude towards smoking is stronger when a person's identification with a film character increases. These findings are consistent with social learning theory, which predicts that attitudes and behaviours are modelled by observing the behaviours of others.

10. Develop a conceptual model for the following case.

    Once given, bonuses are extraordinarily hard to take away without undermining employee morale. The adverse effects of these cuts far outweigh the anticipated savings in dollars. Research has shown that when the reason behind the cuts is explained to employees, morale does not drop.

11. Product placement is a form of advertising in which a company's products and name are intentionally positioned in motion pictures, television programs, radio broadcasts and the like. Product placement can take many forms: verbal mentions in dialogue; actual use by a character or visual displays (for instance, a company logo on a vehicle or billboard). Develop a theoretical framework on this issue, based on a review of the current literature. This framework should include the following:
    a. A specification and definition of an appropriate dependent variable
    b. A conceptual model that describes the relationships between the dependent variable, at least one independent variable, and either a moderating or a mediating variable
    c. A theory on why you would expect these relationships to exist
    d. An appropriate number of testable hypotheses

| **PRACTICE PROJECT** | For the topic you chose to work on for the project in Chapter 4, do the following: |

- Go through the computer-generated bibliography again.
- Define a problem statement that, in your opinion, would be most useful for researchers to investigate.
- Carry out a literature review that would seem to offer the greatest potential for developing a good theoretical framework, using about five to seven references.
- Develop the theoretical framework incorporating its three basic features, as discussed in the chapter.
- Generate a set of testable hypotheses based on the theoretical framework.

Elements of Research Design

LEARNING OBJECTIVES

After completing Chapter 7, you should be able to:

1. Explain what is meant by a research design.

2. Develop an appropriate research design for any given study.

3. Explain why a researcher might be constrained to settle for less than the 'ideal' research design.

4. Demonstrate awareness of the role of the manager in the area of research design.

INTRODUCTION

Up to now you have made a great effort to:

- define the management problem;
- define the research problem;
- develop a research proposal;
- conduct a critical review of the literature;
- document your literature review; and
- (in causal research) develop a theoretical framework and hypotheses.

The next step is to design the research in such a way that the requisite data can be gathered and analyzed to answer your research questions to be able to arrive at a solution for the problem that catalyzed the research project.

THE RESEARCH DESIGN

A **research design** is a blueprint or plan for the collection, measurement and analysis of data, created to answer your research empirical questions.

The various issues involved in the research design and discussed in this chapter are shown comprehensively in Figure 7.1. As may be seen, issues relating to decisions regarding the research strategy (for instance, experiments, surveys, case studies), the extent to which the study is manipulated and controlled by the researcher (extent of researcher interference), location (i.e., the study setting), the level at which the data will be analyzed (unit of analysis), and temporal aspects (the time horizon) are integral to research design. These issues are discussed in this chapter.

As shown in Figure 7.1, each component of the research design offers several critical choice points. Obviously, there is no single design that is superior in all circumstances. Instead, you will have to make choices and create a design that is suitable for the job at hand. The quality of a research design depends on how carefully you choose the appropriate design alternatives, taking into consideration the specific objectives, research questions and constraints of the project, such as access to data, time, and/or money.

In addition to the decisions above regarding the research design, choices have to be made as to the data collection method to be used, the type of sample (sampling design), how variables will be measured (measurement) and how they will be analyzed to test the hypotheses (data analysis). These issues are discussed in subsequent chapters.

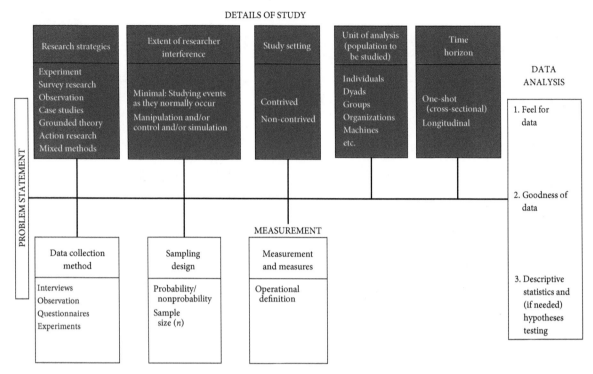

FIGURE 7.1 The research design

RESEARCH STRATEGIES

A strategy is a plan for achieving a certain goal. A *research strategy* will help you to meet your research objective(s) and to answer the research questions of your study. The choice for a particular research strategy will therefore depend on the research objective(s) and (the type of) research questions of your study, but also on your viewpoint on what makes good research and on practical aspects such as access to data sources and time constraints. In this section, we will discuss the following research strategies: experiments, surveys, ethnography, case studies, grounded theory and action research.

Experiments

Experiments are usually associated with causal research and/or a hypothetico-deductive approach to research. The purpose of an experiment is to study causal relationships between variables. Experimental designs are less useful or appropriate for answering exploratory and descriptive research questions.

In an experiment, the researcher *manipulates* the independent variable to study the effect of this manipulation on the dependent variable. In other words, the researcher deliberately changes a certain variable (or certain variables), for instance 'reward system', to establish whether (and to what extent) this change (e.g., different types of reward systems) will produce a change in another variable, in this example 'productivity'. The simplest experimental design is a two-group, post-test-only, randomized experiment, where one group gets a treatment, for instance 'piece wages'. The other group (the comparison group, in this example, the 'hourly wages' group) does not get the treatment. Subjects (workers) are randomly assigned to the groups and hence the researcher is able to determine whether the productivity of the two groups is different after the treatment. Later on in this chapter, we will have more to say about the extent of researcher interference with the study and the study setting. This will help us to make a distinction among field experiments and lab experiments. Chapter 11 discusses lab experiments and field experiments, manipulation, controlling 'nuisance' variables, factors affecting the validity of experiments and various types of experiments in considerable detail.

Under the right circumstances, an experimental design is a very strong design to use. However, experimental designs are not always feasible in an applied research context where the researcher collects information that contributes to solving a management problem. For instance, we do not want (for obvious reasons) to assign customers to a low service quality treatment to study the effect of service quality on customer retention or assign workers to highly stressful situations to investigate the effect of work-related stress on personal and professional relations. In such cases, we may opt for an alternative research strategy to answer the research questions of their study.

Survey Research

A **survey** is a *system* for collecting information from or about people to describe, compare or explain their knowledge, attitudes and behaviour (Fink, 2003). The survey strategy is very popular in applied research contexts, because it allows the researcher to collect quantitative and qualitative data on many types of research questions. Surveys are commonly used in exploratory and descriptive research to collect data about people, events or situations. For instance, surveys are often taken on the subject of consumer decision-making, customer satisfaction, job satisfaction, the use of health services, management information systems and the like. Popular survey instruments are self-administered interviews and structured observation. These instruments are discussed in subsequent chapters. Interviews are discussed in Chapter 8, structured observation in Chapter 9 and self-administered questionnaires in Chapter 10.

Ethnography

Ethnography is a research strategy that has its roots in anthropology. It is a strategy in which the researcher 'closely observes, records, and engages in the daily life of another culture [. . .] and then writes accounts of this culture, emphasizing descriptive detail' (Markus & Fischer, 1986, p. 18). Ethnography involves immersion in the particular culture of the social group that is being studied (such as, for instance, bankers in the City of London), observing behaviour, listening to what is said in conversations and asking questions. It thus aims to generate an understanding of the culture and behaviour of a social group from an 'insider's point of view'. Note that platforms such as facebook are also becoming crucial tools for ethnographers because much social life now exists 'online'.

Participant observation is closely related to **ethnography**. However, different people have different ideas about the exact relationship between the two. Ethnography and participant observation are sometimes used interchangeably in the literature. For some, both ethnography and participant observation are research strategies that involve spending long periods watching people and talking to them about what they are doing, thinking and saying, with the objective of generating an understanding of the social group under study (Delamont, 2004). For others, ethnography is a more inclusive term, whereas participant observation is more specific and related to a particular method of data collection. From this perspective, participant observation is a primary source of ethnographic data. However, it is just one of a number of methods, and rarely the only method, used by a researcher to generate an understanding of a culture or a social group. Along these lines, observation – observing behaviour through a long-term engagement in the field setting where ethnography takes place – is regarded as one of several methods for ethnographic research. Other methods, such as interviews and questionnaires, may also be used to collect data in ethnographic research. We will have more to say about various approaches to observation in Chapter 9.

Case Studies

Case studies focus on collecting information about a specific object, event or activity, such as a particular person, department, business unit or organization. In case studies, the case is the individual, the group, the organization, the event or the situation the researcher is interested in. The idea behind a case study is that in order to obtain a clear picture of a problem one must examine the real-life situation from various angles and perspectives using multiple methods of data collection. Along these lines, one may define a case study as a research strategy that involves an empirical investigation of a particular contemporary phenomenon within its real-life context using multiple methods of data collection (Yin, 2009). It should be noted that case studies may provide both qualitative and quantitative data for analysis and interpretation. As in experimental research, hypotheses can be developed in case studies as well. However, if a particular hypothesis has not been substantiated in even a single other case study, no support can be established for the alternate hypothesis developed.

Grounded Theory

Grounded theory is a systematic set of procedures to develop an inductively derived theory from the data (Strauss & Corbin, 1990). Important tools of grounded theory are theoretical sampling, coding and constant comparison. Theoretical sampling is 'the process of data collection for generating theory whereby the analyst jointly collects, codes and analyzes the data and decides what data to collect next and where to find them, in order to develop his theory as it emerges' (Glaser & Strauss, 1967, p. 45). In constant comparison you compare data (for instance, an interview) to other data (for instance, another interview). After a theory has emerged from this process you compare new data with your theory. If there is a bad fit between data (interviews), or between the data and your theory, then the categories and theories have to be modified until your categories and your theory fit the data. In constant comparison, discrepant and disconfirming cases play an important role in rendering categories and (grounded) theory.

Action Research

Action research is practical and problem-solving in nature. It is based on a cyclic process of action, reflection on the results of action and further action based on this reflection. Action researchers are very often professional practitioners who use this strategy as a means of researching into and changing their own professional behaviour. It is thus often highly participative in nature and it usually involves an examination of the beliefs, values and assumptions that have contributed to the situation that is being investigated. Action research is often used by researchers and practitioners interested in *improving* programs and practices, that is, in formative evaluation. Lewin, who first used the term action research, suggested a spiral with four steps in each coil. Once an idea, problem or opportunity is identified one goes through the following steps: diagnose/investigate, plan, act and reflect/evaluate. Each loop can be regarded as a small experiment or research project, but the process usually continues until the problem is solved. Action research is thus a constantly evolving project with interplay among problem, solution, effects or consequences and new solutions. Note that the cycle has some obvious similarities with a lot of change models. Reservations about the approach include a lack of rigor, objectivity and replicability, its dependency on co-practitioners who have to collaborate, its vulnerability to pressure from stakeholders and the fact that it is time consuming (more often than not, one has to go through several cycles of inquiry).

EXTENT OF RESEARCHER INTERFERENCE WITH THE STUDY

The extent of **interference** by the researcher has a direct bearing on whether the study undertaken is correlational or causal. A correlational study (recall that a correlational study is descriptive in nature, see Chapter 4) is conducted in a natural environment (for instance, a supermarket or the factory floor) with minimal interference by the researcher with the normal flow of events. For example, if a researcher wants to study the factors influencing training effectiveness (a correlational study), all that this researcher has to do is delineate the relevant variables, collect the relevant data and analyze them to come up with the findings. Though there is some disruption to the normal flow of work in the system as the researcher interviews employees and administers questionnaires in the workplace, the researcher's interference in the routine functioning of the system is minimal as compared to that caused during causal studies and experimental designs.

In studies conducted to establish cause-and-effect relationships, the researcher tries to manipulate certain variables so as to study the effects of such manipulation on the dependent variable of interest. In other words, the researcher deliberately changes certain variables in the setting and interferes with the events as they normally occur. As an example, a researcher might want to study the influence of lighting on worker performance; hence he manipulates the lighting in the work situation to varying intensities. Here, there is considerable researcher interference with the natural and normal setting. In other cases, the researcher might even want to create an altogether new artificial setting where the cause-and-effect relationships can be studied by manipulating certain variables and tightly controlling certain others, as in a laboratory. Thus, there could be varying degrees of interference by the researcher in the manipulation and control of variables in the research study, either in the natural setting or in an artificial lab setting.

Let us give examples of research with varying degrees of interference – minimal, moderate and excessive.

MINIMAL INTERFERENCE

Example

A hospital administrator wants to examine the relationship between the perceived emotional support in the system and the stresses experienced by the nursing staff. In other words, she wants to do a correlational study. Here, the administrator/researcher will collect data from the nurses (perhaps through a questionnaire) to indicate how much emotional support they get in the hospital and to what extent they experience stress. (We will learn in a later chapter how to measure these variables.) By correlating the two variables, the answer that is being sought can be found. In this case, beyond administering a questionnaire to the nurses, the researcher has not interfered with the normal activities in the hospital. In other words, researcher interference has been minimal.

MODERATE INTERFERENCE

The same researcher is now no longer content with finding a correlation, but wants to firmly establish a causal connection. That is, the researcher wants to demonstrate that if the nurses had emotional support, this indeed would cause them to experience less stress. If this can be established, then the nurses' stress can definitely be reduced by offering them emotional support. To test the cause-and-effect relationship, the researcher will measure the stress currently experienced by the nurses in three wards in the hospital, and then deliberately manipulate the extent of emotional support given to the three groups of nurses in the three wards for, perhaps, a week, and measure the amount of stress at the end of that period. For one group, the researcher will ensure that a number of lab technicians and doctors help and comfort the nurses when they face stressful events – for example, when they care for patients suffering excruciating pain and distress in the ward. Under a similar setup, for a second group of nurses in another ward, the researcher might arrange only a moderate amount of emotional support, employing only the lab technicians and excluding doctors. The third ward might operate without any emotional support. If the experimenter's theory is correct, then the reduction in the stress levels before and after the one-week period should be greatest for the nurses in the first ward, moderate for those in the second ward, and nil for the nurses in the third ward. Here we find that not only does the researcher collect data from nurses on their experienced stress at two different points in time but she also 'plays with' or manipulates the normal course of events by deliberately changing the amount of emotional support received by the nurses in two wards, while leaving things in the third ward unchanged. Here, the researcher has interfered more than minimally.

EXCESSIVE INTERFERENCE

The above researcher, after conducting the previous experiments, feels that the results may or may not be valid since other external factors might have influenced the stress levels experienced by the nurses. For example, during that particular experimental week, the nurses in one or more wards may not have experienced high levels of stress because there were no serious illnesses or deaths in the ward. Hence, the emotional support received might not be related to the level of stress experienced. The researcher might now want to make sure that such extraneous factors as might affect the cause-and-effect relationship are controlled. So she might take three groups of medical students, put them in different rooms, and confront all of them with the same stressful task. For example, she might ask them to describe in the minutest detail, the procedures in performing surgery on a patient who has not responded to chemotherapy and keep bombarding them with more and more questions even as they respond. Although all are exposed to the same intensive questioning, one group might get help from a doctor who voluntarily offers clarification and help when students stumble. In the second group, a doctor might be nearby, but might offer clarification and help only if the group seeks it. In the third group, there is no doctor present and no help is available. In this case, not only is the support manipulated, but even the setting in which this experiment is conducted is artificial inasmuch as the researcher has taken the subjects away from their normal environment and put them in a totally different setting. Here, the researcher has intervened maximally with the normal setting, the participants, and their duties. In Chapter 11, we will see why such manipulations are necessary to establish cause-and-effect relationships beyond any doubt.

In summary, the extent of researcher interference is related to whether the research questions are correlational or causal in nature and to the importance of establishing a causal relationship beyond any doubt what so ever.

STUDY SETTING: CONTRIVED AND NONCONTRIVED

As we have just seen, business research can be done in the natural environment where events proceed normally (i.e., in **noncontrived settings**) or in artificial, **contrived settings**. Exploratory and descriptive (correlational) studies are invariably conducted in noncontrived settings, whereas most causal studies are done in contrived lab settings.

Studies done in noncontrived settings are called **field studies**. Studies conducted to establish cause-and-effect relationships using the same natural environment in which the subjects under study (employees, consumers, managers and the like) normally function are called **field experiments**. Here, as we have seen earlier, the researcher does interfere with the natural occurrence of events inasmuch as the independent variable is manipulated. For example, a manager wanting to know the effects of pay on performance should raise the salary of employees in one unit, decrease the pay of employees in another unit and leave the pay of the employees in a third unit untouched. Here there is a tampering with, or manipulating of, the pay system to establish a cause-and-effect relationship between pay and performance, but the study is still conducted in the natural setting and hence is called a field experiment.

Experiments done to establish a cause-and-effect relationship beyond the possibility of the least doubt require the creation of an artificial, contrived environment in which all the extraneous factors are strictly controlled. Similar subjects are chosen carefully to respond to certain manipulated stimuli. These studies are referred to as **lab experiments**. Let us give some further examples to understand the differences among a field study (a noncontrived setting with minimal researcher interference), a field experiment (noncontrived setting but with researcher interference to a moderate extent) and a lab experiment (a contrived setting with researcher interference to an excessive degree).

Example

FIELD STUDY

A bank manager wants to analyze the relationship between interest rates and bank deposit patterns of clients. She tries to correlate the two by looking at deposits into different kinds of accounts (such as savings, certificates of deposit, golden passbooks and interest-bearing checking accounts) as interest rates change. This is a field study where the bank manager has merely taken the balances in various types of account and correlated them to the changes in interest rates. Research here is done in a noncontrived setting with no interference with the normal work routine.

FIELD EXPERIMENT

The bank manager now wants to determine the cause-and-effect relationship between the interest rate and the inducement it offers to clients to save and deposit money in the bank. She selects four branches within a 60-mile radius for the experiment. For one week only, she advertises the annual rate for new certificates of deposit received during that week in the following manner: the interest rate will be 9% in one branch, 8% in another and 10% in the third. In the fourth branch, the interest rate remains unchanged at 5%. Within the week, she will be able to determine the effects, if any, of interest rates on deposit mobilization.

The above is a field experiment since nothing but the interest rate is manipulated, with all activities occurring in the normal and natural work environment. Hopefully, all four branches chosen will be more or less compatible in size, number of depositors, deposit patterns and the like, so that the interest–savings relationships are not influenced by some third factor. But it is possible that some other factors might affect the findings. For example, one of the areas may have more retirees who may not have additional disposable income to deposit, despite the attraction of a good interest rate. The banker may not have been aware of this fact while setting up the experiment.

LAB EXPERIMENT

The banker in the previous example may now want to establish the causal connection between interest rates and savings, beyond a doubt. Because of this, she wants to create an artificial environment and trace the true cause-and-effect relationship. She recruits 40 students who are all business majors in their final year of study and are more or less of the same age. She splits them into four groups and gives each one of them chips that count for $1000, which they are told they might utilize to buy their needs, or save for the future, or both. She offers them, by way of incentive, interest on what they save but manipulates the interest rates by offering a 6% interest rate on savings for group 1, 8% for group 2, 9% for group 3 and keeps the interest at the low rate of 1% for group 4.

Here, the manager has created an artificial laboratory environment and has manipulated the interest rates for savings. She has also chosen subjects with similar backgrounds and exposure to financial matters (business students). If the banker finds that the savings by the four groups increase progressively, keeping in step with the increasing rates of interest, she will be able to establish a cause-and-effect relationship between interest rates and the disposition to save.

In this lab experiment with the contrived setting, the researcher interference has been maximal, inasmuch as the setting is different, the independent variable has been manipulated and most external nuisance factors such as age and experience have been controlled.

Experimental designs are discussed more fully in Chapter 11. However, the above examples show us that it is important to decide the various design details before conducting the research study, since one decision criterion might have an impact on others. For example, if one wants to conduct an exploratory or a descriptive study, then the necessity for the researcher to interfere with the normal course of events will be minimal. However, if causal connections are to be established, experimental designs need to be set up either within a setting where the events normally occur (a field experiment) or in an artificially created laboratory setting (a lab experiment).

In summary, we have thus far made a distinction among (1) field studies, where various factors are examined in the natural setting in which daily activities go on as normal with minimal researcher interference, (2) field experiments, where cause-and-effect relationships are studied with some amount of researcher interference, but still in the natural setting where events continue in the normal fashion and (3) lab experiments, where the researcher explores cause-and-effect relationships, not only exercising a high degree of control but also in an artificial and deliberately created setting. In Chapter 11, we will see the advantages and disadvantages of using contrived and noncontrived settings for establishing cause-and-effect relationships.

UNIT OF ANALYSIS: INDIVIDUALS, DYADS, GROUPS, ORGANIZATIONS, CULTURES

The **unit of analysis** refers to the level of aggregation at which information is analyzed and conclusions are drawn. If, for instance, the problem statement focuses on how to raise the motivational levels of employees in general, then we are interested in individual employees in the organization and have to find out what we can do to raise their motivation. Here the unit of analysis is the individual. We will be looking at the data gathered from each individual and treating each employee's response as an individual data source. If the researcher is interested in studying two-person interactions, then several two-person groups, also known as *dyads*, will become the unit of analysis. Analysis of husband–wife interactions in families and supervisor–subordinate relationships in the workplace are good examples of dyads as the unit of analysis. However, if the problem statement is related to group effectiveness or if we want to compare two groups (e.g., departments), then the unit of analysis will be at the group level. In other words, even though we may gather relevant data from all individuals comprising, say, six groups, we aggregate the individual data into group data so as to see the differences among the six groups. If we are comparing different departments in the organization, then the data analysis will be done at the departmental level – that is, the individuals in the department will be treated as one unit – and comparisons made by treating the department as the unit of analysis.

Our research question determines the appropriate unit of analysis. For example, if we wish to study group decision-making patterns, we will probably be examining such aspects as group size, group structure, cohesiveness and the like, in trying to explain the variance in group decision-making. Here, our main interest is not in studying individual decision-making but *group* decision-making, and we will be studying the dynamics that operate in several different groups and the factors that influence group decision-making. In such a case, the unit of analysis will be groups.

As our research question addresses issues that move away from the individual to dyads, and to groups, organizations and even nations, so also does the unit of analysis shift from individuals to dyads, groups, organizations and nations. The characteristic of these 'levels of analysis' is that the lower levels are subsumed within the higher levels. Thus, if we study buying behaviour, we have to collect data from, say, 60 individuals, and analyze the data. If we want to study group dynamics, we may need to study, say, six or more groups, and then analyze the data gathered by examining the patterns in each of the groups. If we want to study cultural differences among nations, we will have to collect data from different countries and study the underlying patterns of culture in each country. Some critical issues in cross-cultural research are discussed in later chapters.

Individuals do not have the same characteristics as groups (e.g., structure, cohesiveness), and groups do not have the same characteristics as individuals (e.g., IQ, stamina). There are variations in the perceptions, attitudes and behaviours of people in different cultures. Hence, the nature of the information gathered, as well as the level at which data are aggregated for analysis, are integral to decisions made on the choice of the unit of analysis.

It is necessary to decide on the unit of analysis even as we formulate the research question, since the data collection methods, sample size and even the variables included in the framework may sometimes be determined or guided by the level at which data are aggregated for analysis.

Let us examine some research scenarios that would call for different units of analysis.

Example

INDIVIDUALS AS THE UNIT OF ANALYSIS

The Chief Financial Officer of a manufacturing company wants to know how many of the staff would be interested in attending a three-day seminar on making appropriate investment decisions. For this purpose, data will have to be collected from each individual staff member and the unit of analysis is the individual.

DYADS AS THE UNIT OF ANALYSIS

Having read about the benefits of mentoring, a human resources manager wants to first identify the number of employees in three departments of the organization who are in mentoring relationships, and then find out what the jointly perceived benefits (i.e., by both the mentor and the one mentored) of such a relationship are. Here, once the mentor and the mentored pairs are identified, their joint perceptions can be obtained by treating each pair as one unit. Hence, if the manager wants data from a sample of 10 pairs, he will have to deal with 20 individuals, a pair at a time. The information obtained from each pair will be a data point for subsequent analysis. Thus, the unit of analysis here is the dyad.

GROUPS AS THE UNIT OF ANALYSIS

A manager wants to see the patterns of usage of the newly installed information system (IS) by the production, sales and operations personnel. Here, three groups of personnel are involved and information on the number of times the IS is used by each member in each of the three groups, as well as other relevant issues, will be collected and analyzed. The final results will indicate the mean usage of the system per day or month for each group. Here, the unit of analysis is the group.

DIVISIONS AS THE UNIT OF ANALYSIS

Procter & Gamble wants to see which of its various divisions (soap, paper, oil, etc.) have made profits of over 12% during the current year. Here, the profits of each of the divisions will be examined and the information aggregated across the various geographical units of the division. Hence, the unit of analysis will be the division, at which level the data will be aggregated.

INDUSTRY AS THE UNIT OF ANALYSIS

An employment survey specialist wants to see the proportion of the workforce employed by the health care, utilities, transportation and manufacturing industries. In this case, the researcher has to aggregate the data relating to each of the subunits comprised in each of the industries and report the proportions of the workforce employed at the industry level. The health care industry, for instance, includes hospitals, nursing homes, mobile units, small and large clinics and other health care providing facilities. The data from these subunits will have to be aggregated to see how many employees are employed by the health care industry. This will need to be done for each of the other industries.

COUNTRIES AS THE UNIT OF ANALYSIS

The Chief Financial Officer (CFO) of a multinational corporation wants to know the profits made during the past five years by each of the subsidiaries in England, Germany, France and Spain. It is possible that there are many regional offices of these subsidiaries in each of these countries. The profits of the various regional centres for each country have to be aggregated and the profits for each country for the past five years provided to the CFO. In other words, the data will now have to be aggregated at the country level. As can be easily seen, the data collection and sampling processes become more cumbersome at higher levels of units of analysis (industry, country) than at the lower levels (individuals and dyads). It is obvious that the unit of analysis has to be clearly identified as dictated by the research question. Sampling plan decisions will also be governed by the unit of analysis. For example, if I compare two cultures, for instance those of India and the United States – where my unit of analysis is the country – my sample size will be only two, despite the fact that I shall have to gather data from several hundred individuals from a variety of organizations in the different regions of each country, incurring huge costs. However, if my unit of analysis is individuals (as when studying the buying patterns of customers in the southern part of the United States), I may perhaps limit the collection of data to a representative sample of a hundred individuals in that region and conduct my study at a low cost!

It is now even easier to see why the unit of analysis should be given serious consideration even as the research question is being formulated and the research design planned.

TIME HORIZON: CROSS-SECTIONAL VERSUS LONGITUDINAL STUDIES

Cross-sectional Studies

A study can be undertaken in which data are gathered just once, perhaps over a period of days or weeks or months, in order to answer a research question. Such studies are called **one-shot** or **cross-sectional studies** (see the following example).

The purpose of the studies in the two following examples was to collect data that would be pertinent to finding the answer to a research question. Data collection at one point in time was sufficient. Both were cross-sectional designs.

Example	Example 1 Data were collected from stock brokers between April and June of last year to study their concerns in a turbulent stock market. Data with respect to this particular research had not been collected before, nor will they be collected again for this research.
	Example 2 A drug company wanting to invest in research for a new obesity (reduction) pill conducted a survey among obese people to see how many of them would be interested in trying the new pill. This is a one-shot or cross-sectional study to assess the likely demand for the new product.

Longitudinal Studies

In some cases, however, the researcher might want to study people or phenomena at more than one point in time in order to answer the research question. For instance, the researcher might want to study employees' behaviour before and after a change in the top management, so as to know what effects the change accomplished. Here, because data are gathered at two different points in time, the study is not cross-sectional or of the one-shot kind, but is carried longitudinally across a period of time. Such studies, as when data on the dependent variable are gathered at two or more points in time to answer the research question, are called **longitudinal studies**.

Example

Example 1   A marketing manager is interested in tracing the pattern of sales of a particular product in four different regions of the country on a quarterly basis for the next two years. Since data will be collected several times to answer the same issue (tracing pattern of sales), the study falls into the longitudinal category.

Example 2   In 2002, Sturges, Guest, Conway and Davey published the results of a two-wave longitudinal study investigating the relationship between career management and organizational commitment among graduates in the first ten years at work. Data were collected at two points in time 12 months apart. The results of this study showed that high organizational commitment predicts the practice of career management activities by graduates to further their career within the organization. On the other hand, low commitment was closely associated with behaviour aimed at furthering their career outside the organization. The results also pointed out that graduates who manage their own careers receive more career management help from their employer. This suggests that there may be the potential for employers to create a 'virtuous circle' of career management in which individual and organizational activities complement each other.

Longitudinal studies take more time and effort and cost more than cross-sectional studies. That is why most studies are cross-sectional in nature. Nevertheless, longitudinal studies will be necessary if a manager wants to keep track of certain factors (e.g., sales, advertising effectiveness, etc.) over a period of time to assess improvements, or to detect possible causal connections (sales promotions and actual sales data; frequency of drug testing and reduction in drug usage, etc.). Though more expensive, such longitudinal studies might offer some good insights.

MIXED METHODS

Earlier (in Chapter 4), we explained that qualitative studies are often carried out to better understand the nature of a problem. Extensive interviews with many people might have to be undertaken to get a handle on the situation and understand the phenomenon. When the data reveal some pattern regarding the phenomenon of interest, theories are developed and hypotheses formulated. Other methods, such as an experimental method, for instance, are subsequently used to test these hypotheses. Along these lines, combinations of qualitative and quantitative methods are used in many studies.

Mixed methods research aims to answer research questions that cannot be answered by 'qualitative' or 'quantitative' approaches alone. Mixed methods research focuses on collecting, analyzing and mixing both quantitative and qualitative data in a single study or series of studies. A mixed methods approach is increasingly advocated within business research. The attractiveness of this approach is that it allows researchers to combine inductive and deductive thinking, to use more than one research method to address the research problem, and to solve this problem using different types of data. On the other hand, a mixed methods approach complicates the research design and therefore requires clear presentation to allow the reader to sort out its different components.

Example

Henry Mintzberg interviewed managers to explore the nature of managerial work. Based on the analysis of his interview data, he formulated theories of managerial roles, the nature and types of managerial activities and so on. These have been tested in different settings through both interviews and questionnaire surveys.

Triangulation is a technique that is also often associated with using mixed methods. The idea behind triangulation is that one can be more confident in a result if the use of different methods or sources leads to the same results. Triangulation requires that research is addressed from multiple perspectives. Several kinds of triangulation are possible:

- Method triangulation: using multiple methods of data collection and analysis.
- Data triangulation: collecting data from several sources and/or at different time periods.
- Researcher triangulation: multiple researchers collect and/or analyze the data.
- Theory triangulation: multiple theories and/or perspectives are used to interpret and explain the data.

TRADE-OFFS AND COMPRO-MISES	This concludes the discussion on the basic design issues regarding the research strategy, extent of researcher interference, study setting, unit of analysis and the time horizon. The researcher determines the appropriate decisions to be made in the study design based on the research perspective of the investigator, the research objective(s), research questions, the extent of rigor desired and practical considerations. Sometimes, because of the time and costs involved, a researcher might be constrained to settle for less than the 'ideal' research design. For instance, the researcher might have to conduct a cross-sectional instead of a longitudinal study, do a field study rather than an experimental design, choose a smaller rather than a larger sample size and so on, thus suboptimizing the research design decisions and settling for a lower level of scientific rigor because of resource constraints. This trade-off between rigor and practical considerations will be a deliberate and conscious decision made by the manager/researcher and will have to be explicitly stated in the research report. Compromises so made also account for why management studies are not entirely scientific, as discussed in Chapter 2. Mixed methods research focuses on collecting, analyzing and mixing both quantitative and qualitative data in a single study or series of studies. As stated above, a mixed methods approach complicates the research design and therefore requires clear presentation to allow the reader to sort out its different components. Regardless of the complexity of the design, the researcher always has to be very clear about each aspect discussed in this chapter before embarking on data collection.
Now do Exercises 7.1, 7.2, 7.3, and 7.4.

EXERCISE 7.1	A foreman thinks that the low efficiency of the machine tool operators is directly linked to the high level of fumes emitted in the workshop. He would like to prove this to his supervisor through a research study.

1. Would this be a causal or a correlational study? Why?
2. Is this an exploratory, a descriptive or a causal study? Why?
3. What kind of a study would this be: field study, lab experiment or field experiment? Why?
4. What would be the unit of analysis? Why?
5. Would this be a cross-sectional or a longitudinal study? Why?

EXERCISE 7.2	You want to examine how exposure to thin or heavy models in advertisements influences a person's self-esteem. You believe that the effect of exposure to models in advertisements depends on the extremity of the model's thinness or heaviness. Discuss the design decisions that you as a researcher will make to investigate this issue, giving reasons for your choices.

EXERCISE 7.3	You want to investigate the specific effects of specific emotions on customers' behavioural responses to failed service encounters across industries. Discuss the design decisions that you as a researcher will make to investigate this issue, giving reasons for your choices.

You are interested in how person–organization fit relates to employees' affective commitment and intention to stay with an organization during the early stages of a strategic organizational change.

MANAGERIAL
IMPLICATIONS

Knowledge about research design issues helps the manager to understand what the researcher is attempting to do. The manager also understands why the reports sometimes indicate data analytic results based on small sample sizes, when a lot of time has been spent in collecting data from several scores of individuals, as in the case of studies involving groups, departments or branch offices.

One of the important decisions a manager has to make before starting a study pertains to how rigorous the study ought to be. Knowing that more rigorous research designs consume more resources, the manager is in a position to weigh the gravity of the problem experienced and decide what kind of design will yield acceptable results in an efficient manner. For example, the manager might decide that knowledge of which variables are associated with employee performance is good enough to enhance performance results and there is no need to ferret out the cause. Such a decision would result not only in economy in resources but also cause the least disruption to the smooth flow of work for employees and preclude the need for collecting data longitudinally. Knowledge of interconnections among various aspects of the research design helps managers to call for the most effective study, after weighing the nature and magnitude of the problem encountered, and the type of solution desired.

One of the main advantages in fully understanding the difference between causal and correlational studies is that managers do not fall into the trap of making implicit causal assumptions when two variables are only associated with each other. They realize that *A* could cause *B*, or *B* could cause *A*, or both *A* and *B* could covary because of some third variable.

Knowledge of research design details also helps managers to study and intelligently comment on research proposals and on research reports.

SUMMARY

- **Learning objective 1: Explain what is meant by a research design.** A research design is a blueprint or plan for the collection, measurement and analysis of data, created to answer your research questions. Issues relating to decisions regarding the research strategy (for instance, experiments, surveys, case studies), the extent of researcher interference, location (i.e., the study setting), the level at which the data will be analyzed (unit of analysis) and temporal aspects (the time horizon) are integral to research design.

- **Learning objective 2: Develop an appropriate research design for any given study.** Each component of the research design offers several critical choice points. There is no single design that is superior in all circumstances. Instead, the researcher will have to make choices and create a design that is suitable for the job at hand. The researcher determines the appropriate decisions to be made in the study design based on the research perspective of the investigator, the research objective(s), research questions, the extent of rigor desired and practical considerations.

- **Learning objective 3: Explain why a researcher might be constrained to settle for less than the 'ideal' research design.** Sometimes, because of the time and costs involved, a researcher might be constrained to settle for less than the 'ideal' research design. For instance, the researcher might have to conduct a field study rather than an experimental design or choose a smaller rather than a larger sample size thus sub-optimizing the research design decisions and settling for a lower level of scientific rigor because of resource constraints. This trade-off between rigor and practical considerations should be a deliberate and conscious decision made by the researcher.

- **Learning objective 4: Demonstrate awareness of the role of the manager in the area of research design.** Knowledge about research design issues helps the manager to understand what the researcher is attempting to do and to study and intelligently comment on research proposals and on research reports.

Instructors can visit the companion website at **www.wiley.com/go/bougie/researchmethods forbusiness8e** for **Case Study: The effect of calorie information on food consumption.**

DISCUSSION QUESTIONS

1. What are the basic research design issues? Describe them in some detail.

2. Why is it important to consider basic design issues before conducting the study and even as early as at the time of formulating the research question?

3. Is a field study totally out of the question if one is trying to establish cause-and-effect relationships?

4. 'A field study is often more useful than a lab experiment'. Discuss this statement.

5. Why is the unit of analysis an integral part of the research design?

6. Discuss the interrelationships among the research questions of a study (exploratory, descriptive, causal), study setting (noncontrived or contrived), researcher interference, research strategy and time horizon of study.

7. Below are three scenarios. Indicate how the researcher should proceed in each case; that is, determine the following, giving reasons:
   a. Type of research question (exploratory, descriptive or causal).
   b. The extent of researcher interference.
   c. The study setting.
   d. The research strategy.
   e. The time horizon for the study.
   f. The unit of analysis.

Scenario 1

A specific department within an organization has a high turnover rate; employees of this department have a shorter average tenure than those of other departments in the company. Skilled workers are leaving and the worker population contains a high percentage of novice workers. Ms Joyce Lynn has no idea what is going on and wants to know more about what is happening.

Scenario 2

Mr Paul Hodge, the owner of several restaurants on the East Coast, is concerned about the wide differences in their profit margins. He would like to try some incentive plans for increasing the efficiency levels of those restaurants that lag behind. But before he actually does this, he would like to be assured that the idea will work. He asks a researcher to help him on this issue.

Scenario 3

A manager is intrigued as to why some people seem to derive joy from work and get energized by it, while others find it troublesome and frustrating.

Interviews

LEARNING OBJECTIVES

After completing Chapter 8, you should be able to:

1. Differentiate primary from secondary data collection methods.

2. Plan, design and carry out a personal interview.

3. Plan, design and carry out a group interview.

4. Discuss the advantages and disadvantages of interviewing.

INTRODUCTION

Having discussed a number of basic issues in research design in the previous chapter, we will now turn to *primary data collection methods* – or ways in which data collected from original sources for the specific purpose of this study can be gathered. Data collection methods are an integral part of research design, as shown in the shaded portion of Figure 8.1.

The aim of this chapter is to introduce a commonly used method of primary data collection: interviewing. Different types of interviews are discussed and ways in which to structure and carry out interviews are explained. The chapter starts with an introduction to primary data collection methods.

PRIMARY DATA COLLECTION METHODS

Since business is largely a social phenomenon, much of the information needed to make decisions in the work setting has to come from people – for instance, from employees, consumers, managers, investors and/or suppliers. For this reason, interviews, observation and questionnaires are very popular in business research; these methods allow the researcher to collect a wide variety of different sorts of data from human respondents. We discuss these methods in, respectively, Chapters 8, 9 and 10. After we have discussed these non-experimental approaches to the collection of primary data, we discuss *experimental designs* in Chapter 11. In this way, our discussion on primary data collection methods is organized around four principal methods of primary data collection.

A thorough knowledge of the most important methods will help you to evaluate alternative approaches to primary data collection (see Box 8.1 for a further example). As you will understand, the primary data collection decision – which involves the selection of the method(s) of obtaining the information needed – is inter-related with the other steps in the research process. That is why your choice of method(s) will depend on the objective(s) of the study, the research questions and the research strategy. Facilities available, the degree of accuracy required, the type of data required, the time span of the study, the expertise of the reviewer and other costs and resources associated with and available for data gathering will also affect the choice of method(s). Problems researched with the use of *appropriate* methods greatly enhance the value of the study.

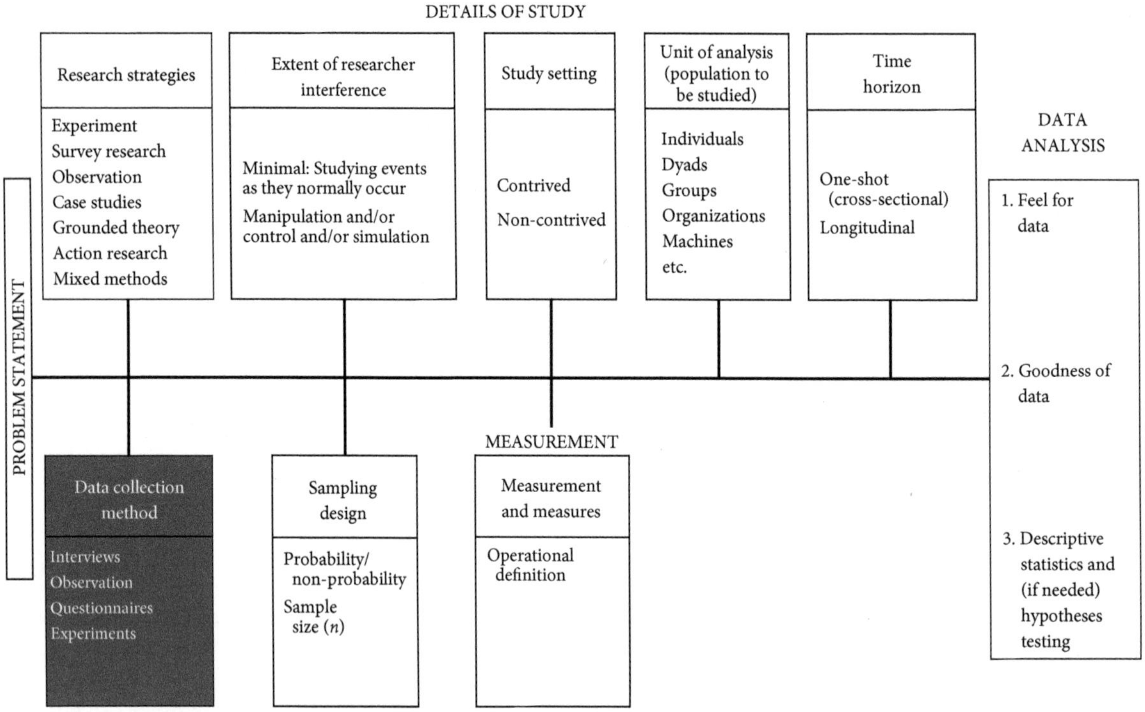

DETAILS OF STUDY

Research strategies	Extent of researcher interference	Study setting	Unit of analysis (population to be studied)	Time horizon
Experiment Survey research Observation Case studies Grounded theory Action research Mixed methods	Minimal: Studying events as they normally occur Manipulation and/or control and/or simulation	Contrived Non-contrived	Individuals Dyads Groups Organizations Machines etc.	One-shot (cross-sectional) Longitudinal

DATA ANALYSIS

1. Feel for data

2. Goodness of data

3. Descriptive statistics and (if needed) hypotheses testing

PROBLEM STATEMENT

Data collection method	Sampling design	Measurement and measures
Interviews Observation Questionnaires Experiments	Probability/ non-probability Sample size (*n*)	Operational definition

MEASUREMENT

FIGURE 8.1   Research design and how data collection methods fit in

---

BOX 8.1   **UNOBTRUSIVE METHODS**

Unobtrusive methods do not require the researcher to interact with the people he or she is studying. Unobtrusive methods are sometimes used by researchers who seek to understand what people actually *do*, instead of what they say they do (as in interviews or in questionnaires). *Internet clickstream data* exemplify unobtrusive data. Nowadays, virtually every commercial website monitors traffic to its site to collect data on its visitors. Based on the observed behaviour of these visitors, it is possible to develop a thorough understanding of the website's customer base. This helps managers to predict likely future behavioural patterns but also to anticipate customers' responses to (future) marketing activities. Like this, clickstream data provide managers with a valuable tool to shape their marketing efforts (cf. Park & Fader, 2004). *Scanner data* (data on sales of consumer goods obtained by scanning bar codes of products in retail outlets) also provide managers with detailed information about the effects of marketing activities (such as price promotions) on sales (cf. Van Heerde, Gupta & Wittink, 2003). Another example of unobtrusive methods is the number of different brands of soft drink cans found in trash bags, which offers a measure of their consumption levels. These unobtrusive sources of data and their use are important in research aimed at understanding behavioural.

INTERVIEWS

Instructors can visit the companion website at **www.wiley.com/go/bougie/researchmethods forbusiness8e** for **Author Video: Interviewing**.

A widely used method of collecting data in business research is to interview respondents to obtain information on an issue of interest. An **interview** is a guided, purposeful conversation between two or more people. There are many different types of interviews. Individual or group interviews may be unstructured or semi-structured, and conducted face to face, by telephone or online.

Unstructured and semi-structured interviews will be discussed first. Some important factors to be borne in mind while interviewing will then be detailed. Next, the advantages and disadvantages of face-to-face interviewing and telephone interviews are considered and then, computer-assisted interviews are described. A discussion on group interviews concludes this chapter. Managerial implications and ethics in interviews and other types of survey research are discussed in Chapter 10 after we have discussed interviews, observation and administering questionnaires in greater detail.

UNSTRUCTURED AND STRUCTURED INTERVIEWS

Unstructured Interviews

Unstructured interviews are so labelled because the interviewer does not enter the interview setting with a planned sequence of questions to be asked of the respondent. At most, the researcher uses a topic list or an interview guide containing a list of things to be sure to ask when talking to the person being interviewed. Interviewees are allowed to respond freely in their own words about the topics the researcher brings to the conversation as well as on topics that they want to bring to the conversation. Informal interviews, where the researcher seizes the opportunity to have a short talk with a stakeholder about issues that are relevant to the project, are a crucial part of many studies.

Semi-structured Interviews

Semi-structured interviews are those conducted when it is known at the outset what information is needed. The content of a semi-structured interview can be prepared in advance, and usually consists of:

- an introduction: the interviewer introduces him- or herself, the purpose of the interview, assures confidentiality, asks permission to record the interview;
- a set of topics (usually questions) in a logical order: first "warm-up" questions (which are easy to answer and non-threatening) and then the main questions covering the purpose of the interview;
- suggestions for probing questions (Box 8.2): follow-up questions that are used when the first answer is unclear or incomplete, the interviewer does not fully understand the answer, or in any other case where the interviewer requires more specific or in-depth information.

BOX 8.2	PROBING TACTICS

- Silence.
- Repeating the answer.
- "So what I hear you saying is . . ."
- "I'm not quite sure I understood . . . Could you . . ."

- "Could you please tell me more about . . ."
- "Could you give an example?"
- "Could you go over that again?"
- "Anything else?"

The same questions will be asked of everybody in the same manner. Sometimes, however, based on the exigencies of the situation, the experienced researcher might take a lead from a respondent's answer and ask other relevant questions not on the interview protocol. Through this process, new factors might be identified, resulting in a deeper understanding. However, to be able to recognize a probable response, the interviewer must comprehend the purpose and goal of each question. This is particularly important when a team of trained interviewers conducts the survey.

Visual aids such as pictures, line drawings, cards and other materials are also sometimes used in conducting interviews. The appropriate visuals are shown to the interviewees, who then indicate their responses to the questions posed. Marketing research, for example, benefits from such techniques in order to capture the likes and dislikes of customers with regard to different types of packaging, forms of advertising and so on. Visual aids, including painting and drawing, are particularly useful when children are the focus of marketing research. Visual aids also come in handy while endeavouring to elicit certain thoughts and ideas that are difficult to express or awkward to articulate.

When a sufficient number of semi-structured interviews has been conducted and adequate information obtained to understand and describe the important factors operating in the situation, the researcher stops the interviews. The information is then tabulated and the data analysed. This helps the researcher to accomplish the task he set out to achieve, such as describing the phenomena, or quantifying them, or identifying the specific problem and evolving a theory of the factors that influence the problem or finding answers to the research question. Much qualitative research is done in this manner.

TRAINING INTERVIEWERS

When several long interviews are to be conducted, it is often not feasible for one individual to conduct all the interviews. A team of trained interviewers then becomes necessary. Interviewers have to be thoroughly briefed about the research and trained in how to start an interview, how to proceed with the questions, how to motivate respondents to answer, what to look for in the answers and how to close an interview. They also need to be instructed about taking notes and coding the interview responses. The tips for interviewing, discussed later, should become a part of their repertoire for interviewing.

Good planning, proper training, offering clear guidelines to interviewers and supervising their work all help in profitably utilizing the interviewing technique as a viable data collection mechanism. Personal interviews provide rich data when respondents spontaneously offer information, in the sense that their answers do not typically fall within a constricted range of responses, as in a questionnaire. However, personal interviews are expensive in terms of time, training costs and resource consumption.

SOME TIPS TO FOLLOW WHEN INTERVIEWING

The information obtained during the interviews should be as free as possible of bias. **Bias** refers to errors or inaccuracies in the data collected. Bias could be introduced by the interviewer, the interviewee or the situation. The interviewer could bias the data if proper trust and rapport are not established with the interviewee, or when the responses are either misinterpreted or distorted or when the interviewer unintentionally encourages or discourages certain types of response through gestures and facial expressions.

Listening attentively to the interviewee, evincing keen interest in what the respondent has to say, exercising tact in questioning, repeating and/or clarifying the questions posed and paraphrasing some of the answers to ensure their thorough understanding goes a long way in keeping alive the interest of the respondent throughout the interview. Recording the responses accurately is equally important.

Interviewees can bias the data when they do not come out with their true opinions but provide information that they think is what the interviewer expects of them or would like to hear. Also, if they do not understand the questions, they may feel diffident or hesitant to seek clarification. They may then answer questions without knowing their importance and thus introduce bias.

Some interviewees may be turned off because of personal likes and dislikes, or the dress of the interviewer or the manner in which the questions are put. They may, therefore, not provide truthful answers, but instead, deliberately offer incorrect responses. Some respondents may also answer questions in a socially acceptable manner rather than indicating their true sentiments.

Biases could be situational as well, in terms of (1) non-participants, (2) trust levels and rapport established and (3) the physical setting of the interview. Non-participation, either because of unwillingness or the inability of the interviewee to participate in the study, can bias data inasmuch as the responses of the participants may be different from those of the non-participants (which implies that a biased, rather than a representative, set of responses is likely to result). Bias also occurs when different interviewers establish different levels of trust and rapport with their interviewees, thus eliciting answers of varying degrees of openness. The actual setting in which the interview is conducted might sometimes introduce bias. Some individuals, for instance, may not feel quite at ease when interviewed at the workplace and therefore may not respond frankly and honestly.

In telephone interviews, when the respondent cannot be reached due to unavailability at that time, callbacks and further contacts should be attempted so that the sample does not become biased (discussed in Chapter 14 on Sampling). The interviewer can also reduce bias by being consistent with the questioning mode as each person is interviewed, by not distorting or falsifying the information received and by not influencing the responses of the subjects in any manner.

The above biases can be minimized in several ways. The following strategies will be useful for the purpose.

Establishing Credibility and Rapport and Motivating Individuals to Respond

The projection of professionalism, enthusiasm and confidence is important for the interviewer. For instance, a manager hiring outside researchers to deal with a problem within an organization would be interested in assessing their abilities and personality predispositions. Researchers must establish rapport with, and gain the confidence and approval of, the hiring client before they can even start their work in the organization. Knowledge, skills, ability, confidence, articulateness and enthusiasm are therefore qualities a researcher must demonstrate in order to establish credibility with the hiring organization and its members.

To obtain honest information from the respondents, the researcher/interviewer should be able to establish rapport and trust with them. In other words, the researcher should be able to make the respondent sufficiently at ease to give informative and truthful answers without fear of adverse consequences. To this end, the researcher should state the purpose of the interview and assure complete confidentiality about the source of the responses. Establishing rapport with the respondents may not be easy, especially when interviewing employees at lower levels. They are likely to be suspicious of the intentions of the researchers; they may believe that the researchers are on the management's 'side', and therefore likely to propose a reduction in the labour force, an increase in the workload and so on. Thus, it is important to ensure that everyone concerned is aware of the researchers' purpose as being one of merely understanding the true state of affairs in the organization. The respondents must be tactfully made to understand that the researchers do not intend to take sides; they are not there to harm the staff, and will provide the results of research to the organization only in aggregates, without disclosing the identity of the individuals. This should encourage the respondents to feel secure about responding.

The researcher can establish rapport by being pleasant, sincere, sensitive and non-evaluative. Evincing a genuine interest in the responses and allaying any anxieties, fears, suspicions and tensions sensed in the situation will help respondents to feel more comfortable with the researchers. If the respondent is told about the purpose of the study and how he or she was chosen to be one of those interviewed, there should be better communication between the parties. Researchers can motivate respondents to offer honest and truthful answers by explaining to them that their contribution will indeed help and that they themselves may stand to gain from such a survey, in the sense that the quality of life at work for most of them may improve significantly.

Certain other strategies in how questions are posed also help participants to offer less biased responses. These are discussed below.

The Questioning Technique

Funnelling   At the beginning of an unstructured interview, it is advisable to ask open-ended questions to get a broad idea and form some impressions about the situation. For example, a question that could be asked would be:

What are some of your feelings about working for this organization?

From the responses to this broad question, further questions that are progressively more focused may be asked as the researcher processes the interviewees' responses and notes some possible key issues relevant to the situation. This transition from broad to narrow themes is called the **funnelling technique**.

Unbiased questions   It is important to ask **unbiased questions** to ensure that you minimize bias in the responses. For example, '*Tell me how you experience your job*' is a better question than, '*Boy, the work you do must be really boring; let me hear how you experience it*'. The latter question is 'loaded' in terms of the interviewer's own perceptions of the job. A loaded question might influence the types of answers received from the respondent. Bias could also be introduced by emphasizing certain words, by tone and voice inflections and through inappropriate suggestions.

Clarifying issues   To make sure that the researcher understands issues as the respondent intends to represent them, it is advisable to restate or rephrase important information given by the respondent. For instance, if the interviewee says, '*There is an unfair promotion policy in this organization; seniority does not count at all – it is the juniors who always get promoted*', the researcher might interject, '*So you are saying that juniors always get promoted over the heads of even capable seniors*'. Rephrasing in this way clarifies the issue of whether or not the respondent considers ability important. If certain things that are being said are not clear, the researcher should seek clarification. For example, if the respondent happens to say, '*The facilities here are really poor; we often have to continue working even when we are dying of thirst*', the researcher might ask if there is no water fountain or drinking water available in the building. The respondent's reply to this might well indicate that there is a water fountain across the hall, but the respondent would like one on his side of the work area as well.

Helping the respondent to think through issues   If the respondent is not able to verbalize her perceptions, or replies, '*I don't know*', the researcher should ask the question in a simpler way or rephrase it. For instance, if a respondent is unable to specify what aspects of the job he dislikes, the researcher might ask the question in a simpler way. For example, the respondent might be asked which task he would prefer to do: serve a customer or do some filing work. If the answer is '*serve the customer*', the researcher might use another aspect of the respondent's job and ask the paired-choice question again. In this way, the respondent can sort out which aspects of the job he likes better than others.

Recording the interview and/or taking notes   The interviews can be recorded if the respondent has no objection. However, recorded interviews might bias the respondents' answers because they know that their answers are being recorded, and their anonymity is not preserved in full. Hence, even if the respondents do not object to being taped, there could be some bias in their responses. Before recording interviews, one should be reasonably certain that such a method of obtaining data is not likely to bias the information received. Any audio or videotaping should always be done only after obtaining the respondent's permission. If the interviews cannot be recorded, it is important that the researcher makes written notes as the interviews are taking place, or as soon as the interview is terminated. The interviewer should not rely on memory, because information recalled from memory is imprecise and often likely to be incorrect. Furthermore, if more than one interview is scheduled for the day, the amount of information received increases, as do possible sources of error in recalling from memory who said what. Information based solely on recall introduces bias into the research.

Review of Tips to Follow When Interviewing

Establishing credibility as able researchers is important for the success of the research project. Researchers need to establish rapport with the respondents and motivate them to give responses relatively free from bias by allaying whatever suspicions, fears, anxieties and concerns they may have about the research and its consequences. This can be accomplished by being sincere, pleasant and non-evaluative. While interviewing, the researcher has to ask broad questions initially and then narrow them down to specific areas, ask questions in an unbiased way, offer clarification when needed and help respondents to think through difficult issues. The responses should be transcribed immediately and should not be trusted to memory and later recall.

Having looked at unstructured and semi-structured interviews and learned something about how to conduct the interviews, we can now discuss face-to-face and telephone interviews.

FACE-TO-FACE AND TELEPHONE INTERVIEWS

Interviews can be conducted either face to face or over the telephone. They may also be computer-assisted. Although most unstructured interviews in business research are conducted face to face, semi-structured interviews may be either face to face or through the medium of the telephone, depending on the level of complexity of the issues involved, the likely duration of the interview, the convenience of both parties and the geographical area covered by the survey. Telephone interviews are best suited when information from a large number of respondents spread over a wide geographic area is to be obtained quickly, and the likely duration of each interview is, say, ten minutes or less. Many market surveys, for instance, are conducted through semi-structured **telephone interviews**. In addition, **computer-assisted telephone interviews (CATI)** are also possible and easy to manage.

Face-to-face interviews and telephone interviews have other advantages and disadvantages. These will now be briefly discussed.

Face-to-Face Interviews: Advantages and Disadvantages

The main advantage of face-to-face or direct interviews is that the researcher can adapt the questions as necessary, clarify doubts and ensure that the responses are properly understood, by repeating or rephrasing the questions. The researcher can also pick up non-verbal cues from the respondent. Any discomfort, stress or problem that the respondent experiences can be detected through frowns, nervous tapping and other body language unconsciously exhibited by her. This would be impossible to detect in a telephone interview.

The main disadvantages of face-to-face interviews are the geographical limitations they may impose on the surveys and the vast resources needed if such surveys need to be done nationally or internationally. The costs of training interviewers to minimize interviewer bias (e.g., differences in questioning methods, interpretation of responses) are also high. Another drawback is that respondents might feel uneasy about the anonymity of their responses when they interact face to face with the interviewer.

Telephone Interviews: Advantages and Disadvantages

The main advantage of telephone interviewing, from the researcher's point of view, is that a number of different people can be reached (if need be, across the country or even internationally) in a relatively short period of time. From the respondents' standpoint, it eliminates any discomfort that some of them might feel in facing the interviewer. It is also possible that most of them might feel less uncomfortable disclosing personal information over the phone than face to face.

A main disadvantage of telephone interviewing is that the respondent could unilaterally terminate the interview without warning or explanation, by hanging up the phone. This is understandable, given the numerous telemarketing calls people are bombarded with on a daily basis. To minimize this type of non-response problem, it is advisable to call the interviewee ahead of time to request participation in the survey, giving an approximate idea of how long the interview will last and setting up a mutually convenient time. Interviewees usually tend to appreciate this courtesy and are more likely to cooperate. It is a good policy not to prolong the interview beyond the time originally stated. As mentioned earlier, another disadvantage of the telephone interview is that the researcher will not be able to see the respondent to read the non-verbal communication.

ADDITIONAL SOURCES OF BIAS IN INTERVIEW DATA

We have already discussed several sources of bias in data collection. Biased data will be obtained when respondents are interviewed while they are extremely busy or are not in good humour. Responses to issues such as strikes, layoffs or the like could also be biased. The personality of the interviewer, the introductory sentence, inflection of the voice and such other aspects could introduce additional bias. Awareness of the many sources of bias will enable interviewers to obtain relatively valid information.

Sampling biases, which include inability to contact persons whose telephone numbers have changed, could also affect the quality of the research data. Likewise, people with unlisted numbers who are not contacted could also bias the sample (discussed in Chapter 14), and, hence, the data obtained. With the introduction of caller ID, it is possible for telephone interviews to be ridden with complexity.

COMPUTER-ASSISTED INTERVIEWING

With computer-assisted interviews (CAI) questions are flashed onto the computer screen and interviewers can enter the answers of the respondents directly into the computer. The accuracy of data collection is considerably enhanced since the software can be programmed to flag the "offbase" or "out-of-range" responses. CAI software also prevents interviewers from asking the wrong questions or in the wrong sequence since the questions are automatically flashed to the respondent in an ordered sequence. This, to some extent, eliminates interviewer-induced bias.

CATI and CAPI

There are two types of computer-assisted interview programs: CATI (computer-assisted telephone interviewing) and CAPI (computer-assisted personal interviewing).

CATI, used in research organizations, is useful inasmuch as responses to surveys can be obtained from people all over the world. The computer prompts the questions with the help of software and the respondent provides the answers. The computer selects the telephone number, dials and places the responses in a file. The data are analysed later. Computerized, voice-activated telephone interviews are also possible for short surveys. Data can also be gathered during field surveys through handheld computers that record and analyse responses.

CAPI has an advantage in that it can be self-administered; that is, respondents can use their own computers to run the program by themselves once they receive the software and enter their responses, thereby reducing errors in recording.

The voice recording system assists CATI programs by recording interviewees' responses. Courtesy, ethics and legal requirements require that the respondents' permission to record be obtained before the interview is recorded.

In sum, the advantages of computer-assisted interviews can be stated simply as quick and more accurate information gathering, plus faster and easier analysis of data. The field costs are low and automatic recording of results is possible. It is efficient in terms of costs.

Software Packages

Field notes taken by interviewers as they collect data generally have to be transcribed, hand-coded, hand-tabulated and so on – all of which are tedious and time-consuming. In the present day, there is a lot of software available that may ease the interviewers' job with regard to these activities.

GROUP INTERVIEWS

Interviews may be conducted on an individual basis, but also on a group basis, where the interviewer puts open questions to a group of participants. The term "focus group" is used for a particular type of group interview, where the topic is clearly defined and there is a focus on facilitating discussion between participants.

Focus Groups

Focus groups consist typically of eight to ten members with a moderator leading the discussions on a particular topic, concept or product. Members are generally chosen on the basis of their familiarity with the topic on which information is sought. For example, women with children may compose a focus group to identify how organizations can help working mothers. Large organizations such as Coca-Cola, Unilever and Nike regularly convene young men and women from around the world to tap them for ideas for a new product.

The focus sessions are aimed at obtaining respondents' impressions, interpretations and opinions, as the members talk about the event, concept, product or service. The moderator plays a vital role in steering the discussions in a manner that draws out the information sought and keeps the members on track.

Focus group discussions on a specific topic at a particular location and at a specified time provide the opportunity for a flexible, free-flowing format for the members. The unstructured and spontaneous responses are expected to reflect the genuine opinions, ideas and feelings of the members about the topic under discussion. Focus groups are relatively inexpensive and can provide fairly dependable data within a short time frame.

Role of the moderator The selection and role of the moderator are critical. The moderator introduces the topic, observes and takes notes and/or records the discussions. The moderator never becomes an integral part of the discussions, but merely steers the group persuasively to obtain all the relevant information, and helps the group members to get through any impasse that might occur. The moderator also ensures that all members participate in the discussion and that no member dominates the group. Someone from the research team may also observe the proceedings through a one-way mirror, listening to the verbal statements and noticing the nonverbal cues of the members.

The nature of data obtained through focus groups It should be noted that although data obtained through these homogeneous group members are less expensive than those obtained through the various other data collection methods, and also lend themselves to quick analysis, the content analysis of the data so obtained provides only qualitative and not quantitative information. Also, since the members are not selected scientifically to reflect the opinions of the population at large (see Chapter 14 on Sampling for more details on this), their opinions cannot be considered to be truly representative. However, when exploratory information is collected as a basis for further scientific research, focus groups serve an important function. Consider, for example, the value of focus groups in exploring the concept of 'intellectual property'. When animated discussions take place, there is a serendipitous flow of new ideas among the group members who discuss the nuances of each thought process. Researchers are thereby helped to obtain valuable insights from the snowballing effects of the discussions.

Videoconferencing If regional variations in responses are expected, several focus groups could be formed, including trained moderators, at different locations. This process is easily facilitated through videoconferencing. By zooming in on a particular member, the non-verbal cues and gestures of that individual can be captured, as and when desired. This also obviates the need for an observer looking through a one-way mirror.

With the great strides that have been made in technological advancement, videoconferencing as a means of gathering information from different groups in distant locations has become rather common these days.

In sum, focus groups are used for:

1. Exploratory studies.

2. Making generalizations based on the information generated by them.

3. Conducting sample surveys.

Focus groups have been credited with enlightening investigators as to why certain products are not doing well, why certain advertising strategies are effective, why specific management techniques do not work and the like.

Expert Panels

'Focus group research' is a generic term for any research that studies how groups of people talk about a clearly defined issue. An **expert panel** is a group of people specifically convened by the researcher to elicit expert knowledge and opinion about a certain issue. The criteria for qualification as an expert are many and varied, but the expert panel usually comprises independent specialists, recognized in at least one of the fields addressed during the panel sessions. Expert panels may thus bring together a wide variety of experts, including scientists, policy makers and community stakeholders.

| **ADVANTAGES AND DISAD- VANTAGES OF INTERVIEWS** | Interviews are one method of obtaining data; they can be either unstructured or semi-structured, and can be conducted face to face, over the telephone or via the computer. Interviews may be conducted on an individual basis, but also on a group basis. Unstructured interviews are usually conducted to obtain definite ideas about what is, and is not, important and relevant to particular problem situations. Semi-structured interviews give more in-depth information about specific variables of interest. To minimize bias in responses, the interviewer must establish rapport with the respondents and ask unbiased questions. The face-to-face interview and that conducted over the telephone have their advantages and disadvantages, and both have their uses in different circumstances. Computer-assisted interviewing is an asset for interviewing and for the analysis of qualitative, spontaneous responses. Computer interactive interviews have become an increasingly important mode of data collection in recent years. |

The advantages and disadvantages of personal or face-to-face and telephone interviews are presented in Table 8.1.

Table 8.1 Advantages and disadvantages of interviews

Mode of Data Collection	Advantages	Disadvantages
Personal or face-to-face interviews	Can establish rapport and motivate respondents.	Takes personal time.
	Can clarify the questions, clear doubts add new questions.	Costs more when a wide geographic region is covered.
	Can read non-verbal cues.	Respondents may be concerned about confidentiality of information given.
	Can use visual aids to clarify points.	
	Rich data can be obtained.	Interviewers need to be trained.
	CAPI can be used and responses entered in a portable computer.	Can introduce interviewer bias.
Telephone interviews	Less costly and speedier than personal interviews.	Non-verbal cues cannot be read.
	Can reach a wide geographic area.	Interviews will have to be kept short.
	Greater anonymity than personal interviews.	Respondents can terminate the interview at any time.
	Can be done using CATI.	

SUMMARY

- **Learning objective 1: Differentiate primary from secondary data collection methods.** Data collection methods are an integral part of research design. Primary data collection methods involve data collection from original sources for the specific purpose of the study. The discussion on primary data collection methods is organized around four principal methods of primary data collection: interviews, observation, administering questionnaires and experiments. The primary data collection decision is interrelated with the other steps in the research process.

- **Learning objective 2: Plan, design and carry out a personal interview.** A commonly used method of collecting data in business research is to interview respondents to obtain information on an issue of interest. An interview is a guided, purposeful conversation between two or more people. There are many different types of interviews. Individual interviews may be unstructured or semi-structured, and conducted face to face, by telephone or online.

- **Learning objective 3: Plan, design and carry out a group interview.** Interviews may be conducted on an individual basis, but also on a group basis, where the interviewer asks open questions of a group of participants. The term 'focus group' is used for a particular type of group interview, where the topic is clearly defined and there is a focus on facilitating discussion between participants. An expert panel is a group of people specifically convened by the researcher to elicit expert knowledge and opinion about a certain issue.

- **Learning objective 4: Discuss the advantages and disadvantages of interviewing.** Problems researched with the use of appropriate methods greatly enhance the value of the study. That is why the choice of method(s) will depend on the objective(s) of the study, the research questions and the research strategy. Other factors, such as facilities available, the degree of accuracy required, the type of data required, the time span of the study, the expertise of the reviewer and costs will also affect the choice of method(s). The advantages and disadvantages of interviews are discussed in the final part of this chapter.

In the next chapter, we discuss observation as a method of collecting data.

Instructors can visit the companion website at **www.wiley.com/go/bougie/researchmethods forbusiness8e** for **Case Study: Kyoto Midtown Shopping Centre**.

DISCUSSION QUESTIONS	1. Describe the different data sources, explaining their usefulness and disadvantages.
	2. As a manager, you have invited a research team to come in, study and offer suggestions on how to improve the performance of your staff. What steps will you take to relieve staff apprehensions and worries even before the research team sets foot in your department?
	3. What is bias, and how can it be reduced during interviews?
	4. Discuss the advantages and disadvantages of personal and telephone interviews.
	5. What are projective techniques and how can they be used profitably?
	6. How has the advancement in technology helped data gathering via interviewing?
	Now do Exercises 8.1 and 8.2.

EXERCISE 8.1	First conduct an unstructured and later a semi-structured interview, to learn about how people use and process information to choose among alternative brands when they are looking for furniture, clothing, household appliances and the like. Select a specific product and ask people, for instance, about the product attributes they consider, and how important these attributes are. Write up the results, and include the formats you used for both stages of the research.

EXERCISE 8.2	Design an interview schedule to assess the 'intellectual capital' as perceived by employees in an organization – the dimensions and elements for which you developed earlier.

Observation

LEARNING OBJECTIVES

After completing Chapter 9, you should be able to:

1. Define observation and discuss how observation may help to solve business problems.

2. Demonstrate the ability to make an informed decision on an appropriate type of observational method for a specific study.

3. Explain the issues related to participant observation and structured observation.

4. Discuss the advantages and disadvantages of observation.

INTRODUCTION

Actions and behaviour of employees, consumers, investors and the like may play an important role in business research. Researchers and managers might be interested in the way workers carry out their jobs, the impact of new manufacturing techniques on employee activity, in how consumers watch commercials, use products or behave in waiting areas or in how a merchant bank trades and operates. A useful and natural technique to collect data on actions and behaviour is observation. Observation involves going into 'the field' – the factory, the supermarket, the waiting room, the office or the trading room – watching what workers, consumers or day traders do, and describing, analysing and interpreting what one has seen.

BOX 9.1

The Internet has extended the concept of observation to include online data collection. For researchers who study online phenomena, social media such as Facebook, Twitter and Instagram have become fieldsites in their own right. For instance, Scaraboto, Rossi and Da Costa (2012) have used online observation to investigate how consumers persuade each other in online communities.

Observational methods are best suited for research requiring non-self-report descriptive data; that is, when behaviour is to be examined without directly asking the respondents themselves. Observational data are rich and uncontaminated by self-report bias. However, observational methods are also time-consuming and challenging in a lot of other ways as you will learn in this chapter. Indeed, they are not without difficulties for the untrained researcher.

This chapter starts with a definition of observation, followed by an overview of observational methods distinguished by four basic dimensions: control, group membership, structure and concealment. Subsequently, we examine two important observational methods, participant observation and structured observation, in more detail. Finally, we discuss advantages and disadvantages of observation.

Example	• Shadowing a Wall Street broker engaged in his daily routine.
Examples of observation discussed in further detail later in this chapter	• Observing in-store shopping behaviour of consumers via a camera. • Sitting in the corner of an office to observe how a merchant bank trader operates. • Working in a plant to study factory life. • Studying the approach skills of sales people disguised as a shopper.

DEFINITION AND PURPOSE OF OBSERVATION

Instructors can visit the companion website at **www.wiley.com/go/bougie/researchmethods forbusiness8e** for **Author Video: Definition and purpose of observation**.

Observation concerns the planned watching, recording, analysis and interpretation of behaviour, actions or events. Various approaches of observation have been used in business research. These may be distinguished by four key dimensions that characterize the way observation is conducted: (1) control (are the observations conducted in an artificial or in a natural setting?), (2) whether the observer is a member of the group that is observed or not (participant versus non-participant observation), (3) structure (to what extent the observation is focused, predetermined, systematic and quantitative in nature) and (4) concealment of observation (are the members of the social group under study told that they are being studied or not?). These key dimensions that distinguish particular methods of observation are discussed next.

FOUR KEY DIMENSIONS THAT CHARACTERIZE THE TYPE OF OBSERVATION

CONTROLLED VERSUS UNCONTROLLED OBSERVATIONAL STUDIES

A distinction can be made between observation conducted in controlled (or artificial) versus uncontrolled (or natural) settings. Observation is often conducted in a natural setting. However, observation is also a potential method of data collection within an experimental, controlled research tradition.

An observational study is said to be high in control when the situation or setting is manipulated or contrived by the researcher; the exposure of subjects (for instance, consumers, employees or investors) to a certain situation or condition (for instance, a specific store layout, specific labour conditions or a certain amount of time pressure) allows the researcher to observe differences between individual behavioural reactions to the situation. Controlled observation may be carried out in a laboratory (for instance, a simulated store environment or trading room) or in the field (for instance, a store).

Controlled observation occurs when observational research is carried out under carefully arranged conditions. **Uncontrolled observation** is an observational technique that makes no attempt to control, manipulate or influence the situation. Events are running their natural course and the researcher observes these events without interfering in the real-life setting. An advantage of uncontrolled observation is that people can be observed in their natural shopping or work environment. A major drawback of uncontrolled observation is, however, that it is usually difficult to untangle the often complex situation since we do not control any factor in this. Accordingly, it is very hard to distinguish *the causes* of events, actions and behaviour.

PARTICIPANT VERSUS NON-PARTICIPANT OBSERVATION

The researcher can play one of two roles while gathering observational data – that of a non-participant or a participant observer. In the case of **non-participant observation**, the researcher is never directly involved in the actions of the actors, but observes them from outside the actors' visual horizon, for instance, via a one-way mirror or a camera.

Participant observation is an approach that has frequently been used in case studies, ethnographic studies and grounded theory studies (see Chapter 7 for a discussion on the relationship between participant observation and ethnography). In participant observation, the researcher gathers data by participating in the daily life of the group or organization under study.

Spradley (1980) has developed a typology to describe a continuum in *the degree of participation* of researchers. The lowest level of participant observation is *passive participation*. Passive participation allows the researcher to collect the required data without becoming an integral part of the (organizational) system. For example, the researcher might sit in the corner of an office and watch and record how a merchant bank trader spends her time. *Moderate participation* occurs when the researcher does not actively participate and only occasionally interacts with the social group under study. In new research settings, in which the researcher is not familiar with the activities, habits and/or the jargon of the group, many researchers begin at the level of moderate participation until a more active role is possible. *Active participation* is when the researcher actually engages in almost everything that the group under study is doing as a means of trying to learn about their behaviour. The researcher may also play the role of the complete participant-observer. In *complete participant observation*, the researcher becomes a member of the social group under study. Complete participant observation involves 'immersion' in the social group under study. For instance, if a researcher wants to study group dynamics in work organizations, then she may join the organization as an employee and observe the dynamics in groups while being a part of the work organization and work groups. Like this, complete participant observation aims to generate an understanding of a social group from an 'insider's point of view' (Hume & Mulcock, 1994).

A famous example of complete participant observation in a business context is Beynon's (1975) study. Beynon spent much of 1967 in Ford's Halewood plant to study factory life and the experience of people who worked at the assembly lines of the Ford Motor Company. Beynon entered the Ford Motor Company and became a member of the social group under study (workers within a car assembly plant) to investigate 'life on the line'.

Example

STRUCTURED VERSUS UNSTRUCTURED OBSERVATIONAL STUDIES

As we have seen, observational studies can be of either the nonparticipant-observer or the participant-observer type. Both of these, again, can be either structured or unstructured. Where the observer has a predetermined set of categories of activities or phenomena planned to be studied, it is a *structured observational study*. Formats for recording the observations can be specifically designed and tailored to each study to suit the goal of that research. **Structured observation** is generally quantitative in nature.

Usually, matters that pertain to the feature of interest, such as the duration and frequency of an event (for instance, how long does it take to get a meal at a fast-food restaurant?), as well as certain activities that precede and follow it, are recorded. Environmental conditions (for instance, labour conditions) and any changes in setting are also noted, if considered relevant. Task-relevant behaviours of the actors, their perceived emotions, verbal and non-verbal communication and the like, may also be recorded. Observations that are recorded in worksheets or field notes are then systematically analysed.

At the beginning of a study, it is also possible that the observer has no definite ideas of the particular aspects that need focus. Observing events as they take place may also be a part of the plan as in many other forms of exploratory and qualitative research. In such cases, the observer will record practically everything that is observed. Such a study will be an *unstructured observational study*. Unstructured observational studies are claimed to be the hallmark of qualitative research. Qualitative data analysis (Chapter 17) is used to analyse and interpret what the researcher has seen.

Unstructured observation may eventually lead to a set of tentative hypotheses that are tested in subsequent research that is deductive in nature. Hence, inductive discovery via observation can pave the way for subsequent theory building and hypotheses testing.

CONCEALED VERSUS UNCONCEALED OBSERVATION

Concealment of observation relates to whether the members of the social group under study are told that they are being investigated. A primary advantage of **concealed observation** is that the research subjects are not influenced by the awareness that they are being observed. Indeed, **reactivity** or the extent to which the observer affects the situation under observation could be a major threat to the validity of the results of observational studies. **Unconcealed observation** is more obtrusive, perhaps upsetting the authenticity of the behaviour under study.

Example **The Hawthorne studies**	A famous example of subject responses to unconcealed observation is the 'Hawthorne effect'. In a relay assembly line, many experiments were conducted that increased lighting and the like, based on the original hypothesis that these would account for increases in productivity. However, as it turned out, the mere fact that people were chosen for the study gave them a feeling of importance that increased their productivity whether or not lighting, heating or other effects were improved, thus the coining of the term the *Hawthorne effect*. **CONCEALED OBSERVATION** To avoid reactivity, McClung, Grove and Hughes (1989) used researchers disguised as shoppers to collect data on the approach skills of salespeople. They decided to employ concealed observation because unconcealed observation could have an effect on the validity of their observations.

Concealed observation has some serious ethical drawbacks. While less reactive, concealed observation raises ethical concerns since it may violate the principles of informed consent, privacy and confidentiality (Burgess, 1989; Lauder, 2003). For this reason, concealed observation may harm the subjects in several ways. However, in some situations, for instance, when a (marketing) researcher watches a service encounter between a bus driver and a bus passenger, the researcher is likely to be less culpable than in other situations, for instance, when the researcher immerses herself in a certain social group such as a specific department within an organization (cf. Grove & Fisk, 1992). Note that there are no strict rules for assessing the ethicality of concealed observational research. Instead, a careful, well-judged assessment of the potential harmful consequences of concealed observational research should be made by the researcher. Frederichs and Ludtke (1975, p. 12) provide an elegant guideline for such an assessment: the research plan 'should be able to justify itself to the members of the scientific community as well as to those involved in the study'.

TWO IMPORTANT APPROACHES TO OBSERVATION	We have just briefly discussed the key dimensions that differentiate various approaches to observation. Two important, distinct approaches to observation are *participant observation* and *structured observation*. The remaining part of this chapter will discuss these two approaches in more detail.

PARTICIPANT OBSERVATION: INTRODUCTION

Earlier in this chapter, we have explained that the researcher can play one of two roles while gathering observational data: that of a non-participant or a participant observer. A key characteristic of participant observation is that the researcher gathers data by participating in the daily life of the group or organization under study. This enables the researcher to learn about the activities of the group under study in a natural setting from an insider's point of view through observing and participating in these activities. When Malinowski introduced this method in his influential work *Argonauts of the Western Pacific*, he argued that it puts the researcher in a position 'to grasp the native's point of view, his relation to life, to realize *his* vision of *his* world' (Malinowksi, 1992, p. 25). Today, this is still regarded as the key objective and one of the main strengths of participant observation. Since the time of Malinowski, the method of participant observation has been thoroughly developed and refined. It is now common to distinguish between two basic ways of conceiving of the method (Zahle, 2012). It may be narrowly identified as participation in the way of life of the social group under study combined with observing what is going on. Or, it may be labelled more broadly to involve not only participation and observation but also the use of other methods such as interviews. In this chapter, we take on a more narrow view of participant observation; we look at participant observation as one of several qualitative research methods aiming to understand the nature of phenomena.

THE PARTICIPATORY ASPECT OF PARTICIPANT OBSERVATION

Participant observation combines the processes of participation and observation. Nonetheless, participant observation should be distinguished from both pure observation and pure participation (Bernard, 1994). **Pure observation** seeks to remove the researcher from the observed actions and behaviour; the researcher is never directly involved in the actions and behaviour of the group under study. **Pure participation** has been described as '**going native**'; the researcher becomes so involved with the group under study that eventually every objectivity and research interest is lost (Jorgensen, 1989; DeWalt & DeWalt, 2002). Within these two extremes, participant observation has been successfully employed by many researchers engaged in business research.

A distinctive feature of participant observation is that the researcher participates in the social group under study. As we have explained earlier in this chapter, the researcher may do so to different extents. The highest degree of participation occurs with *complete participation*. In this case, the researcher lives or works with the subjects under study and tends to assume a pre-established role (for instance, the role of co-worker). In complete participation, the researcher may conceal that she is an observer, behaving as naturally as possible and seeking to become an accepted member of the social group. This technique assures close intimacy with the subjects; the researcher interacts with the subjects and also carries out their activities. A disadvantage of this method is that complete participation may limit freedom of movement outside the adopted role: it is difficult to abandon the role of complete participant as the research proceeds. What's more, the methodological problem of 'going native' may result in a fading research perspective and an increased likelihood of biased research findings. Finally, there are important ethical problems with *concealed* complete participation. Becoming a member of a social group and deliberately deceiving the members of this group is regarded as unethical by many. For these reasons, complete participation has become increasingly rare.

In many situations, observational studies are based on *moderate* participation. In the case of moderate participation, the researcher assumes an intermediate position between being a complete insider (a complete participant) and being a complete outsider (as in non-participation observational studies). In moderate participation, the researcher observes the scene under study, maintaining a certain distance from it and never intervening. Indeed, the role of the researcher is often the role of a passive witness or bystander. Another technique that is sometimes used is 'shadowing'. Shadowing implies that the researcher closely follows a subject (for instance, a manager or a Wall Street broker) engaged in his or her daily routine.

Example	Typical examples of passive participation are observations conducted in service consumption settings, such as in a lecture room, a theatre, a waiting room or a theme park.

In the case of *active* participation, the researcher is not satisfied with the role of the bystander. In this case, the researcher does not conceal that she is an observer but explains the fact that she is an observer to the social group under study right from the start. This allows the researcher to not only observe the everyday activities of the subjects (workers, managers, consumers, brokers), but also to engage in those activities and thus to put them into practice. The goal of active participation is not to become like the subjects, and to immerse in their activities, but to carry out certain activities and hence to acquire a better understanding of their practices.

Example **To what extent should I participate?**	The extent to which the researcher participates depends on a range of factors. For instance, it may be determined by the research questions, ethical considerations, methodological considerations, but also by more practical factors such as by how much the researcher feels happy about participating or by the extent to which either contextual factors or the members of the group under study are willing to let the researcher participate.

THE OBSERVATION ASPECT OF PARTICIPANT OBSERVATION

While participating, the researcher should observe and record, and at a later stage analyse behaviour, actions, interactions, events and the like. Getting started with participant observation and becoming a part of a social group is not without its difficulties. There are several issues that must be addressed. These include choosing a 'site' (a specific department, business unit, plant, supermarket, etc.), gaining permission, the selection of key informants and familiarizing oneself with the research setting (Bernard, 1994).

In most observational studies, gaining access begins with obtaining permission to carry out research from highly ranked people within the organization, preferably from top management. To gain permission to carry out the study, it is important to carefully explain the purpose of the research. If the purpose of the research is understood (and accepted), you will eventually get permission to carry out your research project. You may also benefit from letters of introduction (for instance, from the sponsor of the study) that will ease entry.

Getting permission is only the first step in carrying out participant observation. Becoming an accepted member of the social group under study is the next. Numerous ethnographers have noticed that some members of the social group under study are more open and more likely to approach the researcher early in the fieldwork than others (DeWalt & DeWalt, 2002).

Example **On "deviants" and "professional stranger handlers"**	Agar suggests that the researcher be careful to accept the first people she encounters as key informants, since they are often either 'deviants' or 'professional stranger handlers'. Deviants are 'members who are on the boundaries of the group in some low-status position' (Agar, 1996, p. 136). Association with deviants may alienate the researcher from the rest of the group and provide the researcher with a flawed view on the social group under study. Professional stranger handlers are persons who take it upon themselves to check out the new person and what it is this person is after. 'They can [. . .] quickly improvise some information that satisfies her without representing anything potentially harmful to the group' (Agar, 1996, p. 135).

Experts (e.g. Agar, 1996) recommend that the researcher finds a well-liked and respected person who can act as a sponsor. This 'sponsor' is a group member who is willing to introduce you to the group, to vouch for you and to explain your presence to the other group members.

An essential aspect of participant observation is establishing '**rapport**'. Establishing rapport involves establishing a trusting relationship with the social group under study, by showing respect, being truthful and showing commitment to the well-being of the group or the individual members of the group, so that they feel secure in sharing (sensitive) information with the researcher. Jorgensen (1989) has argued that the degree to which rapport is established influences the degree to which the information that is collected in participant observation is accurate and dependable. In a similar vein, rapport has been referred to as 'the only basis on which really reliable information can be obtained' (Villa Rojas, 1979, p. 59).

	Example
Rapport is built over time. Hanging out with the subjects under study – that is, meeting and chatting with them to develop relationships over an extended period of time – is the process through which the researcher gains trust and establishes rapport with participants (DeMunck & Sobo, 1998). Establishing rapport involves active listening, reciprocity (giving back something to the subjects under study) and confidentiality; the subjects must be assured that they can share personal and sensitive information without their identity being exposed to others.	**How do I establish rapport?**

WHAT TO OBSERVE

A potential problem with observational studies is getting overwhelmed by massive amounts of often disconnected data. For this reason, the researcher should try to keep a certain focus during the various stages of the observation process. Generally speaking, the most important factor in determining what to observe is the aim or purpose of the study. However, '[w]here to begin looking depends on the research question, but where to focus or stop action cannot be determined ahead of time' (Merriam, 1988, p. 97). Werner and Schoepfle (1987) discern three consecutive processes in observation that may provide an increasingly deep understanding of the setting that is being studied: (1) descriptive observation, (2) focused observation and (3) selective observation.

In descriptive observation, the researcher is open to everything that is going on; data are collected that describe the setting, the subjects and the events that are taking place. The example below provides some suggestions for dimensions on which descriptive data might be gathered.

	Example
Spradley (1980) distinguishes the following dimensions on which descriptive data might be collected: • *space* layout of the physical setting such as the factory floor layout; • *objects* physical elements such as office equipment, machines and power tools; • *actors* relevant details of the persons involved; • *feelings, emotions, activities, actions* and *goals* of the actors; • *events* for instance meetings; • *time* or the *time sequence* of events, feelings, actions and the like.	**What to observe in the descriptive observation stage**

The data collected during descriptive observation provide an initial story or narrative account which may serve as a basis for the development of a set of concepts, a theory or even a conceptual framework. The development of concepts, theories and conceptual frameworks is facilitated by a greater focus via focused and selective observation. Focused observation emphasizes observation (often supported by interviews) in which the researcher will concentrate on particular types of feelings, emotions, actions, activities and/or events and look for emerging themes. Finally, in selective observation, the researcher focuses on different types of actions, activities or events and look for regularities in them, while being open to variations from or exceptions to emerging patterns (Emerson, Fretz & Shaw, 1995).

Example	To help researchers decide on what to observe in the focused and selective observation stages, DeWalt and DeWalt (2002) suggest that they:
What to observe in the focused and selective observation stages	• observe events, actions and behaviour and look for a story line; • sort out the regular from the irregular activities; • look for variation in the storyline; • look for negative cases or exceptions; • in case the observation is structured, develop a plan for systematic observation, including an estimate of how many observations will be enough.

The most important method of *capturing data* in participant observation is writing field notes. Notes taken to capture data include records of what is observed, records of informal conversations with the subjects under study and journal notes that are kept on a daily basis. Most researchers write down words, phrases or even whole sentences during the course of the day or the event and write more expanded notes during quieter times. The quality of field notes relies heavily on the level of detail and the accuracy of the description (Schensul, Schensul & LeCompte, 1999). The documentation of observations should therefore be as accurate, complete, detailed and objective as possible. How much is actually written down during the course of the day or the event depends on the quality of the memory of the researcher and the circumstances under which the researcher is working (DeWalt & DeWalt, 2002). Schensul, Schensul and Lecompte (1999) provide a range of characteristics of good field notes. These are summarized in Box 9.2.

BOX 9.2   CHARACTERISTICS OF GOOD FIELD NOTES

Good field notes:

• use exact quotes when possible;
• use pseudonyms to protect confidentiality;
• describe activities in the order in which they occur;
• provide descriptions without inferring meaning;
• include relevant background information to situate the event;

• separate one's own thoughts and assumptions from what one actually observes;
• record the date, time, place and name of researcher on each set of notes.

Schensul, Schensul and LeCompte (1999).

One should be aware of the fact that field notes are a construction of the researcher; it is the researcher who decides what goes into the field notes, the level of detail to include, how much context to include and so on. For this reason, field notes are often regarded as being simultaneously data and data analysis, or as the first step in the process of data analysis (e.g., DeWalt & DeWalt, 2002).

To summarize, participant observation requires many skills, such as commitment, the ability to fit in, tact, the ability to communicate with different members of the social group at their level, patience, the ability to observe, the ability to separate the role of participant from that of observer and so on. Therefore, before committing yourself to participant observation you need to be certain you have the time, resources and skills required to carry out and carry through this exceptionally challenging type of research.

We conclude our discussion of participant observation with some suggestions for conducting participant observation adapted from DeWalt and DeWalt (2002), Merriam (1998) and Wolcott (2001). These suggestions are specified in Box 9.3.

| BOX 9.3 | SUGGESTIONS FOR CONDUCTING PARTICIPANT OBSERVATION |

1. Be unobtrusive in your actions.

2. Become familiar with the setting before collecting other types of data.

3. Be tolerant of ambiguity: this includes being adaptive and flexible.

4. Pay attention, and alternate between a wide (a view of the overall situation) and a narrow (focusing on a single person, activity or interaction) perspective.

5. Look at interactions in the setting: who talks to whom, who is respected and how are decisions made.

6. Listen carefully to conversations, look for key words in conversations, and write these down to prompt later recollection of the conversation.

7. Concentrate on the first and last remarks of a conversation, as these are most easily remembered.

8. Being attentive for a long time is difficult; pay attention off and on. Capitalize on moments of attention.

9. Field work often involves more than observation. It may also involve (informal) interviews and structured interviews, such as questionnaires.

10. Be determined and have faith in yourself.

Adapted from DeWalt and DeWalt (2002), Merriam (1998) and Wolcott (2001).

STRUCTURED OBSERVATION: INTRODUCTION

Structured observation is focused in nature, as it looks selectively at predetermined phenomena. The focus of structured observation is fragmented into small and manageable pieces of information (such as information on behaviour, actions, interactions or events).

There are different levels of structure in structured observation. For instance, the researcher may have decided on the observation categories in a rather precise and mutually exclusive way in advance (highly structured observation) or start with a detailed plan of what will be observed and how, but collect the data in a less systematic or predetermined way (semi-structured observation).

An example of the use of (nonexperimental) structured observation in marketing is the employment of mystery shoppers – thoroughly trained researchers who accurately record employee behaviour using checklists and codes – to gather specific information on service performance. Service providers such as fast-food chains use this particular type of observation to monitor the quality of their service.

Structured observation can also be used to generate numerical data to test hypotheses, as the following example illustrates.

Example

A master's student of Tilburg University, Thomas Perks, is currently engaged in a research project aimed at investigating the effect of GDA labels on the consumption of candy bars. (A GDA label shows the number of calories and grams of sugars, fat, saturates (saturated fat) and salt per portion of food, and expresses these quantities as a percentage of your Guideline Daily Amount.)

To be able to observe the effect of GDA labels on the consumption of candy bars, Thomas is allegedly waiting for his car at a car dealer. In fact, he is observing the behaviour of people who are waiting for their cars, sitting at a large table. To test one of the hypotheses of his study – GDA labels have a negative effect on the consumption of candy bars – he has put two bowls filled with candy bars on this table. In the experimental condition, the candy bars in the bowls contain a GDA-label; in the control condition they do not contain such a label.

In order to minimize possible observer effects, Thomas is keeping a low profile: he avoids eye contact and he smiles politely when people are trying to start a conversation. Nonetheless, he gets engaged in conversations about the weather, computer problems, gas prices and so on every now and then. While Thomas is waiting for his car (observing the behaviour of the subjects under study) he is working on his laptop (keeping a detailed account of the behaviour of the subjects).

Thomas is using a coding scheme that allows him to collect data in a structured way. His coding scheme contains predetermined categories that enable him to systematically generate information on characteristics of the subjects, events and behaviour of the subjects. The categories are closely related to the variables (including a range of confounding variables) in Thomas' conceptual causal model.

THE USE OF CODING SCHEMES IN STRUCTURED OBSERVATION

The development of a coding scheme is a crucial aspect of structured observation. **Coding schemes** contain predetermined categories for recording what is observed. Such schemes come in many forms and shapes. Some of them are very simple; they merely allow the researcher to note whether or not a particular event has taken place. Other schemes are more complex; they include multiple categories, timescales and the like. Note that the development of an adequate coding scheme is never a straightforward task.

The type of coding scheme you will use depends on the information that you want to collect. Again, the research questions of your study serve as the starting point, in this case for the development of a coding scheme. Based on the research questions, sometimes refined via a pilot study, you define the important concepts (variables) in your study and develop a coding scheme that allows you to collect information on these concepts.

The following considerations should be taken into account with regard to the construction of a coding scheme.

- *Focus.* From the coding scheme, it should be clear what is to be observed. For instance, Thomas' coding scheme should help him to establish which aspects of the setting (for instance, how many people are waiting for their car) and which types of behaviour (for instance, the subject is walking through the showroom of the car dealer, the subject is eating a candy bar) are to be observed and recorded.

- *Objective.* The coding scheme and the categories should require little inference or interpretation from the researcher. Clear guidelines and detailed definitions of categories should help the observer to objectively code events, actions and behaviour.

- *Ease of use.* A good coding scheme is easy to use.

- *Mutually exclusive and collectively exhaustive.* Categories in a coding scheme should be mutually exclusive and collectively exhaustive. Categories are mutually exclusive if none of the categories overlap one another. A coding scheme that is collectively exhaustive covers all possibilities (for instance, all the relevant events, actions and behaviour) so that it is always possible to code.

Standard coding schemes may help you to develop your own coding scheme, allowing you to provide an answer to your research questions. In some cases, frequency measures suffice to provide an answer to the research questions. For instance, a researcher who is merely interested in *how often* a manager attends scheduled and unscheduled meetings, answers telephone calls or writes emails may simply wait for these activities to happen and record the incidences on a simple checklist. However, many researchers are not only interested in how often certain events take place, but also in the circumstances under which these events take place. In these cases, the researcher is not only interested in the frequency of certain behaviour, but also in the timing of certain behaviour.

(a) Simple checklist

Event	1	2	3	4
	~~HH~~	//	/	///

(b) Sequence record

Event	1	4	2	4	1	1	3	1	4	2	1

(c) Sequence record on timescale

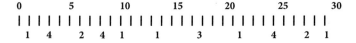

0	5	10	15	20	25	30

1   4   2   4   1   1   3   1   4   2   1

FIGURE 9.1
Alternative ways of coding events

Figure 9.1 illustrates various ways in which the researcher can code events: (a) a **simple checklist** provides information about how often a certain event has occurred; (b) a **sequence record** allows the researcher to collect information on how often an event occurs and about the order in which the events occur; and, finally, (c) a sequence record on a timescale adds a further level of detail, showing the time intervals between the events.

Simple checklists and sequence records are often very useful to the researcher conducting structured observation. Sometimes, however, the researcher may need information about the duration of particular events. In that case the researcher will also code the start and the finish of a certain activity or event.

You have probably noticed by now that structured observation is largely quantitative in nature. Indeed, structured observation allows you to collect quantitative information that may be used to test the hypotheses of your study. The specific instrument for collecting the necessary data is your coding scheme. It is therefore important that your coding scheme is good; in other words, that it is valid and reliable. **Validity** indicates the extent to which observations accurately record the behaviour in which you are interested. **Reliability** refers to the consistency of observations, usually whether two (or more) observers, or the same observer on separate occasions, observing the same event attain the same results.

We have just discussed two important approaches to observation. Of course, there is much more to say about both participant observation and structured observation. If you are interested in learning more about these approaches you may benefit from a range of excellent books and research articles such as, for instance, *Participant Observation: A Guide for Fieldworkers* by DeWalt and DeWalt (2002). We will now conclude this chapter on observation by discussing advantages and disadvantages of observation.

One of the main advantages of observation is its directness. Whereas interviews and questionnaires elicit verbal responses about actions and behaviour from the subjects (which merely allows behaviour to be inferred from these verbal responses), *observation allows the researcher to gather behavioural data without asking questions.* People can be observed in their natural work environment or in the lab setting, and their activities and behaviours or other items of interest can be noted, recorded, analysed, and interpreted.

Apart from the activities performed by the individuals under study, their movements, work habits, the statements made and meetings conducted by them, other – environmental – factors such as layout, work-flow patterns, the closeness of the seating arrangement and the like, can also be noted. In observational studies, it is also relatively easy to discern situational factors such as the weather (hot, cold, rainy), the day of the week (midweek as opposed to Monday or Friday)

ADVANTAGES AND DISADVANTAGES OF OBSERVATION

and other factors that might have a bearing on, for example, productivity, the sales of a product, traffic patterns, absenteeism and the like. These factors can be recorded and meaningful patterns might emerge from this type of data. However, note that it is often very difficult to establish the *specific* effects of situational factors on behaviour and actions of the subjects under study. As we explained earlier in this chapter, it is often difficult to untangle the often complex situation. Accordingly, it is sometimes very difficult to establish *cause-and-effect* relationships between situational factors and events, actions and behaviour.

Another advantage of observation is that it is possible to observe certain groups of individuals – for example, very young children and extremely busy executives – from whom it may be otherwise difficult to obtain information. Children can be observed as to their interests and attention span with various stimuli, such as their involvement with different toys. Such observation would help toy manufacturers, child educators, day-care administrators and others deeply involved in or responsible for children's development, to design and model ideas based on children's interests, which are more easily observed than traced in any other manner. The data obtained through observation of events as they normally occur are generally more reliable and free from respondent bias.

Observation is not without challenges and difficulties. The following drawbacks of observational studies have to be noted. Reactivity (the extent to which the observer affects the situation under study) could be a major threat to the validity of the results of observational studies, because those who are observed may behave differently during the period of the study. Observational research may be particularly vulnerable to reactivity if the observations are confined to a short period of time. In studies of longer duration, the subjects under study will become more relaxed as the study progresses and tend to behave normally, as illustrated in the following passage, provided by Malinowski, who carried out ethnographic field work in Omarkana Trobriand Islands:

> *It must be remembered that the natives saw me constantly every day, they ceased to be interested or alarmed, or made self-conscious by my presence, and I ceased to be a disturbing element in the tribal life which I was to study, altering it by my very approach, as always happens to a newcomer to every savage community. In fact, as they knew that I would thrust my nose into everything, even where a well-mannered native would not dream of intruding, they finished by regarding me as a part and parcel of their life, a necessary evil or nuisance, mitigated by donations of tobacco.*

Malinowski (1992, pp. 7–8)

Researchers doing observational studies often discount the data recorded in the first few days, especially if they seem to be (very) different from what is observed later.

Data observed from the researcher's point of view are likely to be prone to observer biases. For instance, a possible problem in participant observation is that the research perspective fades or even disappears completely because the role that the researcher has adopted in the group has taken over: the researcher has 'gone native'. This may lead to deficient, flawed and biased accounts; there could be recording errors and errors in interpreting activities, behaviours, events and non-verbal cues.

Observation of the happenings day in and day out, over extended periods of time, could also afflict the observer with ennui and could also introduce biases in the recording of the observations.

To minimize observer bias, observers are usually given training on how to observe and what to record. Good observational studies would also establish interobserver reliability. This could also be established during the training of the observers, when videotaped stimuli could be used to determine interobserver reliability. A simple formula can be used for the purpose – dividing the number of agreements among the trainees by the number of agreements and disagreements – thus establishing the reliability coefficient.

Observation is an obvious and appropriate technique to study actions and behaviour. Though moods, feelings and attitudes can be guessed by observing facial expressions and other non-verbal behaviours, the cognitive thought processes of individuals cannot be captured. In other words, it is very difficult to identify reasons behind behaviour of the subjects under study. Observation is therefore often used as a technique to collect data that complement data obtained by other techniques such as interviews.

A practical problem of observation is that it is time-consuming. Many forms of observation require the observer to be physically present, often for prolonged periods of time. For instance, participant observation entails the immersion of the researcher into the social group that is under study for many months and often even years. For this reason, this method of collecting data is not only slow, but also tedious and expensive.

In the following chapter, we turn to another method of collecting data: namely, questionnaires.

SUMMARY

- **Learning objective 1: Define observation and discuss how observation may help to solve business problems.** Actions and behaviour of people may play an important role in business research. A useful and natural technique to collect data on actions and behaviour is observation. Observation concerns the planned watching, recording, analysis, and interpretation of behaviour, actions or events.

- **Learning objective 2: Demonstrate the ability to make an informed decision on an appropriate type of observational method for a specific study.** Various approaches of observation may be distinguished by four key dimensions that characterize the way observation is conducted: (1) control; (2) whether the observer is a member of the group that is observed or not; (3) structure and (4) concealment of observation.

- **Learning objective 3: Explain the issues related to participant observation and structured observation.** Two important, distinct approaches to observation are *participant* and *structured observations*. A key characteristic of participant observation is that the researcher gathers data by participating in the daily life of the group or organization under study. Participant requires many skills, such as commitment, the ability to fit in, tact, the ability to communicate with different members of the social group at their level, patience, the ability to observe, the ability to separate the role of participant from that of observer and so on. Structured observation is focused in nature, as it looks selectively at predetermined phenomena. The focus of structured observation is fragmented into small and manageable pieces of information. The development of a coding scheme is a crucial aspect of structured observation. Coding schemes contain predetermined categories for recording what is observed.

- **Learning objective 4: Discuss the advantages and disadvantages of observation.** One of the main advantages of observation is its directness. Another advantage of observation is that it is possible to observe certain groups of individuals from whom it may otherwise be difficult to obtain information. Drawbacks of observational studies are reactivity, observer bias, and that it is time-consuming, tedious and expensive.

Instructors can visit the companion website at **www.wiley.com/go/bougie/researchmethods forbusiness8e** for **Case Study: Performance Improvement Through Mystery Shopping.**

DISCUSSION QUESTIONS

1. Describe the key purpose of observation.

2. Discuss four dimensions that distinguish various approaches to observation.

3. Under which circumstances would you prefer observation as a method to collect data over other methods of data collection such as interviews and questionnaires?

4. How does participant observation differ from structured observation?

5. Discuss how ethnography and participant observation are related.

6. How does moderate participation differ from complete participation?

7. Although participant observation combines the processes of participation and observation it should be distinguished from both pure observation and pure participation. Explain.

8. What is rapport and how is rapport established in participant observation?

9. Field notes are often regarded as being simultaneously data and data analysis. Why?

10. Is it possible to test hypotheses with structured observation? Why (not)?

11. How does a simple checklist differ from a sequence record on time-scale?

12. 'One of the main advantages of observation is its directness'. Discuss.

13. What is reactivity?

14. A disadvantage of observation is observer bias. Discuss at least two ways of minimizing observer bias.

15. Discuss the ethics of concealed observation.

Now do Exercises 9.1, 9.2, and 9.3.

EXERCISE 9.1

You are investigating the service quality of restaurants. You are collecting primary data through interviews and observation. Your task is to go to a restaurant and collect descriptive observational data on the following factors: *space* (layout of the physical setting), *objects* (physical elements such as equipment, tables, chairs and the like), *actors* (staff and clients) and interactions between staff members and clients.

EXERCISE 9.2

Seek permission from a professor to sit in two sessions of his or her class, and do an unstructured, non-participant-observer study. Give your conclusions on the data, and include in the short report your observation sheets and tabulations.

EXERCISE 9.3

Read all relevant information regarding Thomas Perks' study. From this information, develop a coding scheme to test the effect of GDA labels[1] on the consumption of candy bars (chocolate bars). Do not forget to include categories allowing you to collect data on relevant covariates.

---

[1]GDA labels show the number of calories and grams of sugars, fat, saturates (saturated fats) and salt per portion of food, and expresses these quantities as a percentage of your 'Guideline Daily Amount'.

Administering Questionnaires

LEARNING OBJECTIVES

After completing Chapter 10, you should be able to:

1. Compare and contrast different types of questionnaires.

2. Design questionnaires to tap different variables.

3. Discuss the issues related to cross-cultural research.

4. Discuss the advantages and disadvantages of various data collection methods in survey research.

5. Discuss the advantages of multi-sources and multimethods of data collection.

6. Demonstrate awareness of the role of the manager in primary data collection.

7. Demonstrate awareness of the role of ethics in primary data collection.

INTRODUCTION

In Chapter 7, we have already explained that in business research, three important data collection methods are interviewing, observing people and administering questionnaires. We have discussed interviewing in Chapter 8 and observation in Chapter 9. In this chapter, we will discuss questionnaires and questionnaire design. A **questionnaire** is a preformulated written set of questions to which respondents record their answers, usually within rather closely defined alternatives.

TYPES OF QUESTIONNAIRES

Instructors can visit the companion website at **www.wiley.com/go/bougie/researchmethods forbusiness8e** for **Author Video: Questionnaires**.

Questionnaires are generally designed to collect large numbers of quantitative data. They can be administered personally, distributed electronically or mailed to the respondents. Questionnaires are generally less expensive and time-consuming than interviews and observation, but they also introduce a much larger chance of non-response and non-response error. An overview of the advantages and disadvantages of questionnaires (and other methods of data collection) and a section on when to use each of these methods is provided later in this chapter.

PERSONALLY ADMINISTERED QUESTIONNAIRES

When the survey is confined to a local area, a good way to collect data is to personally administer the questionnaires. The main advantage of this is that the researcher or a member of the research team can collect all the completed responses within a short period of time. Any doubts that the respondents might have on any question can be clarified on the spot. The researcher also has the opportunity to introduce the research topic and motivate the respondents to offer their frank answers. Administering questionnaires to large numbers of individuals at the same time is less expensive and consumes less time than interviewing; equally, it does not require as much skill to administer a questionnaire as it does to conduct interviews. Wherever possible, questionnaires are best administered personally because of these advantages. A disadvantage of personally administered questionnaires is that the researcher may introduce a bias by explaining questions differently to different people; participants may be in fact answering different questions as compared to those to whom the questionnaire was mailed. What's more, personally administered questionnaires take time and a lot of effort. For this reason, electronic questionnaires are widely used these days.

MAIL QUESTIONNAIRES

A mail questionnaire is a self-administered (paper and pencil) questionnaire that is sent to respondents via the mail. This method has long been the backbone of business research, but with the arrival of the Internet, mobile phones and social networks, mail questionnaires have become redundant or even obsolete. Instead, online questionnaires are posted on the Internet or sent via email.

ELECTRONIC AND ONLINE QUESTIONNAIRES

The distribution of electronic or online questionnaires is easy and fast. All you have to do is to email the invitations to complete a survey, post a link on a website or personal blog or use social networks. Online questionnaires are usually created as 'Web forms' with a database to store the answers and statistical software to provide statistical analysis. Until recently, conducting online surveys was a time-consuming and tedious task requiring familiarity with Web authoring programs, HTML codes and/or scripting programs. Today, online survey tools such as Survey Monkey, Qualtrics, Google Forms and Survey Planet make online survey research much easier and more accessible.

Online questionnaires are often used to gain a deeper understanding of consumers' opinions and preferences. A big advantage of online survey research is that it makes the most of the ability of the Internet to provide access to groups and individuals who would be difficult, if not impossible, to reach through other channels. Virtual communities flourish online, and hundreds of thousands of people regularly participate in discussions about almost every conceivable issue and interest (Wright, 2005). A second advantage of online questionnaires is that a wide geographical area can be covered in the survey. A (link to the) questionnaire is sent to the respondents, who can complete it at their convenience, in their homes and at their own pace. The automatic processing of the survey saves further costs, time and energy.

However, there are also important disadvantages to online questionnaires. When conducting online research, researchers often encounter problems with regard to sampling. For instance, self-selection and extremely low response rates make it difficult to establish the representativeness of the sample and to generalize the findings, because those responding to the survey may not at all represent the population they are supposed to (see Box 10.1). Indeed, the return rates of such questionnaires are typically low. A 30% response rate is considered acceptable, and in many cases even exceptional.

Posting invitations to participate in a survey on social networks, discussion groups and chat rooms is often perceived as rude or offensive. This is another drawback of online questionnaires. Many people consider this type of posting to be 'spam', and the researcher may be flooded with emails from angry members of a virtual community. Researchers sending email invitations to participate in a study may face similar issues. An unwanted email is often considered an invasion

BOX 10.1   HOW TO IMPROVE YOUR RESPONSE RATES

Some effective techniques can be employed for improving the rates of response. Sending follow-up mails and keeping the questionnaire brief usually help. Electronic questionnaires are also expected to meet with a better response rate when respondents are notified in advance about the forthcoming survey, and a reputed research organization administers them with its own introductory cover letter. A small monetary incentive is also an effective technique to increase response rates.

of privacy and the invitation for the survey may be deleted, or the researcher may receive email from participants complaining about it (Wright, 2005). Other disadvantages of electronic questionnaires are that any doubts the respondents might have cannot be clarified, the lack of suitable population lists making it virtually impossible to use probability sampling, and the fact that many factors may affect the appearance of online questionnaires. The advantages and disadvantages of personally administered questionnaires, mail questionnaires and electronic questionnaires are presented in Table 10.1.

For most business research, a questionnaire is a convenient data collection mechanism. Survey research, case study research and experimental designs often use questionnaires to collect data on the variables of interest. Because questionnaires are in common use, it is necessary to know how to design them effectively. A set of guidelines for questionnaire construction follows.

Tabel 10.1   Advantages and Disadvantages of Different Questionnaires

Mode of data collection	Advantages	Disadvantages
Personally administered questionnaires	Can establish rapport and motivate respondent.	Explanations may introduce a bias.
	Doubts can be clarified.	Take time and effort.
	Less expensive when administered to groups of respondents.	
	Almost 100% response rate ensured.	
	Anonymity of respondent is high.	
Mail questionnaires	Anonymity is high.	Response rate is almost always low. A 30% rate is quite acceptable.
	Wide geographic regions can be reached.	Cannot clarify questions.
	Token gifts can be enclosed to seek compliance.	Follow-up procedures for non-responses are necessary.
	Respondent can take more time to respond at convenience. Can be administered electronically, if desired.	
Electronic questionnaires	Easy to administer.	Computer literacy is a must.
	Can reach globally.	Sampling issues.
	Very inexpensive.	High non-response.
	Fast delivery.	Not always possible to generalize findings.
	Respondents can answer at their convenience like the mail questionnaire.	Respondent must be willing to complete the survey.
	Automatic processing of answers.	People find invitations via email rude and offensive; emails are deleted or people complain.

GUIDELINES FOR QUESTIONNAIRE DESIGN

Sound questionnaire design principles should focus on three areas. The second relates to the wording of the questions. The first refers to the planning of issues with regard to the goodness of the measures and how the variables will be categorized, scaled and coded after receipt of the responses. The third pertains to the general appearance of the questionnaire. All three are important issues in questionnaire design because they can minimize bias in research. These issues are discussed below. The important aspects are schematically depicted in Figure 10.1.

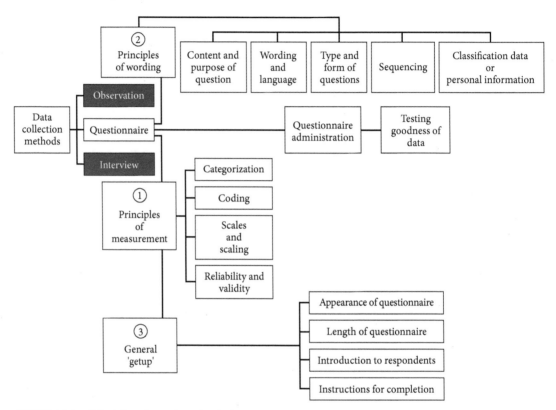

FIGURE 10.1 Principles of questionnaire design

PRINCIPLES OF MEASUREMENT

Principles of measurement ensure that the data collected are related to the research questions driving your empirical research. Remember that is important to collect good (valid) information on the phenomena you are interested in. That is why it is important that you (1) specify and define the phenomena you are interested in, (2) come up with instruments that accurately measure these phenomena, (3) think about the analytic use of your questions, 4) specify the respondents' tasks and (5) asses the quality (reliability and validity) of your instruments.

Validity establishes how well a technique, instrument or process measures a particular concept, and reliability indicates how stably and consistently the instrument taps the variable. In Chapters 12 and 13, we will come back to this very important issue.

PRINCIPLES OF WORDING

The central part of any questionnaire is devoted to the questions you ask. Your respondents should be able to understand your questions in the way you intend, to be willing to answer your questions and to provide their answers in the way called for by the question. An important yet difficult task you have as a researcher is to develop a questionnaire in such a way that respondents understand what you want from them and are happy to provide you with this information. That is why the wording of your questions is important. The principles of wording refer to such factors as:

1. The appropriateness of the content of the questions.

2. How questions are worded and the level of sophistication of the language used.

3. The type and form of questions asked.

4. The sequencing of the questions.

5. The personal data sought from the respondents.

   Each of these is explained below.

Content and Purpose of the Questions

The nature of the variable tapped – subjective feelings or objective facts – will determine what kinds of questions are asked. If the variables tapped are of a subjective nature (e.g. satisfaction, involvement), where respondents' beliefs, perceptions and attitudes are to be measured, the questions should tap the dimensions and elements of the concept. Where objective variables, such as age and educational levels of respondents, are tapped, a single direct question – preferably one that has an ordinal scaled set of categories – is appropriate. Thus, the purpose of each question should be carefully considered so that the variables are adequately measured and yet no superfluous questions are asked.

Language and Wording of the Questionnaire

The language of the questionnaire should approximate the level of understanding of the respondents. The choice of words will depend on their educational level, the usage of terms and idioms in the culture and the frames of reference of the respondents. For instance, even when English is the spoken or official language in two cultures, certain words may be alien to one culture. Terms such as 'working here is a drag' and 'she is a compulsive worker' may not be interpreted the same way in different cultures. Some blue-collar workers may not understand terminology such as 'organizational structure.' Thus, it is essential to word the questions in a way that can be understood by the respondent. If some questions are either not understood or are interpreted differently by the respondent, the researcher will obtain the wrong answers to the questions, and responses will thus be biased. Hence, the questions asked, the language used and the wording should be appropriate to tap respondents' attitudes, perceptions and feelings.

Type and Form of Questions

The type of question refers to whether the question is open-ended or closed. The form of the question refers to whether it is positively or negatively worded.

Open-ended versus closed questions **Open-ended questions** allow respondents to answer them in any way they choose. An example of an open-ended question is asking the respondent to state five things that are interesting and challenging in the job. Another example is asking what the respondents like about their supervisors or their work environment. A third example is to invite their comments on the investment portfolio of the firm.

A **closed question**, in contrast, asks the respondents to make choices among a set of alternatives given by the researcher. For instance, instead of asking the respondent to state any five aspects of the job that she finds interesting and challenging, the researcher might list 10 or 15 aspects that might seem interesting or challenging in jobs and ask the respondents to rank the first five among these in the order of their preference. All items in a questionnaire using a nominal, ordinal, Likert or ratio scale are considered closed.

Closed questions help the respondents to make quick decisions to choose among the several alternatives before them. They also help the researcher to code the information easily for subsequent analysis. Care has to be taken to ensure that the alternatives are mutually exclusive and collectively exhaustive. If there are overlapping categories, or if all possible alternatives are not given (i.e. the categories are not exhaustive), the respondents might get confused and the advantage of their being enabled to make a quick decision is thus lost.

Some respondents may find even well-delineated categories in a closed question rather confining and might avail themselves of the opportunity to make additional comments. This is the reason why many questionnaires end with a final open-ended question that invites respondents to comment on topics that might not have been covered fully or adequately. The responses to such open-ended questions have to be edited and categorized for subsequent data analysis.

Positively and negatively worded questions Instead of phrasing all questions positively, it is advisable to include some negatively worded questions as well, so the tendency in respondents to mechanically circle the points toward one end of the scale is minimized. For example, let us say that a set of six questions is used to tap the variable 'perceived success' on a five-point scale, with 1 being 'very low' and 5 being 'very high' on the scale. A respondent who is not particularly interested in completing the questionnaire is more likely to stay involved and remain alert while answering the questions when positively and negatively worded questions are interspersed in it. For instance, if the respondent has circled 5 for a positively worded question such as, '*I feel I have been able to accomplish a number of different things in my job*', he cannot circle number 5 again to the negatively worded question, '*I do not feel I am very effective in my job*'. The respondent is now shaken out of any likely tendency to mechanically respond to one end of the scale. In case this does still happen, the researcher has an opportunity to detect such bias. A good questionnaire should therefore include both positively and negatively worded questions. The use of double negatives and excessive use of the words 'not' and 'only' should be avoided in negatively worded questions because they tend to confuse respondents. For instance, it is better to say '*Coming to work is not great fun*' than to say '*Not coming to work is greater fun than coming to work*'. Likewise, it is better to say '*The rich need no help*' than to say '*Only the rich do not need help*'.

Double-barrelled questions A question that lends itself to different possible responses to its subparts is called a **double-barrelled question**. Such questions should be avoided and two or more separate questions asked instead. For example, the question '*Do you think there is a good market for the product and that it will sell well?*' could bring a 'yes' response to the first part (i.e. there is a good market for the product) and a 'no' response to the latter part (i.e. it will not sell well for various other reasons). In this case, it would be better to ask two questions: (1) '*Do you think there is a good market for the product?*' and (2) '*Do you think the product will sell well?*' The answers might be 'yes' to both, 'no' to both, 'yes' to the first and 'no' to the second, or 'yes' to the second and 'no' to the first. If we combined the two questions and asked a double-barrelled question, we would confuse the respondents and obtain ambiguous responses. Hence, double-barrelled questions should be eliminated.

Ambiguous questions Even questions that are not double-barrelled might be ambiguously worded and the respondent may not be sure what exactly they mean. An example of such a question is '*To what extent would you say you are happy?*' Respondents might find it difficult to decide whether the question refers to their state of feelings in the workplace, or at home or in general. Thus, responses to **ambiguous questions** have built-in bias inasmuch as different respondents might interpret such items in the questionnaire differently. The result is a mixed bag of ambiguous responses that do not accurately provide the correct answer to the question.

Recall-dependent questions Some questions might require respondents to recall experiences from the past that are hazy in their memory. Answers to such questions might have bias. For instance, if an employee who has had 30 years' service in the organization is asked to state when he first started working in a particular department and for how long, he may not be able to give the correct answers and may be way off in his responses. A better source for obtaining that information would be the personnel records.

Leading questions Questions should not be phrased in such a way that they lead the respondents to give the responses that the researcher would like them to give. An example of such a question is: '*Don't you think that in these days of escalating costs of living, employees should be given good pay rises?*' By asking a **leading question**, we are signalling and pressuring respondents to say 'yes'. Tagging the question to rising living costs makes it difficult for most respondents (unless they are the top bosses in charge of budget and finances) to say, 'No; not unless their productivity increases too!' Another way of asking the question about pay rises to elicit less biased responses would be: '*To what extent do you agree that employees should be given higher pay rises?*' If respondents think that the employees do not deserve a higher pay rise at all, their response will be 'Strongly Disagree'; if they think that respondents should definitely be given a high pay rise, they will respond to the 'Strongly Agree' end of the scale, and the in-between points will be chosen depending on the strength of their agreement or disagreement. In this case, the question is not framed in a suggestive manner as in the previous instance.

Loaded questions Another type of bias in questions occurs when they are phrased in an emotionally charged manner. An example of such a **loaded question** is asking employees: '*To what extent do you think management is likely to be vindictive if the union decides to go on strike?*' The words 'strike' and 'vindictive' are emotionally charged terms, polarizing management and unions. Hence, asking a question such as the above would elicit strongly emotional and highly biased responses. If the purpose of the question is twofold – that is, to find (1) the extent to which employees are in favour of a strike and (2) the extent to which they fear adverse reactions if they do go on strike – then these are the two specific questions that need to be asked. It may turn out that the employees are not strongly in favour of a strike and they also do not believe that management would retaliate if they did go on strike!

Social desirability Questions should not be worded such that they elicit socially desirable responses. For instance, a question such as '*Do you think that older people should be laid off?*' would elicit a response of 'no', mainly because society would frown on a person who said that elderly people should be fired even if they are capable of performing their jobs satisfactorily. Hence, irrespective of the true feelings of the respondent, a socially desirable answer would be provided. If the purpose of the question is to gauge the extent to which organizations are seen as obligated to retain those above 65 years of age, a differently worded question with less pressure toward **social desirability** would be: '*There are advantages and disadvantages to retaining senior citizens in the workforce. To what extent do you think companies should continue to keep the elderly on their payroll?*'

Sometimes certain items that tap social desirability are deliberately introduced at various points in the questionnaire and an index of each individual's social desirability tendency is calculated therefrom. This index is then applied to all other responses given by the individual in order to adjust for social desirability bias (Crowne & Marlowe, 1980; Edwards, 1957).

Length of questions Finally, simple, short questions are preferable to long ones. As a rule of thumb, a question or a statement in the questionnaire should not exceed 20 words, or exceed one full line in print (Horst, 1968; Oppenheim, 1986).

GENERAL APPEARANCE OR 'GETUP' OF THE QUESTIONNAIRE

Not only is it important to address issues of wording and measurement in questionnaire design, but it is also necessary to pay attention to how the questionnaire looks. An attractive and neat questionnaire with appropriate introduction, instructions and well-arrayed set of questions and response alternatives will make it easier for the respondents to answer them. A good introduction, well-organized instructions and neat alignment of the questions are all important. These elements are briefly discussed with examples.

A Good Introduction

A proper introduction that clearly discloses the identity of the researcher and conveys the purpose of the survey is absolutely necessary. It is also essential to establish some rapport with the respondents and motivate them to respond to the questions in the questionnaire wholeheartedly and enthusiastically. Assurance of confidentiality of the information provided by them will allow for less biased answers. The introduction section should end on a courteous note, thanking the respondent for taking the time to respond to the survey. The following is an example of an appropriate introduction.

Example	
Dear Participant	Date

This questionnaire is designed to study aspects of life at work. The information you provide will help us better understand the quality of our work life. Because you are the one who can give us a correct picture of how you experience your work life, I request you to respond to the questions frankly and honestly.

Your response will be kept strictly confidential. Only members of the research team will have access to the information you give. In order to ensure the utmost privacy, we have provided an identification number for each participant. This number will be used by us only for follow-up procedures. The numbers, names and the completed questionnaires will not be made available to anyone other than the research team. A summary of the results will be mailed to you after the data are analysed.

Thank you very much for your time and cooperation. I greatly appreciate the help of your organization and yourself in furthering this research endeavour.

Cordially,
(Sd)
A. Professor, PhD

Organizing Questions, Giving Instructions and Guidance and Good Alignment

Organizing the questions logically and neatly in appropriate sections and providing instructions on how to complete the items in each section will help the respondents to answer them without difficulty. Questions should also be neatly aligned in a way that allows the respondent to complete the task of reading and answering the questionnaire by expending the least time and effort and without straining the eyes.

A specimen of the portion of a questionnaire incorporating the above points follows.

Example	The questions below ask about how you experience your work life. Think in terms of your everyday experiences and accomplishments on the job and put the most appropriate response number for you beside each item, using the scale below.
Section Two: About Work Life	

Strongly Agree 1	Agree 2	Slightly Agree 3	Neutral 4	Slightly Disagree 5	Disagree 6	Strongly Disagree 7

I do my work best when my job assignments are fairly difficult. —

When I have a choice, I try to work in a group instead of by myself. —

In my work assignments, I try to be my own boss. —

I seek an active role in the leadership of a group. —

I try very hard to improve on my past performance at work. —

I pay a good deal of attention to the feelings of others at work. —

I go my own way at work, regardless of the opinions of others. —

I avoid trying to influence those around me to see things my way. —

I take moderate risks, sticking my neck out to get ahead at work. —

I prefer to do my own work, letting others do theirs. —

I disregard rules and regulations that hamper my personal freedom. —

Personal Data

Demographic or personal data could be organized as in the example that follows.

Are you male or female?

☐   Male
☐   Female

What is your age?

_____ years

What is the highest degree or level of school you have completed? If currently enrolled, highest degree received.
☐   No schooling completed
☐   Nursery school to 8th grade
☐   Some high school, no diploma
☐   High school graduate, diploma or the equivalent (for example: GED)
☐   Some college credit, no degree
☐   Trade/technical/vocational training
☐   Associate degree
☐   Bachelor's degree
☐   Master's degree
☐   Professional degree
☐   Doctorate degree (PhD)

How many years have you been with your current organization?

_____ years

How long have you worked in your current position?

_____ years

Example

General Information

Information on Income and Other Sensitive Personal Data

Although demographic information can be sought either at the beginning or at the end of the questionnaire, information of a very private and personal nature such as income, state of health and so on, if considered at all necessary for the survey, should be asked at the end of the questionnaire, rather than the beginning. Also, such questions should be justified by explaining how this information might contribute to knowledge and problem solving, so that respondents do not perceive them to be of an intrusive or prying nature (see example below). Postponing such questions to the end will help reduce respondent bias if the individual is vexed by the personal nature of the question.

Example

Because many people believe that income is a significant factor in explaining the type of career decisions individuals make, the following two questions are very important for this research. Like all other items in this questionnaire, the responses to these two questions will be kept confidential. Please circle the most appropriate number that describes your position.

Roughly, *my total yearly* income before taxes and other deductions is:	Roughly, the *total yearly income* before taxes and other deductions of my *immediate family* – *including* my own job income, income from other sources, and the income of my spouse – is:
1. Less than $36 000	1. Less than $36 000
2. $36 000–50 000	2. $36 000–50 000
3. $50 001–70 000	3. $50 001–70 000
4. $70 001–90 000	4. $70 001–90 000
5. Over $90 000	5. $90 001–120 000
	6. $120 001–150 000
	7. Over $150 000

Open-Ended Question at the End

The questionnaire could include an open-ended question at the end, allowing respondents to comment on any aspect they choose. It should end with an expression of sincere thanks to respondents. The last part of the questionnaire could look as follows.

Example

The questions in the survey may not be all-embracing and comprehensive and may not therefore have afforded you an opportunity to report some things you may want to say about your job, the organization or yourself. Please make any additional comments needed in the space provided.

How did you feel about completing this questionnaire? Check the face in the following diagram that reflects your feelings.

Concluding the Questionnaire

The questionnaire should end on a courteous note, reminding the respondent to check that all the items have been completed, as per the example below.

I sincerely appreciate your time and cooperation. Please check to make sure that you have not skipped any questions inadvertently, and then drop the questionnaire in the locked box, clearly marked for the purpose, at the entrance of your department.

Thank you!

Example

Sequencing of Questions

The sequence of questions in the questionnaire should be such that the respondent is led from questions of a general nature to those that are more specific, and from questions that are relatively easy to answer to those that are progressively more difficult. This funnel approach, as it is called, facilitates the easy and smooth progress of the respondent through the items in the questionnaire. The progression from general to specific questions might mean that the respondent is first asked questions of a global nature that pertain to the issue, and then is asked more incisive questions regarding the specific topic. Easy questions might relate to issues that do not involve much thinking; the more difficult ones might call for more thought, judgment and decision-making in providing the answers.

The way questions are sequenced can also introduce certain biases, frequently referred to as ordering effects. Though randomly placing the questions in the questionnaire reduces any systematic bias in the responses, it is very rarely done, because of subsequent confusion while categorizing, coding and analysing the responses.

In sum, the language and wording of the questionnaire focus on such issues as the type and form of questions asked (i.e. open-ended and closed questions, and positively and negatively worded questions), as well as avoiding double-barrelled questions, ambiguous questions, leading questions, loaded questions, questions prone to tap socially desirable answers and those involving distant recall. Questions should also not be unduly long. Using the funnel approach helps respondents to progress through the questionnaire with ease and comfort.

Administrative and Classification Questions

Administrative questions aim to identify the respondent and in some cases the interviewer, the interview location and interview conditions. These questions are rarely asked of the respondent. They are used to study patterns in the data and possible sources of error. **Classification questions**, also known as personal information or demographic questions, elicit such information as age, educational level and the like that allow respondents answers to be grouped. This allows the researcher to group study patterns in the data, examine differences between groups and so on.

Whether questions seeking personal information should appear at the beginning or at the end of the questionnaire is a matter of choice for the researcher. Some researchers ask for personal data at the end rather than the beginning of the questionnaire. Their reasoning may be that by the time the respondent reaches the end of the questionnaire he or she has been convinced of the legitimacy and genuineness of the questions framed by the researcher and, hence, is more inclined and amenable to share personal information. Researchers who prefer to elicit most of the personal information at the very beginning may argue that once respondents have shared some of their personal history, they may have psychologically identified themselves with the questionnaire, and may feel a commitment to respond. Thus, whether one asks for this information at the beginning or at the end of the questionnaire is a matter of individual choice. However, questions seeking details of income, or other highly sensitive information – if deemed necessary – are best placed at the very end of the questionnaire. Even so, it is a wise policy to ask for such information by providing a range of response options, rather than seeking exact figures. For example, the variables may be tapped as shown below:

Annual income
Less than $20 000
$20 000–30 000
$30 001–40 000
$40 001–50 000
$50 001–70 000
$70 001–90 000
Over $90 000

In surveys, it is advisable to gather certain demographic data such as age, sex, educational level, job level, department and number of years in the organization, even if the research questions not necessitate or include these variables. Such data help to describe the sample characteristics in the report written after data analysis. However, when there are only a few respondents in a department, then questions likely to reveal their identity might render them futile, objectionable and threatening to employees. For instance, if there is only one female in a department, then she might refrain from responding to the question on gender, because it would establish the source of the data; this apprehension is understandable.

To sum up, certain principles of wording need to be followed while designing a questionnaire. The questions asked must be appropriate for tapping the variable. The language and wording used should be such that it is meaningful to the employees. The form and type of questions should be geared to minimize respondent bias. The sequencing of the questions should facilitate the smooth progress of the responses from start to finish. The personal data should be gathered with due regard to the sensitivity of the respondents' feelings and with respect for privacy.

REVIEW OF QUESTIONNAIRE DESIGN

We have devoted a lot of attention to questionnaire design because questionnaires are the most common method of collecting data. The principles of questionnaire design relate to how the questions are worded and measured, and how the entire questionnaire is organized. To minimize respondent bias and measurement errors, all the principles discussed have to be followed carefully.

Questionnaires are most useful as a data collection method, especially when large numbers of people are to be reached in different geographical regions. They are a popular method of collecting data because researchers can obtain information fairly easily, and the questionnaire responses are easily coded. When well-validated instruments are used, the findings of the study benefit the scientific community since the results can be replicated and additions to the theory base made.

There are several ways of administering questionnaires. Questionnaires can be personally administered to respondents, electronically distributed to respondents, a link can be posted on a website, a blog or on your social network account, they can be inserted in magazines, periodicals or newspapers or mailed to respondents. Software is also available to frame subsequent questions based on the subject's response to the preceding question. Companies' websites can also elicit survey responses; for example, reactions to customer service, product utility and the like. Global research is now vastly facilitated by the Internet.

PRETESTING OF STRUCTURED QUESTIONS

Whether it is a structured interview where the questions are posed to the respondent in a predetermined order, or a questionnaire that is used in a survey, it is important to pretest the instrument to ensure that the questions are understood by the respondents (i.e. there is no ambiguity in the questions) and that there are no problems with the wording or measurement. **Pretesting** involves the use of a small number of respondents to test the appropriateness of the questions and their comprehension. This helps to rectify any inadequacies before administering the instrument orally or through a questionnaire to respondents, and thus reduces bias.

It would be good to debrief the results of the pretest and obtain additional information from the small group of participants (who serve the role of a focus group) on their general reactions to the questionnaire and how they felt about completing the instrument.

ELECTRONIC QUESTIONNAIRE AND SURVEY DESIGN

We have explained earlier in this chapter that online surveys are easily designed and administered. Electronic *survey design systems* (for instance, InstantSurvey, Infopoll, SurveyGold, Statpac, SurveyMonkey, SurveyPro, The Survey System), which facilitate the preparation and administration of questionnaires, are particularly useful for online research. Such systems usually include a range of programs enabling the user to design sophisticated questionnaires, computerize the data collection process, check for syntactical or logical errors in the coding and analyse the data collected. More reliable data are likely to result since the respondent can go back and forth and easily change a response, and various on- and off-screen stimuli are provided to sustain respondents' interest.

Even as the survey is in progress, descriptive summaries of the cumulative data can be obtained either on the screen or in printed form. After data collection is complete, a data-editing program identifies missing or out-of-range data (e.g. a 6 in response to a question on a five-point scale). The researcher can set the parameters to either delete missing responses if there are too many of them, or compute the mean of other responses and substitute this figure for the missing response. Such systems also include data analytic programs such as ANOVA, multiple regression and others (discussed later in the book). Randomization of questions and the weighting of respondents to ensure more representative results (in cases where the sample either overrepresents or underrepresents certain population groups – discussed in Chapter 14 on Sampling) are some of the attractive features of survey design systems.

Electronic questionnaires are very popular at the moment, also because electronic nonresponse rates may not be any lower than those for mail questionnaires. With the increased computer literacy, we can expect electronic questionnaire administration to keep on growing in the future.

We have so far discussed instrument development for eliciting responses from subjects within a country. With the globalization of business operations, managers often need to compare the business effectiveness of their subsidiaries in different countries. Researchers engaged in cross-cultural research may attempt to trace the similarities and differences in the behavioural and attitudinal responses of employees, consumers or investors in different cultures. When data are collected through questionnaires and occasionally through interviews, one should pay attention to the measuring instruments and how data are collected, in addition to being sensitive to cultural differences in the use of certain terms. Such research should be tailored to the different cultures, as discussed below.

> **INTERNATIONAL DIMENSIONS OF SURVEYS**

SPECIAL ISSUES IN INSTRUMENTATION FOR CROSS-CULTURAL RESEARCH

Certain special issues need to be addressed while designing instruments for collecting data from multiple countries. Since different languages are spoken in different countries, it is important to ensure that the translation of the instrument to the local language matches accurately to the original language. For this purpose, the instrument should be first translated by a local expert. Supposing a comparative survey is to be done between Japan and the United States, and the researcher is a US national, then the instrument has first to be translated from English to Japanese. Then, another bilinguist should translate it back to English. This back translation, as it is called, ensures vocabulary equivalence (i.e. that the words used have the same meaning). Idiomatic equivalence could also become an issue, where some idioms unique to one language just do not lend themselves for translation to another language. Conceptual equivalence, where the meanings of certain words could differ in different cultures, is yet another issue to which attention has to be paid. For instance, the meaning of the concept 'love' may differ in different cultures. All these issues can be taken care of through good back translation by persons who are fluent with the relevant languages and are also knowledgeable about the customs and usages in the cultures concerned.

The following examples culled from *BusinessWeek* show the pitfalls in cross-cultural advertising and emphasize the need for back translation of messages for idiomatic and conceptual equivalence. Not only is the meaning lost in some advertisement messages by literally translating the English words into the native languages, but in some cases they actually become offensive.

Example

1. Pepsi's 'Come alive with the Pepsi generation' when translated into Chinese means 'Pepsi brings your ancestors from the grave'.

2. Frank Perdue's chicken slogan 'It takes a strong man to make a tender chicken' translates in Spanish to 'It takes an aroused man to make a chicken affectionate'.

3. When American Airlines wanted to advertise its new leather first-class seats to Mexico, its 'Fly in Leather' campaign would have literally translated to 'Fly Naked' in Spanish.

ISSUES IN CROSS-CULTURAL DATA COLLECTION

At least three issues are important for cross-cultural data collection – response equivalence, timing of data collection and the status of the individual collecting the data. Response equivalence is ensured by adopting uniform data collection procedures in the different cultures. Identical methods of introducing the study, the researcher, task instructions and closing remarks, in personally administered questionnaires, provide equivalence in motivation, goal orientation and response attitudes. Timing of data collected across cultures is also critical for cross-cultural comparison. Data collection should be completed within acceptable time frames in the different countries – say within three to four months. If too much time elapses in collecting data in the different countries, much might change during the time interval in any one country or all the countries.

As pointed out as early as 1969 by Mitchell, in interview surveys, the egalitarian-oriented interviewing style used in the West may not be appropriate in societies that have well-defined status and authority structures. Also, when a foreigner comes to collect data, the responses might be biased for fear of portraying the country to a 'foreigner' in an 'adverse light'. The researcher has to be sensitive to these cultural nuances while engaging in cross-cultural research. It is worth while collaborating with a local researcher while developing and administering the research instrument, particularly when the language and customs of the respondents are different from those of the researcher.

Having discussed the various data collection methods, we will now briefly recount the advantages and disadvantages of the three most commonly used methods – interviews, observation and questionnaires – and examine when each method can be most profitably used.

Face-to-face interviews provide rich data, offer the opportunity to establish rapport with the interviewees and help to explore and understand complex issues. Many ideas ordinarily difficult to articulate can also be brought to the surface and discussed during such interviews. On the negative side, face-to-face interviews have the potential for introducing interviewer bias and can be expensive if a large number of subjects are involved. Where several interviewers become necessary, adequate training becomes a necessary first step. Face-to-face interviews are best suited to the exploratory stages of research when the researcher is trying to get an overarching view of the concepts or the situational factors.

Telephone interviews help to contact subjects dispersed over various geographic regions and obtain immediate responses from them. They are, hence, an efficient way of collecting data when one has specific, structured questions to ask, needs the responses quickly and has a sample spread over a wide area. On the negative side, the interviewer cannot observe the non-verbal responses of the respondents, and the interviewee can block the call.

Observational studies help us to comprehend complex issues through direct observation (either as a participant or a non-participant observer) and then, if possible, asking questions to seek clarification on certain issues. The data obtained are rich and uncontaminated by self-report bias. On the negative side, they are expensive, since long periods of observation (usually encompassing several weeks or even months) are required, and observer bias may well be present in the data. Because of the costs involved, very few observational studies are done in business. Henry Mintzberg's (1971) study of managerial work is one of the best-known published works that used an observational data collection method. Observational studies are best suited for research requiring non-self-report descriptive data; that is, when behaviours are to be understood without directly asking the respondents themselves. Observational studies can also capture marketing information such as the in-store buying behaviour of customers.

Personally administering questionnaires to groups of individuals helps to (1) establish rapport with the respondents while introducing the survey, (2) provide clarification sought by the respondents on the spot and (3) collect the questionnaires immediately after they are completed. In that sense, there is a 100% response rate. On the negative side, administering questionnaires personally is expensive, especially if the sample is widely dispersed geographically. Personally administered questionnaires are best suited when data are collected from subjects that are located in close proximity to one another and groups of respondents can be conveniently assembled.

Electronic questionnaires are advantageous when responses to many questions have to be obtained from a sample that is geographically dispersed, or it is difficult or not possible to conduct telephone interviews without much expense. On the negative side, such questionnaires usually have a low response rate and one cannot be sure if the data obtained are unbiased since the non-respondents may be different from those who did respond. The electronic questionnaire survey is best suited (and perhaps the only alternative open to the researcher) when information is to be obtained on a substantial scale through structured questions, at a reasonable cost, from a sample that is widely dispersed geographically.

REVIEW OF THE ADVANTAGES AND DISADVANTAGES OF DIFFERENT DATA COLLECTION METHODS AND WHEN TO USE EACH

Because almost all data collection methods have some bias associated with them, collecting data through multimethods and from multiple sources lends rigor to research. For instance, if the responses collected through interviews, questionnaires and observation are strongly correlated with one another, then we will have more confidence about the goodness of the collected data. If the same question fetches discrepant answers in the questionnaire and during the interview, then an air of uncertainty emerges and we will be inclined to discard both data as being biased.

MULTIMETHODS OF DATA COLLECTION

Likewise, if data obtained from several sources bear a great degree of similarity, we will have stronger conviction in the goodness of the data. For example, if an employee rates his performance as 4 on a five-point scale, and his supervisor gives him a similar rating, we may be inclined to consider him a better than average worker. On the contrary, if he gives himself a 5 on the five-point scale and his supervisor gives him a rating of 2, then we will not know to what extent there is a bias and from which source. Therefore, high correlations among data obtained on the same variable from different sources and through different data collection methods lend more credibility to the research instrument and to the data obtained through these instruments. Good research entails collection of data from multiple sources and through multiple data collection methods. Such research, though, is more costly and time consuming.

Example **The Delphi Technique**	The **Delphi Technique** builds on the idea of using expert panels (discussed in Chapter 8), but seeks to combine expert panel discussions with other research methods such as (email) questionnaires. A panel of experts often answers questionnaires in two or more rounds. In the first round they are asked to answer a series of questions on the likelihood of a future scenario or any other issue about which there is unsure or incomplete knowledge. The contributions from all the experts are then collected, summarized and fed back in the form of a second-round questionnaire. After reviewing the first-round results, the experts assess the same issue once more, taking the opinions of other experts into account. This process goes on until it is stopped by the researcher. The rationale behind this iterative process is that eventually it may lead to a consensus about the issue that is being investigated. The identity of participants is usually not revealed, even after the completion of the final report. This should prevent some experts from dominating others, allow experts to unreservedly express their opinions and encourage them to admit mistakes, if any, by revising their earlier judgments. The Delphi Technique has been widely used for long-run business forecasting.

MANAGERIAL IMPLICATIONS	As a manager, you will perhaps engage consultants to do research and may not be collecting data yourself through interviews, questionnaires or observation. However, some basic knowledge of the characteristics and the advantages and disadvantages of primary methods to data collection will help you to evaluate alternative approaches to primary data collection and to understand why a consultant has opted for a certain method or for a combination of methods. As the sponsor of research, you will be able to decide at what level of sophistication you want data to be collected, based on the complexity and gravity of the situation. Your input will help researchers/consultants to think about their topic list (in interviews), their coding scheme (in observation) or the content of their questions (in questionnaires). As a constant (participant-) observer of all that goes on around you at the workplace, you will be able to understand the dynamics operating in the situation. Also, as a manager, you will be able to differentiate between good and bad questions used in surveys, with sensitivity to cultural variations, not only in scaling but also in developing the entire survey instrument, and in collecting data, as discussed in this chapter.

ETHICS IN DATA COLLECTION	Several ethical issues should be addressed while collecting primary data. As previously noted, these pertain to those who sponsor the research, those who collect the data and those who offer them. The sponsors should ask for the study to be done to better the purpose of the organization, and not for any other self-serving reason. They should respect the confidentiality of the data obtained by the researcher, and not ask for the individual or group responses to be disclosed to them, or ask to see the questionnaires. They should have an open mind in accepting the results and recommendations in the report presented by the researchers.

ETHICS AND THE RESEARCHER

1. Treating the information given by the respondent as strictly confidential and guarding his or her privacy is one of the primary responsibilities of the researcher. If the vice president or some other top executive wishes to take a look at the completed questionnaires, the obligatory need to preserve the confidentiality of the documents should then be pointed out. They should be reminded that prior understanding of this had already been reached with them before starting the survey.

   Also, data for a subgroup of, say, less than ten individuals, should be dealt with tactfully to preserve the confidentiality of the group members. The data can be combined with others, or treated in another unidentifiable manner. It is difficult to sanitize reports to protect sources and still preserve the richness of detail of the study. An acceptable alternative has to be found, since preserving confidentiality is the fundamental goal.

2. Personal or seemingly intrusive information should not be solicited, and if it is absolutely necessary for the project, it should be tapped with high sensitivity to the respondent, offering specific reasons.

3. Whatever the nature of the data collection method, the self-esteem and self-respect of the subjects should never be violated.

4. No one should be forced to respond to the survey and if someone does not want to avail themselves of the opportunity to participate, the individual's desire should be respected. Informed consent of the subjects should be the goal of the researcher. This holds true even when data are collected through mechanical means, such as recording interviews, videotaping and the like.

5. Non-participant observers should be as unintrusive as possible. In qualitative studies, personal values could easily bias the data. It is necessary for the researcher to make explicit his or her assumptions, expectations and biases, so that informed decisions regarding the quality of the data can be made by the manager.

6. Posting invitations to participate in a survey on social networks, discussion groups, and chat rooms is often perceived as 'spam'. Make sure that you are familiar with, and that you act in accordance with, anti-spam legislation and guidelines.

7. There should be absolutely no misrepresentation or distortion in reporting the data collected during the study.

ETHICAL BEHAVIOUR OF RESPONDENTS

1. The subject, once having exercised the choice to participate in a study, should cooperate fully in the tasks ahead, such as responding to a survey.

2. The respondent also has an obligation to be truthful and honest in the responses. Misrepresentation or giving information, knowing it to be untrue, should be avoided.

SUMMARY

- **Learning objective 1: Compare and contrast different types of questionnaires.** Questionnaires are generally designed to collect large numbers of (quantitative) data. They can be administered personally, mailed to the respondents or distributed electronically. When the survey is limited to a local area a good way to collect data is to personally administer the questionnaires. A mail questionnaire is a self-administered (paper and pencil) questionnaire that is sent to respondents via the mail. This method has long been the backbone of business research, but with the arrival of the Internet, mail questionnaires have become redundant or obsolete. Instead, online questionnaires are posted on the Internet or sent via email.

- **Learning objective 2: Design questionnaires to tap different variables.** Sound questionnaire design principles should focus on three areas. The first concerns the wording of the questions; the second refers to the planning of issues with regard to how the variables will be categorized, scaled and coded after the responses are received; and the third pertains to the general appearance of the questionnaire. All three are important issues because they can minimize bias in research.

- **Learning objective 3: Discuss the issues related to cross-cultural research.** With the globalization of business, managers are often interested in similarities and differences in behavioural and attitudinal responses of people (employees, consumers and investors) in different cultures. Surveys should be tailored to the specific needs and features of different cultures. At least three issues are important for cross-cultural data collection – response equivalence, timing of data collection and the status of the individual collecting the data.

- **Learning objective 4: Discuss the advantages and disadvantages of various data collection methods in survey research.** Having discussed the primary data collection methods in survey research (interviews, observation and administering questionnaires), this chapter recounts the advantages and disadvantages of these methods and examines when each method can be most profitably used.

- **Learning objective 5: Discuss the advantages of multisources and multimethods of data collection.** Because almost all data collection methods have some bias associated with them, collecting data through multimethods and from multiple sources lends rigor to research. If data obtained from several sources bear a great degree of similarity, we will have stronger conviction of the goodness of the data.

- **Learning objective 6: Demonstrate awareness of the role of the manager in primary data collection.** Managers often engage consultants to do research and may not be collecting data themselves through interviews, questionnaires or observation. However, some basic knowledge of the characteristics and the advantages and disadvantages of primary methods of data collection will help them to evaluate alternative approaches to primary data collection and/or to understand why a consultant has opted for a certain method or for a combination of methods.

- **Learning objective 7: Demonstrate awareness of the role of ethics in primary data collection.** Several ethical issues should be addressed while collecting primary data. These pertain to those who sponsor the research, those who collect the data and those who offer them.

Instructors can visit the companion website at **www.wiley.com/go/bougie/researchmethods forbusiness8e** for **Case Study: An online shopping questionnaire**.

DISCUSSION QUESTIONS

1. Discuss the advantages and disadvantages of personally administered questionnaires, mail questionnaires and electronic questionnaires.

2. Explain the principles of wording, stating how these are important in questionnaire design, citing examples not in the book.

3. How are multiple methods of data collection and from multiple sources related to the reliability and validity of the measures?

4. 'Every data collection method has its own built-in biases. Therefore, resorting to multimethods of data collection is only going to compound the biases'. How would you critique this statement?

5. 'One way to deal with discrepancies found in the data obtained from multiple sources is to average the figures and take the mean as the value of the variable'. What is your reaction to this?

6. How has the advancement in technology helped data gathering via questionnaires?

Now do Exercises 10.1, 10.2, and 10.3.

David Shen Liang is a business student engaged in a management project for Ocg Business Services (OBS), a supplier of office equipment to a large group of (international) customers. OBS operates in the business-to-business market. David wants to test the following hypotheses:

1. Service quality has a positive effect on customer satisfaction.
2. Price perception has a negative effect on customer satisfaction.

For this purpose he has developed the following questionnaire:

Dear Sir,

My name is David Shen Liang. I am a business student currently engaged in a management project for Ocg Business Services (OBS). I am interested in how satisfied you – as a client of OBS – are about your relationship with OBS. For this purpose I would like you to fill in the following questionnaire. It will take no more than five minutes to fill in the questionnaire. Thank you so much for your time.

Kind regards,

David Shen Liang.

OBS is in an easily accessible location
Strongly disagree -1---2---3---4---5---6---7- Strongly agree

OBS has convenient opening hours
Strongly disagree -1---2---3---4---5---6---7- Strongly agree

OBS delivers fast service
Strongly disagree -1---2---3---4---5---6---7- Strongly agree

OBS informs you on the status of your order
Strongly disagree -1---2---3---4---5---6---7- Strongly agree

OBS provides its services on the agreed time
Strongly disagree -1---2---3---4---5---6---7- Strongly agree

OBS offers a range of products and services that fits your needs
Strongly disagree -1---2---3---4---5---6---7- Strongly agree

The end-products of OBS are sound
Strongly disagree -1---2---3---4---5---6---7- Strongly agree

The facilities of OBS look well-cared for
Strongly disagree -1---2---3---4---5---6---7- Strongly agree

Employees of OBS are helpful and friendly
Strongly disagree -1---2---3---4---5---6---7- Strongly agree

Employees of OBS give good advice
Strongly disagree -1---2---3---4---5---6---7- Strongly agree

Employees of OBS respond to your requests promptly
Strongly disagree -1---2---3---4---5---6---7- Strongly agree

OBS is reliable
Strongly disagree -1---2---3---4---5---6---7- Strongly agree

When a problem occurs, OBS will help you adequately
Strongly disagree -1---2---3---4---5---6---7- Strongly agree

OBS is innovative
Strongly disagree -1---2---3---4---5---6---7- Strongly agree

OBS has your best interests at heart.
Strongly disagree -1---2---3---4---5---6---7- Strongly agree

OBS fully informs you about the products and services it provides within your organization and about everything else you may want to learn from OBS or its employees
Strongly disagree -1---2---3---4---5---6---7- Strongly agree

The price of OBS products is:
Very Low -1---2---3---4---5---6---7- Very high
In general, how satisfied are you about the services you received?
Very satisfied -1---2---3---4---5---6---7- Very dissatisfied

Which services do you miss at Ocg Business Services?

When was your first contact with Ocg? _____ ago.

Are the services of Ocg Business Services of added value to your organization?

[_] Yes, they are.
[_] Irrelevant, the services are not better or worse than those of other providers.
[_] No, I would prefer another provider.

General Questions

Age   ___

Gender   Male/Female

Position

☐ Secretarial   ☐ Management   ☐ Administration
☐ Facility   ☐ Marketing/sales ☐ Project
☐ Engineers   ☐ Purchasing   ☐ Other

This was the final question of this questionnaire.
Thank you very much for your cooperation!

Comment on the foregoing questionnaire. Pay attention to:

- principles of wording;
- the classification data (personal information);
- the general appearance or 'getup' of the questionnaire.

EXERCISE 10.2

A production manager wants to assess the reactions of the blue-collar workers in his department (including foremen) to the introduction of computer-integrated manufacturing (CIM) systems. He is particularly interested to know how they perceive the effects of CIM on:

1. Their future jobs.
2. Additional training that they will have to receive.
3. Future job advancement.

Design a questionnaire for the production manager.

Design a questionnaire that you could use to assess the quality of your on-campus dining facilities. Make sure you can test the following hypotheses:

H$_1$: *There is a positive relationship between the service quality of the on-campus dining facilities and customer loyalty.*

H$_2$: *The relationship between service quality and customer loyalty is mediated by customer satisfaction.*

Experimental Designs

LEARNING OBJECTIVES

After completing Chapter 11, you should be able to:

1. Describe lab experiments and discuss the internal and external validity of this type of experiment.

2. Describe field experiments and discuss the internal and external validity of this type of experiment.

3. Describe, discuss and identify threats to internal and external validity and make a trade-off between internal and external validity.

4. Describe the different types of experimental designs.

5. Discuss when and why simulation might be a good alternative to lab and field experiments.

6. Discuss the role of the manager in experimental designs.

7. Discuss the role of ethics in experimental designs.

INTRODUCTION

In Chapter 7, we examined basic research strategies. We distinguished experimental from non-experimental approaches and explained that experimental designs are typically used in *deductive* research where the researcher is interested in establishing cause-and-effect relationships. In the last three chapters, we discussed non-experimental approaches to primary data collection. In this chapter, we look at experimental designs.

Consider the following three scenarios.

Example

Cause-and-effect relationship after randomization

Scenario A   A manufacturer of luxury cars has decided to launch a global brand communications campaign to reinforce the image of its cars. An 18-month campaign is scheduled that will be rolled out worldwide, with advertising in television, print and electronic media. Under the title 'Bravura', a renowned advertising agency developed three different campaign concepts. To determine which of these concepts is most effective, the car manufacturer wants to test their effects on the brand's image. But how can the car manufacturer test the effectiveness of these concepts?

Scenario B   A study of absenteeism and the steps taken to curb it indicates that companies use the following incentives to reduce it:

14% give bonus days;
39% offer cash;
39% present recognition awards;
4% award prizes;
4% pursue other strategies.

Scenario B
(*continued*)

Asked about their effectiveness,

> 22% of the companies said they were very effective;
> 66% said they were somewhat effective;
> 12% said they were not at all effective.

What does the above information tell us? How do we know what kinds of incentives cause people not to absent themselves? What particular incentive(s) did the 22% of companies that found their strategies to be "very effective" offer? Is there a direct causal connection between one or two specific incentives and absenteeism?

Scenario C

The dagger effect of layoffs is that there is a sharp drop in the commitment of workers who are retained, even though they might well understand the logic of the reduction in the workforce.

> Does layoff really cause employee commitment to drop off, or is something else operating in this situation?

The answers to the questions raised in Scenarios A, B and C might be found by using experimental designs in researching the issues.

In Chapter 7, we touched on experimental designs. In this chapter, we will discuss lab experiments and field experiments in detail. Experimental designs, as we know, are set up to examine possible cause-and-effect relationships among variables, in contrast to correlational studies, which examine the relationships among variables without necessarily trying to establish if one variable causes another.

We have already explained that in order to establish that a change in the independent variable *causes* a change in the dependent variable: (1) the independent and the dependent variable should covary; (2) the independent variable should precede the dependent variable; (3) the researcher should control for the effects of 'extraneous' variables.

The third condition implies that to establish causal relationships between two variables in an organizational setting, several variables that might covary with the dependent variable have to be controlled. This then allows us to say that variable X, and variable X alone, causes the dependent variable Y. However, it is not always possible to control all the covariates while manipulating the causal factor (the independent variable that is causing the dependent variable) in organizational settings, where events flow or occur naturally and normally. It is, however, possible to first isolate the effects of a variable in a tightly controlled artificial setting (the lab setting), and after testing and establishing the cause-and-effect relationship under these tightly controlled conditions, see how generalizable such relationships are to the field setting.

Let us illustrate this with an example.

Example

Suppose a manager believes that staffing the accounting department completely with personnel with M.Acc. (Master of Accountancy) degrees will increase its productivity. It is well nigh impossible to transfer all those without the M.Acc. degree currently in the department to other departments and recruit fresh M.Acc. degree holders to take their place. Such a course of action is bound to disrupt the work of the entire organization inasmuch as many new people will have to be trained, work will slow down, employees will get upset and so on. However, the hypothesis that possession of an M.Acc. degree would cause increases in productivity can be tested in an artificially created setting (i.e. not at the regular workplace) in which an accounting job can be given to three groups of people: those with an M.Acc. degree, those without an M.Acc. degree and a mixed group of those with and without an M.Acc. degree (as is the case in the present work setting). If the first group performs exceedingly well, the second group poorly and the third group falls somewhere in the middle, there will be evidence to indicate that the M.Acc. degree qualification might indeed cause productivity to rise. If such evidence is found, then planned and systematic efforts can be initiated to gradually transfer those without the M.Acc. degree in the accounting department to other departments and recruit others with this degree to this department. It is then possible to see to what extent productivity does, in fact, go up in the department because all the staff members are M.Acc. degree holders.

As we saw earlier, experimental designs fall into two categories: experiments done in an artificial or contrived environment, known as **lab experiments**, and those done in the natural environment in which activities regularly take place, known as **field experiments**.

THE LAB EXPERIMENT

As stated earlier, when a cause-and-effect relationship between an independent and a dependent variable of interest is to be clearly established, then all other variables that might contaminate or confound the relationship have to be tightly controlled. In other words, the possible effects of other variables on the dependent variable have to be accounted for in some way, so that the actual causal effects of the investigated independent variable on the dependent variable can be determined. It is also necessary to manipulate the independent variable so that the extent of its causal effects can be established. The control and manipulation are best done in an artificial setting (the laboratory), where the causal effects can be tested. When control and manipulation are introduced to establish cause-and-effect relationships in an artificial setting, we have laboratory experimental designs, also known as lab experiments.

Because we use the terms control and manipulation, let us examine what these concepts mean.

CONTROL

When we postulate cause-and-effect relationships between two variables X and Y, it is possible that some other factor, say A, might also influence the dependent variable Y. In such a case, it will not be possible to determine the extent to which Y occurred only because of X, since we do not know how much of the total variation in Y was caused by the presence of the other factor A. For instance, a Human Resource Development manager might arrange special training for a set of newly recruited secretaries in creating Web pages, to prove to the VP (his boss) that such training causes them to function more effectively. However, some of the new secretaries might function more effectively than others mainly or partly because they have had previous intermittent experience with using the Web. In this case, the manager cannot prove that the special training alone caused greater effectiveness, since the previous intermittent Web experience of some secretaries is a contaminating factor. If the true effect of the training on learning is to be assessed, then the learners' previous experience has to be controlled. This might be done by not including in the experiment those who already have had some experience with the Web. This is what we mean when we say we have to control the contaminating factors, and we will later see how this is done.

MANIPULATION

To examine the causal effects of an independent variable on a dependent variable, certain manipulations need to be tried. **Manipulation** simply means that we create different levels of the independent variable to assess the impact on the dependent variable. For example, we may want to test the theory that depth of knowledge of various manufacturing technologies is caused by rotating the employees on all the jobs on the production line and in the design department, over a four-week period. Then we can manipulate the independent variable, 'rotation of employees', by rotating one group of production workers and exposing them to all the systems during the four-week period, rotating another group of workers only partially during the four weeks (i.e. exposing them to only half of the manufacturing technologies) and leaving the third group to continue to do what they are currently doing, without any special rotation. By measuring the depth of knowledge of these groups both before and after the manipulation (also known as the treatment), it is possible to assess the extent to which the treatment caused the effect, after controlling the contaminating factors. If deep knowledge is indeed caused by rotation and exposure, the results will show that the third group had the lowest increase in depth of knowledge, the second group had some significant increase and the first group had the greatest gains!

Let us look at another example of how causal relationships are established by manipulating the independent variable.

	Example

Let us say we want to test the effects of lighting on worker production levels among sewing machine operators. To establish a cause-and-effect relationship, we must first measure the production levels of all the operators over a 15-day period with the usual amount of light they work with – say 60 watt lamps. We might then want to split the group of 60 operators into three groups of 20 members each, and while allowing one subgroup to continue to work under the same conditions as before (60 watt electric light bulbs), we might want to manipulate the intensity of the light for the other two subgroups, by making one group work with 75 watt and the other with 100 watt light bulbs. After the different groups have worked with these varying degrees of light exposure for 15 days, each group's total production for these 15 days may be analysed to see if the difference between the pre-experimental and the post-experimental production among the groups is directly related to the intensity of the light to which they have been exposed. If our hypothesis that better lighting increases the production levels is correct, then the subgroup that did not have any change in the lighting (called the **control group**), should have no increase in production and the other two groups should show increases, with those having the most light (100 watts) showing greater increases than those who had the 75 watt lighting.

In the above case, the independent variable, lighting, has been manipulated by exposing different groups to different degrees of changes in it. This manipulation of the independent variable is also known as the **treatment**, and the results of the treatment are called treatment effects.

Let us illustrate how variable X can be both controlled and manipulated in the lab setting through another example.

	Example

Let us say an entrepreneur – the owner of a toy factory – is rather disappointed with the number of plush unicorns produced by his workers, who are paid wages at an hourly rate. He might wonder whether paying them piece rates would increase their production levels. However, before implementing the piece-rate system, he wants to make sure that switching over to the new system would indeed achieve the objective.

In a case like this, the researcher might first want to test the causal relationships in a lab setting, and if the results are encouraging, conduct the experiment later in a field setting.

In designing the lab experiment, the researcher should first think of possible factors affecting the production level of the workers, and then try to control these. Other than piece rates, previous job experience might also influence the rate of production because familiarity with the job makes it easy for people to increase their productivity levels. In some cases, where the jobs are very strenuous and require muscular strength, gender differences may affect productivity. Let us say that for the type of production job discussed earlier, age, gender and prior experience of the employees are the factors that influence the production levels of the employees. The researcher needs to control these three variables. Let us see how this can be done.

Suppose the researcher intends to set up four groups of 15 people each for the lab experiment – one to be used as the control group, and the other three subjected to three different pay manipulations. Now, the variables that may have an impact on the cause-and-effect relationship can be controlled in two different ways: either by matching the groups or through randomization. These concepts are explained before we proceed further.

CONTROLLING THE CONTAMINATING EXOGENOUS OR "NUISANCE" VARIABLES

Matching Groups

One way of controlling the contaminating or 'nuisance' variables is to **match** the various **groups** by picking the confounding characteristics and deliberately spreading them across groups. For instance, if there are 20 women among the 60 members, then each group will be assigned five women, so that the effects of gender are distributed across the four groups. Likewise, age and experience factors can be matched across the four groups, such that each group has a similar mix of individuals in terms of gender, age and experience. Because the suspected contaminating factors are matched across the groups, we can be confident in saying that variable X alone causes variable Y (if, of course, that is the result of the study).

Randomization

Another way of controlling the contaminating variables is to assign the 60 members randomly (i.e. with no predetermination) to the four groups. That is, every member will have a known and equal chance of being assigned to any of these four groups. For instance, we might throw the names of all the 60 members into a hat and draw their names. The first 15 names drawn may be assigned to the first group, the second 15 to the second group and so on, or the first person drawn might be assigned to the first group, the second person drawn to the second group and so on. Thus, in **randomization**, the process by which individuals are drawn (i.e. everybody has a known and equal chance of being drawn) and their assignment to any particular group (each individual could be assigned to any one of the groups set up) are both random. By thus randomly assigning members to the groups we are distributing the confounding variables among the groups equally. That is, the variables of age, sex and previous experience – *the controlled variables* – will have an equal probability of being distributed among the groups.

The process of randomization ideally ensures that each group is comparable to the others, and that all variables, including the effects of age, sex and previous experience, are controlled. In other words, each of the groups will have some members who have more experience mingled with those who have less or no experience. All groups will have members of different age and sex composition. Thus, randomization ensures that if these variables do indeed have a contributory or confounding effect, we have controlled their confounding effects (along with those of other unknown factors) by distributing them across groups. This is achieved because when we manipulate the independent variable of piece rates by having no piece rate system at all for one group (control) and having different piece rates for the other three groups (experimental), we can determine the causal effects of the piece rates on production levels. Any errors or biases caused

Table 11.1   Cause-and-Effect Relationship After Randomization

Groups	Treatment	Treatment effect (% increase in production over pre-piece rate system)
Experimental group 1	$1.00 per piece	10
Experimental group 2	$1.50 per piece	15
Experimental group 3	$2.00 per piece	20
Control group (no treatment)	Old hourly rate	0

by age, sex and previous experience are now distributed equally among all four groups. Any causal effects found will be over and above the effects of the confounding variables.

To make it clear, let us illustrate this with some actual figures, as in Table 11.1. Note that because the effects of experience, sex and age were controlled in all the four groups by randomly assigning the members to them, and the control group had no increase in productivity, it can be reliably concluded from the result that the percentage increases in production are a result of the piece rate (treatment effects). In other words, piece rates are the cause of the increase in the number of toys produced. We cannot now say that the cause-and-effect relationship has been confounded by other 'nuisance' variables, because they have been controlled through the process of randomly assigning members to the groups. Here, we have high internal validity or confidence in the cause-and-effect relationship.

Advantages of randomization   The difference between matching and randomization is that in the former case individuals are deliberately and consciously matched to control the differences among group members, whereas in the latter case we expect that the process of randomization will distribute the inequalities among the groups, based on the laws of normal distribution. Thus, we need not be particularly concerned about any known or unknown confounding factors.

In sum, compared to randomization, matching might be less effective, since we may not know all the factors that could possibly contaminate the cause-and-effect relationship in any given situation, and hence fail to match some critical factors across all groups while conducting an experiment. Randomization, however, will take care of this, since all the contaminating factors will be spread across all groups. Moreover, even if we know the confounding variables, we may not be able to find a match for all such variables. For instance, if gender is a confounding variable, and if there are only two women in a four-group experimental design, we will not be able to match all the groups with respect to gender. Randomization solves these dilemmas as well. Thus, lab experimental designs involve control of the contaminating variables through the process of either matching or randomization, and the manipulation of the treatment.

INTERNAL VALIDITY OF LAB EXPERIMENTS

Internal validity   refers to the confidence we place in the cause-and-effect relationship. In other words, it addresses the question, '*To what extent does the research design permit us to say that the independent variable A causes a change in the dependent variable B?*' As Kidder and Judd (1986) note, in research with high internal validity, we are relatively better able to argue that the relationship is causal, whereas in studies with low internal validity, causality cannot be inferred at all. In lab experiments where cause-and-effect relationships are substantiated, internal validity can be said to be high.

So far we have talked about establishing cause-and-effect relationships within the lab setting, which is an artificially created and controlled environment. You might yourself have been a subject taking part in one of the lab experiments conducted by the psychology or other departments on campus at some time. You might not have been specifically told what cause-and-effect relationships the experimenter was looking for, but you would have been told what is called a 'cover story'. That is, you would have been apprised in general terms of some reason for the study and your role in it, without divulging its true purpose. After the end of the experiment you would also have been debriefed and given a full explanation of the experiment, and any questions you might have had would have been answered. This is how lab experiments are usually conducted: subjects are selected and assigned to different groups through matching or randomization; they are moved to a lab setting; they are given some details of the study and a task to perform; and some kind of questionnaire or other tests are administered both before and after the task is completed. The results of these studies indicate the cause-and-effect relationship between the variables under investigation.

EXTERNAL VALIDITY OR GENERALIZABILITY OF LAB EXPERIMENTS

To what extent are the results found in the lab setting transferable or generalizable to actual organizational or field settings? In other words, if we do find a cause-and-effect relationship after conducting a lab experiment, can we then confidently say that the same cause-and-effect relationship will also hold true in the organizational setting?

Consider the following situation. If, in a lab experimental design, the groups are given the simple production task of screwing bolts and nuts onto a plastic frame, and the results indicate that the groups who were paid piece rates were more productive than those who were paid hourly rates, to what extent can we then say that this would be true of the sophisticated nature of the jobs performed in organizations? The tasks in organizational settings are far more complex, and there might be several confounding variables that cannot be controlled – for example, experience. Under such circumstances, we cannot be sure that the cause-and-effect relationship found in the lab experiment is necessarily likely to hold true in the field setting. To test the causal relationships in the organizational setting, field experiments are carried out. These will now be briefly discussed.

THE FIELD EXPERIMENT	A **field experiment**, as the name implies, is an experiment done in the natural environment in which work (or life) goes on as usual, but treatments are given to one or more groups. Thus, in the field experiment, even though it may not be possible to control all the nuisance variables because members cannot be either randomly assigned to groups, or matched, the treatment can still be manipulated. Control groups can also be set up in field experiments. The experimental and control groups in the field experiment may be made up of the people working at several plants within a certain radius, or from the different shifts in the same plant or in some other way. If there are three different shifts in a production plant, for instance, and the effects of the piece-rate system are to be studied, one of the shifts can be used as the control group, and the two other shifts given two different treatments or the same treatment – that is, different piece rates or the same piece rate. Any cause-and-effect relationship found under these conditions will have wider generalizability to other similar production settings, even though we may not be sure to what extent the piece rates alone were the cause of the increase in productivity, because some of the other confounding variables could not be controlled.
EXTERNAL AND INTERNAL VALIDITY IN EXPERIMENTS	What we just discussed can be referred to as an issue of external validity versus internal validity. **External validity** refers to the extent of generalizability of the results of a causal study to other settings, people or events, and **internal validity** refers to the degree of our confidence in the causal effects (i.e. that variable X causes variable Y). Field experiments have more external validity (i.e. the results are more generalizable to other similar organizational settings), but less internal validity (i.e. we cannot be certain of the extent to which variable X alone causes

variable Y). Note that in the lab experiment, the reverse is true: the internal validity is high but the external validity is rather low. In other words, in lab experiments we can be sure that variable X causes variable Y because we have been able to keep the other confounding exogenous variables under control, but we have so tightly controlled several variables to establish the cause-and-effect relationship that we do not know to what extent the results of our study can be generalized, if at all, to field settings. In other words, since the lab setting does not reflect the 'real-world' setting, we do not know to what extent the lab findings validly represent the realities in the outside world.

TRADE-OFF BETWEEN INTERNAL AND EXTERNAL VALIDITY

There is thus a trade-off between internal validity and external validity. If we want high internal validity, we should be willing to settle for lower external validity and vice versa. To ensure both types of validity, researchers usually try first to test the causal relationships in a tightly controlled artificial or lab setting, and once the relationship has been established, they try to test the causal relationship in a field experiment. Lab experimental designs in the management area have thus far been done to assess, among other things, gender differences in leadership styles and managerial aptitudes. However, gender differences and other factors found in the lab settings are frequently not found in field studies (Osborn & Vicars, 1976). These problems of external validity usually limit the use of lab experiments in the management area. Field experiments are also infrequently undertaken because of the resultant unintended consequences – personnel becoming suspicious, rivalries and jealousies being created among departments and the like.

FACTORS AFFECTING THE VALIDITY OF EXPERIMENTS

Even the best designed lab studies may be influenced by factors that might affect the internal validity of the lab experiment. That is, some confounding factors might still be present that could offer rival explanations as to what is causing the dependent variable. These possible confounding factors pose a threat to internal validity. The seven major threats to internal validity are the effects of history, maturation, (main) testing, selection, mortality, statistical regression and instrumentation, and these are explained below with examples. Two threats to external validity are (interactive) testing and selection. These threats to the validity of experiments are discussed next.

History Effects

Certain events or factors that have an impact on the independent variable–dependent variable relationship might unexpectedly occur while the experiment is in progress, and this history of events would confound the cause-and-effect relationship between the two variables, thus affecting the internal validity. For example, let us say that the manager of a Dairy Products Division wants to test the effects of the 'buy one, get one free' sales promotion on the sale of the company-owned brand of packaged cheese for a week. She carefully records the sales of the packaged cheese during the previous two weeks to assess the effect of the promotion. However, on the very day that her sales promotion goes into effect, the Dairy Farmers' Association unexpectedly launches a multimedia advertisement on the benefits of consuming dairy products, especially cheese. The sales of all dairy products, including cheese, go up in all the stores, including the one where the experiment had been in progress. Here, because of an unexpected advertisement, one cannot be sure how much of the increase in sales of the packaged cheese in question was due to the sales promotion and how much to the advertisement by the Dairy Farmers' Association! The effects of history have reduced the internal validity or the faith that can be placed on the conclusion that the sales promotion caused the increase in sales. The **history effects** in this case are illustrated in Figure 11.1.

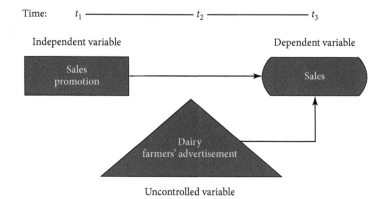

FIGURE 11.1 Illustration of history effects in experimental design

To give another example, let us say a bakery is studying the effects of adding to its bread a new ingredient that is expected to enrich it and offer more nutritional value to children under 14 years of age within 30 days, subject to a certain daily intake. At the start of the experiment, the bakery takes a measure of the health of 30 children through some medical yardsticks. Thereafter, the children are given the prescribed intakes of bread daily. Unfortunately, on day 20 of the experiment, a flu virus hits the city in epidemic proportions affecting most of the children studied. This unforeseen and uncontrollable effect of history, flu, has contaminated the cause-and-effect relationship study for the bakery.

Maturation Effects

Cause-and-effect inferences can also be contaminated by the effects of the passage of time – another uncontrollable variable. Such contamination effects are denoted **maturation effects**. The maturation effects are a function of the processes – both biological and psychological – operating within the respondents as a result of the passage of time. Examples of maturation processes include growing older, getting tired, feeling hungry and getting bored. In other words, there could be a maturation effect on the dependent variable purely because of the passage of time. For instance, let us say that an R&D director contends that increases in the efficiency of workers will result within three months' time if advanced technology is introduced in the work setting. If, at the end of the three months, increased efficiency is indeed found, it will be difficult to claim that the advanced technology (and it alone) increased the efficiency of workers because, with the passage of time, employees will also have gained experience, resulting in better job performance and therefore in improved efficiency. Thus, the internal validity also gets reduced owing to the effects of maturation inasmuch as it is difficult to pinpoint how much of the increase is attributable to the introduction of the enhanced technology alone. Figure 11.2 illustrates the maturation effects in the above example.

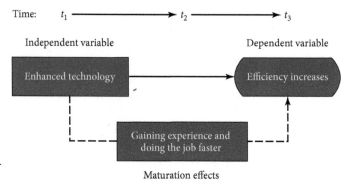

FIGURE 11.2 Illustration of maturation effects on a cause-and-effect relationship

Testing Effects

Frequently, to test the effects of a treatment, subjects are given what is called a pre-test. That is, first a measure of the dependent variable is taken (the **pre-test**), then the treatment is given and after that a second measure of the dependent variable is taken (the **post-test**). The difference between the post-test and the pre-test scores is then attributed to the treatment. However, the exposure of participants to the pre-test may affect both the internal and external validity of the findings. Indeed, the aforementioned process may lead to two types of **testing effects**.

A *main testing effect* occurs when the prior observation (the pre-test) affects *the later observation* (the post-test). Main testing effects typically occur because participants want to be consistent. Let us assume that we have tested the effect of a television commercial (the treatment) on attitudes toward the brand using a pre-test and a post-test. Suppose that no significant difference in attitude toward the brand was found. This finding could lead to the conclusion that the commercial was ineffective. However, an alternative explanation is that our participants tried to be consistent and answered the later questions so that their answers were similar to the answers they gave the first time. The pre-test may thus have affected the results of the experiment. Along these lines, main testing effects are another threat to internal validity.

Interactive testing effects occur when the pre-test affects the participant's *reaction to the treatment* (the independent variable). Again, let's assume that we are testing the effect of a television commercial on attitude toward the brand using a pre-test and a post-test. It is possible that because of the pre-test, the participants watch the television commercial more closely than consumers that do not take part in the experiment. For this reason, any effects that are found may not necessarily be generalizable to the population. Hence, interactive treatment effects are a threat to the external validity of an experiment.

In sum, testing effects may affect both the internal and external validity of our findings. Main testing effects threaten the internal validity, whereas interactive testing effects threaten the external validity.

Selection Bias Effects

Another threat to both the internal and external validity of our findings is the selection of participants. First, we will discuss how selection may affect the external validity of our findings. Then, we will discuss how selection may affect the internal validity.

In a lab setting, the types of participants selected for the experiment may be very different from the types of employees recruited by organizations. For example, students in a university might be allotted a task that is manipulated to study the effects on their performance. The findings from this experiment cannot be generalized, however, to the real world of work, where the employees and the nature of the jobs are both quite different. Thus, subject selection poses a threat to external validity.

The threat to internal validity comes from improper or unmatched selection of subjects for the experimental and control groups. For example, if a lab experiment is set up to assess the impact of the working environment on employees' attitudes toward work, and if one of the experimental conditions is to have a group of subjects work for about two hours in a room with a mildly unpleasant smell, an ethical researcher might disclose this condition to prospective subjects, who may decline to participate in the study. However, some volunteers might be lured through incentives (say, a payment of $70 for the two hours of participation in the study). The volunteers so selected may be quite different from the others (inasmuch as they may come from an environment of deprivation) and their responses to the treatment might be quite different. Such bias in the selection of the subjects might contaminate the cause-and-effect relationships and pose a threat to internal validity as well. Hence, newcomers, volunteers and others who cannot be matched with the control groups pose a threat to internal validity in certain types of experiment. For this reason, randomization or matching groups is highly recommended.

Mortality Effects

Another confounding factor on the cause-and-effect relationship is the **mortality** or attrition of the members in the experimental or control group, or both, as the experiment progresses. When the group composition changes over time across the groups, comparison between the groups becomes difficult, because those who dropped out of the experiment may confound the results. Again, we will not be able to say how much of the effect observed arises from the treatment, and how much is attributable to the members who dropped out, since those who stayed with the experiment may have reacted differently from those who dropped out. Let us see an example.

Example	A sales manager had heard glowing reports about three different training programs that train salespersons in effective sales strategies. All three were of six weeks' duration. The manager was curious to know which one would offer the best results for the company. The first program took the trainees daily on field trips and demonstrated effective and ineffective sales strategies through practical experience. The second program trained groups on the same strategies but indoors in a classroom setting, with lectures, role playing, and answering questions from the participants. The third program used mathematical models and simulations to increase sales effectiveness. The manager chose eight trainees each for the three different programs and sent them to training. By the end of the fourth week, three trainees from the first group, one from the second group and two from the third group had dropped out of the training programs for a variety of reasons, including ill health, family exigencies, transportation problems and a car accident. This attrition from the various groups made it impossible to compare the effectiveness of the various programs. Thus, mortality can also lower the internal validity of an experiment.

Statistical Regression Effects

The effects of **statistical regression** are brought about when the members chosen for the experimental group have extreme scores on the dependent variable to begin with. For instance, if a manager wants to test whether he can increase the 'salesmanship' repertoire of the sales personnel through Dale Carnegie-type programs, he should not choose those with extremely low or extremely high abilities for the experiment. This is because we know from the laws of probability that those with very low scores on a variable (in this case, current sales ability) have a greater probability of showing improvement and scoring closer to the mean on the post-test after being exposed to the treatment. This phenomenon of low scorers tending to score closer to the mean is known as 'regressing toward the mean' (statistical regression). Likewise, those with very high abilities also have a greater tendency to regress toward the mean – they will score lower on the post-test than on the pre-test. Thus, those who are at either end of the continuum with respect to a variable will not 'truly' reflect the cause-and-effect relationship. The phenomenon of statistical regression is thus yet another threat to internal validity.

Instrumentation Effects

Instrumentation effects are yet another source of threat to internal validity. These might arise because of a change in the measuring instrument between pre-test and post-test, and not because of the treatment's differential impact at the end (Cook & Campbell, 1979a). For instance, an observer who is involved in observing a particular pattern of behaviour in respondents before a treatment might start concentrating on a different set of behaviours after the treatment. The frame of measurement of behaviour (in a sense, the measuring instrument) has now changed and will not reflect the change in behaviour that can be attributed to the treatment. This is also true in the case of physical measuring instruments like the spring balance or other finely calibrated instruments that might lose their accuracy due to a loss of tension with constant use, resulting in erroneous final measurement.

In organizations, instrumentation effects in experimental designs are possible when the pre-test is done by the experimenter, treatments are given to the experimental groups and the post-test on measures such as performance is done by different managers. One manager might measure performance by the final units of output, a second manager might take into account the number of rejects as well and a third manager might also take into consideration the amount of resources expended in getting the job done! Here, there are at least three different measuring instruments, if we treat each manager as a performance measuring instrument.

Thus, instrumentation effects also pose a threat to internal validity in experimental design.

IDENTIFYING THREATS TO VALIDITY

Let us examine each of the possible seven threats to validity in the context of the following scenario.

	Example

An organizational consultant wanted to demonstrate to the president of a company, through an experimental design, that the democratic style of leadership best enhances the morale of employees. She set up three experimental groups and one control group for the purpose and assigned members to each of the groups randomly. The three experimental groups were headed by an autocratic leader, a democratic leader and a laissez-faire leader, respectively.

The members in the three experimental groups were administered a pre-test. Since the control group was not exposed to any treatment, they were not given a pre-test. As the experiment progressed, two members in the democratic treatment group got quite excited and started moving around to the other members saying that the participative atmosphere was 'great' and 'performance was bound to be high in this group.' Two members from each of the autocratic and laissez-faire groups left after the first hour saying they had to go and could no longer participate in the experiment. After two hours of activities, a post-test was administered to all the participants, including the control group members, on the same lines as the pre-test.

---

1. *History effects.* The action of the two members in the participative group by way of unexpectedly moving around in an excited manner and remarking that participative leadership is 'great' and the 'performance is bound to be high in this group' might have boosted the morale of all the members in the group. It would be difficult to separate out how much of the increase in morale was due to the participative condition alone and how much to the sudden enthusiasm displayed by the two members.

2. *Maturation effects.* It is doubtful that maturation had any effect on morale in this situation, since the passage of time, in itself, may not have anything much to do with increases or decreases in morale.

3. *Testing effects.* The pre-tests are likely to have sensitized the respondents to both the treatment and the post-test. Thus, main and interactive testing effects exist. However, if all the groups had been given both the pre- and the post-tests, the main testing effects (but not the interactive testing effects!) across all groups would have been taken care of (i.e. nullified) and the post-tests of each of the experimental groups could have been compared with that of the control group to detect the effects of the treatment. Unfortunately, the control group was not given the pre-test, and thus this group's post-test scores were not biased by the pre-test – a phenomenon that could have occurred in the experimental groups. Hence,

it is incorrect, on the face of it, to compare the experimental groups' scores with those of the control group. Interactive testing poses a threat to the external validity of the findings.

4. *Selection bias effects.* Since members were randomly assigned to all groups, selection bias should not have affected the internal validity of the findings. The external validity of the findings should also not have been threatened by selection: there is no reason to assume that the participants selected for the experiment are different from the other employees of the organization.

5. *Mortality effects.* Since members dropped out of two experimental groups, the effects of mortality could affect internal validity.

6. *Statistical regression effects.* Though not specifically stated, we can assume that all the members participating in the experiment were selected randomly from a normally distributed population, in which case the issue of statistical regression contaminating the experiment does not arise.

7. *Instrumentation effects.* Since the same questionnaire measured morale both before and after the treatment for all members, there should not have been any instrumentation bias.

In effect, three of the seven threats to internal validity do apply in this case. The history, main testing and mortality effects are of concern and, therefore, the internal validity will not be high. Interactive testing effects threaten the external validity of the findings.

Example **Internal Validity in Case Studies**	If there are several threats to internal validity even in a tightly controlled lab experiment, it should be quite clear why we cannot draw conclusions about causal relationships from case studies that describe the events that occurred during a particular time. Unless a well-designed experimental study, randomly assigning members to experimental and control groups, and successfully manipulating the treatment indicates possible causal relationships, it is impossible to say which factor causes another. For instance, there are several causes attributed to 'Slice', the soft drink introduced by PepsiCo Inc., not taking off after its initial success. Among the reasons given are: (1) a cutback in advertisements for Slice, (2) operating on the mistaken premise that the juice content in Slice would appeal to health-conscious buyers, (3) PepsiCo's attempts to milk the brand too quickly, (4) several strategic errors made by PepsiCo, (5) underestimation of the time taken to build a brand and the like. While all the above could provide the basis for developing a theoretical framework for explaining the variance in the sales of a product such as Slice, conclusions about cause-and-effect relationships cannot be determined from anecdotal events.

REVIEW OF FACTORS AFFECTING INTERNAL AND EXTERNAL VALIDITY

Whereas internal validity raises questions about whether it is the treatment alone or some additional extraneous factor that causes the effects, external validity raises issues about the generalizability of the findings to other settings.

Interactive testing and **selection effects** may restrict the external validity of our findings. These threats to external validity can be combated by creating experimental conditions that are as close as possible to the situations to which the results of the experiment are to be generalized.

At least seven contaminating factors exist that might affect the internal validity of experimental designs. These are the effects of history, maturation, (main) testing, instrumentation, selection, statistical regression and mortality. It is, however, possible to reduce these biases by enhancing the level of sophistication of the experimental design. Whereas some of the more sophisticated designs, discussed next, help to increase the internal validity of the experimental results, they also become expensive and time consuming.

The different types of experimental design and the extent to which internal and external validity are met in each are discussed next.

<table>
<tr><td>

Let us consider some of the commonly used experimental designs and determine the extent to which they guard against the seven factors that could contaminate the internal validity of experimental results. The shorter the time span of the experiments, the less the chances are of encountering history, maturation and mortality effects. Experiments lasting an hour or two do not usually meet with many of these problems. It is only when experiments are spread over an extended period of, say, several months, that the possibility of encountering more of the confounding factors increases.

</td><td>

TYPES OF EXPERIMENTAL DESIGN AND VALIDITY

</td></tr>
</table>

QUASI-EXPERIMENTAL DESIGNS

Some studies expose an experimental group to a treatment and measure its effects. Such an **experimental design** is the weakest of all designs, and it does not measure the true cause-and-effect relationship. This is so because there is no comparison between groups, nor any recording of the status of the dependent variable as it was prior to the experimental treatment and how it changed after the treatment. In the absence of such control, the study is of no scientific value in determining cause-and-effect relationships. Hence, such a design is referred to as a *quasi-experimental design*. The following three designs are quasi-experimental designs.

Pre-test and Post-test experimental group design

An **experimental group** (without a control group) may be given a pre-test, exposed to a treatment and then given a post-test to measure the effects of the treatment. This can be illustrated as in Table 11.2, where O refers to some process of observation or measurement, X represents the exposure of a group to an experimental treatment and the X and Os in the row are applied to the same specific group. Here, the effects of the treatment can be obtained by measuring the difference between the post-test and the pre-test $(O_2 - O_1)$. Note, however, that testing effects might contaminate both the internal (main testing effects) and external (interactive testing effects) validity of the findings. If the experiment is extended over a period of time, history, mortality and maturation effects may also confound the results.

Post-tests only with experimental and control groups

Some experimental designs are set up with an experimental and a control group, the former alone being exposed to a treatment and not the latter. The effects of the treatment are studied by assessing the difference in the outcomes – that is, the post-test scores of the experimental and control groups. This is illustrated in Table 11.3. Here is a case where the testing effects have been avoided because there is no pre-test, only a post-test. Care has to be taken, however, to make sure that the two groups are matched for all the possible contaminating **'nuisance' variables**. Otherwise, the true effects of the treatment cannot be determined by merely looking at the difference in the post-test scores of the two groups. Randomization would take care of this problem.

Table 11.2   Pre-test and Post-test experimental group design

Group	Pre-test score	Treatment	Post-test score
Experimental group	O_1	X	O_2
	Treatment effect = $(O_2 - O_1)$		

Table 11.3 Post-test only with experimental and control groups

Group	Treatment	Outcome
Experimental group	X	O_1
Control group		O_2
	Treatment effect = $(O_1 - O_2)$	

Mortality (the dropping out of individuals from groups) is a problem for all experimental designs, including this one. It can confound the results, and thus pose a threat to internal validity.

Time Series Design

A time series design (sometimes called an interrupted time series design) differs from the afore-mentioned designs in that it collects data on the same variable at regular intervals (for instance weeks, months or years). A time series design thus allows the researcher to assess the impact of a treatment over time. Figure 11.3 visually describes a time series design. It shows that a series of measurements on the dependent variable is taken before and after the treatment is administered (either by the researcher or naturally).

Figure 11.4 depicts the results of a time series experiment testing the effect of price reduction (in week 4) on sales. The horizontal scale (x-axis) is divided into weeks, and the vertical scale (y-axis) shows the values of sales (the dependent variable) as they fluctuate over a period of nine weeks. Assuming that other factors, such as the other marketing-mix variables and the marketing mix of competitors, stay the same, the impact of the price cut is the difference in sales before and after the change. From Figure 11.4 it is easy to see that there was an increase in sales after the price of the product went down. The question is, however, whether the increase in sales, depicted by the two horizontal lines in Figure 11.4, is significant. Bayesian moving average models (for instance, Box & Jenkins, 1970) are frequently used to test the impact of a treatment on the dependent variable when a time series design is used.

A key problem of time series is history: certain events or factors that have an impact on the independent variable–dependent variable relationship might unexpectedly occur while the experiment is in progress. Other problems are main and interactive testing effects, mortality and maturation.

FIGURE 11.3 Time series design

$$O_1 \quad O_2 \quad O_3 \quad O_4 \quad O_5 \quad X \quad O_6 \quad O_7 \quad O_8 \quad O_9 \quad O_{10}$$

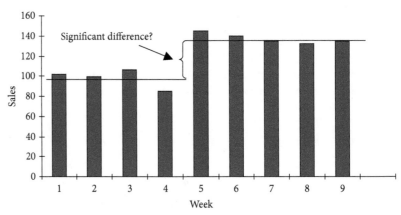

FIGURE 11.4 Effect of price cut in week 4

TRUE EXPERIMENTAL DESIGNS

Experimental designs that include both the treatment and control groups and record information both before and after the experimental group is exposed to the treatment are known as **ex post facto experimental designs**. These are discussed below.

Pre-test and Post-test Experimental and Control Group Design

This design can be visually depicted as in Table 11.4. Two groups – one experimental and the other control – are both exposed to the pre- and post-tests. The only difference between the two groups is that the former is exposed to a treatment whereas the latter is not. Measuring the difference between the differences in the post- and pre-test scores of the two groups gives the net effects of the treatment. Both groups have been exposed to both the pre- and post-tests, and both groups have been randomized; thus we can expect the history, maturation, main testing and instrumentation effects to have been controlled. This is so due to the fact that whatever happened with the experimental group (e.g. maturation, history, main testing and instrumentation) also happened with the control group, and in measuring the net effects (the difference in the differences between the pre- and post-test scores) we have controlled these contaminating factors. Through the process of randomization, we have also controlled the effects of selection bias and statistical regression.

Mortality could, again, pose a problem in this design. In experiments that take several weeks, as in the case of assessing the impact of training on skill development, or measuring the impact of technology advancement on effectiveness, some of the subjects in the experimental group may drop out before the end of the experiment. It is possible that those who drop out are in some way different from those who stay on until the end and take the post-test. If so, mortality could offer a plausible rival explanation for the difference between O_2 and O_1. Interactive testing effects could also cause a problem in this design; the fact that the participants in the experimental group are asked to do a pre-test could make them more sensitive to the manipulation.

Solomon Four-Group Design

To gain more confidence in internal validity in experimental designs, it is advisable to set up two experimental groups and two control groups for the experiment. One experimental group and one control group can be given both the pre- and post-tests, as shown in Table 11.5. The other two groups will be given only the post-test. Here, the effects of the treatment can be calculated in several different ways, as indicated below. To the extent that we come up with almost the same results in each of the different calculations, we can attribute the effects to the treatment. This

Table 11.4   Pre-test and Post-test Experimental and Control Groups

Group	Pre-test	Treatment	Post-test
Experimental group	O_1	X	O_2
Control group	O_3		O_4
	Treatment effect = $[(O_2 - O_1) - (O_4 - O_3)]$		

Table 11.5   Solomon Four-Group Design

Group	Pre-test	Treatment	Post-test
1. Experimental	O_1	X	O_2
2. Control	O_3		O_4
3. Experimental		X	O_5
4. Control			O_6

increases the internal validity of the results of the experimental design. This design, known as the **Solomon four-group design**, is perhaps the most comprehensive and the one with the least number of problems with internal validity.

Solomon four-group design and threats to validity The Solomon four-group design, also known as the four-group six-study design, is a highly sophisticated experimental design. This design controls for all the threats to internal validity, except for mortality (which is a problem for all experimental designs) and also for interactive testing effects. For this reason, the Solomon four-group design is very useful when interactive testing effects are expected.

Treatment effect (E) could be judged by:

$$E = (O_2 - O_1)$$
$$E = (O_2 - O_4)$$
$$E = (O_5 - O_6)$$
$$E = (O_5 - O_3)$$
$$E = \left[(O_2 - O_1) - (O_4 - O_3) \right]$$

If all Es are similar, the cause-and-effect relationship is highly valid.

To be able to calculate the effect of the experimental treatment, an estimate of the prior measurements is needed for Groups 3 and 4. The best estimate of this premeasure is the average of the two pre-tests; that is, $(O_1 + O_3)/2$. Together with the six pre- and post-test observations, the estimates of the premeasures can then be used to generate estimations of the impact of the experimental treatment (E), interactive testing effects (I) and the effects of uncontrolled variables (U). Estimates of these effects are made by comparing the before and after measures of the four groups.

The following equations provide an overview of the potential impact of the experimental treatment (E), interactive testing effects (I) and uncontrolled variables (U) for each group:

Group 1: $(O_2 - O_1) = E + I + U$
Group 2: $(O_4 - O_3) = U$
Group 3: $\left[O_5 - 1/2(O_1 + O_3) \right] = E + U$
Group 4: $\left[O_6 - 1/2(O_1 + O_3) \right] = U$

We can use these equations to estimate the effects of E, I and U by comparing the pre- and post-tests of the groups. For instance, to estimate the effect of the experimental stimulus (E) the results of Groups 3 and 4 are used:

$$\left[O_5 - \frac{1}{2}(O_1 + O_3) \right] - \left[O_6 - \frac{1}{2}(O_1 + O_3) \right] = \left[E + U \right] - U = E$$

To calculate the effect of I (the interactive testing effect), the results of Groups 1 and 3 are used:

$$(O_2 - O_1) - \left[O_5 - \frac{1}{2}(O_1 + O_3) \right] = (E + I + U) - (E + U) = I.$$

Thus, we are able to control for interactive testing effects that threaten the external validity of our findings. Let us now examine how the threats to internal validity are taken care of in the Solomon four-group design.

It is important to note that subjects should be randomly selected and randomly assigned to groups. This removes the statistical regression and selection biases. Group 2, the control group that was exposed to both the pre- and post-tests, helps us to see whether or not history, maturation, (main) testing, instrumentation or regression threatens internal validity. Mortality (the loss of participants during the course of the experiment) is a potential problem for all experimental designs, even for this one.

Thus, the Solomon four-group experimental design guarantees the maximum internal and external validity, ruling out many other rival hypotheses. Where establishing a cause-and-effect relationship is critical for the survival of businesses (e.g. pharmaceutical companies, which often face lawsuits for questionable products) the Solomon four-group design is eminently useful. However, because of the number of subjects that need to be recruited, the care with which the study has to be designed, the time that needs to be devoted to the experiment, and other reasons, the cost of conducting such an experiment is high. For this reason it is rarely used.

Table 11.6 summarizes the threats to validity covered by the different experimental designs. If the subjects have all been randomly assigned to the groups, then selection bias and statistical regression are eliminated in all cases.

Double-Blind Studies

When extreme care and rigor are needed in experimental designs, as in the case of discovery of new medicines that could have an impact on human lives, blind studies are conducted to avoid any bias that might creep in. For example, pharmaceutical companies experimenting with the efficacy of newly developed drugs in the prototype stage ensure that the subjects in the experimental and control groups are kept unaware of who is given the drug, and who the placebo. Such studies are called blind studies.

When Aviron tested and announced the Flu-mist vaccine, neither the subjects nor the researchers who administered the vaccine to them were aware of the 'true' versus the 'placebo' treatment. The entire process was conducted by an outside testing agency, which alone knew who got what treatment. Since, in this case, both the experimenter and the subjects are blinded, such studies are called **double-blind studies**. Since there is no tampering with the treatment in any way, such experimental studies are the least biased.

As mentioned previously, managers rarely undertake the study of cause-and-effect relationships in organizations using experimental designs because of the inconvenience and disruption they cause to the system.

EX POST FACTO DESIGNS

Cause-and-effect relationships are sometimes established through what is called the **ex post facto experimental design**. Here, there is no manipulation of the independent variable in the lab or field setting, but subjects who have already been exposed to a stimulus and those not so

Table 11.6   Major threats to validity in different experimental designs when members are randomly selected and assigned

Types of experimental design	Major threats to validity
1. Pre- and post-tests with one experimental group only	History, maturation, main testing, interactive testing, mortality
2. Pre- and post-tests with one experimental and one control group	Interactive testing, mortality
3. Post-tests only with one experimental and one control group	Mortality
4. Solomon four-group design	Mortality

exposed are studied. For instance, training programs might have been introduced in an organization two years earlier. Some might have already gone through the training while others might not. To study the effects of training on work performance, performance data might now be collected for both groups. Since the study does not immediately follow after the training, but much later, it is an ex post facto design.

More advanced experimental designs such as the completely randomized design, randomized block design, Latin square design and the factorial design are described in the appendix to this chapter, for those students interested in these.

| SIMULATION | An alternative to lab and field experimentation currently being used in business research is simulation. Simulations are aimed at carrying over real-world phenomena into a more controlled environment. A **simulation** can be thought of as an experiment conducted in a specially created setting that very closely represents the natural environment in which activities are usually carried out. |

Although some experiments in which one variable or a few variables are manipulated are sometimes seen as simulations, the more prevalent usage aims to capture 'the bigger picture' (the real world), which is likely to involve many variables. That is why simulations are frequently used by system thinkers. System thinking is a holistic approach to analysis that focuses on the way that a system's constituent parts inter-relate and how systems (such as organizational systems) work over time. A system is a cohesive conglomeration of inter-related an inter-dependent elements or components that is either natural (for instance, an ecosystem) or man-made (e.g. an organization or an industry). Simulations of complex real-world systems imitate the processes of a system to see how it works. Like this, it helps researchers and managers to study the effects of specific interventions on an entire system (instead of on one specific variable) and hence to assess their effects on the real world.

Simulations are also frequently used in the accounting and finance areas. For example, the effectiveness of various analytic review procedures in detecting errors in account balances has been tested through simulations (Knechel, 1986). In the finance area, risk management has been studied through simulations. Simulations have also been used to understand the complex relationships in the financing of pension plans and making important investment decisions (Perrier & Kalwarski, 1989). It is possible to vary several variables (workforce demographics, inflation rates, etc.) singly or simultaneously in such models.

Prototypes of machines and instruments are often the result of simulated models. Simulation has also been used by many companies to test the robustness and efficacy of various products. We are also familiar with flight simulators, driving simulators and even nuclear reactor simulators. Here, the visual patterns presented keep changing in response to the reactions of the individual (the pilot, the driver or the emergency handler) to the previous stimulus presented, and not in any predetermined order. Entire business operations, from office layout to profitability, can be simulated using different prospective scenarios.

| ETHICAL ISSUES IN EXPERIMEN-TAL DESIGN RESEARCH | It is appropriate at this juncture to briefly discuss a few of the many ethical issues involved in doing research, some of which are particularly relevant to conducting lab experiments. The following practices are considered unethical: |

- Putting pressure on individuals to participate in experiments through coercion, or applying social pressure.
- Giving menial tasks and asking demeaning questions that diminish participants' self-respect.
- Deceiving subjects by deliberately misleading them as to the true purpose of the research.
- Exposing participants to physical or mental stress.

- Not allowing subjects to withdraw from the research when they want to.
- Using the research results to disadvantage the participants, or for purposes not to their liking.
- Not explaining the procedures to be followed in the experiment.
- Exposing respondents to hazardous and unsafe environments.
- Not debriefing participants fully and accurately after the experiment is over.
- Not preserving the privacy and confidentiality of the information given by the participants.
- Withholding benefits from control groups.

The last item is somewhat controversial in terms of whether or not it should be an ethical dilemma, especially in organizational research. If three different incentives are offered for three experimental groups and none is offered to the control group, it is a fact that the control group has participated in the experiment with absolutely no benefit. Similarly, if four different experimental groups receive four different levels of training but the control group does not, the other four groups have gained expertise that the control group has been denied. But should this be deemed an ethical dilemma preventing experimental designs with control groups in organizational research? Perhaps not, for at least three reasons. One is that several others in the system who did not participate in the experiment did not benefit either. Second, even in the experimental groups, some would have benefited more than others (depending on the extent to which the causal factor was manipulated). Finally, if a cause-and-effect relationship is found, the system will, in all probability, implement the new-found knowledge sooner or later and everyone will ultimately stand to gain. The assumption that the control group did not benefit from participating in the experiment may not be a sufficient reason not to use lab or field experiments.

Many universities have a 'human subjects committee' to protect the right of individuals participating in any type of research activity involving people. The basic function of these committees is to discharge the moral and ethical responsibilities of the university system by studying the procedures outlined in the research proposals and giving their stamp of approval to the study. The human subjects committee might require the investigators to modify their procedures or inform the subjects fully, if occasion demands it.

Before using experimental designs in research studies, it is essential to consider whether they are necessary at all, and if so, at what level of sophistication. This is because experimental designs call for special efforts and varying degrees of interference with the natural flow of activities. Some questions that need to be addressed in making these decisions are the following:

MANAGERIAL IMPLICATIONS

1. Is it really necessary to identify causal relationships, or would it suffice if the correlates that account for the variance in the dependent variable were known?

2. If it is important to trace the causal relationships, which of the two, internal validity or external validity, is needed more, or are both needed? If only internal validity is important, a carefully designed lab experiment is the answer; if generalizability is the more important criterion, then a field experiment is called for; if both are equally important, then a lab study should be first undertaken, followed by a field experiment (if the results of the former warrant the latter).

3. Is cost an important factor in the study? If so, would a less rather than a more sophisticated experimental design do?

These decision points are illustrated in Figure 11.5.

Though some managers may not be interested in cause-and-effect relationships, a good knowledge of experimental designs could foster some pilot studies to be undertaken to examine whether factors such as bonus systems, piece rates, rest pauses and so on lead to positive

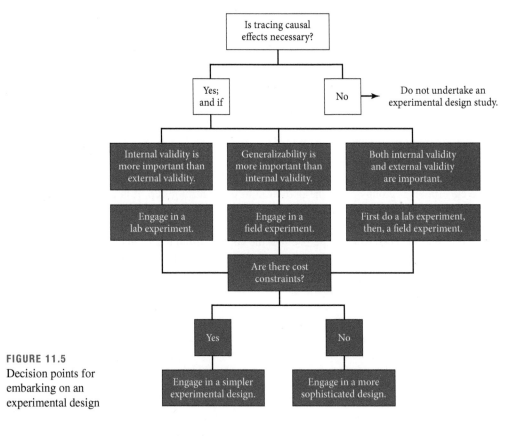

FIGURE 11.5
Decision points for embarking on an experimental design

outcomes such as better motivation, improved job performance and other favourable working conditions at the workplace. Marketing managers could use experimental designs to study the effects on sales of advertisements, sales promotions, pricing and the like. Awareness of the usefulness of simulation as a research tool can also result in creative research endeavours in the management area, as it currently does in the manufacturing side of businesses.

SUMMARY

- **Learning objective 1: Describe lab experiments and discuss the internal and external validity of this type of experiment.** When control and manipulation are introduced to establish cause-and-effect relationships in an artificial setting, we have lab experiments. The goal of the researcher is to keep every variable constant except for the independent variable. Manipulation means that we create different levels of the independent variable to assess the impact on the dependent variable. One way of controlling for contaminating variables is to match the various groups in an experiment. Another way of controlling the contaminating variables is to assign participants randomly to groups. In lab experiments internal validity can be said to be high. On the other hand, the external validity of lab experiments is typically low.

- **Learning objective 2: Describe field experiments and discuss the internal and external validity of this type of experiment.** A field experiment is an experiment done in the natural environment. In the field experiment, it is not possible to control all the nuisance variables. The treatment however can still be manipulated. Control groups can also be set up in field experiments. Cause-and-effect relationships found under these conditions will have a wider generalizability to other similar settings (the external validity is typically high; the internal validity of field experiments is low).

- **Learning objective 3: Describe, discuss and identify threats to internal and external validity and make a trade-off between internal and external validity.** External validity refers to the extent of generalizability of the results of a causal study to other settings. Internal validity refers to the degree of our confidence in the causal effects. Field experiments have more external validity, but less internal validity.

In lab experiments, the internal validity is high but the external validity is low. There is thus a trade-off between internal validity and external validity. Even the best designed lab studies may be influenced by factors affecting the internal validity. The seven major threats to internal validity are the effects of history, maturation, (main) testing, selection, mortality, statistical regression and instrumentation. Two threats to external validity are (interactive) testing and selection.

- **Learning objective 4: Describe the different types of experimental designs.** A quasi-experimental design is the weakest of all designs, and it does not measure the true cause-and-effect relationship. Pre- and post-test experimental group designs, post-tests only with experimental and control groups and time series designs are examples of quasi-experimental designs. True experimental designs that include both treatment and control groups and record information both before and after the experimental group is exposed to the treatment are known as ex post facto experimental designs. Pre- and post-test experimental and control group designs, Solomon four-group designs, and double blind studies are examples of true experimental designs. In ex post facto experimental design, there is no manipulation of the independent variable in the lab or field setting, but subjects who have already been exposed to a stimulus and those not so exposed are studied.

- **Learning objective 5: Discuss when and why simulation might be a good alternative to lab and field experiments.** An alternative to lab and field experimentation, simulation uses a model-building technique to determine the effects of changes.

- **Learning objective 6: Discuss the role of the manager in experimental designs.** Knowledge of experimental designs may help the manager to (engage a consultant to) establish cause-and-effect relationships. Through the analysis of the cause-and effect relationships, it is possible to find answers or solutions to a problem. Experiments may help managers to examine whether bonus systems lead to more motivation, whether piece rates lead to higher productivity or whether price cuts lead to more sales.

- **Learning objective 7: Discuss the role of ethics in experimental designs.** Ethics in experiments refers to the correct rules of conduct necessary when carrying out experimental research. Researchers have a duty to respect the rights and dignity of research participants. This means that they should take certain rules of conduct into account.

Instructors can visit the companion website at **www.wiley.com/go/bougie/researchmethods forbusiness8e** for **Case Study: The moderating effect of involvement in product placement effectiveness**.

DISCUSSION QUESTIONS

1. What are the differences between causal and correlational studies?

2. In what ways do lab experiments differ from field experiments?

3. Define the terms control and manipulation. Describe a possible lab experiment where you would need to control a variable. Include also a variable over which you would have no control but which could affect your experiment.

4. Explain the possible ways in which you can control 'nuisance' variables.

5. What is internal validity and what are the threats it stands exposed to?

6. Explain the concept of 'trade-off between internal validity and external validity'.

7. Explain how the selection of participants may affect both the internal and external validity of your experiments.

8. Explain the difference between main and interactive testing effects. Why is this difference important?

9. History is a key problem in a time series design. Other problems are main and interactive testing effects, mortality and maturation. Explain.

10. Explain why mortality remains a problem even when a Solomon four-group design is used.

11. 'If a control group is a part of an experimental design, one need not worry about controlling other exogenous variables'. Discuss this statement.

12. 'The Solomon four-group design is the answer to all our research questions pertaining to cause-and-effect relationships because it guards against all the threats to internal validity'. Comment.

13. Below is an adapted note from *BusinessWeek* published some time ago. After reading it, apply what you have learned in this chapter, and design a study after sketching the theoretical framework.

The vital role of self-esteem

Why do some people earn more than others? Economists focused on the importance of education, basic skills and work experience – what they called human capital – on increased productivity, and said these were reflected in greater earning power. Researchers also found that self-esteem was instrumental in acquiring human capital.

14. Design a study to examine the following situation:

An organization would like to introduce one of two types of new manufacturing process to increase the productivity of workers, and both involve heavy investment in expensive technology. The company wants to test the efficacy of each process in one of its small plants.

Further Experimental Designs

In this chapter, we discussed different types of experimental design where groups were subjected to one or more treatments and the effects of the manipulation measured. However, we may sometimes wish to assess the simultaneous effects of two or more variables on a dependent variable, and this calls for more complex designs. Among the many advanced experimental designs available, we will examine here the completely randomized design, the randomized block design, the Latin square design and the factorial design.

It would be useful to understand some terms before describing the various designs. The term 'factor' is used to denote an independent variable – for example, price. The term 'level' is used to denote various gradations of the factor – for example, high price, medium price and low price – while making it clear as to what these gradations signify (e.g. high price is anything over \$2 per piece; medium is \$1–2 per piece; low price is anything less than \$1 per piece). 'Treatment' refers to the various levels of the factors. A 'blocking factor' is a preexisting variable in a given situation that might have an effect on the dependent variable in addition to the treatment, the impact of which is important to assess. In effect, a blocking factor is an independent variable that has an effect on the dependent variable, but which pre-exists in a given situation: for example, the number of women and men in an organization; or teenagers, middle-aged men and senior citizens as customers of a store; and so on.

THE COMPLETELY RANDOMIZED DESIGN

Let us say that a bus transportation company manager wants to know the effects of fare reduction by 5, 7 and 10 cents on the average daily increase in the number of passengers using the bus as a means of transportation. He may take 27 routes that the buses usually ply, and randomly assign nine routes for each of the treatments (i.e. reduction of fares by 5, 7 and 10 cents) for a two-week period. His experimental design is shown in Table 11.7, where the Os on the left indicate the number of passengers that used the bus for the two weeks preceding the treatment; X_1, X_2 and X_3 indicate the three different treatments (fare reductions of 5, 7 and 10 cents per mile), and the Os on the right indicate the number of passengers that used the bus as a transportation mode during the two weeks when the fares were reduced. The manager will be able to assess the impact of the three treatments by deducting each of the three Os on the left from its corresponding O on the right. The results of this study will provide the answer to the bus company manager's question.

Table 11.7 Illustration of a Completely Randomized Design

Routes	Number of passengers before	Treatment	Number of passengers after
Group 1 of nine routes	O_1	X_1	O_2
Group 2 of nine routes	O_3	X_2	O_4
Group 3 of nine routes	O_5	X_3	O_6

RANDOMIZED BLOCK DESIGN

In the foregoing case, the bus company manager was interested only in the effects of different levels of price reduction on the increase in the number of passengers in general. He may be more interested, however, in targeting the price reduction on the right routes or sectors. For example, it is likely that the reduction in fares will be more welcome to senior citizens and residents of crowded urban areas where driving is stressful, than to car owners living in the suburbs, who may not be equally appreciative of and sensitive to price reduction. Thus, reductions in fares will probably attract more passengers if targeted at the right groups (i.e. the right blocking factor – the residential areas). In this case, the bus company manager should first identify the routes that fall into the three blocks – those in suburbs, crowded urban areas or residential areas with retirees. Thus, the 27 routes will get assigned to one or other of three blocks and will then be randomly assigned, within the blocks, to the three treatments. The experimental design is shown in Table 11.8.

Through the above randomized block design, not only can the direct effect of each treatment (i.e. the main effect of the level, which is the effect of each type of fare reduction) be assessed, but also the joint effects of price and the residential area route (the interaction effect). For example, the general effect of a 5 cent reduction for all routes will be known by the increase in passengers across all three residential areas, and the general effect of a 5 cent reduction on those in the suburbs alone will also be known by seeing the effects in the first cell. If the highest average daily number of increased passengers is 75 for a 7 cent decrease for the crowded urban area route, followed by an increase of 30 for the retirees' areas for the 10 cent decrease and an increase of five passengers for a 5 cent reduction for the suburbs, the bus company manager can work out a cost–benefit analysis and decide on the course of action to be taken. Thus, the randomized block design is a more powerful technique, providing more information for decision-making. However, the cost of this experimental design will be higher.

LATIN SQUARE DESIGN

Whereas the randomized block design helps the experimenter to minimize the effects of one nuisance variable (variation among the rows) in evaluating the treatment effects, the Latin square design is very useful when two nuisance blocking factors (i.e. variations across both the rows and the columns) are to be controlled. Each treatment appears an equal number of times in any one ordinal position in each row. For instance, in studying the effects of bus fare reduction on passengers, two nuisance factors could be: (1) the day of the week, (a) midweek (Tuesday through Thursday), (b) weekend, (c) Monday and Friday; and (2) the (three) residential localities of the passengers. A three by three Latin square design can be created in this case, to which will be randomly assigned the three treatments (5, 7 and 10 cent fare reductions), such that each treatment occurs only once in each row and column intersection. The Latin square design is shown in Table 11.9. After the experiment is carried out and the net increase in passengers under each treatment calculated, the average treatment effects can be gauged. The price reduction that offers the best advantage can also be assessed.

Table 11.8   Illustration of a Randomized Block Design

Fare reduction	Blocking factor: residential areas		
	Suburbs	Crowded urban areas	Retirement areas
5c	X_1	X_1	X_1
7c	X_2	X_2	X_2
10c	X_3	X_3	X_3

Note that the Xs only indicate various levels of the blocking factor and the Os (the number of passengers before and after each treatment at each level) are not shown, though these measures will be taken.

Table 11.9   Illustration of the Latin Square Design

Residential area	Day of the week		
	Midweek	Weekend	Monday/Friday
Suburbs	X_1	X_2	X_3
Urban	X_2	X_3	X_1
Retirement	X_3	X_1	X_2

Table 11.10   Illustration of a 3 × 3 Factorial Design

Type of bus	Bus fare reduction rates		
	5c	7c	10c
Luxury Express	X_1Y_1	X_2Y_1	X_3Y_1
Standard Express	X_2Y_2	X_1Y_2	X_3Y_2
Regular	X_3Y_3	X_2Y_3	X_1Y_3

A problem with the Latin square design is that it presupposes the absence of interaction between the treatments and blocking factors, which may not always be the case. We also need as many cells as there are treatments. Furthermore, it is an uneconomical design compared to some others.

FACTORIAL DESIGN

Thus far we have discussed experimental designs in the context of examining a cause-and-effect relationship between one independent variable and the dependent variable. The factorial design enables us to test the effects of two or more manipulations at the same time on the dependent variable. In other words, two treatments can be simultaneously manipulated and their single and joint (known as main and interaction) effects assessed. For example, the manager of the bus company might be interested in knowing passenger increases if he used three different types of buses (Luxury Express, Standard Express and Regular) and manipulated both the fare reduction and the type of vehicle used, simultaneously. Table 11.10 illustrates the 3 × 3 factorial design that would be used for the purpose.

Here, two factors are used with three levels in each. The above is completely randomized, since the fares are randomly assigned to one of nine treatment combinations. A wealth of information can be obtained from this design. For example, the bus company manager will know the increase in passengers for each fare reduction, for each type of vehicle, and for the two in combination. Thus, the main effects of the two independent variables, as well as the interactions among them, can be assessed. For this reason, the factorial design is more efficient than several single-factor randomized designs.

It is also statistically possible to control one or more variables through covariance analysis. For example, it may be suspected that even after randomly assigning members to treatments, there is a further 'nuisance' factor. It is possible to statistically block such factors while analysing the data.

Several other complex experimental designs are also available and are treated in books devoted to experimental designs.

Measurement of Variables: Operational Definition

After completing Chapter 12, you should be able to:

1. Explain how variables are measured.

2. Explain when operationalization of variables is necessary.

3. Operationally define (or operationalize) abstract and subjective variables.

INTRODUCTION

Measurement of variables is an integral part of research and an important aspect of research design (see shaded portion in Figure 12.1). Unless the variables are measured in some way, we will not be able to find answers to our research questions. Kaplan (1964) suggested three types of things that can be measured. First, a *direct observable* is some kind of physical phenomenon or feature that can be observed directly, such as the number of people present at a particular place or event. Second, somebody's response to a questionnaire item about the number of people working in an organization is an *indirect observable*; that is, an indirect representation of a characteristic or object. Third, a *construct* is a creation based on observation, but it cannot be observed either directly or indirectly. Examples of constructs are customer satisfaction, job involvement and price consciousness. Although one may able to observe the consequences of customer satisfaction (e.g. positive word-of-mouth communication and customer loyalty) and the antecedents of satisfaction (e.g. employee responsiveness), one cannot observe customer satisfaction itself. The process of translating abstract and subjective constructs into concrete measures is called operationalization. In this process, one needs to make a number of important decisions on how to translate the abstract and subjective construct into a measure. These decisions are discussed in some detail in the next two chapters. In this chapter, will focus on conceptually and operationally defining a construct. Chapter 13 will focus on scaling, reliability and validity.

HOW VARIABLES ARE MEASURED

To assess how satisfied consumers are with our services, to understand how risk-averse day-traders are or to test the hypothesis that workforce diversity affects organizational effectiveness we have to measure. *Measurement* is the assignment of numbers or other symbols to characteristics (or attributes) of objects according to a prespecified set of rules. *Objects* include persons, strategic business units, companies, countries, bicycles, elephants, kitchen appliances, restaurants, shampoo, yogurt and so on. Examples of *characteristics* of objects are arousal-seeking tendency, achievement motivation, organizational effectiveness, shopping enjoyment, length, weight, ethnic diversity, service quality, conditioning effects and taste. It is important that you realize that you cannot measure objects (for instance, a company); you measure characteristics or attributes of objects (for instance, the organizational effectiveness of a company). In a similar fashion, you can measure the length (the attribute) of a person (the object), the weight of an elephant, the arousal-seeking tendency of stockbrokers, the shopping enjoyment of men, the service quality of a restaurant, the conditioning effects of a shampoo and the taste of a certain brand of yogurt. To be able to measure, you need an object and attributes of the object, but you also need a judge. A *judge* is someone who has the necessary knowledge and skills to assess 'the quality' of something, such as the taste of

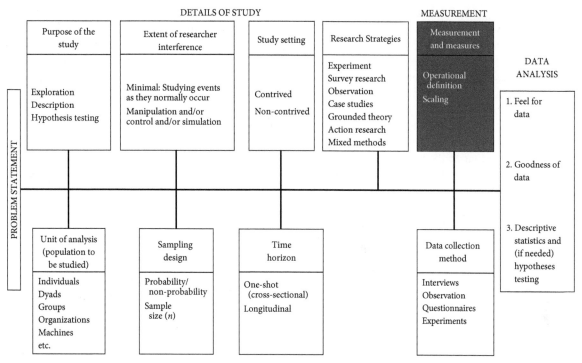

FIGURE 12.1   Research design and where this chapter fits in

yogurt, the arousal-seeking tendency of stockbrokers or the communication skills of students. In many cases, the object and the judge are the same person. For instance, if you want to measure the gender (the attribute) of your employees (the objects), or the shopping enjoyment (the attribute) of men (the objects), you can simply ask the objects (employees and men respectively) to provide you with the necessary details via a self-administered questionnaire. However, it is unlikely that the object has the necessary knowledge and skills to act as a judge when you want to measure the taste (the attribute) of yogurt (the object), the service quality of a restaurant, the communication skills of students or even the managerial expertise of supervisors. In cases like these, the selection of an adequate judge can be rather tricky.

Now do Exercise 12.1.

Identify the object and the attribute. Give your informed opinion about who would be an adequate judge.

a. Price consciousness of car buyers.
b. Self-esteem of dyslexic children.
c. Organizational commitment of school teachers.
d. Marketing orientation of companies.
e. Product quality of mobile phones.

EXERCISE 12.1

Attributes of objects that can be physically measured (direct and indirect observables) by some calibrated instruments pose no measurement problems. For example, the length and width of a rectangular office table can be easily measured with a measuring tape or a ruler. The same is true for measuring the office floor area and for measuring the weight of an elephant (at least to some extent). Data representing several demographic characteristics of office personnel are also easily obtained by asking employees simple, straightforward questions, such as: '*How long have you been working in this organization?*' or '*What is your marital status?*'

The measurement of more abstract and subjective attributes (so-called constructs) is more difficult, however. For instance, it is relatively difficult to measure the level of *achievement motivation* of office clerks, the *shopping enjoyment* of women or the *need for cognition* of students. Likewise, it is not straightforward to test hypotheses on the relationship between workforce diversity, managerial expertise and organizational effectiveness. The problem is that we cannot simply ask questions like *'How diverse is your company's workforce?'* or *'How effective is your organization?'* because of the abstract nature of the variables 'workforce diversity' and 'organizational effectiveness'. Of course, there are solutions to this problem. One of these solutions is discussed next. But let us, before we discuss the solution, summarize the problem.

Certain variables lend themselves to easy measurement through the use of appropriate measuring instruments; for example, physiological phenomena pertaining to human beings, such as blood pressure, pulse rates and body temperature, as well as certain physical attributes such as length and weight. But when we get into the realm of people's subjective feelings, attitudes and perceptions, measurement becomes more difficult because we cannot observe these constructs, either directly or indirectly.

OPERATIONAL DEFINITION (OPERATIONAL-IZATION)

Despite the lack of physical measuring devices to measure the more nebulous constructs, there are ways of tapping these types of variables. One technique is to reduce these constructs to observable behaviour and/or characteristics. In other words, the abstract notions are broken down into observable behaviour or characteristics. For instance, *thirst* is abstract; we cannot observe it. However, we would expect a thirsty person to drink plenty of fluids. In other words, the expected reaction of people to thirst is to drink fluids. If several people say they are thirsty, then we may determine the thirst levels of each of these individuals by the measure of the quantity of fluids that they drink to quench their thirst. We will thus be able to measure their levels of thirst, even though thirst itself is abstract and nebulous. Reduction of abstract concepts to render them measurable in a tangible way is called **operationalization**.

Researchers define abstract and subjective constructs both conceptually and operationally. A conceptual definition tells you what a concept means, an operational definition how it is measured. For instance, a conceptual definition of thirst is 'a sensation of dryness in the mouth and throat, usually associated with a desire for fluids', whereas an operational definition might relate to 'the quantity of fluids that a person drinks'. Operationalizing or operationally defining a construct involves a series of steps.

1. Provide a conceptual definition of the construct.

2. Develop a pool of items that appear to be related or important to the construct. This can be done by reading the literature, talking to experts, brainstorming and pilot studies.

3. Decide on a response format. Very often five-point Likert-scales with end-points labelled 'strongly disagree' and 'strongly agree' are used.

4. Collect data from a representative sample from the population.

5. Select items for your scale using 'item-analysis'. Item analysis is carried out to see if the items in the instrument belong there or not. Each item is examined for its ability to discriminate between those subjects whose total scores are high and those with low scores. Each item is subjected to a test with regard to its discriminative power; the ability to discriminate between the responses of the upper quartile (25%) of respondents, and the responses of the lower quartile. Items with a high discriminative power are then included in the instrument.

6. Test the reliability and validity of the instrument.

We have just reduced the abstract construct *thirst* into observable behaviour by measuring the quantity of fluids people drink to quench their thirst. In a similar way, other abstract constructs such as need for cognition (conceptually defined as the tendency to engage in and enjoy thinking (Cacioppo & Petty, 1982)) can be reduced to observable behaviour and/or characteristics in a similar way. For instance, we would expect individuals with a high need for cognition to prefer complex to simple problems, to find satisfaction in deliberating hard and for long hours and to enjoy tasks that involve coming up with new solutions to problems (examples taken from Cacioppo & Petty, 1982). We may thus identify differences between individuals in need of cognition by measuring to what extent people prefer complex to simple problems, find satisfaction in deliberating hard and for long hours and enjoy tasks that involve coming up with new solutions to problems.

In 1982, Cacioppo and Petty reported four studies to develop and validate a measurement scale to assess need for cognition. In a first study, a pool of 45 items that appeared relevant to need for cognition was generated (based on prior research) and administered to groups 'known to differ in need for cognition'. The results of this study revealed that the 45 items exhibited a high degree of interrelatedness and thus suggested that need for cognition is a *unidimensional* construct (i.e. it does not have more than one main component or dimension; we will come back to this issue further on in this chapter). This finding was replicated in a second study. Two further studies (studies three and four) were carried out to validate the findings of the first two studies. The outcome of this validation process was a valid and reliable need for cognition measure containing 34 items, such as 'I would prefer complex to simple problems', 'I find satisfaction in deliberating hard and for long hours', and 'I really enjoy tasks that involve coming up with new solutions to problems'.

> **Example**
>
> **Operationalizing the construct 'need for cognition'**

Now do Exercise 12.2.

> **EXERCISE 12.2**

a. Either read the paper by Cacioppo and Petty (1982) or read the paper 'An Expanded Conceptualization and a New Measure of Compulsive Buying' by Ridgway, Kukar-Kinney & Monroe (2008) and describe how the authors generated the pool of scale items that appeared relevant to the construct that they were operatioinalizing.

b. Why can't we simply ask to what extent a person has a tendency to engage in and enjoy thinking or to what extent somebody finds him- or herself a compulsive buyer?

c. Why do we need more than one item to measure such constructs?

OPERATIONALIZATION: DIMENSIONS AND ELEMENTS

The examples of thirst and need for cognition illustrate how abstract constructs are operationalized by using observable and measurable elements, such as the amount of drinks people use to quench their thirst, and the extent to which people prefer complex to simple problems. You may have noticed that whereas only one item is needed to measure thirst ('*how many drinks did you use to quench your thirst?*'), 34 items are needed to measure need for cognition. These 34 items are needed because if we used fewer than these 34 items, our measurement scale would probably not represent the entire domain or universe of need for cognition; in other words, our measure would probably not include an adequate and representative set of items (or *elements*). As a consequence, our measure would not be valid. A valid measure of need for cognition thus contains 34 items (at least according to Cacioppo and Petty) even though need for cognition is a *unidimensional* construct.

Whereas some constructs are *unidimensional*, others are not. They have more than one dimension. An example of a construct with more than one dimension is aggression. Aggression has at least two *dimensions*: verbal aggression and physical aggression. That is, aggression might include behaviour such as shouting and swearing at a person (verbal aggression), but also throwing objects, hitting a wall and physically hurting others (physical aggression). A valid measurement scale of aggression would have to include items that measure verbal aggression and items that measure physical aggression. A measurement scale that would only include items measuring physical aggression would not be valid if our aim were to measure aggression. Likewise, a scale that would only include items measuring verbal aggression would also not be a valid measure of aggression. Thus, a valid measurement scale includes quantitatively measurable questions or items (or elements) that adequately represent the entire domain or universe of the construct; if the construct has more than one domain or dimension, we have to make sure that questions that adequately represent these domains or dimensions are included in our measure.

Now do Exercise 12.3.

EXERCISE 12.3	Try to come up with two unidimensional and two multidimensional abstract constructs. Explain why these constructs have either one or more than one dimension.

OPERATIONALIZING THE (MULTIDIMENSIONAL) CONSTRUCT OF ACHIEVEMENT MOTIVATION

Suppose that we are interested in establishing a relationship between gender and achievement motivation. To test this relationship, we will have to measure both gender and achievement motivation. At this point, you will probably understand that whereas measuring gender will not cause any problems, measuring achievement motivation probably will, because the latter construct is abstract and subjective in nature. For this reason we must infer achievement motivation by measuring behavioural facets or characteristics we would expect to find in people with high achievement motivation. Indeed, without measuring these facets or characteristics, we will not be able to arrive at bottom-line statements about the relationship between gender and achievement motivation.

After we have conceptually defined the construct, the next step in the process of measuring abstract constructs such as achievement motivation is to go through the literature to find out whether there are any existing measures of the construct. Both scientific journals and 'scale handbooks' are important sources of existing measures. As a rule, empirical articles published in academic journals provide a detailed description of how specific constructs were measured; information is often provided on what measures were used, when and how these measures were developed, by whom and for how long they have been in use. Scale handbooks are also a useful source of existing measurement scales. Scale handbooks, such as the *Marketing Scales Handbook* or the *Handbook of Organizational Measurement*, provide an exhaustive overview of measurement scales that have appeared in the academic literature. The use of existing measurement scales has several advantages. First, it saves you a lot of time and energy. Second, it allows you to verify the findings of others and to build on the work of others (this is very important in scientific research but impossible if you use measures that differ from those that our predecessors have used!). Hence, if you want to measure something, see if it has been measured before and then use this measure (if it adequately represents your conceptual definition of the construct; adapt it to your specific needs whenever this is needed). Make sure that you document the use of existing measurement scales properly.

Example	*Measures*
Documenting the use of existing measurement scales	*Independent Variables.* To check whether the respondents consider the humor appeal advertisement as amusing and the shock appeal advertisement as shocking, two items on a 7-point scale (amusing/not amusing and shocking/not shocking) were adapted from Soscia et al. (2012).
	Dependent Measures
	Recall. A question adapted from Unnava and Burnkrant (1991) asked the subjects to write down all the social advertisements (and their messages) that they remember seeing.

Moderating variable

To assess the role of the moderating variable on the response of the respondents, perceptions of tabooness were assessed on a 7-point scale (1 = strongly disagree, 7 = strongly agree), where respondents were asked to indicate the extent to which they agreed with the following two statements adapted from Sabri and Obermiller (2012).

1. In my opinion, the topic that is addressed in this advertisement is socially acceptable.

2. It is difficult for me to talk about the topic that is addressed in this advertisement.

There are several measures of achievement motivation available from the literature. But what if there were no existing measures available? In such a case, we would have to develop a measure ourselves; the need for cognition example illustrates how difficult our task would be in such cases.

BOX 12.1   THE POSITIVIST VIEW

You will recall that we earlier pointed out that *business research* cannot be 100% scientific because we often do not have the 'perfect' measuring instruments. That is why, for a positivist, the purpose of science is to stick to what we can observe (and hence, what we can measure). Knowledge of anything beyond that is impossible. Since we cannot directly observe achievement motivation, job satisfaction and service quality, these are not appropriate topics for a scientific study.

Box 12.1 provides the (somewhat exaggerated) viewpoint of the positivist on the measurement of abstract and subjective variables. A pragmatist or a critical realist, operationalizing the construct, nevertheless, is the best way to measure it. Even though it is going to be difficult to develop an adequate measure, they will at least give it a try.

WHAT OPERATIONALIZATION IS NOT

Just as it is important to understand what operationalization is, it is equally important to remember what it is not. An operationalization does not describe the correlates of the concept. For example, success in performance cannot be a dimension of achievement motivation, even though a motivated person is likely to meet with it in large measure. Thus, achievement motivation and performance and/or success may be highly correlated, but we cannot measure an individual's level of motivation through success and performance. Performance and success may have been made possible as a consequence of achievement motivation, but in and of themselves, the two are not measures of it. To elaborate, a person with high achievement motivation might have failed for some reason, perhaps beyond her control, to perform the job successfully. Thus, if we judge the achievement motivation of this person with performance as the yardstick, we will have measured the wrong construct. Instead of measuring achievement motivation – our variable of interest – we will have measured performance, another variable we did not intend to measure nor were interested in.

Thus, it is clear that operationalizing a construct does not consist of delineating the reasons, antecedents, consequences or correlates of the construct. Rather, it describes its observable characteristics in order to be able to measure the construct. It is important to remember this because if we either operationalize the constructs incorrectly or confuse them with other constructs, then we will not have valid measures. This means that we will not have 'good' data, and when we do not have good data, we cannot draw valid conclusions.

REVIEW OF OPERATIONALIZATION

We have thus far examined how to operationally define constructs. Operationalizations are necessary to measure abstract and subjective constructs such as feelings and attitudes. More objective variables such as age or educational level are easily measured through simple, straightforward questions and do not have to be operationalized. We have pointed out that operationalization starts with a conceptual definition of the construct. The next step is to either find or develop an adequate (set of) closed-end question(s) that allow(s) you to measure the construct in a reliable and valid way. Luckily, measures for many constructs that are relevant in business research have already been developed by researchers. While you review the literature in a given area, you might want to particularly note the reference that discusses the instrument used to tap the construct in the study, and read it. The article will tell you when the measure was developed, by whom and for how long it has been in use. If you cannot find or use an existing measure, you have to develop your own measure. To do this, you can follow a process that includes 6 steps: (1) define the construct conceptually, (2) develop a pool of items that are important to the construct, (3) decide on a response format, (4) Collect data, (5) select items for your scale using 'item-analysis' and (6) test the reliability and validity of the measure.

Now do Exercises 12.4, 12.5, and 12.6.

| **EXERCISE 12.4** | Provide conceptual and operational definition of 'service quality'; develop questions that would measure service quality. |

| **EXERCISE 12.5** | Compare your service quality measure to the measure of Zeithaml, Berry and Parasuraman (1996) presented in the *Journal of Retailing*. |

a. How does your measure differ from this measure in terms of dimensions and elements?
b. Would you prefer using your own measure or the measure of Zeithaml, Berry and Parasuraman? Why?

| **EXERCISE 12.6** | Find the paper 'Consumer values orientation for materialism and its measurement: Scale development and validation', written by Marsha Richins and Scott Dawson. |

a. Provide an overview of the dimensions and elements of Richins and Dawson's materialism scale.
b. Use Bruner, Hensel and James' the *Marketing Scales Handbook* or your local (electronic) library to find at least two other materialism scales. Compare the scales you have found with the Richins and Dawson scale.

| **INTERNATIONAL DIMENSIONS OF OPERATIONAL-IZATION** | In conducting transnational research, it is important to remember that certain variables have different meanings and connotations in different cultures. For instance, the term 'love' is subject to several interpretations in different cultures and has at least 20 different interpretations in some countries. Likewise, the concept 'knowledge' is equated with 'jnana' in some Eastern cultures and construed as 'realization of the Almighty'. Thus, it is wise for researchers who come from a country speaking a different language to recruit the help of local scholars to operationalize certain constructs while engaging in cross-cultural research. |

| **SUMMARY** | • **Learning objective 1: Explain how variables are measured.** To collect quantitative data the researcher has to measure. Measurement is the assignment of numbers or other symbols to characteristics (or attributes) of objects according to a prespecified set of rules. There are three types of things that can be measured: (1) direct observables, (2) indirect observables and (3) constructs, creations based on observation that cannot be observed either directly or indirectly. |

- **Learning objective 2: Explain when operationalization of variables is necessary.** Despite the lack of physical measuring devices to measure more nebulous variables, there are ways of tapping these types of variables. One technique is to reduce these abstract notions to observable behaviour and/or characteristics. This is called operationalization. A valid measurement scale includes quantitatively measurable questions or items (or elements) that adequately represent the domain or universe of the construct; if the construct has more than one domain or dimension, the researcher has to make sure that questions that adequately represent these domains or dimensions are included in the measure. An operationalization does not describe the correlates of the concept.

- **Learning objective 3: Operationally define (or operationalize) abstract and subjective variables.** In conducting transnational research, it is important to remember that certain variables have different meanings and connotations in different cultures.

Instructors can visit the companion website at **www.wiley.com/go/bougie/researchmethods forbusiness8e** for **Case Study: The Standard Asian Merchant Bank**.

1. Define measurement.

2. Explain why it is impossible to measure an object.

3. Provide (relevant) measurable attributes for the following objects:
   a. a restaurant;
   b. an investment banker;
   c. a consumer;
   d. a bicycle;
   e. a pair of sunglasses;
   f. a strategic business unit.

4. Why is it wrong to use correlates of a construct to measure that construct?

5. What is meant by operational definition, when is it necessary and why is it necessary?

6. What is the difference between a conceptual definition and an operational definition.

7. Operationalize the following variables:
   a. customer loyalty;
   b. price consciousness;
   c. career success.

8. Is it useful to draw on existing measures to measure abstract and subjective constructs such as customer loyalty? Why (not)?

9. 'Since we cannot directly observe achievement motivation, job satisfaction and service quality, these are not appropriate topics for a scientific study'. Discuss this statement.

DISCUSSION QUESTIONS

Measurement of Variables: Scaling, Reliability and Validity

LEARNING OBJECTIVES

After completing Chapter 13, you should be able to:

1. Describe the characteristics and power of the four types of scales – nominal, ordinal, interval and ratio.

2. Describe and know how and when to use different forms of rating scales.

3. Describe and know how and when to use different forms of ranking scales.

4. Discuss international dimensions of scaling.

5. Describe validity and reliability and how they are established and assess the reliability and validity of a scale.

6. Explain the difference between reflective and formative scales.

INTRODUCTION

In the previous chapter, we have discussed conceptually and operationally defining a construct. This chapter will focus on scaling, reliability and validity. We have already explained that measurement is the assignment of numbers or other symbols to characteristics (or attributes) of objects.

Next, we will examine the types of scales that can be applied to assign numbers to characteristics of objects and subsequently see how we actually apply them. We will first discuss four different types of scales (nominal, ordinal, interval and ratio scales) and point out that the statistical analysis we can perform later on in the research process is directly related to the type of scales we use. We will also discuss two main categories of attitudinal scales (not to be confused with the four different types of scales) – the rating scale and the ranking scale. Then, we will briefly discuss international dimensions of scaling. Finally, we will address two important issues related to the quality of the collected data: reliability and validity of measures.

FOUR TYPES OF SCALES

Instructors can visit the companion website at **www.wiley.com/go/bougie/researchmethods forbusiness8e** for **Author Video: The four types of scales**.

Numbers allow us to perform statistical analyses on the resulting data. To be able to assign numbers to attributes of objects, we need a scale. A **scale** is a tool or mechanism by which individuals are distinguished as to how they differ from one another on the variables of interest to our study. Scaling often involves the creation of a continuum on which our objects are located.

Suppose that we want to measure consumer attitudes toward social media. After we have developed one or more scale items or questions, the next step in measurement is to decide on a scale that allows us to assign numbers to the attribute (attitude toward social media) of our objects (consumers). This allows us to subsequently classify our objects (consumers) in terms of how unfavourable or favourable they are toward social media. One of the many options we have to classify consumers is a **Likert scale**. The Likert scale is a scale designed to examine how strongly respondents agree with a statement (such as '*I enjoy using social media*') on a five-point scale with the following anchors: 1 = Strongly Disagree, 2 = Disagree, 3 = Neither Agree Nor Disagree, 4 = Agree, 5 = Strongly Agree (further on in this chapter we will thoroughly discuss a wide variety of rating and ranking scales, including the Likert scale). Hence, the Likert scale allows us to distinguish consumers in terms of how they differ from one another in their attitude toward social media, each respondent being assigned a number indicating a more or less unfavourable, neutral or more or less favourable.

The million dollar question is: What is the *meaning* of the numbers 1, 2, 3, 4 and 5? Does the scale that we have used allow us for instance to rank our objects (since 2 is more than 1)? Does it allow us to compare differences between objects (in other words is the difference between 1 and 2 the same as the difference between 2 and 3? And does it even allow us to calculate certain statistics such as a mean (or average) and a standard deviation? The answer is: it depends. It depends on the type of scale (i.e. the *basic* scale type) that we have used.

There are four basic types of scales: nominal, ordinal, interval and ratio. Nominal refers to response formats used for classification purposes (e.g. male/female), ordinal to response formats that also allows us to order objects in a meaningful way (e.g. education level), interval to a response format that also has equal intervals on a measurement scale (e.g. degrees Celsius or Fahrenheit) and a ratio scale is similar to an interval scale, but with a real or true zero-point. The degree of sophistication to which the scales are fine-tuned thus increases progressively as we move from the nominal to the ratio scale. That is why information on the variables can be obtained in greater detail when we employ an interval or a ratio scale rather than using nominal or ordinal scales. However, certain variables lend themselves with greater ease to more fine-tuned scaling than others, as we will explain next. Let us now examine each of these four scales in more detail.

NOMINAL SCALE

A **nominal scale** is one that allows the researcher to assign subjects to certain categories or groups. For example, with respect to the variable of gender, respondents can be grouped into two categories – male and female. These two groups can be assigned code numbers 0 and 1 or 1 and 2. These numbers serve as simple and convenient category labels with no intrinsic value, other than to assign respondents to one of two non-overlapping, or mutually exclusive, categories. Note that the categories should also be collectively exhaustive. In other words, there should be no third category into which respondents would normally fall. Thus, nominal scales categorize individuals or objects into mutually exclusive and collectively exhaustive groups. The information that can be generated from nominal scaling is rather limited; the only statistic involved here is the frequency of individuals in each category. The most frequently occurring value is called the *mode*. Other than this marginal information, such scaling tells us nothing more about the two groups. Thus, the nominal scale gives some basic, categorical information.

	Example

Let us take a look at another variable that lends itself to nominal scaling – the nationality of individuals. We could nominally scale this variable in the following mutually exclusive and collectively exhaustive categories.

American	Japanese
Australian	Polish
Chinese	Russian
German	Swiss
Indian	Zambian
Other	

Note that every respondent has to fit into one of the above 11 categories and that the scale allows computation of the numbers and percentages of respondents that fit into them.

Now do Exercise 13.1.

EXERCISE 13.1 | Suggest two variables that would be natural candidates for nominal scales, and set up mutually exclusive and collectively exhaustive categories for each.

ORDINAL SCALE

An **ordinal scale** not only assigns objects (e.g. persons, companies, countries, products and the like) to certain categories, it also allows the researcher to rank order the objects in some meaningful way. The difference with a nominal scale is thus in the possibility of ordering. This can be used when describing and displaying frequencies. The measure of 'educational attainment' in the example illustrates how the response format distinguishes individuals on an ordinal scale; the educational attainment categories can be ordered hierarchically. Note that when data are entered in a statistical software package, numbers are often assigned to the participants' responses. This is called coding the data. For example, we can code 'Less than a high school diploma' with a 1, 'High school degree or equivalent' with a 2, 'Some college, no degree' with a 3 and so on. A major problem arises when these ordinal categories are treated as real numbers. Because the numbers we assign to the categories are essentially arbitrary, attempts to treat them as real numbers lead to arbitrary results that do not make sense at all.

Example | What is the highest degree or level of school you have completed?

- Less than a high school diploma
- High school degree or equivalent
- Some college, no degree
- Associate degree
- Bachelor's degree
- Master's degree
- Doctorate degree (PhD)

Now do Exercise 13.2.

EXERCISE 13.2 | Suggest two variables that would be natural candidates for ordinal scales, and set up mutually exclusive and collectively exhaustive categories for each.

INTERVAL SCALE

In an **interval scale**, or *equal* interval scale, numerically equal distances on the scale represent equal values in the characteristics being measured. Whereas the nominal scale allows us only to qualitatively distinguish objects by categorizing them into mutually exclusive and collectively exhaustive categories sets, and the ordinal scale also allows us to order objects in a meaningful way (e.g. education level), the interval scale also allows us to compare differences between objects: The difference between any two values on an interval scale is identical to the difference between any other two neighbouring values of that scale. The clinical thermometer is a good example of an interval-scaled instrument; it has an arbitrary origin and the magnitude of the difference between 98.6 degrees Fahrenheit (supposed to be the normal body temperature) and 99.6 degrees Fahrenheit is the same as the magnitude of the difference between 104 and 105 degrees. Note, however, that one may not be seriously concerned if one's temperature rises from 98.6 to 99.6, but one is likely to be so when the temperature goes up from 104 to 105 degrees!

The interval scale, then, taps the differences, the order *and* the equality of the magnitude of the differences in the variable. As such, it is a more powerful scale than the nominal and ordinal scales from a statistical point of view, and has for its measures of central tendency the mode, the median and arithmetic mean (the average). Its measures of dispersion are the range, the standard deviation and the variance.

RATIO SCALE

The ratio scale overcomes the disadvantage of the arbitrary origin point of the interval scale, in that it has an absolute (in contrast to an arbitrary) zero point, which is a meaningful measurement point. Thus, the **ratio scale** not only measures the magnitude of the differences between points on the scale but also taps the proportions in the differences. It is the most powerful of the four scales because it has a unique zero origin (not an arbitrary origin) and subsumes all the properties of the other three scales. The weighing balance is a good example of a ratio scale. It has an absolute (and not arbitrary) zero origin calibrated on it, which allows us to calculate the ratio of the weights of two individuals. For instance, a person weighing 250 pounds is twice as heavy as one who weighs 125 pounds. Note that multiplying or dividing both of these numbers (250 and 125) by any given number will preserve the ratio of 2:1. The measure of central tendency of the ratio scale may be either the arithmetic or the geometric mean and the measure of dispersion may be either the standard deviation, or variance, or the coefficient of variation. Some examples of ratio scales are those pertaining to actual age, income and the number of organizations individuals have worked for.

Now do Exercises 13.3 and 13.4.

Measure any three variables on an interval or a ratio scale.	**EXERCISE 13.3**

Mention one variable for each of the four scales in the context of a market survey, and explain how or why it would fit into the scale.	**EXERCISE 13.4**

The properties of the scales, as fine-tuning is increasingly achieved, are summarized in Table 13.1. We may also see from the table how the power of the statistic increases as we move away from the nominal scale (where we group subjects or items under some categories), to the ordinal scale (where we can rank-order the categories), to the interval scale (where we can tap the magnitude of the differences), to the ratio scale (which allows us to measure the proportion of the differences).

Table 13.1 Properties of the Four Scales

Scale	Highlights				Measures of central tendency	Measures of dispersion	Some tests of significance
	Difference	Order	Distance	Unique origin			
Nominal	Yes	No	No	No	Mode	—	χ^2
Ordinal	Yes	Yes	No	No	Median	Semi-interquartile range	Rank-order correlations
Interval	Yes	Yes	Yes	No	Arithmetic mean	Standard deviation, variance, coefficient of variation	t, F
Ratio	Yes	Yes	Yes	Yes	Arithmetic or geometric mean	Standard deviation or variance or coefficient of variation	t, F

Note: The interval scale has an arbitrary starting point. The ratio scale has the natural origin 0, which is meaningful.

You must have surmised by now that some variables, such as gender, can be measured only on the nominal scale, while others, such as temperature, can be measured on an ordinal scale (hot/lukewarm, cold), or the interval scale through a thermometer. Whenever it is possible to use a more powerful scale, it is wise to do so, at least from a statistical point of view.

ORDINAL OR INTERVAL?

Likert scales (discussed later in this chapter) are a commonly used way of measuring opinions and attitudes. They measure the extent to which participants agree or disagree with a given statement, and typically range from 1 (strongly disagree) to 5 (strongly agree) with a neutral point in the middle (e.g. neither agree nor disagree). Whether this scale is ordinal or interval in nature is a subject of much debate. Some people argue that a Likert scale is ordinal in nature. They correctly point out that one cannot assume that all pairs of adjacent levels are equidistant (of the same distance). Nonetheless, Likert scales (and a few other scales, that is, the semantic differential scale and the numerical scale – also discussed later on in this chapter) are generally treated as if they were interval scales, because it allows researchers to calculate averages and standard deviations and to apply other, more advanced statistical techniques (for instance, to test hypotheses).

An example of a Likert scale is provided next. How would you treat this scale?

| Example | Indicate the extent to which you agree with the following statements as they relate to your job, by circling the appropriate number against each, using the scale given below. |

	Strongly Disagree	Disagree	Neither Agree Nor Disagree	Agree	Strongly Agree
	1	2	3	4	5
The following opportunities offered by the job are very important to me:					
a. Interacting with others	1	2	3	4	5
b. Using a number of different skills	1	2	3	4	5
c. Completing a task from beginning to end	1	2	3	4	5
d. Serving others	1	2	3	4	5
e. Working independently	1	2	3	4	5

The specific scaling techniques commonly used in business research can be classified into rating scales and ranking scales. **Rating scales** capture how respondents feel about individual items, measuring positive or negative responses to a question or statement. **Ranking scales** allow participants to compare objects to one another. Specific rating and ranking scales are discussed next.

| RATING SCALES | The following rating scales are often used in business research: |

- Dichotomous scale
- Category scale
- Semantic differential scale
- Numerical scale
- Itemized rating scale
- Likert scale

- Fixed or constant sum rating scale
- Stapel scale
- Graphic rating scale
- Consensus scale

Other scales, such as the Thurstone Equal Appearing Interval Scale, and the multidimensional scale, are less frequently used. We will briefly describe each of the above attitudinal scales.

DICHOTOMOUS SCALE

The **dichotomous scale** is used to elicit a Yes or No answer, as in the example below. Note that a nominal scale is used to elicit the response.

Do you own a car? Yes No	**Example**

CATEGORY SCALE

The **category scale** uses multiple items to elicit a single response, as per the following example. This also uses the nominal scale.

Where in London do you reside?	**Example**
__ East London	
__ South London	
__ West London	
__ North London	
__ Outskirts	

SEMANTIC DIFFERENTIAL SCALE

Several bipolar attributes are identified at the extremes of the scale, and respondents are asked to indicate their attitudes, on what may be called a semantic space, toward a particular individual, object or event on each of the attributes. The bipolar adjectives used might employ such terms as Good–Bad; Strong–Weak; Hot–Cold. The **semantic differential scale** is used to assess respondents' attitudes toward a particular brand, advertisement, object or individual. The responses can be plotted to obtain a good idea of their perceptions. A semantic differential scale is ordinal in nature. However, it is often treated as an interval scale. An example of the semantic differential scale follows.

Responsive	— — — — —	Unresponsive	**Example**
Beautiful	— — — — — —	Ugly	
Courageous	— — — — —	Timid	

NUMERICAL SCALE

The **numerical scale** is similar to the semantic differential scale, with the difference that numbers on a five- or seven-point scale are provided, with bipolar adjectives at both ends, as illustrated below. This scale is also often treated as an interval scale, although it is formally ordinal in nature.

Example	How pleased are you with your new estate agent?

Extremely Pleased   7 6 5 4 3 2 1   Extremely Displeased

ITEMIZED RATING SCALE

A five- or seven-point scale with anchors, as needed, is provided for each item and the respondent states the appropriate number on the side of each item, or circles the relevant number against each item, as per the examples that follow. The responses to the items are then summed. This uses an interval scale.

Example	Respond to each item using the scale below, and indicate your response number on the line by each item.

1	2	3	4	5
Very Unlikely	**Unlikely**	**Neither Unlikely Nor Likely**	**Likely**	**Very Likely**

1	I will be changing my job within the next 12 months.	—
2	I will take on new assignments in the near future.	—
3	It is possible that I will be out of this organization within the next 12 months.	—

Note that the above is a balanced rating scale with a neutral point.

	Not at All Interested 1	Somewhat Interested 2	Moderately Interested 3	Very Much Interested 4
How would you rate your interest in changing current organizational policies?	1	2	3	4

This is an unbalanced rating scale which does not have a neutral point.

The itemized rating scale provides the flexibility to use as many points in the scale as considered necessary (for instance, 4, 5, 7, 9), and it is also possible to use different anchors (e.g. Very Unimportant to Very Important; Extremely Low to Extremely High). When a neutral point is provided, it is a balanced rating scale, and when it is not, it is an **unbalanced rating scale**.

Research indicates that a five-point scale is just as good as any, and that an increase from five to seven or nine points on a rating scale does not improve the reliability of the ratings (Elmore & Beggs, 1975).

The itemized rating scale is frequently used in business research, since it adapts itself to the number of points the researcher wishes to use, as well as the nomenclature of the anchors, as is considered necessary to accommodate the needs of the researcher for tapping the variable.

LIKERT SCALE

The Likert scale is designed to examine how strongly subjects agree or disagree with statements on a five-point scale with the following anchors:

Strongly Disagree	**Disagree**	**Neither Agree nor Disagree**	**Agree**	**Strongly Agree**
1	2	3	4	5

The responses over a number of items tapping a particular concept or variable can be analysed item by item, but it is also possible to calculate a total or summated score for each respondent by summing across items. The summated approach is widely used, and therefore the Likert scale is also referred to as a summated scale.

In the following example, the scores on the second item have to be reversed before calculating the summated score, because a high score on this item reflects an unfavourable attitude to work, whereas a high score on items 1 and 3 reflects a favourable attitude to work. This will lead to high total scores for respondents who have a favourable attitude toward work and to low total scores for respondents who have an unfavourable attitude toward work.

					Example
Using the preceding Likert scale, state the extent to which you agree with each of the following statements:					

My work is very interesting	1	2	3	4	5
I am not engrossed in my work all day	1	2	3	4	5
Life without my work would be dull	1	2	3	4	5

Whether a Likert scale is an ordinal or an interval scale is a subject of much debate. People who treat a Likert scale as an ordinal scale argue that one cannot assume that all pairs of adjacent levels are equidistant. Nonetheless, Likert scales are generally treated as interval scales.

FIXED OR CONSTANT SUM SCALE

The respondents are here asked to distribute a given number of points across various items as per the example below. This is more in the nature of an ordinal scale.

		Example
In choosing a toilet soap, indicate the importance you attach to each of the following five aspects by allotting points for each to total 100 in all.		

Fragrance	—
Colour	—
Shape	—
Size	—
Texture of lather	—
Total points	100

STAPEL SCALE

This scale simultaneously measures both the direction and intensity of the attitude toward the items under study. The characteristic of interest to the study is placed at the centre with a numerical scale ranging, say, from +3 to −3, on either side of the item, as illustrated in the example below. This gives an idea of how close or distant the individual response to the stimulus is. Since this does not have an absolute zero point, this is an interval scale.

Example	State how you would rate your supervisor's abilities with respect to each of the characteristics mentioned below, by circling the appropriate number.

+3	+3	+3
+2	+2	+2
+1	+1	+1
Adopting modern technology	Product innovation	Interpersonal skills
−1	−1	−1
−2	−2	−2
−3	−3	−3

GRAPHIC RATING SCALE

A graphical representation helps the respondents to indicate on this scale their answers to a particular question by placing a mark at the appropriate point on the line, as in the following example. This is an ordinal scale, though the following example might make it look like an interval scale.

Example	On a scale of 1 to 10, how would you rate your supervisor?	–	10 Excellent
		–	
		–	
		–	
		–	
		–	5 Adequate
		–	
		–	
		–	
		–	1 Very bad

This scale is easy to respond to. The brief descriptions on the scale points are meant to serve as a guide in locating the rating rather than representing discrete categories. The **faces scale**, which depicts faces ranging from smiling to sad (illustrated in Chapter 10), is also a graphic rating scale used to obtain responses regarding people's feelings with respect to some aspect – say, how they feel about their jobs.

CONSENSUS SCALE

Scales can also be developed by consensus, where a panel of judges selects certain items, which in its view measure the relevant concept. The items are chosen particularly based on their pertinence or relevance to the concept. Such a **consensus scale** is developed after the selected items have been examined and tested for their validity and reliability. One such consensus scale is the Thurstone Equal Appearing Interval Scale, where a concept is measured by a complex process followed by a panel of judges. Using a pile of cards containing several descriptions of the concept, a panel of judges offers inputs to indicate how close or not the statements are to the concept under study. The scale is then developed based on the consensus reached. However, this scale is rarely used for measuring organizational concepts because of the time necessary to develop it.

OTHER SCALES

There are also some advanced scaling methods such as multidimensional scaling, where objects, people or both, are visually scaled, and a conjoint analysis is performed. This provides a visual image of the relationships in space among the dimensions of a construct.

It should be noted that the Likert or some form of numerical scale is the one most frequently used to measure attitudes and behaviours in business research.

As already mentioned, **ranking scales** are used to tap preferences between two or among more objects or items (ordinal in nature). However, such ranking may not give definitive clues to some of the answers sought. For instance, let us say there are four product lines and the manager seeks information that would help decide which product line should get the most attention. Let us also assume that 35% of the respondents choose the first product, 25% the second and 20% choose each of products three and four as being of importance to them. The manager cannot then conclude that the first product is the most preferred, since 65% of the respondents did not choose that product! Alternative methods used are paired comparisons, forced choice and the comparative scale, which are discussed below.

RANKING SCALES

PAIRED COMPARISON

The **paired comparison** scale is used when, among a small number of objects, respondents are asked to choose between two objects at a time. This helps to assess preferences. If, for instance, in the previous example, during the paired comparisons, respondents consistently show a preference for product one over products two, three and four, the manager can reliably understand which product line demands his utmost attention. However, as the number of objects to be compared increases, so does the number of paired comparisons. The number of paired choices for n objects will be $(n)(n-1)/2$. The greater the number of objects or stimuli, the greater the number of paired comparisons presented to the respondents, and the greater the respondent fatigue. Hence, paired comparison is a good method if the number of stimuli presented is small.

FORCED CHOICE

The **forced choice** enables respondents to rank objects relative to one another, among the alternatives provided. This is easier for the respondents, particularly if the number of choices to be ranked is limited in number.

Rank the following mobile phones that you would like to buy to in the order of preference, assigning 1 to the most preferred choice and 5 to the least preferred.

Apple	—
Samsung	—
Huawei	—
LG	—
Google	—

Example

COMPARATIVE SCALE

The **comparative scale** provides a benchmark or a point of reference to assess attitudes toward the current object, event or situation under study. An example of the use of the comparative scale follows.

| Example | In a volatile financial environment, compared to stocks, how wise or useful is it to invest in Treasury bonds? Please circle the appropriate response. |

More useful		About the same		Less useful
1	2	3	4	5

INTERNATIONAL DIMENSIONS OF SCALING

Apart from sensitivity to operational definition of concepts in other cultures, the issue of scaling also needs to be addressed in cross-cultural research. Different cultures react differently to issues of scaling.

Recent research has shown that people from different countries differ in both their tendency to use the extremes of the rating scale (for instance, 1 and 5 or 1 and 7) and to respond in a socially desirable way (De Jong, 2006). These findings illustrate that analysing and interpreting data that are collected in multiple countries is an extremely challenging undertaking.

GOODNESS OF MEASURES

Now that we have seen how to operationally define variables and apply different scaling techniques, it is important to make sure that the instrument that we develop to measure a particular concept is indeed accurately measuring the variable, and that, in fact, we are actually measuring the concept that we set out to measure. This ensures that in operationally defining perceptual and attitudinal variables, we have not overlooked some important dimensions and elements or included some irrelevant ones. The scales developed can often be imperfect, and errors are prone to occur in the measurement of attitudinal variables. The use of better instruments will ensure more accuracy in results, which in turn will enhance the quality of the conclusions. Hence, in some way, we need to assess the 'goodness' of the measures developed. That is, we need to be reasonably sure that the instruments we use in our research do indeed measure the variables they are supposed to, and that they measure them accurately.

There are two major criteria for evaluating a measurement tool: reliability and validity. Very briefly, **reliability** is a test of how consistently a measuring instrument measures whatever concept it is measuring. **Validity** is a test of how well an instrument that is developed measures the particular concept it is intended to measure. In other words, validity is concerned with whether we measure the right concept, and reliability with stability and consistency of measurement. Validity and reliability of the measure attest to the scientific rigor that has gone into the research study. These two criteria will now be discussed. The various forms of reliability and validity are depicted in Figure 13.1.

VALIDITY

In Chapter 11, we examined the terms *internal validity* and *external validity* in the context of experimental designs. That is, we will be concerned about the issue of the authenticity of the cause-and-effect relationships (internal validity), and their generalizability to the external environment (external validity). For now, we are going to examine the validity of the measuring instrument itself. That is, when we ask a set of questions (i.e. develop a measuring instrument) with the hope that we are tapping the concept, how can we be reasonably certain that we are indeed measuring the concept we set out to measure and not something else? This can be determined by applying certain validity tests.

Several types of validity test are used to test the **goodness of measures** and writers use different terms to denote them. For the sake of clarity, we may group validity tests under three broad headings: content validity, criterion-related validity and construct validity.

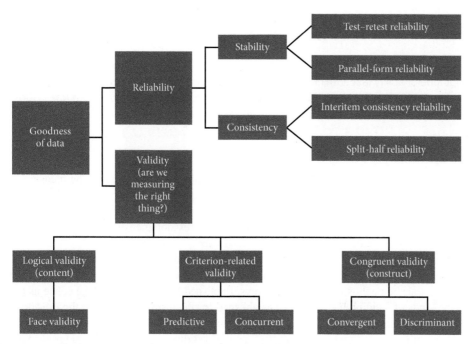

FIGURE 13.1   Testing goodness of measures: forms of reliability and validity

Content Validity

Content validity ensures that the measure includes an adequate and representative set of items that tap the concept. The more the scale items represent the domain or universe of the concept being measured, the greater the content validity. To put it differently, content validity is a function of how well the dimensions and elements of a concept have been delineated.

A panel of judges can attest to the content validity of the instrument. Kidder and Judd (1986) cite the example where a test designed to measure degrees of speech impairment can be considered as having validity if it is so evaluated by a group of expert judges (i.e. professional speech therapists).

Face validity is considered by some a basic and minimum index of content validity. **Face validity** indicates that the items that are intended to measure a concept, do, on the face of it, look like they measure the concept. Some researchers do not see fit to treat face validity as a valid component of content validity.

Criterion-Related Validity

Criterion-related validity is established when the measure differentiates individuals on a criterion it is expected to predict. This can be done by establishing concurrent validity or predictive validity, as explained below.

Concurrent validity is established when the scale discriminates individuals who are known to be different; that is, they should score differently on the instrument, as in the example that follows.

If a measure of work ethic is developed and administered to a group of welfare recipients, the scale should differentiate those who are enthusiastic about accepting a job and glad of an opportunity to be off welfare, from those who do not want to work, even when offered a job. Obviously, those with high work ethic values do not want to be on welfare and yearn for employment to be on their own. Those who are low on work ethic values, on the other hand, might exploit the opportunity to survive on welfare for as long as possible, deeming work to be drudgery. If both types of individual have the same score on the work ethic scale, then the test is not a measure of work ethic, but of something else.

Example

Predictive validity indicates the ability of the measuring instrument to differentiate among individuals with reference to a future criterion.

Example	If an aptitude or ability test administered to employees at the time of recruitment is to differentiate individuals on the basis of their future job performance, then those who score low on the test should be poor performers and those with high scores good performers.

Construct Validity

Construct validity testifies to how well the results obtained from the use of the measure fit the theories around which the test is designed. This is assessed through convergent and discriminant validity, which are explained below.

Convergent validity is established when the scores obtained with two different instruments measuring the same concept are highly correlated.

Discriminant validity is established when, based on theory, two variables are predicted to be uncorrelated, and the scores obtained by measuring them are indeed empirically found to be so. Validity can thus be established in different ways. Published measures for various concepts usually report the kinds of validity that have been established for the instrument, so that the user or reader can judge the 'goodness' of the measure. Table 13.2 summarizes the kinds of validity discussed here.

Some of the ways in which the above forms of validity can be established are through the following:

1. Correlational analysis (as in the case of establishing concurrent and predictive validity or convergent and discriminant validity).

2. Factor analysis, a multivariate technique that confirms the dimensions of the concept that have been operationally defined, as well as indicating which of the items are most appropriate for each dimension (establishing construct validity).

3. The multitrait, multimethod matrix of correlations derived from measuring concepts by different forms and different methods, additionally establishing the robustness of the measure.

In sum, the goodness of measures is established through the different kinds of validity and reliability depicted in Figure 13.1. The results of any research can only be as good as the measures that tap the concepts in the theoretical framework. We need to use well-validated and

Table 13.2   Types of Validity

Validity	Description
Content validity	Does the measure adequately measure the concept?
Face validity	Do 'experts' validate that the instrument measures what its name suggests it measures?
Criterion-related validity	Does the measure differentiate in a manner that helps to predict a criterion variable?
Concurrent validity	Does the measure differentiate in a manner that helps to predict a criterion variable currently?
Predictive validity	Does the measure differentiate individuals in a manner that helps predict a future criterion?
Construct validity	Does the instrument tap the concept as theorized?
Convergent validity	Do two instruments measuring the concept correlate highly?
Discriminant validity	Does the measure have a low correlation with a variable that is supposed to be unrelated to this variable?

reliable measures to ensure that our research is scientific. Fortunately, measures have been developed for many important concepts in business research and their psychometric properties (i.e. the reliability and validity) established by the developers. Thus, researchers can use the instruments already reputed to be 'good', rather than laboriously developing their own measures. When using these measures, however, researchers should cite the source (i.e. the author and reference) so that the reader can seek more information if necessary.

It is not unusual for two or more equally good measures to be developed for the same concept. For example, there are several different instruments for measuring the concept of 'job satisfaction'. One of the most frequently used scales for the purpose, however, is the Job Descriptive Index (JDI) developed by Smith, Kendall and Hulin (1969). When more than one scale exists for any variable, it is preferable to use the measure that has better reliability and validity, and is also more frequently used.

At times, we may also have to adapt an established measure to suit the setting. For example, a scale that is used to measure job performance, job characteristics or job satisfaction in the manufacturing industry may have to be modified slightly to suit a utility company or a health care organization. The work environment in each case is different and the wordings in the instrument may have to be suitably adapted. However, in doing this, we are tampering with an established scale, and it is advisable to test it for the adequacy of the validity and reliability afresh.

A sample of a few measures used to tap some frequently researched concepts in the management and marketing areas is provided in the appendix to this chapter.

Finally, it is important to note that validity is a necessary but not sufficient condition of the test of goodness of a measure. A measure should not only be valid but also reliable. A measure is reliable if it provides consistent results. We will now discuss the concept of reliability.

RELIABILITY

The **reliability** of a measure indicates the extent to which it is without bias (error free) and hence ensures consistent measurement across time and across the various items in the instrument. In other words, the reliability of a measure is an indication of the stability and consistency with which the instrument measures the concept and helps to assess the 'goodness' of a measure.

Stability of Measures

The ability of a measure to remain the same over time – despite uncontrollable testing conditions or the state of the respondents themselves – is indicative of its stability and low vulnerability to changes in the situation. This attests to its 'goodness' because the concept is stably measured, no matter when it is done. Two tests of **stability** are test–retest reliability and parallel-form reliability.

Test–retest reliability   The reliability coefficient obtained by repetition of the same measure on a second occasion is called the **test–retest reliability**. That is, when a questionnaire containing some items that are supposed to measure a concept is administered to a set of respondents, now and again to the same respondents, say several weeks to six months later, then the correlation between the scores obtained at the two different times from one and the same set of respondents is called the test–retest coefficient. The higher it is, the better the test–retest reliability and, consequently, the stability of the measure across time.

Parallel-form reliability   When responses on two comparable sets of measures tapping the same construct are highly correlated, we have **parallel-form reliability**. Both forms have similar items and the same response format, the only changes being the wording and the order or sequence of the questions. What we try to establish here is the error variability resulting from wording and ordering of the questions. If two such comparable forms are highly correlated (say 8 and above), we may be fairly certain that the measures are reasonably reliable, with minimal error variance caused by wording, ordering or other factors.

Internal Consistency of Measures

The **internal consistency** of measures is indicative of the homogeneity of the items in the measure that taps the construct. In other words, the items should 'hang together as a set', and be capable of independently measuring the same concept so that the respondents attach the same overall meaning to each of the items. This can be seen by examining whether the items and the subsets of items in the measuring instrument are correlated highly. Consistency can be examined through the interitem consistency reliability and split-half reliability tests.

Interitem consistency reliability   The **interitem consistency reliability** is a test of the consistency of respondents' answers to all the items in a measure. To the degree that items are independent measures of the same concept, they will be correlated with one another. The most popular test of interitem consistency reliability is Cronbach's coefficient alpha (Cronbach, 1946), which is used for multipoint-scaled items, and the Kuder–Richardson formulas (Kuder & Richardson, 1937), used for dichotomous items. The higher the coefficients, the better the measuring instrument.

Split-half reliability   **Split-half reliability** reflects the correlations between two halves of an instrument. The estimates will vary depending on how the items in the measure are split into two halves. Split-half reliabilities may be higher than Cronbach's alpha only in the circumstance of there being more than one underlying response dimension tapped by the measure and when certain other conditions are met as well (for complete details, refer to Campbell, 1976). Hence, in almost all cases, Cronbach's alpha can be considered a perfectly adequate index of the inter-item consistency reliability.

REFLECTIVE VERSUS FORMATIVE MEASUREMENT SCALES

At this moment, it is important to come back to the contention that the items of a multi-item measure should hang together as a set and be capable of independently measuring the same concept (it may give you a headache right now, but it most certainly will save you an even bigger headache in your future career as a researcher, so bear with us). The fact is that the items that measure a concept should not always hang together: this is only true for reflective, but not for formative, scales.

WHAT IS A REFLECTIVE SCALE?

In a **reflective scale**, the items (all of them!) are expected to correlate. Unlike the items used in a formative scale, discussed next, each item in a reflective scale is assumed to share a common basis (the underlying construct of interest). Hence, an increase in the value of the construct will translate into an increase in the value for all the items representing the construct. An example of a reflective scale is the Attitude Toward the Offer scale developed by Burton and Lichtenstein (1988). This is a six-item, nine-point summated ratings scale measuring a person's attitude about a certain product offered at a certain price. The scale is composed of five bipolar adjectives (unfavourable–favourable; bad–good; harmful–beneficial; unattractive–attractive; poor–excellent) and one disagree–agree item (introduced by the stem: 'I like this deal'), measured on a nine-point graphic scale. Indeed, we would expect that a more favourable attitude toward the offer would translate into an increase in the value of all the six items representing attitude toward the offer. Hence, we would expect all the six items to correlate. Note that the direction of 'causality' is from the construct to the items.

WHAT IS A FORMATIVE SCALE AND WHY DO THE ITEMS OF A FORMATIVE SCALE NOT NECESSARILY HANG TOGETHER?

A **formative scale** is used when a construct is viewed as an explanatory combination of its indicators (Fornell, 1987; Fornell & Bookstein, 1982). Take the Job Description Index (Smith, Kendall & Hulin, 1969), a composite measure purporting to evaluate job satisfaction. This measure includes five dimensions: type of work (18 items), opportunities for promotion (9 items), satisfaction with supervision (18 items), co-workers (18 items) and pay (9 items). The five dimensions are seen as the five defining characteristics of job satisfaction.

The five dimensions are translated into 72 observable and measureable elements such as 'Good opportunity for advancement', 'Regular promotions', 'Fairly good chance for promotion', 'Income adequate for normal expenses', 'Highly paid', and 'Gives sense of accomplishment'. The idea is that we would expect the first three items ('Good opportunity for advancement', 'Regular promotions', and 'Fairly good chance for promotion') to be correlated (after all, they all aim to measure one particular dimension of job satisfaction, that is, 'opportunities for promotion'). However, these items do not necessarily correlate with the items that measure 'Pay' (a second dimension), such as 'Income adequate for normal expenses' and 'Highly paid', because the dimension 'Good opportunities for advancement' is not necessarily related to the dimension 'Pay'. Indeed, a first worker may have a very good salary but no opportunities for promotion, a second worker may have very good opportunities for promotion but a very poor salary and a third worker may have a very good salary and very good opportunities for promotion.

Likewise, we would expect the items 'Income adequate for normal expenses' and 'Highly paid' to be correlated to each other (since both items measure pay), but we would not necessarily expect these items to correlate with the item 'Gives sense of accomplishment' (because this last item does not measure pay but another dimension of the Job Description Index).

In summary, the Job Description Index includes five dimensions and 72 items. These 72 items are not necessarily related to each other, because the five dimensions they represent do not necessarily hang together.

A scale that contains items that are not necessarily related is called a formative scale. We have already explained that formative scales are used when a construct (such as job satisfaction) is viewed as an explanatory combination of its indicators (promotions, pay, satisfaction with supervision, co-workers and work); that is, when a change in any one of the indicators (dimensions) is expected to change the score of the overall construct, regardless of the value of the other indicators (dimensions). The Job Description Index is formative in nature, since an increase in the value of one of its indicators, such as 'opportunities for promotion', is expected to translate into a higher score for job satisfaction, regardless of the value of the other indicators. Thus, the Job Description Index conceptualizes job satisfaction as the total weighted score across the 72 job satisfaction items, where each item corresponds to a specific independent dimension of job satisfaction.

A good (i.e. a valid) formative scale is one that represents the entire domain of the construct. This means that a valid scale should represent all the relevant aspects of the construct of interest, even if these aspects do not necessarily correlate.

While it makes sense to test the interitem consistency of reflective scales, it does not make sense to test the interitem consistency of formative scales. The reason is that we do not expect the items in a formative scale to be homogeneous; in other words, we do not expect all the items to correlate. For this reason, tests of the consistency of respondents' answers to the items of a formative measure do not tell us anything about the quality of our measuring instrument. Note that there are other methods to assess the goodness of formative scales (see, for instance, Jarvis, MacKenzie & Podsakoff, 2003).

SUMMARY

• **Learning objective 1: Describe the characteristics and power of the four types of scales – nominal, ordinal, interval and ratio.** To be able to assign numbers to attributes of objects we need a scale. A scale is a tool or mechanism by which individuals are distinguished as to how they differ from one another on the variables of interest to our study. Scaling involves the creation of a continuum on which our objects are located. There are four basic types of scales: nominal, ordinal, interval and ratio. The degree of sophistication to which the scales are fine-tuned increases progressively as we move from the nominal to the ratio scale.

- **Learning objective 2: Describe and know how and when to use different forms of rating scales.** In rating scales each object is scaled independently of the other objects under study. The following rating scales are often used in business research: dichotomous scale, category scale, semantic differential scale, numerical scale, itemized rating scale, Likert scale, fixed or constant sum rating scale, Stapel scale, graphic rating scale and consensus scale. The Likert scale or some form of numerical scale is the one most frequently used to measure attitudes and behaviours in business research.

- **Learning objective 3: Describe and know how and when to use different forms of ranking scales.** Ranking scales are used to tap preferences between two or among more objects or items. The paired comparison scale is used when, among a small number of objects, respondents are asked to choose between two objects at a time. The forced choice enables respondents to rank objects relative to one another, among the alternatives provided. The comparative scale provides a benchmark or a point of reference to assess attitudes toward the current object, event or situation under study.

- **Learning objective 4: Discuss international dimensions of scaling.** Different cultures react differently to issues of scaling. What's more, recent research has shown that people from different countries differ in both their tendency to use the extremes of the rating scale (for instance, 1 and 5 or 1 and 7) and to respond in a socially desirable way. These findings illustrate that analysing and interpreting data that are collected in multiple countries is a challenging task.

- **Learning objective 5: Describe validity and reliability and how they are established and assess the reliability and validity of a scale.** Reliability is a test of how consistently a measuring instrument measures whatever concept it is measuring. Validity is a test of how well an instrument that is developed measures the particular concept it is intended to measure. Several types of validity test are used to test the goodness of measures. Content validity ensures that the measure includes an adequate and representative set of items that tap the concept. Criterion-related validity is established when the measure differentiates individuals on a criterion it is expected to predict. Construct validity testifies to how well the results obtained from the use of the measure fit the theories around which the test is designed. Two tests of stability are test–retest reliability and parallel-form reliability. The internal consistency of measures is indicative of the homogeneity of the items in the measure that taps the construct.

- **Learning objective 6: Explain the difference between reflective and formative scales.** The items that measure a concept should not always hang together: this is only true for reflective, but not for formative, scales. In a reflective scale, the items (all of them!) are expected to correlate. A formative scale is used when a construct is viewed as an explanatory combination of its indicators.

> Instructors can visit the companion website at **www.wiley.com/go/bougie/researchmethods forbusiness8e** for **Case Study: The Standard Asian Merchant Bank**.

DISCUSSION QUESTIONS	

1. Describe the four types of scales.

2. How is the interval scale more sophisticated than the nominal and ordinal scales?

3. Why is the ratio scale considered to be the most powerful of the four scales?

4. Briefly describe the difference between rating scales and ranking scales and indicate when the two are used.

5. Why is it important to establish the 'goodness' of measures and how is this done?

6. Describe the difference between formative and reflective scales.

7. Explain why it does not make sense to assess the internal consistency of a formative scale.

8. 'The job involvement measure described in the appendix is reflective in nature'. Comment on this statement.

9. Construct a semantic differential scale to assess the properties of a particular brand of coffee or tea.

10. Whenever possible, it is advisable to use instruments that have already been developed and repeatedly used in published studies, rather than developing our own instruments for our studies. Do you agree? Discuss the reasons for your answer.

11. 'A valid instrument is always reliable, but a reliable instrument may not always be valid'. Comment on this statement.

Now do Exercises 13.5 and 13.6.

Develop and name the type of measuring instrument you would use to tap the following:

EXERCISE 13.5

a. Which brands of toothpaste are consumed by how many individuals?
b. Among the three types of exams – multiple choice, essay type and a mix of both – which is the one preferred most by students?
c. To what extent do individuals agree with your definition of accounting principles?
d. How much people like an existing organizational policy.
e. The age of employees in an organization.
f. The number of employees in each of the 20 departments of a company.

'The SERVQUAL-scale described in the appendix is formative in nature'. Comment on this statement. Explain why it does not make sense to assess the interitem consistency of this scale.

EXERCISE 13.6

Examples of Some Measures

Some of the measures used in business research can be found in the *Marketing Scales Handbook* by Bruner, Hensel and James. The latest volumes (5, 6 and 7) are the only ones available at this time. The earlier volumes in the series are no longer being published but revised versions of their scale reviews are in the database. Volume 5 contains reviews of scales published in scholarly marketing articles between 2002 and 2005. Volume 6 has reviews that were reported in articles from 2006 to 2009. Volume 7 is the newest book and covers 2010 and 2011. To be included in these volumes, the scales had to be composed of three or more items, have empirical evidence of their psychometric quality and have been treated by their users as reflective measures rather than formative. Other useful (but somewhat outdated) sources are the *Handbook of Organizational Measurement* by Price and Mueller (1986) and the *Michigan Organizational Assessment Package* published by the Institute of Survey Research in Ann Arbor, Michigan. Several measures can also be seen in Psychological Measurement Yearbooks and in other published books. A sample of measures from the accounting, finance, management and marketing areas is provided in this appendix.

MEASURES FROM BEHAVIOURAL FINANCE RESEARCH

Below is a sample of scales used to measure variables related to behavioural finance research.

Information overload

Information Overload Measure (on a scale of 1 to 6, from strongly disagree to strongly agree)

1.	There were too many different options to consider.	_____
2.	This decision required a great deal of thought.	_____
3.	This was a difficult decision.	_____
4.	I found this decision to be overwhelming.	_____
5.	It was difficult to comprehend all of the information available to me.	_____
6.	This task was stressful.	_____
7.	It was a relief to make a decision.	_____

Source: Agnew, J. R. & Szykman, L. R. (2010) Asset allocation and information overload: The influence of information display, asset choice, and investor experience. *Journal of Behavioral Finance*, 6(2), 57–70. Reproduced with permission.

Orientation Towards Finance: Interest in Financial Information

Interest in Financial Information Measure (on a scale of 1 to 5, from strongly disagree to strongly agree)

I never read the financial pages of my newspaper *(reverse coding)*.	_____
I try to keep track of general economic trends.	_____
I am not attracted by the financial part of life *(reverse coding)*.	_____
I regularly look for interesting investment opportunities for my money.	_____
I am interested in the evolution of currency rates.	_____

Source: Loix, E., Pepermans, R., Mentens, C., Goedee, M. & Jegers, M. (2005) Orientation toward finances: Development of a measurement scale. *Journal of Behavioral Finance*, 6(4), 192–201. Reproduced with permission.

MEASURES FROM MANAGEMENT ACCOUNTING RESEARCH

Below is a sample of scales used to measure variables related to management accounting research.

Formality of performance evaluation:

My superior does not explicitly document work objectives in writing.	1 2 3 4 5	My superior explicitly documents work objectives in writing.
When judging my performance, my superior uses his/her personal judgment of my performance.	1 2 3 4 5	When judging my performance, my superior relies on objective information from the information system.
My pay is based on my superior's personal judgment of my performance.	1 2 3 4 5	My pay is based on objective information from the information system.

Source: Hartmann, F. & Slapničar, S. (2012) The perceived fairness of performance evaluation: The role of uncertainty. *Management Accounting Research*, 23(1), 17–33. Reproduced with permission.

Organizational performance (measured on a scale of 1 to 5, from strongly disagree to strongly agree):

Your company performance on return on investment is better than your competitors.	_____
Your company performance on gross margin is better than your competitors.	_____
Your company performance on customer satisfaction is better than your competitors.	_____
Your company performance on quality of product/service is better than your competitors.	_____
Your company performance on employee productivity is better than your competitors.	_____

Source: Lee, C. & Yang, H. (2011). Organization structure, competition and performance measurement systems and their joint effects on performance. *Management Accounting Research*, 22(2), 84–104. Reproduced with permission.

MEASURES FROM MANAGEMENT RESEARCH

Below is a sample of scales used to measure variables related to management research.

Job Involvement

	Strongly Disagree	Disagree	Neither Agree nor Disagree	Agree	Strongly Agree
1. My job means a lot more to me than just money.	1	2	3	4	5
2. The major satisfaction in my life comes from my job.	1	2	3	4	5
3. I am really interested in my work.	1	2	3	4	5
4. I would probably keep working even if I didn't need the money.	1	2	3	4	5
5. The most important things that happen to me involve my work.	1	2	3	4	5
6. I will stay overtime to finish a job, even if I am not paid for it.	1	2	3	4	5
7. For me, the first few hours at work really fly by.	1	2	3	4	5
8. I actually enjoy performing the daily activities that make up my job.	1	2	3	4	5
9. I look forward to coming to work each day.	1	2	3	4	5

Source: White, J. K., & Ruh, R. A. (1973) Effects of personal values on the relationship between participation and job attitudes. *Administrative Science Quarterly*, 18(4), 509. Reproduced with permission.

Participation in Decision-making

	Not at all	Very little	Somewhat	To a moderate extent	To a large extent
1. In general, how much say or influence do you have on how you perform your job?	1	2	3	4	5
2. To what extent are you able to decide how to do your job?	1	2	3	4	5
3. In general, how much say or influence do you have on what goes on in your work group?	1	2	3	4	5
4. In general, how much say or influence do you have on decisions that affect your job?	1	2	3	4	5
5. My superiors are receptive and listen to my ideas and suggestions.	1	2	3	4	5

Source: White, J. K., & Ruh, R. A. (1973) Effects of personal values on the relationship between participation and job attitudes. *Administrative Science Quarterly*, 18(4), 509. Reproduced with permission.

Career Salience

Strongly Disagree	Disagree	Slightly Disagree	Neutral	Slightly Agree	Agree	Strongly Agree
1	2	3	4	5	6	7

1	My career choice is a good occupational decision for me.	_____
2	My career enables me to make significant contributions to society.	_____
3	The career I am in fits me and reflects my personality.	_____
4	My education and training are not tailored for this career.	_____
5	I don't intend changing careers.	_____
6	All the planning and thought I gave to pursuing this career are a waste.	_____
7	My career is an integral part of my life.	_____

Source: Sekaran, U. (1986) *Dual-Career Families: Contemporary Organizational and Counseling Issues*. San Francisco: Jossey-Bass. Reproduced with permission.

MEASURES FROM MARKETING RESEARCH

Below is a sample of some scales used to measure commonly researched concepts in marketing. Bruner and Hensel have done extensive work since 1992 in documenting and detailing several scores of scales in marketing research. For each scale examined, they have provided the following information:

1. Scale description

2. Scale origin

3. Samples in which the scale was used

4. Reliability of the scale

5. Validity of the scale

6. How the scale was administered

7. Major findings of the studies using the scale

The interested student should refer to the five volumes of *Marketing Scales Handbook* by G. C. Bruner and P. J. Hensel (Volume 1 and 2); G. C. Bruner, P. J. Hensel and K. E. James published by the American Marketing Association (Volume 1, 2 and 3) and Thomson (Volume 4 and 5). The first volume covers scales used in articles published in the 1980s, and second volume covers scales used in articles published from 1990 to 1993. The third volume covers the period from 1994 to 1997. The fourth volume covers marketing scales that were reported in articles published from 1998 to 2001. The fifth volume covers the period from 2001 to 2005.

Complaint Success Likelihood

The likelihood of the complaint being successful (5-point scale with end-points labeled 'very unlikely' and 'very likely'):

At the moment of the service failure, how likely was it that the service provider would. . .

. . .take appropriate action to take care of your problem if you reported the incident?   _____

. . .solve your problem and give better service to you in the future if you reported the incident?   _____

. . .be more careful in the future and everyone would benefit if you reported the incident.   _____

Source: Bougie, R., Pieters, R., & Zeelenberg, M. (2003) Angry customers don't come back, they get back: The experience and behavioral implications of anger and dissatisfaction in services. *Journal of the Academy of Marketing Science*, 31, 377–393. Reproduced with permission.

SERVQUAL: A Multidimensional Scale to Capture Customer Perceptions and Expectations of Service Quality

Reliability items:

1. When XYZ Company promises to do something by a certain time, it does so.
2. When you have a problem, XYZ Company shows a sincere interest in solving it.
3. XYZ Company performs the service right the first time.
4. XYZ Company provides its services at the time it promises to do so.
5. XYZ Company keeps customers informed about when services will be performed.

Responsiveness items:

1. Employees in XYZ Company give you prompt service.
2. Employees in XYZ Company are always willing to help you.
3. Employees in XYZ Company are never too busy to respond to your request.

Assurance items:

1. The behaviour of employees in XYZ Company instils confidence in you.
2. You feel safe in your transactions with XYZ Company.
3. Employees in XYZ Company are consistently courteous with you.
4. Employees in XYZ Company have the knowledge to answer your questions.

Empathy items:

1. XYZ Company gives you individual attention.
2. XYZ Company has employees who give you individual attention.
3. XYZ Company has your best interests at heart.
4. Employees of XYZ Company understand your specific needs.

Tangibles items:

1. XYZ Company has modern-looking equipment.

2. XYZ Company's physical facilities are visually appealing.

3. XYZ Company's employees appear neat.

4. Materials associated with the service (such as pamphlets or statements) are visually appealing at XYZ Company.

5. XYZ Company has convenient business hours.

Source: Parasuraman, A., Zeithaml, V. A., & Berry, L. L. (1988) SERVQUAL: A multi-item scale for measuring consumer perceptions of service quality. *Journal of Retailing* 64(1) (Spring). Reproduced with permission.

Role Ambiguity (Salesperson)

Very False						Very True
1	2	3	4	5	6	7
1. I feel certain about how much authority I have in my selling position.						—
2. I have clearly planned goals for my selling job.						—
3. I am sure I divide my time properly while performing my selling tasks.						—
4. I know my responsibilities in my selling position.						—
5. I know exactly what is expected of me in my selling position.						—
6. I receive lucid explanations of what I have to do in my sales job.						—

Source: Modified from Rizzo, J. R., House, R. J., & Lirtzman, S. L. (1970) Role conflict and role ambiguity in complex organizations. *Administrative Science Quarterly*, 15, 156.

Sampling

LEARNING OBJECTIVES

After completing Chapter 14, you should be able to:

1. Define sampling, sample, population, element, sampling unit and subject.

2. Discuss statistical terms in sampling.

3. Describe and discuss the sampling process.

4. Compare and contrast specific probability sampling designs.

5. Compare and contrast specific non-probability sampling designs.

6. Discuss precision and confidence and the trade-off between precision and confidence.

7. Discuss how hypotheses can be tested with sample data.

8. Discuss the factors to be taken into consideration for determining sample size and determine the sample size for any given research project.

9. Discuss sampling in qualitative research.

10. Discuss the role of the manager in sampling.

INTRODUCTION

Experimental designs and surveys are useful and powerful in finding answers to research questions through data collection and subsequent analyses, but they can do more harm than good if the population is not correctly targeted. That is, if data are not collected from the people, events or objects that can provide the correct answers to solve the problem, the research will be in vain. The process of selecting the right individuals, objects or events as representatives for the entire population is known as **sampling**, which we will examine in some detail in this chapter (see shaded portion in Figure 14.1).

The *reasons* for using a sample, rather than collecting data from the entire population, are self-evident. In research investigations involving several hundreds and even thousands of elements, it would be practically impossible to collect data from, or test, or examine, every element. Even if it were possible, it would be prohibitive in terms of time, cost and other resources. Study of a sample rather than the entire population is also sometimes likely to produce more reliable results. This is mostly because fatigue is reduced and fewer errors therefore result in collecting data, especially when a large number of elements is involved. In a few cases, it would also be impossible to use the entire population to gain knowledge about, or test, something. Consider, for instance, the case of electric light bulbs. In testing the life of bulbs, if we were to burn every single bulb produced, there would be none left to sell! This is known as *destructive sampling*.

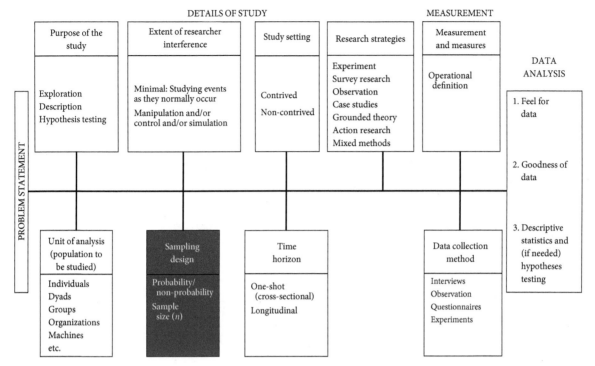

FIGURE 14.1   The research process and where this chapter fits in

POPULATION, ELEMENT, SAMPLE, SAMPLING UNIT AND SUBJECT

In learning how representative data (i.e. as reflected in the universe) can be collected, a few terms, as described below, have first to be understood.

POPULATION

The **population** refers to the entire group of people, events or things of interest that the researcher wishes to investigate. It is the group of people, events or things of interest for which the researcher wants to make inferences (based on sample statistics). For instance, if the CEO of a computer firm wants to know the kinds of advertising strategies adopted by computer firms in the Silicon Valley, then all computer firms situated there will be the population. If an organizational consultant is interested in studying the effects of a four-day work week on the white-collar workers in a telephone company in Ireland, then all white-collar workers in that company will make up the population. If regulators want to know how patients in nursing homes run by a company in France are cared for, then all the patients in all the nursing homes run by them will form the population. If, however, the regulators are interested only in one particular nursing home run by that company, then only the patients in that specific nursing home will form the population.

ELEMENT

An **element** is a single member of the population. If 1000 blue-collar workers in a particular organization happen to be the population of interest to a researcher, each blue-collar worker therein is an element. If 500 pieces of machinery are to be approved after inspecting a few, there will be 500 elements in this population. Incidentally, a census is a count of all elements in the human population.

SAMPLE

A **sample** is a subset of the population. It comprises some members selected from it. In other words, some, but not all, elements of the population form the sample. If 200 members are drawn from a population of 1000 blue-collar workers, these 200 members form the sample for the study. That is, from a study of these 200 members, the researcher will draw conclusions about the entire population of 1000 blue-collar workers. Likewise, if there are 145 in-patients in a hospital and 40 of them are to be surveyed by the hospital administrator to assess their level of satisfaction with the treatment received, then these 40 members will be the sample.

A sample is thus a subgroup or subset of the population. By studying the sample, the researcher aims and should be able to draw conclusions that are generalizable to the population of interest.

SAMPLING UNIT, UNIT OF OBSERVATION AND UNIT OF ANALYSIS

Suppose that you are interested in the views of the British public on the Brexit. You are thinking about using a cross-sectional design, with the aim of obtaining a representative sample by taking a cross section of the population. You plan to obtain a sample using multistage sampling (discussed later on in this chapter). Your sampling method involves three stages of random sampling: (1) a random sample of postal districts in the United Kingdom, (2) within each district a random sample of private households and (3) one adult selected at random in each household.

A **sampling unit** can be defined as the 'who' or 'what' that is sampled. It is the element or set of elements that is available for selection in some stage of the sampling process. In the above example, a sampling unit is involved at each stage, with units nested within each other at successive stages. The postal districts would be referred to as the primary sampling unit, the households the secondary sampling unit and the adults in a household the ultimate sampling unit. Note that not all sampling methods are as complex as the above-mentioned multistage sampling; that is why many samples contain only one sampling unit. For instance, if you were conducting research using a sample of stockbrokers, a single stockbroker would be the sampling unit.

The **unit of observation**, sometimes referred to as the unit of measurement, can be defined as the level at which your data are measured or collected. For instance, if one adult is selected random from a household, and that adult is asked to provide his or her views on the Brexit, the unit of observation is the adult. The unit of observation thus refers to the level at which you collect your data.

The **unit of analysis** refers to the level at which information is analysed and conclusions are drawn. In the above example, the unit of analysis was the adult. In sum, the unit of analysis refers to the level at which you draw your conclusions, whereas the unit of observation refers to the level at which you collect your data. The unit of analysis and the sampling unit might be the same (as in the above example), but need not be the same. For instance, in the context of a certain research project, sampling units could be students and units of analysis cohorts of students, if cohorts are compared. Students can also be both the sampling units and the units of analysis if students are compared.

SUBJECT

A **subject** is a single member of the sample, just as an element is a single member of the population. If 200 members from the total population of 1000 blue-collar workers form the sample for the study, then each blue-collar worker in the sample is a subject. As another example, if a sample of 50 machines from a total of 500 machines is to be inspected, then every one of the 50 machines is a subject, just as every single machine in the total population of 500 machines is an element.

When we sample, our subjects (employees, consumers and the like) provide us with *responses*. For instance, a consumer responding to a survey question may give a response of '3'. When we examine the responses that we get for our entire sample, we make use of *statistics*. In Chapter 15, we will explain that there is a wide variety of statistics we can use, such as the mean, the median or the mode. The reason we sample, however, is that we are interested in the characteristics of the population we sample from. If we study the entire population and calculate the mean or the standard deviation, then we don't refer to this as a statistic. Instead, we call it a *parameter* of the population.

PARAMETERS

The characteristics of the population such as μ (the population mean), σ (the population standard deviation) and σ^2 (the population variance) are referred to as its *parameters*. The central tendencies, the dispersions and other statistics in the sample of interest to the research are treated as approximations of the central tendencies, dispersions and other parameters of the population. As such, all conclusions drawn about the sample under study are generalized to the population. In other words, the sample statistics – X (the sample mean), S (the standard deviation) and S^2 (the variation in the sample) – are used as estimates of the population parameters μ, σ and σ^2. Figure 14.2 shows the relationship between the sample and the population.

REPRESENTATIVENESS OF SAMPLES

Instructors can visit the companion website at **www.wiley.com/go/bougie/researchmethods forbusiness8e** for **Author Video: Representativeness of samples**.

If you want to generalize your findings to the population from which it was selected, the sample must be representative. A representative sample is a sample that reflects the population accurately. In other words, a representative sample is a miniature of the population from which it is drawn.

NORMALITY OF DISTRIBUTIONS

Attributes or characteristics of the population are generally normally distributed. For instance, when attributes such as height and weight are considered, most people will be clustered around the mean, leaving only a small number at the extremes who are either very tall or very short, very heavy or very light and so on, as indicated in Figure 14.3. If we are to estimate the population characteristics from those represented in a sample with reasonable accuracy, the sample has to be chosen so that the distribution of the characteristics of interest follows the same pattern of normal distribution in the sample as it does in the population. From the central limit theorem, we know that the sampling distribution of the sample mean is normally distributed. As the **sample size** n increases, the means of the random samples taken from practically any population approach a normal distribution with mean μ and standard deviation σ. In sum, irrespective of whether or not the attributes of the population are normally

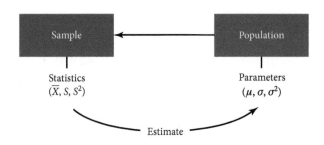

FIGURE 14.2 The relationship between sample and population

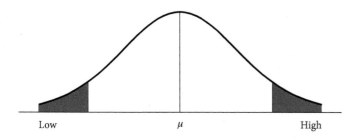

FIGURE 14.3   Normal distribution in a population

distributed, if we take a sufficiently *large number* of samples and *choose* them with care, we will have a sampling distribution of the means that has normality. This is the reason why two important issues in sampling are the sample size (n) and the sampling design, as discussed later.

When the properties of the population are not over-represented or under-represented in the sample, we have a representative sample. When a sample consists of elements in the population that have extremely high values on the variable we are studying, the sample mean X will be far higher than the population mean μ. If, in contrast, the sample subjects consist of elements in the population with extremely low values on the variable of interest, the sample mean will be much lower than the true population mean μ. If our sampling design and sample size are right, however, the sample mean X will be within close range of the true population mean μ. Thus, through appropriate sampling design, we can ensure that the sample subjects are not chosen from the extremes, but are truly representative of the properties of the population. The more representative of the population the sample is, the more generalizable are the findings of the research. Recall that generalizability is one of the hallmarks of scientific research, as we saw in Chapter 2.

While, in view of our concern about generalizability, we may be particular about choosing representative samples for most research, some cases may not call for such regard to generalizability. For instance, at the exploratory stages of fact finding, we may be interested only in 'getting a handle' on the situation, and therefore limit the interview to only the most conveniently available people. The same is true when time is of the essence, and urgency in getting information overrides a high level of accuracy in terms of priority. For instance, a film agency might want to find out quickly the impact on the viewers of a newly released film shown the previous evening. The interviewer might question the first 20 people leaving the theater after seeing the film and obtain their reactions. On the basis of their replies, she may form an opinion as to the likely success of the film. As another example, a restaurant manager might want to find the reactions of customers to a new item added to the menu to determine whether or not it has been a popular and worth while addition. For this purpose, the first 15 people who chose the special item might be interviewed, and their reactions obtained. In such cases, having instant information may be more gainful than obtaining the most representative facts. It should, however, be noted that the results of such convenient samples are not reliable and can never be generalized to the population.

THE SAMPLING PROCESS

Sampling is the *process* of selecting a sufficient number of the right elements from the population, so that a study of the sample and an understanding of its properties or characteristics make it possible for us to generalize such properties or characteristics to the population elements. The major steps in sampling include:

1. Define the population.

2. Determine the sample frame.

3. Determine the sampling design.

4. Determine the appropriate sample size.

5. Execute the sampling process.

DEFINING THE POPULATION

Sampling begins with precisely defining the target population. The target population must be defined in terms of elements, geographical boundaries and time. For instance, for a banker interested in saving habits of blue-collar workers in the mining industry in the United States, the target population might be all blue-collar workers in that industry throughout the country. For an advertising agency interested in reading habits of elderly people, the target population might be the German population aged 50 and over. These examples illustrate that the research objective and the scope of the study play a crucial role in defining the target population.

DETERMINING THE SAMPLE FRAME

The **sampling frame** is a (physical) representation of all the elements in the population from which the sample is drawn. The payroll of an organization would serve as the sampling frame if its members are to be studied. Ideally, a sampling frame is a complete and correct list of the population elements. However, practical circumstances often make such a list incorrect and incomplete. For instance, the names of members who have recently left the organization or dropped out of the university, as well as members who have only recently joined the organization or the university, may not appear in the organization's payroll or the university registers on a given day. How much inaccuracy you can accept in your sampling frame is a matter of judgment.

When the sampling frame does not exactly match the population *coverage error* occurs. In some cases, the researcher might recognize this problem and not be too concerned about it, because the discrepancy between the target population and the sampling frame is small enough to ignore. However, in most cases, the researcher should deal with this error by either redefining the target population in terms of the sampling frame, screening the respondents with respect to important characteristics to ensure that they meet the criteria for the target population or adjusting the collected data by a weighting scheme to counterbalance the coverage error.

DETERMINING THE SAMPLING DESIGN

There are two major types of sampling design: probability and non-probability sampling. In **probability sampling**, the elements in the population have some known, non-zero chance or probability of being selected as sample subjects. In **non-probability sampling**, the elements do not have a known or predetermined chance of being selected as subjects. Probability sampling designs are used when the representativeness of the sample is of importance in the interests of wider generalizability. When time or other factors, rather than generalizability, become critical, non-probability sampling is generally used. Each of these two major designs has different sampling strategies. Depending on the extent of generalizability desired, the demands of time and other resources and the purpose of the study, different types of probability and non-probability sampling design are chosen.

The choice of the sampling procedure is a very important one. Therefore, this chapter will elaborately discuss the different types of sampling designs, bearing in mind the following points in the determination of the choice:

- What is the relevant target population of focus to the study?
- What exactly are the parameters we are interested in investigating?
- What kind of a sampling frame is available?
- What costs are attached to the sampling design?
- How much time is available to collect the data from the sample?

DETERMINING THE SAMPLE SIZE

Is a sample size of 40 large enough? Or do you need a sample size of 75, 180, 384 or 500? Is a large sample better than a small sample; that is, is it more representative? The decision about how large the sample size should be can be a very difficult one. We can summarize the factors affecting decisions on sample size as:

1. The research objective.

2. The extent of precision desired (the confidence interval).

3. The acceptable risk in predicting that level of precision (confidence level).

4. The amount of variability in the population itself.

5. The cost and time constraints.

6. In some cases, the size of the population itself.

Thus, how large your sample should be is a function of these six factors. We will have more to say about sample size later on in this chapter, after we have discussed sampling designs.

EXECUTING THE SAMPLING PROCESS

The following two examples illustrate how, in the final stage of the sampling process, decisions with respect to the target population, the sampling frame, the sample technique and the sample size have to be implemented.

Example

A satisfaction survey was conducted for a computer retailer in New Zealand. The objective of this survey was to improve internal operations and thus to retain more customers. The survey was transactional in nature; service satisfaction and several related variables were measured following a service encounter (i.e. a visit to the retailer). Hence, customer feedback was obtained while the service experience was still fresh. To obtain a representative sample of customers of the computer retailer (*the target population*), every tenth person, leaving one out of ten randomly selected stores, in randomly selected cities, in randomly selected regions, was approached during a one-week period (*the sampling technique*). Trained interviewers that were sent out with standardized questionnaires approached 732 customers leaving the stores (*the sample size*).

A young researcher was investigating the antecedents of salesperson performance. To examine his hypotheses, data were collected from chief sales executives in the United Kingdom (*the target population*) via mail questionnaires. The sample was initially drawn from a published business register (*the sampling frame*), but supplemented with respondent recommendations and other additions, in a *judgment sampling methodology*. Before distributing the questionnaires, the young researcher called each selected company to obtain the name of the chief sales executive, who was contacted and asked to participate in the study. The questionnaires were subsequently distributed to chief sales executives of 450 companies (*the sample size*). To enhance the response rate, pre-addressed and stamped envelopes were provided, anonymity was assured and a summary of the research findings as an incentive to the participants was offered. Several follow-up procedures, such as telephone calls and new mailings, were planned in order to receive as many responses as possible.

| BOX 14.1 | NON-RESPONSE AND NON-RESPONSE ERROR |

A failure to obtain information from a number of subjects included in the sample (non-response) may lead to non-response error. **Non-response error** exists to the extent that those who did respond to your survey are different from those who did not on (one of the) characteristics of interest in your study. An important source of non-response are refusals. The rate of refusals depends, among other things, on the length of the survey, the data collection method and the patronage of the research. Hence, a decrease in survey length, in the data collection method (personal interviews instead of mail questionnaires), and the auspices of the research often improve the overall return rate. Personalized cover letters, a small incentive for participating in the study and an advance notice that the survey is taking place may also help you to increase the response rate. Nonetheless, it is almost impossible to entirely avoid non-response in surveys. In these cases, you may have to turn to methods to deal with non-response error, such as generalizing the results to the respondents only or statistical adjustment (weighting the data by observable variables).

| PROBABILITY SAMPLING |

When elements in the population have a known, non-zero chance of being chosen as subjects in the sample, we resort to a probability sampling design. Probability sampling is used when the researcher wants to generalize the research findings to the population. Probability sampling can be either unrestricted (simple random sampling) or restricted (complex probability sampling) in nature.

UNRESTRICTED OR SIMPLE RANDOM SAMPLING

In the **unrestricted probability sampling** design, more commonly known as **simple random sampling**, every element in the population has a *known and equal* chance of being selected as a subject. Let us say there are 1000 elements in the population, and we need a sample of 100. Suppose we were to drop pieces of paper in a hat, each bearing the name of one of the elements, and draw 100 of those from the hat with our eyes closed. We know that the first piece drawn will have a 1/1000 chance of being drawn, the next one a 1/999 chance of being drawn and so on. In other words, we know that the probability of any one of them being chosen is 1 in the number of the population, and we also know that each single element in the hat has the same or equal probability of being chosen. We certainly know that computers can generate random numbers and one does not have to go through the tedious process of pulling out names from a hat!

When we thus draw the elements from the population, it is most likely that the distribution patterns of the characteristics we are interested in investigating in the population are also likewise distributed in the subjects we draw for our sample. This sampling design, known as simple random sampling, has the least bias and offers the most generalizability. However, this sampling process could become cumbersome and expensive; in addition, an entirely updated listing of the population may not always be available. For these and other reasons, other probability sampling designs are often chosen instead.

RESTRICTED OR COMPLEX PROBABILITY SAMPLING

As an alternative to the simple random sampling design, several **complex probability sampling (restricted probability)** designs can be used. These probability sampling procedures offer a viable, and sometimes more efficient, alternative to the unrestricted design we just discussed. Efficiency is improved in that more information can be obtained for a given sample size using some of the complex probability sampling procedures than the simple random sampling design. The five most common complex probability sampling designs – systematic sampling, stratified random sampling, cluster sampling, area sampling and double sampling – will now be discussed.

Systematic Sampling

The **systematic sampling** design involves drawing every nth element in the population starting with a randomly chosen element between 1 and n.

To draw a systematic sample, you can follow the steps below:

1. Identify the number of elements in the population.

2. Identify the sampling ratio (n = population size/size of the desired sample).

3. Identify a random start.

4. Draw the sample by choosing every nth element.

Systematic sampling requires a full list of the population. Getting such a list is often difficult. The procedure is exemplified below.

> If we wanted a sample of 35 households from a total population of 260 houses in a particular locality, then we could sample every seventh house starting from a random number from 1 to 7. Let us say that the random number was 7, then houses numbered 7, 14, 21, 28 and so on, would be sampled until the 35 houses were selected. The one problem to be borne in mind in the systematic sampling design is the probability of a systematic bias creeping into the sample. In the above example, for instance, let us say that every seventh house happened to be a corner house. If the focus of the research study conducted by the construction industry was to control 'noise pollution' experienced by residents through the use of appropriate filtering materials, then the residents of corner houses may not be exposed to as much noise as the houses that are in between. Information on noise levels gathered from corner house dwellers might therefore bias the researcher's data. The likelihood of drawing incorrect conclusions from such data is thus high. In view of the scope for such systematic bias, the researcher must consider the plans carefully and make sure that the systematic sampling design is appropriate for the study, before deciding on it.

Example

Stratified Random Sampling

While sampling helps to estimate population parameters, there may be identifiable subgroups of elements within the population that may be expected to have different parameters on a variable of interest to the researcher. For example, to the human resources management director interested in assessing the extent of training that the employees in the system feel they need, the entire organization will form the population for study. But the extent, quality and intensity of training desired by middle-level managers, lower-level managers, first-line supervisors, computer analysts, clerical workers and so on will be different for each group. Knowledge of the kinds of differences in needs that exist for the different groups will help the director to develop useful and meaningful training programs for each group in the organization. Data will therefore have to be collected in a manner that will help the assessment of needs at each subgroup level in the population. The unit of analysis then will be at the group level and the stratified random sampling process will come in handy.

Stratified random sampling, as its name implies, involves a process of stratification or segregation, followed by random selection of subjects from each stratum. The population is first divided into mutually exclusive groups that are relevant, appropriate and meaningful in the context of the study. For instance, if the president of a company is concerned about low motivational levels or high absenteeism rates among the employees, it makes sense to stratify the population of organizational members according to their job levels. When the data are collected and the analysis is done, we may find that, contrary to expectations, it is the middle-level managers that are not motivated. This information will help the president to focus on action at the right level and devise better methods to motivate this group. Tracing the differences in the parameters of the subgroups within a population would not be possible without the stratified random sampling procedure. If either the simple random sampling or the systematic sampling procedure were used in a case like this, then the high motivation at some job levels and the low motivation at other levels would cancel each other out, thus masking the real problems that exist at a particular level or levels.

Stratification also helps when research questions such as the following are to be answered:

1. Are the machinists more accident prone than clerical workers?

2. Are Hispanics more loyal to the organization than Native Americans?

Stratifying customers on the basis of life stages, income levels and the like to study buying patterns and stratifying companies according to size, industry, profits and so forth to study stock market reactions are common examples of the use of stratification as a sampling design technique.

Stratification is an efficient research sampling design; that is, it provides more information with a given sample size. Stratification should follow the lines appropriate to the research question. If we are studying consumer preferences for a product, stratification of the population could be by geographical area, market segment, consumers' age, consumers' gender or various combinations of these. If an organization contemplates budget cuts, the effects of these cuts on employee attitudes can be studied with stratification by department, function or region. Stratification ensures homogeneity within each stratum (i.e. very few differences or dispersions on the variable of interest within each stratum), but heterogeneity (variability) between strata. In other words, there will be more between-group differences than within-group differences.

Proportionate and disproportionate stratified random sampling Once the population has been stratified in some meaningful way, a sample of members from each stratum can be drawn using either a simple random sampling or a systematic sampling procedure. The subjects drawn from each stratum can be either proportionate or disproportionate to the number of elements in the stratum. For instance, if an organization employs 10 top managers, 30 middle managers, 50 lower-level managers, 100 supervisors, 500 clerks and 20 secretaries, and a stratified sample of about 140 people is needed for some specific survey, the researcher might decide to include in the sample 20 percent of members from each stratum. That is, members represented in the sample from each stratum will be *proportionate* to the total number of elements in the respective strata. This would mean that two from the top, six from the middle and ten from the lower levels of management would be included in the sample. In addition, 20 supervisors, 100 clerks and 4 secretaries would be represented in the sample, as shown in the third column of Table 14.1. This type of sampling is called a **proportionate stratified random sampling** design.

Table 14.1 Proportionate and Disproportionate Stratified Random Sampling

Job level	Number of elements	Number of subjects in the sample	
		Proportionate sampling (20 percent of the elements)	Disproportionate sampling
Top management	10	2	7
Middle-level management	30	6	15
Lower-level management	50	10	20
Supervisors	100	20	30
Clerks	500	100	60
Secretaries	20	4	10
Total	710	142	142

In situations like the one above, researchers might sometimes be concerned that information from only two members at the top and six from the middle levels would not truly reflect how all members at those levels would respond. Therefore, a researcher might decide, instead, to use a **disproportionate stratified random sampling** procedure. The number of subjects from each stratum would now be altered, while keeping the sample size unchanged. Such a sampling design is illustrated in the far right-hand column in Table 14.1. The idea here is that the 60 clerks might be considered adequate to represent the population of 500 clerks; seven out of ten managers at the top level might also be considered representative of the top managers and likewise 15 out of the 30 managers at the middle level. This redistribution of the numbers in the strata might be considered more appropriate and representative for the study than the previous proportionate sampling design.

Disproportionate sampling decisions are made either when some stratum or strata are too small or too large, or when there is more variability suspected within a particular stratum. As an example, the educational levels among supervisors, which may be considered to influence perceptions, may range from elementary school to master's degrees. Here, more people will be sampled at the supervisory level. Disproportionate sampling is also sometimes done when it is easier, simpler and less expensive to collect data from one or more strata than from others.

In summary, stratified random sampling involves stratifying the elements along meaningful levels and taking proportionate or disproportionate samples from the strata. This sampling design is more efficient than the simple random sampling design because, for the same sample size, each important segment of the population is better represented, and more valuable and differentiated information is obtained with respect to each group.

Cluster Sampling

Cluster samples are samples gathered in groups or chunks of elements that, ideally, are natural aggregates of elements in the population. In **cluster sampling**, the target population is first divided into clusters. Then, a random sample of clusters is drawn and for each selected cluster either all the elements or a sample of elements are included in the sample. Cluster samples offer more heterogeneity within groups and more homogeneity among groups – the reverse of what we find in stratified random sampling, where there is homogeneity within each group and heterogeneity across groups.

A specific type of cluster sampling is **area sampling**. In this case, clusters consist of geographic areas such as counties, city blocks or particular boundaries within a locality. If you wanted to survey the residents of a city, you would get a city map, take a sample of city blocks and select respondents within each city block. Sampling the needs of consumers before opening a 24-hour convenience store in a particular part of town would involve area sampling. Location plans for retail stores, advertisements focused specifically on local populations and TV and radio programs beamed at specific areas could all use an area sampling design to gather information on the interests, attitudes, predispositions and behaviours of the local area people.

Area sampling is less expensive than most other probability sampling designs, and it is not dependent on a sampling frame. A city map showing the blocks of the city is adequate information to allow a researcher to take a sample of the blocks and obtain data from the residents therein. Indeed, the key motivation for cluster sampling is cost reduction. The unit costs of cluster sampling are much lower than those of other probability sampling designs of simple or stratified random sampling or systematic sampling. However, cluster sampling exposes itself to greater bias and is the least generalizable of all the probability sampling designs, because most naturally occurring clusters in the organizational context do not contain heterogeneous elements. In other words, the conditions of intracluster heterogeneity and intercluster homogeneity are often not met.

For these reasons, the cluster sampling technique is not very common in organizational research. Moreover, for marketing research activities, naturally occurring clusters, such as clusters of residents, buyers, students or shops, do not have much heterogeneity among the elements. As stated earlier, there is more intracluster homogeneity than heterogeneity in such clusters. Hence, cluster sampling, though less costly, does not offer much efficiency in terms of precision or confidence in the results. However, cluster sampling offers convenience. For example, it is easier to inspect an assortment of units packed inside, say, four boxes (i.e. all the elements in the four clusters) than to open 30 boxes in a shipment in order to inspect a few units from each at random.

Single-stage and multistage cluster sampling We have thus far discussed single-stage cluster sampling, which involves the division of the population into convenient clusters, randomly choosing the required number of clusters as sample subjects and investigating all the elements in each of the randomly chosen clusters. Cluster sampling can also be done in several stages and is then known as **multistage cluster sampling**. For instance, if we were to do a national survey of the average monthly bank deposits, cluster sampling would first be used to select the urban, semi-urban and rural geographical locations for study. At the next stage, particular areas in each of these locations would be chosen. At the third stage, banks within each area would be chosen. In other words, multistage cluster sampling involves a probability sampling of the primary sampling units; from each of these primary units, a probability sample of the secondary sampling units is then drawn; a third level of probability sampling is done from each of these secondary units, and so on, until we have reached the final stage of breakdown for the sample units, when we sample every member in those units.

Double Sampling

This plan is resorted to when further information is needed from a subset of the group from which some information has already been collected for the same study. A sampling design where initially a sample is used in a study to collect some preliminary information of interest, and later a subsample of this primary sample is used to examine the matter in more detail, is called **double sampling**. For example, a structured interview might indicate that a subgroup of the respondents has more insight into the problems of the organization. These respondents might be interviewed again and asked additional questions. This research adopts a double sampling procedure.

REVIEW OF PROBABILITY SAMPLING DESIGNS

There are two basic probability sampling plans: the unrestricted or simple random sampling and the restricted or complex probability sampling plans. In the simple random sampling design, every element in the population has a known and equal chance of being selected as a subject. The complex probability plan consists of five different sampling designs. Of these five, the cluster sampling design is probably the least expensive as well as the least dependable, but is used when no list of the population elements is available. The stratified random sampling design is probably the most efficient, in the sense that for the same number of sample subjects, it offers precise and detailed information. The systematic sampling design has the built-in hazard of possible systematic bias. Area sampling is a popular form of cluster sampling, and double sampling is resorted to when information in addition to that already obtained by using a primary sample has to be collected using a subgroup of the sample.

NON-PROBABILITY SAMPLING

In **non-probability sampling** designs, the elements in the population do not have any probabilities attached to their being chosen as sample subjects. This means that the findings from the study of the sample cannot be confidently generalized to the population. In probability samples, a sample is selected to represent the population. However, it cannot be said to be representative for the population. As stated earlier, researchers may, at times, be less concerned about generalizability than obtaining some preliminary information in a quick and inexpensive way. They might then resort to non-probability sampling. Sometimes non-probability sampling is the only way to obtain data, as discussed later.

Some of the non-probability sampling plans are more dependable than others. Non-probability sampling designs, which fit into the broad categories of convenience sampling and purposive sampling, are discussed next.

CONVENIENCE SAMPLING

As its name implies, **convenience sampling** refers to the collection of information from members of the population who are conveniently available to provide it. The researcher knows how many subjects (consumers, employees, light bulbs) to include in the sample and continues the process until the required sample size has been reached. Convenience sampling is cheap and easy to conduct, but there is no way of telling how representative the research results are. It is often used to obtain some quick information. In the process, you might sometimes discover that your research results are so indisputable that there is no incentive to collect further information.

PURPOSIVE SAMPLING

Instead of obtaining information from those who are most readily or conveniently available, it might sometimes become necessary to obtain information from specific target groups. The sampling here is confined to specific types of people who can provide the desired information, either because they are the only ones who have it, or they conform to some criteria set by the researcher. This type of sampling design is called **purposive sampling**, and the two major types of purposive sampling – judgment sampling and quota sampling – will now be explained.

Judgment Sampling

Judgment sampling involves the choice of subjects who are most advantageously placed or in the best position to provide the information required. For instance, if a researcher wants to find out what it takes for women managers to make it to the top, the only people who can give first-hand information are the women who have risen to the positions of presidents, vice presidents and important top-level executives in work organizations. They could reasonably be expected to have expert knowledge by virtue of having gone through the experiences and processes themselves, and might perhaps be able to provide good data or information to the researcher. Thus, the **judgment sampling** design is used when a limited number or category of people have the information that is sought. In such cases, any type of probability sampling across a cross section of the entire population is purposeless and not useful.

Judgment sampling may curtail the generalizability of the findings, due to the fact that we are using a sample of experts who are conveniently available to us. However, it is the only viable sampling method for obtaining the type of information that is required from very specific pockets of people who alone possess the needed facts and can give the information sought. In organizational settings, and particularly for market research, opinion leaders who are very knowledgeable are included in the sample. Enlightened opinions, views and knowledge constitute a rich data source.

Judgment sampling calls for special efforts to locate and gain access to the individuals who do have the requisite information. As already stated, this sampling design may be the only useful one for answering certain types of research question.

Quota Sampling

Quota sampling, a second type of purposive sampling, ensures that certain groups are adequately represented in the study through the assignment of a quota. Generally, the quota fixed for each subgroup is based on the total numbers of each group in the population. However, since this is a non-probability sampling plan, the results are not generalizable to the population.

Quota sampling can be considered a form of proportionate stratified sampling, in which a predetermined proportion of people are sampled from different groups, but on a convenience basis. For instance, it may be surmised that the work attitude of blue-collar workers in an organization is quite different from that of white-collar workers. If there are 60 percent blue-collar workers and 40 percent white-collar workers in this organization, and if a total of 30 people are to be interviewed to find the answer to the research question, then a quota of 18 blue-collar workers and 12 white-collar workers will form the sample, because these numbers represent 60 percent and 40 percent of the sample size. The first 18 conveniently available blue-collar workers and 12 white-collar workers will be sampled according to this quota. Needless to say, the sample may not be totally representative of the population; hence the generalizability of the findings will be restricted. However, the convenience it offers in terms of effort, cost and time makes quota sampling attractive for some research efforts. Quota sampling also becomes a necessity when a subset of the population is underrepresented in the organization – for example, minority groups, foremen and so on. In other words, quota sampling ensures that all the subgroups in the population are adequately represented in the sample. Quota samples are basically stratified samples from which subjects are selected non-randomly.

In a workplace (and society) that is becoming increasingly heterogeneous because of the changing demographics, quota sampling can be expected to be used more frequently in the future. For example, quota sampling can be used to gain some idea of the buying predispositions of various ethnic groups, to get a feel of how employees from different nationalities perceive the organizational culture, and so on.

Although quota sampling is not generalizable like stratified random sampling, it does offer some information, based on which further investigation, if necessary, can proceed. That is, it is possible that the first stage of research will use the non-probability design of quota sampling, and once some useful information has been obtained, a probability design will follow. The converse is also entirely possible. A probability sampling design might indicate new areas for research, and non-probability sampling designs might be used to explore their feasibility.

REVIEW OF NON-PROBABILITY SAMPLING DESIGNS

There are two main types of non-probability sampling design: convenience sampling and purposive sampling. Convenience sampling is the least reliable of all sampling designs in terms of generalizability, but sometimes it may be the only viable alternative when quick and timely information is needed, or for exploratory research purposes. Purposive sampling plans fall into two categories: judgment and quota sampling designs. Judgment sampling, though restricted in generalizability, may sometimes be the best sampling design choice, especially when there is a limited population that can supply the information needed. Quota sampling is often used on considerations of cost and time and the need to adequately represent minority elements in the population. Although the generalizability of all non-probability sampling designs is very restricted, they have certain advantages and are sometimes the only viable alternative for the researcher.

Table 14.2 summarizes the probability and non-probability sampling designs discussed thus far, and their advantages and disadvantages. Figure 14.4 offers some decision choice points as to which design might be useful for specific research goals.

Table 14.2   Probability and Non-Probability Sampling Designs

Sampling design	Description	Advantages	Disadvantages
Probability sampling			
1. Simple random sampling	All elements in the population are considered and each element has an equal chance of being chosen as the subject.	High generalizability of findings.	Not as efficient as stratified sampling.
2. Systematic sampling	Every nth element in the population is chosen starting from a random point in the sampling frame.	Easy to use if sampling frame is available.	Systematic biases are possible.
3. Stratified random sampling (Str.R.S.) Proportionate Str.R.S. Disproportionate Str.R.S.	Population is first divided into meaningful segments; thereafter subjects are drawn in proportion to their original numbers in the population. Based on criteria other than their original population numbers.	Most efficient among all probability designs. All groups are adequately sampled and comparisons among groups are possible.	Stratification must be meaningful. More time consuming than simple random sampling or systematic sampling. Sampling frame for each stratum is essential.
4. Cluster sampling	Groups that have heterogeneous members are first identified; then some are chosen at random; all the members in each of the randomly chosen groups are studied.	In geographic clusters, costs of data collection are low.	The least reliable and efficient among all probability sampling designs since subsets of clusters are more homogeneous than heterogeneous.
5. Area sampling	Cluster sampling within a particular area or locality.	Cost-effective. Useful for decisions relating to a particular location.	Takes time to collect data from an area.
6. Double sampling	The same sample or a subset of the sample is studied twice.	Offers more detailed information on the topic of study.	Original biases, if any, will be carried over. Individuals may not be happy responding a second time.
Non-probability sampling			
7. Convenience sampling	The most easily accessible members are chosen as subjects.	Quick, convenient, less expensive.	Not generalizable at all.
8. Judgment sampling	Subjects selected on the basis of their expertise in the subject investigated.	Sometimes, the only meaningful way to investigate.	Generalizability is questionable; not generalizable to entire population.
9. Quota sampling	Subjects are conveniently chosen from targeted groups according to some predetermined number or quota.	Very useful where minority participation in a study is critical.	Not easily generalizable.

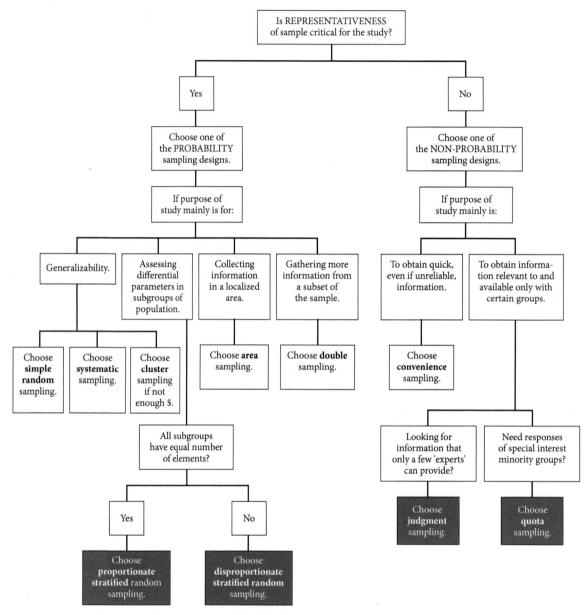

FIGURE 14.4 Choice points in sampling design

<table>
<tr><td>

INTERMEZZO:
EXAMPLES OF
WHEN CERTAIN
SAMPLING
DESIGNS
WOULD BE
APPROPRIATE

</td><td>

SIMPLE RANDOM SAMPLING

This sampling design is best when the generalizability of the findings to the whole population is the main objective of the study. Consider the following two examples.

</td></tr>
</table>

The human resources director of a company with 82 people on its payroll has been asked by the vice president to consider formulating an implementable flextime policy. The director feels that such a policy is not necessary since everyone seems happy with the 9-to-5 hours, and no one has complained. Formulating such a policy now, in the opinion of the director, runs the risk of creating domestic problems for the staff and scheduling problems for the company. She wants, however, to resort to a simple random sampling procedure to do an initial survey, and, with the results, convince the VP that there is no need for flextime, and urge him to drop the matter. Since simple random sampling offers the greatest generalizability of the results to the entire population, and the VP needs to be convinced, it is important to resort to this sampling design.

Example

The regional director of sales operations of a medium-sized company, which has 20 retail stores in each of its four geographical regions of operation, wants to know what types of sales gimmicks worked best for the company overall during the past year. This is to help formulate some general policies for the company *as a whole* and prioritize sales promotion strategies for the coming year. Instead of studying each of the 80 stores, some *dependable* (i.e. *representative* and *generalizable*) information can be had, based on the study of a few stores drawn through a simple random sampling procedure. That is, each one of the 80 stores would have an equal chance of being included in the sample, and the results of the study would be the most generalizable. A simple random sampling procedure is recommended in this case since the policy is to be formulated for the company as a whole. This implies that the most representative information has to be obtained that can be generalized to the entire company. This is best accomplished through this design.

It has to be noted that in some cases, where *cost* is a primary consideration (i.e. resources are limited), and the number of elements in the population is very large and/or geographically dispersed, the simple random sampling design may not be the most desirable, because it could become quite expensive. Thus, both the criticality of generalizability and considerations of cost come into play in the choice of this sampling design.

STRATIFIED RANDOM SAMPLING

This sampling design, which is the most efficient, is a good choice when differentiated information is needed regarding various strata within the population, which are known to differ in their parameters. See the following examples.

The director of human resources of a manufacturing firm wants to offer stress management seminars to the personnel who experience high levels of stress. He conjectures that three groups are most prone to stress: the workmen who constantly handle dangerous chemicals, the foremen who are held responsible for production quotas, and the counsellors who, day in and day out, listen to the problems of the employees, internalize them and offer them counsel, with no idea of how much they have really helped the clients. To get a feel for the experienced level of stress within each of the three groups and the rest of the firm, the director might stratify the sample into four distinct categories: (1) the workmen handling the dangerous chemicals, (2) the foremen, (3) the counsellors and (4) all the rest. He might then choose a *disproportionate random sampling* procedure (since group (3) can be expected to be very small, and groups (2) and (1) are much smaller than group (4)).

Example

This is the only sampling design that would allow the designing of stress management seminars in a meaningful way, targeted at the right groups.

If, in the earlier example, the regional director had wanted to know which sales promotion gimmick offered the best results for *each* of the geographical areas, so that different sales promotion strategies (according to regional preferences) could be developed, then the 80 stores would first be stratified on the basis of the geographical region, and then a representative sample of stores would be drawn from each of the geographical regions (strata) through a simple random sampling procedure. In this case, since each of the regions has 20 stores, a proportionate stratified random sampling process (say, five stores from each region) would be appropriate. If, however, the northern region had only three stores, the southern had 15, and the eastern and western regions had 24 and 38 stores, respectively, then a *disproportionate stratified random sampling* procedure would be the right choice, with all three stores in the northern region being studied, because of the small number of elements in that population. If the sample size was retained at 20, then the north, south, east and west regions would probably have samples respectively of three, four, five and eight. It is interesting to note that sometimes when stratified random sampling might seem logical, it might not really be necessary. For example, when test-marketing results show that Cubans, Puerto Ricans and Mexicans perceive and consume a particular product the same way, there is no need to segment the market and study each of the three groups using a stratified sampling procedure.

SYSTEMATIC SAMPLING

If the sampling frame is large, and a listing of the elements is conveniently available in one place (as in the telephone directory, company payroll, chamber of commerce listings, etc.), then a systematic sampling procedure will offer the advantages of ease and quickness in developing the sample, as illustrated by the following example.

Example

An administrator wants to assess the reactions of employees to a new and improved health benefits scheme that requires a modest increase in the premiums to be paid by the employees for their families. The administrator can assess the enthusiasm for the new scheme by using a systematic sampling design. The company's records will provide the sampling frame, and every *n*th employee can be sampled. A stratified plan is not called for here since the policy is for the entire company.

BOX 14.2   NOTE

Systematic sampling is inadvisable where systematic bias can be anticipated to be present. For example, systematic sampling from the personnel directory of a company (especially when it has an equal number of employees in each department), which lists the names of the individuals department-wise, with the head of the department listed first, and the secretary listed next, has inherent bias. The possibility of systematic bias creeping into the data cannot be ruled out in this case, since the selection process may end up picking each of the heads of the department or the departmental secretaries as the sample subjects. The results from such a sample will clearly be biased and not generalizable, despite the use of a probability sampling procedure. Systematic sampling will have to be scrupulously avoided in cases where known systematic biases are possible.

CLUSTER SAMPLING

This sampling design is most useful when a heterogeneous group is to be studied at one time. Two examples are offered as follows.

A human resources director is interested in knowing why staff resign. Cluster sampling will be useful in this case for conducting exit interviews of all members completing their final papers in the human resources department on the same day (cluster), before resigning. The clusters chosen for interview will be based on a simple random sampling of the various clusters of personnel resigning on different days. The interviews will help to understand the reasons for turnover of a heterogeneous group of individuals (i.e. from various departments), and the study can be conducted at a low cost.

Example

A financial analyst wishes to study the lending practices of banks in the Netherlands. All the banks in each city will form a cluster. By randomly sampling the clusters, the analyst will be able to draw conclusions on the lending practices.

AREA SAMPLING

Area sampling is best suited when the goal of the research is confined to a particular locality or area, as per the example below.

A telephone company wants to install a public telephone outlet in a locality where crime is most rampant, so that victims can have access to a telephone. Studying the crime statistics and interviewing the residents in a particular area will help to choose the right location for installation of the phone.

Example

DOUBLE SAMPLING

This design provides added information at minimal additional expenditure. See the example below.

In the previous exit interview example, some individuals (i.e. a subset of the original cluster sample) might have indicated that they were resigning because of philosophical differences with the company's policies. The researcher might want to do an in-depth interview with these individuals to obtain further information regarding the nature of the policies disliked, the actual philosophical differences and why these particular issues were central to the individuals' value systems. Such additional detailed information from the target group through the double sampling design could help the company to look for ways of retaining employees in the future.

Example

CONVENIENCE SAMPLING

This non-probability design, which is unrestricted, cheap and easy to conduct, is often used to obtain some 'quick' information to get a 'feel' for the phenomenon or variables of interest. See the example below.

The accounts executive has established a new accounting system that maximally utilizes computer technology. Before making further changes, he would like to get a feel for how the accounting clerks react to the new system without making it seem that he has doubts about its acceptability. He may then 'casually' talk to the first five accounting personnel that walk into his office, trying to gauge their reactions.

Example

BOX 14.3	**NOTE**

Convenience sampling should be resorted to in the interests of expediency, with the full knowledge that the results are not generalizable to the population.

JUDGMENT SAMPLING: ONE TYPE OF PURPOSIVE SAMPLING

A judgment sampling design is used where the collection of 'specialized informed inputs' on the topic area researched is vital, and the use of any other sampling design would not offer opportunities to obtain the specialized information, as per the example that follows.

Example	A pharmaceutical company wants to trace the effects of a new drug on patients with specific health problems (muscular dystrophy, sickle cell anaemia, rheumatoid arthritis, etc.). It then contacts such individuals and, with a group of voluntarily consenting patients, tests the drug. This is a judgment sample because data are collected from appropriate special groups.

QUOTA SAMPLING: A SECOND TYPE OF PURPOSIVE SAMPLING

This sampling design allows for the inclusion of *all* groups in the system researched. Thus, groups who are small in number are not neglected, as per the example below.

Example	A company is considering operating an on-site kindergarten facility. But before taking further steps, it wants to get the reactions of four groups to the idea: (1) employees who are parents of kindergarten-age children, and where both are working outside of the home, (2) employees who are parents of kindergarten-age children, but where one of them is *not* working outside of the home, (3) single parents with kindergarten-age children and (4) all those without children of kindergarten age. If the four groups are expected to represent 60 percent, 7 percent, 23 percent and 10 percent, respectively, in the population of 420 employees in the company, then a quota sampling will be appropriate to represent the four groups.

BOX 14.4	**NOTE**

The last group in the above example should also be included in the sample since there is a possibility that they may perceive this as a facility that favours only the parents of kindergarten children, and therefore resent the idea. It is easy to see that resorting to quota sampling would be important in a case such as this.

In effect, as can be seen from the discussions on sampling designs thus far, *decisions on which design to use* depend on many factors, including the following:

1. Extent of prior knowledge in the area of research undertaken.

2. The main objective of the study – generalizability, efficiency, knowing more about subgroups within a population, obtaining some quick (even if unreliable) information, etc.

3. Cost considerations – is exactitude and generalizability worth the extra investment of time, cost and other resources in resorting to a more, rather than less, sophisticated sampling design? Even if it is, is suboptimization because of cost or time constraints called for? (See also Figure 14.4.)

The advantages and disadvantages of the different probability and non-probability sampling designs are listed in Table 14.2.

In sum, choosing the appropriate sampling plan is one of the more important research design decisions the researcher has to make. The choice of a specific design will depend broadly on the goal of research, the characteristics of the population and considerations of cost.

Having discussed the various probability and non-probability sampling designs, we now need to focus attention on the second aspect of the sampling design issue – the sample size. Suppose we select 30 people from a population of 3000 through a simple random sampling procedure. Will we be able to generalize our findings to the population with confidence, since we have chosen a probability design that has the most generalizability? What is the sample size required to make reasonably precise generalizations with confidence? What do precision and confidence mean? These issues will be considered now.

> **ISSUES OF PRECISION AND CONFIDENCE IN DETERMINING SAMPLE SIZE**

A reliable and valid sample should enable us to generalize the findings from the sample to the population under investigation. In other words, the sample statistics should be reliable estimates and reflect the population parameters as closely as possible within a narrow margin of error. No sample statistic (X, for instance) is going to be *exactly* the same as the population parameter (μ), no matter how sophisticated the probability sampling design is. Remember that the very reason for a probability design is to increase the probability that the sample statistics will be as close as possible to the population parameters. Though the point estimate X may not accurately reflect the population mean, μ, an interval estimate can be made within which μ will lie, with probabilities attached – that is, at particular confidence levels. The issues of confidence interval and confidence level are addressed in the following discussions on precision and confidence.

PRECISION

Precision refers to how close our estimate is to the true population characteristic. Usually, we estimate the population parameter to fall within a range, based on the sample estimate. For example, let us say that from a study of a simple random sample of 50 of the total 300 employees in a workshop, we find that the average daily production rate per person is 50 pieces of a particular product ($\overline{X} = 50$). We might then (by doing certain calculations, as we shall see later) be able to say that the true average daily production of the product (μ) lies anywhere between 40 and 60 for the population of employees in the workshop. In saying this, we offer an interval estimate, within which we expect the true population mean production to be ($\mu = 50 \pm 10$). The narrower this interval, the greater the precision. For instance, if we are able to estimate that the population mean will fall anywhere between 45 and 55 pieces of production ($\mu = 50 \pm 5$) rather than 40 and 60 ($\mu = 50 \pm 10$), then we have more precision. That is, we now estimate the mean to lie within a narrower range, which in turn means that we estimate with greater exactitude or precision.

Precision is a function of the range of variability in the sampling distribution of the sample mean. That is, if we take a number of different samples from a population, and take the mean of each of these, we will usually find that they are all different, are normally distributed and have a dispersion associated with them. The smaller this dispersion or variability, the greater the probability that the sample mean will be closer to the population mean. We need not necessarily take several different samples to estimate this variability. Even if we take only one sample of 30 subjects from the population, we will still be able to estimate the variability of the sampling distribution of the sample mean. This variability is called the standard error, denoted by $S_{\bar{X}}$. The standard error is calculated by the following formula:

$$S_{\bar{X}} = \frac{S}{\sqrt{n}}$$

where S is the standard deviation of the sample, n is the sample size, and $S_{\bar{X}}$ indicates the standard error or the extent of precision offered by the sample.

Note that the standard error varies inversely with the square root of the sample size. Hence, if we want to reduce the standard error given a particular standard deviation in the sample, we need to increase the sample size. Another noteworthy point is that the smaller the variation in the population, the smaller the standard error, which in turn implies that the sample size need not be large. Thus, low variability in the population requires a smaller sample size.

In sum, the closer we want our sample results to reflect the population characteristics, the greater the precision we should aim at. The greater the precision required, the larger the sample size needed, especially when the variability in the population itself is large.

CONFIDENCE

Whereas precision denotes how close we estimate the population parameter based on the sample statistic, **confidence** denotes how *certain* we are that our estimates will really hold true for the population. In the previous example of production rate, we know we are more precise when we estimate the true mean production (μ) to fall somewhere between 45 and 55 pieces than somewhere between 40 and 60. However, we may have more confidence in the latter estimation than in the former. After all, anyone can say with 100 percent certainty or confidence that the mean production (μ) will fall anywhere between zero and infinity! Other things being equal, the narrower the range, the lower the confidence. In other words, there is a trade-off between precision and confidence for any given sample size, as we shall see later in this chapter.

In essence, confidence reflects the level of certainty with which we can state that our estimates of the population parameters, based on our sample statistics, will hold true. The level of confidence can range from 0 to 100 percent. A 95 percent confidence is the conventionally accepted level for most business research, most commonly expressed by denoting the significance level as $p \leq 0.05$. In other words, we say that at least 95 times out of 100 our estimate will reflect the true population characteristic.

SAMPLE DATA, PRECISION AND CONFIDENCE IN ESTIMATION

Precision and confidence are important issues in sampling because when we use sample data to draw inferences about the population, we hope to be fairly 'on target', and have some idea of the extent of possible error. Because a point estimate provides no measure of possible error, we do an interval estimation to ensure a *relatively accurate* estimation of the population parameter. Statistics that have the same distribution as the sampling distribution of the mean are used in this procedure, usually a z or a t statistic.

For example, we may want to estimate the mean dollar value of purchases made by customers when they shop at department stores. From a sample of 64 customers sampled through a systematic sampling design procedure, we may find that the sample mean $\bar{X} = 105$, and the sample standard deviation $S = 10. \bar{X}$, the sample mean, is a point estimate of μ, the population mean. We could construct a confidence interval around X to estimate the range within which μ will fall. The standard error $S_{\bar{X}}$ and the percentage or level of confidence we require will determine the width of the interval, which can be represented by the following formula, where K is the t statistic for the level of confidence desired.

$$\mu = X \pm KS$$

We already know that:

$$S_{\bar{X}} = \frac{S}{\sqrt{n}}$$

Here,

$$S_{\bar{X}} = \frac{10}{\sqrt{64}} = 1.25$$

From the table of critical values for t in any statistics book (see Table II, columns 5, 6 and 8, in the statistical tables given toward the end of this book), we know that:

For a 90 percent confidence level, the K value is 1.645.

For a 95 percent confidence level, the K value is 1.96.

For a 99 percent confidence level, the K value is 2.576.

If we desire a 90 percent confidence level in the above case, then $\mu = 105 \pm 1.645\,(1.25)$ (i.e. $\mu = 105 \pm 2.056$). μ thus falls between 102.944 and 107.056. These results indicate that using a sample size of 64, we could state with 90 percent confidence that the true population mean value of purchases for all customers would fall between \$102.94 and \$107.06. If we now want to be 99 percent confident of our results without increasing the sample size, we necessarily have to sacrifice precision, as may be seen from the following calculation: $\mu = 105 \pm 2.576\,(1.25)$. The value of μ now falls between 101.78 and 108.22. In other words, the width of the interval has increased and we are now less precise in estimating the population mean, though we are a lot more confident about our estimation. It is not difficult to see that if we want to maintain our original precision while increasing the confidence, or maintain the confidence level while increasing precision, or we want to increase both the confidence and the precision, we need a larger sample size.

In sum, the sample size, n, is a function of:

1. the variability in the population;

2. precision or accuracy needed;

3. confidence level desired;

4. type of sampling plan used – for example, simple random sampling versus stratified random sampling.

TRADE-OFF BETWEEN CONFIDENCE AND PRECISION

We have noted that if we want more precision, or more confidence, or both, the sample size needs to be increased – unless, of course, there is very little variability in the population itself. However, if the sample size (n) cannot be increased, for whatever reason – say, we cannot afford the costs of increased sampling – then, with the same n, the only way to maintain the same level of precision is to forsake the confidence with which we can predict our estimates. That is, we

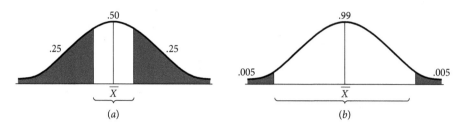

FIGURE 14.5 Illustration of the trade-off between precision and confidence. (a) More precision but less confidence; (b) more confidence but less precision.

reduce the confidence level or the certainty of our estimate. This trade-off between precision and confidence is illustrated in Figure 14.5(a) and (b). Figure 14.5(a) indicates that 50 percent of the time the true mean will fall within the narrow range indicated in the figure, the 0.25 in each tail representing the 25 percent non-confidence, or the probability of making errors, in our estimation on either side. Figure 14.5(b) indicates that 99 percent of the time we expect the true mean μ to fall within the much wider range indicated in the figure and there is only a 0.005 percent chance that we are making an error in this estimation. That is, in Figure 14.5(a), we have more precision but less confidence (our confidence level is only 50 percent). In Figure 14.5(b), we have high confidence (99 percent), but then we are far from being precise – that is, our estimate falls within a broad interval range.

It thus becomes necessary for researchers to consider at least four aspects while making decisions on the sample size needed to do the research:

1. How much precision is really needed in estimating the population characteristics of interest – that is, what is the *margin* of allowable error?

2. How much confidence is really needed – that is, how much *chance* can we take of making errors in estimating the population parameters?

3. To what extent is there *variability* in the population on the characteristics investigated?

4. What is the *cost–benefit* analysis of increasing the sample size?

SAMPLE DATA AND HYPOTHESIS TESTING

So far we have discussed sample data as a means of estimating the population parameters, but sample data can also be used to test hypotheses about population values rather than simply to estimate population values. The procedure for this testing incorporates the same information as in interval estimation, but the goals behind the two methods are somewhat different.

Referring to the earlier example of the average dollar value purchases of customers in a department store, instead of trying to estimate the average purchase value of the store's customers with a certain degree of accuracy, let us say that we now wish to determine whether or not customers expend the same average amount in purchases in Department Store A as in Department Store B. From Chapter 6, we know that we should first set the null hypothesis, which will state that there is no difference in the dollar values expended by customers shopping at the two different stores. This is expressed as:

$$H_0 : \mu_A - \mu_B = 0$$

The alternate hypothesis of differences will be stated non-directionally (since we have no idea whether customers buy more at Store A or Store B) as:

$$H_A : \mu_A - \mu_B \neq 0$$

If we take a sample of 20 customers from each of the two stores and find that the mean dollar value purchases of customers in Store A is 105 with a standard deviation of 10, and the corresponding figures for Store B are 100 and 15, respectively, we see that:

$$X_A - X_B = 105 - 100 = 5$$

whereas our null hypothesis had postulated no difference (difference = 0). Should we then conclude that our alternate hypothesis is to be accepted? We cannot say! To determine this we must first find the probability or likelihood of the two group means having a difference of 5 in the context of the null hypothesis or a difference of 0. This can be done by converting the difference in the sample means to a t statistic and seeing what the probability is of finding a t of that value. The t distribution has known probabilities attached to it (see Table II (t distribution) in the statistical tables given toward the end of the book). Looking at the t distribution table, we find that, with two samples of 20 each (the degrees of freedom become $(n_1 + n_2) - 2 = 38$), for the t value to be significant at the 0.05 level, the critical value should be around 2.021 (see t distribution table column 6 against $v40$). We need to use the two-tailed test since we do not know whether the difference between Store A and Store B will be positive or negative. For even a 90 percent probability, it should be at least 1.684 (see the number to the left of 2.021). The t statistic can be calculated for testing our hypothesis as follows:

$$t = \frac{(\bar{X}_1 - \bar{X}_2) - (\mu_1 - \mu_2)}{S_{\bar{X}_1 - \bar{X}_2}}$$

$$S_{\bar{X}_1 - \bar{X}_2} = \sqrt{\frac{n_1 s_1^2 + n_2 s_2^2}{(n_1 + n_2 - 2)}\left(\frac{1}{n_1} + \frac{1}{n2}\right)}$$

$$= \sqrt{\frac{(20 \times 10^2) + (20 \times 15^2)}{20 + 20 - 2}\left(\frac{1}{20} + \frac{1}{20}\right)}$$

$$t = \frac{(\bar{X}_A - \bar{X}_B) - (\mu_A - \mu_B)}{4.136}$$

We already know that

$$\bar{X}_A - \bar{X}_B = 5 \text{ (the difference in the means of the two stores)}$$

and

$$\mu_A - \mu_B = 0 \text{ (from our null hypothesis)}$$

Then

$$t = \frac{5 - 0}{4.136} = 1.209$$

This t value of 1.209 is way below the value of 2.021 (for 40 degrees of freedom for a two-population t-test, the closest to the actual 38 degrees of freedom [$(20 + 20) - 2$]) required for the conventional 95 percent probability, and even for the 90 percent probability, which requires a value of 1.684. We can thus say that the difference of 5 that we found between the two stores is not significantly different from 0. The conclusion, then, is that there is no significant difference between how much customers buy (dollars expended) at Department Store A and Department Store B. We will thus accept the null hypothesis and reject the alternative.

Sample data can thus be used not only for estimating the population parameters, but also for testing hypotheses about population values, population correlations, and so forth, as we will see more fully in Chapter 16.

THE SAMPLE SIZE

Both sampling design and the sample size are important to establish the representativeness of the sample for generalizability. If the appropriate sampling design is not used, a large sample size will not, in itself, allow the findings to be generalized to the population. Likewise, unless the sample size is adequate for the desired level of precision and confidence, no sampling design, however sophisticated, will be useful to the researcher in meeting the objectives of the study. Hence, sampling decisions should consider both the sampling design and the sample size.

DETERMINING THE SAMPLE SIZE

Now that we are aware of the fact that the sample size is governed by the extent of precision and confidence desired, how do we determine the sample size required for our research? The procedure can be illustrated through an example.

Example

Suppose a manager wants to be 95 percent confident that the expected monthly withdrawals in a bank will be within a confidence interval of ±$500. Let us say that a study of a sample of clients indicates that the average withdrawals made by them have a standard deviation of $3500. What would be the sample size needed in this case?

We noted earlier that the population mean can be estimated by using the formula:

$$\mu = \bar{X} \pm K S_{\bar{X}}$$

Since the confidence level needed here is 95 percent, the applicable K value is 1.96 (t table). The interval estimate of ±$500 will have to encompass a dispersion of (1.96 × standard error). That is,

$$500 = 1.96 \times S_{\bar{X}} \bar{X}$$

We already know that:

$$S_{\bar{X}} = \frac{S}{\sqrt{n}}$$

$$255.10 = \frac{3500}{\sqrt{n}}$$

$$n = 188$$

The sample size indicated above is 188. However, let us say that this bank has a total clientele of only 185. This means we cannot sample 188 clients. We can, in this case, apply a correction formula and see what sample size would be needed to have the same level of precision and confidence given the fact that we have a total of only 185 clients. The correction formula is as follows:

$$S_{\bar{X}} = \frac{S}{\sqrt{n}} \times \sqrt{\frac{N-n}{N-1}}$$

where N is the total number of elements in the population, n is the sample size to be estimated, $S_{\bar{X}}$ is the standard error of the estimate of the mean and S is the standard deviation of the sample mean.

Applying the correction formula, we find that:

$$255.10 = \frac{3500}{\sqrt{n}} \times \sqrt{\frac{185-n}{184}}$$

$$n = 94$$

We would now sample 94 of the total 185 clients.

To understand the impact of precision and/or confidence on the sample size, let us try changing the confidence level required in the bank withdrawal example, which needed a sample size of 188 for a confidence level of 95 percent. Let us say that the bank manager now wants to be 99 percent sure that the expected monthly withdrawals will be within the interval of ±$500. What will be the sample size now needed?

$S_{\bar{x}}$ will now be:

$$\frac{500}{2.576} = 194.099$$

$$194.099 = \frac{3500}{\sqrt{n}}$$

$$n = 325$$

The sample has now to be increased 1.73 times (from 188 to 325) to increase the confidence level from 95 to 99 percent!

Try calculating the sample size if the precision has to be narrowed down from $500 to $300 for a 95 percent and a 99 percent confidence level! Your answers should show the sample sizes needed as 523 and 902, respectively. These results dramatically highlight the costs of increased precision, confidence or both. It is hence a good idea to think through how much precision and confidence one really needs, before determining the sample size for the research project.

Krejcie and Morgan (1970) greatly simplified the sample size decision by providing a table that under certain circumstances ensures a good decision model. Note that the guidelines of Krejcie and Morgan are only valid for confidence intervals for proportions, when the desired margin of error is 0.05 and when the normal curve is a reasonably good approximation of the sampling distribution of the proportion. The table is also limited to cases where the level of confidence of 95 percent or the hypothesis test is two-sided with a level of significance of 5 percent. So the table is not valid for means; for proportions in cases where the normal approximation does not work; for levels of confidence other than 95 percent; and for margins of error other than 0.05. Table 14.3 provides Krejcie and Morgan's guidelines for sample size decisions. The interested student is advised to read Krejcie and Morgan (1970) as well as Cohen (1969) for decisions on sample size.

Table 14.3 Sample Size for a Given Population Size

N	S	N	S	N	S
10	10	220	140	1200	291
15	14	230	144	1300	297
20	19	240	148	1400	302
25	24	250	152	1500	306
30	28	260	155	1600	310
35	32	270	159	1700	313
40	36	280	162	1800	317

(continued)

N	S	N	S	N	S
45	40	290	165	1900	320
50	44	300	169	2000	322
55	48	320	175	2200	327
60	52	340	180	2400	331
65	56	360	186	2600	335
70	59	380	191	2800	338
75	63	400	196	3000	341
80	66	420	201	3500	346
85	70	440	205	4000	351
90	73	460	210	4500	354
95	76	480	214	5000	357
100	80	500	217	6000	361
110	86	550	226	7000	364
120	92	600	234	8000	367
130	97	650	242	9000	368
140	103	700	248	10000	370
150	108	750	254	15000	375
160	113	800	260	20000	377
170	118	850	265	30000	379
180	123	900	269	40000	380
190	127	950	274	50000	381
200	132	1000	278	75000	382
210	136	1100	285	1000000	384

SAMPLE SIZE AND TYPE II ERRORS

With a larger sample, the probability of making a Type II errors (discussed in Chapter 16) increases. That is, we would accept the findings of our research, when in fact we should reject them. In other words, with a very large sample size, even weak relationships (say a correlation of 0.10 between two variables) might reach significance levels, and we could be inclined to believe that these significant relationships found in the sample were indeed true of the population, when in reality they may not be. That, however, does not at all imply that a large sample is necessarily a bad thing. The larger the sample, the more precise the estimate (other things equal): the margin of error of the confidence interval gets smaller. One should therefore take into account all the costs: the costs of making a type I error, of making a type II error, of getting a less precise estimate and of gathering a larger sample. If one properly interprets a hypothesis test, the larger probability of making a type II error for a given level of significance is a feature, not a bug. In sum, if the cost to obtain a larger sample is negligible, a larger sample is better than a small sample because it leads to a more precise estimate.

STATISTICAL AND PRACTICAL SIGNIFICANCE

Another point to consider, even with the appropriate sample size, is whether statistical significance is more relevant than practical significance. For instance, a correlation of 0.25 may be statistically significant, but since this explains only about 6 percent of the variance (0.25^2), how meaningful is it in terms of practical utility?

RULES OF THUMB

Roscoe (1975) proposes the following rules of thumb for determining sample size:

1. Sample sizes larger than 30 and less than 500 are appropriate for most research.

2. Where samples are to be broken into subsamples (males/females, juniors/seniors, etc.), a minimum sample size of 30 for each category is necessary.

3. In multivariate research (including multiple regression analyses), the sample size should be several times (preferably ten times or more) as large as the number of variables in the study.

4. For simple experimental research with tight experimental controls (matched pairs, etc.), successful research is possible with samples as small as 10 to 20 in size.

EFFICIENCY IN SAMPLING

Efficiency in sampling is attained when, for a given level of precision (standard error), the sample size could be reduced, or for a given sample size (n), the level of precision could be increased. Some probability sampling designs are more efficient than others. The simple random sampling procedure is not always the most efficient plan to adopt; some other probability sampling designs are often more efficient. A stratified random sampling plan is often the most efficient, and a disproportionate stratified random sampling design has been shown to be more efficient than a proportionate sampling design in many cases. Cluster sampling is less efficient than simple random sampling because there is generally more homogeneity among the subjects in the clusters than is found in the elements in the population. Multistage cluster sampling is more efficient than single-stage cluster sampling when there is more heterogeneity found in the earlier stages. There is often a trade-off between time and cost efficiencies (as achieved in non-probability sampling designs) and precision efficiencies (as achieved in many probability sampling plans). The choice of a sampling plan thus depends on the objectives of the research, as well as on the extent and nature of efficiency desired.

BOX 14.5   SAMPLING ISSUES IN ONLINE RESEARCH

When conducting online surveys, researchers often encounter problems with respect to sampling (Wright, 2005). Establishing a sampling frame when researching an online community presents a real challenge. Membership of online communities is based on common interests and little information is required when registering to use these communities, if registration is required at all (Andrews, Nonnecke, & Preece, 2003; Couper, 2000). Due to the *lack of an adequate sampling frame*, many online survey invitations are published in the form of a link on websites or in other media, which leads to non-probability samples and in many cases to sample selection bias. *Self-selection* bias is a major limitation of online survey research. In any given online community, there are individuals who are more likely than others to complete an online survey. The tendency of some individuals to respond to an invitation to participate in an online survey, while others ignore it, may lead to a systematic bias. Finally, the *response rates* of online surveys are generally very low. These sampling issues in online research often hinder researchers' ability to generalize their findings.

Sampling for qualitative research is as important as sampling for quantitative research. Qualitative sampling begins with precisely defining the *target population*. As a sampling technique, qualitative research generally uses *non-probability sampling* as it does not aim to draw statistical inference. *Purposive sampling* is one technique that is often employed in qualitative investigation: subjects are selected on the basis of expertise in the subject that is being investigated. It is important that the subjects are chosen in such a way that they reflect the diversity of the population.

SAMPLING AS RELATED TO QUALITATIVE STUDIES

One form of purposive sampling is *theoretical sampling*, introduced by Glaser and Strauss (1967) in their work on grounded theory. The term **grounded theory** expresses the idea that theory will emerge from data through an iterative process that involves repeated sampling, collection of data and analysis of data until 'theoretical saturation' is reached. *Theoretical saturation* is reached when no new information about the subject emerges in repeated cases. Theoretical sampling may or may not begin with purposive sampling, but the sampling of additional subjects is directed by the emerging theoretical framework. According to Glaser, theoretical sampling takes place when 'the analyst jointly collects, codes, and analyses his data and decides what data to collect next and where to find them, in order to develop his theory as it emerges' (1978, p. 36).

Because it is impossible to predict when theoretical saturation is reached, you cannot determine how many subjects will need to be sampled at the beginning of your study. Instead, the general rule in qualitative research is that you continue to sample until you are not getting any new information or are no longer gaining new insights. Note that the sample size will, therefore, at least partly, depend on the heterogeneity of the population.

BOX 14.6	**SAMPLING IN CROSS-CULTURAL RESEARCH**

Just as in instrument development and data collection, while engaging in cross-cultural research one has to be sensitive to the issue of selecting matched samples in the different countries. The nature and types of organizations studied, whether subjects are from rural or urban areas, and the types of sampling design used, should all be similar in the different countries to enable true comparisons.

MANAGERIAL IMPLICATIONS

Awareness of sampling designs and sample size helps managers to understand why a particular method of sampling is used by researchers. It also facilitates understanding of the cost implications of different designs, and the trade-off between precision and confidence vis-à-vis the costs. This enables managers to understand the risk they take in implementing changes based on the results of the research study. While reading research reports or journal articles, this knowledge also helps managers to assess the generalizability of the findings and analyse the implications of trying out the recommendations made therein in their own system.

SUMMARY

- **Learning objective 1: Define sampling, sample, population, element, sampling unit and subject.** In learning how representative data can be collected, a few terms have to be understood. The population refers to the entire group of people, events or things of interest that the researcher wishes to investigate. An element is a single member of the population. A sample is a subset of the population. The sampling unit is the element or set of elements that is available for selection in some stage of the sampling process. A subject is a single member of the sample, just as an element is a single member of the population.

- **Learning objective 2: Discuss statistical terms in sampling.** Sampling units provide the researcher with *responses*. When researchers examine the responses they get for their entire sample, they make use of *statistics*. The characteristics of the population are referred to as its *parameters*. When the properties of the population are not overrepresented or underrepresented in the sample, we have a representative sample.

- **Learning objective 3: Describe and discuss the sampling process.** Sampling is the *process* of selecting a sufficient number of the right elements from the population, so that a study of the sample and an understanding of its properties make it possible for the researcher to generalize such properties to the population elements. The major steps in sampling include: (1) defining the population; (2) determining the sample frame; (3) determining the sampling design; (4) determining the appropriate sample size; and (5) executing the sampling process.

- **Learning objective 4: Compare and contrast specific probability sampling designs.** In probability sampling, elements in the population have a known, non-zero chance of being chosen as subjects in the sample. Probability sampling can be either unrestricted (simple random sampling) or restricted (complex probability sampling) in nature.

- **Learning objective 5: Compare and contrast specific non-probability sampling designs.** In non-probability sampling designs, the elements in the population do not have any probabilities attached to their being chosen as sample subjects. This means that the findings from the study of the sample cannot be confidently generalized to the population. There are two main types of non-probability sampling design: convenience sampling and purposive sampling.

- **Learning objective 6: Discuss precision and confidence and the trade-off between precision and confidence.** A reliable and valid sample enables the researcher to generalize the findings from the sample to the population under study. That is why sample statistics should be reliable estimates and reflect the population parameters as closely as possible. Precision and confidence are important issues in sampling because sample data are used to draw inferences about the population; one hopes to be pretty 'on target'. Precision and confidence are related to sample size: if one wants to maintain the original precision while increasing the confidence, or maintain the confidence level while increasing precision, or one wants to increase both the confidence and the precision, one needs a larger sample size.

- **Learning objective 7: Discuss how hypotheses can be tested with sample data.** Sample data can thus be used not only for estimating the population parameters, but also for testing hypotheses. We will have more to say about this in Chapter 16.

- **Learning objective 8: Discuss the factors to be taken into consideration for determining sample size and determine the sample size for any given research project.** It is a good idea to think through how much precision and confidence one really needs, before determining the sample size for the research project. Too large a sample size could become a problem inasmuch as we would then be prone to committing Type II errors. Efficiency in sampling is attained when, for a given level of precision (standard error), the sample size could be reduced, or for a given sample size (n), the level of precision could be increased.

- **Learning objective 9: Discuss sampling in qualitative research.** Qualitative sampling begins with precisely defining the *target population*. Qualitative research generally uses *non-probability sampling* as it does not aim to draw statistical inference. *Purposive sampling* is one technique that is often employed in qualitative research. It is important that the subjects are chosen in such a way that they reflect the diversity of the population. One form of purposive sampling is *theoretical sampling*. Because it is impossible to predict when theoretical saturation is reached, it is impossible to determine how many subjects will need to be sampled at the beginning of one's study.

- **Learning objective 10: Discuss the role of the manager in sampling.** Awareness of sampling designs and sample size decisions helps managers to understand why particular methods of sampling are used by researchers. In the next two chapters, we will see how the data gathered from a sample of respondents in the population are analysed to test the hypotheses generated and find answers to the research questions. It facilitates understanding of the cost implications of different designs, and the trade-off between precision and confidence in relation to the costs. It enables managers to understand the risk they take in implementing changes based on the results of a research study. Finally, it helps managers to assess the generalizability of the findings of a study.

Instructors can visit the companion website at **www.wiley.com/go/bougie/researchmethods forbusiness8e** for **Case Study: Banks start image repair over financial crisis.**

1. Identify the relevant population for the following research foci, and suggest the appropriate sampling design to investigate the issues, explaining *why* they are appropriate. Wherever necessary, identify the sampling frame as well.

    a. A company wants to investigate the initial reactions of heavy soft-drink users to a new 'all natural' soft drink.

    b. A hospital administrator wants to find out if the single parents working in the hospital have a higher rate of absenteeism than parents who are not single.

    c. A researcher would like to assess the extent of pilferage in the materials storage warehouses of manufacturing firms.

    d. The director of human resources wants to investigate the relationship between drug abuse and dysfunctional behaviour of blue-collar workers in a particular plant.

    e. A marketer wants to generate some ideas on how women differ from men in acquiring product knowledge about cars.

2. a. Explain why cluster sampling is a probability sampling design.

    b. What are the advantages and disadvantages of cluster sampling?

    c. Describe a situation where you would consider the use of cluster sampling.

3. a. Explain what precision and confidence are and how they influence sample size.

    b. Discuss what is meant by the statement: 'There is a trade-off between precision and confidence under certain conditions'.

4. The use of a convenience sample used in organizational research is correct because all members share the same organizational stimuli and go through almost the same kinds of experience in their organizational life. Comment.

5. 'Use of a sample of 5000 is not necessarily better than one of 500'. How would you react to this statement?

6. Non-probability sampling designs ought to be preferred to probability sampling designs in some cases. Explain with an example.

7. Because there seems to be a trade-off between accuracy and confidence for any given sample size, accuracy should always be considered more important than precision. Explain with reasons why you do or do not agree.

8. Overgeneralizations give rise to much confusion and other problems for researchers who try to replicate the findings. Explain what is meant by this.

9. Double sampling is probably the least used of all sampling designs in organizational research. Do you agree? Provide reasons for your answer.

10. Why do you think the sampling design should feature in a research proposal?

Now do Exercises 14.1, 14.2, 14.3, 14.4, 14.5 and 14.6.

For the situations presented in Exercises 14.1 to 14.6, indicate what would be the relevant population and the most appropriate sampling design. Make sure you discuss the reasons for your answers.

A medical inspector wants to estimate the overall average monthly occupancy rates of the cancer wards in 80 different hospitals that are evenly located in the northwestern, southeastern, central and southern suburbs of New York City.

A magazine article suggested that 'Consumers aged 35 to 44 will soon be the nation's biggest spenders, so advertisers must learn how to appeal to this over-the-thrill crowd'. If this suggestion appeals to an apparel manufacturer, what should the sampling design be to assess the tastes of this group?

EXERCISE 14.2

The McArthur Co. produces special vacuum cleaners for conveniently cleaning the inside of cars. About a thousand of these, with stamped serial numbers, are produced every month and stored serially in a stockroom. Once a month an inspector does a quality control check on 50 of these. When he certifies them as to quality, the units are released from the stockroom for sale. The production and sales managers, however, are not satisfied with the quality control check since, quite often, many of the units sold are returned by customers because of various types of defect. What would be the most useful sampling plan to test the 50 units?

EXERCISE 14.3

A consultant had administered a questionnaire to some 285 employees using a simple random sampling procedure. As she looked at the responses, she suspected that two questions might not have been clear to the respondents. She would like to know if her suspicion is well-founded.

EXERCISE 14.4

The executive board of a relatively small university located in Europe wants to determine the attitude of their students toward various aspects of the university. The university, founded in 1928, is a fully accredited government-financed university with 11000 students. The university specializes in the social sciences and humanities and has five faculties, six service departments, eight research centres and two graduate schools. The executive board has asked you to come up with a sampling plan. Develop a sampling plan and pay attention to the following aspects: target population, the sampling frame, the sample technique and the sample size.

EXERCISE 14.5

T-Mobile is a mobile network operator headquartered in Bonn, Germany. The company has enlisted your help as a consultant to develop and test a model on the determinants of subscriber churn in the German mobile telephone market. Develop a sampling plan and pay specific attention to the following aspects.

Define the target population. Discuss in as much detail as possible the sampling frame and the sampling design that you would use. Give reasons for your choice.

EXERCISE 14.6

Quantitative Data Analysis

LEARNING OBJECTIVES

After completing Chapter 15, you should be able to:

1. Demonstrate the ability to get data ready for quantitative analysis.

2. Describe the various processes by which one can get a feel for the data in a study.

3. Describe the means by which the reliability and validity of measures can be assessed.

After quantitative data have been collected, the next step is to analyze them to answer our research questions. However, before we can start analyzing the data, some preliminary steps need to be completed. These help to ensure that the data are accurate, complete and suitable for further analysis. This chapter addresses these preliminary steps in detail. Subsequently, general guidelines are provided for calculating and displaying basic descriptive statistics.

The easiest way to illustrate data analysis is through a case. We will therefore introduce the Excelsior Enterprises case first.

Example

Excelsior Enterprises is a medium-sized company, manufacturing and selling instruments and supplies needed by the health care industry, including blood pressure instruments, surgical instruments, dental accessories and so on. The company, with a total of 360 employees working three shifts, is doing reasonably well but could do far better if it did not experience employee turnover at almost all levels and in all departments. The president of the company called in a research team to study the situation and to make recommendations on the turnover problem.

Since access to those who had left the company would be difficult, the research team suggested to the president that they talk to the current employees and, based on their input and a literature survey, try to get at the factors influencing employees' intentions to stay with, or leave, the company. Since past research has shown that intention to leave (ITL) is an excellent predictor of actual turnover, the president concurred.

The team first conducted an unstructured interview with about 50 employees at various levels and from different departments. Their broad statement was: 'We are here to find out how you experience your work life. Tell us whatever you consider is important for you in your job, as issues relate to your work, the environment, the organization, supervision, and whatever else you think is relevant. If we get a good handle on the issues involved, we may be able to make appropriate recommendations to management to enhance the quality of your work life. We would just like to talk to you now, and administer a questionnaire later'.

Each interview typically lasted about 45 minutes, and notes on the responses were written down by the team members. When the responses were tabulated, it became clear that the issues most frequently brought up by the respondents, in one form or another, related to three main areas: the job (employees said the jobs were dull or too complex; there was lack of freedom to do the job as one wanted to, etc.), perceived inequities (remarks such as 'I put much more in my work than I get out of it'); and burnout (comments such as 'there is so much work to be done that by the end of the day we are physically and emotionally exhausted'; 'we feel the frequent need to take time off because of exhaustion'; etc.).

A literature survey confirmed that these variables were good predictors of intention to leave and subsequent turnover. In addition, job satisfaction was also found to be an important predictor of intention to leave. A theoretical framework was developed based on the interviews and the literature survey, and four hypotheses (stated later) were developed.

Next, a questionnaire was designed incorporating well-validated and reliable measures for job enrichment, perceived equity, burnout, job satisfaction and intention to leave. Perceived equity was measured by five survey items: (1) 'I invest more in my work than I get out of it'; (2) 'I exert myself too much considering what I get back in return'; (3) 'For the efforts I put into the organization, I get much in return' (reversed); (4) 'If I take into account my dedication, the company ought to give me better training'; and (5) 'In general, the benefits I receive from the organization outweigh the effort I put in it' (reversed). Job enrichment was measured on a four-item Likert scale: (1) 'The job is quite simple and repetitive' (reversed); (2) 'The job requires me to use a number of complex or higher-level skills'; (3) 'The job requires a lot of cooperative work with other people'; and (4) 'The job itself is not very significant or important in the broader scheme of things' (reversed). Participants responded to these items on a five-point scale, ranging from 'I disagree completely' (1) to 'I agree completely' (5). Burnout was measured with *The Burnout Measure Short Version* (BMS). The *BMS* includes ten items that measure levels of physical, emotional and mental exhaustion of the individual. Respondents are asked to rate the frequency with which they experience each of the items appearing in the questionnaire (e.g. being tired or helpless) on a scale ranging from 1 ('never') to 5 ('always'). Job satisfaction was measured by a single-item rating of 'satisfaction with your current job', using a five-point 'not at all–very much' scale. Intention to leave was measured using two survey items: 'With what level of certainty do you intend to leave this organization within the next year for another type of job?' (item 1) 'for a similar type of job?' (item 2). Participants indicated on a four-point rating scale their level of certainty. Demographic variables such as age, education, gender, tenure, department and work shift were also included in the questionnaire.

The questionnaire was administered personally to 174 employees who were chosen on a disproportionate stratified random sampling basis. The responses were entered into the computer. Thereafter, the data were submitted for analysis to test the following hypotheses, which were formulated by the researchers:

H$_1$: *Job enrichment has a negative effect on intention to leave.*
H$_2$: *Perceived equity has a negative effect on intention to leave.*
H$_3$: *Burnout has a positive effect on intention to leave.*
H$_4$: *Job satisfaction mediates the relationship between job enrichment, perceived equity and burnout on intention to leave.*

It may be pertinent to point out here that the four hypotheses derived from the theoretical framework are particularly relevant for finding answers to the turnover issue. The results of testing the hypotheses will certainly offer insights into how much of the variance in intention to leave can be explained by the independent variables, and what corrective action, if any, needs to be taken.

Although many researchers use online tools for creating and administering surveys as well as managing and analysing the data these days, traditional paper and pencil techniques still remain one of the most used methods to collect quantitative data. In one way or another, after data are obtained through questionnaires, they need to be coded, keyed in and edited. That is, a

GETTING THE DATA READY FOR ANALYSIS

categorization scheme has to be set up before the data can be typed in. Then, outliers, inconsistencies and blank responses, if any, have to be handled in some way. Each of these stages of data preparation is discussed below.

CODING AND DATA ENTRY

The first step in data preparation is data coding. **Data coding** involves assigning a number to the participants' responses so they can be entered into a database. In Chapter 10, we discussed the convenience of electronic surveys for collecting questionnaire data; such surveys facilitate the entry of the responses directly into the computer without manual keying in of the data. However, if, for whatever reason, this cannot be done, then it is perhaps a good idea to use a coding sheet first to transcribe the data from the questionnaire and then key in the data. This method, in contrast to flipping through each questionnaire for each item, avoids confusion, especially when there are many questions and a large number of questionnaires as well.

Coding the Responses

In the Excelsior Enterprises questionnaire, we have 22 items measuring perceived equity, job enrichment, burnout, job satisfaction and intention to leave, and six demographic variables, as shown in Figure 15.1, a sample questionnaire.

The responses of this particular employee (participant #1 in the data file) to the first 22 questions can be coded by using the actual number circled by the respondent (1, 2, 3, 1, 4, 5, 1, 3, 3, etc.). Coding the demographic variables is somewhat less obvious. For instance, tenure is a special case, because it is a two-category variable. It is possible to use a coding approach that assigns a 1 = part-time and a 2 = full-time. However, using 0 = part-time and 1 = full-time (this is called *dummy coding*) is by far the most popular and recommended approach because it makes our lives easier in the data analysis stage. Hence, we code tenure (full-time) with 1 for participant #1. Work shift (third shift) can be coded 3, department (production) 2, and age 54. Gender can be coded 0 (male) . Finally, education (less than high school) can be coded 1.

At this stage you should also think about how you want to code non-responses. Some researchers leave non-responses blank, others assign a '9', a '99' or a '.' . All the approaches are fine, as long as you code all the non-responses in the same way.

Human errors can occur while coding. At least 10 percent of the coded questionnaires should therefore be checked for coding accuracy. Their selection may follow a systematic sampling procedure. That is, every *n*th form coded could be verified for accuracy. If many errors are found in the sample, all items may have to be checked.

Data Entry

After responses have been coded, they can be entered into a database. Raw data can be entered through any software program. For instance, the SPSS Data Editor, which looks like a spreadsheet and is shown in Figure 15.2, can enter, edit and view the contents of the data file.

Each row of the editor represents a case or observation (in this case a participant of our study – 174 in the Excelsior Enterprises study), and each column represents a *variable* (here variables are defined as the different items of information that you collect for your cases; there are thus 28 variables in the Excelsior Enterprises questionnaire).

It is important to always use the first column for identification purposes; assign a number to every questionnaire, write this number on the first page of the questionnaire and enter this number in the first column of your data file. This allows you to compare the data in the data file with the answers of the participants, even after you have rearranged your data file.

Then, start entering the participants' responses into the data file.

Circle the number that represents your feelings at this particular moment best. There are no right or wrong answers. Please answer every question.

	I disagree completely				I agree completely
1. I invest more in my work than I get out of it	①	2	3	4	5
2. I exert myself too much considering what I get back in return	1	②	3	4	5
3. For the efforts I put into the organization, I get much in return	1	2	③	4	5
4. If I take into account my dedication, the company ought to give me better training	①	2	3	4	5
5. In general, the benefits I receive from the organization outweigh the effort I put in it	1	2	3	④	5

	I disagree completely				I agree completely
6. My job is quite simple and repetitive	1	2	3	4	⑤
7. My job requires me to use a number of complex or higher-level skills	①	2	3	4	5
8. My job requires a lot of cooperative work with other people	1	2	③	4	5
9. My job itself is not very significant or important in the broader scheme of things	1	2	③	4	5

When you think about your work, how often do you feel the following:

	Never				Always
10. Tired	1	2	③	4	5
11. Disappointed with people	1	②	3	4	5
12. Hopeless	①	2	3	4	5
13. Trapped	1	②	3	4	5
14. Helpless	①	2	3	4	5
15. Depressed	1	②	3	4	5
16. Weak/Sickly	1	②	3	4	5
17. Insecure/A failure	1	②	3	4	5
18. Sleep difficulties	①	2	3	4	5
19. "I have had it"	1	2	③	4	5

	Not at all				Very much
20. To what extent are you satisfied with your current job?	1	2	3	4	⑤

With what level of certainty do you intend to leave this organization within the next year:

	Very uncertain			Very certain
21. ...for another type of job?	①	2	3	4
22. ...for a similar type of job?	1	②	3	4

Finally we would like you to provide some background information.

23. Do you have a part-time or a full-time job at Excelsior Enterprises?
O   Part-time
⊗   Full-time

24. What shift do you currently work?
O   First shift (1)
O   Second shift (2)
⊗   Third shift (3)

25. What is your department?

O	Marketing (1)	O	Maintenance (4)	O	Finance (7)
⊗	Production (2)	O	Servicing (5)	O	Personnel (8)
O	Sales (3)	O	Public Relations (6)	O	Accounting (9)

26. What is your age?
<u> 54 </u>

FIGURE 15.1   Sample questionnaire

27. What is your gender
⊗ Male
o Female

28. What is the highest level of education you have completed?
⊗ Less than High School (1)
o High School/GED Equivalent (2)
o College Degree (3)
o Masters Degree (4)
o Doctoral Degree (5)

THIS WAS THE FINAL QUESTION OF THIS QUESTIONNAIRE.
THANK YOU VERY MUCH FOR YOUR COOPERATION!

FIGURE 15.1 *(Continued)*

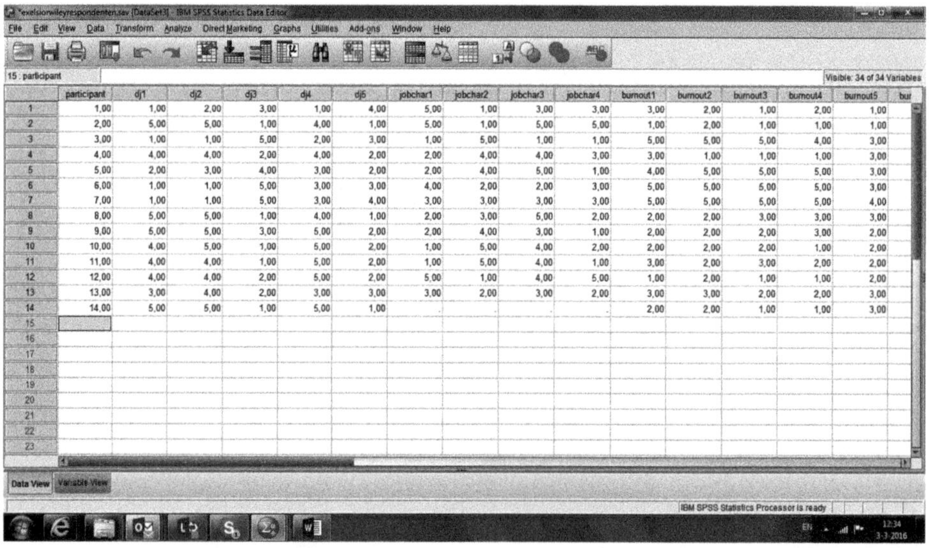

	participant	dj1	dj2	dj3	dj4	dj5	jobchar1	jobchar2	jobchar3	jobchar4	burnout1	burnout2	burnout3	burnout4	burnout5	bur
1	1,00	1,00	2,00	3,00	1,00	4,00	5,00	1,00	3,00	3,00	3,00	2,00	1,00	2,00	1,00	
2	2,00	5,00	5,00	1,00	4,00	1,00	5,00	1,00	5,00	5,00	1,00	2,00	1,00	1,00	1,00	
3	3,00	1,00	1,00	5,00	2,00	3,00	1,00	5,00	1,00	1,00	5,00	5,00	5,00	4,00	3,00	
4	4,00	4,00	4,00	2,00	4,00	2,00	2,00	4,00	4,00	3,00	3,00	1,00	1,00	1,00	3,00	
5	5,00	2,00	3,00	4,00	3,00	2,00	2,00	4,00	5,00	1,00	4,00	5,00	5,00	5,00	3,00	
6	6,00	1,00	1,00	5,00	3,00	3,00	4,00	2,00	2,00	3,00	5,00	5,00	5,00	5,00	3,00	
7	7,00	1,00	1,00	5,00	3,00	4,00	3,00	3,00	3,00	3,00	5,00	5,00	5,00	5,00	4,00	
8	8,00	5,00	5,00	1,00	4,00	1,00	2,00	3,00	5,00	2,00	2,00	2,00	3,00	3,00	3,00	
9	9,00	5,00	5,00	3,00	5,00	2,00	2,00	4,00	3,00	1,00	2,00	2,00	2,00	3,00	2,00	
10	10,00	4,00	5,00	1,00	5,00	2,00	1,00	5,00	4,00	2,00	2,00	2,00	2,00	1,00	2,00	
11	11,00	4,00	4,00	1,00	5,00	2,00	1,00	5,00	4,00	1,00	3,00	2,00	3,00	2,00	2,00	
12	12,00	4,00	4,00	2,00	5,00	2,00	5,00	1,00	4,00	5,00	1,00	2,00	1,00	1,00	2,00	
13	13,00	3,00	4,00	2,00	3,00	3,00	3,00	2,00	3,00	2,00	3,00	3,00	2,00	2,00	3,00	
14	14,00	5,00	5,00	1,00	5,00	1,00	.	.	.	.	2,00	2,00	1,00	1,00	3,00	
15																
16																
17																
18																
19																
20																
21																
22																
23																

FIGURE 15.2 The SPSS Data Editor

EDITING DATA

After the data are keyed in, they need to be edited. For instance, the blank responses, if any, have to be handled in some way, and inconsistent data have to be checked and followed up. **Data editing** deals with detecting and correcting illogical, inconsistent or illegal data and omissions in the information returned by the participants of the study.

An example of an *illogical response* is an **outlier** response. An outlier is an observation that is substantially different from the other observations. An outlier is not always an error even though data errors (entry errors) are a likely source of outliers. Because outliers have a large impact on the research results, they should be investigated carefully to make sure that they are correct. You can check the dispersion of nominal and/or ordinal variables by obtaining minimum and maximum values and frequency tables. This will quickly reveal the most obvious outliers. For interval and ratio data, visual aids (such as a scatterplot or a boxplot) are good methods to check for outliers.

Inconsistent responses are responses that are not in harmony with other information. For instance, a participant in our study might have answered the perceived equity statements as in Figure 15.3. Note that all the answers of this employee indicate that the participant finds that the

	I disagree completely				I agree completely
1. I invest more in my work than I get out of it	①	2	3	4	5
2. I exert myself too much considering what I get back in return	1	②	3	4	5
3. For the efforts I put into the organization, I get much in return	①	2	3	4	5
4. If I take into account my dedication, the company ought to give me better training	①	2	3	4	5
5. In general, the benefits I receive from the organization outweigh the effort I put in it	1	2	3	4	⑤

FIGURE 15.3   Example of a possible inconsistent answer

benefits she receives from the organization balance the efforts she puts into her job, except for the answer to the third statement. From the other four responses we might infer that the participant in all probability feels that, for the efforts she puts into the organization, she *does* get much in return and has made a mistake in responding to this particular statement. The response to this statement could then be edited by the researcher.

It is, however, possible that the respondent deliberately indicated that she does not get much in return for the efforts she puts into the organization. If such were to be the case, we would be introducing a bias by editing the data. Hence, great care has to be taken in dealing with inconsistent responses such as these. Whenever possible, it is desirable to follow up with the respondent to get the correct data, even though this is an expensive solution.

Illegal codes are values that are not specified in the coding instructions. For example, a code of '6' in question 1 (I invest more in my work than I get out of it) would be an illegal code. The best way to check for illegal codes is to have the computer produce a frequency distribution and check it for illegal codes.

Not all respondents answer every item in the questionnaire. *Omissions* may occur because respondents did not understand the question, did not know the answer, or were not willing to answer the question.

If a substantial number of questions – say, 25 percent of the items in the questionnaire – have been left unanswered, it may be a good idea to throw out the questionnaire and not include it in the data set for analysis. In this event, it is important to mention the number of returned but unused responses due to excessive missing data in the final report submitted to the sponsor of the study. If, however, only two or three items are left blank in a questionnaire with, say, 30 or more items, we need to decide how these blank responses are to be handled.

One way to handle a blank response is to ignore it when the analyses are done. This approach is possible in all statistical programs and is the default option in most of them. A disadvantage of this approach is that, of course, it will reduce the sample size, sometimes even to an inappropriate size, whenever that particular variable is involved in the analyses. Moreover, if the missing data are not missing completely at random, this method may bias the results of your study. For this reason, ignoring the blank responses is best suited to instances in which we have gathered a large amount of data, the number of missing data is relatively small and relationships are so strong that they are not affected by the missing data (Hair, Anderson, Tatham & Black, 1995).

An alternative solution would be to look at the participant's pattern of responses to other questions and, from these answers, deduce a logical answer to the question for the missing response. A second alternative solution would be to assign to the item the mean value of the responses of all those who have responded to that particular item. In fact, there are many ways of handling blank responses (see Hair et al., 1995), each of them having its own particular advantages and disadvantages.

Note that if many of the respondents have answered 'don't know' to a particular item or items, further investigation may well be worthwhile. The question might not have been clear or, for some reason, participants could have been reluctant or unable to answer the question.

DATA TRANSFORMATION

Data transformation, a variation of data coding, is the process of changing the original numerical representation of a quantitative value to another value. Data are typically changed to avoid problems in the next stage of the data analysis process. For example, economists often use a logarithmic transformation so that the data are more evenly distributed. If, for instance, income data, which are often unevenly distributed, are reduced to their logarithmic value, the high incomes are brought closer to the lower end of the scale and provide a distribution closer to a normal curve.

Another type of data transformation is reverse scoring. Take, for instance, the perceived inequity measure of the Excelsior Enterprises case. Perceived inequity is measured by five survey items: (1) 'I invest more in my work than I get out of it'; (2) 'I exert myself too much considering what I get back in return'; (3) 'For the efforts I put into the organization, I get much in return' (reversed); (4) 'If I take into account my dedication, the organization ought to give me a better practical training'; and (5) 'In general, the benefits I receive from the organization outweigh the effort I put in' (reversed). For the first, second and fourth items, a score indicating high agreement would be negative, but for the third and fifth questions, a score indicating high agreement would be positive. To maintain consistency in the meaning of a response, the first, second and fourth items have to be reverse scored (note that we are measuring equity and not inequity). In this case, a 5 ('I completely agree') would be transformed to a 1 ('I completely disagree'), a 4 to a 2 and so forth.

Data transformation is also necessary when several questions have been used to measure a single concept. In such cases, scores on the original questions have to be combined into a single score (but only *after* we have established that the interitem consistency is satisfactory (see Testing goodness of data, later on in this chapter). For instance, because five items have been used to measure the concept 'perceived equity', a new 'perceived equity' score has to be calculated from the scores on the five individual items (but only after items 1, 2 and 4 have been reverse coded). This involves calculating the summed score (per case/participant) and then dividing it by the number of items (five in this case). For example, our employee #1 has circled, respectively, 1, 2, 3, 1 and 4 on the five participation in decision-making questions; his (employee #1 is a man) scores on the items, once items 1, 2 and 4 have been reverse coded, are 5, 4, 3, 5 and 4. The combined score on perceived equity would be $5 + 4 + 3 + 5 + 4 = 21/5 = 4.2$). This combined score is included in a new column in SPSS. It is easy to compute the new variables, using the *Compute* dialog box, which opens when the *Transform* icon is chosen (Figure 15.4).

Note that it is useful to set up a scheme for categorizing the responses such that the several items measuring a concept are all grouped together. If the questions measuring a concept are not contiguous but scattered over various parts of the questionnaire, care has to be taken to include all the items without any omission or wrong inclusion.

GETTING A FEEL FOR THE DATA

We can acquire a feel for the data by obtaining a visual summary or by checking the central tendency and the dispersion of a variable. We can also get to know our data by examining the relation between two variables. In Chapter 13, we explained that different statistical operations on variables are possible, depending on the level at which a variable is measured. Table 15.1 summarizes the relationship between scale type, data analysis and methods of obtaining a visual summary for variables.

Table 15.1 shows that, depending on the scale of our measures, the mode, median or mean, and the semi-interquartile range, standard deviation or variance will give us a good idea of how the participants in our study have reacted to the items in the questionnaire. These statistics can be easily obtained and will indicate whether the responses range satisfactorily over the scale. If the response to each individual item in a scale does not have a good spread (range) and shows very

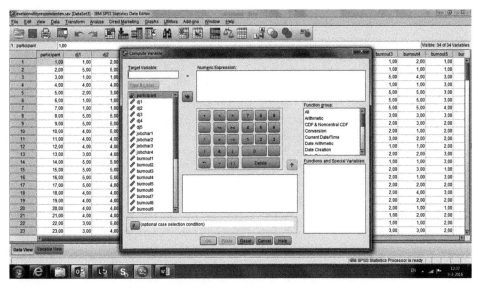

FIGURE 15.4   Transforming data with SPSS

Table 15.1   Scale Type, Data Analysis and Methods of Obtaining a Visual Summary for Variables

Scale	Examples	Measures of central tendency . . . *for a single variable*	Measures of dispersion . . . *for a single variable*	Visual summary . . . *for a single variable*	Measure of relation . . . *between variables*	Visual summary of relation . . . *between variables*
Nominal	Social security number, gender	Mode	–	Bar chart, pie chart	Contingency table (Cross-tab)	Stacked bars, Clustered bars
Ordinal	Satisfaction rating on a 5-point scale (1 = not satisfied at all; 5 = extremely satisfied)	Median	Semi-interquartile range	Bar chart, pie chart	Contingency table (Cross-tab)	Stacked bars, Clustered bars
Interval		Arithmetic mean	Minimum, maximum, standard deviation, variance, coefficient of variation	Histogram, scatterplot, box-and-whisker plot	Correlations	Scatterplots
Ratio	Age, Sales	Arithmetic or geometric mean	Minimum, maximum, standard deviation, variance, coefficient of variation	Histogram, scatterplot, box-and-whisker plot	Correlations	Scatterplots

little variability, then the researcher may suspect that the particular question was probably not properly worded. Biases, if any, may also be detected if the respondents have tended to respond similarly to all items – that is, they have stuck to only certain points on the scale. Remember that if there is no variability in the data, then no variance can be explained! Getting a feel for the data is thus the necessary first step in all data analysis. Based on this initial feel, further detailed analyses may be undertaken to test the goodness of the data.

Researchers go to great lengths to obtain the central tendency, the range, the dispersion and other statistics for every single item measuring the dependent and independent variables, especially when the measures for a concept are newly developed.

Descriptive statistics for a single variable are provided by frequencies, measures of central tendency and dispersion. These are now described.

FREQUENCIES

Frequencies simply refer to the number of times various subcategories of a certain phenomenon occur, from which the percentage and the cumulative percentage of their occurrence can be easily calculated.

Excelsior Enterprises: Frequencies The frequencies for the number of individuals in the various departments for the Excelsior Enterprises sample are shown in Output 15.1. It may be seen therefrom that the greatest number of individuals in the sample came from the production department (28.1 percent), followed by the sales department (25.3 percent). Only three individuals (1.7 percent) came from public relations, and five individuals each from the finance, maintenance and accounting departments (2.9 percent from each). The low numbers in the sample in some of the departments are a function of the total population (very few members) in those departments.

From the frequencies obtained for the other variables (results not shown here), it was found that 79.9 percent of the respondents were men and 20.1 percent women; about 62 percent worked the first shift, 20 percent the second shift and 18 percent the third shift. About 16 percent of the respondents worked part time and 84 percent full time. About 8 percent had less than a high school diploma, 39 percent a high school diploma, 32 percent a college degree, 20 percent a master's degree and 1 percent had doctoral degrees.

We thus have a profile of the employees in this organization, which is useful for describing the sample in the 'methods' section of the written report (see Chapter 19). Other instances where frequency distributions would be useful are when: (1) a marketing manager wants to know how many units (and what proportions or percentages) of each brand of coffee are sold in a particular region during a given period; (2) a tax consultant wishes to keep count of the number of times different sizes of firms (small, medium, large) are audited by the IRS; and (3) the financial analyst wants to keep track of the number of times the shares of manufacturing, industrial and utility companies lose or gain more than ten points on the New York Stock Exchange over a six-month period.

Bar Charts and Pie Charts

Frequencies can also be visually displayed as bar charts, histograms or pie charts. Bar charts, histograms and pie charts help us to understand our data.

Excelsior Enterprises: Bar chart Figure 15.5 provides a graphic representation of the results listed in the table in Output 15.1.

Frequency distributions, bar charts, histograms and pie charts provide a great deal of basic information about the data. Measures of central tendency and dispersion will help us to further understand our data. These are discussed next.

MEASURES OF CENTRAL TENDENCY AND DISPERSION

There are three **measures of central tendency:** the mean, the median and the mode. **Measures of dispersion** include the range, the standard deviation, the variance (where the measure of central tendency is the mean) and the interquartile range (where the measure of central tendency is the median).

Measures of Central Tendency

The mean The **mean**, or the *average*, is a measure of central tendency that offers a general picture of the data without unnecessarily inundating one with each of the observations in a data set. For example, the production department might keep detailed records on how many units of a

OUTPUT 15.1

FREQUENCIES

From the menus, choose:

Analyze
> *Descriptive Statistics*
> *Frequencies*
> [Select the relevant variables]

Choose needed:
> Statistics . . .
> Charts . . .
> Format [for the order in which the results are to be displayed]

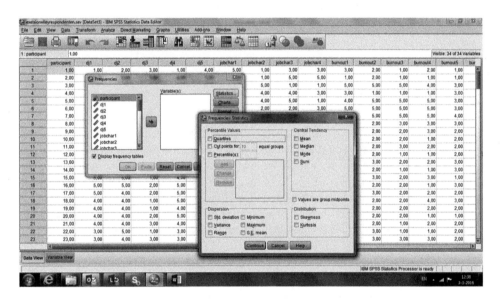

OUTPUT: RESPONDENT'S DEPARTMENT

	Frequency	Percent	Valid percent	Cumulative percent
Marketing	13	7.5	7.5	7.5
Production	49	28.1	28.1	35.6
Sales	44	25.3	25.3	60.9
Finance	5	2.9	2.9	63.8
Servicing	34	19.5	19.5	83.3
Maintenance	5	2.9	2.9	86.2
Personnel	16	9.2	9.2	95.4
Public Relations	3	1.7	1.7	97.1
Accounting	5	2.9	2.9	100.0
Total	174	100.0	100.0	100.0

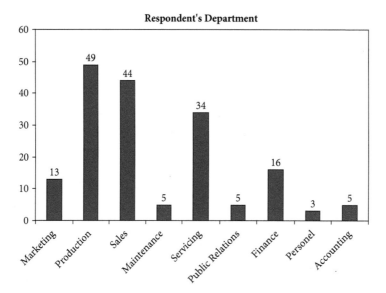

FIGURE 15.5 Bar chart of categories of employees

product are being produced each day. However, to estimate the raw materials inventory, all that the manager might want to know is how many units per month, *on average*, the department has been producing over the past six months. This measure of central tendency – that is, the *mean* – might offer the manager a good idea of the quantity of materials that need to be stocked.

The mean or average of a set of, say, ten observations, is the sum of the ten individual observations divided by ten (the total number of observations).

The median The **median** is the *central item* in a group of observations when they are arrayed in either an ascending or a descending order. Let us take an example to examine how the median is determined as a measure of central tendency.

The mode In some cases, a set of observations does not lend itself to a meaningful representation through either the mean or the median, but can be signified by the *most frequently occurring phenomenon*. For instance, in a department where there are 5 people with a college degree, 1 with a high school diploma, 1 with a doctoral degree and 10 with a master's degree, the most frequently occurring group – the **mode** – is a master's degree. Neither a mean nor a median is calculable or applicable in this case (please think about the reason for this for a few moments). There is also no way of indicating any measure of dispersion.

We have illustrated how the mean, median and the mode can be useful measures of central tendency, based on the type of data we have. We will now examine dispersion.

| Example | Let's say the annual salaries of nine employees in a department are as follows: $65 000, $30 000, $25 000, $64 000, $35 000, $63 000, $32 000, $60 000 and $61 000. The mean salary here works out to be about $48 333, but the median is $60 000. That is, when arrayed in ascending order, the figures will be as follows: $25 000, $30 000, $32 000, $35 000, $60 000, $61 000, $63 000, $64 000, $65 000, and the figure in the middle is $60 000. If there is an even number of employees, then the median will be the average of the middle two salaries. |

Measures of Dispersion

Apart from knowing that the measure of central tendency is the mean, median or mode (depending on the type of available data), one would also like to know about the variability that exists in a set of observations. Like the measure of central tendency, the measure of dispersion is also unique to nominal and interval data.

Two sets of data might have the same mean, but the dispersions could be different. For example, if Company A sold 30, 40 and 50 units of a product during the months of April, May and June, respectively, and Company B sold 10, 40 and 70 units during the same period, the average units sold per month by both companies is the same – 40 units – but the variability or the *dispersion* in the latter company is larger.

The three measurements of dispersion connected with the mean are the range, the variance and the standard deviation, which are explained below.

Range Range refers to the extreme values in a set of observations. The range is between 30 and 50 for Company A (a dispersion of 20 units), while the range is between 10 and 70 units (a dispersion of 60 units) for Company B. Another more useful measure of dispersion is the variance.

Variance The **variance** is calculated by subtracting the mean from each of the observations in the data set, taking the square of this difference and dividing the total of these by the number of observations. In the above example, the variance for each of the two companies is:

$$\text{Variance for Company A} = \frac{(30-40)^2 + (40-40)^2 + (50-40)^2}{3} = 66.7$$

$$\text{Variance for Company B} = \frac{(10-40)^2 + (40-40)^2 + (70-40)^2}{3} = 600$$

As we can see, the variance is much larger in Company B than Company A. This makes it more difficult for the manager of Company B to estimate how many goods to stock than it is for the manager of Company A. Thus, variance gives an indication of how dispersed the data in a data set are.

Standard deviation The **standard deviation**, which is another measure of dispersion for interval and ratio scaled data, offers an index of the spread of a distribution or the variability in the data. It is a very commonly used measure of dispersion, and is simply the square root of the variance. In the case of the above two companies, the standard deviation for Companies A and B would be $\sqrt{66.7}$ and $\sqrt{600}$ or 8.167 and 24.495, respectively.

The mean and standard deviation are the most common descriptive statistics for interval and ratio scaled data. The standard deviation, in conjunction with the mean, is a very useful tool because of the following statistical rules, in a normal distribution:

1. Practically all observations fall within three standard deviations of the average or the mean.

2. More than 90 percent of the observations are within two standard deviations of the mean.

3. More than half of the observations are within one standard deviation of the mean.

Other measures of dispersion When the *median* is the measure of central tendency, percentiles, deciles and quartiles become meaningful. Just as the median divides the total realm of observations into two equal halves, the *quartile* divides it into four equal parts, the *decile* into ten and the *percentile* into 100 equal parts. The percentile is useful when huge masses of data, such as the GRE or GMAT scores, are handled. When the area of observations is divided into 100 equal parts, there are 99 percentile points. Any given score has a probability of 0.01 that it will fall in any one of those points. If John's score is in the 16th percentile, it indicates that 84 percent of those who took the exam scored better than he did, while 15 percent did worse.

Oftentimes we are interested in knowing where we stand in comparison to others – are we in the middle, in the upper 10 or 25 percent, or in the lower 20 or 25 percent, or where? For instance, if in a company-administered test, Mr Chou scores 78 out of a total of 100 points, he may be unhappy if he is in the bottom 10 percent among his colleagues (the test-takers), but may be reasonably pleased if he is in the top 10 percent, despite the fact that his score remains the same. His standing in relation to the others can be determined by the central tendency median and the percentile he falls in.

The measure of dispersion for the median, the **interquartile range**, consists of the middle 50 percent of the observations (i.e. observations excluding the bottom and top 25 percent quartiles). The interquartile range is very useful when comparisons are to be made among several groups. For instance, telephone companies can compare long-distance charges of customers in several areas by taking samples of customer bills from each of the cities to be compared. By plotting the first and third quartiles and comparing the median and the spread, they can get a good idea of where billings tend to be highest, to what extent customers vary in the frequency of use of long-distance calls and so on. This is done by creating a box-and-whisker plot for each area. The box-and-whisker plot is a graphic device that portrays central tendency, percentiles and variability. A box is drawn, extending from the first to the third quartile, and lines are drawn from either side of the box to the extreme scores, as shown in Figure 15.6(a). Figure 15.6(b) has the median represented by a dot within each box. Side-by-side comparisons of the various plots clearly indicate the highest value, the range and the spread for each area or city. For a fuller discussion on this, refer to Salvia (1990).

In sum, we have illustrated how the mean, median and the mode can be useful measures of central tendency, depending on the type of available data. Likewise, we have shown how the standard deviation (and variance, which is the square of standard deviation), and the interquartile range are useful measures of dispersion. Obviously, there is no measure of dispersion associated with the mode.

RELATIONSHIPS BETWEEN VARIABLES

In a research project that includes several variables, beyond knowing the descriptive statistics of the variables, we would often like to know how one variable is related to another. That is, we would like to see the nature, direction and significance of the *bivariate* relationships of the variables used in the study (i.e. the relationship between any two variables among the variables tapped in the study).

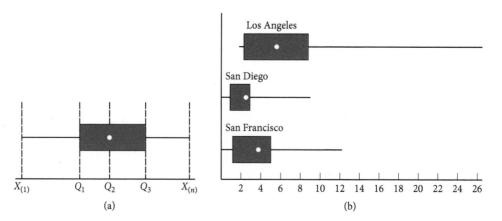

FIGURE 15.6   (a) Box-and-whisker plot; (b) comparison of telephone bills in three cities

Non-parametric tests are available to assess the relationship between variables measured on a nominal or an ordinal scale. Spearman's rank correlation and Kendall's rank correlation are used to examine relationships between two ordinal variables. A **correlation matrix** is used to examine relationships between interval and/or ratio variables.

Relationship Between Two Nominal Variables: χ^2 Test

We might sometimes want to know if there is a relationship between two nominal variables or whether they are independent of each other. As examples: (1) Is viewing a television advertisement of a product (yes/no) related to buying that product by individuals (buy/don't buy)? (2) Is the type of job done by individuals (white-collar job/blue-collar job) a function of the colour of their skin (white/non-white)? Such comparisons are possible by organizing data by groups or categories and seeing if there are any statistically significant relationships. For example, we might collect data from a sample of 55 individuals whose colour of skin and nature of jobs, culled from a frequency count, might be illustrated as in Table 15.2 in a two-by-two contingency table. Just by looking at Table 15.2, a clear pattern seems to emerge that those who are white hold white-collar jobs. Only a few of the non-whites hold white-collar jobs. Thus, there does seem to be a relationship between the colour of the skin and the type of job handled; the two do not seem to be independent. This can be statistically confirmed by the **chi-square (χ^2) test** – a non-parametric test – which indicates whether or not the observed pattern is due to chance. As we know, non-parametric tests are used when normality of distributions cannot be assumed as in nominal or ordinal data. The χ^2 test compares the expected frequency (based on probability) and the observed frequency, and the χ^2 statistic is obtained by the formula:

$$\chi^2 = \Sigma \frac{(Oi - Ei)^2}{Ei}$$

where χ^2 is the chi-square statistic; Oi is the observed frequency of the ith cell; and Ei is the expected frequency. The χ^2 statistic with its level of significance can be obtained for any set of nominal data through computer analysis.

Thus, in testing for differences in relationships among nominally scaled variables, the χ^2 (chi-square) statistic comes in handy. The null hypothesis would be set to state that there is no significant relationship between two variables (colour of skin and nature of the job, in the above example), and the alternate hypothesis would state that there is a significant relationship.

The chi-square statistic is associated with the degrees of freedom (df), which denote whether or not a significant relationship exists between two nominal variables. The number of degrees of freedom is one less than the number of cells in the columns and rows. If there are four cells (two in a column and two in a row), then the number of degrees of freedom would be 1: $[(2 - 1) \times (2 - 1)]$. The chi-square statistic for various df is provided in Table III in the statistical tables toward the end of the book.

The χ^2 statistic can also be used for multiple levels of two nominal variables. For instance, one might be interested to know if four groups of employees – production, sales, marketing and R&D personnel – react to a policy in four different ways (i.e. with no interest at all, with mild interest, moderate interest and intense interest). Here, the χ^2 value for the test of independence

Table 15.2 Contingency Table of Skin Colour and Job Type

Skin colour	White collar	Blue collar	Total
White	30	5	35
Non-white	2	18	20
Total	32	23	55

is generated by cross-tabulating the data in 16 cells – that is, classifying the data in terms of the four groups of employees and the four categories of interest. The degrees of freedom here will be 9: [(4 − 1 × (4 − 1)].

The χ^2 test of significance thus helps us to see whether or not two nominal variables are related. Besides the χ^2 test, other tests, such as the *Fisher exact probability test* and the *Cochran Q test* are used to determine the relationship between two nominally scaled variables.

Correlations

A Pearson correlation matrix will indicate the direction, strength and significance of the bivariate relationships among all the variables that were measured at an interval or ratio level. The correlation is derived by assessing the variations in one variable as another variable also varies. For the sake of simplicity, let us say we have collected data on two variables – price and sales – for two different products. The volume of sales at every price level can be plotted for each product, as shown in the scatter diagrams in Figure 15.7(a) and (b).

Figure 15.7(b) indicates a discernible pattern of how the two factors vary simultaneously (the trend of the scatter is that of a downward straight line), whereas Figure 15.7(a) does not. Looking at the scatter diagram in Figure 15.7(b), it would seem there is a direct negative correlation between price and sales for this product. That is, as the price increases, sales of the product drop consistently. Figure 15.7(a) suggests no interpretable pattern for the other product.

A correlation coefficient that indicates the strength and direction of the relationship can be computed by applying a formula that takes into consideration the two sets of figures – in this case, different sales volumes at different prices.

Theoretically, there could be a perfect positive correlation between two variables, which is represented by 1.0 (plus 1), or a perfect negative correlation which would be −1.0 (minus 1). However, neither of these will be found in reality when assessing correlations between any two variables expected to be different from each other.

While the correlation could range between −1.0 and +1.0, we need to know if any correlation found between two variables is significant or not (i.e. if it has occurred solely by chance or if there is a high probability of its actual existence). As we know, a significance of $p = 0.05$ is the generally accepted conventional level in social science research. This indicates that 95 times out of 100, we can be sure that there is a true or significant correlation between the two variables, and there is only a 5 percent chance that the relationship does not truly exist. If there is a correlation of 0.56 (denoted as $r = 0.56$) between two variables A and B, with $p < 0.01$, then we know that there is a positive relationship between the two variables and the probability of this not being true is 1 percent or less. That is, over 99 percent of the time we would expect this correlation to exist. The correlation of 0.56 also indicates that the variables explain the variance in one another to the extent of 31.4 percent (0.56^2).

FIGURE 15.7 (a) Scatter diagram with no discernible pattern; (b) scatter diagram indicating a downward or negative slope

We do not know which variable *causes* which, but we do know that the two variables are associated with each other. Thus, a hypothesis that postulates a significant positive (or negative) relationship between two variables can be tested by examining the correlation between the two.

The Pearson correlation coefficient is appropriate for interval- and ratio-scaled variables, and the Spearman Rank or the Kendall's tau coefficients are appropriate when variables are measured on an ordinal scale. Any bivariate correlation can be obtained by clicking the relevant menu, identifying the variables, and seeking the appropriate parametric or non-parametric statistics.

Descriptive statistics such as maximum, minimum, means, standard deviations and variance were obtained for the interval-scaled items of the Excelsior Enterprises study. The procedure is shown in Output 15.2.

EXCELSIOR ENTERPRISES: DESCRIPTIVE STATISTICS PART 1

The results presented in the table in Output 15.2 indicate that:

- there are missing observations for every item except for the items pe1, pe2, pe3, burnout10, itl1 and itl2;

- there are illegal codes for items jobchar1 (a 6 has been entered in at least one cell), burnout3 (again, a 6 has been entered in at least one cell) and itl2 (a 5 has been entered in at least one cell);

- the responses to each individual item have a good spread.

OUTPUT 15.2

DESCRIPTIVE STATISTICS: CENTRAL TENDENCIES AND DISPERSIONS

From the menus, choose:
Analyze
   Descriptive Statistics
   Descriptives
   [Select the variables]
   Statistics . . .
   [Choose the relevant statistics needed]

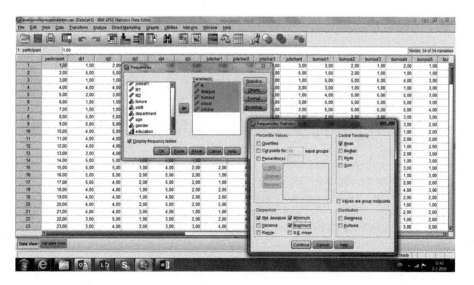

(Continued)

(Continued)

OUTPUT

	pe1	pe2	pe3	pe4	pe5	jobchar1	jobchar2	jobchar3	jobchar4	burnout1	burnout2
N valid	174	174	174	171	171	172	173	173	173	171	171
N missing	0	0	0	3	3	2	1	1	1	3	3
Mean	2.385	2.270	2.523	2.491	2.552	3.526	3.428	3.549	3.462	2.468	2.444
Std deviation	1.023	0.980	1.126	0.916	0.999	1.097	1.035	1.097	1.081	1.238	1.041
Variance	1.047	0.961	1.268	0.840	0.997	1.204	1.072	1.203	1.169	1.533	1.084
Minimum	1	1	1	1	1	1	1	1	1	1	1
Maximum	5	5	5	5	5	6	5	5	5	5	5

	burnout3	burnout4	burnout5	burnout6	burnout7	burnout8	burnout9	burnout10	job sat	itl1	itl2
N valid	171	171	173	173	173	173	173	174	173	174	174
N missing	3	3	1	1	1	1	1	0	1	0	0
Mean	2.462	2.532	2.734	2.665	2.584	2.688	2.798	2.270	2.931	2.569	2.615
Std deviation	1.144	1.356	1.028	1.064	1.146	1.129	0.988	1.021	1.169	0.828	0.903
Variance	1.309	1.356	1.057	1.131	1.314	1.274	0.976	1.042	1.367	0.686	0.816
Minimum	1	1	1	1	1	1	1	1	1	1	1
Maximum	6	5	5	5	5	5	5	4	5	4	5

Appropriate actions were taken to correct the illegal entries. A further inspection of the missing data revealed that every participant answered either all or the vast majority of the questions. Therefore, no questionnaires were thrown out. Missing data will be ignored during subsequent analyses.

From here, we can proceed with further detailed analyses to test the goodness of our data.

TESTING THE GOODNESS OF MEASURES

The reliability and validity of the measures can now be tested.

RELIABILITY

Instructors can visit the companion website at **www.wiley.com/go/bougie/researchmethods forbusiness8e** for **Author Video: Reliability**.

As discussed in Chapter 13, the reliability of a measure is established by testing for both consistency and stability. Consistency indicates how well the items measuring a concept hang together as a set. Cronbach's alpha is a reliability coefficient that indicates how well the items in a set are positively correlated to one another. Cronbach's alpha is computed in terms of the average intercorrelations among the items measuring the concept. The closer Cronbach's alpha is to 1, the higher the internal consistency reliability.

Another measure of consistency reliability used in specific situations is the split-half reliability coefficient. Since this reflects the correlations between two halves of a set of items, the coefficients obtained will vary depending on how the scale is split. Sometimes split-half reliability is obtained to test for consistency when more than one scale, dimension or factor is assessed. The items across each of the dimensions or factors are split, based on some predetermined logic (Campbell, 1976). In almost every case, Cronbach's alpha is an adequate test of internal consistency reliability. You will see later in this chapter how Cronbach's alpha is obtained through computer analysis.

As discussed in Chapter 13, the stability of a measure can be assessed through parallel form reliability and test–retest reliability. When a high correlation between two similar forms of a measure (see Chapter 13) is obtained, parallel form reliability is established. Test–retest reliability can be established by computing the correlation between the same tests administered at two different time periods.

Excelsior Enterprises: Checking the Reliability of the Multi-Item Measures

Because perceived equity, burnout, job enrichment and intention to leave were measured with multi-item scales, the consistency of the respondents' answers to the scale items has to be tested for each measure. In Chapter 13, we explained that Cronbach's alpha is a popular test of inter-item consistency. Table 15.3 provides an overview of Cronbach's alpha for the four variables. This table shows that the alphas were all well above 0.60.

In general, reliabilities less than 0.60 are considered to be poor, those in the 0.70 range, acceptable, and those over 0.80 good. Thus, the internal consistency reliability of the measures used in this study can be considered to be acceptable for the intention to leave measure and good for the other measures.

It is important to note that all the negatively worded items in the questionnaire should first be reversed before the items are submitted for reliability tests. Unless all the items measuring a variable are in the same direction, the reliabilities obtained will be incorrect.

A sample of the result obtained for the Cronbach's alpha test for job enrichment, together with instructions on how it is obtained, is shown in Output 15.3.

The reliability of the job enrichment measure is presented in the first table in Output 15.3. The second table provides an overview of the alphas if we take one of the items out of the measure. For instance, it is shown that if the first item (Jobchar1) is taken out, Cronbach's alpha of the new three-item measure will be 0.777. This means that the alpha will go down if we take item 1 out of our measure. Likewise, if we take out item 2, our alpha will go down and become 0.788. Note that even if our alpha would increase if we would take out one of the items, we would not take it out for two reasons. First, our alpha is above 0.7 so we do not have to take any remedial actions. Second, if we would take one of the items out, the *validity* of our measure would probably decrease. The items (all of them) were included in the original measure for a reason!

If, however, our Cronbach's alpha was too low (under 0.60), then we could use this table to find out which of the items would have to be removed from our measure to increase the inter-item consistency. Note that, usually, taking out an item, although improving the reliability of our measure, affects the validity of our measure in a negative way.

Table 15.3   Reliability of the Excelsior Enterprises Measures

Variable	Number of items	Cronbach's alpha
Perceived equity	5	0.882
Job enrichment	4	0.844
Burnout	10	0.813
Intention to leave	2	0.749

OUTPUT 15.3

RELIABILITY ANALYSIS

From the menus, choose:

Analyze
  Scale
  Reliability Analysis . . .
  [Select the variables constituting the scale]
  Choose *Model Alpha* [this is the default option]
  Click on *Statistics*.
  Select *Scale* if item deleted under *Descriptives*

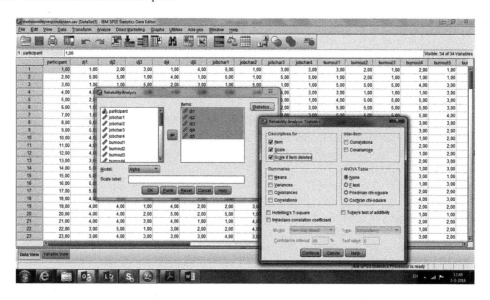

OUTPUT

Reliability statistics	
Cronbach's alpha	Number of items
0.844	4

Item-total statistics

	Scale mean if item deleted	Scale variance if item deleted	Corrected item-total variation	Cronbach's alpha if item deleted
Jobchar1	10,4393	7,143	,735	,777
Jobchar2	10,5318	7,483	,714	,788
Jobchar3	10,4104	7,639	,620	,828
Jobchar4	10,4971	7,554	,652	,814

Now that we have established that the inter-item consistency is satisfactory for perceived equity, job enrichment, burnout and intention to leave, the scores on the original questions can be combined into a single score. For instance, a new 'perceived equity' score can be calculated from the scores on the five individual 'perceived equity' items (but only after items 1, 2 and 4 have been reverse coded). Likewise, a new 'job enrichment' score can be calculated from the scores on the four individual 'job enrichment' items, and so on. We have already explained that this involves calculating the summed score (per case/participant) and then dividing it by the number of items.

VALIDITY

Factorial validity can be established by submitting the data for factor analysis. The results of factor analysis (a multivariate technique) will confirm whether or not the theorized dimensions emerge. Recall from Chapter 12 that measures are developed by first delineating the dimensions so as to operationalize the concept. Factor analysis reveals whether the dimensions are indeed tapped by the items in the measure, as theorized. **Criterion-related validity** can be established by testing for the power of the measure to differentiate individuals who are known to be different (refer to discussions regarding concurrent and predictive validity in Chapter 13). **Convergent validity** can be established when there is a high degree of correlation between two different sources responding to the same measure (e.g. both supervisors and subordinates respond similarly to a perceived reward system measure administered to them). **Discriminant validity** can be established when two distinctly different concepts are not correlated to each other (e.g. courage and honesty; leadership and motivation; attitudes and behaviour). Convergent and discriminant validity can be established through the multitrait multimethod matrix, a full discussion of which is beyond the scope of this book. The student interested in knowing more about factor analysis and the multitrait multimethod matrix can refer to books on those subjects. When well-validated measures are used, there is no need, of course, to establish their validity again for each study. The reliability of the items can, however, be tested.

Once the new scores for perceived equity, job enrichment, burnout and intention to leave have been calculated, we are ready to further analyse the data. Descriptive statistics such as maximum, minimum, means, standard deviations and variance can now be obtained for the multi-item, interval-scaled independent and dependent variables. What's more, a correlation matrix can also be obtained to examine how the variables in our model are related to each other.

> **EXCELSIOR ENTERPRISES: DESCRIPTIVE STATISTICS PART 2**

This will help us to answer important questions such as:

- *How big is the problem?* In other words, to what extent are the employees of Excelsior Enterprises inclined to leave? What is the average inclination to leave?

- *What is the nature of the problem?* Compare, for instance, the histograms provided in Figure 15.8. The average ITL is the same in both cases. However, the graphs show us that in the first hypothetical histogram ITL is 'fairly normally' distributed.[1] In the second hypothetical histogram, the distribution is clearly not normal. In fact, it looks bimodal (with two peaks indicative of two modes). The first distribution suggests that most of the respondents are neither bent on leaving nor staying. The bimodal distribution, on the other hand, suggests that one group of employees is not inclined to leave at all, whereas another group is determined to leave the organization.[2]

---

[1] Note that there are objective tests to decide whether or not a distribution is normal, for instance the Kolmogorov–Smirnov test and the Shapiro–Wilk test.

[2] 'Normally distributed data' is one of the assumptions of *parametric data*; this assumption is unmistakably violated in the second histogram. An excellent discussion on the assumptions of parametric data and on what to do if the assumptions are violated is provided by Andy Field in his book *Discovering Statistics Using SPSS* (Field, 2009).

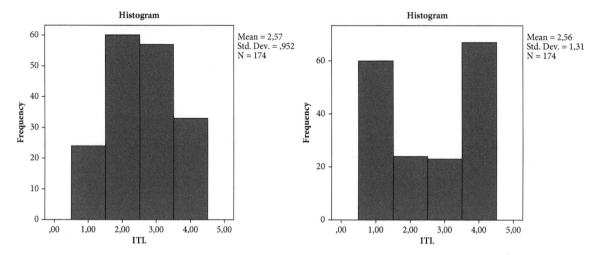

FIGURE 15.8 Two hypothetical histograms of 'intention to leave'

Descriptive statistics will also help us to answer the following questions:

- Are the employees satisfied with their jobs?
- What are the employees' perceptions on job enrichment?
- How many employees have which degrees of burnout?
- Is there much variance in the extent to which employees perceive the relationship with the company as equitable?
- What are the relationships between perceived equity, burnout, job enrichment, job satisfaction and intention to leave?

The answers to these questions will help us (together with the results of our hypotheses tests) to make informed decisions on how we can best solve the problem.

Descriptive statistics such as maximum, minimum, means, standard deviations and variance were obtained for the interval-scaled independent and dependent variables in the Excelsior Enterprises study. The results are shown in Table 15.4. It may be mentioned that all variables except ITL were tapped on a five-point scale. ITL was measured on a four-point scale.

From the results, it may be seen that the mean of 2.59 on a four-point scale for ITL indicates that Excelsior Enterprises has a problem with regard to turnover. The minimum of 1 reveals that there are some employees who do not intend to leave at all, and the maximum of 4 reveals that some are seriously considering leaving. Job satisfaction is about average (2.91 on a five-point scale). The mean on perceived equity is rather low (2.44 on a five-point scale), as is the mean on experienced burnout (2.57). Finally, the job is perceived as somewhat enriched (3.49). Table 15.4 also points out that the variance for all the variables is rather high, indicating that participants' answers are not always very close to the mean on all the variables.

Table 15.4 Descriptive Statistics for Independent and Dependent Variables

	N	**Minimum**	**Maximum**	**Mean**	**Std deviation**	**Variance**
ITL	174	1.00	4.00	2.589	0.769	0.592
Job satisfaction	173	1.00	5.00	2.931	1.169	1.367
Perceived equity	174	1.00	4.60	2.444	0.883	0.694
Burnout	174	1.20	4.60	2.566	0.681	0.463
Jobchar	173	1.00	5.00	3.491	0.888	0.789

Table 15.5   Frequency Table Intention to Leave

	Frequency	Percentage	Valid percentage	Cumulative percentage
1.00	9	5.2	5.2	5.2
1.50	16	9.2	9.2	14.4
2.00	33	19.0	19.0	33.3
2.50	40	23.0	23.0	56.3
3.00	39	22.4	22.4	78.7
3.50	27	15.5	15.5	94.3
4.00	10	5.7	5.7	100.0
Total	174	100.0	100.0	

Table 15.5 provides a more detailed account of employees' intentions to leave. This table shows that a large group of employees seriously considers leaving Excelsior Enterprises! Testing our hypotheses will improve our understanding of *why* employees consider leaving Excelsior Enterprises and will provide us with useful tools to reduce employees' intentions to leave the company.

The Pearson correlation matrix obtained for the five interval-scaled variables is shown in Table 15.6. From the results, we see that the intention to leave is, as would be expected, significantly negatively correlated to job satisfaction, perceived equity, and job enrichment. That is, the intention to leave is low if job satisfaction and equitable treatment are experienced, and the job is enriched. However, when individuals experience burnout (physical and emotional exhaustion), their intention to leave does not increase (this relationship is not significant; we will have more to say about this in the next chapter). Job satisfaction is positively correlated to perceived equity and an enriched job and negatively correlated to burnout and ITL. These correlations are all in the expected direction. It is important to note that the correlations between the independent variables does not exceed 0.272 for this sample. This is an important finding, because if correlations between the *independent variables* were very high (say, 0.75 and above), we might run into a *collinearity* problem in our regression analysis.

Table 15.6   Correlations Between Independent and Dependent Variables

	Intention to leave	Job satisfaction	Perceived equity	Burnout	Job enrichment
Intention to leave	1	−0.703	−0.384	0.037	−0.426
Sig. (two-tailed)		0.000	0.000	0.629	0.000
N	174	173	174	174	173
Job satisfaction	−0.703	1	.280	−0.242	0.268
Sig. (two-tailed)	0.000		0.000	0.001	0.000
N	173	173	173	173	172
Perceived equity	−0.384	0.280	1	0.089	0.272
Sig. (two-tailed)	0.000	0.000		0.241	0.000
N	174	173	174	174	173
Burnout	0.037	−0.242	0.089	1	0.028
Sig. (two-tailed)	0.629	0.000	0.241		0.719
N	174	173	174	174	173
Job enrichment	−0.426	0.268	0.272	0.028	1
Sig. (two-tailed)	0.000	0.000	0.000	0.719	
N	173	172	173	173	173

After we have obtained descriptive statistics for the variables in our study, we can test our hypotheses. Hypothesis testing is discussed in the next chapter.

SUMMARY

- **Learning objective 1: Demonstrate the ability to get data ready for quantitative analysis.** After quantitative data have been collected, the next step is to analyse them to answer the research questions. However, before the data can be analyzed, they need to be coded, keyed in and edited. A categorization scheme has to be set up before the data can be typed in. Then, outliers, inconsistencies and blank responses, if any, have to be handled in some way. Data transformation, the next step, is a variation of data coding; it is the process of changing the original numerical representation of a quantitative value to another value. Data are typically changed to avoid problems in the next stage of the data analysis process. Data transformation is also necessary when several questions have been used to measure a single concept.

- **Learning objective 2: Describe the various processes by which one can get a feel for the data in a study.** The researcher can acquire a feel for the data by obtaining a visual summary or by checking the central tendency and the dispersion of a variable. One can also get to know the data by examining the relation between two variables.

- **Learning objective 3: Describe the means by which the reliability and validity of measures can be assessed.** The reliability of a measure is established by testing for both consistency and stability. Consistency indicates how well the items measuring a concept hang together as a set. Cronbach's alpha is a reliability coefficient that indicates how well the items in a set are correlated to one another. Another measure of consistency reliability used in specific situations is the split-half reliability coefficient. Factorial validity can be established by submitting the data for factor analysis. Criterion-related validity can be established by testing for the power of the measure to differentiate individuals who are known to be different. Convergent validity can be established when there is a high degree of correlation between two different sources responding to the same measure. Discriminant validity can be established when two distinctly different concepts are not correlated to each other.

> Instructors can visit the companion website at **www.wiley.com/go/bougie/researchmethods forbusiness8e** for **Case Study: The Subway Family**.

DISCUSSION QUESTIONS

1. What activities are involved in getting the data ready for analysis?

2. What does coding the data involve?

3. Data editing deals with detecting and correcting illogical, inconsistent or illegal data in the information returned by the participants of the study. Explain the difference between illogical, inconsistent and illegal data.

4. How would you deal with missing data?

5. What is reverse scoring and when is reverse scoring necessary?

6. There are three measures of central tendency: the mean, the median and the mode. Measures of dispersion include the range, the standard deviation and the variance (where the measure of central tendency is the mean), and the interquartile range (where the measure of central tendency is the median). Describe these measures and explain which of these measures you would use to provide an overview of (a) nominal, (b) ordinal and (c) interval data?

7. A researcher wants to provide an overview of the gender of the respondents in his sample. The gender is measured like this: What is your gender? ☐ Male ☐ Female. What is the best way to provide an overview of the gender of the respondents?

8. Consider the following reliability analysis for the variable customer differentiation. What could you conclude from it?

Reliability analysis-scale (alpha)

Item-total statistics

	Scale Mean if item deleted	Scale Variance if item deleted	Corrected Item-total correlation	Alpha if item deleted
CUSDIF1	10.0405	5.4733	0.2437	0.7454
CUSDIF2	9.7432	5.0176	0.5047	0.3293
CUSDIF3	9.6486	5.3754	0.4849	0.3722

Reliability coefficients

N of Cases = 111.0   N of Items = 3

Alpha = 0.5878

The following data are available:

Respondent	Age	Exam mark	Paper mark	Sex	Year in college	IQ
1	21	87	83	M	2	80
2	19	83	80	M	1	100
3	23	85	86	M	4	98
4	21	81	75	F	1	76
5	21	81	75	F	3	82
6	20	67	68	F	3	99
7	26	75	88	F	2	120
8	24	92	78	F	4	115
9	26	78	92	M	4	126
10	30	89	95	F	3	129
11	21	72	80	F	1	86
12	19	81	65	M	2	80
13	17	75	77	M	1	70
14	19	76	85	F	1	99
15	35	80	83	F	3	99
16	27	75	60	F	2	60
17	21	85	80	M	3	89
18	27	79	75	M	4	70
19	21	90	93	F	3	140

Respondent	Age	Exam mark	Paper mark	Sex	Year in college	IQ
20	22	97	95	M	3	165
21	21	90	82	M	2	115
22	19	87	86	F	3	119
23	32	95	90	M	2	120
24	19	68	57	F	3	89

Note: Maximum exam mark = 100, Maximum paper mark = 100, Sex: M = male, F = female, Year in college: 1 = Freshman; 2 = Sophomore; 3 = Junior; 4 = Senior.

1. Data handling
   a. Enter the data in SPSS. Save the file to your USB flashdrive. Name the file 'resmethassignment1'.
   b. Provide appropriate variable labels, value labels and scaling indications to the variables.

2. Descriptives
   a. Use Analyse, Descriptive statistics, Descriptives to summarize metric variables.
   b. Use Analyse, Descriptive statistics, Frequencies to summarize non-metric variables.
   c. Create a pie-chart for Year in college.
   d. Create a histogram for IQ and include the normal distribution.
   e. Make a scatter plot with IQ on the x-axis and exam grade on the y-axis. What do you conclude?
   f. Recode the sex variable such that it is 1 for females and 0 for males.
   g. Make a scatter plot with sex on the x-axis and IQ on the y-axis. What do you conclude?
   h. Compute the mean IQ for males and for females. Conclusion?
   i. Create a new dummy variable, IQdum, which is 1 if the IQ is larger than or equal to 100, and 0 otherwise.

Quantitative Data Analysis: Hypothesis Testing

LEARNING OBJECTIVES

After completing Chapter 16, you should be able to:

1. Discuss type I errors, type II errors and statistical power.

2. Test hypotheses using the appropriate statistical technique.

3. Describe data mining and operations research.

4. Describe useful software packages for quantitative data analysis.

In Chapter 6, we discussed the steps to be followed in hypothesis development and testing. These steps are:

1. State the null and the alternate hypotheses.

2. Determine the level of significance desired ($p = 0.05$, or more, or less).

3. Choose the appropriate statistical test depending on the type of scales that have been used (nominal, ordinal, interval or ratio).

4. See if the output results from computer analysis indicate that the significance level is met. When the resultant value is larger than the critical value, the null hypothesis is rejected, and the alternate accepted. If the calculated value is less than the critical value, the null hypothesis is accepted and the alternate hypothesis rejected.

In this chapter, we will discuss hypothesis testing. First, we will pay attention to type I errors, type II errors and statistical power. Then, we will discuss various univariate and bivariate statistical tests that can be used to test hypotheses. Finally, we will come back to the Excelsior Enterprises case and test the hypotheses that were developed in the previous chapter.

In Chapter 6, we explained that the hypothetico-deductive method requires hypotheses to be falsifiable. For this reason, null hypotheses are developed. These null hypotheses (H_0) are thus set up to be rejected in order to support the alternate hypothesis, termed H_A.

The null hypothesis is presumed true until statistical evidence, in the form of a hypothesis test, indicates otherwise. The required statistical evidence is provided by **inferential statistics**, such as regression analysis or MANOVA. Inferential statistics help us to draw conclusions (or to make inferences) *about the population* from a sample.

The purpose of hypothesis testing is to determine *accurately* if the null hypothesis can be rejected in favour of the alternate hypothesis. Based on the sample data the researcher can reject the null hypothesis (and therefore accept the alternate hypothesis) *with a certain degree of confidence*: there is always a risk that the inference that is drawn about the population is incorrect.

There are two kinds of (or two ways in which a conclusion can be incorrect), classified as type I and type II errors. A **type I error**, also referred to as alpha (α), is the probability of rejecting the null hypothesis when it is actually true. In the Excelsior Enterprises example introduced in Chapter 15, a type I error would occur if we concluded, based on the data, that burnout affects intention to leave when, in fact, it does not. The probability of type I error, also known as the *significance level*, is determined by the researcher. Typical significance levels in business research are 5 percent (<0.05) and 1 percent (<0.01).

A **type II error**, also referred to as beta (β), is the probability of failing to reject the null hypothesis given that the alternate hypothesis is actually true; for example, concluding, based on the data, that burnout does not affect intention to leave when, in fact, it does. The probability of type II error is inversely related to the probability of type I error: the smaller the risk of one of these types of error, the higher the risk of the other type of error.

A third important concept in hypothesis testing is statistical power (1 − β). **Statistical power**, or just power, is the probability of correctly rejecting the null hypothesis. In other words, power is the probability that statistical significance will be indicated if it is present.

Statistical power depends on:

1. Alpha (α): The statistical significance criterion used in the test. If alpha moves closer to zero (for instance, if alpha moves from 5 to 1 percent), then the probability of finding an effect when there is an effect decreases. This implies that the lower the α (i.e. the closer α moves to zero) the lower the power; the higher the alpha, the higher the power.

2. Effect size: The effect size is the size of a difference or the strength of a relationship *in the population*: a large difference (or a strong relationship) in the population is more likely to be found than a small difference (similarity, relationship).

3. The size of the sample: At a given level of alpha, increased sample sizes produce more power, because increased sample sizes lead to more accurate parameter estimates. Thus, increased sample sizes lead to a higher probability of finding what we were looking for. However, increasing the sample size can also lead to too much power, because even very small effects will be found to be statistically significant.

Along these lines, there are four interrelated components that affect the inferences you might draw from a statistical test in a research project: the power of the test, the alpha, the effect size and the sample size. Given the values for any three of these components, it is thus possible to calculate the value of the fourth. Generally, it is recommended to establish the power, the alpha and the required precision (effect size) of a test first, and then, based on the values of these components, determine an appropriate sample size.

BOX 16.1

The focus of business research is usually on type I error. However, power (e.g. to determine an appropriate sample size) and, in some situations, type II error (e.g. if you are testing the effect of a new drug) must also be given serious consideration.

CHOOSING THE APPROPRIATE STATISTICAL TECHNIQUE

Instructors can visit the companion website at **www.wiley.com/go/bougie/researchmethods forbusiness8e** for **Author Video: Choosing the appropriate statistical technique.**

After you have selected an acceptable level of statistical significance to test your hypotheses, the next step is to decide on the appropriate method to test the hypotheses. The choice of the appropriate statistical technique largely depends on the number of (independent and dependent) variables you are examining and the scale of measurement (metric or non-metric) of your variable(s). Other aspects that play a role are whether the assumptions of parametric tests are met and the size of your sample.

Univariate statistical techniques are used when you want to examine two-variable relationships. For instance, if you want to examine the effect of gender on the number of candy bars that students eat per week, univariate statistics are appropriate. If, on the other hand, you are interested in the relationships between many variables, such as in the Excelsior Enterprises case, *multivariate statistical techniques* are required. The appropriate univariate or multivariate test largely depends on the measurement scale you have used, as Figure 16.1 illustrates.

Univariate techniques:

Testing a hypothesis on a single mean:

Metric data:	One sample t-test
Non-metric data:	Chi-square

Testing hypotheses about two related means

Independent samples

Metric data:	Independent samples *t*-test
Non-metric data:	Chi-square
	Mann–Whitney *U*-test

Related samples

Metric data	Paired samples *t*-test
Non-metric data:	Chi-square
	Wilcoxon
	McNemar

Testing hypotheses about several means

Metric data:	One-way analysis of variance
Non-metric data:	Chi-square

Multivariate techniques:

One metric dependent variable

Analysis of variance and covariance

Multiple regression analysis

Conjoint analysis

One non-metric dependent variable

Discriminant analysis

Logistic regression

More than one metric dependent variable

Multivariate analysis of variance

Canonical correlation

FIGURE 16.1   Overview of univariate and multivariate statistical techniques

282 CHAPTER 16 Quantitative Data Analysis: Hypothesis Testing

Chi-square analysis was discussed in the previous chapter. This chapter will discuss the other techniques listed in Figure 16.1. Note that some techniques are discussed more elaborately than others. A detailed discussion of all these techniques is beyond the scope of this book.

TESTING A HYPOTHESIS ABOUT A SINGLE MEAN

The **one sample *t*-test** is used to test the hypothesis that the mean of the *population* from which a sample is drawn is equal to a comparison standard. Assume that you have read that the average student studies 32 hours a week. From what you have observed so far, you think that students from your university (the population from which your sample will be drawn) study more. Therefore, you ask 20 classmates how long they study in an average week. The average study time per week turns out to be 36.2 hours, 4 hours and 12 minutes more than the study time of students in general. The question is: is this a coincidence?

In the above example, the *sample* of students from your university differs from the typical student. What you want to know, however, is whether your fellow students come from a different population than the rest of the students. In other words, did you select a group of motivated students by chance? Or is there a "true" difference between students from your university and students in general?

In this example the null hypothesis is:

H_0: *The number of study hours of students from our university is equal to the number of study hours of students in general.*

The alternate hypothesis is:

H_1: *The number of study hours of students from our university differs from the number of study hours of students in general.*

The way to decide whether there is a significant difference between students from your university and students in general depends on three aspects: the value of the sample mean (36.2 hours); the value of the comparison standard (32 hours); and the degree of uncertainty concerning how well the sample mean represents the population mean (the standard error of the sample mean).

Along these lines, the following formula is used to compute the *t*-value:

$$t_{n-1} = \frac{X - \mu}{s / \sqrt{n}}$$

Assume that the observed standard deviation is 8. Hence, the *t*-statistic becomes:

$$t = \frac{36.2 - 32}{8 / \sqrt{20}} = 2.438$$

Having calculated the *t*-statistic, we can now compare the *t*-value with a standard table of *t*-values with $n - 1$ degrees of freedom to determine whether the *t*-statistic reaches the threshold of statistical significance. When the *t*-statistic is larger than the appropriate table value, the null hypothesis (no significant difference) is rejected.

Our *t*-statistic (2.438) is larger than the appropriate table value (1.729). This means that the difference between 36.2 and 32 is statistically significant. The null hypothesis must thus be rejected: there is a significant difference in study time between students from our university and students in general. Note that the critical-value approach has often been used in the past, because most researchers did not have the computing power available to obtain observed significance

| BOX 16.2 | HOW DOES THIS WORK IN SPSS? |

Under the Analyse menu, choose Compare Means, then One-Sample T Test. Move the dependent variable into the 'Test Variable(s)' box. Type in the value you wish to compare your sample to in the box called 'Test Value'.

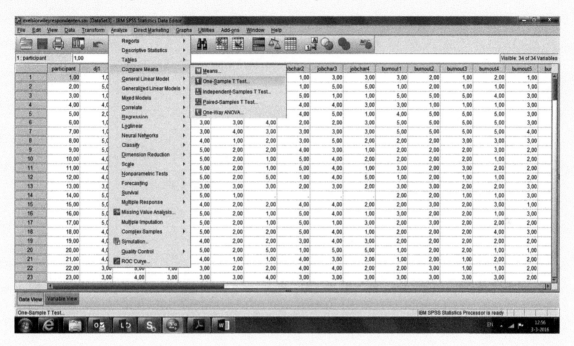

levels (p-values). Nowadays one can easily obtain p-values via statistical software packages such as SPSS, Stata or Qualtrics (discussed later in this chapter). Because p-values are often considered to be more informative than the test statistic, the American Psychological Association, the American Economic Association and others recommend to use the p-value approach when conducting hypothesis tests whenever possible. The p-value, or calculated probability, is the probability of finding the observed, or more extreme, results when the null hypothesis (for instance, in this example 'The number of study hours (. . .) is equal (. . .)') is true. If the observed p-value is larger than 0.05, we cannot reject the null hypothesis. For pedagogical reasons, we will use a critical value approach throughout this chapter.

TESTING HYPOTHESES ABOUT TWO RELATED MEANS

We can also do a **(paired samples)** *t*-test to examine the differences in the same group before and after a treatment. For example, would a group of employees perform better *after* undergoing training than they did *before?* In this case, there would be two observations for each employee, one before the training and one after the training. We would use a paired samples *t*-test to test the null hypothesis that the average of the differences between the before and after measure is zero.

BOX 16.3   HOW DOES THIS WORK IN SPSS?

Under the Analyse menu, choose Compare Means, then Paired-Samples T Test. Move each of the two variables whose means you want to compare to the 'Paired Variables' list.

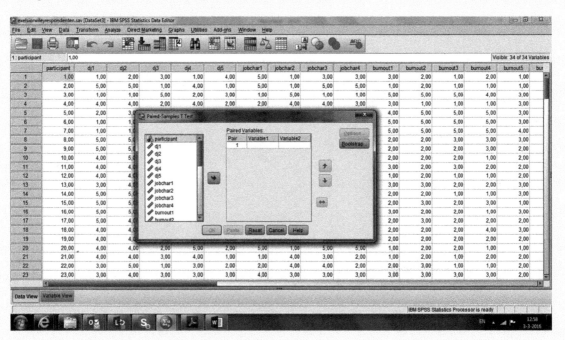

Example	A university professor was interested in the effect of her teaching program on the performance of her students. For this reason, ten students were given a math test in the first week of the semester and their scores were recorded. Subsequently, the students were given an equivalent test during the last week of the semester. The professor now wants to know whether the students' math scores have increased.

Table 16.1 depicts the scores of students on the math test in the first and in the last week of the semester.

To find out if there is a significant difference in math scores we need a test statistic. The test statistic is the average difference/$s_{difference}/\sqrt{n}$.

In this example we get: 22.5/13.79412/$\sqrt{10}$.

Having calculated the t-statistic, we can now compare the t-value with a standard table of t-values with $n - 1$ degrees of freedom to determine whether the t-statistic reaches the threshold of statistical significance. Again, when the t-statistic is larger than the appropriate table value, the null hypothesis (no significant difference) is rejected.

Our t-statistic is larger than the appropriate table value (1.83). This means that the difference between 70 and 57.5 is statistically significant. The null hypothesis must thus be rejected: there is a significant increase in math score.

Table 16.1   Math Scores of Ten Students in the First and Last Week of the Semester

Student	Math scores		
	Score first week	Score last week	Difference
1	55	75	+20
2	65	80	+15
3	70	75	+5
4	55	60	+5
5	40	45	+5
6	60	55	−5
7	80	75	−5
8	35	70	+35
9	55	75	+20
10	60	90	+30
Average score	57.5	70	22.5

BOX 16.4   HOW DOES THIS WORK IN SPSS?

Under the Analyse menu, choose Non-parametric Tests, then Related Samples. Choose 'Automatically compare observed data to hypothesized' as the objective of your analysis, 'Wilcoxon matched-pair signed-rank (2 samples)', under 'Settings' and move the variables you want to compare into the 'Test Fields' box.

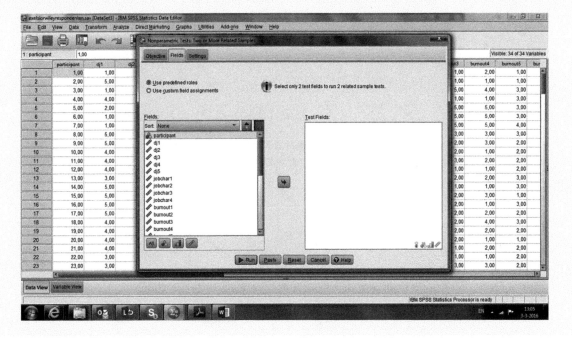

The **Wilcoxon signed-rank test** is a non-parametric test for examining significant differences between two related samples or repeated measurements on a single sample. It is used as an alternative to a paired samples *t*-test when the population cannot be assumed to be normally distributed.

McNemar's test is a non-parametric method used on nominal data. It assesses the significance of the difference between two dependent samples when the variable of interest is dichotomous. It is used primarily in before–after studies to test for an experimental effect.

In the following example, a researcher wants to determine whether the use of a new training method (called CARE) has an effect on the performance of athletes. Counts of individual athletes are given in Table 16.2. The performance (average/good) before the treatment (the new training method) is given in the columns (244 athletes delivered an average performance before they trained with the CARE method, whereas 134 athletes delivered a good performance before they adopted this method). You can find the performance after the treatment (average/good) in the rows (190 athletes delivered an average performance after using the new training method, while the number of athletes that delivered a good performance increased to 188).

The cells of Table 16.2 can be represented by the letters a, b, c and d. The totals across rows and columns are marginal totals ($a + b$, $c + d$, $a + c$ and $b + d$). The grand total is represented by n, as shown in Table 16.3.

McNemar's test is a rather straightforward technique to test marginal homogeneity. *Marginal homogeneity* refers to equality (or the lack of a significant difference) between one or more of the marginal row totals and the corresponding marginal column totals. In this example, marginal homogeneity implies that the row totals are equal to the corresponding column totals, or

$$a + b = a + c$$
$$c + d = b + d$$

Marginal homogeneity would mean there was no effect of the treatment. In this case it would mean that the new training method would not affect the performance of athletes.

The McNemar test uses the χ^2 distribution, based on the formula: $(|b - c| - 1)^2/(b + c)$. χ^2 is a statistic with 1 degree of freedom [(# rows − 1) × (# columns −1)]. The marginal frequencies are *not* homogeneous if the χ^2 result is significant at $p < 0.05$.

The χ^2 value in this example is:

$$(|78 - 132| - 1)^2)/(78 + 132) = 53^2 / 210 = 13.376$$

Table 16.2 Performance of Athletes Before and After New Training Method

		Before		
		average	good	totals
	average	112	78	190
After	good	132	56	188
	totals	244	134	378

Table 16.3 A More Abstract Representation of Table 16.2

		Before		
		average	good	totals
	average	a	b	$a + b$
After	good	c	d	$c + d$
	totals	$a + c$	$b + d$	n

BOX 16.5   **HOW DOES THIS WORK IN SPSS?**

Under the Analyse menu, choose Non-parametric Tests, then Related Samples. Choose 'Automatically compare observed data to hypothesized' as the objective of your analysis, 'McNedmar's test (2 samples)', under 'Settings' and move the variables you want to compare into the 'Test Fields' box.

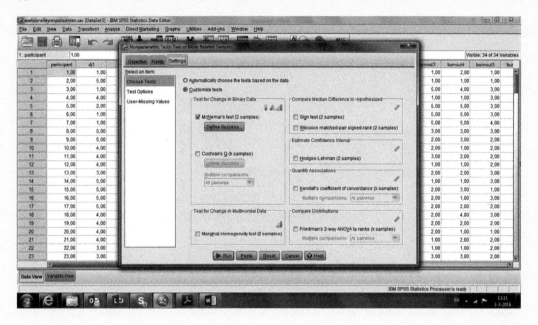

The table of the distribution of chi-square, with 1 degree of freedom, reveals that the difference between samples is significant at the 0.05 level: the critical value of chi-square is 3.841. Since 13.376 computed for the example above exceeds this value, the difference between samples is significant. Hence, we can conclude that the new training method has a positive effect on the performance of athletes.

Note that if b and/or c are small ($b + c < 20$), then χ^2 is not approximated by the chi-square distribution. Instead a *sign test* should be used.

TESTING HYPOTHESES ABOUT TWO UNRELATED MEANS

There are many instances when we are interested to know whether two groups are different from each other on a particular interval-scaled or ratio-scaled variable of interest. For example, would men and women press their case for the introduction of flextime at the workplace to the same extent, or would their needs be different? Do MBAs perform better in organizational settings than business students with only a bachelor's degree? Do individuals in urban areas have a different investment pattern for their savings than those in semi-urban areas? Do CPAs perform better than non-CPAs in accounting tasks? To find answers to such questions, an **independent samples *t*-test** is carried out to see if there are any significant differences in the means for two groups in the variable of interest. That is, a **nominal** variable that is split into two subgroups (e.g. smokers and non-smokers; employees in the marketing department and those in the accounting department; younger and older employees) is tested to see if there is a significant mean difference between the two split groups on a dependent variable, which is measured on an **interval** or **ratio scale** (for instance, extent of well-being; pay; or comprehension level).

| BOX 16.6 | HOW DOES THIS WORK IN SPSS? |

Under the Analyse menu, choose Compare Means, then Independent Samples T Test. Move the dependent variable into the 'Test Variable(s)' box. Move the independent variable (i.e. the variable whose values define the two groups) into the 'Grouping Variable' box. Click 'Define Groups' and specify how the groups are defined (for instance, 0 and 1 or 1 and 2).

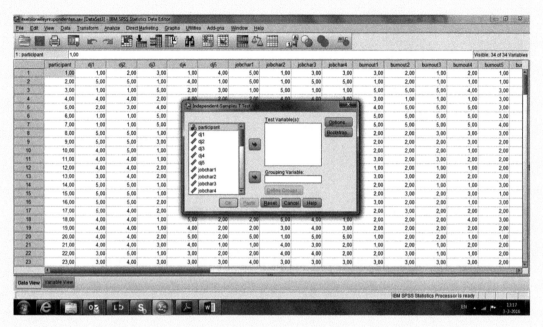

TESTING HYPOTHESES ABOUT SEVERAL MEANS

Whereas the (independent samples) t-test indicates whether or not there is a significant mean difference in a dependent variable between two groups, an analysis of variance (**ANOVA**) helps to examine the significant mean differences among more than two groups on an interval or ratio-scaled dependent variable. For example, is there a significant difference in the amount of sales by the following four groups of salespersons: those who are sent to training schools; those who are given on-the-job training during field trips; those who have been tutored by the sales manager; and those who have had none of the above? Or is the rate of promotion significantly different for those who have assigned mentors, choose their own mentors and have no mentors in the organizational system?

The results of ANOVA show whether or not the means of the various groups are significantly different from one another, as indicated by the F statistic. The F statistic shows whether two sample variances differ from each other or are from the same population. The F distribution is a probability distribution of sample variances and the family of distributions changes with changes in the sample size. Details of the F statistic may be seen in Table IV in the statistical tables toward the end of the book.

When significant mean differences among the groups are indicated by the F statistic, there is no way of knowing from the ANOVA results alone where they lie; that is, whether the significant difference is between Groups A and B, or between B and C, or A and C and so on. It is therefore unwise to use multiple t-tests, taking two groups at a time, because the greater the number of t-tests done, the lower the confidence we can place on results. For example, three t-tests done simultaneously decrease the confidence level from 95 to 86 percent $(0.95)^3$.

BOX 16.7	HOW DOES THIS WORK IN SPSS?

Under the Analyse menu, choose Compare Means, then One-Way ANOVA. Move the dependent variable into the 'Dependent List'. Move the Independent variable (i.e. the variable whose values define the groups) into the 'Factor' box. Click OK.

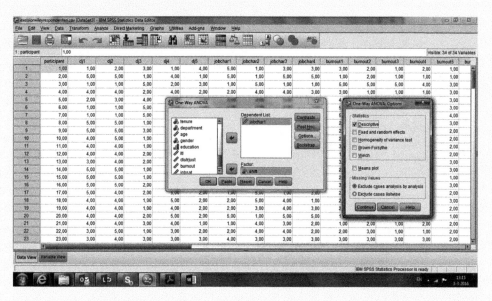

However, several tests, such as Scheffe's test, Duncan Multiple Range test, Tukey's test and Student–Newman–Keul's test are available and can be used, as appropriate, to detect where exactly the mean differences lie.

REGRESSION ANALYSIS

Simple **regression analysis** is used in a situation where one independent variable is hypothesized to affect one dependent variable. For instance, assume that we propose that the propensity to buy a product depends only on the perceived quality of that product.[1] In this case we would have to gather information on perceived quality and propensity to buy a product. We could then plot the data to obtain some first ideas on the relationship between these variables.

From Figure 16.2 we can see that there is a linear relationship between perceived quality and propensity to buy the product. We can model this linear relationship by a *least squares function*.

A simple linear regression equation represents a straight line. Indeed, to summarize the relationship between perceived quality and propensity to buy, we can draw a straight line through the data points, as in Figure 16.3.

We can also express this relationship in an equation:

$$Y_i = \beta_0 + \beta_1 X_{1i} + \varepsilon_i$$

---

[1] In reality, any effort to model the effect of perceived quality on propensity to buy a product without careful attention to other factors that affect propensity to buy would cause a serious statistical problem ('omitted variables bias').

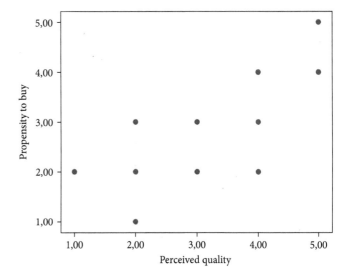

FIGURE 16.2 Scatter plot of perceived quality versus propensity to buy

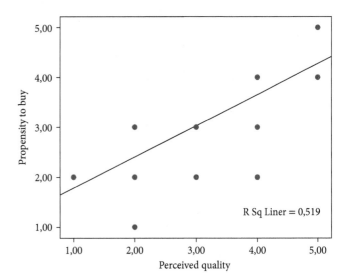

FIGURE 16.3 Regression of propensity to buy on perceived quality

The parameters β_0 and β_1 are called regression coefficients. They are the intercept (β_0) and the slope (β_1) of the straight line relating propensity to buy (Y) to perceived quality (X_1). The slope can be interpreted as the number of units by which propensity to buy would increase if perceived quality increased by a unit. The error term denotes the error in prediction or the difference between the estimated propensity to buy and the actual propensity to buy.

In this example, the intercept (β_0) was not significant whereas the slope (β_1) was. The unstandardized regression coefficient β_1 was 0.832. Recall that the unstandardized regression coefficient represents the amount of change in the dependent variable (propensity to buy in this case) for a one-unit change in the independent variable (perceived quality). Hence, the regression coefficient β_1 indicates that the propensity to buy increases by 0.832 (on a five-point scale) for a one unit change in perceived quality. In other words, the propensity to buy for consumer A, who appraises perceived quality with a 4 (on a five-point scale) is *estimated* to be 0.832 units higher (on a five-point scale) than the propensity to buy for consumer B, who appraised perceived quality with a 3 (on a five-point scale).

The coefficient of determination, R^2, provides information about the goodness of fit of the regression model: it is a statistical measure of how well the regression line approximates the real data points. R^2 is the percentage of variance in the dependent variable that is explained by the variation in the independent variable. If R^2 is 1, the regression model using perceived quality perfectly predicts propensity to buy. In other words, the regression model fits the data perfectly. On the other hand, if R^2 is 0, none of the variation in propensity to buy can be attributed to the independent variable, perceived quality. In this case, the R^2 for the model is 0.519. This means that almost 52 percent of the variation in propensity to buy is explained by variation in perceived quality.

The basic idea of **multiple regression analysis** is similar to that of simple regression analysis. Only in this case, we use more than one independent variable to explain variance in the dependent variable. Multiple regression analysis is a multivariate technique that is used very often in business research. The starting point of multiple regression analysis is, of course, the conceptual model (and the hypotheses derived from that model) that the researcher has developed in an earlier stage of the research process.

Multiple regression analysis provides a means of objectively assessing the degree and the character of the relationship between the independent variables and the dependent variable: the regression coefficients indicate the relative importance of each of the independent variables in the prediction of the dependent variable. For example, suppose that a researcher believes that the variance in performance can be explained by four independent variables, A, B, C and D (say, pay, task difficulty, supervisory support and organizational culture). When these variables are jointly

BOX 16.8   HOW DOES THIS WORK IN SPSS?

Under the Analyse menu, choose Regression, then Linear. Move the dependent variable into the 'Dependent' box. Move the independent variables into the 'Independent(s)' list and click OK.

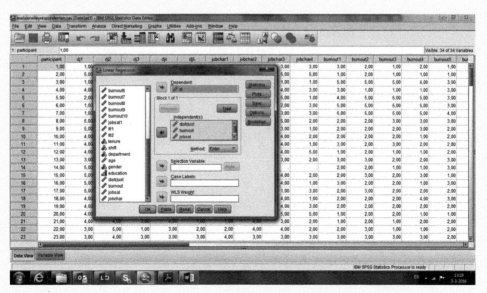

regressed against the dependent variable in an effort to explain the variance in it, the sizes of the individual regression coefficients indicate how much an increase of one unit in the independent variable would affect the dependent variable, assuming that all the other independent variables remain unchanged. What's more, the individual correlations between the independent variables and the dependent variable collapse into what is called a *multiple r* or multiple correlation coefficient. The square of multiple *r*, *R*-square, or R^2 as it is commonly known, is the amount of variance explained in the dependent variable by the predictors.

Standardized Regression Coefficients

Standardized regression coefficients (or beta coefficients) are the estimates resulting from a multiple regression analysis performed on variables that have been standardized (a process whereby the variables are transformed into variables with a mean of 0 and a standard deviation of 1). This is usually done to allow the researcher to compare the relative effects of independent variables on the dependent variable, when the independent variables are measured in different units of measurement (e.g. income measured in dollars and household size measured in number of individuals).

Regression with Dummy Variables

A **dummy variable** is a variable that has two or more distinct levels, which are coded 0 or 1. Dummy variables allow us to use nominal or ordinal variables as independent variables to explain, understand or predict the dependent variable.

Suppose that we are interested in the relationship between work shift and job satisfaction. In this case, the variable 'work shift', which has three categories (see the Excelsior Enterprises case), would have to be coded in terms of two dummy variables, since one of the three categories should serve as the reference category. This might be done as shown in Table 16.4. Note that the third shift serves as the reference category.

Next, the dummy variables D_1 and D_2 have to be included in a regression model. This would look like this:

$$Y_i = \beta_0 + \beta_1 D_{1i} + \beta_{2i} D_{2i} + \varepsilon_i$$

In this example workers from the third shift have been selected as the reference category. For this reason, this category has not been included in the regression equation. For workers in the third shift, D_1 and D_2 assume a value of 0, and the regression equation thus becomes:

$$Y_i = \beta_0 + \varepsilon_i$$

For workers in the first shift the equation becomes:

$$Y_i = \beta_0 + \beta_1 D_{1i} + \varepsilon_i$$

Table 16.4 Recoding Work Shift into Dummy Codes

Work shift	Original code	Dummy D_1	Dummy D_2
First shift	1	1	0
Second shift	2	0	1
Third shift	3	0	0

The coefficient β_1 is the difference in predicted job satisfaction for workers in the first shift, as compared to workers in the third shift. The coefficient β_2 has the same interpretation. Note that any of the three shifts could have been used as a reference category.

Now do Exercises 16.1 and 16.2.

Provide the equation for workers in the second shift.	**EXERCISE 16.1**

Use the data of the Excelsior Enterprises case to estimate the effect of work shift on job satisfaction.	**EXERCISE 16.2**

Multicollinearity

Multicollinearity is an often encountered statistical phenomenon in which two or more independent variables in a multiple regression model are highly correlated. In its most severe case (if the correlation between two independent variables is equal to 1 or −1), multicollinearity makes the estimation of the regression coefficients impossible. In all other cases it makes the estimates of the regression coefficients unreliable.

The simplest and most obvious way to detect multicollinearity is to check the correlation matrix for the independent variables. The presence of high correlations (most people consider correlations of 0.70 and above high) is a first sign of sizeable multicollinearity. However, when multicollinearity is the result of complex relationships among several independent variables, it may not be revealed by this approach. More common measures for identifying multicollinearity are therefore the *tolerance value* and the *variance inflation factor* (*VIF* – the inverse of the tolerance value). Box 16.9 explains how you can produce tolerance and VIF values using SPSS. These measures indicate the degree to which one independent variable is explained by the other independent variables. A common cutoff value is a tolerance value of 0.10, which corresponds to a VIF of 10.

Note that multicollinearity is *not* a serious problem if the purpose of the study is to predict or forecast future values of the dependent variable, because even though the estimations of the regression coefficients may be unstable, multicollinearity does not affect the reliability of the forecast. However, if the objective of the study is to reliably estimate the individual regression coefficients, multicollinearity is a problem. In this case, we may use one or more of the following methods to reduce it:

- Reduce the set of independent variables to a set that are not collinear (but note that this may lead to omitted variable bias, which is also a serious problem).
- Use more sophisticated ways to analyse the data, such as ridge regression.
- Create a new variable that is a composite of the highly correlated variables.

Testing Moderation Using Regression Analysis: Interaction Effects

Earlier in this book we described a moderating variable as a variable that modifies the original relationship between an independent variable and the dependent variable. This means that the effect of one variable (X_1) on Y depends on the value of another variable, the moderating variable (X_2). Such *interactions* are included as *the product* of two variables in a regression model.

Suppose that we have developed the following hypothesis:

H$_1$: *The students' judgment of the university's library is affected by the students' judgment of the computers in the library.*

BOX 16.9   HOW DOES THIS WORK IN SPSS?

Under the Analyse menu, choose Regression, then Linear. Move the dependent variable into the 'Dependent' box. Move the independent variables into the 'Independent(s)' list. Select 'Statistics' by clicking the button on the right-hand side. Select 'Collinearity diagnostics' and click continue. Then click OK.

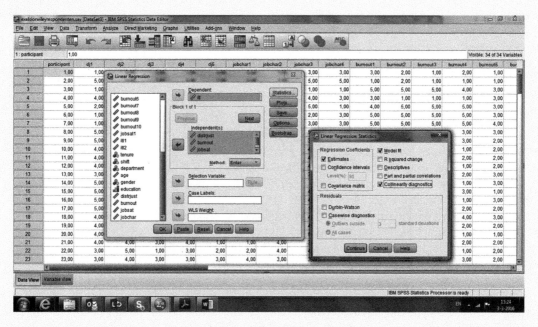

Now suppose that we also believe that, even though this relationship will hold for all students, it will be nonetheless contingent on laptop ownership. That is, we believe that the relationship between the judgment of computers in the library and the judgment of the library is affected by laptop ownership (indeed laptop ownership is a *dummy variable*). Therefore, we hypothesize that:

H₂: *The relationship between the judgment of the library and judgment of computers in the library is moderated by laptop ownership.*

The relationship between the judgment of the library and judgment of computers in the library can be modelled as follows:

$$Y_i = \beta_0 + \beta_1 X_{1i} + \varepsilon_i \tag{1}$$

We have also hypothesized that the effect of X_1 on Y depends on X_2. This can be modelled as follows:

$$\beta_1 = \gamma_0 + \gamma_1 X_{2i} \tag{2}$$

Adding the second equation into the first one leads to the following model:

$$Y_i = \beta_0 + \gamma_0 X_{1i} + \gamma_1 \left(X_{1i} \cdot X_{2i} \right) + \varepsilon_i \tag{3}$$

This last model states that the slope of the relationship between the independent variable (judgment of computers in the library: X_1) and the dependent variable (judgment of the library: Y) varies according to the level of the moderating variable (laptop possession: X_2). In other words, the relationship between the independent and the dependent variable is a function of variable X_2.

Although this model allows us to test moderation, the following model is better (because it also helps us to account for differences in starting level between laptop owners and students who do not own a laptop):

$$Y_i = \beta_0 + \gamma_0 X_{1i} + \gamma_1 (X_{1i} \cdot X_{2i}) + \gamma_2 X_{2i} + \varepsilon_i \tag{4}$$

Because model (4) includes a direct effect of X_2 on Y, it allows us to differentiate between *pure moderation* and *quasi moderation* (compare Sharma, Durand & Gur-Arie, 1981), as explained next.

If $\gamma_1 = 0$ and $\gamma_2 \neq 0$, X_2 is not a moderator but simply an independent predictor variable. If $\gamma_1 \neq 0$, X_2 is a moderator. Model (4) allows us to differentiate between pure moderators and quasi moderators as follows: if $\gamma_1 \neq 0$ and $\gamma_2 = 0$, X_2 is a pure moderator. That is, X_2 moderates the relationship between X_1 and Y, but it has no direct effect on Y. In other words, in this case the *effect* of judgment of computers in the library on judgment of the library is different for the two groups (the line representing this relationship has a different slope); the starting level is the same however (there are no differences in the intercept). If $\gamma_1 \neq 0$ and $\gamma_2 \neq 0$, X_2 is a quasi moderator. That is, X_2 moderates the relationship between X_1 and Y, but it also has a direct effect on Y (different slope and different intercept).

Suppose that data analysis leads to the following model:

$$\hat{Y}_i = 4.3 + 0.4 X_{1i} - 0.01 X_{2i} - 0.2 (X_{1i} \cdot X_{2i}) \tag{5}$$

where $\beta_0 \neq 0$, $\gamma_0 \neq 0$, $\gamma_1 \neq 0$ and $\gamma_2 = 0$.

Based on the results we can conclude that: (1) the judgment of computers in the library has a positive effect on the judgment of the library and (2) that this effect is moderated by laptop possession: if a student has no laptop $(X_{2i} = 0)(X_{2i} = 0)$ the *marginal* effect is 0.4; if the student has a laptop $(X_{2i} = 1)(X_{2i} = 1)$ the *marginal* effect is 0.2. Thus, laptop possession has a negative moderating effect.

Now do Exercises 16.3, 16.4 and 16.5.

Why could it be important to differentiate between quasi moderators and pure moderators?

EXERCISE 16.3

Is laptop possession a pure moderator or a quasi moderator? Explain.

EXERCISE 16.4

Provide a logical explanation for the negative moderating effect of laptop possession.

EXERCISE 16.5

The previous example shows that dummy variables can be used to allow the effect of one independent variable on the dependent variable to change depending on the value of the dummy variable. It is, of course, also possible to include metric variables as moderators in a model. In such cases, the procedure to test moderation is exactly the same as in the previous example.

In this section, we have explained how moderation can be tested with regression analysis. Note that it is also possible to test mediation with regression analysis. We will explain this later on in this chapter using the Excelsior Enterprises data.

OTHER MULTIVARIATE TESTS AND ANALYSES

We will now briefly describe five other multivariate techniques: discriminant analysis, logistic regression, conjoint analysis, multivariate analysis of variance (MANOVA) and canonical correlations.

Discriminant Analysis

Discriminant analysis (Box 16.10) helps to identify the independent variables that discriminate a nominally scaled dependent variable of interest – say, those who are high on a variable from those who are low on it. The linear combination of independent variables indicates the discriminating function showing the large difference that exists in the two group means. In other words, the independent variables measured on an interval or ratio scale discriminate the groups of interest to the study.

BOX 16.10	**HOW DOES THIS WORK IN SPSS?**

Under the Analyse menu, choose Classify, then Discriminant. Move the dependent variable into the 'Grouping' box.

Move the independent variables into the 'Independent(s)' list and click OK.

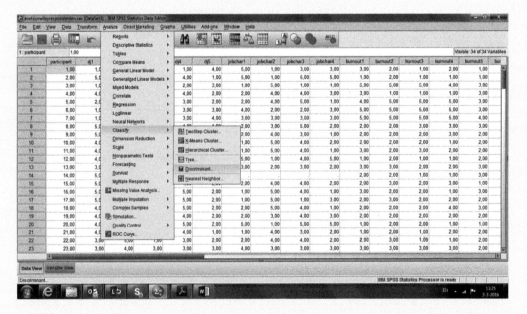

Logistic Regression

Logistic regression (Box 16.11) is also used when the dependent variable is non-metric. However, when the dependent variable has only two groups, logistic regression is often preferred because it does not face the strict assumptions that discriminant analysis faces and because it is very similar to regression analysis. Although regression analysis and logistic regression analysis are very different from a statistical point of view, they are very much alike from a practical viewpoint. Both methods produce prediction equations and in both cases the regression coefficients measure the predictive capability of the independent variables. Thus, logistic regression allows the researcher to predict a discrete outcome, such as 'will purchase the product/will not purchase the product', from a set of variables that may be continuous, discrete or dichotomous.

Conjoint Analysis

Conjoint analysis is a statistical technique that is used in many fields including marketing, product management and operations research. Conjoint analysis requires participants to make a series of trade-offs. In marketing, conjoint analysis is used to understand how consumers develop preferences for products or services. Conjoint analysis is built on the idea that consumers evaluate the value of a product or service by combining the value that is provided by each attribute. An attribute is a general feature of a product or service, such as price, product quality or delivery speed. Each attribute has specific levels. For instance, for the attribute 'price', levels might be €249, €279 and €319. Along these lines, we might describe a mobile phone using the attributes 'memory', 'battery life', 'camera' and 'price'. A specific mobile phone would be described as follows: memory, 12 GB; battery life, 24 hours; camera 8 megapixels; and price €249.

BOX 16.11   **HOW DOES THIS WORK IN SPSS?**

Under the Analyse menu, choose Regression, then Binary Logistic. Move the dependent variable into the 'Dependent' box. Move the independent variables into the 'Covariate(s)' list and click OK.

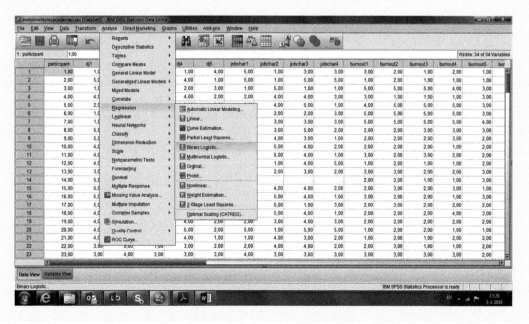

Conjoint analysis takes these attribute and level descriptions of products and services and uses them by asking participants to make a series of choices between different products. For instance:

Would you choose phone X or phone Y?

	Phone X	Phone Y
Memory	12 GB	16 GB
Battery life	24 hours	12 hours
Camera	8 megapixels	16 megapixels
Price	€249	€319

By asking for enough choices, it is possible to establish how important each of the levels is relative to the others; this is known as the utility of the level. Conjoint analysis is traditionally carried out with some form of multiple regression analysis. More recently, the use of hierarchical Bayesian analysis has become widespread to develop models of individual consumer decision-making behaviour.

Two-Way ANOVA

Two-way ANOVA can be used to examine the effect of two non-metric independent variables on a single metric dependent variable. Note that, in this context, an independent variable is often referred to as a factor and this is why a design that aims to examine the effect of two non-metric independent variables on a single metric dependent variable is often called a *factorial design*. The factorial design is very popular in the social sciences. Two-way ANOVA enables us to examine main effects (the effects of the independent variables on the dependent variable) but also interaction effects that exist between the independent variables (or factors). An interaction effect exists when the effect of one independent variable (or one factor) on the dependent variable depends on the level of the other independent variable (factor).

MANOVA

MANOVA is similar to ANOVA, with the difference that ANOVA tests the mean differences of more than two groups on *one* dependent variable, whereas MANOVA tests mean differences among groups across *several* dependent variables simultaneously, by using sums of squares and cross-product matrices. Just as multiple t-tests would bias the results (as explained earlier), multiple ANOVA tests, using one dependent variable at a time, would also bias the results, since the dependent variables are likely to be interrelated. MANOVA circumvents this bias by simultaneously testing all the dependent variables, cancelling out the effects of any intercorrelations among them.

In MANOVA tests (Box 16.12), the independent variable is measured on a nominal scale and the dependent variables on an interval or ratio scale.

The null hypothesis tested by MANOVA is:

$$H_0 : \mu_1 = \mu_2 = \mu_3 = \dots \mu_n$$

The alternate hypothesis is:

$$H_A : \mu_1 \neq \mu_2 \neq \mu_3 \neq \dots \mu_n$$

BOX 16.12   HOW DOES THIS WORK IN SPSS?

Under the Analyse menu, choose General Linear Model, then Multivariate. Move the dependent variables into the 'Dependent' box. Move the independent variables into the 'Fixed Factor(s)' list. Select any of the dialog boxes by clicking the buttons on the right-hand side.

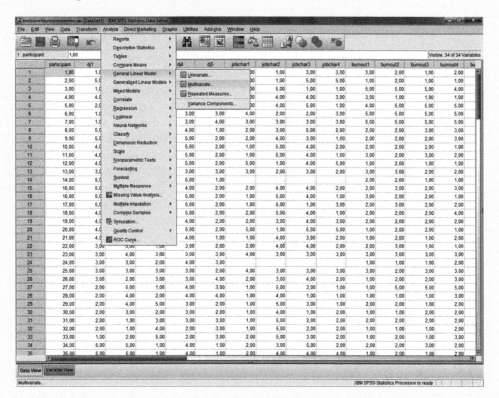

Canonical Correlation

Canonical correlation examines the relationship between two or more dependent variables and several independent variables; for example, the correlation between a set of job behaviours (such as engrossment in work, timely completion of work and number of absences) and their influence on a set of performance factors (such as quality of work, the output and rate of rejects). The focus here is on delineating the job behaviour profiles associated with performance that result in high-quality production.

In sum, several univariate, bivariate and multivariate techniques are available to analyse sample data. Using these techniques allows us to generalize the results obtained from the sample to the population at large. It is, of course, very important to use the correct statistical technique to test the hypotheses of your study. We have explained earlier in this chapter that the choice of the appropriate statistical technique depends on the number of variables you are examining, on the scale of measurement of your variable(s), on whether the assumptions of **parametric tests** are met and on the size of your sample.

The following hypotheses were generated for this study, as stated earlier:

H_1: *Job enrichment has a negative effect on intention to leave.*

H_2: *Perceived equity has a negative effect on intention to leave.*

H_3: *Burnout has a positive effect on intention to leave.*

H_4: *Job satisfaction mediates the relationship between job enrichment, perceived equity and burnout on intention to leave.*

These hypotheses call for the use of mediated regression analysis (all the variables are measured at an interval level). The results of these tests and their interpretation are discussed below.

To test the hypothesis that job satisfaction mediates the effect of perceived justice, burnout and job enrichment on employees' intentions to leave three regression models were estimated, following Baron and Kenny (1986): model 1, regressing job satisfaction on perceived justice, burnout and job enrichment; model 2, regressing intention to leave on perceived justice, burnout and job enrichment; and model 3, regressing employees' intentions to leave on perceived justice, burnout, job enrichment and job satisfaction. Separate coefficients for each equation were estimated and tested. To establish mediation the following conditions must hold: perceived justice, burnout and job enrichment must affect job satisfaction in model 1; perceived justice, burnout and job enrichment must be shown to have an impact on employees' intention to leave in model 2; and job satisfaction must affect employees' intention to leave in model 3 (while controlling for perceived justice, burnout and job enrichment). If these conditions all hold in the predicted direction, then the effect of perceived justice, burnout and job enrichment must be less in model 3 than in model 2. *Perfect mediation* holds if perceived justice, burnout and job enrichment have no effect on intention to leave (in other words, the effect of these variables on intention to leave is no longer significant) when the effect of job satisfaction is controlled for (model 3); *partial mediation* is established if perceived justice, burnout and job enrichment still affect intention to leave in model 3.

The *R*-square of the first regression model (model 1) was 0.172 and the model was statistically significant. In this model perceived equity, burnout and job enrichment were all significant predictors of job satisfaction. The *R*-square of the second regression model (model 2) was 0.264 and this model was also statistically significant. Model 2, as depicted in Table 16.5 indicated that perceived equity and job enrichment affected employees' intention to leave, whereas burnout did not.

The *R*-square of the last model (model 3) was 0.577 and again the model was statistically significant. In this model, job satisfaction was a significant predictor of intention to leave. Perceived equity and job enrichment were significant predictors of intention to leave when job satisfaction was controlled for. The effect of perceived equity and job enrichment on intention to leave was less in the third model than in the second model. Thus, all conditions for *partial* mediation were met for perceived equity and job enrichment.

Follow-up analyses were performed to test for the indirect effect of perceived equity and job enrichment on intention to leave via job satisfaction. Baron and Kenny (1986) provide an approximate significance test for the *indirect* effect of perceived justices and burnout on employees' intentions. The path from, respectively, perceived equity and job enrichment to job satisfaction is denoted a and its standard error s_a; the path from job satisfaction to intention to leave is denoted b and its standard error s_b. The product ab is the estimate of the indirect effect of perceived equity and job enrichment on employees' intentions to leave. The standard error of ab is:

$$SE_{ab} = \sqrt{b^2 s_a^2 + a^2 s_b^2 + s_a^2 s_b^2}$$

Table 16.5 Mediation Analysis

Step 1 model, with job satisfaction as the dependent variable

	Coefficient	p-value
Constant	2.329	0.000
Perceived equity	0.343	0.001
Burnout	−0.454	0.000
Job enrichment	0.269	0.005

Model fit = 0.172

Step 2 model, with intention to leave (ITL) as the dependent variable

	Coefficient	p-value
Constant	4.094	0.000
Perceived equity	−0.270	0.000
Burnout	0.075	0.315
Job enrichment	−0.299	0.000

Model fit = 0.264

Step 3 model, including job satisfaction as an independent variable and with ITL as the dependent variable

	Coefficient	p-value
Constant	5.019	0.000
Perceived equity	−0.131	0.009
Burnout	−0.103	0.089
Job enrichment	−0.187	0.000
Job satisfaction	−0.408	0.000

Model fit = 0.577

Note: Parameters are unstandardized regression weights, with significance levels of *t*-values. Two-sided tests. $N = 174$.

The ratio ab/SE_{ab} can be interpreted as a z statistic. Indirect effects of perceived equity (-3.246, $p < 0.01$) and burnout (-2.743, $p < 0.01$) were both significant.

BOX 16.13   **RESEARCH REALITY**

A method of testing mediation and moderation that is becoming more and more popular is *bootstrapping* (Bullock, Green & Ha, 2010; Preacher, Rucker & Hayes, 2007; Shrout & Bolger, 2002). Bootstrapping is a statistical method based on building a sampling distribution for a statistic by resampling from the data at hand. A big advantage of bootstrapping is that no assumptions about the shape of the sampling distribution of the statistic are necessary when conducting inferential tests. Two software packages that are often used to bootstrap are Mplus and AMOS.

OVERALL INTERPRETATION AND RECOMMENDATIONS TO THE PRESIDENT

From the results of the hypothesis tests, it is clear that perceived equity and job enrichment affect employees' intentions to leave through job satisfaction. From the descriptive results, we have already seen that the mean on perceived equity is rather low (2.44 on a five-point scale).

The mean of job enrichment is clearly higher (3.49 on a five-point scale), but it is still below the standards of the company. Hence, if retention of employees is a top priority for the president, it is important to formulate policies and practices that help to enhance equity perceptions and to redesign jobs in such a way that they are more challenging to the employees. Whatever is done to improve employees' perceptions of equity and to enrich the jobs of employees will improve job satisfaction and thus help employees to think less about leaving and induce them to stay.

The president would therefore be well advised to rectify inequities in the system, if they really exist, or to clear misperceptions of inequities if this is actually the case.

To enrich jobs of employees, the president may want to keep the following goals in mind:

- Reduce repetitive work.
- Increase the employee's feelings of recognition and achievement.
- Provide opportunities for employee advancement (promotions into jobs requiring more skills).
- Provide opportunities for employee growth (an increase in skills and knowledge without a job promotion).

The fact that only 57.7 percent of the variance in 'intention to leave' was explained by the four independent variables considered in this study still leaves more than 40 percent unexplained. In other words, there are other additional variables that are important in explaining ITL that have not been considered in this study. Further research might be necessary to explain more of the variance in ITL, if the president wishes to pursue the matter further.

Now do Exercises 16.6, 16.7 and 16.8.

EXERCISE 16.6

Discuss: What do the unstandardized coefficients and their p-values in the first model imply? In other words, what happens to job satisfaction if perceived justice, burnout and job enrichment change by one unit?

EXERCISE 16.7

Provide the tolerance values and the variance inflation factors for all the independent variables in model 1. Discuss: Do we have a multicollinearity problem?

EXERCISE 16.8

Does work shift moderate the relationship between job satisfaction and intention to leave for Excelsior Enterprises employees?

We have now seen how different hypotheses can be tested by applying the appropriate statistical tests in data analysis. Based on the interpretation of the results, the research report is then written, making necessary recommendations and discussing the pros and cons of each, together with cost–benefit analysis.

BIG DATA MINING AND OPERATIONS RESEARCH

Some companies however are successfully using data mining as a strategic tool for reaching new levels of business intelligence. Using algorithms to analyse (big) data in a meaningful way, **data mining** is the process of discovering patterns in (large) data sets. The overall goal of data mining is to extract *information* (data that helps to resolve uncertainty with respect to a topic of interest) from data sets. In the 1960s, terms like data fishing, data dredging and data mining were often used to refer to the bad practice (at least in the eyes of many) of analysing data without a a-priori hypotheses. The term *data mining* reappeared with the influx of the Internet and social media, generally with more positive connotations, because it is very often associated with big data. At the risk of repeating ourselves, where the term big data is used to describe a large volume of structured and unstructured data, data mining is the process of semi-automatically analysing large databases to find patterns in such data.

Operations research (OR) or *management science* (MS) is another sophisticated tool used to simplify and thus clarify certain types of complex problem that lend themselves to quantification. OR uses higher mathematics and statistics to identify, analyse and ultimately solve intricate problems of great complexity faced by the manager. It provides an additional tool to the manager by using quantification to supplement personal judgment. Areas of problem solving that easily lend themselves to OR include those relating to inventory, queuing, sequencing, routing and search and replacement. OR helps to minimize costs and increase efficiency by resorting to *decision trees*, *linear programming*, *network analysis* and *mathematical models*.

By using the wide variety of tools and techniques available for solving problems of differing magnitude, executives, managers and others entrusted with responsibility for results at various levels of the organization can find solutions to various concerns merely by securing access to available data and analysing them.

There is a wide variety of analytical software that may help you to analyse your data. Based on your specific needs, your research problem and/or your conceptual model, you might consider the following software packages:

> **SOME SOFTWARE PACKAGES USEFUL FOR DATA ANALYSIS**

- **LISREL**: from Scientific Software International;
- **MATLAB®**: from the MathWorks, Inc.;
- **Mplus**: developed by Linda and Bengt Muthén;
- **Qualtrics**: a private research software company;
- **SAS/STAT**: from SAS Institute;
- **SPSS**: from SPSS Inc.;
- **SPSS AMOS**: from SPSS Inc.;
- **Stata**: from Stata Corporation.

LISREL is designed to estimate and test structural equation models. Structural equation models are complex, statistical models of linear relationships among latent (unobserved) variables and manifest (observed) variables. You can also use LISREL to carry out exploratory factor analysis and confirmatory factor analysis.

MATLAB is a computer program that was originally designed to simplify the implementation of numerical linear algebra routines. It is used to implement numerical algorithms for a wide range of applications.

Mplus is a statistical modelling program that offers researchers a wide choice of models, estimators and algorithms. Mplus allows the analysis of a wide variety of data such as cross-sectional and longitudinal data, single-level and multilevel data and data that come from different populations with either observed or unobserved heterogeneity. In addition, Mplus has extensive capabilities for Monte Carlo simulation studies.

Qualtrics was founded in 2002. The program allows users to do many kinds of online data collection and data analysis, employee evaluations, website feedback, marketing research and customer satisfaction and loyalty research.

SAS is an integrated system of software products, capable of performing a broad range of statistical analyses such as descriptive statistics, multivariate techniques and time series analyses. Because of its capabilities, it is used in many disciplines, including medical sciences, biological sciences, social sciences and education.

SPSS (Statistical Package for the Social Sciences) is a data management and analysis program designed to do statistical data analysis, including descriptive statistics such as plots, frequencies, charts and lists, as well as sophisticated inferential and multivariate statistical procedures like analysis of variance (ANOVA), factor analysis, cluster analysis and categorical data analysis.

SPSS AMOS is designed to estimate and test structural equation models.

Stata is a general-purpose statistical software package that supports various statistical and econometric methods, graphics and enhanced features for data manipulation, programming and matrix manipulation.

SUMMARY	• **Learning objective 1: Discuss type I errors, type II errors and statistical power.** The null hypothesis is presumed true until statistical evidence, in the form of a hypothesis test, indicates otherwise. The required statistical evidence is provided by inferential statistics. There are two kinds of errors (two ways in which a conclusion can be incorrect), classified as type I and type II errors. A type I error, also referred to as alpha (α), is the probability of rejecting the null hypothesis when it is actually true. A type II error, also referred to as beta (β), is the probability of failing to reject the null hypothesis given that the alternate hypothesis is actually true. A third important concept in hypothesis testing is statistical power $(1 - \beta)$. Statistical power is the probability of correctly rejecting the null hypothesis. In other words, power is the probability that statistical significance will be indicated if it is present.
	• **Learning objective 2: Test hypotheses using the appropriate statistical technique.** After the researcher has selected an acceptable level of statistical significance to test the hypotheses, the next step is to decide on the appropriate method to test them. The choice of the appropriate statistical technique largely depends on the number of (independent and dependent) variables and the scale of measurement (metric or non-metric) of these variables. Other aspects that play a role are whether the assumptions of parametric tests are met and the size of the sample.
	• **Learning objective 3: Describe useful software packages for quantitative data analysis.** There is a wide variety of analytical software that may help researchers to analyse their data. Based on one's specific needs, the research problem and/or the conceptual model, one might consider software packages such as LISREL, MATLAB, Qualtrics or SPSS, to name a few.

> Instructors can visit the companion website at **www.wiley.com/go/bougie/researchmethods forbusiness8e** for **Case Study: Perceptions of Organizational Attractiveness**.

DISCUSSION QUESTIONS	1. What kinds of biases do you think could be minimized or avoided during the data analysis stage of research?
	2. When we collect data on the effects of treatment in experimental designs, which statistical test is most appropriate to test the treatment effects?
	3. A tax consultant wonders whether he should be more selective about the class of clients he serves so as to maximize his income. He usually deals with four categories of clients: the very rich, rich, upper middle class and middle class. He has records of each and every client served, the taxes paid by them and how much he has charged them. Since many particulars in respect of the clients vary (number of dependants, business deductibles, etc.), irrespective of the category they belong to, he would like an appropriate analysis to be done to see which among the four categories of clientele he should choose to continue to serve in the future. *What kind of analysis should be done in this case and why?*
	4. What is bootstrapping and why do you think that this method is becoming more and more popular as a method of testing for moderation and mediation?

Now do Exercises 16.9, 16.10, and 16.11.

Open the file 'resmethassignment1' (you created this file doing the exercise from the previous chapter). Answer the following questions.

EXERCISE 16.9

a. Is the exam grade significantly larger than 75?
b. Are there significant differences in the exam grade for men and women?
c. Is there a significant difference between the exam grade and the paper grade?
d. Are there significant differences in the paper grade for the four year groups?
e. Is the sample representative for the IQ level, for which it is known that 50 percent of the population has an IQ below 100, and 50 percent has an IQ of 100 or higher?
f. Obtain a correlation matrix for all relevant variables and discuss the results.
g. Do a multiple regression analysis to explain the variance in paper grades using the independent variables of age, sex (dummy coded) and IQ, and interpret the results.

Tables 16.A to 16.D summarize the results of data analyses of research conducted in a sales organization that operates in 50 different cities of the country and employs a total sales force of about 500. The number of salespersons sampled for the study was 150.

EXERCISE 16.10

a. Interpret the information contained in each of the tables in as much detail as possible.
b. Summarize the results for the CEO of the company.
c. Make recommendations based on your interpretation of the results.

Table 16.A   Means, Standard Deviations, Minimum and Maximum

Variable	Mean	Std. deviation	Minimum	Maximum
Sales (in 1000s of $)	75.1	8.6	45.2	97.3
No of salespersons	25	6	5	50
Population (in 100s)	5.1	0.8	2.78	7.12
Per capita income (in 1000s of $)	20.3	20.1	10.1	75.9
Advertising (in 1000s of $)	10.3	5.2	6.1	15.7

Table 16.B   Correlations Among the Variables

	Sales	Salespersons	Population	Income	Ad. expenditure
Sales	1.0				
No. of salespersons	0.76	1.0			
Population	0.62	0.06	1.0		
Income	0.56	0.21	0.11	1.0	
Ad. expenditure	0.68	0.16	0.36	0.23	1.0

All figures above 0.15 are significant at $p = 0.05$.
All figures above 0.35 are significant at $p \leq 0.001$.

Table 16.C Results of One-Way ANOVA: Sales by Level of Education

Source of variation	Sums of squares	df	Mean squares	F	Significance of F
Between groups	50.7	4	12.7	3.6	0.01
Within groups	501.8	145	3.5		
Total	552.5	150			

Table 16.D Results of Regression Analysis

Multiple R	0.65924		
R-square	0.43459		
Adjusted R-square	0.35225		
Standard error	0.41173		
df	(5.144)		
F	5.278		
Sig.	0.000		
Variable	Beta	t	Sig. t
Training of salespersons	0.28	2.768	0.0092
No. of salespersons	0.34	3.55	0.00001
Population	0.09	0.97	0.467
Per capita income	0.12	1.200	0.089
Advertisement	0.47	4.54	0.00001

EXERCISE 16.11 Visit David Kenny's website (http://davidakenny.net/cm/mediate.htm) and search for a link to SPSS and SAS macros that can be downloaded for tests of indirect effects.

Qualitative Data Analysis

LEARNING OBJECTIVES

After completing Chapter 17, you should be able to:

1. Discuss three important steps in qualitative data analysis: data reduction, data display and drawing conclusions.

2. Discuss how reliability and validity have a different meaning in qualitative research in comparison to quantitative research and explain how reliability and validity are achieved in qualitative research.

3. Compare and contrast content analysis, narrative analysis and analytic induction.

4. Describe the characteristics of big data and explain why big data holds many promises for organizations and managers.

INTRODUCTION

Qualitative data are data in the form of words. Examples of qualitative data are interview notes, transcripts of focus groups, answers to open-ended questions, transcriptions of video recordings, accounts of experiences with a product on the Internet, news articles and the like. Qualitative data can come from a wide variety of primary sources and/or secondary sources, such as individuals, focus groups, company records, government publications and the Internet. The analysis of qualitative data is aimed at making valid inferences from the often overwhelming amount of collected data.

THREE IMPORTANT STEPS IN QUALITATIVE DATA ANALYSIS

The analysis of qualitative data is not easy. The problem is that, in comparison with quantitative data analysis, there are relatively few well-established and commonly accepted rules and guidelines for analysing qualitative data. Over the years, however, some general approaches for the analysis of qualitative data have been developed. The approach discussed in this chapter is largely based on work of Miles and Huberman (1994). According to them, there are generally three steps in qualitative data analysis: data reduction, data display and the drawing of conclusions.

The first step in qualitative data analysis is concerned with data reduction. **Data reduction** refers to the process of selecting, coding and categorizing the data. **Data display** refers to ways of presenting the data. A selection of quotes, a matrix, a graph or a chart illustrating patterns in the data may help the researcher (and eventually the reader) to understand the data. In this way, data displays may help you to draw conclusions based on patterns in the reduced set of data.

Having identified these general stages, it should be noted that qualitative data analysis is not a step-by-step, linear process but rather a continuous and iterative process. For instance, **data coding**

BOX 17.1	**THE INTERNET AS A SOURCE OF TEXTUAL INFORMATION**

Earlier in this book, we explained that you can search the Internet for books, journals articles, conference proceedings, company publications and the like. However, the Internet is more than a mere source of documents; it is also a rich source of textual information for qualitative research. For instance, there are many *social networks* on the Internet structured around products and services such as computer games, mobile telephones, movies, books and music. Through an analysis of these social networks researchers may learn a lot about the needs of consumers, about the amount of time consumers spend in group communication or about the social network that underlies the virtual community. In this way, social networks on the Internet may provide researchers and marketing and business strategists with valuable, strategic information.

The possibilities for qualitative research on the Internet are unlimited, as the following example illustrates. In an effort to find out what motivates consumers to construct *protest websites*, Ward and Ostrom (2006) examined and analysed protest websites. A content analysis revealed that consumers construct complaint websites to demonstrate their power, to influence others and to gain revenge on the organization that betrayed them. This example illustrates how the Internet can be a valuable source of rich, authentic qualitative information. With increasing usage of the Internet, it will undoubtedly become even more important as a source of qualitative and quantitative information.

---

may help you simultaneously to develop ideas on how the data may be displayed, as well as to draw some preliminary conclusions. In turn, preliminary conclusions may feed back into the way the raw data are coded, categorized and displayed.

Example	Qualitative research may involve the repeated sampling, collection and analysis of data. As a result, qualitative data analysis may already start after some of the data have been collected.

This chapter will discuss the three important steps in qualitative data analysis – data reduction, data display and drawing and verifying conclusions – in some detail. To illustrate these steps in qualitative data analysis, we will introduce a case. We will use the case, by means of boxes throughout the chapter, to illustrate key parts of the qualitative research process.

DATA REDUCTION

Instructors can visit the companion website at **www.wiley.com/go/bougie/researchmethods forbusiness8e** for **Author Video: Data reduction.**

Qualitative data collection produces large amounts of data. The first step in data analysis is therefore the reduction of data through coding and categorization. **Coding** is the analytic process through which the qualitative data that you have gathered are reduced, rearranged and integrated to form theory. The purpose of coding is to help you to draw meaningful conclusions about the data. *Codes* are labels given to units of text which are later grouped and turned into categories. Coding is often an iterative process; you may have to return to your data repeatedly to increase your understanding of the data (i.e. to be able to recognize patterns in the data, to discover connections between the data and to organize the data into coherent categories).

CASE	Instigations of Customer Anger

Introduction

Suppose that you are in a fashion shop and that you have just found a clothing item that you like. You go to the counter to pay for the item. At the counter you find a shop assistant who is talking to a friend on her mobile phone. You have to wait. You wait for a couple of minutes, but the shop assistant is in no hurry to finish the call.

This event may make you angry. Waiting for service is a common cause of anger: the longer the delay, the angrier customers tend to be (Taylor, 1994).

Research Objective

Prior research in marketing has applied appraisal theory to understand why anger is experienced in such situations (e.g. Folkes, Koletsky & Graham, 1987; Nyer, 1997; Taylor, 1994). Appraisal refers to the process of judging the significance of an event for personal well-being. The basic premise of appraisal theory is that emotions are related to the interpretations that people have about events: people may differ in the specific appraisals that are elicited by a particular event (for instance, waiting for service), but the same patterns of appraisal give rise to the same emotions. Most appraisal theories see appraisals as being a cause of emotions (Parrott, 2001). Along these lines, appraisal theory has been used to understand why anger is experienced in service settings.

Although appraisal theory provides useful insights into the role of cognition in emotional service encounters, recent research suggests that, although they are clearly associated with anger, none of the aforementioned appraisals is a necessary or sufficient condition for anger to arise (Kuppens, VanMechelen, Smits & DeBoeck, 2003; Smith & Ellsworth, 1987). What's more, for the specific purpose of avoiding customer anger, appraisal theory is too abstract to be diagnostic for services management. That is, service firm management may benefit more from a classification of incidents that are considered to be unfair (for instance, waiting for service and core service failures), than from the finding that unfair events are generally associated with customer anger.

In other words, to be able to avoid customer anger, it is crucial that service firm management knows what specific precipitating events typically elicit this emotion in customers. After all, it is easier to manage such events than the appraisals that may or may not be associated with these particular events.

Therefore, this study investigates events that typically instigate customer anger in services. This study builds on a rich tradition of research in psychology that has specified typical instigations of anger in everyday life. In addition, it builds on research

in marketing that has identified and classified service failures, retail failures and behaviours of service firms that cause customers to switch services (Bitner, Booms & Tetreault, 1990; Keaveney, 1995; Kelley, Hoffman & Davis, 1993).

Method

Procedure. Following related research in marketing, the critical incident technique (CIT) was used to identify critical behaviours of service providers that instigate customer anger (e.g. Bitner, Booms & Tetreault, 1990; Keaveney, 1995; Kelley, Hoffman & Davis, 1993; Mangold, Miller & Brockway, 1999). Critical incidents were collected by 30 trained research assistants, who were instructed to collect 30 critical incidents each. In order to obtain a sample representative of customers of service organizations, they were instructed to collect data from a wide variety of people. Participants were asked to record their critical incidents on a standardized form in the presence of the interviewer. This has several advantages, such as availability of the interviewer to answer questions and to provide explanations.

Questionnaire. Participants were asked to record their answers on a standardized questionnaire, which was modelled after previous applications of CIT in services (e.g. Keaveney, 1995; Kelley, Hoffman & Davis, 1993). The questionnaire began by asking participants to indicate which of 30 different services they had purchased during the previous six-month period. Next, participants were asked to recall the last negative incident with a service provider that made them feel angry. They were asked to describe the incident in detail by means of open-ended questions. The open-ended questions were 'What service are you thinking about?', 'Please tell us, in your own words, what happened. Why did you get angry?', and 'Try to tell us exactly what happened: where you were, what happened, what the service provider did, how you felt, what you said, and so forth'.

Sample. Critical incidents were defined as events, combinations of events or series of events between a customer and a service provider that caused customer anger. The interviewers collected 859 incidents. The participants (452 males, 407 females) represented a cross section of the population. Their ages ranged between 16 and 87 with a mean age of 37.4. Approximately 2 percent of the participants had less than a completed high school education, whereas 45.1 percent had at least a bachelor's degree. The reported incidents covered more than 40 different service businesses, including banking and insurance, personal transportation (by airplane, bus, ferry, taxi or train), hospitals, physicians, and dentists, repair and utility services, (local) government and the police, (virtual) stores, education and child care, entertainment, hospitality, restaurants, telecommunication companies, health clubs, contracting firms, hairdressers, real-estate agents, driving schools, rental companies and travel agencies. On average, the negative events that participants reported had happened 18 weeks earlier.

Coding begins with selecting the coding unit. Indeed, qualitative data can be analysed at many levels. Examples of coding units include words, sentences, paragraphs and themes. The smallest unit that is generally used is the word. A larger, and often more useful, unit of content analysis is the theme: 'a single assertion about a subject' (Kassarjian, 1977, p. 12). When you are using the theme as a coding unit, you are primarily looking for the expression of an idea (Minichiello, Aroni, Timewell & Alexander, 1990). Thus, you might assign a code to a text unit of any size, as long as that unit of text represents a single theme or issue. Consider, for instance, the following critical incident:

> After the meal I asked for the check. The waitress nodded and I expected to get the check. After three cigarettes there was still no check. I looked around and saw that the waitress was having a lively conversation with the bartender.

This critical incident contains two themes:

1. The waitress does not provide service at the time she promises to: 'The waitress nodded and I expected to get the check. After three cigarettes there was still no check'.

2. The waitress pays little attention to the customer: she is not late because she is very busy; instead of bringing the check, she is engaged in a lively conversation with the bartender.

Accordingly, the aforementioned critical incident was coded as: 'delivery promises' (that were broken) and 'personal attention' (that was not provided).

This example illustrates how the codes 'delivery promises' and 'personal attention' help to reduce the data to a more manageable amount. Note that proper coding not only involves reducing the data but also making sure that no relevant data are eliminated. Hence, it is important that the codes 'delivery promises' and 'personal attention' capture the meaning of the coded unit of text.

BOX 17.2   **DATA ANALYSIS**

Unit of analysis Since the term 'critical incident' can refer to either the overall story of a participant or to discrete behaviours contained within this story, the first step in data analysis is to determine the appropriate unit of analysis (Kassarjian, 1977). In this study, *critical behaviour* was chosen as the unit of analysis.

For this reason, 600 critical incidents were coded into 886 critical behaviours. For instance, a critical incident in which a service provider does not provide prompt service and treats a customer in a rude manner was coded as containing two critical behaviours ('unresponsiveness' and 'insulting behaviour').

Categorization is the process of organizing, arranging and classifying coding units. Codes and categories can be developed both inductively and deductively. In situations where there is no theory available, you must generate codes and categories inductively from the data. In its extreme form, this is what has been called **grounded theory** (see Chapter 7).

In many situations, however, you will have a preliminary theory on which you can base your codes and categories. In these situations you can construct an initial list of codes and categories from the theory, and, if necessary, change or refine these during the research process as new codes and categories emerge inductively (Miles & Huberman, 1994). The benefit of the adoption of existing codes and categories is that you are able to build on and/or expand prevailing knowledge.

BOX 17.3   DATA ANALYSIS

Categorization Qualitative data analysis was used to examine the data (Kassarjian, 1977). As a first step, two judges coded critical incidents into critical behaviours. Next, (sub)categories were developed based on these critical behaviours. Two judges (A and B) independently developed mutually exclusive and exhaustive categories and subcategories for responses 1 to 400 (587 critical behaviours). Two other trained judges (C and D) independently sorted the critical behaviours into the categories provided by judges A and B. Finally, a fifth, independent judge (E) carried out a final sort.

As you begin to organize your data into categories and subcategories you will begin to notice patterns and relationships between the data. Note that your list of categories and subcategories may change during the process of analysing the data. For instance, new categories may have to be identified, definitions of categories may have to be changed and categories may have to be broken into subcategories. This is all part of the iterative process of qualitative data analysis.

BOX 17.4   RESULTS

Categories Participants reported a wide range of critical behaviours that made them angry. Some of these behaviours were closely related to the *outcome* of the service process (e.g. 'My suitcase was heavily damaged'). Other behaviours were related to *service delivery* (e.g. 'For three days in a row I tried to make an appointment [. . .] via the telephone. The line was always busy') or *interpersonal relationships* (e.g. 'She did not stir a finger. She was definitely not intending to help me'). Finally, customers got angry because of *inadequate responses to service failures* (e.g. 'He did not even apologize' or 'He refused to give me back my money'). These four specific behaviour types represent the four overarching categories of events that instigate customer anger.

Two of these categories were further separated into, respectively, three categories representing service delivery or procedural failures ('unreliability', 'inaccessibility' and 'company policies') and two categories representing interpersonal relationships or interactional failures ('insensitive behaviour' and 'impolite behaviour'). The main reason for this was that the categories 'procedural failures' and 'interactional failures' would otherwise be too heterogeneous with respect to their composition and, more importantly, with respect to ways of avoiding or dealing with these failures. For instance, avoiding anger in response to unreliability (not performing in accordance with agreements) will most likely call for a different – and maybe even opposite – approach than avoiding anger in response to company policies (performing in accordance with company rules and procedures), even though these failures are both procedural; that is, related to service delivery.

Sometimes you may want to capture the number of times a particular theme or event occurs, or how many respondents bring up certain themes or events. Quantification of your qualitative data may provide you with a rough idea about the (relative) importance of the categories and subcategories.

BOX 17.5

Table 17.1 indicates that 'price agreements that were broken' (category 'unreliability', subcategory 'pricing') was mentioned 12 times as a cause of anger. Hence, broken price agreements represent 1.35 percent of the total number of critical behaviours (886) and 2 percent of the total number of the reported critical incidents (600). The sixth column indicates that nine participants mentioned broken price agreements as the sole cause of their anger, whereas three participants mentioned at least one additional critical behaviour (column 7).

Table 17.1 Instigations of Anger in Service Consumption Settings

(Sub)category	(Sub)category definition	No. of behaviours	No. of behaviours in % of behaviours	No. of behaviours in % of incidents	No. of behaviours in single-factor incidents	No. of behaviours in multi-factor incidents	Example(s)
Procedural failures							
Unreliability	*Service firm does not perform the service dependably.*	*156*	*17.61*	*26.00*	*73*	*83*	
Delivery promises	Service provider does not provide services at the time it promises to do so.	104	11.74	17.33	42	62	Wait for appointment with dentist, physician or hairdresser, or on a plane, train or taxi.
Service provision	Service provider does not provide the service that was agreed upon.	40	4.52	6.67	22	18	Client receives different car than agreed upon with car rental company or different apartment than agreed upon with travel agent. Bicycle repairers, car mechanics or building contractors carry out different work than agreed upon or work that was not agreed upon with their clients.
Pricing	Price agreements are broken.	12	1.35	2.00	9	3	'After a party we called a cab. We were with a party of five. A van would take us home for a fixed, low price. However, upon arrival, the driver asked the regular clock price'.
Inaccessibility	*Customers experience difficulties with engaging in the service process.*	*47*	*5.30*	*7.83*	*17*	*30*	
Communicative inaccessibility	Inaccessibility via telephone, fax, email and/or the Internet.	26	2.93	4.33	9	17	'For three days in a row I tried to make an appointment with my physician via the telephone. The line was always busy'.
Physical inaccessibility of service elements	Customers experience difficulties with accessing a certain element or part of the service.	12	1.35	2.00	4	8	Check-in counter of an airline company, cash-point of a supermarket, service desk of a holiday resort or baggage claim at an airport.

Physical inaccessibility of service provider	Difficult physical accessibility of service provider because of inconvenient locations or opening hours.	9	1.02	1.50	4	5	'It was three o'clock on a Saturday afternoon and the dry cleaner was already closed'.
Company policies	*Service provider's rules and procedures or the execution of rules and procedures by service staff is perceived to be unfair.*	76	8.57	12.67	45	31	
Rules and procedures	Inefficient, ill-timed and unclear rules and procedures.	66	7.45	11.00	38	28	'It turned out that the [Cystic Fibrosis] foundation used unfair procedures for assigning families with cystic fibrosis to vacations. For example, some families were invited for years in a row even though this is not allowed'. 'Only two days before our wedding my wife was ordered to leave the country by the immigration office'. 'I went to the local administration to report a change of address. At the same time I wanted to apply for a parking license. In that case you must draw a number for the change of address first and later on you must draw a second number for the parking license. I got angry and asked why on earth that was necessary'.
Inflexible service staff	Service staff does not adapt rules and procedures to reflect individual circumstances of customer.	10	1.12	1.67	7	3	'It was an exceptionally hot day. The second-class compartments of the train were overcrowded. To avoid the bad atmosphere I went to a first-class compartment. When the guard came he sent us away. At that moment I flew into a rage'.
Interactional failures							
Impolite behaviour	*Service provider behaves rudely.*	84	9.48	14.00	46	38	

(continued)

Table 17.1 Continued

(Sub)category	(Sub)category definition	No. of behaviours	No. of behaviours in % of behaviours	No. of behaviours in % of incidents	No. of behaviours in single-factor incidents	No. of behaviours in multi-factor incidents	Example(s)
Insulting behaviour	Service provider is behaving offensively.	32	3.61	5.33	15	17	'The physician was getting fluid out of my knee. This was rather painful, so I told him that it hurt. He directly stopped even though there was some fluid left. When I asked him why he had stopped he said "because you are such a moaner". That's no way to treat people'.
Not taking client seriously	Service provider does not take client seriously.	28	3.16	4.67	15	13	'For some time I was hearing strange noises when I was driving my car. Again and again they [garage] fobbed me off with "Yes, dear . . ." and "Yes, love . . ." Eventually they had to replace the engine'.
Dishonesty	Service provider tries to earn money in an improper manner.	16	1.81	2.67	10	6	'After we went to the theater, we took a cab. The driver made a huge detour. I was mad because this was a plain rip-off'.
Discrimination	Person or group is treated unfairly, usually because of prejudice about race, ethnic group, age group or gender.	8	0.90	1.33	6	2	'I was refused access to the bar because of my race, even though I was immaculately dressed. They literally told me that they did not care for my kind of people'.
Insensitive behaviour	Service provider does not make an effort to appreciate the customer's needs and/or pays little attention to customers or their belongings.	195	22.01	32.50	76	119	

Category	Description					Example
Unresponsiveness	Unresponsive staff does not provide prompt service to customers or does not respond to customers' requests at all.	80	9.03	13.33	33	47	'I went to a cash desk [of a drugstore] but the salesperson walked away. At another cash desk two persons were helping one client. One of them looked at me but did not show any intention to help me. It took forever before I was finally served'. 'I asked a girl to help me find the right size [clothes] for my grandson. She did not stir a finger. She was definitely not intending to help me'.
Incomplete/incorrect information	Service provider withholds information from client or provides incomplete, imprecise or incorrect information.	61	6.88	10.17	21	40	'Our plane was not there. I got mad because they did not tell us why or what to do'.
Inaccuracy with personal data	Service provider handles personal information of client rather carelessly.	16	1.81	2.67	5	11	'I was looking for a summer job and signed up at an employment agency. When I asked them about the state of affairs a couple of weeks later, I found out that I had not been signed up yet. They told me that they had lost my application form'.
Personal attention	Service provider pays little attention to the customer.	15	1.69	2.50	8	7	'After the meal I asked for the check. The waitress nodded and I expected to get the check. After three cigarettes there was still no check. I looked around and saw that the waitress was having a lively conversation with the bartender'.
Impersonal treatment	Service provider does not provide tailor-made solutions.	9	1.02	1.50	3	6	'I got angry because she [hairdresser] did not cut my hair the way I had asked her to . . .' 'The mortgage counselor was very dominant during the conversation. My own point of view was not sufficiently addressed'.

(continued)

Table 17.1 Continued

(Sub)category	(Sub)category definition	No. of behaviours	No. of behaviours in % of behaviours	No. of behaviours in % of incidents	No. of behaviours in single-factor incidents	No. of behaviours in multi-factor incidents	Example(s)
Inconvenience	Customer ends up in inconvenient or uncomfortable situation, often leading to physical distress.	8	0.90	1.33	2	6	'After landing [airplane], we had to stay in our seats for 1.5 hours. It was very uncomfortable'.
Privacy matters	Service provider invades or disregards a person's privacy.	3	0.34	0.50	2	1	'The welfare worker left the door open during our private conversation'.
Irresponsible behaviour	Service staff behaves irresponsibly.	3	0.34	0.50	2	1	'The schoolteacher let my very young children walk to their homes on their own when I was a little late to pick them up'.
Outcome failures	*Quality of core service itself.*	*191*	*21.56*	*31.84*	*76*	*115*	
Service mistakes	Small or big mistakes, which may cause damage to the customer or belongings of the customer.	115	12.98	18.50	47	68	'The waitress brought the wrong meal'. 'The physician prescribed the wrong medicine'. 'As a consequence of the operation I will not be able to ever walk again'. 'My suitcase was heavily damaged'.
Defective tangibles	Inoperative, broken, badly prepared or unsatisfactory tangibles.	35	3.95	5.83	6	29	'My cash card was not working'. 'After three weeks the coffee machine [bought in shop] broke down'. 'The food was cold'. 'We booked a very expensive holiday. However, the hotel was an old, dirty, run-down slum, with holes in the carpeting. The swimming pool was unpainted and 95 centimeters deep. The dining room looked like a stable'.

Category	Description						Examples
Billing errors	Customers are mis-charged for services.	25	2.82	4.17	10	15	
High prices	Service provider's prices are considered to be too high relative to an internal reference price or relative to prices of competitors.	16	1.81	2.67	13	3	'I ordered two drinks at the bar. I had to pay €12. That is really an absurd price!' 'The price of the DVD-player was €1250. At another store it was only €900'.
Inadequate responses to service failures		*137*	*15.46*	*22.83*	*10*	*127*	
Interactional unfairness	Service employees' interpersonal behaviour during the service recovery.	80	9.03	13.33	4	76	'He [waiter] did not even apologize'.
Outcome unfairness	The outcome of the service recovery.	37	4.17	6.17	5	32	'I did not receive the newspaper. I called them on the phone and they promised that I would receive the newspaper that same day. Nothing happened'. 'He [hairdresser] refused to give me back my money'.
Procedural unfairness	The perceived fairness of the service recovery process.	20	2.26	3.33	1	19	'Recently I bought a house. After moving in I noticed that the bathroom tap was defective. The contractor admitted that it was the firm's responsibility. However, it took forever before they took action. Only after the chief executive of the company intervened did they cover the expenses'.

DATA DISPLAY

According to Miles and Huberman (1994), data display is the second major activity that you should go through when analysing your qualitative data. **Data display** involves taking your reduced data and displaying them in an organized, condensed manner. Along these lines, charts, matrices, diagrams, graphs, frequently mentioned phrases and/or drawings may help you to organize the data and to discover patterns and relationships in the data so that the drawing of conclusions is eventually facilitated.

In our example, a matrix was considered to be the appropriate display to bring together the qualitative data. The selected data display technique may depend on researcher preference, the type of data set and the purpose of the display. A matrix is, by and large, descriptive in nature, as the aforementioned example illustrates. Other displays, such as networks or diagrams, allow you to present causal relationships between concepts in your data.

BOX 17.6 DATA ANALYSIS

In our study into events that typically elicit customer anger in service consumption settings, we developed a matrix to organize and arrange the qualitative data. This allowed us to extract higher order themes from the data: we were able to combine the 28 subcategories into seven categories and four 'super-categories.' The seven categories were 'unreliability', 'inaccessibility,' and 'company policies' (procedural failures); 'insensitive behaviour' and 'impolite behaviour' (interactional failures); 'outcome failures'; and 'inadequate responses to service failures.' These categories and subcategories are defined in the second column of Table 17.1. The eighth column provides typical examples of critical behaviour per subcategory.

Table 17.1 illustrates how data display organizes qualitative information in a way that helps you to draw conclusions. Categories and corresponding subcategories of events that typically instigate anger are presented in column 1 and defined in column 2. Column 3 provides information on how many times specific themes were mentioned by the participants. Column 4 provides information about how many times a specific theme was mentioned as a percentage of the total number of themes (885). Column 5 contains the percentage of participants that mentioned a specific category or subcategory. Columns 6 and 7 provide an overview of the distribution of incidents over one- or multifactor incidents. Column 8 provides (verbatim) examples of critical behaviours, attitudes and manners of service providers.

DRAWING CONCLUSIONS

Conclusion drawing is the 'final' analytical activity in the process of qualitative data analysis. It is the essence of data analysis; it is at this point where you answer your research questions by determining what identified themes stand for, by thinking about explanations for observed patterns and relationships, or by making contrasts and comparisons.

BOX 17.7 DISCUSSION

The identification of precipitating events of anger is critical to understanding this emotion. What's more, for service firm management, it is important to understand what critical behaviours from their side typically elicit anger in customers. For this reason, this exploratory study investigated precipitating events of customer anger in services.

The results of this study provide an adequate, unambiguous representation of precipitating events of customer anger and expand existing (appraisal) theories of antecedents of customer anger. Specifically, seven event categories were found to instigate anger, including unreliability, inaccessibility and company policies (the procedural failures), insensitive behaviour and impolite behaviour (the interactional failures), outcome failures and inadequate responses to service failures. Each of these events was found to be a sufficient cause of customer anger. However, the compound incidents that were reported by the participants in this study suggest that critical behaviours of service providers may also interact in their effects on customer anger.

The foregoing findings imply certain extensions to service marketing research. Researchers have previously examined the effects of core service failures and waiting for service on anger. However, this study shows that the antecedents of anger are not limited to these two factors. For service firm management, the seven categories suggest areas in which managers might take action to prevent customer anger. For example, the finding that inaccessibility of services causes customers to get angry suggests that service providers may benefit from being easily accessible for consumers. The finding that customer anger may be caused by insensitivity and impoliteness of service staff implies that hiring the right people, adequate training of service employees and finding ways to motivate service staff to adequately perform services also reduces customer anger.

The present results partly converge with prior studies that have categorized dissatisfying experiences with service firm employees (Bitner, Booms & Tetreault, 1990) and retail failures (Kelley, Hoffman & Davis, 1993). Besides these similarities, there are important differences with the aforementioned studies as well. For instance, incidents reported by the participants of this study include difficulties with engaging in the service process and unfair rules and procedures (company policies). These behaviours, which account for more than 20 percent of the reported anger-provoking incidents, did not come forward as unfavourable behaviours of service providers in earlier research. This shows how the classification scheme developed here builds on and extends earlier models of service and retail failures.

RELIABILITY AND VALIDITY IN QUALITATIVE RESEARCH

It is important that the conclusions that you have drawn are verified in one way or another. That is, you must make sure that the conclusions that you derive from your qualitative data are plausible, reliable and valid.

Reliability and validity have a slightly different meaning in qualitative research in comparison to quantitative research. Reliability in qualitative data analysis includes category and interjudge reliability. **Category reliability** 'depends on the analyst's ability to formulate categories and present to competent judges definitions of the categories so they will agree on which items of a certain population belong in a category and which do not' (Kassarjian, 1977, p. 14). Thus, category reliability relates to the extent to which judges are able to use category definitions to classify the qualitative data. Well-defined categories will lead to higher category reliability and eventually to higher interjudge reliability (Kassarjian, 1977), as discussed next. However, categories that are defined in a very broad manner will also lead to higher category reliability. This can lead to the oversimplification of categories, which reduces the relevance of the research findings. For instance, McKellar (1949) in an attempt to classify instigations of anger distinguished between *need situations* and *personality instigations*. Need situations were defined as 'any interference with the pursuit of a personal goal', such as missing a bus. Personality situations included the imposition of physical or mental pain or the violation of personal values, status and possession. This classification, which focuses on whether an anger-provoking event can be classified as a personality situation or a need situation, will undoubtedly lead to high category and interjudge reliability, but it seems to be too broad to be relevant to service firm management trying to avoid customer anger. Therefore, Kassarjian (1977) suggests that the researcher must find a balance between category reliability and the relevance of categories. **Interjudge reliability** can be defined as a degree of consistency between coders processing the same data (Kassarjian, 1977). A commonly used measure of interjudge reliability is the percentage of coding agreements out of the total number of coding decisions. As a general guideline, agreement rates at or above 80 percent are considered to be satisfactory.

Earlier in this book, **validity** was defined as the extent to which an instrument measures what it purports to measure. In this context, however, validity has a different meaning. It refers to the extent to which the research results (1) accurately represent the collected data (internal validity) and (2) can be generalized or transferred to other contexts or settings (external validity). Two methods that have been developed to achieve validity in qualitative research are:

- Supporting generalizations by counts of events. This can address common concerns about the reporting of qualitative data: that anecdotes supporting the researcher's theory have been selected, or that too much attention has been paid to a small number of events, at the expense of more common ones.

- Ensuring representativeness of cases and the inclusion of deviant cases (cases that may contradict your theory). The selection of deviant cases provides a strong test of your theory.

Triangulation, discussed in Chapter 7, is a technique that is also often associated with reliability and validity in qualitative research. Finally, you can also enhance the validity of your research by providing an in-depth description of the research project. Anyone who wishes to transfer the results to another context is then responsible for judging how valid such a transfer is.

BOX 17.8   RELIABILITY AND VALIDITY

A rigorous classification system should be 'intersubjectively unambiguous' (Hunt, 1983), as measured by interjudge reliability. The interjudge reliability averaged 0.84, and no individual coefficients were lower than 0.80. The content validity of a critical incident classification scheme is regarded as satisfactory if themes in the confirmation sample are fully represented by the categories and subcategories developed in the classification sample. In order to determine whether the sample size was appropriate, two confirmation samples (hold-out samples from the original 859 samples) of 100 new incidents (299 critical behaviours) were sorted into the classification scheme with an eye to developing new categories. No new categories emerged, indicating that the set of analysed critical incidents forms an adequate representation of the precipitating events of anger in services.

SOME OTHER METHODS OF GATHERING AND ANALYSING QUALITATIVE DATA

CONTENT ANALYSIS

Content analysis is an observational research method that is used to systematically evaluate the symbolic contents of all forms of recorded communications (Kolbe & Burnett, 1991). Content analysis can be used to analyse newspapers, websites, advertisements, recordings of interviews and the like. The method of content analysis enables the researcher to analyse (large amounts of) textual information and systematically identify its properties, such as the presence of certain words, concepts, characters, themes or sentences. To conduct a content analysis on a text, the text is coded into categories and then analysed using conceptual analysis or relational analysis.

Conceptual analysis establishes the existence and frequency of concepts (such as words, themes or characters) in a text. Conceptual analysis analyses and interprets text by coding the text into manageable content categories. **Relational analysis** builds on conceptual analysis by examining the relationships among concepts in a text.

The results of conceptual or relational analysis are used to make inferences about the messages within the text, the effects of environmental variables on message content, the effects of messages on the receiver and so on. Along these lines, content analysis has been used to analyse press coverage of election campaigns, to assess the effects of the content of advertisements on consumer behaviour and to provide a systematic overview of tools that online media use to encourage interactive communication processes.

NARRATIVE ANALYSIS

A narrative is a story or 'an account involving the narration of a series of events in a plotted sequence which unfolds in time' (Denzin, 2000). **Narrative analysis** is an approach that aims to elicit and scrutinize the stories we tell about ourselves and their implications for our lives. Narrative data are often collected via interviews. These interviews are designed to encourage the participant to describe a certain incident in the context of his or her life history. In this way, narrative analysis differs from other qualitative research methods; it is focused on a process or temporal order, for instance, by eliciting information about the antecedents and consequences of a certain incident in order to relate this incident to other incidents. Narrative analysis has thus been used to study impulsive buying (Rook, 1987), customers' responses to advertisements (Mick & Buhl, 1992), and relationships between service providers and consumers (Stern, Thomson & Arnould, 1998).

ANALYTIC INDUCTION

Another (more general) strategy of qualitative data analysis is analytic induction. Analytic induction is an approach to qualitative data analysis in which universal explanations of phenomena are sought by the collection of (qualitative) data until no cases that are inconsistent with a hypothetical explanation of a phenomenon are found. Analytic induction starts with a (rough) definition of a problem ('why do people use marijuana' is a famous example), continues with a hypothetical explanation of the problem (e.g. 'people use marijuana for pleasure'), and then proceeds with the examination of cases (e.g. the collection of data via in-depth interviews). If a case is inconsistent with the researcher's hypothesis (e.g. 'I use marijuana for health reasons'), the researcher either redefines the hypothesis or excludes the 'deviant' case that does not confirm the hypothesis. Analytic induction involves inductive – rather than deductive – reasoning, allowing for the modification of a hypothetical explanation for phenomena throughout the process of doing research.

Now that we have discussed data analysis, it is time to say a few words about *big data*. 'Big data' is a popular term nowadays that is commonly used to describe the exponential growth and availability of data from digital sources inside and outside the organization. The term originally related to the volume of data that could not be processed and analysed (efficiently) by traditional methods and tools. The original definition of big data focused on structured data, but most researchers and practitioners have come to realize that a lot of information resides in massive, unstructured or semi-structured data, such as texts (think weblogs, Twitter and Facebook), images, clickstreams and/or videos. New technologies have the ability to measure, record and combine such data and that is why big data has great potential for making fast advances in many academic disciplines and improving decision making in organizations.

| BIG DATA |

The main characteristics of big data are its *volume*, its *variety* and its *velocity*, where volume refers to the amount of data, variety refers to the many different types of data and velocity refers to the pace at which data become available from business processes, social networks, mobile devices and the like. Occasionally, additional 'V's are put forward, most notably *veracity*, which refers to the biases, noise and abnormality that are often present in big data.

Big data holds many promises for organizations and managers. However, it also provides them with new challenges and dilemmas, for instance, with regard to how big data should be managed, processed and analysed. That is why many organizations find it difficult to successfully exploit the value in big data.

- **Learning objective 1: Discuss three important steps in qualitative data analysis: data reduction, data display and drawing conclusions.** Qualitative data are data in the form of words. There are generally three steps in qualitative data analysis: data reduction, data display and the drawing of conclusions. Data reduction refers to the process of selecting, coding and categorizing the data. Data display refers to ways of presenting the data. Data displays may help the researcher to draw conclusions based on patterns in the reduced set of data.

| SUMMARY |

- **Learning objective 2: Discuss how reliability and validity have a different meaning in qualitative research in comparison to quantitative research and explain how reliability and validity are achieved in qualitative research.** Reliability and validity have a slightly different meaning in qualitative research in comparison to quantitative research. Reliability in qualitative data analysis includes category and interjudge reliability. Category reliability relates to the extent to which judges are able to use category definitions to classify the qualitative data. Interjudge reliability can be defined as a degree of consistency between coders processing the same data. Two methods that have been developed to achieve validity in qualitative research are (1) supporting generalizations by counts of events, and (2) ensuring representativeness of cases and the inclusion of deviant cases. Triangulation is a technique that is also often associated with reliability and validity in qualitative research.

- **Learning objective 3: Compare and contrast content analysis, narrative analysis and analytic induction.** Content analysis is an observational research method that enables the researcher to analyse textual information and systematically identify its properties, such as the presence of certain words, concepts, characters, themes or sentences. Narrative analysis is an approach that aims to elicit and scrutinize the stories we tell about ourselves and their implications for our lives. Narrative data are often collected via interviews. Analytic induction is an approach to qualitative data analysis in which universal explanations of phenomena are sought by the collection of (qualitative) data until no cases that are inconsistent with a hypothetical explanation of a phenomenon are found.

- **Learning objective 4: Describe the characteristics of big data and explain why big data holds many promises for organizations and managers.** New technologies have the ability to measure, record and combine large amounts of data that reside in massive, unstructured or semi-structured data, such as texts, images, clickstreams and/or videos. That is why big data has great potential for making fast advances in many academic disciplines and improving decision making in organizations. The main characteristics of big data are its volume, its variety and its velocity. Occasionally, additional 'V's are put forward, most notably veracity.

> Instructors can visit the companion website at **www.wiley.com/go/bougie/researchmethods forbusiness8e** for **Case study: The Prevalence of Anger in Service Consumption Settings**.

DISCUSSION QUESTIONS	

1. What is qualitative data? How do qualitative data differ from quantitative data?

2. Describe the main steps in qualitative data analysis.

3. Define reliability and validity in the context of qualitative research.

4. How can you assess the reliability and validity of qualitative research?

5. What is grounded theory?

6. How does narrative analysis differ from content analysis?

7. Why is analytic induction inductive (rather than deductive) in nature?

Conclusions

LEARNING OBJECTIVES

After completing Chapter 18, you should be able to:

1. Describe the characteristics of conclusions.

2. Explain an argument.

3. Compare and contrast deductive and ampliative arguments.

4. Discuss the difference between valid and invalid arguments and good and bad arguments.

5. Discuss incorrect or flawed forms of reasoning known as fallacies.

6. Draw conclusions based on research results.

INTRODUCTION

Business research always starts with a specific aim. Applied research can be done when a manager proactively aims to assess how the organization (business unit, department) is performing on a certain aspect (for instance, employee satisfaction, corporate image, the IT infrastructure), how competitors are positioning their products in a certain market segment or, for instance, how attractive a certain industry is in the long run. More often, research is done when a manager is unhappy with the existing situation (e.g. market share is low, customers are not satisfied or employee turnover is high) and wants to achieve a specific desired situation (a higher market share, more satisfied customers, less employee turnover) but he does not know how, hence research is needed. Based on the data that you have collected as a researcher and the analysis of these data, you will ultimately be able to develop an informed judgement regarding (a solution to) the manager's problem. In other words, you will be able to draw conclusions. For instance, your conclusions might relate to how satisfied or dissatisfied employees are with the organization, how attractive a certain industry is in the long run, how competitors are positioning their products in a certain market segment or how the client organization is able to improve its market share (customer satisfaction, employee turnover and the like). After you have drawn your conclusions and developed recommendations based on these conclusions, you have achieved your objective as a researcher. Thus, you have contributed to solving the problem of the client organization.

Your conclusions are built on the data you have collected. To draw good conclusions, you need good (accurate, reliable and valid) data. That is why – earlier in this book – we paid attention to issues such as research design, the reliability and validity of measuring instruments, representative samples and, for example, the use of multiple judges when analysing qualitative data. However, apart from good data, you need good arguments to draw good conclusions. An argument is a set of statements that includes a conclusion and evidence that supports the conclusion. In order to convince others of your conclusions, it is important that your arguments are good and that you argue in the right way. For this reason, we discuss different types of arguments later on in this chapter. First, however, we turn to conclusions.

CONCLUSIONS AND RECOMMENDATIONS: WHERE YOUR JOURNEY AS A RESEARCHER ENDS	Drawing conclusions and providing recommendations to the client organization is the last stage of the research process. In a certain sense, the conclusions you draw are the climax of your research project. In your conclusions chapter, you explain what your results mean for the client organization and how your findings can be applied to inform evidence-based decision-making and practice. This is how your conclusions bring back the attention to the organizational problem that catalysed the research project. With the development of conclusions and recommendations, you have made your contribution as a researcher to solving the organizational problem. This is where your journey as a researcher ends; with the conclusions and recommendations, you give the project back to the manager. So many people, including the manager, are particularly interested in your conclusions and recommendations chapter. Remember this when you are in the process of writing your research report. This chapter is what your research has been all about. Your research proposal, your critical review of the literature, your research design and the collection and analysis of the data all served a bigger purpose: being able to draw strong conclusions and providing useful recommendations.

WRITING DOWN YOUR CONCLUSIONS

For many researchers, writing down their conclusions is not easy. A good place to start thinking about what should be in your conclusions chapter is the problem of the client organization. As explained earlier in this chapter, applied research can be done when a manager wants to know how the organization is performing on a certain aspect or, for instance, how attractive its industry is in the long run. Another reason to do research is that a manager wants to change something in the organization but does not know how. Based on the data you collected as a researcher and the analysis of these data, you can develop an informed judgement regarding the problem of the organization. For instance, if the objective of your research was to identify the factors that influence employee motivation (because the client organization wants to increase employee motivation), the conclusions you present should be focused on these factors. That is why, in your conclusions chapter, you should make *claims* regarding how the client organization can (best) improve the motivation of its employees. Obviously, to convince the client organization of your viewpoint, you should also substantiate your viewpoint. In other words, you need to provide '*evidence*' (research results) that supports your conclusions. Hence, you might want to take a look at your data and ensure that you have all the information you need to be able to draw conclusions prior to writing your conclusions chapter.

Remember that your research is intended to inform thinking, decision-making and/or action of client organizations. It is therefore important that your conclusions are unambiguous and are not misleading. It is also important that you take into account the audience of the research report when you are writing down your conclusions. You should think about which issues are important to them and how you can best communicate these issues.

The limitations of your study relate to those issues in your research design or methodology that impacted or influenced the reliability and validity of your findings (the evidence). Describe the limitations of your study to inform your audience about the weaknesses of your study. Many researchers are hesitant to do this because they think doing so highlights the flaws in their research and makes the research look bad. But this is not the case. Describing the limitations of your study actually makes a positive impression on your audience because it stresses that you can think objectively and critically about your own research. More importantly, it ensures that the conclusions you present are an objective and honest representation of what you have found in your research.

BOX 18.1 SUGGESTIONS FOR WRITING YOUR CONCLUSIONS CHAPTER

- Keep your audience in mind.
- Make claims!
- Make sure that your claims are supported by the data that you have collected.
- Discuss what your results mean for the client organization. How could your findings be applied to solve the problem?
- Discuss your conclusions in order of most to least relevant.
- State whether your results are in line with the findings of previous research. If they are not, provide explanations (such explanations are probably related to the specific context of the client organization).
- Discuss any inconclusive results and explain them as best you can. Suggest additional research to clarify these results.

- Briefly describe the limitations of your research. Note that many researchers are hesitant to do this because they think that highlighting the weaknesses in their research makes the research report weaker. But it is not true. Describing the limitations of the research creates a positive impression as it makes it clear that you have an in-depth understanding of your topic and you have reported objectively. The limitations of your research may stimulate future research. Make suggestions for such research.
- If your research is exploratory, suggest future research that can be carried out to build on your findings.

DIFFERENT WAYS OF LOOKING AT CONCLUSIONS

There are two important different ways of looking at **conclusions**. The first one (and by far our favourite way) is that they represent the researcher's informed judgement about (how) the organizational problem (can best be solved); how attractive its industry is, how satisfied its customers are or how the motivation of its employees can (best) be improved, depending on the (type of) problem that set off the research process. Along these lines, the researcher presents his or her judgement(s) in the form of one or more claims in the conclusions chapter. For instance, a researcher might claim: 'The organization will benefit from enhancing participation in decision-making in order to improve employee motivation'. To convince the client organization of the need to improve participation in decision-making, the researcher needs to provide 'evidence' (see Box 18.2) supporting the claim. This is how conclusions provide the foundation for evidence-based decision-making and practice.

BOX 18.2 ON THE RELATIONSHIP BETWEEN DATA, INFORMATION AND EVIDENCE

The term *data* originates from the Latin word *dare*, which means to give. Data are thus 'given things'. The responses from your participants are data. The term *information* applies when the data are meaningful to someone and/or if they are collected with a specific aim or purpose (a research purpose) in mind. If information is used to convince someone of a certain point of view, the term *evidence* applies.

For instance, the responses to questions of a group of employees to specific questions measuring employee motivation can be entered into a database. We can acquire a feel for these data by obtaining visual summaries and by checking central tendencies and dispersions. The term information refers to data that are meaningful to someone and help that person

to achieve a certain goal or to reduce uncertainty about something (e.g. for a manager who wants to know how motivated his employees are data with regard to employee motivation represent information). Evidence is information that is used to support a certain claim or conclusion; in other words, information that is used to convince someone of a certain claim or point of view. For instance, if the argument is that 'Employees of organization XYZ are extremely motivated. That is why they are performing better than most employees in other organizations', then the information on employee motivation has become evidence supporting the claim or conclusion that employees of organization XYZ are performing better than most employees in other organizations.

EXERCISE 18.1	A researcher has collected quantitative data on employee satisfaction for a client organization. She has found that the satisfaction of employees averages 4.7 on a 5-point scale with end-points anchored by 'not at all satisfied' (1) and 'very satisfied' (5).

    a. Provide an example of a claim that the researcher might make based on these data.

    b. Explain why the above data might represent information to some people, whereas it might represent evidence to some people.

BOX 18.3   **WHAT CONCLUSIONS ARE NOT: A SET OF CLAIMS NOT BACKED UP BY EVIDENCE**

Every time a conclusion is drawn (a claim is made), check whether you can find the evidence that supports that claim. Where there is no evidence, (1) find the evidence and provide it, (2) remove the claim or (3) explicitly explain that you are speculating.

A second way to look at conclusions (and not our favourite way) is that your conclusions provide an answer to your research questions. Indeed, because your conclusions are based on the data that you have collected, you will often get the advice to answer your research questions in the conclusions chapter. There is nothing wrong with that. However, the results of your research do not simply add up to conclusions. As we have argued before, an important question that should be answered in the conclusions chapter is: 'What do my results *mean*?' That is why your conclusions chapter should not merely provide a summary of your research results, but should also provide an interpretation of these results. Along these lines, a conclusions chapter includes a discussion of what the results mean for the client organization and how the results can be applied to solve the problem that has set off the research project.

BOX 18.4   **WHAT CONCLUSIONS ARE NOT: ANOTHER OVERVIEW OR A SUMMARY OF THE RESEARCH RESULTS**

Conclusions are based on data (or better, on evidence); therefore, research results play an important role in a conclusions chapter. However, the research results themselves do not add up to conclusions and the reporting or summary of results cannot substitute for drawing conclusions.

CHARACTERISTICS OF CONCLUSIONS

The results of your research and the subsequent conclusions might be delicate, in conflict with vested interests and, in some cases, even a potential source of reputational damage. For example, your research might reveal that the financial position of the client organization is vulnerable, that its IT infrastructure is not up to par or even that the company policy during a certain period of time has been irresponsible and blameworthy. Remember that there is always someone responsible for the financial position of an organization, the IT infrastructure or the company policy, so your research results and conclusions might be potentially harmful to people working for your client organization. This may lead to 'requests' to (a) omit certain results, (b) to emphasize other results or (c) to provide a toned-down version of the research report. It is important to resist such pressure and to arm yourself against it.

BOX 18.5	**WHAT CONCLUSIONS ARE NOT: AN OPPORTUNITY TO PRESENT THE CONCLUSIONS THE CLIENT ORGANIZATION WAS HOPING FOR**

Every now and then the findings of a study may be unpalatable to the client organization or a specific person within that organization. As a consequence, people may react defensively to the conclusions of your study. There may even be pressure from stakeholders to highlight certain results and omit other results.

It is not always easy to deal with such pressure. However, it is important to present the correct results (all of them) and to draw conclusions only from the evidence, even if the conclusions are awkward. Apart from the ethical issues involved, the credibility of the research and the researcher is at stake here.

If your research is action-oriented, the implementation of the recommendations you provide might ask for considerable investments in terms of time, money and other resources. Suppose that you conclude that your client organization will benefit from improving the responsiveness of its employees in order to enhance customer satisfaction. If the client organization follows your advice and starts a training program to improve the responsiveness of its employees, it should invest in this training in terms of time and money. It is often impossible to revoke such investments. Therefore, it is important that your conclusions do not mislead and that you explain how you have arrived at your conclusions on the basis of the data that you have collected.

BOX 18.6	**WHAT CONCLUSIONS ARE NOT: AN OPPORTUNITY TO PRESENT THE CONCLUSIONS YOU WERE HOPING FOR**

Throughout your career as a researcher, you will find out that the results of your research efforts are sometimes rather disappointing. The model that you have carefully built does not explain much variation in the dependent variable, the effects

that you were expecting to find are not there, your theory cannot be confirmed. Irrespective of what you were hoping to find, the conclusions must provide a true reflection of the results of your research.

Drawing strong conclusions is not easy. Strong conclusions are based on strong data. The data you have gathered may have come from many different sources and subjects. What's more, they should be relevant to the specific context of the client organization. Therefore, you will need to synthesize. To synthesize (we already discussed this in Chapter 5 about a critical review of the literature) is to combine two or more elements to form a new whole. To convince the client organization of your viewpoint on how to solve the problem, you will also need to be able to develop strong arguments, which is also far from easy as you will learn later on in this chapter. Finally, when you are writing down your conclusions for an audience, you need to make sure that what you write is clear and coherent; the overall message or argument you are conveying should hang together and be consistent. Pay close attention to your target audience when writing down your conclusions. Think about what they want to know (for instance, how can you best solve our specific problem or how attractive is a specific market segment), which matters are important to communicate and how you can best make your point. Use language that is understandable and be open and honest regarding the limitations of your research and the degree of certainty of your conclusions.

BOX 18.7	**WHAT CONCLUSIONS ARE NOT: NEW ISSUES OR IDEAS**

Your conclusions chapter should not contain new information. This means that you should not come up with topics (for instance, in the form of research results, explanations for certain findings or theory) that have not been discussed earlier in your research report.

Now that we have presented different ways of looking at conclusions and some important characteristics of conclusions, we will turn to arguments. As you will soon find out, arguments play an important role in the development of strong conclusions. We will start our discussion on arguments with a description and a definition of an argument and discuss different types of arguments and argumentation models. Finally, we will provide a brief overview of incorrect or flawed forms of reasoning that are relevant in a research setting.

DEVELOPING AN ARGUMENT

With the development of an argument, one tries to convince others of their own point of view by asserting what they want others to believe and by presenting evidence in its favour. When evidence is provided for a certain point of view (for instance, with regard to the best solution to a problem), we have the basis for an argument in its favour. Note that there is an important difference between arguing for a certain point of view and merely asserting it. Suppose that you believe an organization will benefit from employing a diverse workforce and that you want to convince someone of this. You could simply state something like 'The organization will benefit from employing a diverse workforce!'. While this assertion may persuade *some* people to think that workforce diversity is important (even though you have not offered any reasons why they should), it may not convince others. If, in addition you were to offer reasons for employing a diverse workforce, then you would be developing an argument. For instance, you might state: 'My research results show that workforce diversity has a positive effect on organizational effectiveness. That is why the organization will benefit from employing a diverse workforce'. This is an argument in favour of the assertion that the organization will benefit from employing a diverse workforce.

An **argument** is thus a set of statements that includes the following:

1. A conclusion (or claim) – which is the main point the argument is trying to establish.;

2. Premises ('the evidence') – which support the conclusion.

This is how the collection of data, drawing conclusions and the development of an argument are related.

Let us see an example. Suppose that you have collected the following data on employee satisfaction for three different departments in an organization: Department A that is being led by Amber, department B, led by Bob, and department C, led by Caroline. Suppose that the average employee satisfaction in these three departments (measured on a 5-point scale with end-points anchored by 'very dissatisfied [1]' and 'very satisfied' [5]) was 3.6 (department A), 3.9 (department B) and 4.3 (department C), respectively.

Table 18.1   Results of Employee Satisfaction Survey

Department	Head of department	Employee satisfaction
A	Amber	3.1
B	Bob	3.6
C	Caroline	4.3

Suppose that data analysis has shown that the averages are significantly different. Based on these results, you might state: 'The average employee satisfaction is higher in department C than in departments A and B'. If you were to use these research results to contribute to the development of an argument and to draw a conclusion, your data would become evidence (you will hopefully remember that we have explained earlier in this chapter how evidence can be distinguished from information and data).

Now let us assume that you have developed the following argument:

'The average employee satisfaction is higher in department C than in departments A and B. Therefore: Caroline is a better boss than Amber and Bob'.

This is an argument in support of the conclusion that Caroline is a better boss than Amber and Bob. Notice however, that it's being an argument does *not* necessarily mean that it is a *good* argument.

Do you think that the above argument is a good argument? Why or why not?	**EXERCISE 18.2**

Notice also the fact that an argument is not a good argument does *not* mean that the evidence or the conclusion is untrue; it simply means that the evidence does not provide strong support for the conclusion. We will come back to the above example later in this chapter, after the discussion of different types of arguments.

In sum, this section has explained that when you are developing an argument you are giving someone reasons for believing something, provided that the premises are true (the evidence is good). Arguments have a structure that allows someone to see how a statement made is supported by reasons. The statement that is made is called the conclusion (and sometimes claim) and the statements on which it is based are called premises (or evidence). The premises or evidence contain an answer to the question, 'This is interesting, but why should I believe you?' If you do not provide reasons for your conclusions, people may very well reject them. In the next section, we will be answering the question of what makes the difference between good and bad arguments. We will also differentiate between two types of arguments: deductive and ampliative arguments.

What is the evidence and conclusions in the following argument?	**EXERCISE 18.3**

Workforce diversity has a positive effect on organizational effectiveness.

The effect of workforce diversity on organizational effectiveness is more positive if a manager has the expertise to manage diversity in the right way.

Managers of organization XYZ have the experience to manage workforce diversity.

Therefore: Organization XYZ will benefit from having a diverse workforce.

DIFFERENT TYPES OF ARGUMENTS

In arguments, the idea is that evidence supports the conclusion and that the conclusion is supported by evidence. The term *good* when we talk about 'a good argument' describes how well the premises support the conclusion. In other words, 'good' describes the relationship between the premises and the conclusion in terms of strength of the support.

In some cases, the relationship between the premises and the conclusion is perfect. Perfect means that if the premises are true, then the conclusion *must be* true. In other words, the conclusion is *guaranteed* by the premises. In such cases, the argument is said to be *valid*.

A famous example of a valid argument is given as follows:

All men are mortal (the first premise)

John is a man (the second premise)

Therefore, John is mortal (the conclusion)

As you can see, the relationship between the premises and the conclusion is perfect. The first premise states that all objects classified as 'men' have the attribute 'mortal'. The second premise states that 'John' is a 'man'; in other words, John is a member of the group 'men'. The conclusion then *must be* that 'John is mortal'; he acquires this attribute from his classification as a 'man'.

The type of reasoning used here is called *deductive reasoning* (not to be confused with deductive research). In deductive reasoning, if the premises are true, then the conclusion must be true. Deductive arguments are either valid or invalid. In a valid argument, the conclusion follows from the premises; in an invalid argument, the conclusion does not follow from the premises (even though the premises and the conclusions might be true).

Consider the following argument:

All mobile phones produced after 2018 have a capacity of 16 GB or more.

My mobile phone has a capacity of 32 GB.

Therefore: My mobile phone was produced after 2018.

This above argument is invalid. The conclusion does not follow from the premises. Even though the premises are true, the conclusion may be false; the fact that mobile phones made after 2018 may have a capacity of 16 GB or more does not mean that mobile phones made before 2018 cannot have a capacity of 16 GB or more. This is how the conclusion does not logically follow from the premises.

EXERCISE 18.4

All organizations are agile.

The Museum of Modern Art is an organization.

Therefore: The Museum of Modern Art is agile.

a. Write down what you take to be the premise or premises of the argument.
b. Write down what you think to be the conclusion or conclusions of the argument.
c. Are the premises true?
d. Is the argument deductive in nature? Why or why not?
e. Is the argument valid? Why or why not?

In real life, most arguments are not deductive. That is, the relationship between the premises and the conclusion is *less than perfect*. A less-than-perfect relationship is not necessarily a bad relationship however. Less-than-perfect arguments can be either good or bad (and sometimes even awful), *depending on how well the premises support the conclusion*. Good arguments support (even though they do not guarantee) their conclusion and bad arguments do not. When the relationship between the premises and the conclusion is less than perfect, the type of reasoning used is called ampliative (and sometimes inductive reasoning).

If the relationship between the premises and the conclusion is less than perfect, we may benefit from using an argumentation model that includes more than merely premises and conclusions. Arguing that deductive arguments (and perfect relationships) often lack practical value, the British philosopher Stephen Toulmin proposed a broader argumentation model containing six interrelated parts for analysing arguments. Toulmin's model takes conclusions as a starting point and emphasizes that conclusions are often based on probability (strong relationships) rather than on certainty (perfect relationships). Hence, the model is particularly useful when arguments are not deductive but ampliative (or inductive). Again, in *ampliative reasoning*, the premises support (but do not guarantee) the conclusion.

BOX 18.8	**WHAT RESEARCH DOES NOT DO**

Research improves the odds of making a correct decision. It does *not* guarantee success. The value of research can (and must) be seen over the long run, where an increase in the number of good decisions is manifested in improved bottom-line performance (Lehmann, Gupta & Steckel, 1998).

We often need ampliative reasoning when we build our conclusions based on the results of research (see Box 18.8). Therefore, we will examine Toulmin's model in more detail. We will start discussion of six parts of this model:

1. **The conclusion (often referred to as 'the claim')** For example, if a person tries to convince somebody that he is a British citizen, the conclusion could be 'Harry is a British citizen'.
2. **The premise (or evidence)** The premise serves as the foundation for the conclusion. For example, the person claiming that Harry is a British citizen can support his conclusion with the following evidence: 'He was born in Bermuda'.

   Because the relation between the conclusion ('Harry is a British citizen') and the evidence ('He was born in Bermuda') is not perfect – the evidence does not *guarantee* the conclusion – we may benefit from using additional four parts to assess the quality (the goodness) of the argument.
3. **The warrant** In order to move from the evidence 'Harry was born in Bermuda' to the conclusion 'He is a British citizen', a warrant is needed to bridge the gap between the two. The warrant provides the underlying connection between the conclusion and evidence and explains why the evidence supports the conclusion. For instance, one might argue that 'A man born in Bermuda will generally be a British citizen'.

   A backing A backing is needed when the warrant itself is not convincing enough. The backing explains why the warrant is a rational one. For example, if the opposing party (e.g. your thesis supervisor) does not deem the warrant 'A man born in Bermuda will generally be a British citizen' as credible, you may need to supply legal provisions: 'The British Parliament Acts explicitly state that…'. Obviously, research results can also serve as a backing.

   Given that the warrant does not have 'total justifying force' (take note of the term *generally*) the conclusion that Harry is a British citizen must be *qualified*, it follows 'presumably', 'possibly' or maybe even 'impossibly'. Qualifiers add nuance and specificity to arguments and account for counter-arguments. They thus address potential objections or restrictions to the conclusion.
4. **Qualifiers** These are words or phrases expressing the degree of certainty concerning the conclusion. Such words or phrases include 'probably', 'possible', 'impossible', 'certainly', 'presumably', 'as far as the evidence goes' and sometimes 'necessarily'. Note that the conclusion 'Harry is definitely a British citizen' has a greater degree of certainty than the conclusion that 'He is presumably a British citizen'.
5. **Counter-arguments (rebuttal)** Counter-arguments address potential objections to the conclusion and/ or recognize the restrictions that may be applied to the conclusion. For instance, a counter-argument to the conclusion that 'Harry is a British citizen' may be 'A man born in Bermuda will legally be British, unless his parents are Dutch or he has changed his nationality'.

The first three elements 'conclusion', 'premise' and 'warrant' are considered the essential components of practical arguments, while 'backing', 'qualifiers' and rebuttal' may not be needed in some arguments.

One the Importance of Using the Correct Type of Argumentation

Let us now return to the example in Section 'Developing an Argument' where we developed the following argument: 'The average employee satisfaction in department C is higher than the average employee satisfaction in departments A and B. Therefore: Caroline is a better boss than Amber and Bob'. Let us check whether this argument is a good argument.

When you are evaluating an argument, you should know whether it is to be deductive or (merely) ampliative. If an argument is portrayed as a deductive argument but careful consideration of the argument reveals that the premises do not guarantee the conclusion (the conclusion could be false even though the premises are true), it is often a good reason to reject the argument as a bad argument. In an ampliative argument, however, to notice that the truth of the premises does not guarantee the conclusion is simply to notice that the argument is an ampliative argument. So knowing the type of argument is essential to know the tools to use to evaluate whether or not it is a good argument.

A careful consideration of the argument 'The average employee satisfaction in department C is higher than the average employee satisfaction in departments A and B. Therefore: Caroline is a better boss than Amber and Bob' reveals that it is supposed to be ampliative; the fact that the employee satisfaction is higher in department C than in departments A and B does not *guarantee* the conclusion that Caroline is a better boss than Amber and Bob. Other factors might also play a role. Nonetheless, the argument is portrayed as if it were a deductive argument (no backing is provided and rebuttals and qualifiers are lacking). Hence, this argument is not a good argument.

EXERCISE 18.5

Use a warrant, a backing, counter-arguments, and qualifiers to improve the argument 'The average employee satisfaction in department C is higher than the average employee satisfaction in departments A and B. Therefore: Caroline is a better boss than Amber and Bob'.

INCORRECT OR FLAWED FORMS OF REASONING

Some ways of arguing appear to be good, but upon closer inspection they do not support their conclusions. These incorrect or flawed forms of reasoning are known as fallacies. Some fallacies are common enough to have received their own particular labels. In what follows, we present some common types of fallacies that typically pop up in a research context. Acquaintance with these fallacies will help you to avoid them in your arguments as a researcher. What's more, it will also help you to point out fallacies in others' arguments. You can find a rather complete overview of logical fallacies on the website 'Logically Fallacious': https://www.logicallyfallacious.com/tools/lp/Bo/LogicalFallacies.

- *Alleged certainty*: Asserting a conclusion without evidence or premises through a statement that makes the conclusion appear certain when in fact it is not. For instance: 'Everybody knows that . . .' or 'Scholars everywhere recognize the need to . . .'.

- *Appeal to common belief*: When the claim that most (or many) people – in general or a particular group – accept a belief as true is presented as evidence for the claim. For instance: 'A lot of people believe in autocratic leadership. Therefore, autocratic leadership must be a good thing'.

- *Argument by repetition*: Repeating a conclusion, research findings or a premise over and over again in place of better supporting evidence. For instance: 'Customer satisfaction is quite low. Indeed, the clients of organization XYZ are not happy. They are thus unsatisfied about the organization'.

- *Blind authority argument*: Asserting that a proposition is true solely on the authority making the claim (extreme cases also ignore any counter evidence no matter how strong this evidence is). For example: 'Authority X asserts that an ABC-policy is of the utmost importance. That is why organization Z will benefit from adopting an ABC-policy'.

- *Begging the question (circular reasoning)*: A form of reasoning in which a circle is created; the conclusion is supported by the premises, which are supported by the conclusion. Like this, no useful information is being provided. For example: 'The reason every organization wants to be agile is because being agile is extremely popular'.

- *Cherry picking (ignoring inconvenient data, suppressed evidence, fallacy of incomplete evidence, argument by selective observation, argument by half-truth, ignoring the counter evidence, one-sided assessment, one-sidedness)*: When one presents only a select evidence in order to convince the audience and other evidence that would go against the conclusion is withheld.

- *Does not follow (non-sequitur)*: The conclusion does not follow logically from the evidence or premises. For example: 'If all planets revolve around the sun and the earth revolves around the sun, then the earth is a planet'. This conclusion is incorrect on the basis of the rules of logic.

- *False cause*: This argument equates sequence with causality. Because event A was followed by event B, the first caused the second. For instance: 'After Bill became CEO, the company enjoyed unprecedented growth and success. That is why Bill is a great CEO'.

- *Hasty generalization*: A conclusion based on a small sample size, rather than looking at statistics that are much more in line with the typical or average situation. For instance: 'Organization ABC has never invested in any marketing activity whatsoever. This organization is more than a hundred years old and still flourishing. Therefore, engaging in marketing activities really can't be that important'.

- *Regression to the mean*: Ascribing a cause where none exists in situations where natural fluctuations exist while failing to account for these natural fluctuations. For example, 'Naomi's parents are very tall, that is why Naomi will be at least as tall as her parents or even taller'. The thing is that children of tall parents are usually smaller than their parents (and children of small parents are usually taller than their parents). In this fallacy, one ignores the idea that in a consecutive series of measurements, the statistical probability of a phenomenon will tend to the average.

- *Sunk-cost fallacy*: Costs already made (effort, money or time) are used as an argument to decide to continue with a project or process. For instance: 'We have to finish the project because we have already invested millions in it'.

MANAGERIAL IMPLICATIONS

Recommendations provided by the researcher to solve the problem are based on the conclusions that the researcher has drawn. In turn, the conclusions are based on the collected data. Strong conclusions are based on strong data. But strong data do not necessarily lead to strong conclusions; if the arguments provided by the researcher are bad, then the conclusions might still be bad and sometimes even misleading. Therefore, good arguments play an important role in drawing conclusions. Hence, it is important for a manager being able to distinguish between good and bad data, good and bad arguments and good and bad conclusions. Knowledge on how to draw conclusions, good and bad arguments and different types of arguments helps the manager to recognize the value of the conclusions presented in the research report and the recommendations based on these conclusions. This helps the manager to make an informed decision as to whether or not to follow the recommendations of the researcher.

SUMMARY	

- **Learning objective 1: Describe the characteristics of conclusions.** Drawing conclusions and providing recommendations to the client organization is the last stage of the research process. A good place to start thinking about what should be in your conclusions chapter is the problem of the client organization. In your conclusions chapter, you will often make *claims* regarding what the organization wants to know or how the client organization can (best) solve the problem. To convince the client organization of your viewpoint, you will also have to provide reasons for your claims. In other words, you need to provide '*evidence*' (research results) that supports your conclusions. It is important that your conclusions are unambiguous and are not misleading. It is also important that you take into account the audience of the research report when you are writing down your conclusions. The limitations of your study relate to those issues in your research design or methodology that impacted or influenced the reliability and validity of your findings (the evidence). Describe the 'limitations' of your study to inform your audience about the weaknesses of your study. This makes your research report stronger. An important characteristic of conclusions is that the results of your research and the subsequent conclusions might be delicate, in conflict with vested interests and, in some cases, even a potential source of reputational damage. If your research is action-oriented, the implementation of the recommendations you provide might ask for considerable investments in terms of time, money and other resources.

- **Learning objective 2: Explain what an argument is.** An argument is a set of statements that includes (1) a conclusion (or claim), which is the main point the argument is trying to establish, and (2) premises ('the evidence') that support the conclusion.

- **Learning objective 3: Compare and contrast deductive and ampliative arguments and discuss these two types of arguments.** In deductive reasoning, if the premises are true, then the conclusion must be true. Deductive arguments are either valid or invalid. In real life, most arguments are not deductive. The relationship between the premises and the conclusion is less than perfect. A less-than-perfect relationship is not necessarily a bad relationship however. Less-than-perfect arguments are ampliative (or inductive). In ampliative reasoning, the premises support (but do not guarantee) the conclusion.

- **Learning objective 4: Discuss the differences between valid and invalid arguments and good and bad arguments.** Deductive arguments are either valid or invalid. In a valid argument, the conclusion follows from the premises; in an invalid argument, the conclusion does not follow from the premises. Ampliative (or inductive) arguments can be either good or bad, depending on how well the premises support the conclusion. Good arguments support their conclusion and bad arguments do not.

- **Learning objective 5: Discuss incorrect or flawed forms of reasoning known as fallacies.** Some ways of arguing appear to be good, but upon closer inspection they do not support their conclusions. These incorrect or flawed forms of reasoning are known as fallacies. Common types of fallacies include alleged certainty, appeal to common belief, argument by repetition, blind authority argument, begging the question (circular reasoning), cherry picking, does not follow (non-sequitur), false cause, hasty generalization, regression to the mean and the sunk-cost fallacy.

- **Learning objective 6: Draw strong conclusions based on strong research results and strong arguments.** The exact content of your conclusions and recommendations chapter depends on the type of research you have done. In general, some suggestions for writing your conclusions chapter are as follows: Keep your audience in mind; make claims; make sure that your claims are supported by the data that you have collected; discuss what your results mean for the client organization; discuss your conclusions in order of most to least relevant; state whether your results are in line with the findings of previous research; discuss any inconclusive results and explain them as best you can and suggest additional research to clarify these results; briefly describe the limitations of your research; if your research is exploratory in nature, suggest future research that can be carried out to build on your findings.

1. An organization wants to reduce staff turnover. A researcher who was hired by the organization developed the following research objective: 'To provide an overview of possible approaches to reducing staff turnover'.
   a. What type of data would you collect and how would you collect these data?
   b. Provide an example of a conclusion that you would be able to draw based on these data.
   c. Provide an example of an argument that you would develop to convince the client organization of this conclusion.
   d. Discuss whether this argument is deductive or ampliative.

2. You have just finished a research report on customer satisfaction for a specific client organization. Your research objective was to provide an overview of possible ways to improve customer satisfaction. The following table provides a brief overview of your research results.

Factors	Average (on a 5-point likert scale)	Beta-coefficient (regression analysis)
Independent variables		
Employee responsiveness	4.1	0.454
Empathy	3.6	0.312
Reliability	2.8	0.238
Assurance	4.3	0.116 (not significant)
Tangibles	3.3	0.387
Dependent variable		
Satisfaction	4.0	–

Note: All the variables were measured on 5-point Likert scales. 1 = not satisfied at all, 5 = very satisfied; 1 = not at all responsive, 5 = very responsive, etc.

   a. Develop an argument based on these research results.
   b. Is the argument deductive or ampliative? Why?

3. Consider the following argument:

   If people get paid well, then they will not leave the organization.

   George gets paid well.

   Therefore: George will not leave the organization.

   a. Write down what you take to be the premise or premises of the argument.
   b. Write down what you think to be the conclusion or conclusions of the argument.
   c. Is the argument deductive or ampliative? Why?
   d. Is the argument good? Why or why not?

4. Provide your own examples of flawed arguments or flawed forms of reasoning. Use the following fallacies:
   a. Alleged uncertainty
   b. Blind authority argument
   c. Does not follow (non-sequitur)

5. Consider the following argument:

   'Organization X has already been investing heavily in project Y. More investment is needed to complete the project, otherwise it will be lost. Therefore, more investments in the project are justified'.

   Is the argument good/valid? Why or why not?

6. The following text is taken from a conclusions chapter of an MBA thesis.

With regard to market-entry, this paper sought to understand how competitive advantage is derived by posing the theoretical question "What does literature state regarding business-level strategies to create competitive advantage for firms within the industry?". This question was answered in the theoretical chapter by providing Porters (1980) Competitor analysis framework which included the two important dimensions of 'How a firm competes' and its 'resources'. Given the complex nature and number of possible dimensions on how an education firm competes, Chen's (1996) theory on market commonality which describes multiple point competition was also provided. Lastly, to reduce the numerous possible competition points the Hill framework was provided to focus analysis on order winning criteria instead of order qualifying.

The two empirical questions focusing on Porter's dimensions of 'how a firm competes' and 'resources' posed were; "What are the resources and capabilities of current firms that produce competitive advantage?", and "How, and on which dimensions, do current firms compete to achieve their objectives?". The answer to the first question was provided in the results section illustrating that the total resources of the 123 firms within the sample group analyzed (representing ~40% of all Grade 7+ students) was approximately $820 million/annum. The share of revenue by these firms deviates along several lines. Schools offering boarding programs gain significantly greater revenues, firms in less dense population areas face less competition, are more likely to offer boarding, and more likely to hold a higher average tuition rate. Schools focused on the primary competitive dimensions of 'Single-Sex' and 'Special-Needs' have, in general, higher tuition rates. Beyond the primary competitive dimension, the secondary dimension also plays a large role with the best example being firms competing primarily along 'Academic' and secondarily along offering "IB Programs" & "STEM" specialties hold the ability to charge 20-40% higher rents.

The second question on how firms compete identified 9 primary, and 74 secondary, competition dimensions. Focusing on primary, this paper identified 5 of these dimensions as unique to specific regions. The remaining 4 categories of 'Academics', 'Single-Sex', 'Facilities', and 'Values' represents over 90% of how firms most commonly compete.

Discuss these conclusions.

The Research Report

LEARNING OBJECTIVES

After completing Chapter 19, you should be able to:

1. Describe the characteristics of a well-written research report that is tailored to the needs of a specific audience.

2. Write a thorough and complete research report.

3. Describe the characteristics of a good oral presentation and deliver a good oral presentation.

INTRODUCTION

The key purpose of any research report is to offer a clear description of what has been done in the various stages of the research process. Hence, a research report may possibly include information on the formulation of the problem statement, a critical review of the literature, the development of a theoretical framework, the collection of data, the analysis of the data and the interpretation of the results.

When researchers describe what has been done in the research, they may benefit from keeping the hallmarks of scientific research in mind. For instance, the researcher started the research with a definite aim or purpose. It is imperative to inform the reader about the specific aim or purpose of the research project as soon as possible; that is, in the introductory section of the research report. The researcher should also keep the criterion of replicability in mind; a research report is well written when a colleague researcher is able to replicate the research after reading the report. It is also important that the results of the study and the recommendations for solving the problem are objectively and effectively communicated to the sponsor, so that the suggestions made are accepted and implemented. Otherwise, all the effort hitherto expended on the investigation would have been in vain. Writing the report concisely, convincingly and with clarity is perhaps as important as conducting a rigorous research study. Indeed, a well-thought-out written report and oral presentation are critical.

The exact contents and organization of both modes of communication – the written report and the oral presentation – depend on the purpose of the research study and the audience to which it is targeted. The relevant aspects of the written report and oral presentation are discussed in this chapter.

THE WRITTEN REPORT

The written report starts with a description of the management problem and the research problem (research objective and research questions). This allows the reader to quickly become familiar with 'the why' of the research project. The written report should also allow the reader to weigh the facts and arguments presented therein, to examine the results of the study, to reflect on the conclusions and recommendations and eventually to implement the acceptable recommendations presented in the report, with a view to closing the gap between the existing state of affairs and the desired state. To achieve its goal, the written report has to focus on the issues discussed below.

THE PURPOSE OF THE WRITTEN REPORT

Research reports can have different purposes and hence the form of the written report will vary according to the situation. It is important to identify the purpose of the report, so that it can be tailored accordingly. If the purpose is simply to offer details on some specific areas of interest requested by a manager, the report can be very narrowly focused and provide the desired information to the manager in a brief format, as in the example below. A different form of report will be prescribed in some cases, where a manager asks for several alternative solutions or recommendations to rectify a problem in a given situation. Here the researcher provides the requested information and the manager chooses from among the alternatives and makes the final decision. In this case, a more detailed report that includes a conceptual background and a theoretical framework, the methodology used for data analyses and alternative solutions based on the conclusions drawn therefrom will have to be provided. How each alternative helps to improve the problem situation will also have to be discussed. The advantage and disadvantages of each of the proposed solutions, together with a cost–benefit analysis in terms of dollars and/or other resources, will also have to be presented to help the manager make the decision.

Yet another type of report might require the researcher to identify the problem and provide the final solution as well. That is, the researcher might be called in to study a situation, determine the nature of the problem and offer a report of the findings, conclusions and recommendations. Such a report has to be very comprehensive, following the format of a full-fledged study, as detailed later in this chapter. A fourth kind of research report is the very scholarly publication presenting the findings of a basic study that one usually finds published in academic journals.

Example	
A simple descriptive report	If a study is undertaken to understand, in detail, certain factors of interest in a given situation (variations in production levels, composition of employees and the like), then a report describing the phenomena of interest, in the manner desired, is all that is called for.

If a study is undertaken to understand, in detail, certain factors of interest in a given situation (variations in production levels, composition of employees and the like), then a report describing the phenomena of interest, in the manner desired, is all that is called for.

For instance, let us say a human resources manager wants to know how many employees have been recruited during the past 18 months in the organization, their gender composition, educational level and the average proportion of days that these individuals have absented themselves since recruitment. A simple report giving the desired information would suffice.

In this report, a statement of the purpose of the study will be first given (e.g. 'It was desired that a profile of the employees recruited during the past 18 months in the company, and an idea of their rate of absenteeism be provided. This report offers those details'). The methods or procedures adopted to collect the data will then be given (e.g. 'The payroll of the company and the personal files of the employees were examined'). Finally, a narration of the actual results, reinforced by visual tabular and graphical forms of representation of the data, will be provided. Frequency distributions, cross-tabulations and other data will be presented in a tabular form, and illustrations will include bar charts (for gender), pie charts (to indicate the proportions of individuals at various educational levels) and so on. This section will summarize the data and may look as follows:

A total of 27 employees were recruited during the past 18 months, of whom 45% are women and 55% are men. Twenty percent have a master's degree, 68% a bachelor's degree, and 12% a high school diploma. The average proportion of days that these employees remained absent during the past 18 months is six.

These details provide the information required by the manager. It may, however, be a good idea to provide a further gender-wise breakdown of the mean proportion of days of absence of the employees in an appendix, even though this information might not have been specifically requested. If considered relevant, a similar breakdown can also be furnished for people at different job levels.

A short simple report of the type discussed above is provided in Report 1 in the appendix to this chapter.

The president of a tire company wants several recommendations to be made on planning for the future growth of the company, taking into consideration the manufacturing, marketing, accounting and financial perspectives. In this case, only a broad objective is stated: corporate growth. There may currently be several impediments that retard growth. One has to carefully examine the situation to determine the obstacles to expansion and how these may be overcome through strategic planning from production, marketing, management, financial and accounting perspectives. Identification of the problems or impediments in the situation would call for intensive interviews, literature review, industry analysis, formulation of a theoretical perspective, generation of several hypotheses to come up with different alternative solutions, data gathering, data analysis and then exploration of alternative ways of attaining corporate growth through different strategies. To enable the president to evaluate the alternatives proposed, the pros and cons of implementing each of the alternative solutions, and a statement of the costs and benefits attached to each, would follow.

This report will be more elaborate than the previous one, detailing each of the steps in the study, emphasizing the results of data analysis, and furnishing a strong basis for the various recommendations. The alternatives generated and the pros and cons of each in a report such as this are likely to follow the format of Report 2 in the appendix. Report 3 in the appendix relates to basic research on an issue that was examined by a researcher.

As we can see, the contents and format of a report will depend on the purpose of the study and the needs of the sponsors to whom it is submitted.

Example

A situation where a comprehensive report, offering alternative solutions, is needed

THE AUDIENCE FOR THE WRITTEN REPORT

The organization of a report, its length, focus on details, data presentation and illustrations will, in part, be a function of the audience for whom it is intended. The letter of transmittal of the report will clearly indicate to whom the report is being sent. An executive summary placed at the beginning will offer (busy) executives just the right amount of vital details – usually in less than one page. This will help the managers to quickly grasp the essentials of the study and its findings, and turn to the pages that offer more detailed information on aspects that are of special interest to them.

Some managers are distracted by data presented in the form of tables and feel more comfortable with graphs and charts, while others want to see 'facts and figures.' Both tables and figures are visual forms of representation and need to be presented in reports. Which of these are to be prominently highlighted in the report and which relegated to an appendix is a function of the awareness of the idiosyncrasies of the ultimate user of the report. If a report is to be handled by different executives, with different orientations, it should be packaged such that they know where to find the information that meets their preferred mode of information processing. The length, organization and presentation modes of the report will, among other things, depend at least in part on the target audience. Some businesses might also prescribe their own format for report writing. In all cases, a good report is a function of the audience for whom it is intended and its exact purpose. As we have seen, some reports may have to be long and detailed, and others brief and specific.

Sometimes, the findings of a study may be unpalatable to the executive (e.g. the organizational policies are outdated and the system is very bureaucratic), or may reflect poorly on management, tending to make them react defensively (e.g. the system has an ineffective top-down approach). In such cases, tact should be exercised in presenting the conclusions without compromising on the actual findings. That is, while there is no need to suppress the unpleasant findings, they can be presented in a non-judgemental, non-fault-finding or finger-pointing manner, using objective data and facts that forcefully lead to, and convince the managers of the correctness of, the conclusions drawn. If this is not done, the report will be read defensively, the recommendations will not be accepted and the problem will remain unsolved.

CHARACTERISTICS OF A WELL-WRITTEN REPORT

Despite the fact that report writing is a function of the purpose of the study and the type of audience to which it is presented and accordingly has to be tailored to meet both, certain basic features are integral to all written reports. Clarity, conciseness, coherence, the right emphasis on important aspects, meaningful organization of paragraphs, smooth transition from one topic to the next, apt choice of words and specificity are all important features of a good report. The report should, to the extent possible, be free of technical or statistical jargon unless it happens to be of a technical or statistical nature. Care should also be taken to eliminate grammatical and spelling errors.

Any assumptions made by the researcher should be clearly stated in the report and facts, rather than opinions, provided. The report should be organized in a manner that enhances the meaningful and smooth flow of materials, as the reader progresses through it. Indeed, every reader loves to read a well-built 'story'. The balance between the academic standpoint and the writing of a good story is not always easy to find though; some trial and error is often needed.

The importance of the appearance of the report and its readability cannot be overemphasized. Appropriate headings and subheadings help organize the report in a logical manner and allow the reader to follow the transitions easily. A double-spaced, typed report with wide margins on all sides enables the reader to make notes/comments while perusing the contents.

CONTENTS OF THE RESEARCH REPORT

A research report has a title page, an executive summary (in the case of applied research) or an abstract (in the case of basic research), a preface, a table of contents and sometimes a copy of the authorization to conduct the study.

All reports should have an introductory section detailing the management problem, the purpose of the study and the research questions (the research problem), giving some background of what it relates to and setting the stage for what the reader should expect in the rest of the report. The body of the report should contain a conceptual background, details regarding the framework of the study and hypotheses (in case of deductive research), the sampling design, data collection methods, analysis of data and the results obtained. The final part of the report should present the findings and draw conclusions. If recommendations have been called for, they will be included with a cost–benefit analysis provided with respect to each. Such information clarifies the net advantages of implementing each of the recommendations. The details provided in the report should be such as to convince the reader of the thoroughness of the study and induce confidence in accepting the results and the recommendations made. Every professional report should also point out the limitations of the study (e.g. in sampling, data collection and the like). A list of references cited in the report should then follow.

Appendices, if any, should be attached to the report. A report on the factors influencing the upward mobility of women in accounting firms can be found in Report 3 of the appendix to this chapter. We will now discuss the different parts of the report.

THE TITLE AND THE TITLE PAGE

The title of your research report (together with the abstract or management summary) permits potential readers to obtain a first idea of your study and to decide whether they want to read your report in its entirety. For this reason, you may decide to come up with a descriptive title that accurately reflects the contents of your research or that indicates the methodology used in the research. Examples of descriptive titles are: 'The Impact of Venture Capital Investments on Public Firm Stock Performance'; 'Compulsive Buying: An Exploration into Self-Esteem and Money Attitudes'; and 'How Advertising Really Works: A Meta-Analysis.' Hence, a descriptive title may inform potential readers about the contents of the research, the method that was used, the results of the research report and the like.

A good title also grabs attention and entices people to read the research report in its entirety. References to well-known (literary) quotes, proverbs or popular movie and song titles are only some of the possibilities you have to stand out. 'Scents and sensibility: When do (in) congruent ambient scents influence product evaluations?' is an excellent example of a title that is both informative and persuasive. Indeed, do not be afraid to use a subtitle. If you have a catchy title, but feel it does not provide enough information, use it to clarify the contents of your research.

In addition to the title of the project, the title page will also indicate further relevant information. Note that it is important that you are familiar with your institution's rules and recommendations about what should be included here. You may need to enter your name, your student number, the name of your institution, department, sponsors, supervisor(s), the date of your final report and so on.

THE EXECUTIVE SUMMARY OR ABSTRACT

An executive summary or abstract of your research report is placed on the page immediately following the title page. The executive summary is a brief account of the entire research study. It provides an overview and highlights the following important information related to it: the management problem, the research problem, data collection methods used, design results of data analysis, conclusions and recommendations, with suggestions for their implementation.

The executive summary is probably the first part of your research report that is read by the sponsors of your study. They will use it to get an initial idea (the results) of your study. The executive summary will be brief – and is usually restricted to one page or less in length.

An example of a management summary of a study of customer satisfaction with the website of a Dutch investment bank follows.

The aim of this study was to determine the variables that drive website user satisfaction in the Dutch investment banking industry. The results of this study aim to help Peeters & Co.'s Structured Products (SP) desk to improve the quality of its website. The following problem statement was formulated:	**Example** **Management summary**

'What elements are of importance in driving website user satisfaction in the Dutch investment banking industry and how can the results of this study be used to ensure users spend more time on the website of the SP desk and use it as their main information source?'

Based on a literature review and exploratory interviews, a conceptual model of website user satisfaction was constructed. The conceptual model includes website user satisfaction and its expected (hypothesized) antecedents: information quality, system quality, interactivity and system design quality. To examine the effect of the independent variables on website user satisfaction, an online survey was used. The results of this survey showed that the current level of user satisfaction with the website of the SP desk is below Peeters & Co.'s standards. Furthermore, the results showed that the variables information quality, system quality, interactivity and system design quality all have a linear and positive influence on website user satisfaction.

Based on the results of this study, it is recommended that the SP desk improves the information quality and interactivity of its website. Information quality can be improved by including more relevant content on the website and by making the information on the website more transparent, objective and up to date. Interactivity can be improved by improving customer support and by including customization options and financial tools on the website.

TABLE OF CONTENTS

The logic of the structure of your research report becomes evident not only through an apt choice of words in the titles of the sections, but also as a result of the arrangement of the different components of the work. For the reader, the table of contents serves as a guide through your research report. The table of contents usually lists the important headings and subheadings in the report with page references. A separate list of tables and figures should also be listed in the table of contents. Your institution may have guidelines or recommendations about the form the contents pages should take. An example of the guidelines of the TIAS School for Business and Society is provided next.

Example **TIAS School for Business and Society guidelines for the table of contents**	The table of contents contains the headings and subheadings of the chapters and sections of your research project, with the numbers of the pages on which these chapters and sections begin. The outer cover page and management summary are not entered in the table of contents and therefore the first item to be listed is the preface. The minimum content of the table of contents should be the preface, each chapter or main division title, each appendix and the bibliography. All headings should correspond exactly in wording, arrangement, punctuation and capitalization with the headings as they appear in the body of the dissertation. A main heading or chapter title is given entirely in capitals and begins at the left-hand margin of the page. Main subheadings should be indented and typed in upper and lower case. Subordinate subheadings should also be indented. Chapters, sections of chapters and subsections and so on are numbered using Arabic numerals in a decimal sequence. Thus, the third subsection of the second section of chapter three is numbered 3.2.3. The number of the page on which the division begins in the text of the management project is given in the table of contents in Arabic numerals flush with the right-hand margin of the page. Double-spacing is used except for overrun lines, which are single-spaced.

LIST OF TABLES, FIGURES AND OTHER MATERIALS

If the research report contains charts, figures, maps, tables, photographs or other types of material, each series of these should be listed separately in an appropriate list on the page or pages immediately following the table of contents. Each such list should appear on a separate page. In format, such lists should follow the general style of the table of contents.

The number of the item is given at the left-hand margin of the page under the appropriate column headings entitled, 'Charts', 'Figures', 'Maps', 'Tables' or 'Photographs'. This is followed by the title of the item, given exactly as it appears in the text of the research report. The number of the page on which the item appears in the body of the research report is given flush with the right-hand margin of the page. Tables, figures and so on should be numbered according to their chapter and position in the chapter. Thus, Figure 2.10 is the tenth figure in Chapter 2.

PREFACE

The preface is used primarily to mention matters of background necessary for an understanding of the subject that do not logically fit into the text. Items such as the following may also be mentioned here unless they are more extensively considered in the body of the research report: why the report has been written (e.g. Management Project Report for . . .), reason for the selection of the subject, difficulties encountered along the way and so on. It is customary to include a brief expression of the author's appreciation of help and guidance received in the research. Note that the preface is not the same as an introduction, which is a part of the main body of the research report.

THE AUTHORIZATION LETTER

A copy of the letter of authorization from the sponsor of the study approving the investigation and detailing its scope is sometimes attached at the beginning of the research report. The authorization letter makes clear to the reader that the goals of the study have the full blessing of the organization.

THE INTRODUCTORY SECTION

The layout of the *first chapter* is more or less standard. This chapter could contain, in the following order:

1. Introduction (§1.1).

2. Reason for the research (description of the problem)(§1.2).

3. Research objective and research questions (§1.3).

4. The scope of the study (§1.4).

5. Research method (approach) (§1.5).

6. Managerial relevance (§1.6).

7. Structure and division of chapters in the research report (§1.7).

The introductory section starts with a short introduction providing background information on why and how the study was initiated. The introduction is followed by a section describing the objective of the research project and a section providing the research questions. Brief (!) descriptions of the scope of the study, the research method and the managerial relevance of the study are also provided in the introductory section. The last section offers an overview of the structure and division of chapters in the research report.

THE BODY OF THE REPORT

The central part of a research report usually has two large sections: a *theoretical* part and an *empirical* part. The theoretical part contains an in-depth exploration and a clear explication of the relevant literature. The exact nature of this part depends on the type of study you have done (exploratory, descriptive or causal – see Chapter 5, Box 5.2 for an example). It documents the relevant instruments provided in earlier research that may help you to describe what you aim to describe (when your research is descriptive in nature) or relevant findings from earlier research (when your research is exploratory or causal in nature) and should be selective, goal oriented, thorough and critical – a literature review is more than just a summary of the literature! The literature review can be concluded with a theoretical framework and a number of hypotheses, which will be tested in the empirical part of your study (only if your research is deductive and causal in nature). Avoid elaborations that will ultimately not contribute to a better understanding of the problem and/or solutions to the problem.

The design details – such as sampling and data collection methods, as well as the time horizon, the field setting and the unit of analysis – and the results of the study are described in the empirical part of the research report. The information provided here should enable the reader to replicate the research. In the case of experiments, the empirical part should therefore at the very least contain the components 'participants', 'material', and 'method'. In the case of survey research, you should include the components 'participants', 'method', and, if relevant, 'material'.

The 'participants' section clarifies who took part in the research, the number of participants and how and why participants were selected. The section 'material' describes the instruments (such as stimuli and measurement scales) that were used and their functions. The description should be detailed enough to allow another researcher to replicate your research at a later stage. Stimuli can, for example, be a series of product packages that you showed your participants during an experiment. This part also informs the reader about the measurement scales that were used in the research. If an existing measurement scale (to measure a construct from your conceptual model) is used, the source of the material should be mentioned. Self-developed measurement scales should be tested for validity and internal consistency. For existing and previously published scales, a mention of a coefficient of internal consistence usually suffices (e.g. Cronbach's alpha). The 'method' section provides a step-by-step description of the execution of the research. Again, it is important that the full course of the research that was followed by the participants is given in enough detail to allow another person to carry out an exact replication of the research.

In the 'results' part of the research report, the data are presented that were uncovered through your empirical research and subsequent data analysis. In this part you do not come forward with an explanation for the results yet or the implications that follow from the results; this information should be offered in the final part of the report. At this place you provide a well-organized and understandable overview of the results of your study, using the appropriate procedures for statistical analysis. The specific form in which you present your results depends on the type of research. It is customary in descriptive statistics always to process information in tables or graphs (e.g. means, standard deviations, number of subjects per cell and so on) and to include statistical tests in the text. A few of the various ways in which data can be pictorially presented in written reports and oral presentations are illustrated in Figure 19.1.

Note that all relevant results should be reported: that is, also those that contradict your hypotheses. However, avoid an overflow of numbers and figures in your text. Only include the most relevant statistical data; incorporate the rest of the results in the appendices.

THE FINAL PART OF THE REPORT

Instructors can visit the companion website at **www.wiley.com/go/bougie/researchmethods forbusiness8e** for **Author Video: The final part of the report**.

The aim of this part of the research report is to interpret the results of the research with regard to the research questions. This is a very important aspect of the research report. Readers (managers) often skip the method section and move straight to the conclusions of the research. For this reason, the discussion should stand on its own and should form a whole with a beginning and an ending. Include the following aspects in your discussion:

1. The main findings of your research.

2. The conclusions.

3. Recommendations for implementation and a cost–benefit analysis of these recommendations.

4. The limitations of your study and suggestions for future research following up on your research project.

REFERENCES

Immediately after the final part of the research report, starting on a fresh page, a list of the references cited in the literature review and in other places in the report will be given. The format of the references has been discussed and illustrated in the appendix to Chapter 5. Footnotes, if any in the text, are referenced either separately at the end of the report or at the bottom of the page where the footnote occurs.

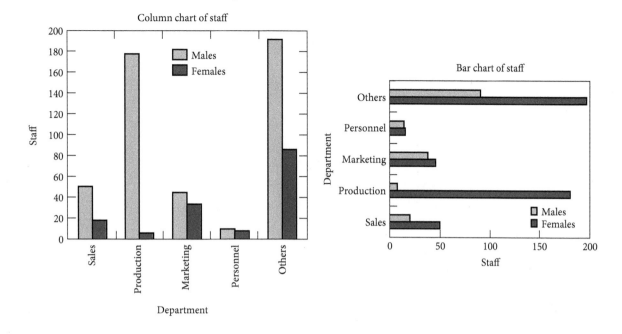

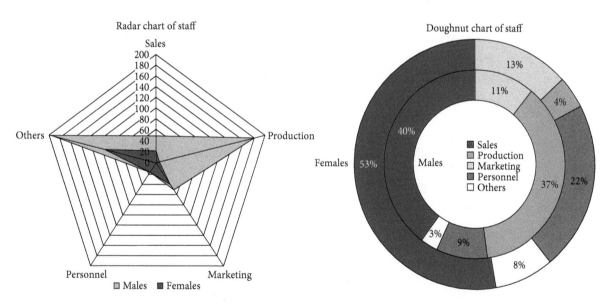

FIGURE 19.1   Pictorial representation of data

APPENDIX

The appendix, which comes last, is the appropriate place for the organization chart, newspaper clippings or other materials that substantiate the text of the report, detailed verbatim narration of interviews with members and whatever else might help the reader follow the text. It should also contain a copy of the questionnaire administered to the respondents. If there are several appendices, they should be referenced as Appendix A, Appendix B and so on and appropriately labelled.

The above will make clear that the table of contents (mentioned earlier), following the title page and the letter of transmittal, will look somewhat as indicated below, with some possible variations.

Example	Preface
Table of contents	• Introduction to your research report
	• Introduction
	• Definition of the management problem
	• Research objective(s)
	• Research questions
	• The scope of the study
	• Research method
	• Managerial relevance
	• Structure of the research report
	• Conceptual background and theoretical framework
	• Research design
	• Results
	• Conclusions
	• Recommendations
	• Limitations of study and suggestions for further research
	• References
	• Appendices

ORAL PRESENTATION

Usually organizations (and instructors in classes) require about a 20-minute oral presentation of the research project, followed by a question-and-answer session. The oral presentation calls for considerable planning. Imagine a study that spanned several months having to be presented in 20 minutes to a live audience! Those who have not read the report at all or at best only superficially, have to be convinced that the recommendations made therein will indeed prove to be beneficial to the organization. All this will have to be effectively accomplished in the matter of a few minutes.

The challenge is to present the important aspects of the study so as to hold the interest of the audience, while still providing detailed information, which may drive many to ennui. Different stimuli (charts, short movies, pictorial and tabular depiction, etc.) have to be creatively provided to the audience to sustain their interest throughout the presentation. To make all this possible, time and effort have to be expended in crafting, planning, organizing and rehearsing the presentation.

Check out the information provided on the TEDx Speaker Guide (www.ted.com) or review the 'TEDx Illustrated Guide for Speakers' document (http://storage.ted.com/tedx/manuals/IllustratedTEDxSpeakerGuide.pdf) for some guiding principles on how to draft and deliver a compelling talk.

Slides are often helpful for the audience – even though they are not necessary for every talk. Images, photos, graphs and infographics help you to sustain the interest of your audience. They also help you to discuss and explain the research project coherently, without reading from prepared notes.

Factors irrelevant to the written report, such as dress, mannerisms, gestures, voice modulation and the like, take on added importance in oral presentations. Speaking audibly, clearly, without distracting mannerisms and at the right speed for the audience to comprehend is vital for holding their attention. Varying the length of the sentences, establishing eye contact, tone variations, voice modulation and the rate of flow of information make all the difference to audience receptivity. That is why it is very important that you rehearse. The contents of the presentation, timing and the style of delivery should be practiced in detail. Keep rehearsing until you feel comfortable about your presentation.

DECIDING ON THE CONTENT

Because a lot of material has to be covered in, perhaps, a 20-minute presentation, it becomes necessary to decide on the points to focus on and the importance to be given to each. Remembering that the listener absorbs only a small proportion of all that he or she has heard, it is important to determine what the presenter would like the listener to walk away with, and then organize the presentation accordingly.

Obviously, the problem investigated, the results found, the conclusions drawn, the recommendations made and the ways in which they can be implemented are of vital interest to organizational members and need to be emphasized during the presentation. The design aspects of the study, details of the sample, data collection methods, details of data analysis and the like can be mentioned in passing to be picked up at the question-and-answer session by interested members.

However, depending on the type of audience, it may become necessary to put more stress on the data analytic aspects. For example, if the presentation is being made to a group of statisticians in the company, or in a research methods class, the data analyses and results will receive more time than if the project is being presented to a group of managers whose main interest lies in the solution to the problem and implementation of the recommendations. Thus, the time and attention devoted to the various components of the study will require adjustment, depending on the audience.

VISUAL AIDS

Graphs, charts and tables help to drive home the points one wishes to make much faster and more effectively, true to the adage that a picture is worth a thousand words. Visual aids provide a captivating sensory stimulus that sustains the attention of the audience. Slides, flip charts and handout materials also help the audience to easily follow the points of the speaker's focus. The selection of specific visual modes of presentation will depend, among other things, on the size of the room, the availability of a good screen for projection and the cost constraints of developing sophisticated visuals. Visuals that present side-by-side comparisons of the existing and would-be state of affairs via graphs or pie charts drive home the points made much more forcefully than elaborate and laborious verbal explanations.

Integrated multimedia presentations using PowerPoint, Prezi and other visuals are quite common in this technological age. When planning a presentation using PowerPoint or Prezi, it is important to ensure before the presentation starts that the related equipment is properly hooked up and tested so that the presentation can go smoothly without interruptions.

THE PRESENTER

An effective presentation is also a function of how 'unstressed' the presenter is. The speaker should establish eye contact with the audience, speak audibly and understandably and be sensitive to the non-verbal reactions of the audience. Strict adherence to the time frame and concentration on the points of interest to the audience are critical aspects of presentation. A display of extreme nervousness throughout the presentation, stumbling for words, fumbling with the notes or audiovisuals, speaking inaudibly and/or with distracting mannerisms, straying away from the main focus of the study and exceeding the time limit all detract from effectiveness. One should also not minimize the importance of the impression created on the audience by dress, posture, bearing and the confidence with which one carries oneself. Such simple things as covering the materials on the visuals until they need to be exhibited and voice modulation, help to focus the attention of the audience on the discussion.

THE PRESENTATION

The opening remarks set the stage for riveting the attention of the audience. Certain aspects such as the problem investigated, the findings, the conclusions drawn, the recommendations made and their implementation are, as previously mentioned, important aspects of the presentation. The speaker should drive home these points at least three times – once in the beginning, again when each of these areas is covered and finally, while summarizing and bringing the presentation to a conclusion.

HANDLING QUESTIONS

Concentrated and continuous research on the research topic over a considerable period of time indisputably makes the presenter more knowledgeable about the project than anyone else in the audience. Hence, it is not difficult to handle questions from the members with confidence and poise. It is important to be non-defensive when questions are posed that seemingly find fault with some aspect of the research. Openness to suggestions also helps, as the audience might, at times, come up with some excellent ideas or recommendations that the researcher might not have thought of. Such ideas must always be acknowledged graciously. If a question or a suggestion from a member in the audience happens to be flawed, it is best addressed in a non-judgemental fashion.

The question-and-answer session, when handled well, leaves the audience with a sense of involvement and satisfaction. Questioning should be encouraged and responded to with care. This interactive question-and-answer session offers an exciting experience both to the audience and to the presenter.

As may be readily seen, a 20-minute presentation and a short question-and-answer session thereafter do call for substantial planning, anticipation of audience concerns, psychological preparedness and good impression management skills.

Reporting has to be done in an honest and straightforward manner. It is unethical to fail to report findings that are unpalatable to the sponsors or that reflect poorly on management. As suggested earlier, it is possible to be tactful in presenting such findings without withholding or distorting information to please the sponsors. Internal researchers, in particular, will have to find ways of presenting unpopular information in a tactful manner. It is also important to state the limitations of the study – and practically every study has some limitation – so that the audience is not misled.

- **Learning objective 1: Describe the characteristics of a well-written research report that is tailored to the needs of a specific audience.** The written report should allow the reader to weigh the facts and arguments presented therein, to examine the results of the study, to reflect on the conclusions and recommendations and to implement the recommendations presented, with a view to solving the problem that catalysed the research project. Despite the fact that report writing is a function of the purpose of the study and the type of audience to which it is presented and accordingly has to be tailored to meet both, certain basic features are integral to all written reports. Clarity, conciseness, coherence and the right emphasis on important aspects are examples of characteristics of a well-written research report.

- **Learning objective 2: Write a thorough and complete research report.** The exact content and organization of the written report depend on the purpose of the research study and the audience to which it is targeted. In general, a research report has a title page, an executive summary or an abstract, a preface, a table of contents and (sometimes) a copy of the authorization to conduct the study. The introductory section details the problem studied, the purpose of the study and the research questions, giving some background of what it relates to and setting the stage for what the reader should expect in the rest of the report. The body of the report contains a conceptual background, the theoretical framework of the study and hypotheses, if any, the sampling design, data collection methods, analysis of data and the results obtained. The final part of the report should present the findings, conclusions and recommendations (for further research). A list of references cited in the report should then follow. Appendices should be attached to the report.

- **Learning objective 3: Describe the characteristics of a good oral presentation and deliver a good oral presentation.** Usually organizations require about a 20-minute oral presentation of the research project, followed by a question-and-answer session. The oral presentation calls for considerable planning: time and effort have to be expended in crafting, planning, organizing and rehearsing the presentation. Because a lot of material has to be covered, it becomes necessary to decide on the points to focus on and the importance to be given to each. The problem investigated, the results found, the conclusions drawn, the recommendations made and the ways in which they can be implemented are of vital interest to organizational members and need to be emphasized during the presentation.

Instructors can visit the companion website at **www.wiley.com/go/bougie/researchmethods forbusiness8e** for **Case Study: The Jupiter Consumer Electronics Chain**.

1. Discuss the purpose and contents of the executive summary.
2. What are the similarities and differences between basic and applied research reports?
3. How have technological advancements helped in writing and presenting research reports?
4. Why is it necessary to specify the limitations of the study in the research report?
5. What aspects of a class research project would be stressed by you in the written report and in the oral presentation?

Now do Exercises 19.1 and 19.2.

Critique Report 3 in the appendix. Discuss it in terms of good and bad research, suggesting how the study could have been improved, what aspects of it are good and how scientific it is.

Give a title to and write the introductory section of any study you might like to conduct.

Examples

<table>
<tr><td>

**REPORT 1:
SAMPLE OF
A REPORT
INVOLVING
A DESCRIPTIVE
STUDY**

</td><td>

Sekras Company

TO: Mr L. Raiburn, Chairman
Strategic Planning Committee
FR: Joanne Williams
Public Relations Officer
RE: Report requested by Mr Raiburn

Attached is the report requested by Mr Raiburn. If any further information or clarification is needed, please let me know.

Encl: Report

</td></tr>
</table>

REPORT FOR THE STRATEGIC PLANNING COMMITTEE

Introduction

Vice President Raiburn, Chairman of the Strategic Planning Committee, requested two pieces of information:

1. The sales figures of the top five retailers in the country.

2. Customers' ideas of what improvements can be made to Sekras to enhance their satisfaction. For this purpose, he desired that a quick survey of the company's customers be done to elicit their opinions.

Method Used for Obtaining the Requisite Information

Figures of sales of the top five retailers in the country were obtained from *BusinessWeek*, which periodically publishes many kinds of industry statistics.

To obtain customers' inputs on improvements that could be made by the company, a short questionnaire (specimen in Appendix A) was mailed to 300 of our credit card customers – 100 who had most frequently used the card in the last 18 months, 100 who most infrequently used it during the same period and 100 average users. Questionnaires in three different colors were sent to the three groups. Respondents were offered a complimentary magnet for responses received within a week. The questionnaire asked for responses to three questions:

1. What are some of the things you like best about shopping at Sekras?

2. What are some of the things that you dislike and would like to see improved at Sekras? Please explain in as much detail as possible.

3. What are your specific suggestions for making improvements to enhance the quality of our service to customers like you?

Findings

Sales figures of the top five retailers Information regarding sales of the top five retailers in 2015 and 2018 is provided in Table 19.1.

As can be seen, Wal-Mart and Home Depot retained their top positions in 2018. Kroger (a supermarket chain with 2532 grocery stores in 32 states) which was not among the top five in 2015, occupied the third place in 2018, whereas Costco (an international chain of membership warehouses, primarily under the 'Costco Wholesale' name) occupied the fourth place. Target (the company's stores offer men's and women's clothing, home furnishings, electronic products, sports products, toys and entertainment products) retained the fifth position in 2018. Sears, Roebuck and Kmart did not find a place among the top five retailers during 2018. It may be observed that even though Wal-Mart increased its sales by about 1.33 times during the three-year period, its share among the top five did not increase.

Customer suggestions for improvements Of the 300 surveys sent out, 225 were received, a 75 percent response rate. Of the 100 most frequent users of our credit card to whom questionnaires were sent, 80 responded; among the most infrequent users, 60 responded; and among the average users, 85 responded.

About 75 percent of the respondents were women. The majority of the customers were between the ages of 35 and 55 (62 percent).

TABLE 19.1 Comparative Sales Figures of the Five Top Retail Companies During 2015 and 2018

Top retailers in 2015			Top retailers in 2018		
Company	Sales in billions of $	Share among top five	Company	Sales in billions of $	Share among top five
Wal-Mart Stores	191.33	54.7%	Wal-Mart Stores	256.0	53.4%
Home Depot	45.74	13.1%	Home Depot	73.10	15.2%
Sears, Roebuck	40.94	11.7%	Kroger	56.40	11.8%
Kmart	36.50	10.3%	Costco	47.15	9.8%
Target	35.51	10.2%	Target	46.80	9.8%

Source: Businessweek

The responses to the three open-ended questions were analysed. The information needed by the Committee on the suggested improvements is tabulated (see Table 19.2). Responses to the other two questions on features liked by the customers and their specific suggestions for improvement, are provided in the two tables in the appendix. The following are suggestions received from one or two respondents only:

1. Have more water fountains on each floor.
2. The pushcarts could be lighter, so they will be less difficult to push.
3. More seats for resting after long hours of shopping would help.
4. Prices of luxury items are too high.

From looking at Table 19.2, it can be seen that the most dissatisfaction stems from (1) out-of-stock small appliances and (2) inability to locate store assistants who could guide customers in locating what they need (44 percent each). The need for child care services is expressed by 38 percent of the customers. Twenty percent also indicate that the cafeteria should cater to tastes for international spicy type of foods. The next two important items pertain to the temperature (18 percent) and billing mistakes (16 percent). Some customers (16 percent) also wish the store was open 24 hours.

The rest of the suggestions were offered by less than 10 percent of the customers and, hence, can perhaps be attended to later.

TABLE 19.2 Suggested Areas for Improvement

Features	Frequent users no.	Medium users no.	Infrequent users no.	Total no.	%
1. Small appliances such as mixers, blenders are often not in stock. This is irritating.	30	48	22	100	44
2. The cafeteria serves only bland, uninteresting food. How about some spicy international food?	26	14	5	45	20
3. Often, we are unable to locate where the items we want are!	3	6	14	23	10
4. It would be nice if you could have a child care service so we can shop without distractions.	28	32	25	85	38
5. It is often difficult to locate an assistant who can help us with answers to our questions.	29	49	22	100	44
6. I wish it were a 24-hour store.	17	13	7	37	16
7. Sometimes, there is a mistake in billing. We have to make some telephone calls before charges are corrected. This is a waste of our time.	4	12	14	20	16
8. Allocate some floor space for kids to play video games.	2	—	4	6	2
9. Import more Eastern apparel like the kimono, sarees, sarongs.	—	8	4	12	5
10. Regulate the temperature better; often, it is too cold or too hot.	15	12	17	44	18

A note of caution is in order at this juncture. We are not sure how representative our sample is. We thought that a mix of high, average and infrequent users of our credit card would provide us with some useful insights. If a more detailed study obtaining information from a sample of all the customers who come to the store is considered necessary, we will initiate it quickly. In the meantime, we are also interviewing a few of the customers who shop here daily. If we find anything of significance from these interviews, we will inform you.

Improvements Indicated by These Suggestions

Based on the current sample of customers who have responded to our survey, the following improvements and actions seem called for:

1. Small appliances need to be adequately stocked (44% complained about this). An effective reorder inventory system has to be developed for this department to minimize customer dissatisfaction and avoid loss of sales for lack of sufficient stock. The research team can help in this, if requested.

2. Customers seem to need help to locate store items and would appreciate help from store assistants (44 percent expressed this need). If providing assistance is a primary concern, it

would be a good idea to have liveried store personnel with badges to indicate they are there to assist customers. During idle hours, if any (when there are no customers seeking help), these individuals can be deployed as shelf organizers.

3. Need for child care has been expressed by more than a third of our customers (38 percent). It would be a good idea to earmark a portion of the front of the building for parents to drop off their children while shopping. The children will have to be supervised by a trained child care professional recruited by the organization. An assistant could be recruited later if needed. From the cost–benefit analysis in Exhibit 7, it may be seen that this additional expenditure will pay off multifold in sales revenue and at the same time, create a fund of goodwill for the company.

4. Adding to the variety of foods served in the cafeteria (a need expressed by 20 percent) is at once a simple and a complex matter. We need further ideas and details as to what types of food need to be added. This information can be obtained through a short survey, if Mr Raiburn so desires.

5. Billing errors should not occur (16 percent indicated this). The billing department should be warned that such mistakes should be avoided and should not recur. Performance assessment should be tied to such mistakes.

6. Regulation of temperature (16 percent identified this) is easy. This, in fact, could be immediately attended to by the engineering department personnel.

I hope this report contains all the information sought by Mr Raiburn. As stated earlier, if the non-credit card customers also have to be sampled, this can be easily arranged.

TO: Mr Charles Orient, CEO, Lunard Manufacturing Company
FR: Alex Ventura, Senior Researcher, Beam Research Team
RE: Suggestions on alternative ways of cutting costs in anticipation of recession.

Enclosed is the report requested by Mr Orient. If any additional Information or clarification is needed, please let me know.
   Encl: Report

> **REPORT 2: SAMPLE OF A REPORT OFFERING ALTERNATIVE SOLUTIONS AND EXPLAINING THE PROS AND CONS OF EACH ALTERNATIVE**

REPORT ON ALTERNATIVE WAYS OF HANDLING RECESSIONARY TIMES WITHOUT MASSIVE LAYOFFS

Introduction

The Beam Research Team was asked to suggest alternative ways of tiding over the anticipated recession of the next several months, when a slowdown of the economy is expected. A recent article in *BusinessWeek* entitled 'Hunkering Down in a Hurry' indicated that executives in a large number of companies are slashing costs mostly through layoffs and restructuring. Mr Orient wanted the Beam Research Team to suggest other alternatives besides layoffs.

   This report provides five alternatives citing the advantages and disadvantages of each.

Method Used for Developing the Alternatives

The team studied the economic indicators and the published industry analyses, read the Federal Reserve Board Chairman's speeches, examined the many ways in which companies cut costs during non-recessionary periods as well as recessions and, based on these, suggests the following five alternatives.

Alternatives suggested:

1. A moratorium on all capital expenditure.

2. Hiring freeze.

3. Recovery of bad debts through sustained efforts.

4. Trimming of operating expenditure with substantial reduction in travel and entertainment expenditure.

5. Discontinuance of the manufacture of low-profit-margin products.

Advantages and Disadvantages of Each of the Above

Itemized details of the cost–benefit analysis for each of the above suggestions are furnished in the appendix. We give only the net benefits for each alternative here.

Moratorium on all capital expenditure It makes good sense to desist from all capital expenditure since manufacture of most of the items will slow down during recession. Except for parts for existing machines, there is no need to buy capital equipment and all proposals in this regard should be shelved.

This strategy will cut down expenditure to the extent of 7–10 percent of revenue. See appendix for full details. A reserve fund can be created to catch up with future orders when the economy returns to normal.

Hiring freeze The annual increase in the strength of staff during the past four years has been about 15 percent. With a slowdown of the economy, a hiring freeze in all branch offices will save over $10 million annually.

This might initially result in some extra workload for the staff and cause some job dissatisfaction, but once they get used to it and the impact of the actual recession hits them, employees will be thankful for the job they have. It will be a good idea to explain in advance the reasons for the hiring freeze to the employees so that they understand the motive behind the company's policy and appreciate having been informed.

Recovery of bad debts through aggressive efforts Bad debts of the company have been on the increase over the past three years and no intensive efforts to recover them seem to have been made hitherto.

We suggest that collection agents who have successfully recovered bad debts for other companies be hired immediately. Such agents may have to be paid more than other collection agents, but the extra cost will be well worth it. About a billion dollars can be collected within a few weeks of their being on the job and this will help the financial cash flow of the company.

Trimming of operating expenditure Several operating expenses can be cut down – the travel expenses of managers in particular – as shown in Exhibit 4 of the appendix. Videoconferencing costs much less and is quicker and should be encouraged for most of the meetings and negotiations. This alone will result in savings of more than $175000 per month.

Another way of considerably curtailing expenditure is to restrict entertainment expenses only for such purposes and to such managers as actively promote the business of the company or are essential for public relations.

These changes will have a negative impact on morale, but managers understand the economic situation and will adjust to the new system once the initial mental resistance wears off.

Eliminating the manufacture of low-margin products   The team found from a detailed study of the company records of manufacturing, sales and profits figures for the various products that all the items listed in Exhibit 5 of the appendix have very low profit margins. It is evident from the data provided that considerable time and effort are expended in manufacturing and selling these items.

It will be useful to phase out the manufacture of these items and divert the resources to the high-profit items suggested in Exhibit 6. From the cost–benefit analysis in Exhibit 7, it may be seen that several billions can be saved through this strategy.

It is possible to put into effect all of the five alternatives above and handle the onslaught of the recession with confidence.

FACTORS AFFECTING THE UPWARD MOBILITY OF WOMEN IN PUBLIC ACCOUNTING

> **REPORT 3: EXAMPLE OF AN ABRIDGED BASIC RESEARCH REPORT**

Introduction

A substantial number of women have entered the public accounting profession in the past 15 years or so. However, less than 4 percent of the partners in the big eight accounting firms are women, indicating a lack of upward mobility for women in the accounting profession. Against the backdrop of the fact that the women students perform significantly better during their academic training than their male counterparts, it is unfortunate that their intellectual ability and knowledge remain underutilized during their professional careers. The recent costly litigation and discrimination suits filed make it imperative for us to study the factors that affect the upward mobility of women and examine how the situation can be rectified.

A Brief Literature Review

Studies of male and female accounting majors indicate that the percentage of women accounting students has increased severalfold since 1977 (Kurian, 1998). Based on the analysis of longitudinal data collected over a 15-year period, Mulcher, Turner and Williams (2000) found that female students' grades in senior accounting courses were significantly higher than those of the male students. This higher level of academic performance has been theorized as being due to the higher need and desire that women have to achieve and overcome stereotypes (Messing, 2000), having higher career aspirations (Tinsley et al., 1999) or having a higher aptitude for accounting (Jones & Alexander, 2001; Riley, 2001). Empirical studies by Fraser, Lytle and Stolle (1998) and Johnson and Meyer (1999), however, found no significant differences in personality predispositions or behavioural traits among male and female accounting majors.

Several surveys of women accountants in the country pinpoint three major factors that hinder women's career progress in the public accounting field (see, for instance, Kaufman, 1986; Larson, 1999; Walkup & Fenman, 2001). They are: (1) the long hours of work demanded by the profession (a factor that conflicts with family demands); (2) failure to be entrusted with responsible assignments; and (3) discrimination. In sum, the lack of upward mobility seems to be due to factors over which the organization has some control.

Research Question

Do long work hours, failure to be handed greater responsibilities and discrimination account for the lack of upward mobility of women in public accounting?

Theoretical Framework

The variance in the dependent variable, upward mobility, can be explained by the three independent variables: long hours of work, not handling greater responsibilities and discrimination. As women are expected to and do indeed, take on responsibility for household work and childrearing, they are not able to work beyond regular work hours at the workplace. This creates the wrong impression among higher-ups in the organization that women are less committed to their work. Because of this perception, they are not entrusted with significant responsibilities. This further hinders their progress as they are not afforded exposure to the intricacies of accounting practices as much as men. Hence, women are overlooked at the time of promotion.

Deliberate discriminatory practices due to sex-role stereotypes, as evidenced in the well-known case of *Hopkins vs. Price Waterhouse & Co.*, also arrest women's progress. If women are not valued for their potential and are expected to conform to sex-typed behaviour (which confines them to inconspicuous roles), their chances of moving up the career ladder are significantly reduced.

Thus, the three independent variables considered here would significantly explain the variance in the upward mobility of women in public accounting. The impracticability of putting in long hours of work, lack of opportunities to handle greater responsibilities and sex-role stereotyping all negatively impact upward mobility.

Hypotheses

If women spend more hours on the job after regular work hours, they will be given greater responsibilities.

If women are entrusted with higher levels of responsibility, they will have more opportunities to move up in the organization.

If women are not expected to conform to stereotypical behaviour, their chances for upward mobility will increase.

All three independent variables will significantly explain the variance in women CPAs' upward mobility.

Method Section

Study design In this cross-sectional correlational field study, data on the three independent variables and the dependent variable were collected from women CPAs in several public accounting organizations in the country through mail questionnaires.

Population and sample The population for the study comprised all women CPAs in the country. A systematic sampling procedure was first used to select 30 cities from the various regions of the country, from which a sample of accounting firms would be drawn. Then, through a simple random sampling procedure, five CPA firms from each of the cities were chosen for the study. Data were collected from all the women in each of the firms so chosen. The total sample size was 300 and responses were received from 264 women CPAs, for an 88 percent response rate for the mail questionnaires, which is pretty good. The unit of analysis was the individuals who responded to the survey.

All respondents had, as expected, the CPA degree. Their ages ranged from 28 to 66. About 60 percent of the women were over 45 years of age. The average number of children in the house below the age of 13 was two. The average number of years of work in the organization was 15 and the average number of organizations worked for was two. The average number of hours spent daily at home on office-related matters was 1.4.

Variables and measures   All demographic variables such as age, number of years in the organization, number of other organizations in which the individual had worked, number of hours spent at home on office-related matters and number of children in the house and their ages were tapped by direct single questions.

Upward mobility. This dependent variable indicates the extent to which individuals are expected to progress in their career during the succeeding three to ten years. Hall (1986) developed four items to measure this variable, a sample item being: 'I see myself being promoted to the next level quite easily'. The measure is reported to have convergent and discriminant validity and Cronbach's alpha for the four items for this sample was 0.86.

Sex-role stereotyping. This independent variable was measured using Hall and Humphreys' (1972) eight-item measure. An example item is: 'Men in this organization do not consider women's place to be primarily in the home'. Cronbach's alpha for the measure for this sample was 0.82.

Responsibilities assigned. This was tapped by three items from Sonnenfield and McGrath (1983), which asked respondents to indicate their levels of assigned responsibility to (a) make important decisions, (b) handle large accounts and (c) account for the annual profits of the firm. Cronbach's alpha for the three items was 0.71 for this sample.

Data collection method   Questionnaires were mailed to 300 women CPAs in the United States. After two reminders, 264 completed questionnaires were received within a period of six weeks. The high return rate of 88% can be attributed to the shortness of the questionnaire and perhaps the motivation of the women CPAs to respond to a topic close to their heart.

Questionnaires were not electronically administered for various reasons, including the advantage it afforded to the busy respondents to reply without switching on the computer.

Data analysis and results   After determining the reliabilities (Cronbach's alpha) for the measures for this sample, frequency distributions for the demographic variables were obtained. These may be seen in Exhibit 1. Then a Pearson correlation matrix was obtained for the four independent and dependent variables. This may be seen in Exhibit 2. It is to be noted that no correlation exceeded 0.6.

Each hypothesis was then tested. The correlation matrix provided the answer to the first three hypotheses. The first hypothesis stated that the number of hours put in beyond work hours on office-related matters would be positively correlated to the responsibilities assigned. The correlation of 0.56 ($p < 0.001$) between the number of hours spent on office work beyond regular work hours and the entrusted responsibilities substantiates this hypothesis.

The second hypothesis stated that if women were given higher responsibilities, their upward mobility would improve. The positive correlation of 0.59 ($p < 0.001$) between the two variables substantiates this hypothesis. That is, the greater the entrusted responsibilities, the higher are the perceived chances of being promoted.

The third hypothesis indicated that sex-role stereotyping would be negatively correlated to upward mobility. The correlation of -0.54 ($p < 0.001$) substantiates this hypothesis as well. That is, the greater the expected conformity to stereotyped behaviour, the less the chances of upward mobility.

To test the fourth hypothesis that the number of hours spent beyond regular work hours on job-related matters, assignment of higher responsibilities and expectations of conformity with stereotyped behaviour will significantly explain the variance in perceived upward mobility, the three independent variables were regressed against the dependent variable. The results, which are shown in Exhibit 3, indicate that this hypothesis is also substantiated. That is, the R^2 value of 0.43 at a significance level of $p < 0.001$, with df (3.238), confirms that 43 percent of the variance in upward mobility is significantly explained by the three independent variables.

Discussion of results The results of this study confirm that the variables considered in the theoretical framework are important. By focusing solely on the number of hours worked, ignoring the quality of work done, the organization is perhaps not harnessing the full potential and encouraging the development of the talents of the women CPAs adequately. It seems worth while to remedy this situation.

It would be useful if the top executives were to assign progressively higher levels of responsibility to women. This would utilize their abilities fully and, in turn, enhance the effectiveness of the firm. If executives are helped to modify their mental attitudes and sex-role expectations, they should tend to expect less stereotypical behaviour and encourage the upward mobility of women CPAs. Knowing women bring a different kind of perspective to organizational matters (Smith, 1999; Vernon, 2001), it is quite possible that having them as partners of the firm will enhance the organizational effectiveness as well.

Recommendations It is recommended that a system be set up to assess the value of the contributions of each individual in discharging his or her duties and use that, rather than the number of hours of work put in, as a yardstick for promotion.

Second, women CPAs should be given progressively more responsibility after they have served three to five years in the system. Assigning a mentor to train them will facilitate smooth functioning of the firm.

Third, a short seminar should be organized for executives to sensitize them to the adverse effects of sex-role stereotyping at the workplace. This will help them to beneficially utilize the talents of women CPAs. If viewed as professionals with career goals and aspirations, rather than in stereotyped ways, women CPAs will be enabled to handle more responsibilities and advance in the system. The organization also stands to benefit from their contributions.

In conclusion, it would be worth while for public accounting firms to modify their mental orientations toward and expectations of, women CPAs. It is a national waste if their potential is not fully tapped and utilized.

A Final Note to Students

If you have enjoyed learning about research and built up a repertoire of research skills, you are prepared and ready for your professional life. Earlier in the book we have explained how research helps managers to get a grip on issues, concerns and conflicts within the company or in its environment, to take effective decisions and to develop effective courses of action. As you must have realized from these and other discussions in this book, research is an integral part of organizational reality that helps businesses to continuously improve and grow progressively.

Though you may not have become an *expert* researcher after one semester of coursework, and perhaps a research project, we are sure you would have gained an intelligent appreciation of, and an adequate depth of knowledge for, business research – great assets in dealing effectively with consultants. The ability to discriminate between the good and the not-so-good research will also be invaluable to you in sifting through the materials you will undoubtedly read in the practitioner and academic journals in your professional life as managers. And, more important, as you get deluged by all the information from various sources, including the Internet, newspapers, talk shows and the like, you will be better able to evaluate the validity of the messages and judge them for what they truly represent. You are thus armed to handle the information overload that one faces in today's information age.

If you have satisfactorily met the chapter objectives, you can be confident that you have taken a giant step toward becoming even more effective as a manager.

Research is the excitement of exploring avenues for problem solving, and as a manager you will find the research knowledge and skills you have now acquired to be extremely useful. Research, when applied with good common sense, yields the desired results.

We wish you success in your personal, academic and professional careers!

— ROGER BOUGIE AND UMA SEKARAN

Statistical Tables

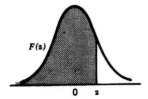

Table I   Cumulative Normal Probabilities

z	F(z)	z	F(z)
0.00	0.5000000	0.28	0.6102612
0.01	0.5039894	0.29	0.6140919
0.02	0.5079783	0.30	0.6179114
0.03	0.5119665	0.31	0.6217195
0.04	0.5159534	0.32	0.6255158
0.05	0.5199388	0.33	0.6293000
0.06	0.5239222	0.34	0.6330717
0.07	0.5279032	0.35	0.6368307
0.08	0.5318814	0.36	0.6405764
0.09	0.5358564	0.37	0.6443088
0.10	0.5398278	0.38	0.6480273
0.11	0.5437953	0.39	0.6517317
0.12	0.5477584	0.40	0.6554217
0.13	0.5517168	0.41	0.6590970
0.14	0.5556700	0.42	0.6627573
0.15	0.5596177	0.43	0.6664022
0.16	0.5635595	0.44	0.6700314
0.17	0.5674949	0.45	0.6736448
0.18	0.5714237	0.46	0.6772419
0.19	0.5753454	0.47	0.6808225
0.20	0.5792597	0.48	0.6843863
0.21	0.5831662	0.49	0.6879331
0.22	0.5870604	0.50	0.6914625
0.23	0.5909541	0.51	0.6949743
0.24	0.5948349	0.52	0.6984682
0.25	0.5987063	0.53	0.7019440
0.26	0.6025681	0.54	0.7054015
0.27	0.6064199	0.55	0.7088403

(continued)

(continued)

z	F(z)	z	F(z)
0.56	0.7122603	0.98	0.8364569
0.57	0.7156612	0.99	0.8389129
0.58	0.7190427	1.00	0.8413447
0.59	0.7224047	1.01	0.8437524
0.60	0.7257469	1.02	0.8461358
0.61	0.7290691	1.03	0.8484950
0.62	0.7323711	1.04	0.8508300
0.63	0.7356527	1.05	0.8531409
0.64	0.7389137	1.06	0.8554277
0.65	0.7421539	1.07	0.8576903
0.66	0.7453731	1.08	0.8599289
0.67	0.7485711	1.09	0.8621434
0.68	0.7517478	1.10	0.8643339
0.69	0.7549029	1.11	0.8665005
0.70	0.7580363	1.12	0.8686431
0.71	0.7611479	1.13	0.8707619
0.72	0.7642375	1.14	0.8728568
0.73	0.7673049	1.15	0.8749281
0.74	0.7703500	1.16	0.8769756
0.75	0.7733726	1.17	0.8789995
0.76	0.7763727	1.18	0.8809999
0.77	0.7793501	1.19	0.8829768
0.78	0.7823046	1.20	0.8849303
0.79	0.7852361	1.21	0.8868606
0.80	0.7881446	1.22	0.8887676
0.81	0.7910299	1.23	0.8906514
0.82	0.7938919	1.24	0.8925123
0.83	0.7967306	1.25	0.8943502
0.84	0.7995458	1.26	0.8961653
0.85	0.8023375	1.27	0.8979577
0.86	0.8051055	1.28	0.8997274
0.87	0.8078498	1.29	0.9014747
0.88	0.8105703	1.30	0.9031995
0.89	0.8132671	1.31	0.9049021
0.90	0.8159399	1.32	0.9065825
0.91	0.8185887	1.33	0.9082409
0.92	0.8212136	1.34	0.9098773
0.93	0.8238145	1.35	0.9114920
0.94	0.8263912	1.36	0.9130850
0.95	0.8289439	1.37	0.9146565
0.96	0.8314724	1.38	0.9162067
0.97	0.8339768	1.39	0.9177356

(continued)

z	F(z)	z	F(z)
1.40	0.9192433	1.82	0.9656205
1.41	0.9207302	1.83	0.9663750
1.42	0.9221962	1.84	0.9671159
1.43	0.9236415	1.85	0.9678432
1.44	0.9250663	1.86	0.9685572
1.45	0.9264707	1.87	0.9692581
1.46	0.9278550	1.88	0.9699460
1.47	0.9292191	1.89	0.9706210
1.48	0.9305634	1.90	0.9712834
1.49	0.9318879	1.91	0.9719334
1.50	0.9331928	1.92	0.9725711
1.51	0.9344783	1.93	0.9731966
1.52	0.9357445	1.94	0.9738102
1.53	0.9369916	1.95	0.9744119
1.54	0.9382198	1.96	0.9750021
1.55	0.9394292	1.97	0.9755808
1.56	0.9406201	1.98	0.9761482
1.57	0.9417924	1.99	0.9767045
1.58	0.9429466	2.00	0.9772499
1.59	0.9440826	2.01	0.9777844
1.60	0.9452007	2.02	0.9783083
1.61	0.9463011	2.03	0.9788217
1.62	0.9473839	2.04	0.9793248
1.63	0.9484493	2.05	0.9798178
1.64	0.9494974	2.06	0.9803007
1.65	0.9505285	2.07	0.9807738
1.66	0.9515428	2.08	0.9812372
1.67	0.9525403	2.09	0.9816911
1.68	0.9535213	2.10	0.9821356
1.69	0.9544860	2.11	0.9825708
1.70	0.9554345	2.12	0.9829970
1.71	0.9563671	2.13	0.9834142
1.72	0.9572838	2.14	0.9838226
1.73	0.9581849	2.15	0.9842224
1.74	0.9590705	2.16	0.9846137
1.75	0.9599408	2.17	0.9849966
1.76	0.9607961	2.18	0.9853713
1.77	0.9616364	2.19	0.9857379
1.78	0.9624620	2.20	0.9860966
1.79	0.9632730	2.21	0.9864474
1.80	0.9640697	2.22	0.9867906
1.81	0.9648521	2.23	0.9871263

(continued)

(continued)

z	F(z)	z	F(z)
2.24	0.9874545	2.49	0.9936128
2.25	0.9877755	2.50	0.9937903
2.26	0.9880894	2.51	0.9939634
2.27	0.9883962	2.52	0.9941323
2.28	0.9886962	2.53	0.9942969
2.29	0.9889893	2.54	0.9944574
2.30	0.9892759	2.55	0.9946139
2.31	0.9895559	2.56	0.9947664
2.32	0.9898296	2.57	0.9949151
2.33	0.9900969	2.58	0.9950600
2.34	0.9903581	2.59	0.9952012
2.35	0.9906133	2.60	0.9953388
2.36	0.9908625	2.70	0.9965330
2.37	0.9911060	2.80	0.9974449
2.38	0.9913437	2.90	0.9981342
2.39	0.9915758	3.00	0.9986501
2.40	0.9918025	3.20	0.9993129
2.41	0.9920237	3.40	0.9996631
2.42	0.9922397	3.60	0.9998409
2.43	0.9924506	3.80	0.9999277
2.44	0.9926564	4.00	0.9999683
2.45	0.9928572	4.50	0.9999966
2.46	0.9930531	5.00	0.9999997
2.47	0.9932443	5.50	0.9999999
2.48	0 9934309		

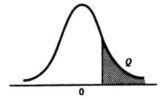

Table II   Upper Percentage Points of the *t* Distribution

v	$Q = 0.4$ $2Q = 0.8$	0.25 0.5	0.1 0.2	0.05 0.1	0.025 0.05	0.01 0.02	0.005 0.01	0.001 0.002
1	0.325	1.000	3.078	6.314	12.706	31.821	63.657	318.31
2	0.289	0.816	1.886	2.920	4.303	6.965	9.925	22.326
3	0.277	0.765	1.638	2.353	3.182	4.541	5.841	10.213
4	0.271	0.741	1.533	2.132	2.776	3.747	4.604	7.173
5	0.267	0.727	1.476	2.015	2.571	3.365	4.032	5.893
6	0.265	0.718	1.440	1.943	2.447	3.143	3.707	5.208
7	0.263	0.711	1.415	1.895	2.365	2.998	3.499	4.785
8	0.262	0.706	1.397	1.860	2.306	2.896	3.355	4.501
9	0.261	0.703	1.383	1.833	2.262	2.821	3.250	4.297
10	0.260	0.700	1.372	1.812	2.228	2.764	3.169	4.144
11	0.260	0.697	1.363	1.796	2.201	2.718	3.106	4.025
12	0.259	0.695	1.356	1.782	2.179	2.681	3.055	3.930
13	0.259	0.694	1.350	1.771	2.160	2.650	3.012	3.852
14	0.258	0.692	1.345	1.761	2.145	2.624	2.977	3.787
15	0.258	0.691	1.341	1.753	2.131	2.602	2.947	3.733
16	0.258	0.690	1.337	1.746	2.120	2.583	2.921	3.686
17	0.257	0.689	1.333	1.740	2.110	2.567	2.898	3.646
18	0.257	0.688	1.330	1.734	2.101	2.552	2.878	3.610
19	0.257	0.688	1.328	1.729	2.093	2.539	2.861	3.579
20	0.257	0.687	1.325	1.725	2.086	2.528	2.845	3.552
21	0.257	0.686	1.323	1.721	2.080	2.518	2.831	3.527
22	0.256	0.686	1.321	1.717	2.074	2.508	2.819	3.505
23	0.256	0.685	1.319	1.714	2.069	2.500	2.807	3.485
24	0.256	0.685	1.318	1.711	2.064	2.492	2.797	3.467
25	0.256	0.684	1.316	1.708	2.060	2.485	2.787	3.450
26	0.256	0.684	1.315	1.706	2.056	2.479	2.779	3.435
27	0.256	0.684	1.314	1.703	2.052	2.473	2.771	3.421
28	0.256	0.683	1.313	1.701	2.048	2.467	2.763	3.408
29	0.256	0.683	1.311	1.699	2.045	2.462	2.756	3.396
30	0.256	0.683	1.310	1.697	2.042	2.457	2.750	3.385
40	0.255	0.681	1.303	1.684	2.021	2.423	2.704	3.307
60	0.254	0.679	1.296	1.671	2.000	2.390	2.660	3.232
120	0.254	0.677	1.289	1.658	1.980	2.358	2.617	3.160
∞	0.253	0.674	1.282	1.645	1.960	2.326	2.576	3.090

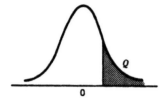

TABLE III Upper Percentage Points of the χ^2 Distribution

Q υ	0.995	0.990	0.975	0.950	0.900	0.750	0.500
1	392704.10^{-10}	157088.10^{-9}	982069.10^{-9}	393214.10^{-8}	0.0157908	0.1015308	0.454937
2	0.0100251	0.0201007	0.0506356	0.102587	0.210720	0.575364	1.38629
3	0.0717212	0.114832	0.215795	0.351846	0.584375	1.212534	2.36597
4	0.206990	0.297110	0.484419	0.710721	1.063623	1.92255	3.35670
5	0.411740	0.554300	0.831211	1.145476	1.61031	2.67460	4.35146
6	0.675727	0.872085	1.237347	1.63539	2.20413	3.45460	5.34812
7	0.989265	1.239043	1.68987	2.16735	2.83311	4.25485	6.34581
8	1.344419	1.646482	2.17973	2.73264	3.48954	5.07064	7.34412
9	1.734926	2.087912	2.70039	3.32511	4.16816	5.89883	8.34283
10	2.15585	2.55821	3.24697	3.94030	4.86518	6.73720	9.34182
11	2.60321	3.05347	3.81575	4.57481	5.57779	7.58412	10.3410
12	3.07382	3.57056	4.40379	5.22603	6.30380	8.43842	11.3403
13	3.56503	4.10691	5.00874	5.89186	7.04150	9.29906	12.3398
14	4.07468	4.66043	5.62872	6.57063	7.78953	10.1653	13.3393
15	4.60094	5.22935	6.26214	7.26094	8.54675	11.0365	14.3389
16	5.14224	5.81221	6.90766	7.96164	9.31223	11.9122	15.3385
17	5.69724	6.40776	7.56418	8.67176	10.0852	12.7919	16.3381
18	6.26481	7.01491	8.23075	9.39046	10.8649	13.6753	17.3379
19	6.84398	7.63273	8.90655	10.1170	11.6509	14.5620	18.3376
20	7.43386	8.26040	9.59083	10.8508	12.4426	15.4518	19.3374
21	8.03366	8.89720	10.28293	11.5913	13.2396	16.3444	20.3372
22	8.64272	9.54249	10.9823	12.3380	14.0415	17.2396	21.3370
23	9.26042	10.19567	11.6885	13.0905	14.8479	18.1373	22.3369
24	9.88623	10.8564	12.4011	13.8484	15.6587	19.0372	23.3367
25	10.5197	11.5240	13.1197	14.6114	16.4734	19.9393	24.3366
26	11.1603	12.1981	13.8439	15.3791	17.2919	20.8434	25.3364
27	11.8076	12.8786	14.5733	16.1513	18.1138	21.7494	26.3363
28	12.4613	13.5648	15.3079	16.9279	18.9392	22.6572	27.3363
29	13.1211	14.2565	16.0471	17.7083	19.7677	23.5666	28.3362
30	13.7867	14.9535	16.7908	18.4926	20.5992	24.4776	29.3360
40	20.7065	22.1643	24.4331	26.5093	29.0505	33.6603	39.3354
50	27.9907	29.7067	32.3574	34.7642	37.6886	42.9421	49.3349
60	35.5346	37.4848	40.4817	43.1879	46.4589	52.2938	59.3347
70	43.2752	45.4418	48.7576	51.7393	55.3290	61.6983	69.3344
80	51.1720	53.5400	57.1532	60.3915	64.2778	71.1445	79.3343
90	59.1963	61.7541	65.6466	69.1260	73.2912	80.6247	89.3342
100	67.3276	70.0648	74.2219	77.9295	82.3581	90.1332	99.3341
Z_Q	−2.5758	−2.3263	−1.9600	−1.6449	−1.2816	−0.6745	0.0000

(continued)

Q							
v	0.250	0.100	0.050	0.025	0.010	0.005	0.001
1	1.32330	2.70554	3.84146	5.02389	6.63490	7.87944	10.828
2	2.77259	4.60517	5.99147	7.37776	9.21034	10.5966	13.816
3	4.10835	6.25139	7.81473	9.34840	11.3449	12.8381	16.266
4	5.38527	7.77944	9.48773	11.1433	13.2767	14.8602	18.467
5	6.62568	9.23635	11.0705	12.8325	15.0863	16.7496	20.515
6	7.84080	10.6446	12.5916	14.4494	16.8119	18.5476	22.458
7	9.03715	12.0170	14.0671	16.0128	18.4753	20.2777	24.322
8	10.2188	13.3616	15.5073	17.5346	20.0902	21.9550	26.125
9	11.3887	14.6837	16.9190	19.0228	21.6660	23.5893	27.877
10	12.5489	15.9871	18.3070	20.4831	23.2093	25.1882	29.588
11	13.7007	17.2750	19.6751	21.9200	24.7250	26.7569	31.264
12	14.8454	18.5494	21.0261	23.3367	26.2170	28.2995	32.909
13	15.9839	19.8119	22.3621	24.7356	27.6883	29.8194	34.528
14	17.1170	21.0642	23.6848	26.1190	29.1413	31.3193	36.123
15	18.2451	22.3072	24.9958	27.4884	30.5779	32.8013	37.697
16	19.3688	23.5418	26.2962	28.8454	31.9999	34.2672	39.252
17	20.4887	24.7690	27.5871	30.1910	33.4087	35.7185	40.790
18	21.6049	25.9894	28.8693	31.5264	34.8053	37.1564	42.312
19	22.71578	27.2036	30.1435	32.8523	36.1908	38.5822	43.820
20	23.8277	28.4120	31.4104	34.1696	37.5662	39.9968	45.315
21	24.9348	29.6151	32.6705	35.4789	38.9321	41.4010	46.797
22	26.0393	30.8133	33.9244	36.7807	40.2894	42.7956	48.268
23	27.1413	32.0069	35.1725	38.0757	41.6384	44.1813	49.728
24	28.2412	33.1963	36.4151	39.3641	42.9798	45.5585	51.179
25	29.3389	34.3816	37.6525	40.6465	44.3141	46.9278	52.620
26	30.4345	35.5631	38.8852	41.9232	45.6417	48.2899	54.052
27	31.5284	36.7412	40.1133	43.1944	46.9630	49.6449	55.476
28	32.6205	37.9159	41.3372	44.4607	48.2782	50.9933	56.892
29	33.7109	39.0875	42.5569	45.7222	49.5879	52.3356	58.302
30	34.7998	40.2560	43.7729	46.9792	50.8922	53.6720	59.703
40	45.6160	51.8050	55.7585	59.3417	63.6907	66.7659	73.402
50	56.3336	63.1671	67.5048	71.4202	76.1539	79.4900	86.661
60	66.9814	74.3970	79.0819	83.2976	88.3794	91.9517	99.607
70	77.5766	85.5271	90.5312	95.0231	100.425	104.215	112.317
80	88.1303	96.5782	101.879	106.629	112.329	116.321	124.839
90	98.6499	107.565	113.145	118.136	124.116	128.299	137.208
100	109.141	118.498	124.342	129.561	135.807	140.169	149.449
z_Q	+0.6745	+1.2816	+1.6449	+1.9600	+2.3263	+2.5758	+3.0902

This table is taken from Table 8 of the *Biometrika Tables for Statisticians*, Vol. 1 (1st ed), edited by E. S. Pearson and H. O. Hartley. Reproduced with the kind permission of E. S. Pearson and the trustees of *Biometrika*.

Table IV Percentage Points of the F Distribution: Upper 5% Points

v_2 \ v_1	1	2	3	4	5	6	7	8	9	10	12	15	20	24	30	40	60	120	∞
1	161.4	199.5	215.7	224.6	230.2	234.0	236.8	238.9	240.5	241.9	243.9	245.9	248.0	249.1	250.1	251.1	252.2	253.3	254.3
2	18.51	19.00	19.16	19.25	19.30	19.33	19.35	19.37	19.38	19.40	19.41	19.43	19.45	19.45	19.46	19.47	19.48	19.49	19.50
3	10.13	9.55	9.28	9.12	9.01	8.94	8.89	8.85	8.81	8.79	8.74	8.70	8.66	8.64	8.62	8.59	8.57	8.55	8.53
4	7.71	6.94	6.59	6.39	6.26	6.16	6.09	6.04	6.00	5.96	5.91	5.86	5.80	5.77	5.75	5.72	5.69	5.66	5.63
5	6.61	5.79	5.41	5.19	5.05	4.95	4.88	4.82	4.77	4.74	4.68	4.62	4.56	4.53	4.50	4.46	4.43	4.40	4.36
6	5.99	5.14	4.76	4.53	4.39	4.28	4.21	4.15	4.10	4.06	4.00	3.94	3.87	3.84	3.81	3.77	3.74	3.70	3.67
7	5.59	4.74	4.35	4.12	3.97	3.87	3.79	3.73	3.68	3.64	3.57	3.51	3.44	3.41	3.38	3.34	3.30	3.27	3.23
8	5.32	4.46	4.07	3.84	3.69	3.58	3.50	3.44	3.39	3.35	3.28	3.22	3.15	3.12	3.08	3.04	3.01	2.97	2.93
9	5.12	4.26	3.86	3.63	3.48	3.37	3.29	3.23	3.18	3.14	3.07	3.01	2.94	2.90	2.86	2.83	2.79	2.75	2.71
10	4.96	4.10	3.71	3.48	3.33	3.22	3.14	3.07	3.02	2.98	2.91	2.85	2.77	2.74	2.70	2.66	2.62	2.58	2.54
11	4.84	3.98	3.59	3.36	3.20	3.09	3.01	2.95	2.90	2.85	2.79	2.72	2.65	2.61	2.57	2.53	2.49	2.45	2.40
12	4.75	3.89	3.49	3.26	3.11	3.00	2.91	2.85	2.80	2.75	2.69	2.62	2.54	2.51	2.47	2.43	2.38	2.34	2.30
13	4.67	3.81	3.41	3.18	3.03	2.92	2.83	2.77	2.71	2.67	2.60	2.53	2.46	2.42	2.38	2.34	2.30	2.25	2.21
14	4.60	3.74	3.34	3.11	2.96	2.85	2.76	2.70	2.65	2.60	2.53	2.46	2.39	2.35	2.31	2.27	2.22	2.18	2.13
15	4.54	3.68	3.29	3.06	2.90	2.79	2.71	2.64	2.59	2.54	2.48	2.40	2.33	2.29	2.25	2.20	2.16	2.11	2.07
16	4.49	3.63	3.24	3.01	2.85	2.74	2.66	2.59	2.54	2.49	2.42	2.35	2.28	2.24	2.19	2.15	2.11	2.06	2.01
17	4.45	3.59	3.20	2.96	2.81	2.70	2.61	2.55	2.49	2.45	2.38	2.31	2.23	2.19	2.15	2.10	2.06	2.01	1.96
18	4.41	3.55	3.16	2.93	2.77	2.66	2.58	2.51	2.46	2.41	2.34	2.27	2.19	2.15	2.11	2.06	2.02	1.97	1.92
19	4.38	3.52	3.13	2.90	2.74	2.63	2.54	2.48	2.42	2.38	2.31	2.23	2.16	2.11	2.07	2.03	1.98	1.93	1.88
20	4.35	3.49	3.10	2.87	2.71	2.60	2.51	2.45	2.39	2.35	2.28	2.20	2.12	2.08	2.04	1.99	1.95	1.90	1.84
21	4.32	3.47	3.07	2.84	2.68	2.57	2.49	2.42	2.37	2.32	2.25	2.18	2.10	2.05	2.01	1.96	1.92	1.87	1.81
22	4.30	3.44	3.05	2.82	2.66	2.55	2.46	2.40	2.34	2.30	2.23	2.15	2.07	2.03	1.98	1.94	1.89	1.84	1.78
23	4.28	3.42	3.03	2.80	2.64	2.53	2.44	2.37	2.32	2.27	2.20	2.13	2.05	2.01	1.96	1.91	1.86	1.81	1.76
24	4.26	3.40	3.01	2.78	2.62	2.51	2.42	2.36	2.30	2.25	2.18	2.11	2.03	1.98	1.94	1.89	1.84	1.79	1.73
25	4.24	3.39	2.99	2.76	2.60	2.49	2.40	2.34	2.28	2.24	2.16	2.09	2.01	1.96	1.92	1.87	1.82	1.77	1.71
26	4.23	3.37	2.98	2.74	2.59	2.47	2.39	2.32	2.27	2.22	2.15	2.07	1.99	1.95	1.90	1.85	1.80	1.75	1.69
27	4.21	3.35	2.96	2.73	2.57	2.46	2.37	2.31	2.25	2.20	2.13	2.06	1.97	1.93	1.88	1.84	1.79	1.73	1.67
28	4.20	3.34	2.95	2.71	2.56	2.45	2.36	2.29	2.24	2.19	2.12	2.04	1.96	1.91	1.87	1.82	1.77	1.71	1.65
29	4.18	3.33	2.93	2.70	2.55	2.43	2.35	2.28	2.22	2.18	2.10	2.03	1.94	1.90	1.85	1.81	1.75	1.70	1.64
30	4.17	3.32	2.92	2.69	2.53	2.42	2.33	2.27	2.21	2.16	2.09	2.01	1.93	1.89	1.84	1.79	1.74	1.68	1.62
40	4.08	3.23	2.84	2.61	2.45	2.34	2.25	2.18	2.12	2.08	2.00	1.92	1.84	1.79	1.74	1.69	1.64	1.58	1.51
60	4.00	3.15	2.76	2.53	2.37	2.25	2.17	2.10	2.03	1.99	1.92	1.84	1.75	1.70	1.65	1.59	1.53	1.47	1.39
120	3.92	3.07	2.68	2.45	2.29	2.17	2.09	2.02	1.96	1.91	1.83	1.75	1.66	1.61	1.55	1.50	1.43	1.35	1.25
∞	3.84	3.00	2.60	2.37	2.21	2.10	2.01	1.94	1.88	1.83	1.75	1.67	1.57	1.52	1.46	1.39	1.32	1.22	1.00

Upper 2.5% Points

v_2 \ v_1	1	2	3	4	5	6	7	8	9	10	12	15	20	24	30	40	60	120	∞
1	647.8	799.5	864.2	899.6	921.8	937.1	948.2	96.67	93.33	968.6	976.7	984.9	993.1	997.2	1001	1006	1010	1014	1018
2	38.51	39.00	39.17	39.25	39.30	39.33	39.36	39.37	39.39	39.40	39.41	39.43	39.45	39.46	39.46	39.47	39.48	39.49	39.50
3	17.44	16.04	15.44	15.10	14.88	14.73	14.62	14.54	14.47	14.42	14.34	14.25	14.17	14.12	14.08	14.04	13.99	13.95	13.90
4	12.22	10.65	9.98	9.60	9.36	9.20	9.07	8.98	8.90	8.84	8.75	8.66	8.56	8.51	8.46	8.41	8.36	8.31	8.26
5	10.01	8.43	7.76	7.39	7.15	6.98	6.85	6.76	6.68	6.62	6.52	6.43	6.33	6.28	6.23	6.18	6.12	6.07	6.02
6	8.81	7.26	6.60	6.23	5.99	5.82	5.70	5.60	5.52	5.46	5.37	5.27	5.17	5.12	5.07	5.01	4.96	4.90	4.85
7	8.07	6.54	5.89	5.52	5.29	5.21	4.99	4.90	4.82	4.76	4.67	4.57	4.47	4.42	4.36	4.31	4.25	4.20	4.14
8	7.57	6.06	5.42	5.05	4.82	4.65	4.53	4.43	4.36	4.30	4.20	4.10	4.00	3.95	3.89	3.84	3.78	3.73	3.67
9	7.21	5.71	5.08	4.72	4.48	4.32	4.20	4.10	4.03	3.96	3.87	3.77	3.67	3.61	3.56	3.51	3.45	3.39	3.33
10	6.94	5.46	4.83	4.47	4.24	4.07	3.95	3.85	3.78	3.72	3.62	3.52	3.42	3.37	3.31	3.26	3.20	3.14	3.08
11	6.72	5.26	4.63	4.28	4.04	3.88	3.76	3.66	3.59	3.53	3.43	3.33	3.23	3.17	3.12	3.06	3.00	2.94	2.88
12	6.55	5.10	4.47	4.12	3.89	3.73	3.61	3.51	3.44	3.37	3.28	3.18	3.07	3.02	2.96	2.91	2.85	2.79	2.72
13	6.41	4.97	4.35	4.00	3.77	3.60	3.48	3.39	3.31	3.25	3.15	3.05	2.95	2.89	2.84	2.78	2.72	2.66	2.60
14	6.30	4.86	4.24	3.89	3.66	3.50	3.38	3.29	3.21	3.15	3.05	2.95	2.84	2.79	2.73	2.67	2.61	2.55	2.49
15	6.20	4.77	4.15	3.80	3.58	3.41	3.29	3.20	3.12	3.06	2.96	2.86	2.76	2.70	2.64	2.59	2.52	2.46	2.40
16	6.12	4.69	4.08	3.73	3.50	3.34	3.22	3.12	3.05	2.99	2.89	2.79	2.68	2.63	2.57	2.51	2.45	2.38	2.32
17	6.04	4.62	4.01	3.66	3.44	3.28	3.16	3.06	2.98	2.92	2.82	2.72	2.62	2.56	2.50	2.44	2.38	2.32	2.25
18	5.98	4.56	3.95	3.61	3.38	3.22	3.10	3.01	2.93	2.87	2.77	2.67	2.56	2.50	2.44	2.38	2.32	2.26	2.19
19	5.92	4.51	3.90	3.56	3.33	3.17	3.05	2.96	2.88	2.82	2.72	2.62	2.51	2.45	2.39	2.33	2.27	2.20	2.13
20	5.87	4.46	3.86	3.51	3.29	3.13	3.01	2.91	2.84	2.77	2.68	2.57	2.46	2.41	2.35	2.29	2.22	2.16	2.19
21	5.83	4.42	3.82	3.48	3.25	3.09	2.97	2.87	2.80	2.73	2.64	2.53	2.42	2.37	2.31	2.25	2.18	2.11	2.04
22	5.79	4.38	3.78	3.44	3.22	3.05	2.93	2.84	2.76	2.70	2.60	2.50	2.39	2.33	2.27	2.21	2.14	2.08	2.00
23	5.75	4.35	3.75	3.41	3.18	3.02	2.90	2.81	2.73	2.67	2.57	2.47	2.36	2.30	2.24	2.18	2.11	2.04	1.97
24	5.72	4.32	3.72	3.38	3.15	2.99	2.87	2.78	2.70	2.64	2.54	2.44	2.33	2.27	2.21	2.15	2.08	2.01	1.94
25	5.69	4.29	3.69	3.35	3.13	2.97	2.85	2.75	2.68	2.61	2.51	2.41	2.30	2.24	2.18	2.12	2.05	1.98	1.91
26	5.66	4.27	3.67	3.33	3.10	2.94	2.82	2.73	2.65	2.59	2.49	2.39	2.28	2.22	2.16	2.09	2.03	1.95	1.88
27	5.63	4.24	3.65	3.31	3.08	2.92	2.80	2.71	2.63	2.57	2.47	2.36	2.25	2.19	2.13	2.07	2.00	1.93	1.85
28	5.61	4.22	3.63	3.29	3.06	2.90	2.78	2.69	2.61	2.55	2.45	2.34	2.23	2.17	2.11	2.05	1.98	1.91	1.83
29	5.59	4.20	3.61	3.27	3.04	2.88	2.76	2.67	2.59	2.53	2.43	2.32	2.21	2.15	2.09	2.03	1.96	1.89	1.81
30	5.57	4.18	3.59	3.25	3.03	2.87	2.75	2.65	2.57	2.51	2.41	2.31	2.20	2.14	2.07	2.01	1.94	1.87	1.79
40	5.42	4.05	3.46	3.13	2.90	2.74	2.62	2.53	2.45	2.39	2.29	2.18	2.07	2.01	1.94	1.88	1.80	1.72	1.64
60	5.29	3.93	3.34	3.01	2.79	2.63	2.51	2.41	2.33	2.27	2.17	2.06	1.94	1.88	1.82	1.74	1.67	1.58	1.48
120	5.15	3.80	3.23	2.89	2.67	2.52	2.39	2.30	2.22	2.16	2.05	1.94	1.82	1.76	1.69	1.61	1.53	1.43	1.31
∞	5.02	3.69	3.12	2.79	2.57	2.41	2.29	2.19	2.11	2.05	1.94	1.83	1.71	1.64	1.57	1.48	1.39	1.27	1.00

(continued)

Upper 1% Points

v_2 \ v_1	1	2	3	4	5	6	7	8	9	10	12	15	20	24	30	40	60	120	∞
1	4052	4999.5	5403	5625	5764	5859	5928	5982	6022	6056	6106	6157	6209	6235	6261	6287	6313	6339	6366
2	98.50	99.00	99.17	99.25	99.30	99.33	99.36	99.37	99.39	99.40	99.42	99.43	99.45	99.46	99.47	99.47	99.48	99.49	99.50
3	34.12	30.82	29.46	28.71	28.24	27.91	27.67	27.49	27.35	27.23	27.05	26.87	26.69	26.60	26.50	26.41	26.32	26.22	26.13
4	21.20	18.00	16.69	15.98	15.52	15.21	14.98	14.80	14.66	14.55	14.37	14.20	14.02	13.93	13.84	13.75	13.65	13.56	13.46
5	16.26	13.27	12.06	11.39	10.97	10.67	10.46	10.29	10.16	10.05	9.89	9.72	9.55	9.47	9.38	9.29	9.20	9.11	9.02
6	13.75	10.92	9.78	9.15	8.75	8.47	8.26	8.10	7.98	7.87	7.72	7.56	7.40	7.31	7.23	7.14	7.06	6.97	6.88
7	12.25	9.55	8.45	7.85	7.46	7.19	6.99	6.84	6.72	6.62	6.47	6.31	6.16	6.07	5.99	5.91	5.82	5.74	5.65
8	11.26	8.65	7.59	7.01	6.63	6.37	6.18	6.03	5.91	5.81	5.67	5.52	5.36	5.28	5.20	5.12	5.03	4.95	4.86
9	10.56	8.02	6.99	6.42	6.06	5.80	5.61	5.47	5.35	5.26	5.11	4.96	4.81	4.73	4.65	4.57	4.48	4.40	4.31
10	10.04	7.56	6.55	5.99	5.64	5.39	5.20	5.06	4.94	4.85	4.71	4.56	4.41	4.33	4.25	4.17	4.08	4.00	3.91
11	9.65	7.21	6.22	5.67	5.32	5.07	4.89	4.74	4.63	4.54	4.40	4.25	4.10	4.02	3.94	3.86	3.78	3.69	3.60
12	9.33	6.93	5.95	5.41	5.06	4.82	4.64	4.50	4.39	4.30	4.16	4.01	3.86	3.78	3.70	3.62	3.54	3.45	3.36
13	9.07	6.70	5.74	5.21	4.86	4.62	4.44	4.30	4.19	4.10	3.96	3.82	3.66	3.59	3.51	3.43	3.34	3.25	3.17
14	8.86	6.51	5.56	5.04	4.69	4.46	4.28	4.14	4.03	3.94	3.80	3.66	3.51	3.43	3.35	3.27	3.18	3.09	3.00
15	8.68	6.36	5.42	4.89	4.56	4.32	4.14	4.00	3.89	3.80	3.67	3.52	3.37	3.29	3.21	3.13	3.05	2.96	2.87
16	8.53	6.23	5.29	4.77	4.44	4.20	4.03	3.89	3.78	3.69	3.55	3.41	3.26	3.18	3.10	3.02	2.93	2.84	2.75
17	8.40	6.11	5.18	4.67	4.34	4.10	3.93	3.79	3.68	3.59	3.46	3.31	3.16	3.08	3.00	2.92	2.83	2.75	2.65
18	8.29	6.01	5.09	4.58	4.25	4.01	3.84	3.71	3.60	3.51	3.37	3.23	3.08	3.00	2.92	2.84	2.75	2.66	2.57
19	8.18	5.93	5.01	4.50	4.17	3.94	3.77	3.63	3.52	3.43	3.30	3.15	3.00	2.92	2.84	2.76	2.67	2.58	2.49
20	8.10	5.85	4.94	4.43	4.10	3.87	3.70	3.56	3.46	3.37	3.23	3.09	2.94	2.86	2.78	2.69	2.61	2.52	2.42
21	8.02	5.78	4.87	4.37	4.04	3.81	3.64	3.51	3.40	3.31	3.17	3.03	2.88	2.80	2.72	2.64	2.55	2.46	2.36
22	7.95	5.72	4.82	4.31	3.99	3.76	3.59	3.45	3.35	3.26	3.12	2.98	2.83	2.75	2.67	2.58	2.50	2.40	2.31
23	7.88	5.66	4.76	4.26	3.94	3.71	3.54	3.41	3.30	3.21	3.07	2.93	2.78	2.70	2.62	2.54	2.45	2.35	2.26
24	7.82	5.61	4.72	4.22	3.90	3.67	3.50	3.36	3.26	3.17	3.03	2.89	2.74	2.66	2.58	2.49	2.40	2.31	2.21
25	7.77	5.57	4.68	4.18	3.85	3.63	3.46	3.32	3.22	3.13	2.99	2.85	2.70	2.62	2.54	2.45	2.36	2.27	2.17
26	7.72	5.53	4.64	4.14	3.82	3.59	3.42	3.29	3.18	3.09	2.96	2.81	2.66	2.58	2.50	2.42	2.33	2.23	2.13
27	7.68	5.49	4.60	4.11	3.78	3.56	3.39	3.26	3.15	3.06	2.93	2.78	2.63	2.55	2.47	2.38	2.29	2.20	2.10
28	7.64	5.45	4.57	4.07	3.75	3.53	3.36	3.23	3.12	3.03	2.90	2.75	2.60	2.52	2.44	2.35	2.26	2.17	2.06
29	7.60	5.42	4.54	4.04	3.73	3.50	3.33	3.20	3.09	3.00	2.87	2.73	2.57	2.49	2.41	2.33	2.23	2.14	2.03
30	7.56	5.39	4.51	4.02	3.70	3.47	3.30	3.17	3.07	2.98	2.84	2.70	2.55	2.47	2.39	2.30	2.21	2.11	2.01
40	7.31	5.18	4.31	3.83	3.51	3.29	3.12	2.99	2.89	2.80	2.66	2.52	2.37	2.29	2.20	2.11	2.02	1.92	1.80
60	7.08	4.98	4.13	3.65	3.34	3.12	2.95	2.82	2.72	2.63	2.50	2.35	2.20	2.12	2.03	1.94	1.84	1.73	1.60
120	6.85	4.79	3.95	3.48	3.17	2.96	2.79	2.66	2.56	2.47	2.34	2.19	2.03	1.95	1.86	1.76	1.66	1.53	1.38
∞	6.63	4.61	3.78	3.32	3.02	2.80	2.64	2.51	2.41	2.32	2.18	2.04	1.88	1.79	1.70	1.59	1.47	1.32	1.00

Glossary

Action research A research strategy aimed at initiating change processes, with an incremental focus, for narrowing the gap between the desired and actual states.

Alternate hypothesis An educated conjecture that sets the parameters one expects to find. The alternate hypothesis is tested to see whether or not the null is to be rejected.

Ambiguous questions Questions that are not clearly worded and are likely to be interpreted by respondents in different ways.

ANOVA Stands for analysis of variance, which tests for significant mean differences in variables among multiple groups.

Applied research Research conducted in a particular setting with the specific objective of solving an existing problem in the situation.

Area sampling Cluster sampling within a specified area or region; a probability sampling design.

Argument A set of statements that includes a conclusion (or a claim) and premises ('the evidence') which support the conclusion.

Basic research Research conducted to generate knowledge and understanding of phenomena (in the work setting) that adds to the existing body of knowledge (about organizations and management theory).

Bias Any error that creeps into the data. Biases can be introduced by the researcher, the respondent, the measuring instrument, the sample, and so on.

Bibliography A listing of books, articles, and other relevant materials, alphabetized according to the last name of the authors, referencing the titles of their works, and indicating where they can be located.

Big data Term commonly used to describe the exponential growth and availability of data from digital sources inside and outside the organization.

Canonical correlation A statistical technique that examines the relationship between two or more dependent variables and several independent variables.

Case study Focuses on collecting information about a specific object, event or activity, such as a particular business unit or organization.

Categorization The process of organizing, arranging, and classifying coding units (in qualitative data analysis).

Category (in qualitative data analysis) A group of coding units that share some commonality.

Category reliability The extent to which judges are able to use category definitions to classify qualitative data.

Category scale A scale that uses multiple items to seek a single response.

Causal study A research study conducted to establish cause-and-effect relationships among variables.

Chi-square test A nonparametric test that establishes the independence or otherwise between two nominal variables.

Classification data Personal information or demographic details of the respondents such as age, marital status, and educational level.

Closed questions Questions with a clearly delineated set of alternatives that confine the respondents' choice to one of them.

Cluster sampling A probability sampling design in which the sample comprises groups or chunks of elements with intragroup heterogeneity and intergroup homogeneity.

Coding The analytic process through which the qualitative data that you have gathered are reduced, rearranged, and integrated to form theory (compare Data coding).

Coding scheme Contains predetermined categories for recording what is observed. Such schemes come in many forms and shapes.

Combination of an information and a consensus problem There is little or no knowledge about how the problem can be solved, but there is also insufficient agreement about what the problem is and/or about the constraints that the solution must meet.

Comparative scale A scale that provides a benchmark or point of reference to assess attitudes, opinions, and the like.

Complex probability sampling Several probability sampling designs (such as systematic and stratified random), which offer an alternative to the cumbersome, simple random sampling design.

Computer-assisted telephone interviews (CATI) Interviews in which questions are prompted onto a PC monitor that is networked into the telephone system, to which respondents provide their answers.

Concealed observation Members of a social group under study are not told that they are being observed.

Concealment of observation Relates to whether the members of the social group under study are told that they are being observed.

Conceptual analysis Establishes the existence and frequency of concepts (such as words, themes, or characters) in a text.

Conclusion The researcher's informed judgement about (how) the organizational problem (can best be solved).

Concurrent validity Relates to criterion-related validity, which is established at the same time the test is administered.

Confidence The probability estimate of how much reliance can be placed on the findings; the usual accepted level of confidence in social science research is 95%.

Conjoint analysis A multivariate statistical technique used to determine the relative importance respondents attach to attributes and the utilities they attach to specific levels of attributes.

Consensus problem There is sufficient knowledge about how to solve the problem, but due to, for example, conflicting interests or different value systems, beliefs or ethical standpoints, every viable solution to the problem is blocked.

Consensus scale A scale developed through consensus or the unanimous agreement of a panel of judges as to the items that measure a concept.

Constant sum rating scale A scale where the respondents distribute a fixed number of points across several items.

Construct validity Testifies to how well the results obtained from the use of the measure fit the theories around which the test was designed.

Constructionism An approach to research that is based on the idea that the world as we know it is fundamentally mental or mentally constructed. Constructionists aim to understand the rules people use to make sense of the world by investigating what happens in people's minds.

Content analysis An observational research method that is used to systematically evaluate the symbolic contents of all forms of recorded communication.

Content validity Establishes the representative sampling of a whole set of items that measures a concept, and reflects how well the dimensions and elements thereof are delineated.

Contextual factors Factors relating to the organization under study such as the background and environment of the organization, including its origin and purpose, size, resources, financial standing, and the like.

Contrived setting An artificially created or "lab" environment in which research is conducted.

Control group The group that is not exposed to any treatment in an experiment.

Controlled observation Controlled observation occurs when observational research is carried out under carefully arranged conditions.

Convenience sampling A nonprobability sampling design in which information or data for the research are gathered from members of the population conveniently accessible to the researcher.

Convergent validity That which is established when the scores obtained by two different instruments measuring the same concept, or by measuring the concept by two different methods, are highly correlated.

Correlation matrix A correlation matrix is used to examine relationships between interval and/or ratio variables.

Correlational study A research study conducted to identify the important factors associated with the variables of interest.

Criterion-related validity That which is established when the measure differentiates individuals on a criterion that it is expected to predict.

Criterion variable The variable of primary interest to the study, also known as the dependent variable.

Critical literature review A step-by-step process that involves the identification of published and unpublished work from secondary data sources on the topic of interest, the evaluation of this work in relation to the problem, and the documentation of this work.

Critical realism A school of thought combining the belief in an external reality (an objective truth) with the rejection of the claim that this external reality can be objectively measured. The critical realist is critical of our ability to understand the world with certainty.

Cross-sectional study A research study for which data are gathered just once (stretched though it may be over a period of days, weeks, or months) to answer the research question.

Data coding In quantitative research data coding involves assigning a number to the participants' responses so they can be entered into a database.

Data display Taking the reduced qualitative data and displaying them in an organized, condensed manner.

Data editing Data editing deals with detecting and correcting illogical, inconsistent, or illegal data and omissions in the information returned by the participants of the study.

Data mining Helps to trace patterns and relationships in the data stored in the data warehouse.

Data reduction Breaking down data into manageable pieces.

Data transformation The process of changing the original numerical representation of a quantitative value to another value.

Data warehouse A central repository of all information gathered by the company.

Deductive reasoning In deductive reasoning if the premises are true, then the conclusion must be true. Deductive arguments are either valid or invalid.

Deductive research A research approach aimed at testing theory.

Delphi technique A forecasting method that uses a cautiously selected panel of experts in a systematic, interactive manner.

Dependent variable *See* Criterion variable.

Descriptive statistics Statistics such as frequencies, the mean, and the standard deviation, which provide descriptive information about a set of data.

Descriptive study A research study that describes the variables in a situation of interest to the researcher.

Dichotomous scale Scale used to elicit a Yes/No response, or an answer to two different aspects of a concept.

Directional hypothesis An educated conjecture as to the direction of the relationship, or differences among variables, which could be positive or negative, or more or less, respectively.

Discriminant analysis A statistical technique that helps to identify the independent variables that discriminate a nominally scaled dependent variable of interest.

Discriminant validity That which is established when two variables are theorized to be uncorrelated, and the scores obtained by measuring them are indeed empirically found to be so.

Disproportionate stratified random sampling A probability sampling design that involves a procedure in which the number of sample subjects chosen from various strata is not directly proportionate to the total number of elements in the respective strata.

Double-barreled question Refers to the improper framing of a question that should be posed as two or more separate questions, so that the respondent can give clear and unambiguous answers.

Double-blind study A study where neither the experimenter nor the subjects are aware as to who is given the real treatment and who the placebo.

Double sampling A probability sampling design that involves the process of collecting information from a set of subjects twice – such as using a sample to collect preliminary information, and later using a subsample of the primary sample for more information.

Dummy variable A variable that has two or more distinct levels, which are coded 0 or 1.

Efficiency in sampling Attained when the sampling design chosen either results in a cost reduction to the researcher or offers a greater degree of accuracy in terms of the sample size.

Electronic questionnaire Online questionnaire administered when a microcomputer is hooked up to computer networks.

Element A single member of the population.

Epistemology Theory about the nature of knowledge or how we come to know.

Ethics Code of conduct or expected societal norms of behavior.

Ethnography A research process in which the anthropologist closely observes, records, and engages in the daily life of another culture and then writes accounts of this culture, emphasizing descriptive detail.

Evidence information used to convince someone of a certain point of view.

Exogenous variable A variable that exerts an influence on the cause-and-effect relationship between two variables in some way, and needs to be controlled.

Experimental design A study design in which the researcher might create an artificial setting, control some variables, and manipulate the independent variable to establish cause-and-effect relationships.

Experimental group The group exposed to a treatment in an experimental design.

Expert panel A group of people specifically convened by the researcher to elicit expert knowledge and opinion about a certain issue.

Exploratory research A research study where very little knowledge or information is available on the subject under investigation.

Ex post facto experimental design Studying subjects who have already been exposed to a stimulus and comparing them to those not so exposed, so as to establish cause-and-effect relationships (in contrast to establishing cause-and-effect relationships by manipulating an independent variable in a lab or a field setting).

External consultants Research experts outside the organization who are hired to study specific problems to find solutions.

External validity The extent of generalizability of the results of a causal study to other field settings.

Faces scale A particular representation of the graphic scale, depicting faces with expressions that range from smiling to sad.

Face-to-face interview Information gathering when both the interviewer and interviewee meet in person.

Face validity An aspect of validity examining whether the item on the scale, on the face of it, reads as if it indeed measures what it is supposed to measure.

Factorial validity That which indicates, through the use of factor analytic techniques, whether a test is a pure measure of some specific factor or dimension.

Field experiment An experiment done to detect cause-and-effect relationships in the natural environment in which events normally occur.

Field study A study conducted in the natural setting with a minimal amount of researcher interference in the flow of events in the situation.

Fixed rating scale *See* Constant sum rating scale.

Focus group A group consisting of eight to ten members randomly chosen, who discuss a product or any given topic for about two hours with a moderator present, so that their opinions can serve as the basis for further research.

Forced choice Elicits the ranking of objects relative to one another.

Formative scale Used when a construct is viewed as an explanatory combination of its indicators.

Frequencies The number of times various subcategories of a phenomenon occur, from which the percentage and cumulative percentage of any occurrence can be calculated.

Fundamental research *See* Basic research.

Funneling technique The questioning technique that consists of initially asking general and broad questions, and gradually narrowing the focus thereafter to more specific themes.

Generalizability The applicability of research findings in one setting to others.

Going native The researcher/observer becomes so involved with the group under study that eventually every objectivity and research interest is lost.

Goodness of measures Attests to the reliability and validity of measures.

Graphic rating scale A scale that graphically illustrates the responses that can be provided, rather than specifying any discrete response categories.

Grounded theory A systematic set of procedures to develop an inductively derived theory from the data.

History effects A threat to the internal validity of the experimental results, when events unexpectedly occur while the experiment is in progress and contaminate the cause-and-effect relationship.

Hypothesis A tentative, yet testable, statement that predicts what you expect to find in your empirical data.

Hypothetico-deductive method A seven-step research process of identifying a broad problem area, defining the problem statement, developing hypotheses, determining measures, data collection, data analysis, and the interpretation of data.

Independent samples *t*-test Test that is done to see if there are significant differences in the means for two groups in the variable of interest.

Independent variable A variable that influences the dependent or criterion variable and accounts for (or explains) its variance.

Inductive or ampliative reasoning In inductive or ampliative reasoning the premises support (but do not guarantee) the conclusion.

Inductive research A research approach where we observe specific phenomena and on this basis arrive at general conclusions.

Inferential statistics Statistics that help to establish relationships among variables and draw conclusions therefrom.

Information problem A particular type of action problem where there is clarity and agreement on what the problem is and the constraints of the solution. In contrast to routine problems however, it is *not* clear how the problem can (best) be solved.

Instrumentation effects The threat to internal validity in experimental designs caused by changes in the measuring instrument between the pretest and the posttest.

Inter item consistency reliability A test of the consistency of responses to all the items in a measure to establish that they hang together as a set.

Interjudge reliability The degree of consistency between coders processing the same (qualitative) data.

Internal consistency Homogeneity of the items in the measure that tap a construct.

Internal consultants Research experts within the organization who investigate and find solutions to problems.

Internal validity of experiments Attests to the confidence that can be placed in the cause-and-effect relationship found in experimental designs.

Interval scale A multipoint scale that taps the differences, the order, and the equality of the magnitude of the differences in the responses.

Intervening variable A variable that surfaces as a function of the independent variable, and helps in conceptualizing and explaining the influence of the independent variable on the dependent variable.

Interview A data collection method in which the researcher asks for information verbally from the respondents.

Itemized rating scale A scale that offers several categories of response, out of which the respondent picks the one most relevant for answering the question.

Judgment sampling A purposive, nonprobability sampling design in which the sample subject is chosen on the basis of the individual's ability to provide the type of special information needed by the researcher.L

Lab experiment An experimental design set up in an artificially contrived setting where controls and manipulations are introduced to establish cause-and-effect relationships among variables of interest to the researcher.

Leading questions Questions phrased in such a manner as to lead the respondent to give the answers that the researcher would like to obtain.

Likert scale An interval scale that specifically uses the five anchors of *Strongly Disagree, Disagree, Neither Disagree nor Agree, Agree*, and *Strongly Agree*.

Literature review A step-by-step process that involves the identification of published and unpublished work from secondary data sources on the topic of interest, the evaluation of this work in relation to the problem, and the documentation of this work.

Loaded questions Questions that elicit highly biased emotional responses from subjects.

Logistic regression A specific form of regression analysis in which the dependent variable is a nonmetric, dichotomous variable.

Longitudinal study A research study for which data are gathered at several points in time to answer a research question.

Manipulation How the researcher exposes the subjects to the independent variable to determine cause-and-effect relationships in experimental designs.

MANOVA A statistical technique that is similar to ANOVA, with the difference that ANOVA tests the mean differences of more than two groups on *one* dependent variable, whereas MANOVA tests mean differences among groups across *several* dependent variables simultaneously, by using sums of squares and cross-product matrices.

Match groups A method of controlling known contaminating factors in experimental studies, by deliberately spreading them equally across the experimental and control groups, so as not to confound the cause-and-effect relationship.

Maturation effects A threat to internal validity that is a function of the biological, psychological, and other processes taking place in the respondents as a result of the passage of time.

McNemar's test A nonparametric method used on nominal data. It assesses the significance of the difference between two dependent samples when the variable of interest is dichotomous.

Mean The average of a set of figures.

Measure of central tendency Descriptive statistics of a *data set* such as the mean, median, or mode.

Measure of dispersion The variability in a set of observations, represented by the range, variance, standard deviation, and the interquartile range.

Measurement The assignment of numbers or other symbols to characteristics (or attributes) of objects according to a prespecified set of rules.

Median The central item in a group of observations arranged in an ascending or descending order.

Mediating variable A variable that surfaces as a function of the independent variable, and helps in conceptualizing and explaining the influence of the independent variable on the dependent variable.

Mode The most frequently occurring number in a data set.

Moderating variable A variable on which the relationship between two other variables is contingent. That is, if the moderating variable is present, the theorized relationship between the two variables will hold good, but not otherwise.

Mortality The loss of research subjects during the course of the experiment, which confounds the cause-and-effect relationship.

Multicollinearity A statistical phenomenon in which two or more independent variables in a multiple regression model are highly correlated.

Multiple regression analysis A statistical technique to predict the variance in the dependent variable by regressing the independent variables against it.

Multistage cluster sampling A probability sampling design that is a stratified sampling of clusters.

Narrative analysis A qualitative approach that aims to elicit and scrutinize the stories we tell about ourselves and their implications for our lives.

Nominal scale A scale that categorizes individuals or objects into mutually exclusive and collectively exhaustive groups, and offers basic, categorical information on the variable of interest.

Noncontrived setting Research conducted in the natural environment where activities take place in the normal manner (i.e., the field setting).

Nondirectional hypothesis An educated conjecture of a relationship between two variables, the directionality of which cannot be guessed.

Nonparametric test A hypothesis test that does not require certain assumptions about the population's distribution, such as that the population follows a normal distribution.

Nonparticipant observation The researcher is never directly involved in the actions of the actors, but observes them from outside the actors' visual horizon, for instance via a one-way mirror or a camera.

Nonprobability sampling A sampling design in which the elements in the population do not have a known or predetermined chance of being selected as sample subjects.

Nonresponse error Exists to the extent that those who did respond to your survey are different from those who did not on (one of the) characteristics of interest in your study. Two important sources of non-response are not-at-homes and refusals.

Nuisance variable A variable that contaminates the cause-and-effect relationship.

Null hypothesis The conjecture that postulates no differences or no relationship between or among variables.

Numerical scale A scale with bipolar attributes with five points or seven points indicated on the scale.

Objectivity Interpretation of the results on the basis of the results of data analysis, as opposed to subjective or emotional interpretations.

Observation The planned watching, recording, analysis, and interpretation of behavior, actions, or events.

One sample *t*-test A test that is used to test the hypothesis that the mean of the population from which a sample is drawn is equal to a comparison standard.

One-shot study *See* Cross-sectional study.

Ontology The philosophical study of what can be said to exist.

Open-ended questions Questions that the respondent can answer in a free-flowing format without restricting the range of choices to a set of specific alternatives suggested by the researcher.

Operationalizing Reduction of abstract concepts to render them measurable in a tangible way.

Operations research A quantitative approach taken to analyze and solve problems of complexity.

Ordinal scale A scale that not only categorizes the qualitative differences in the variable of interest, but also allows for the rank-ordering of these categories in a meaningful way.

Outlier An observation that is substantially different from the other observations.

Paired comparisons Respondents choose between two objects at a time, with the process repeated with a small number of objects.

Paired samples *t*-test Test that examines the differences in the same group before and after a treatment.

Parallel-form reliability That form of reliability which is established when responses to two comparable sets of measures tapping the same construct are highly correlated.

Parametric test A hypothesis test that assumes that your data follow a specific distribution.

Parsimony Efficient explanation of the variance in the dependent variable of interest through the use of a smaller, rather than a larger number of independent variables.

Participant observation In participant observation the researcher gathers data by participating in the daily life of the group or organization under study.

Population The entire group of people, events, or things that the researcher desires to investigate.

Positivism A school of thought employing deductive laws and quantitative methods to get at the truth. For a positivist, the world operates by laws of cause and effect that one can discern if one uses a scientific approach to research.

Posttest A test given to the subjects to measure the dependent variable after exposing them to a treatment.

Pragmatism A viewpoint on research that does not take on a particular position on what makes good research. Pragmatists feel that research on both objective, observable phenomena and subjective meanings can produce useful knowledge, depending on the research questions of the study.

Precision The degree of closeness of the estimated sample characteristics to the population parameters, determined by the extent of the variability of the sampling distribution of the sample mean.

Predictive validity The ability of the measure to differentiate among individuals as to a criterion predicted for the future.

Predictor variable *See* Independent variable.

Pretest A test given to subjects to measure the dependent variable before exposing them to a treatment.

Pretesting survey questions Test of the understandability and appropriateness of the questions planned to be included in a regular survey, using a small number of respondents.

Primary data Data collected first-hand for subsequent analysis to find solutions to the problem researched.

Probability sampling The sampling design in which the elements of the population have some known chance or probability of being selected as sample subjects.

Problem definition A definition of the difference between the actual and desired situation.

Problem statement A problem statement includes both a statement of the research objective(s) and the research question(s).

Proportionate stratified random sampling A probability sampling design in which the number of sample subjects drawn from each stratum is proportionate to the total number of elements in the respective strata.

Pure observation Seeks to remove the researcher from the observed actions and behavior; the researcher is never directly involved in the actions and behavior of the group under study.

Pure participation The researcher becomes so involved with the group under study that eventually every objectivity and research interest is lost.

Pure research *See* Basic research.

Purposiveness in research The situation in which research is focused on solving a well-identified and defined problem, rather than aimlessly looking for answers to vague questions.

Purposive sampling A nonprobability sampling design in which the required information is gathered from special or specific targets or groups of people on some rational basis.

Qualitative data Data that are not immediately quantifiable unless they are coded and categorized in some way.

Questionnaire A preformulated written set of questions to which the respondent records the answers, usually within rather closely delineated alternatives.

Quota sampling A form of purposive sampling in which a predetermined proportion of people from different subgroups is sampled.

Randomization The process of controlling the nuisance variables by randomly assigning members among the various experimental and control groups, so that the confounding variables are randomly distributed across all groups.

Range The spread in a set of numbers indicated by the difference in the two extreme values in the observations.

Ranking scale Scale used to tap preferences between two or among more objects or items.

Rapport A trusting relationship with the social group under study, by showing respect, being truthful, and showing commitment to the well-being of the group or the individual members of the group, so that they feel secure in sharing (sensitive) information with the researcher

Rating scale Scale with several response categories that evaluate an object on a scale.

Ratio scale A scale that has an absolute zero origin, and hence indicates not only the magnitude, but also the proportion, of the differences.

Reactivity The extent to which the observer affects the situation under observation.

Recall-dependent question Question that elicits from the respondents information that involves recall of experiences from the past that may be hazy in their memory.

Reference list A list that includes details of all the citations used in the literature review and elsewhere in the paper or report.

Reflective scale Each item in a reflective scale is assumed to share a common basis (the underlying construct of interest).

Regression analysis Used in a situation where one or more metric independent variable(s) is (are) hypothesized to affect a metric dependent variable.

Relational analysis Builds on conceptual analysis by examining the relationships among concepts in a text.

Reliability Attests to the consistency and stability of the measuring instrument.

Replicability The extent to which a re-study is made possible by the provision of the design details of the study in the research report.

Representativeness of the sample The extent to which the sample that is selected possesses the same characteristics as the population from which it is drawn.

Research An organized, systematic, critical, scientific inquiry or investigation into a specific problem, undertaken with the objective of finding answers or solutions thereto.

Research design A blueprint or plan for the collection, measurement, and analysis of data, created to answer your research questions.

Research objective The purpose or objective of the study explains why the study is being done. Providing a solution to a problem encountered in the work setting is the purpose of the study in most applied research.

Research proposal A document that sets out the purpose of the study and the research design details of the investigation to be carried out by the researcher.

Research question(s) Specify *what* you want to learn about the topic. They guide and structure the process of collecting and analyzing information to help you to attain the purpose of your study. In other words, research questions are the translation of the problem of the organization into a specific need for information.

Researcher interference The extent to which the person conducting the research interferes with the normal course of work at the study site.

Restricted probability designs *See* Complex probability sampling.

Rigor The theoretical and methodological precision adhered to in conducting research.

Sample A subset or subgroup of the population.

Sample size The actual number of subjects chosen as a sample to represent the population characteristics.

Sampling The process of selecting items from the population so that the sample characteristics can be generalized to the population. Sampling involves both design choice and sample size decisions.

Sampling frame A (physical) representation of all the elements in the population from which the sample is drawn.

Sampling unit The element or set of elements that is available for selection in some stage of the sampling process.

Scale A tool or mechanism by which individuals, events, or objects are distinguished on the variables of interest in some meaningful way.

Scientific investigation A step-by-step, logical, organized, and rigorous effort to solve problems.

Secondary data Data that already exist and do not have to be collected by the researcher.

Selection effects The threat to internal validity that is a function of improper or unmatched selection of subjects for the experimental and control groups.

Semantic differential scale Usually a seven-point scale with bipolar attributes indicated at its extremes.

Sequence record A sequence record allows the researcher conducting an observational study to collect information on how often an event occurs.

Simple checklist Checklist used in structured observation that provides information about how often a certain event has occurred.

Simple random sampling A probability sampling design in which every single element in the population has a known and equal chance of being selected as a subject.

Simulation A model-building technique for assessing the possible effects of changes that might be introduced in a system.

Social desirability The respondents' need to give socially or culturally acceptable responses to the questions posed by the researcher even if they are not true.

Solomon four-group design The experimental design that sets up two experimental groups and two control groups, subjecting one experimental group and one control group to *both* the pretest and the posttest, and the other experimental group and control group to *only* the posttest.

Split-half reliability The correlation coefficient between one half of the items measuring a concept and the other half.

Stability of a measure The ability of the measure to repeat the same results over time with low vulnerability to changes in the situation.

Standard deviation A measure of dispersion for parametric data; the square root of the variance.

Standardized regression coefficients (or beta coefficients) The estimates resulting from a multiple regression analysis performed on variables that have been standardized (a process whereby the variables are transformed into variables with a mean of 0 and a standard deviation of 1).

Stapel scale A scale that measures both the direction and intensity of the attributes of a concept.

Statistical power $(1 - \beta)$ The probability of correctly rejecting the null hypothesis.

Statistical regression The threat to internal validity that results when various groups in the study have been selected on the basis of their extreme (very high or very low) scores on some important variables.

Stratified random sampling A probability sampling design that first divides the population into meaningful, nonoverlapping subsets, and then randomly chooses the subjects from each subset.

Structured interviews Interviews conducted by the researcher with a predetermined list of questions to be asked of the interviewee.

Structured observation Form of observation where the observer has a predetermined set of categories of activities or phenomena planned to be studied.

Subject A single member of the sample.

Survey A *system* for collecting information from or about people to describe, compare, or explain their knowledge, attitudes, and behavior.

Systematic sampling A probability sampling design that involves choosing every *n*th element in the population for the sample.

Technical or **routine problem** A particular type of action problem where there is clarity and agreement on what the problem is and the constraints of the solution. There is also sufficient knowledge and experience on how to solve the problem, either within or outside the organization.

Telephone interview The information-gathering method by which the interviewer asks the interviewee *over the telephone*, rather than face to face, for information needed for the research.

Test–retest reliability A way of establishing the stability of the measuring instrument by correlating the scores obtained through its administration to the same set of respondents at two different points in time.

Testability The ability to subject the data collected to appropriate statistical tests, in order to substantiate or reject the hypotheses developed for the research study.

Testing effects The distorting effects on the experimental results (the posttest scores) caused by the prior sensitization of the respondents to the instrument through the pretest.

Theoretical framework A logically developed, described, and explained network of associations among variables of interest to the research study.

Treatment The manipulation of the independent variable in experimental designs so as to determine its effects on a dependent variable of interest to the researcher.

Two-way ANOVA A statistical technique that can be used to examine the effect of two nonmetric independent variables on a single metric dependent variable.

Type I error (α) The probability of rejecting the null hypothesis when it is actually true.

Type II error (β) The probability of failing to reject the null hypothesis given that the alternative hypothesis is actually true.

Unbalanced rating scale An even-numbered scale that has no neutral point.

Unbiased questions Questions posed in accordance with the principles of wording and measurement, and the right questioning technique, so as to elicit the least biased responses.

Unconcealed observation Members of a social group under study are told that they are being observed.

Uncontrolled observation An observational technique that makes no attempt to control, manipulate, or influence the situation.

Unit of analysis The level of aggregation of the data collected during data analysis.

Unobtrusive methods Methods that do not require the researcher to interact with the people he or she is studying.

Unrestricted probability sampling *See* Simple random sampling.

Unstructured interviews Interviews conducted with the primary purpose of identifying some important issues relevant to the problem situation, without prior preparation of a planned or predetermined sequence of questions.

Unstructured observation Form of observation that is used when the observer has no definite ideas of the particular aspects that need focus.

Validity Evidence that the instrument, technique, or process used to measure a concept does indeed measure the intended concept.

Variable Anything that can take on differing or varying values.

Variance Indicates the dispersion of a variable in the data set, and is obtained by subtracting the mean from each of the observations, squaring the results, summing them, and dividing the total by the number of observations.

Wilcoxon signed-rank test A nonparametric test used to examine differences between two related samples or repeated measurements on a single sample. It is used as an alternative to a paired samples *t*-test when the population cannot be assumed to be normally distributed.

Bibliography

Abbott, C. C. (1966) *Basic Research in Finance: Needs and Prospects*. Charlottesville, VA: University Press.

Abdel-khalik, A. R. & Ajinkya, B. B. (1979) *Empirical Research in Accounting: A Methodological Viewpoint*. Sarasota, FL: American Accounting Association.

Agar, M. (1996) *The Professional Stranger: An Informal Introduction to Ethnography*, 2nd ed. New York: Academic Press.

Amabile, T. M., Hill, K. G., Hennessey, B. A. & Tighe, E. M. (1994) The work preference inventory: Assessing intrinsic and extrinsic motivational orientations. *Journal of Personality and Social Psychology*, 66, 950–967.

American Psychological Association (2009) *Publication Manual of the American Psychological Association*, 6th ed. Washington, DC.

Andrews, D., Nonnecke, B. & Preece, J. (2003) Electronic survey methodology: A case study in reaching hard-to-involve Internet users. *International Journal of Human–Computer Interaction*, 16 (2), 185–210.

Angell, R. C. & Freedman, R. (1966) The use of documents, records, census materials, and indices. In L. Festinger & D. Katz (Eds.), *Research Methods in the Behavioral Sciences*. New York: Holt, Rinehart and Winston.

Baker, R. L. & Schutz, R. E. (Eds.) (1972) *Instructional Product Research*. New York: Van Nostrand.

Balsley, H. L. & Clover, V. T. (1988) *Research for Business Decisions. Business Research Methods*, 4th ed. Columbus, OH: Publishing Horizons.

Baron, R. M. & Kenny, D. A. (1986) The moderator–mediator variable distinction in social psychological research: conceptual, strategic, and statistical considerations. *Journal of Personality and Social Psychology*, 51, 1173–1182.

Barry, H. (1969) Cross-cultural research with matched pairs of societies. *Journal of Social Psychology*, 79, 25–33.

Bending, A. W. (1954) Transmitted information and the length of rating scales. *Journal of Experimental Psychology*, 47, 303–308.

Bentley, T. J. & Forkner, I. H. (1983) *Making Information Systems Work for You: How to Make Better Decisions using Computer-generated Information*. Englewood Cliffs, NJ: Prentice Hall.

Bernard, R. H. (1994) *Research Methods in Anthropology: Qualitative and Quantitative Approaches*, 2nd ed. Walnut Creek, CA: AltaMira Press.

Beynon, H. (1975) *Working for Ford*. London: EP Publishing.

Billings, R. S. & Wroten, S. P. (1978) Use of path analysis in industrial/organizational psychology: Criticisms and suggestions. *Journal of Applied Psychology*, 63(6), 677–688.

Bitner, M. J., Booms, B. H. & Tetreault, M. S. (1990) The service encounter – diagnosing favorable and unfavorable incidents. *Journal of Marketing*, 54, 71–84.

Blank, G. (1989). Finding the right statistic with statistical navigator. *PC Magazine*, March 14, p. 97.

Boot, J. C. G. & Cox, E. B. (1970) *Statistical Analysis for Managerial Decisions*. New York: McGraw-Hill.

Bordens, K. S. & Abbott, B. B. (1988) *Research Design and Methods: A Process Approach*. Mountain View, CA: Mayfield Publishing.

Bougie, R., Pieters, R. & Zeelenberg, M. (2003) Angry customers don't come back, they get back: The experience and behavioral implications of anger and dissatisfaction in services. *Journal of the Academy of Marketing Science*, 31, 377–393.

Box, G. & Jenkins, G. (1970) *Time Series Analysis: Forecasting and Control*. San Francisco: Holden-Day.

Brown, L. D. & Vasarhelyi, M. A. (1985) *Accounting Research Directory: The Database of Accounting Literature*. New York: Markus Wiener Publishing.

Bruner II, G. C., Hensel, P. J. & James, K. E. (2005) *Marketing Scales Handbook*. Chicago: Thomson South-Western Co.

Bullock, J. G., Green, D. P. & Ha, S. E. (2010) Yes, but what's the mechanism? (Don't expect an easy answer). *Journal of Personality and Social Psychology*, 98 (April), 550–558.

Burger, D. (2015, March 12). *EA Tries Selling Video Games That Work*. Retrieved from http://www.bloomberg.com/news/articles/2015-03-12/electronic-arts-delays-game-releases-to-fix-bugs-for-a-change

Burgess, R (Ed.) (1989) *The Ethics of Educational Research*. Lewes: Falmer Press.

Burton, S. & Lichtenstein, D. R. (1988) The effect of ad claims and ad context on attitude toward the advertisement. *Journal of Advertising*, 17, 3–11.

Cacioppo, J. T. & Petty, R. E. (1982) The need for cognition. *Journal of Personality and Social Psychology*, 42, 116–131.

Campbell, A. A. & Katona, G. (1966) The sample survey: A technique for social science research. In L. Festinger & D. Katz (Eds.), *Research Methods in the Behavioral Sciences*. New York: Holt, Rinehart and Winston.

Campbell, D. T. (1976) Psychometric theory. In M. D. Dunnette (Ed.), *Handbook of Industrial and Organizational Psychology*. Chicago: Rand McNally.

Campbell, D. T. & Fiske, D. W. (1959) Convergent and discriminant validation by the multitrait-multimethod matrix. *Psychological Bulletin*, 56, 81–105.

Campbell, D. T. & Stanley, J. C. (1966) *Experimental and Quasi-experimental Designs for Research*. Chicago: Rand McNally.

Cannell, C. F. & Kahn, R. L. (1966) The collection of data by interviewing. In L. Festinger & D. Katz (Eds.), *Research Methods in the Behavioral Sciences*. New York: Holt, Rinehart and Winston.

Carlsmith, M., Ellsworth, P. C. & Aronson, E. (1976) *Methods of Research in Social Psychology*. Reading, MA: Addison-Wesley.

Cattell, R. B. (1966) The screen test for the number of factors. *Multivariate Behavioral Research*, 1, 245–276.

Chein, L. (1959) An introduction to sampling. In C. Selltiz, M. Jahoda, M. Deutsch, & S. W. Cook (Eds.), *Research Methods in Social Relations*. New York: Holt, Rinehart and Winston.

Chicago Manual of Style, 16th ed. (2010) Chicago: University of Chicago Press.

Churchill, G. A. (1987) *Marketing Research: Methodological Foundations*. Chicago: Dryden Press.

Clark, D. & Bank, D. (1998) Microsoft and Sony agree to work together to link consumer-electronic devices. *Wall Street Journal*, April 8, p. B6.

Cohen, J. (1969) *Statistical Power Analysis for the Behavioral Sciences*. New York: Academic Press.

Cohen, J. (1990) Things I have learned (so far). *American Psychologist*, 1304–1312.

Cook, T. D. & Campbell, D. T. (1979a) *Quasi-experimentation: Design and Analysis Issues for Field Settings*. Boston: Houghton-Mifflin.

Cook, T. D. & Campbell, D. T. (1979b) Four kinds of validity. In R. T. Mowday & R. M. Steers (Eds.), *Research in Organizations: Issues and Controversies*. Santa Monica, CA: Goodyear Publishing.

Cooke, A. (2001) *A Guide to Finding Quality Information on the Internet: Selection and Evaluation Strategies*, 2nd ed. London: Library Association.

Coombs, C. H. (1966) Theory and methods of social measurement. In L. Festinger & D. Katz (Eds.), *Research Methods in the Behavioral Sciences*. New York: Holt, Rinehart and Winston.

Cortada, J. W. (1996) *Information Technology as Business History: Issues in the History and Management of Computers*. Westport, CT: Greenwood Press.

Coulter, M. K. (2002) *Strategic Management in Action*. Englewood Cliffs, NJ: Prentice Hall.

Couper, M. P. (2000) Web-based surveys: A review of issues and approaches. *Public Opinion Quarterly*, 64 (4), 464–494.

Cronbach, L. J. (1946) Response sets and test validating. *Educational and Psychological Measurement*, 6, 475–494.

Cronbach, L. J. (1990) *Essentials of Psychological Testing*, 5th ed. New York: Harper & Row.

Cronin, M. J. (1998a) Business secrets of the billion-dollar website. *Fortune*, February 2, p. 142.

Cronin, M. J. (1998b) Ford's Intranet success. *Fortune*, March 30, p. 158.

Crosby, L. A. & Stephens N. (1987) Effects of relationship marketing on satisfaction, retention, and prices in the life insurance industry. *Journal of Marketing Research*, 24, 404–411.

Crowne, D. P. & Marlowe, D. (1980) *The Approval Motive: Studies in Evaluative Dependence*. Westport, CT: Greenwood Press.

Cummings, L. L. (1977) Emergence of the instrumental organization. In P. S. Goodman & J. M. Pennings (Eds.), *New Perspectives on Organizational Effectiveness*. San Francisco, CA: Jossey-Bass, pp. 56–62.

Cummings, T.G. & Worley, C.G. (2015) *Organization Development and Change*. Boston: Cengage Learning.

Davies, G. R. & Yoder, D. (1937) *Business Statistics*. New York: John Wiley & Sons, Inc.

Davis, D. & Cosenza, R. M. (1988) *Business Research for Decision Making*, 2nd ed. Boston: PWS-Kent Publishing.

DeArmond, S., Tye, M., Chen, P. Y., Krauss, A., Rogers, D. A. & Sintek, E. (2006) Age and gender stereotypes: New challenges in a changing workplace and workforce. *Journal of Applied Social Psychology*, 36, 2184–2214.

DeJong, M. (2006) *Response bias in international marketing research*, Doctoral Dissertation, Tilburg University.

Delamont, S. (2004) Ethnography and participant observation. In C. Seale, G. Gobo & J. Gubrium (Eds.) *Qualitative Research Practices*, pp. 217–229. London: Sage.

DeMunck, V. C. & Sobo, E. J. (Eds.) (1998) *Using Methods in the Field: A Practical Introduction and Casebook*. Walnut Creek, CA: AltaMira Press.

Denzin, N. K. (2000) The practices and politics of interpretation. In N. K. Denzin & Y. S. Lincoln (Eds.), *Handbook of Qualitative Research*, 2nd ed. Thousand Oaks, CA: Sage.

DeWalt, K. M. & DeWalt, B. R. (2002) *Participant Observation: A Guide for Fieldworkers*. Walnut Creek, CA: AltaMira Press.

Doran, G. T. (1981). There's a S.M.A.R.T. Way to Write Management's Goals and Objectives. *Management Review*, 70, 35–36.

Douglas, M. & Wildavsky A.B. (1982) *Risk and Culture*. Berkeley: University of California Press.

Drenkow, G. (1987) Data acquisition software that adapts to your needs. *Research and Development*, April, 84–87.

Dubé, L. & Maute, M. (1996) The antecedents of brand switching, brand loyalty and verbal responses to service failure. *Advances in Services Marketing and Management*, 5, 127–151.

Dubé-Rioux, L., Schmitt, B. H. & LeClerc, F. (1988) Consumers' reactions to waiting: When delays affect the perception of service quality. In T. Snull (Ed.), *Advances in Consumer Research*, Volume 16(1).

Edwards, A. L. (1957) *Manual for the Edwards Personal Preference Schedule*. New York: Psychological Corporation.

Elmore, P. E. & Beggs, D. L. (1975) Salience of concepts and commitment to extreme judgements in response pattern of teachers. *Education*, 95(4), 325–334.

Emerson, R., Fretz, R. & Shaw, L. (1995) *Writing Ethnographic Fieldnotes*. Chicago: University of Chicago Press.

Emory, C. W. (1985) *Business Research Methods*, 3rd ed. Homewood, IL: Richard D. Irwin.

Etzioni, A. (1960) Interpersonal and structural factors in the study of mental hospitals. *Psychiatry*, 23, 13–22.

Ferris, K. R. (1988) *Behavioral Accounting Research: A Critical Analysis.* Columbus, OH: Century VII Publishing.

Festinger, L. (1966) Laboratory experiments. In L. Festinger & D. Katz (Eds.), *Research Methods in the Behavioral Sciences.* New York: Holt, Rinehart and Winston.

Festinger, L. & Katz, D. (1966) *Research Methods in the Behavioral Sciences.* New York: Holt, Rinehart and Winston.

Fiedler, F. (1967) *A Theory of Leadership Effectiveness.* New York: McGraw-Hill.

Field, A. (2009) *Discovering Statistics Using SPSS.* Sage Publications.

Fink, A. (2003) *The Survey Kit,* 2nd ed. Thousand Oaks, CA: Sage.

Fishbein, M. (1967) *Readings in Attitude Theory and Measurement.* New York: John Wiley.

Folkes, V. S., Koletsky, S. & Graham, J. L. (1987) A field study of causal inferences and consumer reaction: The view from the airport. *Journal of Consumer Research,* 13, 534–539.

Folkman, J.R. (2006) The Power of Feedback. 35 Principles for Turning Feedback from Others into Personal and Professional Change. Chichester: John Wiley & Sons.

Fornell, C. (1987) A second generation of multivariate analysis: Classification of methods and implications for marketing research. In M. Houston (Ed.), *Review of Marketing.* Chicago, IL: American Marketing Association.

Fornell, C. & Bookstein, F. L. (1982) Two structural equation models: LISREL and PLS applied to consumer exit-voice theory. *Journal of Marketing Research,* 19, 440–452.

Frederichs, J. & Ludtke, H. (1975) *Participant Observation: Theory and Practice.* Lexington, MA: Lexington Books.

French, J. R. P. (1966) Experiments in field settings. In L. Festinger & D. Katz (Eds.), *Research Methods in the Behavioral Sciences.* New York: Holt, Rinehart and Winston.

Garten, J. E. (1998) Why the global economy is here to stay. *Business Week,* March 23, p. 21.

Gaski, J. F. & Etzel, M. J. (1986) The index of consumer sentiment toward marketing. *Journal of Marketing,* 50, 71–81.

Georgopolous, B. S. & Tannenbaum, A. S. (1957) The study of organizational effectiveness. *American Sociological Review,* 22, 534–540.

Glaser, B. (1978) *Theoretical Sensitivity.* Mill Valley, CA: Sociology Press.

Glaser, B. G. & Strauss, A. L. (1967) *The Discovery of Grounded Theory.* Chicago: Aldine.

Gordon, R. A. (1973) An explicit estimation of the prevalence of commitment to a training school, to age 18, by race and by sex. *Journal of the American Statistical Association,* 68, 547–553.

Gorsuch, R. L. (1974) *Factor Analysis.* Philadelphia: Saunders.

Gorsuch, R. L. (1983) *Factor Analysis,* 2nd ed. Philadelphia: Saunders.

Green, P. E., Kedia, P. K. & Nikhil, R. S. (1985) *Electronic Questionnaire Design and Analysis with CAPPA.* Palo Alto, CA: The Scientific Press.

Grove, S. J. & Fisk, R. P. (1992) Observational data collection methods for services marketing: An overview. *Journal of the Academy of Marketing Science,* 20(3), 217–224.

Hair, J. F., Jr., Anderson, R. E., Tatham, R. L. & Black, W. C. (1995) *Multi-variate Data Analysis.* Englewood Cliffs, NJ: Prentice Hall.

Hardy, Q. & Goel, V. (2015, March 26). *Drones Beaming Web Access are in the Stars for Facebook.* Retrieved from http://www.nytimes.com/2015/03/26/technology/drones-beaming-web-access-are-in-the-stars-for-facebook.html

Harnett, D. L. & Horrell, J. F. (1998) *Data, Statistics, and Decision Models with Excel.* New York: John Wiley & Sons, Inc.

Hart, C. (1998) *Doing a Literature Review.* London: Sage.

Heerde, H. van, Leeflang P. S. H. & Wittink, D. R. (2004) Decomposing the sales promotion bump with store data. *Marketing Science,* 23, 317–334.

Heggestad, E. D. & Kanfer, R. (1999) *Individual differences in trait motivation: Development of the motivational trait questionnaire. Poster presented at the Annual Meetings of the Society of Industrial and Organizational Psychology,* Atlanta, Georgia, April.

Hoel, P. G. & Jessen, R. J. (1971) *Basic Statistics for Business and Economics.* New York: John Wiley.

Horst, P. (1968) *Personality: Measurement of Dimensions.* San Francisco: Jossey-Bass.

Hume, L. & Mulcock J. (Eds) (1994) *Anthropologists in the Field: Cases in Participant Observation.* New York: Columbia University Press.

Hunt, S. D. (1983) *Marketing Theory: The Philosophy of Marketing Science.* Homewood, IL: Richard D. Irwin.

IJzermans, M. G. & Van Schaaijk, G. A. F. M. (2007) *Oefening baart kunst. Onderzoeken, argumenteren en presenteren voor juristen.* Den Haag: Boom Juridische uitgevers.

Izard, C. E. (1977) *Human Emotions.* New York: Plenum.

Jarvis, C. B., MacKenzie, S. B. & Podsakoff, P. M. (2003) A critical review of construct indicators and measurement model misspecification in marketing and consumer research. *Journal of Consumer Research,* 30(2), 199–218.

Jorgensen, D. L. (1989) *Participant Observation: Methodology for Human Studies.* Newbury, CA: Sage.

Kanuk, L. & Berenson, C. (1975) Mail surveys and response rates: A literature review. *Journal of Marketing Research,* 12, 440–453.

Kaplan, A. (1979) *The Conduct of Inquiry: Methodology for Behavioral Science.* New York: Harper & Row.

Kapteyn B. (1999) *Probleemoplossing in organisaties.* Houten: Bohn Stafleu van Loghum.

Kassarjian, H. H. (1977) Content-analysis in consumer research. *Journal of Consumer Research,* 4, 8–18.

Katz, D. (1966) *Research Methods in the Behavioral Sciences.* New York: Holt, Rinehart and Winston.

Katz, D. & Kahn, R. L. (1966) *Organizations and the System Concept: The Social Psychology of Organizations.* John Wiley & Sons, Inc. Reprinted in Shafritz, J. & Ott, J. S. (2001) *Classics of Organization Theory.* Fort Worth: Harcourt College Publishers.

Keaveney, S. M. (1995) Customer Switching Behavior in Service Industries – an Exploratory Study. *Journal of Marketing,* 59, 71–82.

Kelley, S. W., Hoffman, K. D. & Davis, M. A. (1993) A typology of retail failures and recoveries. *Journal of Retailing*, 69, 429–452.

Kelly, F. J., Beggs, D. L., McNeil, K. A., Eichelberger, T. & Lyon, J. (1969) *Research Design in the Behavioral Sciences: Multiple Regression Approach*. Carbondale, IL: Southern Illinois University Press.

Kerlinger, R. N. (1986) *Foundations of Behavioral Research*, 3rd ed. New York: Holt, Rinehart and Winston.

Kidder, L. H. & Judd, C. H. (1986) *Research Methods in Social Relations*. New York: Holt, Rinehart and Winston.

Kilmer, B. & Harnett, D. L. (1998) *KADDSTAT: Statistical Analysis Plug-in to Microsoft Excel*. New York: John Wiley.

Kirby, C. (2001) Snail mail's loss could be e-mail's gain. *San Francisco Chronicle*, October 23, p. B1.

Kirk, R. E. (1982) *Experimental Design: Procedures for the Behavioral Sciences*. Belmont, CA: Brooks/Cole.

Kish, L. (1965) *Survey Sampling*. New York: John Wiley.

Kish, L. (1966) Selection of the sample. In L. Festinger & D. Katz (Eds.), *Research Methods in the Behavioral Sciences*. New York: Holt, Rinehart and Winston.

Knechel, W. R. (1986) A simulation study of the relative effectiveness of alternative analytical review procedures. *Decision Sciences*, 17(3), 376–394.

Kolbe, R. H. & Burnett, M. S. (1991) Content analysis research: an examination of applications with directives for improving research reliability and objectivity. *Journal of Consumer Research*, 18, 243–250.

Kornhauser, A. & Sheatsley, P. B. (1959) Questionnaire construction and interview procedure. In C. Sellitz, M. Jahoda, M. Deutsch & S. W. Cook (Eds.), *Research Methods in Social Relations*. New York: Holt, Rinehart and Winston.

Krejcie, R. & Morgan, D. (1970) Determining sample size for research activities. *Educational and Psychological Measurement*, 30, 607–610.

Kuder, G. F. & Richardson, M. W. (1937) The theory of the estimation of test reliability. *Psychometrika*, 2, 151–160.

Kuppens, P., VanMechelen, I., Smits, D. J. M. & DeBoeck, P. (2003) The appraisal basis of anger: Specificity, necessity, and sufficiency of components. *Emotion*, 3(3), 254–269.

Labaw, P. (1980) *Advanced Questionnaire Design*. Cambridge, MA: Abt Books.

Lauder, M. A. (2003) Covert participant observation of a deviant community: Justifying the use of deception. *Journal of Contemporary Religion*, 18(2), 185–196.

Lazarsfeld, P. F. (1935) The art of asking why. *National Marketing Research*, 1, 26–38.

Leedy, P. D. (1985) *Practical Research: Planning and Design*, 3rd ed. New York: Macmillan Publishing.

Lehmann, D. R., Gupta S. & Steckel J.H. (1998) *Marketing Research*. Boston: Addison-Wesley.

Leshin, C. B. (1997) *Management on the World Wide Web*. Englewood Cliffs, NJ: Prentice Hall.

Likert, R. (1932) A technique for the measurement of attitudes. *Archives of Psychology*, No. 140.

Lombardo, M. L., McCall, M. & DeVries, D. L. (1983) *Looking Glass*. Glenview, IL: Scott Foresman, Co.

Lückerath-Rovers, M. (2013) Women on boards and company performance. *Journal of Management and Governance*, 17 (2), 491–509.

Luconi, F. L., Malone, T. W. & Scott Morton, M. S. (1986) Expert systems: The next challenge for managers. *Sloan Management Review*, 27(4), 3–14.

Luftman, J. N. (1996) *Competing in the Information Age: Strategic Alignment in Practice*. New York: Oxford University Press.

Machi, L. E. & McEvoy, B. T. (2009) *The Literature Review: Six Steps to Success*. Thousand Oaks: Corwin Sage.

Malinowski, B. (1992) *Argonauts of the Western Pacific*. New York: Dutton (First Published 1922).

Mandalios, J. (2013) RADAR: An approach for helping students evaluate Internet sources. *Journal of Information Science*, 39, 470–478.

Mangold, W. G., Miller, F. & Brockway, G. R. (1999) Word-of-mouth communication in the service marketplace. *Journal of Services Marketing*, 13, 73–89.

Marascuilo, L. A. & McSweeney, M. (1977) *Nonparametric and Distribution-free Methods for the Social Sciences*. Monterey, CA: Brooks/Cole.

Marcus, G. E. & Fischer, M. M. J. (1986) *Anthropology as Cultural Critique. An Experimental Moment in the Human Sciences*. Chicago: University of Chicago Press.

Martin, M. H. (1998) Smart managing: Best practices, careers, and ideas. *Fortune, February* 2, p. 149.

McClave, J. T. & Benson, P. G. (1988) *Statistics for Business and Economics*, 4th ed. San Francisco: Dellen Publishing Co.

McClung, J., Grove S. J., & Hughes, M. A. (1989) An investigation of the impact and situation as determinants of customers' approach skills in retailing. In P. Bloom et al. (Eds.), *Proceedings: Summer Conference of the American Marketing Association*. Chicago. 92.

McKellar, P. (1949) The emotion of anger in the expression of human aggressiveness. *British Journal of Psychology*, 39, 148–155.

McNeil, K. A., Kelly, F. J. & McNeil, J. T. (1975) *Testing Research Hypotheses using Multiple Linear Regression*. Carbondale, IL: Southern Illinois University Press.

Meltzer, M. E. (1981) *Information: The Ultimate Management Resource*. New York: Amacom.

Menon A. & Varadarajan P.R. (1992) A model of marketing knowledge use within firms. *Journal of Marketing*, 56, 53–71.

Merriam, S. B. (1988). *Case Study Research in Education: A Qualitative Approach*. San Francisco: Jossey-Bass Publishers.

Merton, R. K. & Kendall, P. L. (1955) The focused interview. In P. F. Lazarsfeld & M. Rosenberg (Eds.), *The Language of Social Research*. New York: The Free Press.

Mick, D. & Buhl, C. (1992) A meaning-based model of advertising experiences. *Journal of Consumer Research*, 19, 317–338.

Miles, M. B. & Huberman, A. M. (1994) *Qualitative Data Analysis*, 2nd ed. Thousand Oaks, CA: Sage.

Miller, E. G., Kahn, B., & Luce M. F. (2008) Consumer wait management strategies for negative service events: A coping approach. *Journal of Consumer Research*, 34(5), 635–648.

Minichiello, V., Aroni, R., Timewell, E. & Alexander, L. (1990) *In-depth Interviewing: Researching People*. Melbourne: Longman Cheshire.

Mintzberg, H. (1971) Managerial work: Analysis from observation. *Management Science*, 18, 23, 97–110.

Mitchell, R. E. (1969) Survey materials collected in developing countries: Sampling, measurement, and interviewing obstacles to intra- and international comparisons. In J. Boddewyn (Ed.), *Comparative Management and Marketing*, pp. 232–252. Glenview, IL: Scott, Foresman & Co.

Mittal, B. & Lassar, W. M. (1996) The role of personalization in service encounters. *Journal of Retailing*, 72, 95–109.

Muehling, D. D. (1987) An investigation of factors underlying attitude toward advertising in general. *Journal of Advertising*, 16(1), 32–40.

Murdick, P. G. & Cooper, D. R. (1982) *Business Research: Concepts and Guides*. Columbus, OH: Grid Publishing.

Murray, N. & Hughes, G. (2008) *Writing up your university assignments and research projects: A practical handbook*. New York: McGraw-Hill.

Namboodiri, N. K., Carter, L. F. & Blalock, H. M. (1975) *Applied Multivariate Analysis and Experimental Designs*. New York: McGraw-Hill.

Nasr-Bechwati, N. & Morrin, M. (2003) Outraged consumers: Getting even at the expense of getting a good deal. *Journal of Consumer Psychology*, 13, 440–453.

Norusis, M. J. (1998) *SPSS 8.0 Guide to Data Analysis*. Englewood Cliffs, NJ: Prentice Hall.

Nyer, P. U. (1997) A study of the relationships between cognitive appraisals and consumption emotions. *Journal of the Academy of Marketing Science*, 25, 296–304.

Oliver, R. L. (1996) *Satisfaction: A Behavioral Perspective on the Consumer*. New York: McGraw-Hill.

O'Neil, D., Hopkins, M. M. & Bilimoria, D. (2008) Women's careers at the start of the 21st century: Patterns and paradoxes. *Journal of Business Ethics*, 80, 727–743.

Oppenheim, A. N. (1986) *Questionnaire Design and Attitude Measurement*. Gower Publishing.

Osborn, R. N. & Vicars, W. M. (1976) Sex stereotypes: An artifact in leader behavior and subordinate satisfaction analysis? *Academy of Management Journal*, 19, 439–449.

Parasuraman, A., Drewal G. & Krishnan, D. (2004) *Marketing Research*. Boston: Cengage Learning.

Park, Y. -H. & Fader P. S. (2004) Modeling browsing behavior at multiple web sites. *Marketing Science*, 23, 280–303.

Parrott, W. G. (2001) *Emotions in Social Psychology: Essential Readings*. Philadelphia: Psychology Press.

Payne, S. L. (1951) *The Art of Asking Questions*. Princeton, NJ: Princeton University Press.

Peak, H. (1966) Problems of objective observation. In L. Festinger & D. Katz (Eds.), *Research Methods in the Behavioral Sciences*. New York: Holt, Rinehart and Winston.

Pedhazur, E. J. (1982) *Multiple Regression in Behavioral Research: Explanation and Prediction*, 2nd ed. New York: CBS College Publishing.

Pelosi, M. K., Sandifer, T. M. & Letkowski, J. J. (1998) *Doing Statistics with Excel™ 97: Software Instruction and Exercise Activity Supplement*. New York: John Wiley & Sons, Inc.

Perrier, C. & Kalwarski, G. (1989) Stimulating Simulations: Technique shows relationship between risk, funding. *Pensions and Investment Age, October* 30, 41–43.

Pfeffer, J. (1977) The ambiguity of leadership. *The Academy of Management Review*, 2.

Pope D., Price J. & Wolfers J. (2018) Awareness Reduces Racial Bias. *Management Science*, 64, 4988–4995.

Popper, K. R. (2002a) *The Logic of Scientific Discovery*. London: Routledge.

Popper, K. R. (2002b) *Conjectures and Refutations*. London: Routledge.

Preacher, K. J., Rucker, D. D. & Hayes, A. F. (2007) Addressing moderated mediated hypotheses: Theory, methods, and prescriptions. *Multivariate Behavioral Research*, 42, 185–227.

Price, J. (1997) Handbook of Organizational Measurement. *International Journal of Manpower*, 18(4/5/6), 301–558.

Price, J. L. & Mueller, C. W. (1986) *Handbook of Organizational Measurement*. Marshfield, MA: Pitman.

Rao, C. R. (1973) *Linear Statistical Inference and its Applications*, 2nd ed. New York: John Wiley.

Resta, P. A. (1972) *The Research Report*. New York: American Book Co.

Richins, M. L. & Dawson, S. (1992) Consumer values orientation for materialism and its measurement: Scale development and validation. *Journal of Consumer Research*, 19, 303–316.

Ridgway, N., Kukar-Kinney, M. & Monroe, K. (2018) An expanded conceptualization and a new measure of compulsive buying. *Journal of Consumer Research*, 35, 622–639.

Riley, M. W. & Nelson, E. E. (1974) *Sociological Observation: A Strategy for New Social Knowledge*. New York: Basic Books.

Rizzo, J. R., House, R. J. & Lirtzman, S. L. (1970) Role conflict and role ambiguity in complex organizations. *Administrative Science Quarterly*, 15, 150–163.

Rook, D. W. (1987) The buying impulse. *Journal of Consumer Research*, 14(2), 189–199.

Roscoe, J. T. (1975) *Fundamental Research Statistics for the Behavioral Sciences*, 2nd ed. New York: Holt, Rinehart and Winston.

Runkel, P. J. & McGrath, J. E. (1972) *Research on Human Behavior: A Systematic Guide to Method*. New York: Holt, Rinehart and Winston.

Salvia, A. A. (1990) *Introduction to Statistics*. Philadelphia, PA: Saunders.

Scaraboto, D., Rossi, C. & Costa, D. (2012). How consumers persuade each other: rhetorical strategies of interpersonal influence in online communities. *Brazilian Administration Review*, 9(3), 246–267.

Schein, V. E. (2007) Women in management: Reflections and projections. *Women in Management Review*, 22(1), 6–18.

Schensul, S. L., Schensul, J. J. & LeCompte, M. D. (1999) *Essential Ethnographic Methods: Observations, Interviews, and Questionnaires* (Book 2 in Ethnographer's Toolkit). Walnut Creek, CA: AltaMira Press.

Schmitt, N. W. & Klimoski, R. J. (1991) *Research Methods in Human Resources Management*. Cincinnati, OH: South-Western Publishing.

Sekaran, U. (1983) Methodological and theoretical issues and advancements in cross-cultural research. *Journal of International Business*, Fall, 61–73.

Sekaran, U. (1986) *Dual-career Families: Contemporary Organizational and Counseling Issues*. San Francisco: Jossey-Bass.

Sekaran, U. & Martin, H. J. (1982) An examination of the psychometric properties of some commonly researched individual differences, job, and organizational variables in two cultures. *Journal of International Business Studies*, Spring/Summer, 51–66.

Sekaran, U. & Trafton, R. S. (1978) The dimensionality of jobs: Back to square one. *Twenty-fourth Midwest Academy of Management Proceedings*, pp. 249–262.

Selltiz, C., Jahoda, M., Deutsch, M. & Cook, S. W. (1959) *Research Methods in Social Relations*, rev. ed. New York: Holt, Rinehart, and Winston.

Selltiz, C., Wrightsman, L. S. & Cook, S. W. (1981) *Research Methods in Social Relations*, 4th ed. New York: Holt, Rinehart and Winston.

Shapira, Z. (1995) *Risk Taking: A Managerial Perspective*. New York: Russell Sage Foundation.

Sharma, S., Durand, R. M. & Gur-Arie, O. (1981) Identification and analysis of moderator variables. *Journal of Marketing Research*, 18, 291–300.

Shrout, P. E. & Bolger, N. (2002) Mediation in experimental and nonexperimental studies: New procedures and recommendations. *Psychological Methods*, 7(4), 422–445.

Shurter, R. L., Williamson, J. P. & Broehl, W. G., Jr. (1965) *Business Research and Report Writing*. New York: McGraw-Hill.

Smith, C. A. & Ellsworth, P. C. (1987) Patterns of appraisals and emotions related to taking an exam. *Journal of Personality and Social Psychology*, 52, 475–488.

Smith, C. B. (1981) *A Guide to Business Research: Developing, Conducting, and Writing Research Projects*. Chicago, IL: Nelson-Hall.

Smith, P. C., Kendall, L. & Hulin, C. (1969) *The Measurement of Satisfaction in Work and Retirement*. Chicago: Rand McNally.

Spradley, J. P. (1980) *Participant Observation*. New York: Holt, Rinehart and Winston.

Stanford, D. (2015, March 19). *Scientists are Racing to Build a Better Diet Soda*. Retrieved from http://www.bloomberg.com/news/articles/2015-03-19/coke-pepsi-seek-diet-soda-s-perfect-sweetener

Stern, B. B., Thompson, C. J. & Arnould, E. J. (1998) Narrative analysis of a marketing relationship: The consumer's perspective. *Psychology and Marketing*, 15(3), 195–214.

Stern, N. B. & Stern, R. A. (1996) *Computing in the Information Age*, 2nd ed. New York: John Wiley & Sons, Inc.

Steufert, S., Pogash, R. & Piasecki, M. (1988) Simulation-based assessment of managerial competence: Reliability and validity. *Personnel Psychology*, 41(3), 537–557.

Stone, E. (1978) *Research Methods in Organizational Behavior*. Santa Monica, CA: Goodyear Publishing.

Strauss, A. & Corbin, J. (1990) *Basics of Qualitative Research: Grounded Theory Procedures and Techniques*. Sage Publications.

Sturges, J., Guest, D., Conway, N. & Davey, K. M. (2002) A longitudinal study of the relationship between career management and organizational commitment among graduates in the first ten years at work. *Journal of Organizational Behavior*, 23, 731–748. http://doi: 10.1002/job.164

Super, D. E. (1970) *Work Values Inventory Manual*. Boston, MA: Houghton Mifflin Co.

Taylor, S. (1994) Waiting for service – the relationship between delays and evaluations of service. *Journal of Marketing*, 58, 56–69.

Tomaski, E. A. (1970) *The Computer Revolution: The Executive and the New Information Technology*. New York: Macmillan.

Toulmin S. E. (1958) *The uses of argument*. Cambridge: Cambridge University Press.

Turabian, K. L. (2007) *A Manual for Writers of Term Papers, Theses, and Dissertations*, 7th ed. Chicago: University of Chicago Press.

Turban, E., McLean, E. & Wetherbe, J. (1998) *Informational Technology for Management: Making Connections for Strategic Advantage*. New York: John Wiley & Sons, Inc.

University of Chicago (2010) *The Chicago Manual of Style*, 16th ed. Chicago: University of Chicago Press.

Villa Rojas, A. (1979) Fieldwork in the Mayan region of Mexico. In G. Foster, T. Scudder, E. Colson & R. Kemper (Eds.), *Long-Term Field Research in Social Anthropology*, pp. 45–64. New York: Academic Press.

Ward, J. C. & Ostrom, A. L. (2006) Complaining to the masses: The role of protest framing in customer-created complaint web sites. *Journal of Consumer Research*, 33, 220–230.

Webb, E. J., Campbell, D. T., Schwartz, P. D. & Sechrest, L. (1966) *Unobtrusive Measures: Non-reactive Research in the Social Sciences*. Chicago, IL: Rand McNally.

Werner, O. & Schoepfle, M. G. (1987) *Systematic Fieldwork. Volume 1: Foundations of Ethnography and Interviewing*. Newbury Park, CA: Sage Publications.

Wetherbe, J. C. (1983) *Computer-based Information Systems*. Englewood Cliffs, NJ: Prentice Hall.

What is Plagiarism? (n.d.) Retrieved June 22, 2011, from http://www.plagiarism.org/learning_center/what_is_ plagiarism.html

White, J. K. & Ruh, R. A. (1973) Effects of personal values on the relationship between participation and job attitudes. *Administrative Science Quarterly*, 18(4), 506–514.

Wildstrom, S. H. (1998) Web sites made simpler. *Business Week*, January 26.

Williams, C. T. & Wolfe, G. K. (1979) *Elements of Research: A Guide for Writers*. Sherman Oaks, CA: Alfred Publishing.

Wolcott, H. (2001) *Writing Up Qualitative Research*, 2nd ed. London: Sage.

Wolfers, J. (2015, March 2). *Fewer Women Run Big Companies Than Men Named John*. Retrieved from http://www.nytimes.com/2015/03/03/upshot/fewer-women-run-big-companies-than-men-named-john.html?_r=0&abt=0002&abg=1

Wright, K. B. (2005) Researching internet-based populations: Advantages and disadvantages of online survey research, online questionnaire authoring software packages, and web survey services. *Journal of Computer-Mediated Communication*, http://doi: 10.1111/j.1083-6101.2005.tb00259.x

Yin, R. (2009) *Case Study Research: Design and Methods*, 4th ed. Thousand Oaks, CA: Sage Publications.

Yuchtman, E. & Seashore, S. E. (1967) A system resource approach to organizational effectiveness. *American Sociological Review*, 32, 891–903.

Zahle, J. (2012) Practical knowledge and participant observation. *Inquiry: An Interdisciplinary Journal of Philosophy*, 55, 50–65.

Zeithaml, V. A., Berry, L. L. & Parasuraman, A. (1996) The behavioral consequences of service quality. *Journal of Retailing*, 60, 31–46.

Zetterberg, H. (1955) On axiomatic theories in sociology. In P. F. Lazarsfeld & M. Rosenberg (Eds.), *The Language of Social Research*. New York: The Free Press.

Index